CW01065089

HERDER AND ENLIGHTENMENT POLITICS

Johann Gottfried Herder initiated the modern disciplines of philosophical anthropology and cultural history, including the study of popular culture. He is also remembered as a sharp critic of colonialism and imperialism. But what types of social, economic and political arrangements did Herder envision for modern European societies? *Herder and Enlightenment Politics* provides a radically new interpretation of Herder's political thought, situating his ideas in Enlightenment debates on modern patriotism, commerce and peace. By reconstructing Herder's engagement with Rousseau, Montesquieu, Abbt, Ferguson, Möser, Kant and many other contemporary authors, Eva Piirimäe shows that Herder was deeply interested in the potential for cultural, moral and political reform in Russia, Germany and Europe. Herder probed the foundations of modern liberty, community and peace, developing a distinctive understanding of human self-determination, natural sociability and modern patriotism as well as advocating a vision of Europe as a commercially and culturally interconnected community of peoples.

EVA PIIRIMÄE is Associate Professor of Political Theory at the Johan Skytte Institute of Political Studies, University of Tartu. She has published widely on Enlightenment moral philosophy and political thought. Her research has appeared in journals such as *History of Political Thought, European History of Ideas, Eighteenth-Century Studies* and *Global Responsibility to Protect.* Her recent publications include a co-edited *History of European Ideas* special issue 'Sociability in Enlightenment Thought' (2015) and the co-edited volume *Herder on Empathy and Sympathy* (2020).

IDEAS IN CONTEXT

Edited by David Armitage, Richard Bourke and
Jennifer Pitts

The books in this series will discuss the emergence of intellectual traditions and of related new disciplines. The procedures, aims and vocabularies that were generated will be set in the context of the alternatives available within the contemporary frameworks of ideas and institutions. Through detailed studies of the evolution of such traditions, and their modification by different audiences, it is hoped that a new picture will form of the development of ideas in their concrete contexts. By this means, artificial distinctions between the history of philosophy, of the various sciences, of society and politics, and of literature may be seen to dissolve.

A full list of titles in the series can be found at: www.cambridge.org/IdeasContext

HERDER AND ENLIGHTENMENT POLITICS

EVA PIIRIMÄE

University of Tartu

CAMBRIDGE
UNIVERSITY PRESS

Shaftesbury Road, Cambridge CB2 8EA, United Kingdom

One Liberty Plaza, 20th Floor, New York, NY 10006, USA

477 Williamstown Road, Port Melbourne, VIC 3207, Australia

314–321, 3rd Floor, Plot 3, Splendor Forum, Jasola District Centre, New Delhi – 110025, India

103 Penang Road, #05-06/07, Visioncrest Commercial, Singapore 238467

Cambridge University Press is part of Cambridge University Press & Assessment, a department of the University of Cambridge.

We share the University's mission to contribute to society through the pursuit of education, learning and research at the highest international levels of excellence.

www.cambridge.org
Information on this title: www.cambridge.org/9781009263863

DOI: 10.1017/9781009263825

First published 2023

A catalogue record for this publication is available from the British Library.

Library of Congress Cataloging-in-Publication Data
NAMES: Piirimäe, Eva, author.
TITLE: Herder and enlightenment politics / Eva Piirimäe.
DESCRIPTION: Cambridge ; New York, NY : Cambridge University Press, 2023. | Series: Ideas in context | Includes bibliographical references.
IDENTIFIERS: LCCN 2022052360 (print) | LCCN 2022052361 (ebook) | ISBN 9781009263863 (hardback) | ISBN 9781009263832 (paperback) | ISBN 9781009263825 (epub)
SUBJECTS: LCSH: Herder, Johann Gottfried, 1744-1803–Political and social views. | Enlightenment–Germany. | Political science–Germany–History–18th century. | Philosophy, German–18th century.
CLASSIFICATION: LCC B3051.Z7 P55 2023 (print) | LCC B3051.Z7 (ebook) | DDC 141.0943–dc23/eng/20221213
LC record available at https://lccn.loc.gov/2022052360
LC ebook record available at https://lccn.loc.gov/2022052361

ISBN 978-1-009-26386-3 Hardback

Contents

v

Preface

Cultural history, or the study of culture and popular culture in particular, began in its modern form with Johann Gottfried Herder (1744–1803). Herder's influence is often characterised as 'rays widely cast' (*weitstrahlsinnig*), using an expression coined by Johann Wolfgang von Goethe. Herder's essays of literary criticism, aesthetic theory and philosophy of history were widely read in Germany, and some were rapidly translated into other major European languages. Most importantly, an English translation of Herder's *Ideen zur Philosophie der Geschichte der Menschheit* (*Ideas for a Philosophy of History of Humanity*) appeared as early as 1800 (2nd ed., 1803), followed by Edgar Quinet's French translation in 1827/1828. Although the first complete Russian translation was not published until 1977, Herder was also read far and wide throughout the Russian Empire. Furthermore, although they drew on Herder's ideas, most authors in the nineteenth century no longer cared to mention him by name. In part, this was due to the devastating assessment Herder's philosophical ideas received from Immanuel Kant and Kant's followers. More importantly, however, Herder's ideas were simply quickly absorbed into Europe's common cultural heritage as well as across the Atlantic. One way or another, anyone reading writers such as Samuel Taylor Coleridge, Ralph Waldo Emerson, Edgar Quinet, Victor Hugo or Alexandr Herzen was also, indirectly, reading Herder.[1]

But what were the moral and political implications of Herder's understanding of humanity as a distinctively cultural species? What types of economic, social and political arrangements did Herder himself envision for modern societies? The usual answers to these questions have been heavily polarised. In Herder's rich and complex oeuvre, it is possible to find ideas and arguments that have subsequently come to play an important role in each of

---

[1] For a concise overview of the state of the art in the study of Herder's international reception, see Günter Arnold, Kurt Kloocke and Ernest A. Menze, 'Herder's Reception and Influence', in *A Companion to the Works of Johann Gottfried Herder*, ed. Hans Adler and Wulf Koepke (Rochester, NY, 2009), 391–419.

the hitherto dominant political languages emerging in the nineteenth century – liberalism, conservatism, socialism and anarchism. Using a highly selective reading of his ideas, he can be made a forefather of any of these ideologies. Since the late nineteenth century, however, the main contrast in characterising his thought has been that between 'cosmopolitanism' and 'nationalism', which in turn has often been associated with that between the Enlightenment and Romanticism. Herder has accordingly been presented both as a cosmopolitan democrat and a typical Enlightenment figure, and as a Romantic nationalist and a representative of 'Counter-Enlightenment'. In the late twentieth and early twenty-first century, Herder has also emerged as a 'communitarian', 'republican' and a 'multiculturalist'.

The aim of this book is to stand back from *all* these familiar but misleading labels and try to find a way to describe Herder's political thought contextually. In recent decades, amazing advances have been made in carving out the intellectual contexts of his ideas on language, culture, art and aesthetics. A vast body of scholarship has helped to dissolve the long-lasting shadow that the (post-) Kantian tradition cast upon Herder, restoring Herder to the rank of a first-rate philosopher. It has also demonstrated the extent to which Herder's conception of the human being as involving an inseparable body-soul constitution was informed by the latest developments in natural history and philosophy. The evolution of Herder's political thought, however, is yet to receive the close attention it deserves. This book seeks to remedy this. It begins with Herder's contribution to mid-eighteenth-century debates about possible reforms in modern monarchies and republics and finishes with late eighteenth-century discussions on the significance of the French Revolution and the foundations of international peace in Europe. As will emerge, Herder's penetrating studies of philosophical anthropology, cultural history and popular culture can be seen as essential elements of his distinctive solutions to problems addressed in these debates. Modern patriotism – as a problem and a goal – was a constant source of pondering for him. He probed both the foundations of modern liberty and modern community, developing distinctive understandings of human self-determination and natural sociability as well as putting forward a vision of Europe as a commercially and culturally interconnected community of peoples.

This book is not about the reception of Herder's political ideas. Nevertheless, it seeks to open up new ways of determining his legacy in political theory. Understanding Herder's main concerns in politics, we can hopefully also better differentiate between various appropriations of his ideas. Some lines of political reception are substantively more justified than others.

Acknowledgements

Coming from a small country, Estonia, which regained its independence through the process of a 'singing revolution' from 1987 to 1991, I have always been interested in the moral psychology of patriotism and national sentiment. Is it possible to cultivate a form of patriotism that is compatible with humanitarian concerns and aspirations? What would guarantee its stability as such? One way or another, my academic research has touched on these issues for years. I initially wanted to write a book on the philosophical origins of German nationalism based on my PhD dissertation on Thomas Abbt's (1738–1766) political thought. I wished to add a concluding chapter on Herder. However, I never finished that book and instead immersed myself in researching Herder. I was struck by the depth and complexity of Herder's thinking. I quickly realised that Herder's political ideas were not best approached through the frame of 'nationalism'. Nevertheless, it also became ever more clear to me that Herder was deeply interested in the future of Germany and Europe, and that he came up with a coherent vision of politics.

The person who has contributed most to my growth as a scholar is my PhD supervisor István Hont, who sadly passed away in 2013. I consider myself exceptionally lucky to have been guided by him; István's incisive questions and grand analytical framework transformed my approach to intellectual history. I am also deeply grateful to Michael Sonenscher for his encouragement, support and interest in my work. I have greatly benefited from his advice and suggestions on my manuscript. Alexander Schmidt has been a close friend over the years, and we have collaborated in and discussed each other's research ever since we met in 2001. He, too, took the time to read the entire manuscript, providing valuable advice. I am also thankful for my friendship and discussions with Nigel DeSouza. Nigel's enthusiasm for Herder must be infectious – he has known all along that in order to understand the *human condition* it is Herder's philosophy that one must delve into. I would further like to thank Edward Castleton, Béla

Kapossy, Iain McDaniel, Isaac Nakhimovsky, Mark Somos and Koen Stapelbroek for stimulating conversations, advice and collaboration. I am also very grateful to all the members of the research group on 'The self-determination of peoples in historical perspective' for their willingness to read and discuss the manuscript chapter by chapter. David Ilmar Lepasaar Beecher, Kadi Kähär-Peterson, Hent Kalmo, Kaarel Piirimäe, Andres Reimann, Semyon Reshenin and Juhan Saharov all gave helpful feedback. I would also like to thank Jonathan Clark, Lea Leppik, Liina Lukas, James Pearson and Pärtel Piirimäe for their comments on parts of the manuscript. Needless to say, the faults that the work still has are all mine.

Having immersed myself in Herder studies, I was glad to receive a warm welcome from specialist Herder scholars. The encouragement and support of Wolfgang Proß has meant a lot to me. I have benefited greatly from his magisterial studies and our scholarly correspondence. It has also been an immense pleasure to get to know Marion Heinz and to collaborate with her on the Springer *Encyclopedia of the Philosophy of Law and Social Philosophy* article on Herder. Liina Lukas – another long-term friend – and Johannes Schmidt were truly resourceful co-editors of our joint volume, *Herder on Empathy and Sympathy/Einfühlung und Sympathie im Denken Herders* (2020). Collaborating with them and our contributing authors was a wonderful experience.

It is impossible to list all the numerous conferences and seminars at which I have presented my research over the years. Richard Bourke, Joanna Innes, Béla Kapossy, Shiru Lim, Efraim Podoksik, John Robertson, Alexander Schmidt, Koen Stapelbroek, Mikko Tolonen, Balázs Trencsényi and many others have organised events at which I have had the pleasure to participate. In particular, I am very grateful to Richard Bourke for encouraging me to submit a book proposal to the Ideas in Context series of the Cambridge University Press. Much of this book was written during my sabbatical in the United States during 2016/2017. I am grateful to the Center for European Studies at Harvard University and The Whitney and Betty MacMillan Center for International and Area Studies at Yale University for successively providing me with institutional homes during my sabbatical, and to the Yale Baltic Fellows programme for offering me a fellowship. I greatly benefited from the opportunities to present my work at different research seminars and conferences, and am truly grateful to David Armitage, Eric Nelson and Bradley Woodworth for their inspiration and warm welcomes. The Johan Skytte Institute of Political Studies at the University of Tartu has provided a supportive institutional basis for me over years; I would like to thank Eiki Berg,

Piret Ehin and Vello Pettai among many others for their friendship and collaboration in different research projects.

I would also like to express my gratitude to Alexia Grosjean for her editing help. Elizabeth Friend-Smith at Cambridge University Press has also been a kind and helpful editor. I am further very grateful to the two anonymous readers for Cambridge University Press for their congenial and insightful comments and advice on my book, and to the editors of the Ideas in Context series for their support. A special thanks goes to Kadi Polli, Uku Peterson, Ojārs Spārītis, and the staff of The Museum of the History of Riga and Navigation for their help in tracing down the original piece of art used in the cover image of this book.

I have been incredibly lucky to have grown up in a family with strong academic traditions. My mother, Marika Mikelsaar, has been a constant source of inspiration, and so has my sister, Margit Sutrop. I have always looked up to them as models of combining fulfilling academic careers with having a happy family life. My father Raik-Hiio Mikelsaar (who sadly passed away in spring 2022) and my brother Hannes Mikelsaar have inspired me with their good humour and adventurous spirit. Last but not least, I owe more than I can ever express to my husband and soulmate Pärtel Piirimäe. We have been able to conduct most of our different academic peregrinations together, but even more importantly, we share the same values and so many interests. We have been married for over half our lives by now and have three beloved daughters. This book is dedicated to my family – Pärtel, Ellinor, Maarja-Leen and Ingel.

Chapters 1, 4, 7 and 8 include elements of substantially reworked published material: 'Herder and Cosmopolitanism', in *Critique of Cosmopolitan Reason: Timing and Spacing the Concept of World Citizenship*, ed. Rebecka Lettevall and Kristian Petrov (Oxford, Bern et al.: Peter Lang, 2014), 181–213; 'Philosophy, Sociability and Modern Patriotism: Young Herder between Rousseau and Abbt', published by Taylor & Francis Group in *History of European Ideas*, 41:5 (2015), 640–661, available online: https://www.tandfonline.com/DOI:10.1080/01916599.2014.987561; 'Sociability, Nationalism and Cosmopolitanism in Herder's Early Philosophy of History', *History of Political Thought* 36:3 (2015), 521–559; 'State-Machines, Commerce and the Progress of *Humanität* in Europe: Herder's Response to Kant in "Ideas for the Philosophy of History of Mankind"', in *Commerce and Peace in the Enlightenment*, ed. Béla Kapossy, Isaac Nakhimovsky and Richard Whatmore (Cambridge: Cambridge University Press, 2017), 155–191; 'Human Rights and their Realisation in the World: Herder's Debate with Kant', in *Passions, Politics and the Limits of Society* (*Helsinki Yearbook of Intellectual History*, 1), ed. Heikki Haara, Mikko Immanen and Koen Stapelbroek (Berlin: de Gruyter, 2020), 47–74. I would like to thank the publishers for allowing this material to be incorporated in this book.

The research for this monograph has been funded by the Estonian Research Council personal research grant PRG 942. I gratefully acknowledge this support.

Note on Translations

A substantial number of Herder's texts, including his private letters, remain untranslated into English. Unless otherwise indicated, the translations of citations from these texts and letters are all mine. For other texts, I have used available English translations, whilst sometimes finding it necessary to modify these translations to convey Herder's meaning more precisely. I have mostly preferred translations of complete texts to those of excerpts. In the cases where there is a full English translation of a text available, I do not provide references to German originals, although I do sometimes insert some original German terms in square brackets in citations. However, since the only complete translation of Herder's *Ideen zur Philosophie der Geschichte der Menschheit* is that of T. O. Churchill from 1800/1803, I am providing references also to the German original in *Werke in 3 Bänden* (*HWP*). In cases where there is an English translation of an excerpt available, I give references to both the excerpt and the German original.

Abbreviations

DA = Herder, Johann Gottfried. *Briefe. Gesamtausgabe 1763–1803*, 18 vols., ed. Wilhelm Dobbek and Günter Arnold (Weimar, 1977–2016).

FHA = Herder, Johann Gottfried. *Werke in zehn Bänden*, 10 vols., ed. Günter Arnold, Martin Bollacher, Jürgen Brummack, Christopher Bultmann, Ulrich Gaier, Gunter E. Grimm, Hans Dietrich Irmscher, Regine Otto, Rudolf Smend, Rainer Wisbert, Thomas Zippert and Johannes Wallmann (Frankfurt am Main, 1985–).

HEW = Herder, Johann Gottfried. *Selected Early Works, 1764–1767: Addresses, Essays and Drafts; Fragments on German Literature*, ed. Ernest A. Menze and Karl Menges, trans. Ernest A. Menze and Michael Palma (University Park, 1991).

HWP = Herder, Johann Gottfried. *Werke in 3 Bänden*, 3 in 4 vols., ed. Wolfgang Proß (Munich, 1984–2002).

PW = von Herder, Johann Gottfried. *Philosophical Writings*, ed. and trans. Michael N. Forster (Cambridge, 2002).

SWA = Herder, Johann Gottfried. *Selected Writings on Aesthetics*, ed. and trans. Gregory Moore (Princeton, 2006).

SWS = Herder, Johann Gottfried. *Sämmtliche Werke*, 33 vols., ed. Bernhard Suphan, (Berlin, 1877–1913).

Introduction

In 1819, in his *Athénée Royal* speech 'The Liberty of the Ancients Compared to the Moderns', Benjamin Constant made a plea for a historically grounded political philosophy. The philosophers who advocated the revival of ancient liberty during the French Revolution, Constant suggested, had not recognised the fundamental 'changes brought by two thousand years in the dispositions of mankind'. The liberty of the ancients 'consisted in an active and constant participation in collective power', whereas 'our freedom must consist of peaceful enjoyment and private independence'.[1] For the ancients, political liberty was the central value, while for the moderns, it was civil liberty. The German philosopher Johann Gottfried Herder presented a very similar argument more than half a century before Constant's speech. In a 1765 address entitled 'Do We Still Have the Public and Fatherland of the Ancients?', the twenty-one-year-old school teacher reasoned,

> Do we [still] have a fatherland whose sweet surname is *freedom*? Yes, only we think differently than the ancients when we use the word *freedom*. For them, *freedom* was an untamed audacity, the daring to hold the wheel of state in one's hands, the wilfulness not to suffer any other name above oneself [. . .]. Our people are no longer characterized by the *brazen audacity* of the ancients, there prevails, instead, a finer and more modest *freedom*: the freedom of *conscience*, to be an honest man and a Christian; the *freedom* to enjoy in the shadow of the throne one's dwelling and vineyard in peace and quiet, and to possess the fruit of one's labours, the *freedom* to be the shaper of one's happiness and comfort, the friend of one's intimates and the father and guardian of one's children. That is the *freedom*, the modest *freedom*, that every patriot today desires for himself [. . .].[2]

---

[1] Benjamin Constant, 'The Liberty of the Ancients Compared with That of Moderns', *Political Writings*, ed. and trans. Biancamaria Fontana (Cambridge, 1988), 308–328 (316–317).

[2] Johann Gottfried Herder, 'Do We Still Have the Public and Fatherland of Yore?', in *Selected Early Works, 1764–1767: Addresses, Essays and Drafts; Fragments on German Literature*, ed. Ernest A. Menze and Karl Menges, trans. Ernest A. Menze and Michael Palma (University Park, 1991)

This is a book about Herder's contribution to Enlightenment discussions on the problems and prospects of modern – post-Renaissance – European political societies. As the parallelism between Constant's and Herder's ideas shows, Constant was looking back at a long conversation that was well under way in the middle of the eighteenth century when Herder penned his essay. The rise of novel forms of liberty and an increasingly complex division of labour in their societies was widely registered by eighteenth-century writers. European monarchies were undergoing profound transformations due to the intensification of modern commerce, although their political and social institutions (most importantly, hereditary rule and the division of society into estates) were still retained. Many authors became increasingly concerned about a deepening individualism and social antagonism as well as the persistent international rivalry that was typical of their era. This raised questions about possible political alternatives to these developments as well as moral and political reforms to tackle them. One radical alternative was identified in austere democratic republicanism modelled on ancient polities. To a wide array of thinkers, however, the main question was rather how to stabilise or further enhance modern liberty and prosperity. They thus pondered the guarantees and preconditions of liberty, asking penetrating questions about the relationship between commerce and modern liberty and about the moral psychological foundations of the latter. Did these preconditions also include a certain kind of public spirit, perhaps some form of patriotism? If so, how could this spirit be sustained or regenerated in a society riddled with individualism? And last, but not least, what kind of international implications would this spirit have?[3]

Herder's political thought revolved around the problem of modern patriotism. In his various writings, he in one way or another tackled the following question: Is patriotism – an unselfish commitment to one's country or compatriots – justified, necessary or even possible in contemporary European states? Taking a fresh look at the bulk of Herder's oeuvre – his smaller essays as much as well-known great works – this book offers a reconstruction of the evolution of his political thought as developing in dialogue with the ideas of a number of key thinkers of his time on this

---

(henceforth abbr. as *HEW*), 53–64 (61). (I have modified the translation of the title in the text above.)

[3] For a seminal reconstruction of the early modern political thought around these themes, see István Hont, *Jealousy of Trade: International Competition and the Nation-State in Historical Perspective* (Cambridge, MA, 2005); István Hont, 'The Early Enlightenment Debate on Commerce and Luxury', in *The Cambridge History of Eighteenth-Century Political Thought,* ed. Mark Goldie and Robert Wokler (Cambridge, 2005), 379–418.

theme. Rousseau, Montesquieu, Abbt, Iselin, Moser, Möser, Ferguson, Hume and Kant figure particularly prominently in its analysis. In responding to these thinkers, Herder refined and modified his views on the characteristic dispositions and values of modern societies and the possibility of generating patriotism in them. He insisted on the need for moral and political reforms in all contemporary societies, whilst also tirelessly pointing out that realising the goals of these reforms entailed more than good-willed legislation. Institutions and laws mattered, but more important was the spirit that animated them. For Herder, it was essential for seeks to remedy this to develop a commitment to the common good in order to enable the betterment, stabilisation and pacification of modern European societies. 'Patriotism' (*Vaterlandsliebe, Patriotismus*) was the term he used for this kind of commitment.

In exploring the question of how patriotism could be regenerated in a modern society, Herder pondered the relationship between language, poetry, mores and politics. He raised penetrating questions about the relationship between law and ethics in modern societies, whilst also identifying a gap between the educated elites' professed values and principles, on the one hand, and their actual dispositions and actions, on the other. Paying lip service to the ideal of liberty – whether ancient or modern – was not enough. Herder accordingly came to fear that modern freedom was but a transient achievement disguising an emergent new form of military despotism. He accepted the central role of commerce in modern politics but understood that commerce, too, had become an instrument of power politics. He welcomed the French Revolution but was concerned about the ways in which republican ideas would be implemented in the hostile international environment in which the revolutionary French nation found itself. Herder commented on a vast array of political contexts but dedicated special interest to Russia, the city of Riga and Germany (the Holy Roman Empire) in particular. He also pondered how a new kind of political and international order could be created in Europe (and indeed, the world), which would combine modern liberty with social cohesion, vibrant cultural life, local self-government as well as international peace and humanitarian solidarity. At the end of his life, he specified the moral psychological foundations of this political ideal as 'purified patriotism' (*geläuterte Patriotismus*).

The last decades have witnessed a veritable 'revolution' in Herder studies.[4] An impressive new body of scholarship has carved out Herder's

---

[4] John H. Zammito, Karl Menges and Ernest A. Menze, 'Johann Gottfried Herder Revisited: The Revolution of Scholarship in the Last Quarter Century', *Journal of the History of Ideas*, 71:4 (2010),

highly original and interconnected ideas about epistemology, metaphysics, philosophical anthropology, philosophy of history, language and aesthetics, situating his thinking in various strands of Enlightenment philosophy, natural history and hermeneutics.[5] Several important recent studies have also dissected Herder's moral and political ideas. Sonia Sikka's, Vicki Spencer's and John Noyes's works have all greatly enhanced our understanding of the complexity of Herder's political thought as well as demonstrated his relevance for contemporary philosophical discussions on moral relativism and value pluralism.[6] In different ways, these and several other studies have highlighted Herder's fundamental commitment to individual and cultural self-determination, on the one hand, and international justice, on the other.[7]

Nevertheless, there is still considerable ambiguity in regard to Herder's views on modern European politics. There is also no clear understanding about the major continuities and ruptures in his political thinking, including his ideas on human moral psychology. As we will see in this book, Herder's early embrace of 'modern freedom' was embedded in a penetrating critique of modern society and politics, of which he only became increasingly critical in subsequent years. This raises questions about his

---

661–684; for a comprehensive overview of the most recent state of the art in research on Herder, see Stefan Greif, Marion Heinz and Heinrich Clairmont (eds.), *Herder Handbuch* (Paderborn, 2016). See also the excellent commentaries of the scholarly editions of Herder's collected works, most importantly, Johann Gottfried Herder, *Werke*, ed. Wolfgang Proß, 3 vols. (Munich and Vienna, 1984–2002) (henceforth abbr. as *HWP*) and Johann Gottfried Herder, *Werke in zehn Bänden*, ed. Martin Bollacher et al., 10 vols. in 11 (Frankfurt a. M., 1985–2000) (henceforth abbr. as *FHA*).

5 Wolfgang Proß, 'Nachwort. Herder und die Anthropologie der Aufklärung', in *HWP*, II, 1128–1216; Wolfgang Proß, 'Nachwort. *Natur* und *Geschichte* in Herders *Ideen zur Philosophie der Geschichte der Menschheit*', in *HWP*, III/1, 839–1040; Wolfgang Proß, 'Naturalism, Anthropology, Culture', in *The Cambridge History of Eighteenth-Century Political Thought*, ed. Mark Goldie and Robert Wokler (Cambridge, 2006), 218–247; Hans Adler, *Die Prägnanz des Dunklen: Gnoseologie, Ästhetik, Geschichtsphilosophie bei J.G. Herder* (Hamburg, 1990); Robert E. Norton, *Herder's Aesthetics and the European Enlightenment* (Ithaca and London, 1991); Marion Heinz, *Sensualistischer Idealismus: Untersuchungen zur Erkenntnistheorie und Metaphysik des jungen Herder (1763–1778)* (Hamburg, 1994); John H. Zammito, *Kant, Herder, and the Birth of Anthropology* (Chicago, 2002); Michael N. Forster, *After Herder: Philosophy of Language in the German Tradition* (Oxford, 2010), part One; Kristin Gjesdal, *Herder's Hermeneutics: History, Poetry, Enlightenment* (Cambridge, 2017). See also Adler and Koepke (eds.), *A Companion to the Works*; Anik Waldow and Nigel DeSouza (eds.), *Herder: Philosophy and Anthropology* (Oxford, 2017) and Eva Piirimäe, Liina Lukas and Johannes Schmidt (eds.), *Herder on Empathy and Sympathy/ Einfühlung und Sympathie im Denken Herders* (Leiden, 2020).

6 Sonia Sikka, *Herder on Humanity and Cultural Difference: Enlightened Relativism* (Cambridge, 2011); Vicki Spencer, *Herder's Political Thought: A Study of Language, Culture and Community* (Toronto, 2012); John Noyes, *Herder: Aesthetics against Imperialism* (Toronto, 2015).

7 See also Michael L. Frazer, *The Enlightenment of Sympathy: Justice and the Moral Sentiments in the Eighteenth Century and Today* (Oxford, 2010), ch. 6; Alan Patten, 'The Most Natural State: Herder and Nationalism', *History of Political Thought*, XXXI (2010), 658–689.

alternative vision for modern European societies. Whilst Herder's republican sympathies[8] and principled rejection of European colonialism and imperialism[9] have been explored in considerable depth, the evolution of his ideas on the past, present and future of European states and peoples has remained elusive.[10] Herder's assessment of the role of commerce in European history and in transforming modern societies has not received the attention it deserves. At the same time, contemporary scholars are also rather reluctant to discuss his views on the specific predicament of Germany. Yet, Herder not only consistently discussed what I have characterised as 'the problem of modern patriotism' but also identified himself as a German patriot.[11] Herder's minor writings of the 1770s in which he explores early 'German' mores and politics as well as expresses rather intense German national sentiment are particularly rarely studied in any depth, if at all. Nor is there much engagement with his views on the

[8] Frederick C. Beiser, *Enlightenment, Revolution, and Romanticism: The Genesis of Modern German Political Thought, 1790–1800* (Cambridge, MA, 1992), 189–221; Michael N. Forster, 'Introduction', in Johann Gottfried von Herder, *Philosophical Writings*, ed. Michael N. Forster (Cambridge, 2002) (henceforth abbr. as *PW*), vii–xxxv; Spencer, *Herder's Political Thought*.

[9] Sankar Muthu, *Enlightenment against Empire* (Princeton, 2003), ch. 6; Vicki Spencer, 'Kant and Herder on Colonialism, Indigenous Peoples, and Minority Nations', *International Theory*, 7:2 (2015), 360–392; Wolfgang Proß, 'Kolonialismuskritik aus dem Geist der Geschichtsphilosophie: Raynal, Herder, Dobrizhoffer und der Fall Paraguay', in *Raynal – Herder – Merkel. Transformationen der Antikolonialismusdebatte in der europäischen Aufklärung*, ed. York-Gothart Mix, Hinrich Ahrend (*Germanisch-Romanische Monatsschrift* 79) (Heidelberg, 2017), 17–73; Noyes, *Herder: Aesthetics*.

[10] See, however, important studies on some of his distinct works and their contexts: Alexander Schmidt, 'Scholarship, Morals and Government: Jean-Henri-Samuel Formey's and Johann Gottfried Herder's Responses to Rousseau's First Discourse', *Modern Intellectual History*, 9:2 (2012), 249–274; Wolfgang Proß, 'Geschichtliches Handeln und seine Nemesis: Visionäre Geschichte in der Zeit der Französischen Revolution', in *Gestaltbarkeit der Geschichte*, ed. Kurt Bayertz and Matthias Hoesch (Hamburg, 2019), 81–116.

[11] Unless otherwise specified, I will be using the terms 'people' (with an indefinite article) and 'nation' as synonyms, referring in both cases to distinct cultural peoples (e.g. the English, the French, the Germans). It also needs to be highlighted at the outset that to Herder the terms 'German' (*deutsch*) or 'Germany' (*Deutschland*) carried various kinds of meanings. First and foremost, the term 'German' for Herder was linked to the German language – contemporary 'German' literature was literature in the German language and 'Germany' could accordingly also mean the German-speaking literary public. Second, Herder also used the term 'German' (*deutsch*) to designate the 'peoples' (*deutsche Völker*) described in Tacitus' *De moribus Germanorum*, which included Saxons, Franks, Swabians and many other peoples. When referring to the ancient constitution of these peoples, he designated it as 'ancient German (peoples') constitution' (*alte deutsche Verfassung, deutsche Völkerverfassung*). He also used the term 'German people' both in the singular and in the plural, when discussing the historical population of the Holy Roman Empire. Further, when discussing the history of German literature, Herder regarded Danes and other Scandinavian peoples as a subset of German or 'northern peoples', whilst also underlining a common ancestry of English and German peoples with the Saxon people. Third, 'Germany' for Herder often also denoted the Holy Roman Empire. See the discussion in Markus Hien, *Altes Reich und Neue Dichtung. Literarisch-politisches Reichsdenken zwischen 1750 und 1830* (Berlin, 2015), 182–183.

prospects of Germany (the Holy Roman Empire) and Europe in general in the French Revolution period.

Herder and Nationalism

Herder's criticisms of modern European states and his patriotic commitments were often discussed in tandem in earlier scholarship. Indeed, there is a long-standing debate on Herder's relationship to 'Enlightenment' and 'nationalism' that has not been fully settled to this day. It is worth exploring the history of this debate in some detail here so as to understand the reasons why it gained traction and still lingers on.

The rise of sustained academic interest in Herder's ideas coincided with the establishment of the Second German Empire in 1871. Whereas Rudolf Haym presented a rather balanced (but distinctively neo-Kantian) interpretation of Herder's ideas in his monumental two-volume biography,[12] a strand of scholarship emerged in which Herder was presented as an 'anti-Enlightenment' thinker. Seeking to establish a straightforward connection between German political Romanticism and Herder's ideas, a number of scholars also came to hail Herder's notion of nation (*Volk*, *Nation*) as the foundation of a *völkisch* nationalism, an ideal of pan-Germanism as well as of a distinctively German idea(l) of a 'nation-state' (*Nationalstaat*) now being realised in the Second Empire.[13] Rudolf Unger's comparisons between Johann Georg Hamann and Herder further contributed to the solidification of this line of interpretation.[14] Some views expressed in the early twentieth century were more subtle, whilst still remaining indebted to the new framework that had emerged in the last quarter of the nineteenth century. In his *Cosmopolitanism and the Nation-State* (*Weltbürgertum und Nationalstaat* (1908)), Friedrich Meinecke influentially argued that Herder combined a deep sense of historical individuality with a veneration of the

---

[12] Rudolf Haym, *Herder nach seinem Leben und seinen Werken dargestellt*, 2 vols. (Berlin, 1880–1885; reprint 1958).

[13] For discussion and critical evaluation of this scholarship, see Claus Träger, *Herder Legende des deutschen Historismus* (Berlin, 1979); Otto Dann, 'Herder und die deutsche Bewegung', in *Johann Gottfried Herder, 1744–1803*, ed. Gerhard Sauder (Hamburg, 1987), 308–340; Wolfgang Proß, 'Die Ordnung der Zeiten und Räume. Herder zwischen Aufklärung und "Historismus"', in *Vernunft – Freiheit – Humanität. Über Johann Gottfried Herder und einige seiner Zeitgenossen: Festgabe für Günter Arnold zum 65. Geburtstag*, ed. Claudia Taszus (Eutin, 2008), 9–73 (10–11, 35–53) and Wolfgang Proß, 'Herder zwischen Restauration, Vormärz und Reichsgründung – Zur politischen und anthropologischen Interpretation seines Werkes (1805–1870)', in *Herder und das neunzehnte Jahrhundert*, ed. Liisa Steinby (Heidelberg, 2020), 119–148.

[14] See, most importantly, Rudolf Unger, *Hamann und die Aufklärung: Studien zur Vorgeschichte des romantischen Geistes im 18ten Jahrhundert* (Jena, 1911).

universal ideal of humanity but had 'not yet' achieved an adequate understanding of the nature of the modern state. According to Meinecke, even when Herder 'called for the political autonomy of the nation' in his later philosophy he did so 'in a spirit that was still not that of the modern autonomous state'.[15] Meinecke further elaborated this line of interpretation in his *Historism: The Rise of a Historical Outlook* (1936), casting Herder as a 'father' of the new *historicist* approach to the study of human history and culture, but not an important political thinker.[16] For Meinecke, Herder was simply not enough of a theorist of the 'national state' to be counted as such.

Nevertheless, a flurry of writings in the 1930s and 1940s invested considerable effort into highlighting Herder's contributions to the rise of German *völkisch* nationalism or nationalism more broadly. Even the most sympathetic commentators presented Herder as a critic of 'Western' culture and ideas of democracy who himself accordingly came up with a deeper and distinctively 'German' understanding of the nation (*Volk*) as a clear alternative to the former.[17] The core of this interpretation resurfaced in many general anglophone histories of nationalism after the Second World War; what had changed was the way this interpretation was morally and politically evaluated. Herder's ideas about the importance of language and culture for politics were presented as fostering authoritarian and bellicose political views. According to Elie Kedourie, Herder provided the emerging theory of 'national self-determination' with the crucial element of diversity, which called for the preservation and nurturing of peculiarities and idiosyncrasies, and, in particular, language. As regards the question of self-determination, Kedourie argued, language was subsequently turned into a 'political issue for which men were ready to kill and exterminate each other'.[18]

---

[15] Friedrich Meinecke, *Cosmopolitanism and the National State*, trans. Felix Gilbert (Princeton, NJ, 1970), 29–30.

[16] Compare Meinecke's verdict in *Historism*: 'the supranational movement of the Enlightenment, with its obliteration of all national character, was what he rebelled against; but he was thereby blinded to the specific life that belongs to a modern nation, and failed to realise that the Enlightenment could remodel this, yet could not extinguish it.' Friedrich Meinecke, *Historism: The Rise of a New Historical Outlook*, trans. J. E. Anderson [translation revised by H. D. Schmidt]; with a foreword by Sir Isaiah Berlin (London, 1972; German original 1936), 341–342.

[17] For references and discussion, see Günter Arnold et al., 'Herder's Reception', 401–402. Ideas to a similar effect can also be found in Robert Reinhold Ergang, *Herder and the Foundations of German Nationalism* (New York, 1931); Max Rouché, *La philosophie de l'histoire de Herder* (Paris, 1940) and Hans-Georg Gadamer, *Volk und Geschichte im Denken Herders* (Frankfurt/Main, 1942).

[18] Elie Kedourie, *Nationalism* (Oxford, Cambridge, MA, 1993) (4th edition, 1st edition 1960), 48, 64. Like Kedourie, Liah Greenfeld regarded German ideas about culturally based 'national identity' as encouraging an aggressive attitude towards those excluded from the national community; in her view, 'Germany was ready for Holocaust from the moment that its national identity existed', Liah

A new generation of Herder scholars, by contrast, again emphasised Herder's relative distance from political questions. Inverting Meinecke's value judgements, Isaiah Berlin relied on Meinecke's account of Herder's 'historicism' to defend Herder against associations with aggressive nationalism. Drawing on Meinecke, Berlin even coined the notion of 'Counter-Enlightenment' to capture the various 'proto-Romantic' eighteenth-century trends critically reacting to, and diverging from, what he – following Meinecke – identified as the dominant monistic natural law theories and the 'Enlightenment' encapsulated in the French Encyclopaedist tradition.[19] Berlin believed that Herder's 'cultural nationalism' could be vindicated in its own right as a pacific, apolitical and even anti-political philosophy of cultural belonging.[20] Berlin thus sought to rescue Herder from associations with subsequent German nationalism and power politics, whilst still following earlier German authors (particularly Meinecke) in viewing his ideas as distinct from, and straightforwardly opposed to, mainstream Enlightenment philosophy, including Enlightenment discussions on modern politics. Despite his sympathy for Herder's moral approach (moral pluralism), Berlin did not pay much attention to Herder's interest in modern politics, let alone discuss his ideas on moral and political reforms in Europe. In some sense, Charles Taylor, too, continued the same line of interpretation, when he highlighted Herder's originality and contribution to the rise of the modern ideal of authenticity, thereby casting him with the Romantic ('expressivist') critics of the Enlightenment.[21]

Greenfeld, *Nationalism: Five Roads to Modernity* (Cambridge, MA and London, 1992), 384. Most recently, we encounter arguments to the same effect in Zeev Sternhell, *The Anti-Enlightenment Tradition* (New Haven, 2010), ch. 6. For a recent systematic attempt to settle questions about Herder's relationship to 'nationalism', see Dominic Eggel, Andre Liebich and Deborah Mancini-Griffoli, 'Was Herder a Nationalist?', *The Review of Politics*, 69 (2007), 48–78.

[19] See, most importantly, Avi Lifschitz, 'Between Friedrich Meinecke and Ernst Cassirer: Isaiah Berlin's Bifurcated Enlightenment', in *Isaiah Berlin and the Enlightenment*, ed. L. Brockliss and R. Robertson (Oxford, 2016), 51–66. For the German origins of Berlin's general interpretation, Robert Norton, 'The Myth of the Counter-Enlightenment', *Journal of the History of Ideas*, 68:4 (2007), 635–658 (651–652); cf. Eva Piirimäe, 'Herder, Berlin and the Counter-Enlightenment', *Eighteenth-Century Studies*, 49:1 (2015), 71–76.

[20] See Isaiah Berlin, *Three Critics of the Enlightenment: Vico, Hamann, Herder*, ed. Henry Hardy, with an introduction by J. Israel (Princeton, 2013) [the study of Herder was originally contained in Isaiah Berlin, *Vico and Herder: Two Studies of the History of Ideas* New York, 1976]; Isaiah Berlin, 'The Counter-Enlightenment' [1973], in *Against the Current*, ed. H. Hardy (New York, 1980), 1–24. Originally Berlin used the term 'populism' to characterise Herder's 'form of nationalism', Isaiah Berlin, *Three Critics*, 222f.

[21] See, e.g., Charles Taylor, *Hegel* (Cambridge, 1975), ch. 1; Taylor, *Sources of the Self: The Making of Modern Identity* (Cambridge, 1989), 368–382; Taylor, 'The Importance of Herder', in *Isaiah Berlin: A Celebration*, ed. Edna Margalit and Avishai Margalit (Chicago, 1991), 40–63.

The views of Herder as an 'anti-Enlightenment' or 'Counter-Enlightenment' thinker – and the corresponding accounts of his political views as either 'nationalist', non-existent (apolitical) or even anti-political – have received substantial and justified criticism from a number of authors over a considerable span of time. F. M. Barnard – one of the few post–Second World War scholars focusing specifically on Herder's social and political thought – already sought to qualify the view of Herder's apolitical or anti-political cultural nationalism, highlighting the complexity of his ideas on political legitimacy and participation.[22] The East German literary scholar Claus Träger further uncovered, in the spirit of a 'critique of ideology', how the German Romantics actually found little use in Herder's thought when developing their *political* ideas. It was only the ideologues of the Second German Empire who came to associate Herder with political Romanticism.[23] Frederick Beiser highlighted the *sui generis* republican political theory that Herder offered, defending the view that Herder was a radical rather than conservative political thinker.[24] F. M. Barnard also returned to the topic of Herder's relationship to 'nationalism' and 'conservatism' in his later book. Underlining Herder's fundamentally different understanding of the nature and status of modern states compared to that of political Romantics, Barnard nevertheless sought to demonstrate the political relevance of Herder's cultural ideas. Initially using the term 'nationalism' with a neutral evaluative connotation to characterise Herder's position, Barnard later opted for that of 'nationality', so as to emphasise that Herder's thinking was humanitarian and universalistic rather than narrowly 'nationalist'.[25] In recent decades, Wolfgang Proß has further substantiated this reading by illuminating the wide range of sources for Herder's cosmopolitan thinking as well as putting forward a novel and compelling view of the history of Herder's reception and significance in the nineteenth century (until 1871).[26]

---

[22] See F. M. Barnard, *Herder's Social and Political Thought: from Enlightenment to Nationalism* (Oxford, 1965); F. M. Barnard, 'Introduction', in *J. G. Herder on Social and Political Culture*, ed. F. M. Barnard (London, Cambridge, 1969); F. M. Barnard, *Self-Direction and Political Legitimacy: Rousseau and Herder* (Oxford, 1988).

[23] Träger, *Herder Legende*.

[24] Beiser, *Enlightenment, Revolution*, 209–221. Alongside Barnard's studies, Beiser draws considerably on Wilhelm Dobbek's extensive article 'Johann Gottfried Herders Haltung im politischen Leben seiner Zeit', *Zeitschrift für Ostforschung*, 8 (1959), 321–387.

[25] F. M. Barnard, *Herder on Nationality, Humanity, and History* (Montreal and Kingston, 2003). Compare, however, Horst Dreitzel, 'Herders politische Konzepte', in *Johann Gottfried Herder, 1744–1803*, ed. Gerhard Sauder (Hamburg, 1987), 266–298. Dreitzel draws attention to changes in Herder's attitude to the modern state in the final decade of his life.

[26] See, most importantly, Proß, 'Die Ordnung der Zeiten' and 'Herder zwischen Restauration'.

Yet there are also relatively recent dissenting voices that focus on Herder's conception of patriotism specifically. In a small but widely read study, Maurizio Viroli has highlighted Herder's 'distrust for republican liberty' and the 'anti-political orientation of German patriotism' in general.[27] 'Republican patriots', Viroli maintains, would have easily identified the cause of modern problems in the lack of opportunities for political participation. Herder, however, ignored this aspect in his analysis of modern society. According to Viroli, it was precisely Herder's early rejection of ancient liberty that led him to identify a new object of veneration for modern patriots in a cultural nation. In so doing, 'Herder changed the meaning of republican love of country and recommended another love, perhaps more intense and easier to cultivate, but surely different from the patriotic love of common liberty'. In contrast to the latter, love of the fatherland for Herder was a 'natural inclination, a vital force that reason endeavours to corrupt', not a form of rational love that would emerge as a result of 'a moral training led by reason'.[28] As such, it was 'an exclusive attachment to one's own national culture, an attachment to be protected against cosmopolitanism and cultural assimilation'.[29] No matter how philosophically deep and morally benign Herder's intentions in coining such a way of thinking were, Viroli insists, he must be seen as responsible for initiating a new language and way of thought known as ethno-cultural 'nationalism'. By relinquishing the ideal of ancient liberty and seeking to offer a different remedy to the malaise of modernity, he contributed to the emergence of a novel, and perhaps even the most virulent, variety of such a malaise.

Viroli's interpretation of Herder has been decisively countered by Vicki Spencer. Highlighting what she calls Herder's systematic 'anti-dualism', Spencer shows that Herder's political thought is grounded in his expressivist theory of language. Cultures, for Herder, are not homogenous entities, and the central principles of his political thought are those of cultural (and not necessarily political) self-determination and respect for cultural

---

[27] Maurizio Viroli, *For Love of Country: An Essay on Patriotism and Nationalism* (Oxford, 1997), 113–114. It needs to be pointed out that Viroli does not discuss the newer literature on Herder and is heavily indebted to Ergang's *Herder and the Foundations* in his interpretation of Herder's ideas and their context. Like Kedourie and Greenfeld, Viroli emphasises the potentially exclusionist and even aggressive implications of Herder's allegedly 'apolitical' and 'humanitarian' cultural nationalism.

[28] Viroli, *For Love of Country*, 124. A similar misleading criticism can also be encountered in Erica Benner's otherwise more balanced account in her overview 'The Nation-State', in *Cambridge History of Philosophy in the Nineteenth Century 1790–1870*, ed. Allen W. Wood and Songsuk Susan Hahn (Cambridge, 2012), 699–730 (706–707).

[29] Viroli, *For Love of Country*, 119.

diversity. Herder was firmly opposed to all sorts of aggressive nationalism, including assimilationalist official nationalisms. According to Spencer, Herder thus has far more in common with contemporary communitarianism and multiculturalism than even liberal nationalism.[30] Spencer has also demonstrated Herder's fundamentally republican commitments. Far from ignoring 'the importance of liberty to individual welfare in favour of communal rights', Spencer argues, Herder viewed the two as inextricably linked.[31]

Spencer's claim that Viroli neglects a number of central aspects of Herder's thought can be substantiated. However, as will emerge in this study, there is a deeper problem with the broader interpretative scheme Viroli proposes for understanding the origins of Herder's 'nationalism'. He is right to point out that the young Herder was critical of ancient liberty, but he neither explores Herder's reasons for being so nor does he properly analyse what Herder's ethical outlook actually involves. Indeed, in his assessment of Herder's thought he merely turns Herder's and Constant's distinction between modern and ancient liberty upside down, putting his stakes on 'ancient republican liberty' instead of 'modern liberty'. He does not address the underlying questions about the changed 'dispositions of mankind' and the complex eighteenth-century debates on the problems of modern European societies to which Herder sought to contribute. Instead, he has simply propped up a pseudo-historical contrast between a 'generous and pacific republican patriotism', on the one hand, and an 'exclusivist and aggressive cultural nationalism', on the other.[32]

István Hont, in his *Jealousy of Trade: International Competition and the Nation-State in Historical Perspective*, provides a different perspective on Herder's relationship to nationalism. Offering a brief but highly suggestive sketch of Herder's contribution to broader eighteenth-century debates about modern sovereignty and international commercial rivalry, Hont presents Herder's approach as 'deeply antipolitical and designed to abolish both the state, and its offspring, the pseudopatriotic "political nation"'. According to Hont, Herder developed the idea of the linguistic-cultural nation as an alternative to the latter, 'conjuring up an image of a richly articulated mankind' consisting of diverse national groups, all confident in their identity and hence 'capable of relating to other nations without

---

[30] Spencer, *Herder's Political Thought*, 218; on Spencer's views on Herder's relationship to nationalism, see ibid., 144–157.

[31] Ibid., 159.

[32] See also Veit Bader, 'Review: For Love of Country [Book Review]', *Political Theory*, 27:3 (1999), 379–397.

jealousy and rivalry'.[33] In Hont's view, Herder was not a nationalist but a republican patriot and an astute critic of nationalism. However, when 'transposed back' into the world of intense international rivalry in the nineteenth century, Herder's 'originally critical and antipolitical philosophy of the nation spawned an unpleasantly self-righteous understanding of sovereign statehood'.[34]

Goals and Main Arguments of the Book

This study is much indebted to Hont's analytical framework. However, it takes an even more strongly contextualist approach to Herder's political thought, as its goal is to offer a full-bodied and nuanced historical reconstruction of its evolution. As such, it further differs from most recent discussions of Herder's political ideas, whilst showing some parallels with Noyes's approach.[35] Rather than looking at Herder's political thought as an instance of a certain ideology or 'political language' (Viroli), determining its role in the complex genesis of modern nationalism (Hont) or reconstructing it as one single systematic whole grounded in Herder's deeper philosophical presuppositions,[36] it asks what were his main concerns, ideas and political agenda in his own time and how they evolved over years.

It proposes that reconstructing Herder's serial contributions to eighteenth-century discussions on the moral psychological foundations of, and the possible reforms in, modern societies provides a key to answering these questions. Although Herder never wrote a major political treatise and at no time in his life focused exclusively on politics, there is a deeper consistency in his general political outlook, as expressed in his different essays and philosophical works. Some of his more specific views, at the same time, underwent substantial transformations over the years. The continuities and ruptures in his ideas can best be understood against the backdrop of these discussions or his engagement with specific authors. Political developments and events also prompted him to further probe the implications of his previously developed views. The reception of his thought is a separate topic. However, once we have identified the central themes of his evolving thought, we can also seek to determine the ways in which it resonated with thinkers in the nineteenth century and beyond.

---

[33] Hont, *Jealousy of Trade*, 137; see also ibid., 503–508.   [34] Hont, *Jealousy of Trade*, 141.
[35] Noyes, *Herder: Aesthetics*. Noyes' focus, however, is different from mine; it is on Herder's aesthetics and anti-imperialism rather than on his discussion of modern European politics.
[36] Sikka, *Herder on Humanity*; Spencer, *Herder's Political Thought*.

Debates during the Seven Years' War

One of the central arguments of this study is that the roots of Herder's political agenda lay in the moral and political discussions arising during the Seven Years' War (1756–1763).[37] At this moment, it was becoming particularly apparent both to the political elites as well as the wider public in different European countries that national security was codependent on economic prosperity, which in turn depended on 'modern liberty'. Great Britain had proved particularly successful in this respect in a long-term perspective with its quasi-republican form of government, as had the republican Netherlands. One of the central questions discussed was thus how the possible economic reforms modelled on these countries would tally with the current societal order and political system in a given state and the international system more generally. Would it be possible for continental European monarchies to emulate the commercial success of Britain? Why were the Netherlands experiencing decline, despite their previous spectacular success story? What was to become of the Holy Roman Empire, now that the kingdom of Prussia was emerging as one of Europe's great powers? What chances did Russia have of becoming one such power as well? What were the future prospects for the Utrecht peace settlement and the European 'balance of power'? Questions were also raised about the effects of 'luxury' on civic cohesion and morality, including subjects' capacity to discharge their civic duties. To many, both France and Britain were negative examples in this regard. In different ways, a number of authors already expressed sceptical views about these countries' political stability.

An important theoretical impetus for these debates was provided by Charles de Montesquieu's and Jean-Jacques Rousseau's powerful, yet also in many ways challenging, political visions. Montesquieu's and Rousseau's works provoked numerous authors all over Europe to put forward and defend their alternative political ideas.[38] Herder was among these readers;

---

[37] For these debates in different national contexts, see e.g. Béla Kapossy, *Iselin contra Rousseau: Sociable Patriotism and the History of Mankind* (Basle, 2006); John Shovlin, *The Political Economy of Virtue: Luxury, Patriotism and the Origins of the French Revolution* (Ithaca, 2006); Michael Sonenscher, *Before the Deluge: Public Debt, Inequality, and the Intellectual Origins of the French Revolution* (Princeton and Oxford, 2007) and Michael Sonenscher, *Sans-Culottes: An Eighteenth-Century Emblem in the French Revolution* (Princeton, 2008); Iain McDaniel, *Adam Ferguson in the Scottish Enlightenment: The Roman Past and Europe's Future* (Cambridge, MA and London, 2013).

[38] On German responses to debates inspired by Montesquieu, see Eva Piirimäe, 'Thomas Abbt's "Vom Tode für das Vaterland" (1761) and the French Debates on Monarchical Patriotism', *Trames: Journal of the Humanities and Social Sciences*, 9:4 (2005), 326–347.

it is thus vital to spell out some of the elements of these challenges at the outset. In his monumental *The Spirit of the Laws* (1748) Montesquieu suggested that different political regimes were animated by specific motivational principles, their viability depending upon the preservation of this distinctive principle and the mores supporting it. The latter, according to Montesquieu, originated not only in complex educational and religious systems but were also intricately bound with the political system that they helped to sustain and animate.[39] The principle of republican form of government was love of the laws of one's country, that is, patriotism. In republics patriotism was engendered in such a way (through general laws and by giving vent to the passion for general order) that it became the very spring of government, the prevailing principle of action of all citizens. It was identical to the love of equality in republics because equality was the fundamental principle of republican laws. From the economic perspective, Montesquieu distinguished between landlocked agrarian (military) and maritime commercial republics. In the first, socioeconomic equality was achieved through pervasive equalising legislation (and civic religion that supported it in citizens' perceptions); in the second, the dominant source of income (entrepôt trade) itself had rough equalising effects on citizens' property.[40] Montesquieu's paradigmatic example when discussing republican virtue were the former. In landlocked republics, the initial legislative frameworks particularly strictly regulated citizens' property accumulation and transfer and restrained or prohibited their engagement in commerce. The laws regulated also their spending in general, teaching republicans to 'renounce themselves' so as to preserve social equality.[41]

The constitutive feature of monarchical laws, by contrast, was inequality. Montesquieu highlighted the role of hereditary nobility in guaranteeing the rule of law in modern monarchies and maintained that the motivational principle of monarchies was false honour, the desire for public esteem. Since monarchies were complex societies, honour took a special form in each rank, inspiring an organised form of competition for distinction among peers.[42] This lent an extraordinary moral energy to

---

[39] Charles de Secondat, Baron de Montesquieu, *The Spirit of the Laws* [1748], ed. and trans. Anne M. Cohler, Basia Carolyn Miller and Harold Samuel Stone (Cambridge, 1989), Book XIX provides Montesquieu's most systematic attempt to discuss the relationships between what he called 'principles, mores, and manners of a nation', ibid., 308ff.

[40] Ibid., V: 6, 48; XX: 4, 340.   [41] Ibid., III: 3, 22–23; V: 2–7, 43–50.

[42] Ibid., III: 5–6, 27–28. Montesquieu's 'honour' echoed what many seventeenth-century thinkers, as well as Bernard Mandeville at the beginning of the eighteenth century, designated as 'pride'. Cf. for example Mandeville's statement: 'The more pride [men] have and the greater value they set on [gaining] the esteem of others, the more they'll make themselves acceptable to all they converse

monarchical society, without requiring any intricate and homogeneous systems of education or uniform legal restraints upon people's engagement in commerce or arts. According to Montesquieu, monarchies could continue to exist 'independently of love of the homeland, desire for true glory, self-renunciation, sacrifice of one's dearest interests, and all those heroic virtues we find in the ancients and know only by hearsay'.[43] Competition for false honour animated even the lower ranks, as expressed in their seeking of prestige through luxury and conspicuous consumption.[44] Many of Montesquieu's readers were perplexed: was patriotism, then, at all possible or, indeed, desirable in modern monarchies? Political virtue based on moral or Christian virtue was possible in monarchies, but was there also a separate kind of political virtue distinctive of monarchies? Should not false honour be accepted as a form of 'political virtue' suitable for monarchies? Furthermore, would not many of the reforms advocated for in modern monarchies in fact undermine their very basis – hereditary nobility?

Rousseau's challenges to reform-minded thinkers were even more profound. Many of Rousseau's readers interpreted his philosophy in the 1750s as both a development and critique of Montesquieu's ideas. In the *First Discourse* (1751) – the prize-winning answer to the Dijon academy's question concerning the impact of the progress of the arts and sciences on the purity of morals – Rousseau followed up Montesquieu's association of republican 'virtue' with the austere physical culture of military republics.[45] However, he also provided a highly provocative answer to the academy's question, disputing the positive impact of the arts and science upon morality or even political government. In the *Replies* to his critics Rousseau developed his 'sad system of society' to the full. He elaborated the extent to which the arts and sciences contributed to the emergence of a society based solely on individual interests and exchange of services (commercial society) and disputed the secondary beneficial effects of the arts and sciences on society as a whole. In the *Second Discourse – Discourse on the Origin and the Foundations of Inequality among Men* (1755) – he revealed the reasons for his pessimism and directly addressed the history

with.' Mandeville, *The Fable of the Bees, or the Private Vices, Public Benefits*, ed. and annot. F.B. Kaye [1924], II (2 vols., Indianapolis, 1988), 65.

[43] Montesquieu, *The Spirit of the Laws*, III: 5, 25.

[44] On Montesquieu's concept of monarchy, see Sonenscher, *Before the Deluge*, ch. 3 and Sylvana Tomaselli, 'The Spirit of Nations', in *The Cambridge History of Eighteenth-Century Political Thought*, ed. Mark Goldie and Robert Wokler (Cambridge, 2006), 7–39.

[45] Jean-Jacques Rousseau, 'Discourse on the Sciences and Arts or First Discourse [1751]', in Jean-Jacques Rousseau, *The Discourses and Other Early Political Writings*, ed. and trans. By Victor Gourevitch (Cambridge, 1997), 1–28.

and future of modern monarchies.[46] For Rousseau, moreover, Montesquieu's questions about the viability of various kinds of political regimes laid bare the more fundamental issue of political legitimacy and obligation in modern states. Rousseau did not shy away from asking: how could the people within a given state remain free and what was a modern republic to look like? He gave new validity to the social contract argument in his *The Social Contract* (1762), whilst also paying very close attention to questions of moral psychology. What kind of socioeconomic and moral psychology was a modern republic to be based on, Rousseau asked. Denying human natural sociability, on the one hand, and posing an evocative ideal of the modern democratic republic grounded in a purely artificial 'general will', on the other, Rousseau challenged his contemporaries (and not only them!) to ponder upon the consistency and plausibility of his 'system' whilst also sparking a long-lasting debate on the historical evolution of modern society.[47]

To be sure, there were quite a few authors who sought to defend the distinctiveness of republican and monarchical forms of government and their underlying moral psychological principles. In so doing, many of them also drew on Montesquieu and Rousseau. Herder was not among them. Rather, he at an early point aligned himself with a broad international current of thought underlining the need for monarchies to learn from different republics such as the Swiss republics, on the one hand, and the Netherlands, on the other. Similarly to authors like Thomas Abbt and Isaak Iselin, the young Herder was initially sympathetic to David Hume's idea of a modern 'civilised monarchy', according to which it was impossible for modern European rulers to ignore the value of commerce in contributing to the power of their states; thus even constitutionally unlimited (but patriotic and enlightened) kings would be committed to the rule of law and modern liberty as well as to promoting the arts and sciences,

---

[46] Jean-Jacques Rousseau, 'Discourse on the Origin and Foundations of Inequality Among Men or Second Discourse' ('Second Discourse'), in *The Discourses and Other Early Political Writings*, 111–188.

[47] For an introduction to these debates, see, e.g., Ursula Goldenbaum, 'Einführung', in Jean-Jacques Rousseau, *Abhandlung von dem Ursprunge der Ungleichheit*, trans. M. Mendelssohn, ed. U. Goldenbaum (Weimar, 2000), 1–63 and the contributions in Avi Lifschitz (ed.), *Engaging with Rousseau: Reaction and Interpretation from the Eighteenth Century to the Present* (Cambridge, 2016). The most important recent discussions of Rousseau's 'system' include Frederick Neuhouser, 'Jean-Jacques Rousseau and the Origins of Autonomy', *Inquiry*, 54 (2011), 478–493; Frederick Neuhouser, *Rousseau's Theodicy of Self-Love: Evil, Rationality, and the Drive for Recognition* (Oxford, 2008); István Hont, *Politics in Commercial Society*, ed. Béla Kapossy and Michael Sonenscher (Cambridge, MA, 2015); Michael Sonenscher, *Jean-Jacques Rousseau: The Division of Labour, the Politics of the Imagination and the Concept of Federal Government* (Leiden, 2020).

and trade.[48] Indeed, the central question for these thinkers was whether and how European states could be reformed so that the distinctively modern achievements – e.g. freedom of thought, security in property and economic prosperity – could not only be solidified and expanded but also be combined with the classical republican values of political agency and social cohesion, on the one hand, and the Christian one of peace, on the other.[49] The concerns and ideas characteristic of these authors cannot thus be understood in terms of the supposed opposition between 'monarchism' and 'republicanism', or indeed, monarchical (civil) versus republican (political) liberty. This intellectual movement was intentionally syncretic, including writers with a republican as well as monarchical background.[50] Most thinkers also highlighted the role of modern patriotism in both animating as well as sustaining these reforms. Some of these authors also emphatically underlined the compatibility of patriotism with love of mankind.

Natural Sociability and Cosmopolitan Humanity

My second central thesis concerns the distinctive arguments with which Herder sought to prove the feasibility of his desired political model. Although he rejected Rousseau's specific brand of republicanism, Herder took Rousseau's criticisms of modern society and morality very seriously; his efforts were directed at searching for ways in which patriotism could be revived in a new form in a modern society. The problem was that Rousseau's history of mankind seemed to rule out the possibility of reforming modern societies altogether.

Indeed, in many ways Rousseau helped to revive a long-standing debate on sociability. At the centre of this debate were the constitutive features of human nature or more specifically, the foundations of social order and

---

[48] David Hume, 'Of Civil Liberty', in *Essays Moral, Political, and Literary*, ed. Eugene Miller (Indianapolis, 1985), 88, 92–94; François Marie Arouet de Voltaire, *Le siècle de Louis XIV* (Berlin, 1751), passim. For a broader discussion, see J. G. A. Pocock, *Barbarism and Religion*, 6 vols. (I = *Narratives of Civil Government*) (Cambridge, 1999–2015) and Hont, *Jealousy of Trade*, 8–11; ch. 2.

[49] Cf. Kapossy, *Iselin contra Rousseau*; McDaniel, *Adam Ferguson in the Scottish Enlightenment.*; Sonenscher, *Before the Deluge*; see also Sonenscher, *Sans-Culottes*, 28 and *passim*.

[50] For a good introduction into the topics of republicanism and monarchism in this period, see Hans Blom, John Christian Laursen, and Luisa Simonutti (eds.), *Monarchisms in the Age of Enlightenment: Liberty, Patriotism, and the Common Good* (Toronto, 2007); see also Eva Piirimäe, 'Monarchisms, Republicanisms and Enlightenments', *History of European Ideas*, 36:1 (2010), 125–129.

morality.[51] Put crudely, the question was whether social order could be seen to rest on humans' sociable nature or whether it was based on the second-order effects of humans' fundamentally egoistic dispositions such as the desire for utility or honour (or both). Thinkers' ideas about the possibilities for reforms and the likelihood of their success depended on these more fundamental views. The debate originated in the late sixteenth century and early seventeenth century, when several philosophers voiced Epicurean and sceptical views on the foundations of morality, which in turn elicited various kinds of responses. These responses were often (albeit not exclusively) couched in the form of natural law, whilst also drawing inspiration from various kinds of ancient philosophy,[52] theological thought and/or Biblical history.[53] In the late seventeenth century, a number of authors further exacerbated the Epicurean, Augustinian and sceptical challenge by suggesting that individualism and self-interested behaviour was the defining feature of commercial modernity, yet one that was also the dominant feature of human nature itself.[54] In the first half of the eighteenth century, the Third Earl of Shaftesbury and Francis Hutcheson responded critically to this kind of 'selfish philosophy', including much of the earlier individualist natural law tradition, initiating a wave of thinking about natural human sociability, aesthetic and moral sentiments – all described as distinctively non-selfish by Shaftesbury and Hutcheson. In these theories, love of country was an important example of 'natural' (as opposed to artificial or secondary) human sociability, whilst also representing a norm and a virtue to be embraced by everyone in well-ordered societies, ancient or modern.[55] Further, these ideas were often

---

[51] For a recent survey on the state of art of research on sociability, see Eva Piirimäe and Alexander Schmidt, 'Between Morality and Anthropology: Sociability in Enlightenment Thought', *History of European Ideas*, 41:5 (2015), 571–588.

[52] For discussion, see, e.g., Haakonssen, *Natural Law and Moral Philosophy: From Grotius to the Scottish Enlightenment* (Cambridge, 1996); Richard Tuck, *The Rights of War and Peace: Political Thought and the International Order from Grotius to Kant* (Oxford, 1999); Daniel Carey, *Locke, Shaftesbury, and Hutcheson: Contesting Diversity in the Enlightenment and Beyond* (Cambridge, 2009).

[53] See John Robertson, 'Sacred History and Political Thought: Neapolitan Responses to the Problem of Sociability after Hobbes', *The Historical Journal*, 56:1 (2013), 1–29 and John Robertson, 'Sociability in Sacred Historical Perspective, 1650–1800', in *Markets, Morals, Politics: Jealousy of Trade and the History of Political Thought*, ed. Béla Kapossy, Isaac Nakhimovsky, Sophus A. Reinert, Richard Whatmore (Cambridge, MA, 2018), 53–81.

[54] See, e.g, Nannerl O. Keohane, *Philosophy and the State in France: The Renaissance to the Enlightenment* (Princeton, 1980) and Ed J. Hundert, *The Enlightenment Fable: Bernard Mandeville and the Discovery of Society* (Cambridge, 1994). On the centrality of the question of 'luxury' in early eighteenth-century moral and political debates, see Hont, 'The Early Enlightenment Debate'.

[55] See Eva Piirimäe, 'Dying for the Fatherland: Thomas Abbt's Theory of Aesthetic Patriotism', *History of European Ideas*, 35:2 (2009), 194–208; Béla Kapossy, 'The Sociable Patriot: Isaak Iselin's Protestant Reading of Jean-Jacques Rousseau', *History of European Ideas*, 27:2 (2001), 153–170.

combined with attempts to distinguish true, sociable, patriotism from its corrupt alternatives, first of all, narrow-minded egoistic and bellicose patriotism.[56]

This book will argue that in responding to Rousseau's challenge in the *Second Discourse*, Herder gave a new direction to this debate. In particular, he drew on and himself substantially contributed to the new mid-eighteenth-century work on human psychology, sensibility and physiology. Engaging particularly with Wolfgang Proß's in-depth commentaries on Herder's works,[57] as well as Michael Sonenscher's discussion of mid-eighteenth-century 'historical speculation' about the origins of culture,[58] I trace how Herder's political interests led him to develop and refine his account of human natural sociability. As a young philosopher, Herder already developed a complex philosophical anthropology, combining an epistemologically grounded theory of human adaptation to different geographical and environmental conditions with elements of a fundamentally Stoic-inspired understanding of self-preservation. He came up with a thesis that human societies are formed through language and poetry specifically. The distinctive way of thought, mores (*Sitten*) and laws of a people, he argued, are first articulated in communal singing, a form of original creativity uniting various kinds of human cognitive endeavours (religion, philosophy, arts and sciences) that later came to be separated. In his later years, he also put forward a sophisticated argument for the natural foundations of morality, revisiting the early modern natural law tradition. Indeed, I will argue that the Stoic and early modern traditions of natural law were a considerable source of inspiration for Herder. Herder rejected the more severely individualist and contractarian arguments in this tradition and emphasised the Stoic strands in Grotius and early modern natural law tradition in general.

It is important to see that this emphasis on natural sociability enabled Herder to retain a certain glimmer of hope about the future of Europe even in the most pessimistic period of his life. By the end of the 1760s, Herder was

---

[56] For an example of a theory of sociable patriotism with cosmopolitan overtones, see Isaak Iselin, *Philosophische und Patriotische Träume eines Menschenfreundes* (Freiburg, 1755; Zurich, 1758) and Isaak Iselin, 'Anrede an die im Jahr 1764 zu Schinznach versammelt gewesene Helvetische Gesellschaft', in Isaak Iselin, *Vermischte Schriften* (2 vols., Zurich, 1770), II. Not all thinkers, of course, were convinced that this kind of neat separation was possible, given that many also began to view love of country as an example of expanded self-love, rather than as an example of purely other-regarding virtue. Most prominently, both David Hume and Adam Smith disputed the possibility of such a separation, while acknowledging the largely beneficial effects of a tempered version of patriotism. On Hume's analysis of patriotism, see Annie Stilz, 'Hume, Modern Patriotism, and Commercial Society', *History of European Ideas*, 29:1 (2003), 15–32; on Smith's ideas on this subject, see Hont, *Jealousy of Trade*, 111–112.

[57] See the *HWP* edition.   [58] Sonenscher, *Sans-Culottes*, 164–195.

growing more critical of contemporary European states. Drawing on a number of contemporary philosophical histories of early cultures, Herder contrasted the 'common sense' and mores that were characteristic of savage/ barbarous cultures as well as the sociable kind of civic patriotism of the ancients with the apathy of the subjects of modern states that, mainly for this reason, were veering towards despotism, an idea he borrowed from Adam Ferguson's *Essay on the History of Civil Society* (1767). However, his own (at this stage, rather undeveloped) solution was an alternative *cosmopolitan* view of Europe's exceptional destiny to become a fraternal community of peoples. In the early 1770s, he also came to emphasise the role of Christianity in transforming the 'natural' pattern of European history. Putting forward a sophisticated account of the moral psychology of Christian virtue, Herder came to associate Christianity with a new kind of love of mankind and universalism, musing about its so far unused (and misused) potential for substantially transforming human and inter-group relationships.

Furthermore, Herder's criticisms of modern states did not amount to a rejection of all kinds of commerce. As Sonenscher has shown, some of the mid-eighteenth-century authors defending (like Herder) a rather optimistic idea of human 'perfectibility' also put forward an optimistic account of modern commerce and (moderate) luxury. Whilst rejecting competitive trade and colonial imperialism, they hoped to use the distinctively modern invention of public credit to achieve domestic prosperity and reduce greater inequality, thereby making foreign trade voluntary and reciprocal.[59] This book will argue that these tendencies were reflected in Herder's thinking. Herder generally regarded commerce as a vehicle of communication and exchange between individuals and peoples. During the 1760s he welcomed the ideas of Accarias de Sérionne on the reciprocity of trade, whilst his *Ideas* was a plea for commerce as a source of European 'universal spirit' and common identity as well as a potential vehicle for empowering the 'third estate' in cities to overturn or fundamentally transform the 'state-machines' originating in Carolingian times. In the final decade of his life, he turned to Isaac de Pinto's ideas of public credit as a way of promoting prosperity whilst he also celebrated the reciprocity of trade as an exchange of surpluses at home for those created abroad.[60] To Herder this kind of benign trade was fully compatible with the aspiration of international peace.

---

[59] Ibid., 46.
[60] Johann Gottfried Herder, 'Letters for the Advancement of Humanity (1793–1797) – Tenth Collection', in *PW*, 380–424 (407).

The Uses of History

Thirdly, this study also sheds light on Herder's distinctive understanding of the use of historical knowledge for modern reformers. In the 1770s, Herder developed a theologically framed but idiosyncratic understanding of the history of mankind as a form of 'divine revelation' and gradual ethical formation (*Bildung*) of humanity. As I will try to show, this account was still in many ways compatible with his earlier naturalistic approach. In the 1780s, Herder explicitly came to embed his philosophy of history of mankind in a broader naturalistic framework, viewing human history as part of a more encompassing 'natural process' of the unfolding of divine forces in nature. At the same time, Herder consistently also conceived of himself as a patriotic reformer and insisted that it was a reformer's duty to understand the ways in which various kinds of complex historical processes – cultural, political, economic – influenced the formation and development of national ways of thought and dispositions, which in turn was essential for devising appropriate reforms. He thus simultaneously offered nuanced genealogies of the modern state and politics, on the one hand, and different national characters, on the other.

A substantial part of this study will be devoted to specifying these genealogies. As is well-known, 'national characters' were widely debated in the European republic of letters in the seventeenth and eighteenth centuries.[61] However, as I will argue, there were three particularly prominent sources of inspiration for Herder in his attempts to carve out the historical development of 'national' ways of thought in Europe – Montesquieu, the Scottish Enlightenment, and German discussions on imperial history, more specifically, the historical work of the German historian and lawyer Justus Möser. Montesquieu's *Spirit of the Laws* transformed the discussions on national character by offering several highly significant insights into the different historical trajectories that modern European states had traversed. This further helped to create new awareness of the importance of economic

---

[61] For examples of the widespread use of the category of 'national character' in the eighteenth century, see Robert B. Louden, *The World We Want: How and Why the Ideals of the Enlightenment Still Elude Us* (Oxford, 2007), ch. 4; see also Robert B. Louden, *Kant's Human Being: Essays on His Theory of Human Nature* (Oxford, 2011), ch. 12 and Silvia Sebastiani, 'National Characters and Race: A Scottish Enlightenment Debate', in *Character, Self, and Sociability in the Scottish Enlightenment*, ed. Thomas Ahnert and Susan Manning (New York, 2011), 187–205. Wolfgang Proß has also recently uncovered remarkable parallels between John Barclay's influential *Icon animorum* (1611) and Herder's *This Too a Philosophy*, Wolfgang Proß, '"Diversus cum diversis": John Barclays *Icon animorum* (1614) und Herders *Auch eine Philosophie der Geschichte*', in *Herder on Empathy*, 119–157.

and political history in understanding the prospects for political reform in modern states. Drawing on Montesquieu's framework, but rarely agreeing with Montesquieu's specific historical accounts, the Scottish Enlightenment thinkers provided their own visions of the origins and moral psychological foundations of modern liberty. Similarly, German imperial lawyers and historians pondered the transformations of ancient German freedom after the Germanic conquest of Roman territories and in the Holy Roman Empire.

Although Herder's interest in these kinds of history has previously been registered, there is still considerable ambiguity regarding his precise relationships to these thinkers and traditions. As this book will show, over the course of his life, Herder himself proposed plans for aesthetic, moral and political reforms for various kinds of states. Russia's particular status as an empire and 'half-savage' nation greatly intrigued him in his early years; here he also voiced highly critical views about Catherine II's attempts to create a Montesquieuian monarchy in Russia. Based in the semi-autonomous commercial city of Riga, Herder was particularly interested in Riga's situation in the Russian Empire, and studied new work on the contemporary 'science of commerce'. In the 1770s, Herder seriously engaged with the possibility of regenerating the German national spirit in the Holy Roman Empire. It was also largely in response to Montesquieu's ideas on ancient German freedom that a heated debate was launched in Germany on the concept of German 'national spirit' during the Seven Years' War.[62] Herder followed this debate and provided a distinctive contribution to it by offering a series of highly original reflections on German political, economic and cultural history. In the 1780s, he continued to ponder the themes of German and European history, whilst his specific views underwent several substantial changes.

In the 1770s, Herder initially rejected Montesquieu's account of ancient German freedom and adopted that of Justus Möser, also further developing the latter's ideas about the genesis of what he called European 'state-machines'. At the same time, Herder sought to combine these ideas with the Scottish Enlightenment view that modern 'civilised monarchies' had made an important step towards guaranteeing the rule of law, and engaged closely with David Hume's, William Robertson's and John Millar's histories of modern liberty. I argue that Herder's disparaging remarks on his contemporary philosophers'

---

[62] Nicolas Vazsonyi, 'Montesquieu, Friedrich Carl von Moser and the National Spirit Debate in Germany, 1765–1767', *German Studies Review*, 22:2 (1999), 225–246; Conrad Wiedemann, 'The Germans' Concern about Their National Identity in the Pre-Romantic Era: An Answer to Montesquieu?', in *Concepts of National Identity: An Interdisciplinary Dialogue*, ed. Peter Boerner (Baden-Baden, 1986), 141–152.

ideas in his *This Too a Philosophy* should not be read – as they standardly have been read – as a fundamental rejection of their historical accounts. Although highlighting certain blindspots of these 'Enlightened narratives' (J. G. A. Pocock), most importantly in regard to what he saw as their overly optimistic views on modern virtue and freedom, Herder substantially drew on their ideas in a number of writings. However, he also again engaged seriously with an idiosyncratic Scottish Enlightenment thinker whose assessments of modern politics he endorsed and developed in particular – Adam Ferguson. In the 1770s, Herder was actively pondering the potential for reforms in the Holy Roman Empire, lamenting its backwardness but also searching for a distinctive solution to its problems.

In his controversy with Immanuel Kant on universal history in the 1780s, Herder substantially revised his account of ancient German freedom and the actual foundations of modern liberty. Drawing on Robertson (and via Robertson, Adam Smith), he highlighted the pivotal role of commercial cities in European history. He argued that the basic principles of ancient German freedom were further developed in self-governing Hanseatic cities, and celebrated the latter and the Hanseatic League in general as the cradles of European freedom, prosperity and 'universal spirit'. This allowed Herder to embed his qualified endorsement of the positive aspects of modern civilised monarchies in a sophisticated historical account that emphasised the value of self-government. For Herder, this account showed that modern liberty originally presupposed a degree of self-government and political participation, and thus in all likelihood still did so.

Self-Determination and Purified Patriotism

Fourthly, the study carves out the ways in which Herder described a desirable form of modern patriotism or national spirit whilst also specifying the fundamental values underlying his political model. As already indicated, Herder had no doubt that political institutions mattered but even more important was the 'spirit' that animated them. Cultivating the right 'spirit' could thus also be seen as a first step towards achieving better institutions. I argue that for Herder, it was vital to revive the original unity of religion, philosophy and the arts and sciences. He insisted that the vocation of 'humanitarian' professions – pastors, poets, philosophers (to name just the three most important ones) – was ultimately one and the same. All of them were to provide moral training to humanity so as to improve the quality of moral, social and political life, indeed provide for social and political cohesion. This is not to claim that Herder sought to 'revive' certain historical forms of art or politics. Herder quite quickly came to a conclusion that modern forms of art and self-understanding were fundamentally intertextual and reflective – modern humans, for Herder, had a unique chance to develop something like a historical self-awareness. Human self-determination (*Selbstbestimmung*) for Herder was impossible without this kind of awareness; yet it also entailed an active element of self-formation.

As I seek to show, Herder originally developed his understanding of human 'freedom in bondage' by engaging with the ancient Stoics, Luther and Spinoza but later consciously placed this view in opposition to the Kantian understanding of self-determination. Individual human self-determination for Herder consisted in a 'life according to nature', and a knowing embrace of 'natural law'. The self-determination of peoples entailed 'purified patriotism' based on a recognition of human partiality and fallibility, and a conscious effort to guard against the rise of 'national delusions', particularly those based on the idea of the grandeur of one's political community. The task for moderns specifically was to reconnect with their nation's particular historical linguistic and cultural heritage through self-critical and intertextual forms of national art and public discussion. Herder also suggested that modern humans would need to cultivate a form of 'self-contained national pride' regarding the progress of *Humanität* in their respective countries, one that would motivate them to creatively develop and 'humanise' their various institutions and practices, including the modern state. All these individual and collective kinds of self-determination were encapsulated in Herder's complex conception of modern patriotism.

Herder's theory of purified patriotism had profound implications for political legitimacy. This did not mean, however, that he advocated the revival of some distinct kinds of small-scale human communities. Particularly in current Kant studies, there is still a widespread perception of Herder as primarily a defender of 'the communities of the old *Reich*' or indeed, the oldest and most primitive forms of life.[63] The same view is characteristic of both broader textbook accounts as well as some

---

[63] Reidar Maliks, *Kant's Politics in Context* (Oxford, 2014), 29–32; Allen W. Wood, 'General Introduction', in Immanuel Kant, *Practical Philosophy*, ed. and trans. Mary J. Gregor (Cambridge, 1996), xiii–xxxiii (xxi). Compare, however, Wood's later, more nuanced assessment in Allen W. Wood, 'Herder and Kant on History: Their Enlightenment Faith', in *Metaphysics and the Good: Themes from the Philosophy of Robert Merrihew Adams*, ed. Samuel Newlands and Larry M. Jorgensen (Oxford, 2009), 313–342.

theoretically sophisticated discussions of the origins of nationalism.[64] This book qualifies these views. Herder not only sought to demonstrate the value of different forms of life but also provided a penetrating commentary on modern politics and a positive vision for modern European nations. During the French Revolution, he strongly sympathised with the attempt of the French nation to give itself a 'living constitution'. He also whole-heartedly supported republican principles and advocated a distinctive form of republican or constitutional patriotism as an essential element of his broader conception of purified patriotism. His criticisms were directed at what he saw as different forms of abstract idealism – the Jacobin ideal of direct democracy and Kant's constitutionalist republicanism for 'a nation of devils'. He was also worried that both these conceptions of republican-ism harboured a potential for imperialist misuse.

National self-government became an important value for Herder. By drawing attention to the need for laws to be grounded in ethics, and associating ethics with language and culture, Herder made a clear case against the legitimacy of external intervention as well as colonial and imperial rule. He also powerfully raised the issue of the relationship between states and nations (peoples). Whilst states were often habitually identified with nations, Herder both problematised as well as strengthened this linkage. By affirming the need for political participation and national self-government, he called for the reorganisation of current empires. As we will see, he made a highly original prediction that the modern state-machines would soon collapse thanks to the emancipatory potential of commerce. His emphasis on the value of national self-government could thus also be interpreted as encouragement for a substantial redrawing of state borders in Europe. At the same time, he believed in the responsibility of cultural elites in reforming 'their' current states 'from below'. It was their duty to strive to propose their polity a new 'living constitution'. He also valued federal unions both at the subnational and international level. Herder's historical sympathies lay with the federated Hebrew tribes, the Greek commercial republics (particularly Athens), pre-Christian 'German' peoples and the medieval Hanseatic cities. He linked Christian love of humanity with the ideal of the brotherhood of peoples, and identified the rise of a modern European 'public' in European history, presenting the Hanseatic League as a possible model for a future 'European League'. During the French Revolution and after, he consistently emphasised the need for sentimental moral education in order to further strengthen the

---

[64] See, e.g., Bernard Yack, *Nationalism and the Moral Psychology of Community* (Chicago, 2012), 41.

already existing broader humanitarian alliance of individuals as well as peoples. The ideals of communal and national 'self-government' and 'friendship of peoples' emerged in tandem in his thought. Both these ideals came to resonate with a variety of thinkers in the nineteenth century.

Sketch of Herder's Life

Over the course of his life, Herder became more familiar with a variety of urban contexts in three different political communities – the small town of Mohrungen and the city of Königsberg in East Prussia, the city of Riga in the province of Livland[65] in the Russian Empire, and the town of Bückeburg in the County of Schaumburg-Lippe and the city of Weimar in the Duchy of Saxe-Weimar (both parts of the Holy Roman Empire).[66] Born and raised in East Prussia, Herder received his higher education at the University of Königsberg (1762–1764). Initially a student of medicine, he soon understood that theology was a more suitable subject for him. He also extensively studied philosophy and was mentored by Immanuel Kant. He befriended Kant's friend Johann Georg Hamann, another highly original philosopher. In 1764 he moved to the Baltic seaport and former Hanseatic city of Riga, where he became an assistant teacher (*Kollaborator*) at the Cathedral school. In 1767 he also obtained the post of adjunct pastor at the *Jesuskirche* and *Gertrudkirche*. At that time Riga was the most important city and capital of Livland, one of the two Baltic provinces that Russia had acquired from Sweden in the Great Northern War, which was formally ended with the Peace of Nystad in 1721. The German-speaking nobilities (*Ritterschaften*) and the self-governing cities of the provinces of Livland and Estland had capitulated to Peter the First in 1710 on the condition that their financial system, existing customs border, Lutheran religion, administrative use of the German language, established legal order and institutions of self-government would be preserved. Although Riga thus functioned as a semi-self-governing city during

---

[65] I am following contemporary Baltic historians who opt for using the German names 'Livland' (in the eighteenth century, *Liefland*) and 'Estland' (*Ehstland*) in English, too, to clearly distinguish these two Baltic provinces of Russia (from the eighteenth to early twentieth century) from the medieval and early modern 'Livonia' (*Livland*) that encompassed much of present-day Estonia and Latvia. The province of Livland under Russia encompassed the southern part (roughly a half) of current Estonia and the bulk of the territory of current Latvia. The Duchy of Courland and Semigallia in present-day south-western Latvia was incorporated into the Polish-Lithuanian commonwealth in 1726; it was annexed by the Russian Empire during the Third Partition of Poland in 1795 (then becoming Russia's third Baltic province).

[66] For the most recent detailed biographical overview, see Hans-Peter Nowitzki, 'Biographie', in *Herder Handbuch*, 23–38. See also Robert Thomas Clark, *Herder: His Life and Thought* (Berkeley and Los Angeles, 1955) and Haym, *Herder*.

Herder's time there, there were widespread expectations (and fears) of broader reforms in Riga in this period. Catherine II had ascended to the Russian throne in 1762, and initially pursued an ambitious reform agenda throughout the Russian Empire. Herder welcomed her reform initiative (but not her specific plans), and mused about becoming one of her advisors. Much of his political thought in his early years thus revolved around the prospects of reforming Riga, Livland, and, indeed, Russia in general. He befriended a number of influential representatives of the mercantile patriciate elite in Riga, and was well-informed about, and sympathetic to, their ideas about civic life in and the future prospects of Riga, including their plans for fostering Russia's trade and economic power. Throughout his life, Herder compared the burgher 'common spirit' in the Hanseatic cities with Athenian patriotism.

In 1769 Herder left Riga to accompany Gustav Berens, a member of the influential patriciate and merchant family Berens, on his journey to France and the Netherlands. Herder initially intended to return to Riga and long continued to toy with the idea of becoming a reformer of Livland and/or Russia. During his travels and sojourns in cities like Nantes, Paris, Leiden, Antwerp, Hamburg, Darmstadt and Strasbourg, however, Herder became ever more interested in the moral psychological foundations of the states through which he travelled. He reflected about the ways in which the history of the Holy Roman Empire was different from that of France, and critically commented on the mores and form of government of Holland or Prussia. He never visited Great Britain, but throughout his life, voiced critical comments about its commercial policies. At the end of the 1760s, he grew increasingly pessimistic about the situation of European states, whilst delving ever deeper into the history of the German language and literature. In 1770 he arrived in Strasbourg to undergo an eye operation. There he met and befriended Johann Wolfgang Goethe, with whom he embarked on investigations into the German national character as expressed in folk songs, literature and art, whilst also entering into the debate about the German national spirit and pondering the possibilities of reform in the German states.

From 1771 to 1776 Herder lived in the town of Bückeburg, where Count Friedrich Wilhelm Ernst zu Schaumburg-Lippe offered him the position of Counsellor of the Consistory and Court Chaplain. Impressed by Herder's review of Thomas Abbt's writings after his early and unexpected death, the count invited Herder to succeed Abbt in this office. However, whilst Abbt had become close friends with the count, Herder never did so. He despised the ways in which the imperial count sought to remilitarise society and build a mini-Prussia in his small state; the count's enlightened views of foreign policy (e.g. his rejection of aggressive wars) failed to redeem him in Herder's eyes.[67] Whilst the extent of Herder's supposed 'religious turn' in Bückeburg has remained debatable, his views on German political life as well as modern European politics in general were remarkably critical in this period. During his stay in Bückeburg, he delved into different theological, epistemological and moral problems whilst taking a sustained interest in the history of various kinds of poetry. He also thoroughly studied the history of the Holy Roman Empire, taking particular interest in the transformations of German mores and laws in European history.

In 1776 Goethe procured an invitation to Herder from the Grand Duke of Karl August of Saxe-Weimar-Eisenach (duke from 1775 to 1828) to take up the position of general superintendent of schools and chief pastor of the parish church in Weimar. The grand duke was an enlightened ruler who sought to foster the arts and sciences by becoming a patron of Goethe, Herder and Schiller and generously supporting the University of Jena; indeed, he also developed a close friendship with Goethe. Herder soon became closely involved in reforming the school system in Saxe-Weimar; he also developed further his idea of the responsibilities of a modern preacher. By the late 1770s, Herder was wavering between a somewhat moderated pessimism and some hopefulness regarding the future of 'Germany'. He accepted the invitation of Margrave Karl Friedrich of Baden, one of the leading members of the German League of Princes (*Fürstenbund*) formed in 1785 under the leadership of Frederick Second the Great of Prussia, to draft what he called 'The Idea for the First Patriotic Institute for Germany's Public Spirit' (*Idee zum ersten patriotischen Institut für den Allgemeingeist Deutschlands*). Such an institute, according to Herder, was supposed to serve as a platform for a broader national and cultural consolidation of the Holy Roman Empire. In 1788–1789, Herder visited Italy.

Herder's republican sympathies became evident already before the French Revolution, when he responded highly critically to Kant's political ideas as expressed in *Ideas for a Philosophy of Humanity* (1784–1791). Herder was strongly supportive of the French Revolution during its early stages and passionately criticised the Austro-Prussian interventionism of the early 1790s. This created tensions with his superior, Karl August

---

[67] On Count Schaumburg-Lippe, see C. E. White, 'Scharnhorst's Mentor: Count Wilhelm zu Schaumburg-Lippe and the Origins of the Modern National Army', *War in History*, 24:3 (2017), 258–285.

Grand Duke of Saxe-Weimar, who was an ally of Prussia and participated in the military intervention, as well as with Goethe who supported Karl August and did not share Herder's enthusiasm about the French Revolution. Despite his disappointment in Jacobin rule as well as the ensuing French republican imperialism, Herder remained a supporter of the revolution. At the same time, however, he became increasingly concerned about the future of Germany and German culture in general during the revolutionary and Coalition wars. He died in Weimar in year 1803 at the age of fifty-nine.

Chapter Outline

Let us conclude this introduction with a brief overview of the structure of the book. In general, the book follows a chronological approach. Each chapter reconstructs a major work or a set of chronologically contiguous and thematically interconnected works by Herder in response to another important thinker or an already ongoing debate. In so doing, I attempt to weave into my narrative the views of both his major adversaries and theoretical allies. In terms of specific themes, I follow Herder's own focus, which was influenced by ongoing pan-European debates, on the one hand, and his own life (mainly, his relocations in space and shifts in identity), on the other. I thus also discuss different central themes and political contexts in the order in which they became prominent for Herder.

The chapters in this book can be divided into three clusters. Chapters 1, 2 and 3 discuss Herder's ideas during his Riga period (1764–1769). Here, Herder's main intellectual concerns were greatly influenced by the theoretical visions of Rousseau and Montesquieu and pan-European debates about these visions. The political context he sought to influence, at the same time, was the Russian Empire and, more specifically, the city of Riga in the province of Livland, whilst he also pondered the possibility of German patriotism. Chapters 4, 5 and 6 examine Herder's writings in the 1770s, including those written during his travels in Europe, during his Bückeburg years (1771–1776), and in his early Weimar years. In this period, Herder's political thought developed in particularly close dialogue with the Scottish Enlightenment authors, on the one hand, and the German authors debating the German 'national spirit', on the other. It was also in this period that he delved into theological issues as well as engaged with discussions about the history of poetry. Herder's political focus in these years was on the historical prospects of the Holy Roman Empire and Europe as a whole. Chapters 7 and 8 discuss Herder's major writings in the 1780s and 1790s. Here, his central theoretical adversary was his former academic mentor Immanuel Kant, whilst his political focus remained the same. As Chapter 7 reveals, Herder challenged Kant's account of the origin of modern liberty and his ideas on the prospects of peace in Europe before the outbreak of the French Revolution. In Chapter 8 we see that both Herder and Kant refined and modified their views in response to the French Revolution, whilst their views generally continued to evolve in different directions.

CHAPTER I

Republics, Monarchies and the Philosophy of Human Society

In 1761, in a review article in the *Letters on the Newest Literature* (*Briefe, die neueste Literatur betreffend*), the Berlin philosopher and literary critic Moses Mendelssohn reflected on the situation of political philosophy in Germany:

> Philosophy is at home in Germany . . . . Nor do we lack systems of political science . . . . It is just that our political philosophy still retains an element of timidity, which it will naturally only lay aside in a free state . . . . We must admit, in all fairness, that several Swiss writers were among the first Germans to begin looking at people in the context of a wider political society from a truly philosophical viewpoint.[1]

This is a striking homage to Swiss republican authors by one of the leading lights in the Prussian monarchy during the second half of the eighteenth century. Yet, that same year, Mendelssohn gladly welcomed the young Prussian philosopher Thomas Abbt's *On Dying for the Fatherland* (*Vom Tode für das Vaterland*) (1761) as a work that followed the example set by the Swiss:

> You read the writings of the Swiss with delight? You like the patriotic tone of their essays, one that gives fire, audacity and strength to their thoughts? Then you will be even more pleased by the following work which has similar merits and is born in our fatherland. It deals with dying for the fatherland . . ., a subject that touches you very closely, and certainly is worthy of the pen of a patriot who is at the same time a philosopher [*Weltweiser*].[2]

---

[1] Moses Mendelssohn [Anon.], 'Ueber Iselin, I.: *Philosophische und politische Versuche*. Zurich: Orell 1760: Rezension', *Briefe, die neueste Literatur betreffend* (1760), Literaturbriefe 138, 361–373 (361). (I am adopting the translation of John Zammito of this paragraph in *Kant, Herder*, 33. The rest of the translations from German are mine, if not otherwise indicated.) The works referred to by Mendelssohn were Isaak Iselin's *Philosophical and Patriotic Dreams of a Friend of Mankind* (*Filosofische* [*sic*] *und Patriotische Träume eines Menschenfreundes*) (Freiburg, 1755) and Johann Georg Zimmermann's *On National Pride* (*Von dem Nationalstolze*) (Zurich, 1758).

[2] Moses Mendelssohn, 'Über *Vom Tode für das Vaterland*,' *Briefe, die neueste Literatur betreffend* (1760), Literaturbrief 181, 39–58 (39).

As Moses Mendelssohn noted, the German and Swiss political philosophies were developing in close dialogue with each other in the late 1750s and early 1760s. Their new approach was largely inspired by Montesquieu's *The Spirit of the Laws* (1748) along with, of course, the major 'Swiss thinker'[3] whose ideas were catalytic for further debates: Jean-Jacques Rousseau.[4] As seen in the Introduction, it was not just the merits of republican and monarchical forms of government that were being debated, but more fundamentally, the moral psychological principles and values of modern society, on the one hand, and the possible direction of reforms in modern states, on the other.[5] With the onset of the Seven Years' War, these debates also acquired a very real practical dimension. Thomas Abbt's *On Dying for the Fatherland* is a clear example of a work that was not only embedded in these philosophical discussions but also sought to encourage patriotic fighting in the ongoing war.

From 1762 to 1764 Herder was a student in Königsberg under the close tutorship of Immanuel Kant, who was greatly impressed by Rousseau's ideas.[6] As John Zammito has argued, Herder's early work thus echoed much of Kant's Rousseauian criticism of science and scholars.[7] According to Zammito, in this period Herder also had somewhat exaggerated hopes that Kant would share his own philosophical agenda of turning philosophy into anthropology, whereas it was more likely that Herder derived his rather

---

[3] Geneva was not a member of the Swiss Federation, and hence it is strictly speaking not correct to qualify the Genevan citizen Rousseau as 'Swiss'.

[4] See Kapossy, *Iselin contra Rousseau*. For Rousseau's reception in Germany, see Herbert Jaumann (ed.), *Rousseau in Deutschland: Neue Beiträge zur Erforschung seiner Rezeption* (Berlin and New York, 1995); Goldenbaum, 'Einführung'; Schmidt, 'Scholarship, Morals and Government'.

[5] On these debates, see Simone Zurbuchen, 'Staatstheorie zwischen eidgenössischer Republik und preussischer Monarchie', *Das Achtzehnte Jahrhundert*, 26:2 (Deutsch-schweizerische Kulturtransfer im achtzehnten Jahrhundert) (2002), 145–162; Simone Zurbuchen, 'Theorizing Enlightened Absolutism: The Swiss Republican Origins of Prussian Monarchism', in *Monarchisms in the Age of Enlightenment*, 240–266; Kapossy, *Iselin contra Rousseau*; Eva Piirimäe, 'The Vicissitudes of Noble National Pride: Johann Georg von Zimmermann's (1728–1795) Theory of Patriotism', in *Human Nature as the Basis of Morality and Society in Early Modern Philosophy*, ed. Juhana Lemetti and Eva Piirimäe (*Acta Philosophica Fennica*, vol. 83) (Helsinki, 2007), 121–142.

[6] For Kant's engagement with Rousseau's criticism of the arts and sciences, see Alexander Schmidt, 'Sources of Evil or Seeds of the Good? Rousseau and Kant on Needs, the Arts and the Sciences', in *Engaging with Rousseau*, 33–55. On parallels between Kant's and Rousseau's moral and political philosophy more broadly, see also Nicholas J. H. Dent and Timothy O'Hagan, 'Rousseau on Amour-Propre', *Proceedings of the Aristotelian Society (Supplementary Volume)*, 72:1 (1998), 57–74; Frederick Neuhouser, *Rousseau's Theodicy of Self-Love: Evil, Rationality, and the Drive for Recognition* (Oxford, 2008).

[7] Zammito, *Kant, Herder*, 91–120, 137–177, 214; cf. Forster, 'Introduction', in *PW*, vii–xxxv (xi–xiv). Zammito approvingly quotes Haym's characterisation of Herder as the 'Kantian of the year 1765', see Haym, *Herder*, I, 15. For a detailed and critical reconstruction of the emergence of Haym's reading of Herder's early Kantianism, see John Christian Vivian, 'Der Einfluß David Humes auf den jungen Herder von 1762–1769: unter besonderer Berücksichtigung der Königsberger und Rigaer Jahre' (University of Jena, unpublished PhD thesis, 1993). I am grateful to Alexander Schmidt for bringing this work to my attention.

radical idea that 'the state must be reformed from below' from Kant himself.[8]

It is important to highlight, however, that during these years Herder viewed his mentor's moral and political ideas as representative of broader trends in recent political thought, placing Kant in what he saw as the 'Swiss' tradition of moral and political philosophy. According to Herder, Kant's *Beobachtungen über das Gefühl des Schönen und Erhabenen* (*Observations on the Feelings of the Beautiful and Sublime*) (1764) represented a 'Swiss writing style and Rousseauian way of thought [*Schweizerische Schreib- und Rousseauische Denkart*]', while Rousseau, in turn, was the Swiss thinkers' 'God over all the country [*überall ihr Gott*]'.[9] Furthermore, Kant did not actually offer much of a specific commentary on contemporary debates on politics, nor is there any clear understanding in current scholarship as to what Herder's own position was with regard to broader debates on modern patriotism. We know that Kant shared much of Rousseau's devastating criticism of modern society, but to what extent did Herder really share it? How did he come upon the idea that the state must be reformed from below? What kind of political vision did he put forward at this point? It is the aim of this chapter to find an answer to these questions.

Herder discussed these issues in two early essays that set the scene for his lifelong engagement with the topic of patriotism. The first of them, entitled 'How Philosophy Can Become More Universal and Useful for the Benefit of the People' (henceforth abbreviated as 'Benefit of the People'), was conceived as an answer to a question set by the Berne Patriotic Society's essay competition of 1763.[10] Herder started writing the essay as a student in Königsberg and, after arriving in Riga in November 1764, he continued to work on it there. On 23 April 1765 he reported to Johann Georg Hamann, his friend and mentor in Königsberg: 'For some time I have been absorbed in working out some of my favourite ideas on the subject of how to make philosophy more general and useful for the good of the people. I am

---

[8] Zammito, *Kant, Herder*, 174. Zammito also offers a brief discussion of Abbt's relevance for Herder, focusing mainly on Abbt's controversy with Mendelssohn on the vocation of man, ibid., 163–171.

[9] Herder to J. G. Hamann, Riga 21 May 1765, in *DA*, I, 45.

[10] The German original can be found in Johann Gottfried von Herder, '*Wie die Philosophie zum Besten des Volks allgemeiner und nützlicher werden kann*', in *FHA*, I, 101–134. I will be using Herder, 'How Philosophy Can Become More Universal and Useful for the Benefit of the People', in *PW*, 3–29. This title is given to the essay by Herder's German editor, Ulrich Gaier, and derives from Herder's letter of 23 April 1766 to his friend Johann Georg Hamann (see below). An earlier draft bore the title 'How Can the Truths of Philosophy Become More Universal and Useful for the Benefit of the People?'. This was the original question posed by the Patriotic Society of Berne, Ulrich Gaier, 'Kommentar', in *FHA*, I, 811–1334, 974; cf. Herder, 'Benefit of the People', 3 (footnote 2). For a detailed reconstruction of Herder's argument about philosophy in Herder's different drafts on this theme, see Marion Heinz, '1.2.2 *Philosophie zum Besten des Volks*', in *Herder Handbuch*, 58–71.

currently writing it up, and perhaps can send you more cues [*Winke*] of it soon.'[11] Herder never completed the essay and never mentioned it again to Hamann. The second essay, his voluntary laudation 'Do We Still Have the Public and Fatherland of the Ancients?', was printed in October 1765[12] and focuses directly on patriotism and moral and political philosophy. Although Herder presents himself as a patriot of Riga in this text, the essay is written in a more generic tone, addressing the challenges of modern politics in general. At the same time, as we shall see, his understanding of the role of commerce in modern politics also very much echoed the perspective of the mercantile patriciate in Riga.[13]

Reading Herder's two patriotic essays of 1765 side by side, one is struck by their contrasting tenor. 'Benefit of the People' is highly critical of modern society and politics, speaking in Rousseauian tone of the widespread 'malaise' (*Übel*) in modern times,[14] while 'Do We Still Have the Public' celebrates modern developments, including luxury and modern freedom. This chapter seeks to explain these differences. As I hope to show, these two essays represent a highly interesting intersection between two kinds of debates on Rousseau's moral and political thought in German-speaking countries. Herder entered the debate as a self-avowed 'Rousseauian', engaging with and responding to Rousseau's *First Discourse* and *Emile or On Education* (1762). However, he also soon became aware of economic and political debates that were originally shaped by Montesquieu's *Spirit of the Laws* (1748). In these debates, Rousseau had come to be seen as a defender of austere democratic republicanism modelled on early Greek societies and Sparta. This was not the Rousseau with whom Herder wished to associate himself.

The first section of the chapter discusses Herder's relationship to Rousseau in the 'Benefit of the People'. I argue that Herder here adopted Rousseau's critical attitude to modern society and politics in general, and to modern philosophers in particular, seeking to build on Rousseau's ideas to develop his own political vision. He believed that Rousseau simply had not

---

[11] Herder to J. G. Hamann, Riga, 23 April/4 May 1765, in *DA*, I, 41. Hamann's answer to Herder is quoted in Gaier, 'Kommentar', 969.

[12] Herder, 'Do We Still Have the Public', in *HEW*, 53–64. For the German original, see Herder, 'Haben wir noch jetzt das Publikum und Vaterland der Alten? Eine Abhandlung zur Feier der Beziehung des neuen Gerichtshauses [1765]', in *FHA*, I, 40–56. This speech is the only one of Herder's early works that he published under his own name. See Bernhard Ludwig Suphan, 'Einleitung', in *SWS*, I, xvii; cf. Haym, *Herder*, I, 126.

[13] For Herder's experiences in Riga, see Haym, *Herder* I, 87–130. and Hans Graubner, 'Spätaufklärer im aufgeklärten Riga: Hamann und Herder', *Zeitschrift für Ostforschung*, 35 (1994), 517–533.

[14] Herder, 'Benefit of the People', 18.

yet fully teased out the implications of his moral philosophy for an ethic of citizenship in a modern society. Here, Herder still aligned himself with Kant in hoping that Rousseau might provide guidance for reforming the current societies from below and sought to combine Rousseau's ideas with those of Thomas Abbt. In fact, Herder's precise diagnosis of the evils of modern society already diverged in essential respects from Rousseau, despite his obvious borrowings in terms of style and argument from the latter.[15] While Rousseau emphasised the fundamental antagonism of modern societies, Herder was worried about modern individualism and 'inaction'.

The second section of the chapter discusses 'Do We Still Have the Public'. This essay was conspicuously silent about Rousseau. In it, Herder turned the polemics against a distinct group of Swiss authors whom he perceived to be advocating austere democratic models of republicanism.[16] Some of these thinkers had explicitly drawn on Rousseau. Yet this model was evidently not feasible in modern monarchies and in Herder's view was unsuited to modern conditions in general. Herder gradually realised that this was also the reason why some Swiss authors rejected the idea that patriotism could exist and be justified in modern monarchies, and advocated austere democratic republicanism for their native republics in Switzerland. As I seek to show, Herder properly began to distance himself from Rousseau when he started to follow the debates about modern commerce more closely, engaging more substantially with the ideas of Thomas Abbt, on the one hand, and those of David Hume and Johann Georg Hamann, on the other. This rejection of austere democratic republicanism and embracing of commerce and moderate luxury tallied very well with the ideas of the local elites in Riga, whose views, as we shall see, had been represented in Hamann's youth treatise, *Supplement to Dangueil* [*sic*] (1756).[17] Indeed, as it will emerge, Herder's 'Do We Still Have the Public' is replete with implicit references to these three authors – Abbt, Hume and Hamann. All these authors sought to show that modern monarchies had considerable advantages over ancient republics, whilst also emphasising (albeit to a varying degree) human natural sociability and the compatibility

---

[15] Cf. Zammito, *Kant, Herder*, 176.   [16] Herder, 'Do We Still Have the Public', 43.

[17] Johann Georg Hamann, *Des Herrn von Dangueil* [*sic*] *Anmerkungen über die Vortheile und Nachtheile von Frankreich und Grossbritannien in Ansehung des Handels und der übrigen Quellen von der Macht der Staaten. Auszug eines Werks des Bernardo de Ulloa über die Wiederherstellung der Manufacturen und des Handels in Spanien; Beylage des deutschen Übersetzers* (Mitau, Leipzig, 1756); reprint as 'Beylage zu *Dangeuil* [1756]', *Sämtliche Werke*, ed. J. Nadler, 4 vols. (Vienna, 1949–1956), IV, 225–242. Plumard de Dangeul's treatise in turn was largely based on Josiah Tucker, *Essay on the Advantages and Disadvantages, Which Respectively Attend France and Great Britain with Regard to Trade* (London 1749; new edition 1750).

of patriotism with the spirit of commerce. This shift is also clearly reflected in Herder's judgement about the greatest philosophers of his time. In November 1768, Herder accordingly wrote to Kant: 'I was more averse to Hume when I was still daydreaming with Rousseau. Yet as it gradually became clear to me that, in whatever way, man is still, and must be, a social animal (*ein geselliges Thier*), I came to appreciate the man who can most properly be called a philosopher of human society.'[18]

1.1   Between Rousseau and Abbt

Herder's lead question in 'Benefit of the People' was posed specifically with a view towards the status and future of contemporary philosophy: 'How can philosophy be reconciled with humanity and politics so that it also really serves the latter?' This question, Herder explained, was the 'most useful and most appropriate for our economic-political era', yet also one 'over which *Plato, Rousseau, Hume*, and *Shaftesbury* pondered very deeply and plunged into doubt' (6).[19]

Herder's question about reconciling philosophy with humanity and politics was a rephrased version of the Berne Patriotic Society's prize question of 1763 about the 'ways in which the truths of philosophy could be made more general and more useful for the good of humanity and society'.[20] The founding of the Berne Patriotic Society in 1762 had been part of a wider initiative in Switzerland during the Seven Years' War. It was a philosophical counterpart to the Berne Economic Society, established in 1759, and Helvetian Society in Bad Schinznach, set up in 1761/1762,[21]

---

[18] Herder to Immanuel Kant, November 1768, in *DA*, I, 119. For Herder's intellectual debts to Hamann and his engagement with Hume in this period, see Vivian, 'Der Einfluß David Humes' and below. Frederick Beiser also discusses Hamann's impact on Herder in this early period, but overstates the influence of Hamann's critical attitude to 'Aufklärung' upon Herder, *Enlightenment, Revolution*, 192–197.

[19] In this section, parenthetical page numbers refer to Herder, 'Benefit of the People'.

[20] Herder's wording of the question reveals that Herder himself shared the Pyrrhonism he ascribed to other thinkers – what Herder edited out of the initial question posed by the Berne Patriotic Society was precisely that philosophy possessed 'the truths', Zammito, *Kant, Herder*, 173. Herder made a reference to another of the essay questions posed by the Berne Patriotic Society in 1763 (*Which was probably the happiest people in history?*) in his 'This Too a Philosophy for the Formation of Humanity: A Contribution to Many Contributions of the Century [1774]', in *PW*, 272–358 (296).

[21] Kapossy, *Iselin contra Rousseau*, 155. For a broad overview and discussion of economic and patriotic societies all over Europe (including the Berne Economic Society), see Koen Stapelbroek and Jani Marjanen (eds.), *The Rise of Economic Societies in the Eighteenth Century: Patriotic Reform in Europe and North America* (Basingstoke, 2012).

which aimed to engage the most prominent philosophers in Europe in a collaborative effort to form a philosophically justified approach for a Christian legislator to follow.[22] Indeed, this initiative found wide resonance in other German-speaking countries as well. Information about the Berne Patriotic Society's essay competition was disseminated to German readers by Moses Mendelssohn and through his and Friedrich Nicolai's *Letters*. By that time, Mendelssohn had also become an affiliated member of the Patriotic Society.[23] Essay questions were also published in Johann Georg Hamann's small journal in Königsberg.[24]

Recent scholarship has highlighted the ways in which Herder in 'Benefit of the People' addressed the most fundamental epistemological questions. Herder had already, in his 'Essay on Being' (1764), sketched a novel philosophical programme, calling for an 'anthropocentric turn' in epistemology, whereby, as Heinz and Clairmont have put it, 'pointless attempts to solve the problem of truth as the central task of classical epistemology are to be renounced in favor of metareflection on which kind of certainty is possible for which kind of subject'.[25] Now, in the 'Benefit of the People', he delved into the reasons for fighting for philosophy and its status among other branches of knowledge. These reasons had to do with philosophy's 'function' (*Gebrauch*) and 'application' (*Anwendung*), and required its repositioning with regard to mathematics and physics, on the one hand, and theology and political science, on the other. According to Herder, all cognition had to be traced back to the fundamental human body-soul constitution as its source and origin.[26]

It is important to see, however, that Herder also wished to contribute to an ongoing political debate. In rephrasing the question asked by the Berne Patriotic Society, Herder did not fail to recognise that the question was inspired by the challenge posed by Rousseau's famous criticism of the arts

---

[22] Kapossy, *Iselin contra Rousseau*, 155; Ulrich Im Hof, 'Mendelssohn und Iselin', in *Moses Mendelssohn und die Kreise seiner Wirksamkeit*, ed. Michael Albrecht et al. (Tübingen, 1994), 61–92 (62–65).

[23] Moses Mendelssohn, 'Von einer patriotischen Gesellschaft in der Schweiz, zum Besten der Sittenlehre und der Gesetzgebungswissenschaft. Gedanken darüber, Preisfragen dieser Gesellschaft für das Jahr 1763', *Briefe, die neueste Literatur betreffend* (1762), Literaturbrief 123, 169–182; Mendelssohn, 'Nachricht', *Briefe, die neueste Literatur betreffend* (1763), Literaturbrief 262, 136–140. For Mendelssohn's critical views on Rousseau, see Goldenbaum, 'Einführung', 9. St., 2 March 1764.

[24] *Königsbergsche gelehrte und politische Zeitungen*, 9, 2 March 1764.

[25] Marion Heinz and Heinrich Clairmont, 'Herder's Epistemology', in *A Companion to the Works*, 42–64 (49–50). On this seminal essay, see the recent collection of articles in John Noyes (ed.), *Herder's Essay on Being: A Translation and Critical Commentary* (Rochester, 2019).

[26] See Heinz, '1.2.2 *Philosophie zum Besten des Volks*', 61–64.

and sciences. One of the central issues of dispute among the Bernese reformers was precisely Rousseau's moral and political thought.[27] Although there were prominent members who rejected the sceptical premises of Rousseau's arguments,[28] the majority supported Rousseau and hoped to recruit him for the society's cause. Despite Rousseau's own reservations and warnings about the society's agenda, they read Rousseau as remaining fundamentally committed to the goal of improving modern society and as sharing their own loyalty to a Protestant vision of modern commercial republicanism.[29] In a similar vein, I suggest, Herder initially saw direct political relevance in Rousseau's fundamental revision of philosophy: he was hoping to make use of some central ideas of Rousseau in developing a new kind of philosophical reform programme for a modern society. Indeed, Herder presented Rousseau as 'our patriotic friend of humanity', whose 'great theme is all too closely related with mine' (8). The task was not to better disseminate certain 'philosophical truths' but to achieve a new kind of self-knowledge, which would also include a fundamental awareness of our natural sociability and capacity to act as a citizen. As we shall see, given that Rousseau in fact had a very pessimistic view of human nature and did not believe that it was possible to revive patriotic sentiments in a corrupt society, Herder's argument was bound to get stuck at some point.

1.1.1   Similarities with Rousseau

Some of the philosophical premises of Herder's argument in 'Benefit of the People' are remarkably close to Rousseau's, reflecting his initial admiration for Rousseau. First of all, he not only echoed much of Rousseau's criticism of the arts and sciences in the *First Discourse* and *Emile* but also accepted his basic distinction between 'natural' and 'vain curiosity'.[30] Herder flatly rejected the idea espoused by various contemporary critics of Rousseau that curiosity or pursuit of intellectual pleasure can be seen as the first

---

[27] See Im Hof, 'Mendelssohn und Iselin', in *Moses Mendelssohn*, 67.

[28] Most importantly, Isaak Iselin consistently tried to convince the other members of the Patriotic Society of Rousseau's underlying scepticism, and even dedicated his famous anti-Rousseauian *Philosophische Muthmassungen über die Geschichte der Menschheit* (Frankfurt and Leipzig, 1764) to his friends in the Patriotic Society, Kapossy, *Iselin contra Rousseau*, 179. We will return to discussions about Rousseau's 'Second Discourse' in Chapter 2.

[29] See the highly interesting reconstruction of this discussion in Kapossy, *Iselin contra Rousseau*, 180–201.

[30] Rousseau, 'First Discourse', 16–17; cf. Jean-Jacques Rousseau, 'Observations [to Stanislas, King of Poland]', in *The Discourses*, 32–51 (33) and Rousseau, *Emile, or On Education*, ed. and trans. by Allan Bloom (New York, 1979), 80–83, 204–205, 229–230.

impetus of the human soul or even the 'basis of all pleasure' (16).[31] While curiosity was answerable for our humanity as such – it was a drive that had 'changed the needs of the animal into the needs of a human being' – it originated in the most fundamental drive of self-preservation. Only by serving this drive did it lead to true happiness. 'Finer curiosity', by contrast, was essentially limitless and as such a form of vain pleasure-seeking (16). This applied to philosophy, too: 'As soon as our soul transcends the bounds of need,' Herder argued, it becomes 'insatiable in the desire for excess' (11).[32] 'Clinging to creations of our own reason', at the same time, we give up 'the habit of lively regard for the creations of nature and society' (11). All we would end up doing was fighting over mere abstractions or simply *words* (4). 'The highest degree of *philosophical ability* cannot at all coexist with the highest level of the healthy understanding,' Herder wrote, 'and thus the dissemination of the former becomes harmful for the people' (11). Far from enjoying increasing happiness in pursuing ever higher abstract ideas, Herder argued, philosophers doom themselves to unresolvable disputes and finally, boredom (16).

Herder also shared Rousseau's emphasis on the sentimental foundations of morality, disputing philosophy's contribution to forming or supporting the morality of the people.[33] Nature has given us moral sensations, 'voices of conscience', but not principles. Everything that *principles* and maxims of moral theory tell us, Herder claimed, is already known by 'each person, implicitly and obscurely'. What moves us to act is precisely this kind of obscure knowledge in which the sensuous and affective components are combined. Making this knowledge distinct, moral philosophy would only 'teach our understanding', giving us new reasons for moral action, yet without enhancing our power to act. Abstract thought as such was incapable of moving people to act. Furthermore, moral philosophy would also be unable to fight our 'prejudices, corruptions, bad dispositions', only creating 'for itself labyrinths, in order to make itself a guiding thread' (11). The principles would need to be applied to particular cases, which philosophers were often unable to do. Ordinary people, not accustomed to philosophical thinking, were thus fully justified in regarding the philosophical moral principles as nothing but 'venerable barbarism of words' (14). As a result of abstract reasoning, Herder summed up his argument, neither nature's command to 'live, reproduce, and die' nor the state's command to 'act' can be fulfilled by scholars. 'We lose the

---

[31] See Chapter 2 for Iselin's use of this idea in his refutation of Rousseau's 'Second Discourse'.
[32] Cf. Rousseau, 'First Discourse', 6–9, 16–17 and Rousseau, *Emile*, 80–81.
[33] Rousseau, 'First Discourse', 28; *Emile*, 235, 253–257.

honorable name of a patriotic people if we want to be scholars', was Herder's stern Rousseauian conclusion (11).

Similarly, Herder's positive programme built directly on Rousseau's. Indeed, in a number of passages Herder simply summarised the principles of 'negative education' outlined in Rousseau's *Emile* (22–25).[34] For Herder, Rousseau prepared the ground for working out 'the method of "preserving for the human spirit its natural strength in full vivacity, and of being able to apply it to each case"' (11). Herder's own goal, now, was to set a kind of 'negative Logic' into operation, one that would direct the people back to 'healthy understanding's well':

> Where else is this Logic than in the writings of our patriotic friend of humanity Rousseau? His great theme is all too closely related with mine: he has proved to everyone who has human eyes which have not been weakened by the philosophical telescope 'that for the benefit of the human people no development of the higher powers of the soul is desirable', and I have had to prove that for the people *in the state* of these creatures still nearer to nature than scholars, no development of the philosophical powers of the soul is desirable. (12, emphasis added)

As we see from this strange-sounding distinction between 'the human people' and 'the people in the state', Herder understood that Rousseau's programme of education in *Emile* was meant to be a philosophical and moral one – it was essentially a thought experiment of how to cultivate healthy reasoning in a single individual in as great isolation as possible from the corrupting influence of society. Yet for Herder it should not stop at that. Herder reserved the task of drafting a civic form of education along the same lines to himself.

But how did Herder conceive of the relationship between the state and the people? Did he take Rousseau as his guide in this context, too? Without further mentioning Rousseau, Herder proceeded to discuss the possible alternative of purely political patriotism:

---

[34] Cf. Rousseau, *Emile*, 86–96. The following passage in *Emile* captures the core of this education:

> If children jumped all at once from the breast to the age of reason, the education they are given might be suitable for them. But according to the natural progress, they need an entirely contrary one. They ought to do nothing with their soul until all of its faculties have been developed, because while the soul is yet blind, it cannot perceive the torch you are presenting to it or follow the path reason maps out across the vast plain of ideas, a path which is so faint even to the best of eyes. Thus, the first education ought to be purely negative. It consists not at all in teaching virtue or truth but in securing the heart from vice and the mind from error. (Ibid., 93)

So push forth, O people, into the holy places of philosophy. Tear down all the idols, and construct there state buildings, assemblies where instead of philosophical nonsense the healthy understanding counsels the state, humanity. Tear from the philosophers their Diogenes-capes and teach them pillars of the state. No, O republic!, by means of this devastation you plunge yourself into the jaws of barbarism; to avoid a small harm, you drown yourself in the Euripus. [. . .] Only philosophy can be the antidote to all the evil into which the philosophical curiosity has plunged us (18).

The rigid contrast between unpolitical 'cosmopolitan' philosophy (the chief example of which is the Cynic philosopher Diogenes of Synope) and political patriotism propounded in this citation is of course inspired by Rousseau's thought.[35] Herder here seems to have thought that Rousseau, too, was on his side in rejecting these two extreme options.

However, many other readers received a different message. In his *First Discourse* and *Replies to my Critics*, Rousseau maintained that real social cohesion was possible only in purely political societies such as Sparta. The 'happy ignorance' of the Spartans was matched by the 'wisdom of their laws'. The balance between the body and mind that the Spartan citizens had enjoyed was a product of political artifice.[36] In his 'Epistle dedicatory' to the Second *Discourse* and the *Discourse on Political Economy*,[37] Rousseau insisted that peoples 'in the long run' are 'what governments make them be'.[38] In a good political regime man's corruption would be forestalled despite the necessary rise of inequality and vain desires (*amour-propre*) at some point of historical development. The fundamental feature of such a regime according to Rousseau was the 'happy' combination of 'the equality which nature [has] established between men, and the inequality which they have instituted'.[39] Indeed, to many of Rousseau's readers, his considered view was clear: although Rousseau denied advocating 'overthrowing existing society, burning Libraries and all books, destroying Colleges and Academies', or 'reducing men to making do with the bare necessities', he seemed to counsel abandoning modern societies based on luxury.[40]

---

[35] It is noteworthy that Kant regarded Rousseau himself as a 'subtle Diogenes', see Sonenscher, *Before the Deluge*, 177. Herder may have been aware of this comparison.

[36] Rousseau, 'First Discourse', 11; cf. Rousseau, 'Last Reply', in *The Discourses*, 63–85 (73–74). For discussion, see Kapossy, *Iselin contra Rousseau*, 75f.

[37] On Rousseau's intellectual development, see Helena Rosenblatt, *Rousseau and Geneva. From the 'First Discourse' to the 'Social Contract,' 1749–1762* (Cambridge, 1997).

[38] Jean-Jacques Rousseau, 'Discourse on Political Economy [1755]', in *Rousseau: The Social Contract*, 3–38 (13).

[39] Rousseau, 'Second Discourse', 114.

[40] Rousseau, 'Last Reply', 84–85; cf. Rousseau's view of luxury: 'luxury supports States as Carytides support the palaces they adorn: or rather, as do the beams used to prop up rotting buildings, and

We will see later how, in his 'Do We Still Have the Public', Herder came to criticise a number of authors who developed this line of austere republicanism in Rousseau. Herder's move in 'Benefit of the People' was to dismiss this solution by sleight of hand. He indicated simply that contemporary states 'transplanted [...] into finer circumstances' could no longer be transformed into austere republics. Substituting modern arts, sciences and philosophy with political patriotism would only plunge corrupt society into the worst kind of barbarism, thus it was necessary to search for a different kind of solution. As one might expect from a student of Kant, Herder seems to have read Rousseau's *Emile*, and maybe also *The Social Contract*, as pointing towards a way of reconciling individual human happiness and virtue with a happy society and political freedom. Political transformation, in his view, would start 'from below', through moral reform: 'instead of politics,' he argued, philosophy should 'form the patriot, the citizen who actually acts' (19; cf. 25). Human beings educated in the right way would learn to withstand the tyrants of opinion and honour and thus come to lead independent, active and patriotic lives (23). He also did not regard it as contradictory to endorse the ideal of a 'philosophical peasant'[41] – one that Rousseau, too, had positively endorsed, but as a contrast to lives led under monarchies[42] – counselling philosophers to learn 'the way of farmers' who, so admirably, were the 'freest of people', despising the 'tyrant of honor', and to 'refine this picture into an ideal' (23).[43]

1.1.2   *Divergence from Rousseau*

Despite this substantial overlap between Herder's and Rousseau's views, there were notable differences in their emphases and other premises. The two thinkers clearly differed in their understanding of the level of corruption embodied in modern societies. Rousseau saw the French monarchy, and indeed, the city of Paris, as the (negative) model of modern commercial society, while Herder was 'speaking to Germans' and 'as a German' (8), drawing solely on his first-hand experience of the Baltic commercial

---

which often only succeed in toppling them. Wise and prudent men, abandon any house that is being propped up'. Ibid., 70.

[41]   Johann Caspar Hirzel, *Die Wirtschaft eines Philosophischen Bauers* (Zurich, 1761).

[42]   On Rousseau's admiration for this work, see Kapossy, *Iselin contra Rousseau*, 192–194.

[43]   It needs to be pointed out that this ideal was of course completely at odds with the actual agrarian conditions in Prussia and the province of Livland in the Russian Empire, Herder's new home territory, where the vast majority of peasants were serfs.

towns of Königsberg and Riga. Although he shared Rousseau's emphasis on the sentimental foundations of morality, Herder almost completely neglected Rousseau's discussion of *amour-propre* and his more detailed suggestions in *Emile* as to how it might be possible to give the latter a positive turn through combining it with the sentiment of pity.[44] The crux of Rousseau's moral education in *Emile* – the one emphasising mutual equal recognition as the key idea of modern morality – is also lacking. There is no echo of Rousseau's insistence that 'natural education' would teach humans to see that 'society depraves and perverts men', making them mutually deceptive towards one another.[45] Rousseau's counsel of making Emile 'inclined to esteem each individual but despise the multitude'[46] was also in clear tension with Herder's fundamental starting point: respect for, and attention to, the actual common 'people'.

The difference between their views, however, ran even deeper, as is revealed in their understanding of the role and power of philosophy in society. For Rousseau, corruption resulted from human desires as they developed within society, hence affecting all aspects of human activity, including philosophy.[47] While Rousseau accepted the possibility, and need, for 'a few privileged souls' to engage in philosophy and hoped that they would be invited to counsel ruling potentates, he was acutely aware that philosophers themselves were prone to vanity and deceit.[48] Herder, by contrast, did not share such worries to any significant degree: it was not the entanglement of philosophers in webs of mutual deception and aggressive competition for individual rank and honour in society but their fighting over corporate rank and honour against other branches of knowledge and their overall isolation from 'society', understood as the 'people', that he was complaining about.

As actual members of society, however, philosophers could potentially come to understand their responsibility towards society as well as the true nature of the 'philosophical spirit'. Hence Herder's central thesis in the

---

[44] Rousseau, *Emile*, 235–236; for discussion, see Dent and O'Hagan, 'Rousseau on *Amour-propre*'; Neuhouser, *Rousseau's Theodicy of Self-Love* and Sonenscher, *Jean-Jacques Rousseau*.

[45] Rousseau, *Emile*, 237.   [46] Ibid., 237.

[47] Cf. Rousseau's striking concession to his opponents: '*All the reproofs levelled at Philosophy attack the human mind. I concede it.*' Rousseau, 'Last Reply', 83. For a detailed analysis of Rousseau's genealogy of the arts and sciences, and their integral part in commercial society, see Kapossy, *Iselin contra Rousseau*, 65–75. For a summary of Rousseau's account of the development of *amour-propre* in human history, see Chapter 2.

[48] As for himself, he declared: 'I want nothing to do with a deceitful profession in which one believes one is doing much for wisdom while doing everything for vanity.' Rousseau, 'Observations', 35 (footnote), cf. Rousseau, 'First Discourse', 27.

essay: reversing modern corruption is still possible because 'philosophy with a philosophical spirit' can act as an antidote to the false kind of philosophy. Herder did not thus advocate the renunciation of 'thinking' or 'enlightenment'; what he rejected was a particular, unsociable, variety of philosophical thinking, namely speculative reasoning. Even in modern circumstances of increasing luxury it was possible to attempt to create a new kind of educational programme that would benefit all (19). In earlier times, Herder argued, it had been necessary to guard against ambition and stubbornness in particular; now it was the softness that resulted from luxury that was corrupting the common people. Herder wrote: 'Our time is not a time of strictness but of luxury, and what was appropriate for other times is perhaps contrary to our manner of thought. Times of rough simplicity have virtues and vices of strength, we have virtues and vices of weakness.' (25) It was possible to reverse modern corruption and develop distinctively modern virtues by strengthening humans' independent moral judgement and by reminding them of their own nature as patriots and citizens.

1.1.3   Thomas Abbt's Modern Monarchical Patriotism

From where might Herder have derived inspiration for this more optimistic thinking about the role of a new kind of philosophy in modern societies? One crucial model for him in this respect was Thomas Abbt's moral and political philosophy.[49] Through his two works on patriotism, *Dying for the Fatherland* (1761) and *On Merit* (1765), the young university lecturer at Frankfurt/Oder and Rinteln and, subsequently, *Hof- und Regierungsrat* of Count of Schaumburg-Lippe in Bückeburg had substantially contributed to the debate on modern patriotism. He was also an active participant in broader literary debates: already in 1761, following the publication of his first treatise on fatherland that Mendelssohn had lauded in his review, Mendelssohn and Friedrich Nicolai recruited him to join their group of anonymous reviewers in their *Letters on the Newest Literature*. Abbt quickly became a regular correspondent to *Letters* and, as Herder later confessed, Abbt was the 'closest and dearest' of all the

---

[49] Cf. Zammito, *Kant, Herder*, 163–165. The importance of Abbt for the development of Herder's ideas is widely recognised in scholarship. See, e.g., Haym, *Herder*, I, 137–144; Viroli, *For Love of Country*, 111–124; Benjamin Redekop, *Enlightenment and Community: Lessing, Abbt, Herder, and the Quest for a German Public* (Montreal, London, 2000). However, almost no attention has been paid to the ways in which Abbt's philosophy of patriotism served as a model for Herder.

different writers for this journal to him.[50] Let us thus summarise some of Abbt's contributions to debates on modern patriotism in his two main works so as to determine their precise significance for the young Herder's evolving views on modern patriotism.[51]

In his first work, *Dying for the Fatherland*, Abbt argued that patriotism was possible and highly necessary in modern states in general and in his contemporary Prussia in particular. He defended modern monarchies from criticism by republicans, while also rejecting Montesquieu's conception of modern monarchy.[52] Abbt accepted the political participation of 'the people' in common deliberation as an advantage enjoyed by the ancient republics but argued that there were definitive advantages in modern monarchical states, too: they were larger, externally more secure and internally more stable.[53] Abbt's main argument here was that the rule of law could be guaranteed through the monarchs' commitment to this principle, based on their growing understanding of the true foundations of their own power.[54] He accepted the 'growth of luxuries' and of the population in modern monarchies as necessary and in themselves positive but lamented their impact on people's morals, including their willingness to fight and die for their fatherland.[55] In his second book *On Merit* (1765), Abbt qualified his account, indicating that true freedom required not only limited government but also the possibility of having a say about the laws or at least of participating in legislation through electing one's representatives. Nevertheless, he was convinced that modern monarchies offered ample opportunities for cultivating virtue.[56]

In both works, Abbt insisted that the key to moral reform was to enlighten human beings about their own nature, to draw their attention to the feelings that they already possessed, but which for various reasons had been weakened or stultified. Patriotism for Abbt was a primary example of sociable passions. It enabled one to fulfil one's moral duty of making oneself 'more perfect as the final aim of the creation, but also as a means for the good of the whole'.[57] Drawing on the moral philosophy of

---

[50] Johann Gottfried Herder to Christoph Friedrich Nicolai, Riga, 19 February 1767, in *DA*, I, 71.

[51] The following summary of Abbt's political philosophy draws on Piirimäe, 'Dying for the Fatherland' and Piirimäe, 'Thomas Abbt (1738–1766) and the Philosophical Genesis of German Nationalism' (Cambridge University, unpublished Ph.D. thesis, 2006).

[52] Piirimäe, 'Thomas Abbt', 265–266.

[53] Thomas Abbt, 'Vom Tode für das Vaterland', in *Aufklärung und Kriegserfahrung. Klassische Zeitzeugen zum Siebenjährigen Krieg*, ed. Johannes Kunisch (Bibliothek der Geschichte und Politik, 9) (Frankfurt/Main, 1996), 589–650, 971–1008 (603–604).

[54] Ibid., 597–602.   [55] Ibid., 591, 595, passim.

[56] See Piirimäe, 'Thomas Abbt', 63–67, 241–248.   [57] Ibid., 616.

the Third Earl of Shaftesbury and Alexander Baumgarten, Abbt developed an original theory of the moral psychology of patriotism. Emphasising the pleasure humans gain from order (as the basis for feelings for what is beautiful and good), he qualified patriotism as an instance of these feelings, and in the case of particularly strong feelings of love for fatherland, as a form of enthusiasm.[58]

In a review article written a year after the publication of *Dying for the Fatherland*, Abbt also connected patriotic enthusiasm to the rebirth of German literature and the German cultural nation as a whole – foreshadowing Herder's central theme in his subsequent *Fragments on the German Literature* (1766–1768).[59] Germans had already shown excellence in world wisdom, whilst new opportunities were arising thanks to a new kind of political situation. Ideally, Abbt envisioned Germans aligning themselves behind Frederick the Great as a source of national and linguistic pride as well as moral inspiration. Berlin could become the 'capital city' where the 'leading lights' would speak truth from their 'heated breasts', while 'others would join them, asserting their right that they, too, are Germans'.[60] Following Shaftesbury, Abbt furthermore emphasised the logical priority of the reform of moral taste over that of aesthetic taste. A right kind of aesthetic taste, Abbt argued, would only follow on from recognising the operation of the moral principles in one's breast, by experiencing admiration and enthusiasm.[61] At the same time, German philosophy, too, could take the lead in delving into the philosophical foundations of moral and political reform, thus claiming for Germans, in particular, the honour of being 'worldly-wise' by their very national character.[62]

Abbt's *On Merit* (1765) sought to develop a distinctive kind of analytical approach to moral phenomena by combining both the consequentialist perspectives embraced by Claude-Adrien Helvétius with the aesthetic ones developed by Shaftesbury, Alexander Baumgarten and Mendelssohn.[63] A 'distinct' [*deutliche*] idea of merit', Abbt suggested, could be achieved by searching for common characteristics [*Merkmale*] in historical examples of merit, as well as the 'judgements of the contemporaries', while separating

---

[58] Ibid., 644. For discussion, see Piirimäe, 'Dying for the Fatherland', 204.
[59] Anon. [Abbt, Thomas], 'Einige allgemeine Anmerkungen über das Genie der Deutschen und den Zustand der deutschen Litteratur', *Briefe, die neueste Literatur betreffend* XV (1762), Literaturbrief 245, 53–62 (56–57). On *Fragments*, see Chapter 2.
[60] Anon. [Abbt], 'Einige allgemeine Anmerkungen', 56–57.   [61] Piirimäe, 'Thomas Abbt', 196.
[62] This importance of this idea for Herder is also highlighted by Heinz, '1.2.2 *Philosophie zum Besten des Volks*', 63.
[63] Piirimäe, 'Thomas Abbt', 211–241.

the concept's essential components from the unessential ones 'through one's own reflection'.[64] The clarified notions thus achieved, however, had to be reworked into 'ideals', beautiful ideas, which would then be able to motivate the people.[65] The task of a patriotic writer was to follow the ancients who 'never wanted to convince the audience by appealing to the understanding alone, but who always were bent to transform the will, too'. They hence had to 'paint in strong images' and to focus on particular situations that called for action.[66]

Abbt specified voluntary and unselfish benevolence as an essential component of merit.[67] While embracing sensationalism and emphasising human capacity for sympathy (the 'good heart'), he identified 'thinking' as an essential precondition for 'true goodness' or benevolence.[68] Benevolence was grounded in a reflective aesthetic endorsement of humans' 'good heart', while its constancy was guaranteed through association with knowledge and the love of order. The main goal of Abbt's *On Merit*, however, was to provide a classification of different ranks of 'merit' as well as to specify the relationship of different professions to these ranks in modern society.[69] Abbt emphasised that a basic degree of 'mere merit' was attainable for everybody: 'healthy understanding instead of genius, patience [...] rather than courage, good heart instead of benevolence are sufficient for that'.[70] By using these faculties and virtues to benefit their relatives, friends, neighbours, fellow citizens and fellow subjects, ordinary men and women could become respectable members of society. In Abbt's view, this kind of public spirit was compatible with Christianity, but not with exaggerated religious piety.[71]

In delineating this view of modern sociable patriotism Abbt indicated his position with regard to debates concerning the compatibility of modern commerce with virtue. He insisted that even though self-interest was the main motivation for private people's economic activity, it could be complemented and contained through human interactions based on healthy understanding and what he called 'good heart'. Plenty of merchants and

---

[64] Thomas Abbt, 'Vom Verdienste', in Abbt, *Vermischte Werke*, 6 vols., (Frankfurt und Leipzig, 1783), I:1, 5, 11–12.

[65] Abbt, 'Vom Verdienste', 5.

[66] Anon. [Abbt], 'Über *Patriotische Vorstellungen und sichere Mittel, arme Staaten zu bereichern*,' *Briefe, die neueste Literatur betreffend* (1762), XV, Literaturbrief 253, 137–160 (142).

[67] Abbt, 'Vom Verdienste', 11.

[68] For reconstructions of Abbt's analysis of the historical genesis of morality in society, see Piirimäe, 'Thomas Abbt', 218–223 and Avi Lifschitz, 'Genesis for Historians: Thomas Abbt on Biblical and Conjectural Accounts of Human Nature', *History of European Ideas* (special issue: *Sociability in Enlightenment Thought*, ed. Eva Piirimäe and Alexander Schmidt), 41 (5) 605–618.

[69] For a more detailed account of his classification, see Piirimäe, 'Thomas Abbt', 232–240.

[70] Abbt, 'Vom Verdienste', 216.   [71] Ibid., 277.

manufacturers had shown generosity and public spirit, especially in times of great need, thereby approximating ruling potentates themselves in terms of the merit that they had earned through their actions. For the ancients, the market place had never solely existed for doing business but equally for giving counsel and rendering other freely given services. It was the increase in personal comforts and privatism (*Gemächlichkeit*) that had dissolved this habit, but there was no reason why it could not be recreated in modern times.[72] Abbt elsewhere specified Swiss civic thinking and 'English public spirit' as his ideal models in this respect; his own goal, too, was to spread a 'generally useful way of thought' that any 'private person' could exhibit and cultivate in his circle.[73] When writing to the educated public Abbt indicated that a particularly useful form of public writing would be one aiming to provide enlightenment to the 'common man', namely the intellectually less-developed vast majority of the general public.[74]

1.1.4   Abbt's Inspiration for Herder

Herder digested the message of Abbt's *On Merit* while writing 'Benefit of the People' in summer 1765. In his review of *On Merit*, which was published in September 1765,[75] Herder celebrated Abbt as the 'philosopher of the good German healthy understanding', one whose 'half philosophical and half political' approach and 'human' writing style has demonstrated why 'metaphysics has become a distinctively German field'.[76] Herder later reiterated some of the central views expressed in the review in his *On Thomas Abbt's Writings*, explicitly rejecting the title of 'scholar' when portraying Abbt and instead characterising him as 'a *philosopher of the human being, of the citizen, of the common man*'.[77] Herder

---

[72] Ibid., 313. Abbt directed these musings directly against Rousseau's critique of modern society and his alternative system in *Emile*, see 'Vom Verdienste', 305–321. For discussion, see Piirimäe, 'Thomas Abbt', 166–170.

[73] Abbt [anon.], 'Über *Patriotische Vorstellungen*', 141; Abbt, 'Vom Verdienste', 217–221, 313.

[74] Abbt, 'Vom Verdienste', 277.

[75] Johann Gottfried Herder, 'Über *Vom Verdienste*', in *SWS*, I, 79–81 (orig. *Königsbergsche gelehrte und politische Zeitungen auf das Jahr 1765*. Rostock und Greifswald (73 Stück, 13. September)).

[76] Ibid., 79–81.

[77] The most striking evidence of young Herder's admiration for Abbt is his literary obituary to Abbt, 'Über Thomas Abbts Schriften. Der Torso einem Denkmal, an seinem Grabe errichtet. Erstes Stück' [1768], in *FHA*, II, 565–608; English translation: 'On Thomas Abbt's Writings (1768) [selections concerning psychology]', in *PW*, 167–177 (173). Compare also Herder's positive verdict of Abbt in *Fragments*: 'Abbt's Schriften sind für die deutschen Original: der gute gesunde Menschen- und Bürgerverstand, der in ihnen herrschet, ist das Erbstück unsrer Nation: die analytische Auflösung der Begriffe ist die beste Methode deutscher Philosophie; die Laune seiner Schreibart, die statt der französischen Charaktere, und der brittischen erdachten Beispiele, durch Geschichte lehrt, nährt unseren Geist, und seine

admired both Abbt's 'sensuous attentiveness' directed to different 'points' and 'sides' of an object, and his making the latter 'comprehensible through the *number* of its characterizing marks'. As a result, Herder argued, Abbt was able to 'persuade [*überreden*] to the point of obviousness'.[78] Thereby, Abbt came upon concepts that he 'felt deeply', while '[thinking] them with effort' and '[expressing] them with difficulty'.[79] Herder described Abbt's imagination as 'rich, fecund, rhapsodic and in a noble way, unrestrained' but immediately qualified it as possessing the rare quality of 'remaining a sister of truth'.[80] Furthermore, Abbt's 'strong feeling for the beautiful, the human and ethical' always guaranteed that the affective component of cognition remained lively in his thinking and hence his 'aesthetic taste, [. . .] human and moral judgement, [was] founded on sensation, not on rules as with unfeeling teachers of ethics or art'.[81]

In 'Benefit of the People' we see Herder first elaborating on this kind of 'patriotic philosophy', demanding from any philosopher precisely what he saw as the virtues and method of Abbt as a writer. 'A philosophy of the healthy human understanding' should 'talk to the people in its language, in its manner of thought, in its sphere', while 'its manner of thought' should be 'lively, not distinct – certain, not proving' (19).[82] Tacitly following Abbt's notion of patriotism as based on human natural sociability, Herder associated the formative power of the philosophy of 'healthy understanding' with the fact that the people already 'are human beings and patriots'. Thus the philosopher 'who is a human being, citizen, and a wise man' should consult 'the human being, the patriot, the philosopher within himself' and appear before himself as 'in a higher tribunal', so as to determine the possible role of philosophy in society (21). If the philosopher were to truly follow this route, Herder argued, he would become an 'honorable bard among his brothers' (19), 'teaching the people to act without thinking, to be virtuous without knowing it, to be citizens without pondering about the fundamental principles of the state, to be Christians without understanding a theological metaphysics' (22).[83]

In contrast to Abbt, however, Herder developed his own account of moral sentiments along more radically anti-intellectualist lines. While

---

Schreibart unsere Einbildungskraft.' Johann Gottfried Herder, 'Über die neuere deutsche Literatur I. Fragment 18', in *FHA*, I, 149–160 (244).

[78] Herder, 'On Thomas Abbt's Writings', 174.   [79] Ibid., 174.   [80] Ibid., 175.

[81] Ibid., 175.

[82] I have modified Forster's translation, as I believe that 'distinct' captures the meaning of 'deutlich' more precisely than 'clear'.

[83] I will return to Herder's understanding of modern philosopher-bards in Chapters 2 and 5.

Abbt reserved the terms 'virtue' or 'true goodness' for the sublime morality of benevolence [*Wohlwollen*] and associated the latter with philosophical reflection, Herder decisively proclaimed abstract concepts unnecessary for the morality [*Moral*] of the people. People's God-given sentiments, he maintained, can be moulded into healthy moral judgement and dispositions towards virtue without resorting to abstract reasoning about world order or moral principles. Thereby Herder was beginning to develop what became an important theme of his moral philosophy in the later 1760s regarding 'mores' [*Sitten*] as the central embodiment of morality and hence emphasising the possibility of virtue in every period of human history.[84] At the same time, Herder acknowledged that in the modern age of luxury and refinement it was impossible to do without abstract concepts altogether. Society was diversified and divided into different ranks, just like Christian religion itself showing a high level of abstraction – this necessarily had an impact on morality. Thus, philosophers had to learn these concepts from their own hearts, so as to reinforce the sentiments that people already possessed. This would prevent these few abstract concepts from becoming a 'collection of barbaric words' or 'foreign obligations' and they would instead be 'preached to the conscience' by 'impressing' in people 'an image which never dies out, and without any help from art' (24).

In a fragmentary section towards the end of the essay, Herder also spelled out his hopes about the impact that this kind of patriotic and human education would have on politics. In particular, he pointed to the important role of socialising in people's education. Herder, like Abbt and in stark contrast to Rousseau, laid great emphasis on the education of not only men but also of women. Although he distinguished between men's and women's education, he emphatically called for women to be educated through 'books', 'better household tutors' and 'more socializing between sexes' (26).[85] Indeed, Herder even went as far as to emphasise the crucial role of women's thinking in the moral transformation of society in general: philosophers would have to 'know the *fair* [part of the] people' in order to enrich philosophy with their 'finest ideas' (27–28).

---

[84] For the pivotal role of Abbt's *Zweifel über die Bestimmung des Menschen* (1764) in the development of this position, see Marion Heinz, 'Die Bestimmung des Menschen: Herder contra Mendelssohn', in *Philosophie der Endlichkeit: Festschrift für Erich Christian Schröder zum 65. Geburtstag*, ed. Beate Niemeyer and Dirk Schütze (Würzburg, 1991), 263–285 and Marion Heinz, 'Historismus oder Metaphysik? Zu Herders Bückeburger Geschichtsphilosophie', in *Johann Gottfried Herder: Geschichte und Kultur*, ed. Martin Bollacher (Würzburg, 1994), 75–85; see also Zammito, *Kant, Herder*, 165–171. We will return to the topic of 'moral instincts' and 'mores' in Chapter 3.

[85] For Rousseau's (and Kant's) radically different views on women and their role in society, see Zammito, *Kant, Herder*, 120–135; cf. Sonenscher, *Sans-Culottes*, 156–164, 195–201.

While thus calling for more sociability between different ranks and sexes, Herder simultaneously affirmed fundamental human freedom and a contract-like relationship between the people and the rulers:

> Each human being is free and independent from others. All societies are contracts, and if these are destroyed on one side, then they also cease to hold on the other side etc. I must indeed exist in society etc. But one must keep faith etc. (25).

Although these ideas may be inspired by Rousseau's summary of *The Social Contract* at the end of *Emile*,[86] Herder's argument throughout the essay was radically different from Rousseau's, presupposing human natural sociability. In contrast to Rousseau in *Social Contract*, the 'people' for Herder did not emerge through social contract. He described 'family spirit' (*Familiengeist*)[87] as the constitutive element of republican city-based communities, arguing that this spirit can and must spread all over a bigger community as well, and be embraced as a virtue as soon as the people understood that all parties in society (including their rulers) were bound by this kind of family spirit and faithfulness to 'contract'. This is what Herder seems to have meant in the following shorthand:

> Does this not lead to the discontentment of the people? No! [...] If one educates citizens as a patriot. – This fire spreads, reproduces itself etc. In republics it is etc. And society. Education too early. Books. Abbt. Also Sermons. Family spirit etc. As soon as I understand that I am connected etc. (26).

For Herder, human sociability was a precondition for patriotic education. Sociable patriotism, in turn, supported freedom and good government. It was not simply a foundation of political loyalty but could also be regarded as providing the hope to preserve, or at least regain, basic stability in cases where criticism of, and perhaps even resistance to, government was needed. Since there was always a danger that the rulers might betray the 'contract' between them and the people, the people were justified in demanding loyalty to this contract.

Herder never finished his 'Benefit of the People'. It is possible that he began to realise the serious tensions that existed between Rousseau's cultural criticism and his ideas of 'human education', on the one hand,

---

[86] Cf. Rousseau, *Emile*, 460: 'Since the people are the people before electing the king, what made it so if not a social contract? Therefore the social contract is the basis of every civil society, and the nature of the society it forms must be sought in the nature of this transaction.'

[87] It is likely that Herder derives this notion from Johann Georg Hamann who discussed the same concept and term in *Des Herrn von Dangueil Anmerkungen*, 391. On the significance of this work for Herder, see Section 1.2.2.

and a notion of modern sociable patriotism as well as a patriotic philosophy of 'healthy understanding', on the other. As an attempt to combine these different strands of thinking, however, the essay suited the agenda of the Berne *Patriotic Society*. Although the young Herder's underlying moral philosophy was more radically anti-intellectualist than that of most other advocates of sociable and aesthetic patriotism, he clearly shared their fundamental commitment to the ideal of reforming the state 'from below'. Human and civic philosophy were to be developed in tandem.

1.2   Ancients and Moderns

Later on in 1765, Herder wrote the piece 'Do We Still Have the Public and Fatherland of the Ancients', which we cited in the Introduction. This piece, essentially a written speech, celebrated the inauguration of a new court building in Riga and commemorated Catherine II of Russia's visit to Riga in 1764.[88] It was actually not presented orally on this occasion but was first published in October 1765 and reprinted in 1768.[89] The essay is divided into two sections, the first dealing with the idea of the 'public', including the character of ancient and modern peoples, while the second is devoted to the idea of 'fatherland' – the appropriate moral and civic ideals in these contexts.[90] In the first part of the essay, Herder offered a comparative account of the ways in which 'the public' was formed in the ancient and modern periods – either in terms of various kinds of art performed in shared space, public institutions, and open dialogue and persuasion (ancient politics) or through the medium of print and oration (modern politics). This served as a background to a broader question on how a nation that had lost its public institutions could still have a 'fatherland' in some other sense.[91] While thus approaching his overall topic with a certain nostalgia, Herder in the second half of the essay came up with a nuanced contrast between ancient republics and modern monarchies. Eager to impress the Russian Empress Catherine, Herder highlighted the advantages of modern monarchies and empires, rejecting

---

[88] On Herder's views on Catherine's reform agenda, see Chapter 3.
[89] Bernhard Ludwig Suphan, 'Einleitung', in *SWS*, I, xvii; cf. Haym, *Herder*, I, 126.
[90] For the subsequent debate in Germany in the last quarter of the century, see Alexander Schmidt, 'The Liberty of the Ancients? Friedrich Schiller and Aesthetic Republicanism', *History of Political Thought*, 30:2 (2009), 286–314. Herder published another essay on the same theme thirty years later (1795), see Herder, 'Haben wir noch jetzt die Vaterland und Publikum der Alten?', in *FHA*, VII (*Briefe zu Beförderung der Humanität*, ed. Hans Dietrich Irmscher), 301–338. I discuss this essay in Chapter 8.
[91] Noyes, *Herder: Aesthetics*, 71.

and criticising austere democratic republicans for reserving patriotism to republics only. Let us have a closer look at whom he had in mind here, and why he held it important to challenge these views.

Having admired the 'Rousseauian' way of thought in his 'Benefit of the People', Herder now singled out a group of contemporary Swiss authors as his opponents: 'It always causes wonder that the Swiss, today, have taken up the *fashion* of sketching political systems patterned on the revised standards of Greek states; of these I call particular attention to [Mably's] the *dialogues of Phocion*, [Wegelin's] the *observations on Lycurgus*, and [Iselin's] the *Patriotic Dreams*' (55).[92] In fact Herder's Swiss admirers of the Greeks were a rather varied group of authors and the publication dates of the works he referred to covered a span of ten years. In 1765 when Herder wrote these words, Iselin, for example, certainly no longer admired the Greeks in the same way, as we will see in Chapter 2. However, Herder made specific reference to his *Patriotic Dreams of a Friend of Mankind* (1755), and this work had indeed painted a favourable picture of early Greek societies as described by Homer and Hesiod. While this did not mean that Iselin in this early work was an admirer of Rousseau,[93] Mably and Wegelin not only admired the early Greeks, but also stood quite close to Rousseau. Mably's mature works were often compared with Rousseau's political thought – indeed, Constant, too, in his speech on ancient and modern liberty highlighted Mably in particular as the philosopher who had failed to understand the nature and characteristic values of modern society.[94] Mably, who was not Swiss but French, had in fact been acquainted with Rousseau since the early 1740s. Mably's *Conversations* focused on international relations, advocating a league of virtue between republican

---

[92] In this section, the parenthetical page numbers refer to Herder, 'Do We Still Have the Public'. The original titles of the works mentioned in the quotation are Gabriel Bonnot Abbé de Mably, *Entretiens de Phocion, sur le rapport de la morale avec la politique* (Amsterdam, 1763). Johann Jakob Wegelin, *Politische und moralische Betrachtungen über die spartanische Gesetz-Gebung des Lykurgus* (Lindau, 1763); Isaak Iselin, *Philosophische und Patriotische Träume eines Menschenfreundes* (Freiburg, 1755; Zurich, 1758).

[93] On the contrary, as Béla Kapossy has shown, Iselin's *Patriotic Dreams* offered a passionate critique of Rousseau's *First Discourse*, putting forward a theory of republican patriotism anchored in Christian sociability. Iselin argued that early Greek societies proved the compatibility of wealth and virtue; love was the driving principle of all human activities (including the arts and sciences) within them, while the inequality and increasing distribution of labour between the individuals did not corrupt the morals of the people. In particular, Iselin emphasised the absence of foreign trade in this model of economy, thus indicating that corrupting luxury was induced by the latter. Kapossy, *Iselin contra Rousseau*, 85–94. As Kapossy has shown, Iselin's *Über die Geschichte der Menschheit* (1764) was an impassioned defence of a fusion of republican and monarchical values and institutions.

[94] Constant, 'The Liberty of the Ancients', 318–320.

states, a position to which Rousseau was sympathetic yet never came to embrace wholeheartedly.[95] What made Mably sound similar to Rousseau was his particular admiration for Sparta and his analysis of the foundations of love of country in certain 'basic virtues' that were supported by rigid laws regulating private property.[96] Yet in contrast to Rousseau (and like Iselin), Mably held on to the idea of human natural sociability, while also emphasising love of honour as an important source of moral motivation. Tellingly, Mably's work had also won the Berne *Patriotic Society* essay competition in 1762.[97] Mably's moralistic philosophy of international relations, as well as his morally more optimistic conception of human motivation, were probably also the reasons why his work so impressed the Bernese.

The third Swiss work to which Herder referred was Johann Jacob Wegelin's *Political and Moral Observations on the Spartan Legislation of Lycurgus*. Wegelin, a close associate of the Zurich circle of the followers of Johann Jacob Bodmer, was one of the leading advocates of anti-commercial city-based military republicanism in Switzerland. Wegelin's work on Lycurgus was an attempt to show the continuing relevance of this political model in modern conditions. Aligning himself explicitly with Rousseau's political ideas, Wegelin wanted to explore the ways in which Lycurgus had been able to prevent the development of selfish passions such as greed or pleasure-seeking, while giving full vent to the passions of love of honour and fatherland.[98] In his explanation of Spartan patriotism, Wegelin (like Mably) revealed himself to be a faithful follower of the 'Greek tradition in republican thought'.[99] He emphasised frugal living and the abolition of private property as the key conditions for sustaining patriotism. He also praised the arrangement in which 'families were no

---

[95] Sonenscher, *Before the Deluge*, 23–24, 240. For a subtle comparison of Mably's and Rousseau's thought bringing out a number of major differences between them, see ibid., 239–253. Cf. Johnson Kent Wright, *A Classical Republican in Eighteenth-Century France: The Political Thought of Mably* (Stanford, 1997).

[96] 'There is not, and there cannot be, any love for one's country without temperance, love of labour, love of glory, or respect for the gods. In a state where those virtues are wanting, the citizen, wrapped up in his own concerns, looks upon himself as a stranger in the midst of his countrymen.' Gabriel Bonnot de Mably, *Phocion's Conversations or the Relation between Morality and Politics* [1763] (London, 1769), 131.

[97] Mendelssohn, 'Nachricht', *Briefe, die neueste Literatur betreffend*, Literaturbrief 262, 137–138.

[98] Wegelin, *Politische und moralische Betrachtungen*, 38.

[99] For the idea that there are two traditions of republicanism, one originating in Greece and one in Rome, see Eric Nelson, *The Greek Tradition in Republican Thought* (Cambridge, 2005). In Nelson's account, it is distinctive of ancient Greek authors (and accordingly their followers) to emphasise egalitarian property regulation (particularly equal distribution of land) as the essential feature of republicanism and a precondition of republican virtue.

more like true little states than in other forms of government', arguing that this enabled the citizens to truly dedicate themselves to the republic as well as to organise proper public education for the children.[100] Like Mably, he also sought to demonstrate the humanitarian dimension of ancient republicanism as a whole, presenting both republican Rome and, on some occasions, even Sparta as allies of the freedom of all peoples. At the same time, he described the contemporary British political system as an example of the successful adaptation of the Spartan constitution in the modern setting.

1.2.1 Abbt's Review of Wegelin

It is highly likely that Herder's generalisation about the 'newest' Swiss tendencies was prompted by his having read Abbt's review of Wegelin's *Observations on Lycurgus* in *Letters on the Newest Literature*. At the very time (from 4 April to 2 May) that Herder was reporting to Hamann about working on 'Benefit of the People', Abbt published a devastating criticism of Wegelin's work.[101] Although Abbt's review essay was anonymous, Herder probably correctly surmised its author. It is very likely that reading this essay made Herder rethink his views of Rousseau's politics and thus appreciate the pessimistic implications of the latter's rejection of natural sociability. Siding with Abbt's defence of natural sociability and his corresponding criticism of Swiss radical democratic republicanism, Herder came to acknowledge some of the advantages of modern societies in 'Do We Still Have the Public'.

In his review, Abbt highlighted the sources of Wegelin's argument: 'Rousseau, Sparta, and the British are the three things that the author is almost ridiculously enamoured of'.[102] For Abbt, this attempted synthesis was nothing but a misguided dogmatic application of Montesquieu's theory of the three forms of government.[103] In criticising Wegelin's

---

[100] Wegelin, *Politische und moralische Betrachtungen*, 19.

[101] Abbt (anon.), 'Über [J. J. Wegelin (anon.),] *Politische und moralische Betrachtungen über die Spartanische Gesetzgebung des Lykurgus*', *Briefe, die neueste Literatur betreffend*, XXII (1765), Literaturbriefe 320–322, 93–146; cf. the discussion of Wegelin's work and Abbt's review in Schmidt, 'The Liberty of the Ancients', 301–302. There was also a pre-story to Abbt's review of Wegelin. In all likelihood Wegelin was the author of one of the most critical anonymous reviews of Abbt's *On Dying for the Fatherland* in the early 1760s in *Freymüthige Nachrichten Von Neuen Büchern, und andern zur Gelehrtheit gehörigen Sachen*, Achtzehnter Jahrgang, Zürich 1761, XXXIII. Stück, Mittwochs, am 19. Augustmonath, 1761, 258ff. For a summary of this review and the reactions to it by the Prussian enlightened circles, see Kapossy, *Iselin contra Rousseau*, 146–149 and Zurbuchen, 'Staatstheorie zwischen eidgenössischer Republik', 145–162.

[102] Anon. [Abbt], 'Über *Politische und moralische Betrachtungen*', 107.   [103] Ibid., 109.

idealised conception of Spartan government, Abbt insisted on a broader point: the entire Spartan regime had attempted to do away with human nature and natural principles of human interaction. Equality was unnatural, as sustaining it required the most drastic measures.[104] This clearly showed that the Spartan constitution went 'against the will of God', and that 'for each society that develops naturally, God has prescribed rich and poor'.[105] Moreover, the celebrated Spartan equality was in fact a highly limited one, based on nothing but patricians' pride and consciousness of their privileges.[106] Abbt concluded his review by ironically approving of Wegelin's association of Emile's educational plan with the Spartan constitution: 'surely the protégé of Rousseau must be as rich as a Spartan, insofar as he must have servants taking care of him, as well as parents who support him and his mentor, just like the Spartan had to have slaves'.[107]

Abbt's criticism of the Spartan constitution as well as its modern admirers signalled his position on sociability, commerce and patriotism. Abbt was not a critic of ancient republicanism *tout court* but only attempted to show the limitations of a certain type of republicanism that was based on political artifice rather than human nature. Ancient virtue still remained the most remarkable example of what human nature was capable of, just like ancient arts, eloquence, and politics provided ample examples of true human *sensus communis*. Luxury certainly engendered moral corruption, yet the solution was not to ban it but to learn to use its positive aspects for enhancing national wealth and security, while its negative effects had to be curbed through moral education and a political system that would reward true human merit. Nothing in modern limited monarchies with their large territories and complex societies ruled out this kind of education and self-reform, while the Christian religion was a powerful force supporting it.

---

[104] Ibid., 133.
[105] Ibid., 124f. David Hume's verdict: 'ancient policy was violent, and contrary to the more natural and usual course of things. It is well known with what peculiar laws SPARTA was governed, and what a prodigy that republic is justly esteemed by every one, who has considered human nature as it has displayed itself in other nations, and other ages.' David Hume, 'Of Commerce', in *Essays Moral, Political, and Literary*, ed. Eugene Miller (Indianapolis, 1985), 253–267 (259).
[106] Anon. [Abbt], 'Über *Politische und moralische Betrachtungen*', 125. See also Abbt's highly interesting comparison between the Spartan patriciate and the nobility of the northern European peoples, ibid., 121–122.
[107] Ibid., 140.

1.2.2   Herder's Critique of the Swiss 'Grecianism'

In his 'Do We Still Have the Public', Herder elaborated on exactly the same themes, declaring that his approach was to compare the best examples of the ancient public and fatherland with modern ones. Introducing the theme of 'the fatherland' specifically, he clarified his aims: rather than venturing 'upon the special *regions* of *Montesquieu's* legislature to search after his mainsprings [*Triebfeder*] of the various present forms of government', he would like to enquire whether the modern people 'no longer have a fatherland with regard to *honor, utility, freedom, courage, and religion*' (59).

In addition to Abbt's influence, that of David Hume's *Essays* is also clearly palpable in Herder's essay. While Hume's assessment of modern society was far from a jubilant one, his comparisons between ancient and modern (society, economy, politics, religion, arts and sciences) conveyed a basic message of the advantages of modern refinement. Most importantly, Herder followed Hume's characterisation of the modern age as one of trade, commerce, and growing refinement in arts as well as sociability, while his conception of modern monarchy and the international system also paralleled Hume's idea of 'civilised monarchy' and 'balance of power'.[108]

These ideas were also highly welcome in Herder's local context of the city of Riga, as he must have first heard from his mentor Johann Georg Hamann in Königsberg. Hamann had initially worked as a home tutor in various Curonian manor houses from 1753 to 1756 and had during this time befriended several important burghers in Riga, including an ambitious merchant and president of the court of trade (*Handelsgericht*) named Johann Christoph Berens. In 1756, Hamann became a home tutor for Berens's younger brother Georg and in this period also translated Louis-Joseph Plumard de Dangeul's treatise on commerce into German, supplying a lengthy commentary to it. Advocating the usefulness of commerce and the idea of commercial nobility, Plumard de Dangeul sided with the defenders of modern refinement and commerce; the young Hamann wholeheartedly agreed with him, celebrating the civilising, pacifying and equalising power of commerce as well as emphatically stipulating the compatibility of what he called 'family spirit' or 'patriotism' with '*esprit*

---

[108] David Hume, 'Of Civil Liberty' and 'Of the Rise of Arts and Sciences', in *Essays*, 87–96 and 111–137. On Herder's continuing engagement with Hume's *Essays*, see Schmidt, 'Scholarship, Morals and Government', 265–268 and Chapters 4 and 5.

de commerce.[109] In so doing, both Plumard de Dangeul and Hamann rejected the Machiavellian and Mandevillian accounts of human nature and accordingly also disputed the exclusively 'selfish' foundations of the commercial spirit.[110] In 1757, Johann Christoph Berens commissioned Hamann to travel to England so as to present Riga merchants as potentially valuable trading partners there. Little is known about Berens's plans specifically, but his broader goal had been to achieve a special status for Riga as a kind of 'commercial republic' in the Russian Empire so that Riga's own merchant fleet would have a relationship of 'neutrality' towards Britain and Prussia.[111] Hamann's efforts led to no tangible result, whereas in London he experienced a religious revelation and lost interest in debates on modern commerce. However, as we will see below, Herder had clearly read Hamann's *Supplement* and it was most likely also Hamann who had already introduced Hume's political essays to Herder when he was studying in Königsberg.[112]

The combined inspiration that Herder derived from Abbt, Hume and Hamann is initially evident in Herder's verdict on ancient republicanism. In a way, Herder even radicalised their positions, unequivocally emphasising the advantages of modern civilised monarchies (rather than some form of modern republicanism) over ancient republics.[113] Ancient (Greek) democracy and popular government, based on entrusting the people with deliberative and judicial tasks, Herder maintained, had become extinct (55–56).[114] The celebrated equality of the ancients was possible only because their societies were undifferentiated, the citizens [*Bürger*] being 'soldiers, farmers, and members of the council of state at the same time'

---

[109] [Hamann], *Des Herrn von Dangueil Anmerkungen*, 125–135. For discussion, see Vivian, 'Der Einfluß David Humes', 166–183; Christoph Meineke, '"Die Vortheile unserer Vereinigung": Hamanns Dangeuil-Beylage im Lichte der Debatte um den handeltreibenden Adel', *Johann Georg Hamann: Religion und Gesellschaft*, ed. M. Beetz and R. Andre (Halle, 2012), 46–71. On the beginning of Herder's friendship with Hamann in Königsberg and his engagement with Dangeul, see Vivian, 'Der Einfluß David Humes', 155–166, 183–184.

[110] [Hamann], *Des Herrn von Dangueil Anmerkungen*, 144–147.

[111] See Rainis Bičevskis and Aija Taimņa, 'Johann Georg Hamanns kameralwissenschaftliche Studien und Johann Christoph Berens' Vision von Riga: ein utopisches Projekt aus der zweiten Hälfte des achtzehnten Jahrhunderts', *Forschungen zur baltischen Geschichte*, 8 (2013), 127–144.

[112] Vivian, 'Der Einfluß David Humes', 158–160, 183–184.

[113] Abbt, in his *Of Dying*, already acknowledged that monarchies harboured a greater potential for the abuse of power than republics, as everything depended on one individual, while he in *On Merit* came to advocate a form of republican monarchy, see Piirimäe, 'Thomas Abbt', 54, 63–66.

[114] Rousseau was in fact also critical of the deliberative aspect of ancient democracy and insisted on a distinction between sovereignty and government. For discussion, see Sonenscher, *Jean-Jacques Rousseau*, 4–5 and passim; Richard Tuck, *The Sleeping Sovereign: The Invention of Modern Democracy* (Cambridge, 2015), 141–142. It needs to be pointed out that in all likelihood Herder was not familiar with Rousseau's *Lettres écrites de la montagne* (1764).

(57, 55). (Translation modified.)[115] In modern times, by contrast, people who engaged in farming, martial activity, and generally also government were distinguished from the burgher estate [Bürger], which in turn consisted of artisans and merchants (57). In ancient times, state and military matters were primitive enough for anyone to be able to take up the office – either military or political – without special training. But this also necessarily entailed abuses, since powerful, yet uneducated and superstitious, people were highly dependent on orators, oracles and priests who in fact manipulated their ignorance in their selfish interests (55–57).

Like Abbt and Hume, Herder regretted certain features of modern society – notably, the lack of occasions and venues for the people to gather and the disappearance of the oratory art (57–58).[116] Nevertheless, Herder was adamant that patriotism continued to be a moral duty in modern times, too. As John Vivian has suggested, here he also very clearly picked up Hamann's specific point in *Supplement to Dangeuil*. Denying patriotism to moderns, Herder argued, would amount to renouncing all hope for humane politics, hence clarifying the link between radical democratic republicanism and *selfish* political philosophy:

> Only a *Helvétius* who claims to find only selfish drives in man, a *Mandeville* who transforms us into mere *bees*, a *Machiavelli*, who creates that monster of a despot who sucks the blood [of the people] through tax collectors, *vampires* and *leeches*, only these base and cold misanthropes deprive us of the gentle sensation of patriotism; and each rotten soul that tears itself away from the fatherland and after the Ptolemaic scheme of the world makes the self's terrestrial clod the centre of the whole, will deprive itself of this gentle sentiment (61). (Translation modified.)[117]

Patriotism, Herder argued, was at a deeper level a natural feeling, the existence of which is best proven in the meritorious deeds of reformist rulers like Peter the Great or any public authorities diligently doing their duty. It was also inherent in the idea of any public institution, such as the court house, the opening of which he was celebrating in this piece. Yet, as in 'Benefit of the People', he also insisted that patriotism was simultaneously a principle and duty that enabled the people to hold their rulers in

---

[115] Cf. David Hume, 'Of Commerce', 253–267 (259) and Abbt, 'Vom Tode für das Vaterland', 598, 603–604.

[116] For a discussion of these arguments, see Redekop, *Enlightenment*, 126–129, 181–182; cf. Noyes, *Herder: Aesthetics*, 72–73.

[117] Cf. J. G. Hamann, *Des Herrn Dangeuil Anmerkungen*, 368. The similarities between Herder's ideas in this paragraph and those of J. G. Hamann in *Dangeuil* have been pointed out by John Vivian, 'Der Einfluß David Humes', 183.

check by expecting and demanding patriotism from them too. Herder conceded to Montesquieu and austere democratic republicans that patriotism was stronger in ancient times when it was inculcated through a 'political religion', when '*freedom* was an untamed *audacity*, the daring to hold the wheel of state in one's hands' and when 'the youth cried out in the heat of battle the name of *fatherland* as once heroic knights-errants called out the name of the invisible princess for whom they sacrificed themselves' (61–62). But this kind of patriotism was typical of primitive and martial people, which regarded political participation and patriotic honour as the most desirable goods in life.[118] Modern patriotism, by contrast, was based on natural feelings and the true idea of human flourishing, and hence did not require intricate political artifice and constant self-sacrifice in maintaining it. What was required was first of all the formation of patriots and citizens through public speaking and writing. There also had to be time for deliberation and delay in public discussion: decisions were not taken in the heat of passion but had to 'unfold in the repose of an open, quiet soul' (58). The true model of modern public speaking was Christian preaching, one that would recite 'neither dry *lessons*, nor *duties*' but would 'rouse the heart' and present each case with an 'urgent, practical intensity' [*dringende, praktische Fülle*] (58).

Rejecting the ideals of austere democratic republicanism, Herder emphasised the compatibility of Christianity, foreign trade, and religious tolerance, setting up 'Holland' (the Netherlands) and 'England' (Britain) as his chief examples of 'flourishing countries' in this respect (60). In his view, monarchies, too, could and did already emulate these models by guaranteeing freedom. Instead of democratic republicans' ideals of political participation and austere virtue, Herder presented security of property and private happiness as the key components of freedom. Modern freedom, he explained in the paragraph that we cited in the Introduction, was a more moderate kind of freedom that could also be guaranteed by a benevolent ruler (61). As such it was perfectly compatible with the monarchical form of government or, indeed, empire, since the people could enjoy it 'from the hands' of their 'just' rulers and it did not matter whether the rule of law was guaranteed by one or many (60).[119] Explicitly paraphrasing and referring to Abbt's *Dying for the Fatherland* in this context, Herder also advanced a more specific point: not only was freedom possible in a monarchy but monarchical patriots were also capable of dying for this freedom. The private nature of modern freedom did not exclude the

---

[118] Cf. Hume, 'Of Commerce', 259.   [119] Cf. Hume, 'Of Civil Liberty', 92–93.

sweetness and dignity of dying for the fatherland. Indeed, one could argue that it was instead the 'word *fatherland, monarch, empress*' that would be 'the sound of victory [to a patriot], impassioning his vein, stirring his heart, steadying his hands, and protecting his chest with an iron armor' (60). The idea of the *fatherland* could continue to be a 'wellspring of merit' and an 'inspiration of the wise and [a] reward of effort' in modern times just like in ancient ones (62).[120]

1.3 Conclusion

In 1771 Isaak Iselin published a review of Herder's 'On Thomas Abbt's Writings'. Voicing his sympathy with Abbt's and Herder's shared understanding of the vocation of philosophy, Iselin also pointed to something like their special intellectual congeniality:

> The writings of the late Thomas Abbt can surely be seen as a most remarkable case in the German literature. The treatise [Herder's treatise] that aims to evaluate this extraordinary phenomenon is an even more rare meteorite. The author must be a very special kind of genius. He is perhaps the only one in the whole of Germany who is able to replace Abbt for us, to make the same mistakes, easily to overhaul him in these or other things, perhaps even to be more original than his favourite writer [Abbt] himself was. Deep insights into the human soul, commendable views of the true vocation of philosophy. [. . .] Yet we also find almost as many illusory rather than thorough-going thoughts, and a number of dark affected and far-fetched ideas.[121]

As we have seen, Herder attempted to combine ideas derived from Abbt (and Hume) with those of Rousseau as early as in 1765. He initially embraced a rather more optimistic reading of Rousseau's moral philosophy. This kind of reading was also typical of a number of members of the Berne *Patriotic Society*. At a deeper level, the Bernese (like Herder) at the same time diverged from Rousseau's radical cultural criticism and pessimism about the possible reform of modern monarchies. However, like Iselin himself, Herder soon realised that Rousseau in fact put forward an *unsociable* account of human nature, which did not give much hope that individuals could improve their society from below. Herder

---

[120] Cf. Hume, 'The Rise of Arts and Sciences', 124–125; Hume, 'Of Refinement in the Arts', 268–280 (274).

[121] Isaak Iselin, 'Herder, J.G. *Über Thomas Abbts Schriften; Der Torso Von Einem Denkmal Auf Seinem Grabe Errichtet. Rezension*', *Allgemeine Deutsche Bibliothek* (*Anhang zu dem ersten bis zwölften Bände*) (1771), 626–630 (626).

accordingly began to criticise models of austere democratic republicanism inspired by Rousseau.

In so doing, Herder seems to have absorbed many of the new ideas about the compatibility of commerce and patriotism circulating in Riga in this period. He encountered them in the youth work of his mentor Johann Georg Hamann, and sought to synthesise Hamann's (and Hume's) views with those of Abbt. As Iselin recognised in his comment, Herder also derived from Abbt and Hume his understanding of the vocation of philosophy. Herder had, already in his early essay on patriotism, spelled out the characteristic features of his ideal of politics – a distinctively modern kind of polity in which the citizens would be enjoying 'modern freedom', prosperity and peace, while being animated by natural sociability and feelings of patriotism. It is with the view to this political model that Herder distanced himself from a more austere variety of Swiss Rousseauianism, one that he also characterised as Swiss 'Grecianism', and set out to develop a new, and in his view distinctively 'German' and 'modern', philosophy of patriotism.

Yet, as Iselin observed, Herder also followed Abbt in developing a number of 'dark affected' ideas. What he mainly had in view here was probably Herder's anti-intellectualism that in the next years developed into a new form of aesthetics and literary and linguistic patriotism. As Chapter 2 will show, in this development, too, Herder's engagement with Rousseau played an important role.

CHAPTER 2

Rousseau and the Origins of the 'Current Malaise of the World'

As we saw in Chapter 1, Herder was initially strongly drawn to Rousseau's educational ideas and anti-intellectualist criticism of modern moral philosophy but rejected what he saw as a strand of Rousseau-inspired 'Grecianism' in Swiss political thought. However, Rousseau had also put forward a challenging account of early human history in his *Second Discourse*. In April 1768, Herder reflected on his relationship to Rousseau in a letter he wrote to Johann Georg Hamann:

> I never succeeded, even while I was still a keen Rousseauian, in discovering his [Rousseau's] solution to the central knot, How did it come about that man passed from the state of nature into the current malaise of the world [*das jetzige Uebel der Welt*]? If his nature contained the locked treasure-trove of abilities, of inclinations and so forth, which had to remain locked for the sake of his felicity, why did God give him this germ of error? How did it begin to sprout? I remember to have asked Kant, the great student of Rousseau, about this once, but he responded like Uncle *Toby* Shandy.[1]

This chapter traces the ways in which Herder in the mid-1760s attempted to respond to Rousseau's ideas on the genealogy of the 'current malaise of the world'. As the citation above reveals, Herder realised from an early point that Rousseau's conjectural history did not allow one to see how it was possible for human culture and society to develop in a healthy manner. From a theological point of view, it was difficult to reconcile Rousseau's account with God's universal benevolence, unless one emphasised man's fallen nature or, alternatively, identified a moment in human history when

---

[1] Herder to J. G. Hamann, Riga, April 1768, in *DA*, I, 97. The translation of this citation (with a small modification) is from Noyes, *Herder: Aesthetics*, 332. Noyes clarifies the allusion to Uncle Toby Shandy as follows: 'In vol. 3, chap. 41, Sterne writes: "There is no cause but one, replied my uncle Toby, – why one man's nose is longer than another's, but because God pleases to have it so." Lawrence Sterne, *The Life and Opinions of Tristram Shandy, Gentleman* (New York: Derby and Jackson, 1857), 199'. [Unless otherwise indicated, all translations from German or French in this chapter are mine.]

an equivalent of the Fall took place. Herder was by no means prepared to endorse a strong version of the thesis of man's fallen nature, nor did he endorse any of the ancient or secular parallels of this understanding of human nature.

For Herder it was instead essential to show that even in his current pathological state, the human being remained as much a 'divine' (*Geschöpf Gottes*) as a 'human creation' (*Geschöpf des Menschen*). In the same letter to Hamann, Herder articulated this view in theological terms, arguing that an authentically 'Oriental' and 'Jewish' rather than 'Northern' and 'Christian' reading of the book of Genesis could drive home this point. While the latter would 'debase' the human senses and sensuality as the sources of error, the former would emphasise the positive openness of the human constitution. In such an authentic reading, he suggested, the tree of the knowledge of good and evil would be understood as

> the risk that the human being has taken in seeking to step outside his limits, to expand himself [*sich zu erweitern*], to collect knowledge, to enjoy foreign fruits, to imitate other creatures, to elevate reason [*die Vernunft zu erhöhen*] and to embody the place [*Sammelplatz*] where *all* instincts, *all* abilities, *all* enjoyment is collected, to be like God (no longer an animal), and to know.[2]

The potential for development and improvement thus necessarily involved the 'risk' of becoming corrupted. This was, in a nutshell, Herder's answer to Rousseau. As Wolfgang Proß has argued, in this interpretation of the tree of knowledge of good and evil Herder also already outlined the presuppositions of what came to be his own distinctive approach in *Fragments on Recent German Literature* (1767; revised version of the first collection 1768). In contrast to Hamann who viewed a combination of theology and philology as the sole way of tackling the probem of evil, Herder set out to provide a historical reconstruction of the ways in which humans have 'created instruments of knowledge' for themselves in different cultures.[3] While he initially sought to provide an all-encompassing theological, philosophical and philological view of the origins of human language and literature, he in the second edition of *Fragments* focused solely on 'Ethopöie' (*ethopoeia*), the question about the origins of distinct cultural traditions.[4]

This chapter will reconstruct the ideas Herder developed during his time in Riga regarding the earliest history of humanity. Its more specific

[2] Herder to J. G. Hamann, Riga, April 1768, in *DA*, I, 99.
[3] Proß, 'Anmerkungen [*Über die neuere deutsche Literatur*]', in *HWP*, I, 730.   [4] Ibid., 731.

aim is to determine what significance this endeavour had for the evolution of his views on modern patriotism, as spelled out in *Fragments*.[5] In this work, Herder provided a comprehensive 'patriotic' assessment of the current situation of the German language and literature, focusing on the essays in *Letters on the Newest Literature*.[6] He also provided a history of German literature as a broad field of 'higher learning',[7] and compared various individual German authors and works with those in Hebrew, Greek and Latin. Thereby, Herder hoped not only to spotlight the distinctive features of the German language and literature but also to provide guidance for an aesthetic, moral and political regeneration in Germany. Further, in this collection of essays of literary criticism, he included excerpts from several smaller essays (sometimes in a revised form) on fundamental questions about the origins of poetry, language and even society. My goal is to explain why he did so.

Previous scholarly discussions have mainly focused on Herder's evolving historicism, aesthetics or philosophical hermeneutics as set out in these early essays.[8] However, as I hope to show, his theory of German linguistic and literary patriotism rested on a philosophical history of humanity, which he devised in dialogue with several other such histories. Although Rousseau was not his sole target in *Fragments*, Herder provided a response and alternative to Rousseau's account of early human history as described in *Second Discourse*. Indeed, as we will see, Herder directly contributed to

[5] Johann Gottfried Herder, 'Über die neueste Literatur. Fragmenten. Eine Beilage zu den *Briefen, die neueste Literatur betreffend*' (three collections), in *FHA*, I, 161–540; second edition in *FHA*, I, 541–650 and Herder, 'Über die neueste Literatur. Fragmente', in *HWP*, I, 65–354. The most extensive English translation of selections from the first edition of *Fragments* is: Herder, 'On Recent German Literature: the First [and Second and Third] Collection', in *HEW*, 85–234; a selection of translations from the first edition can also be found in Herder, 'Fragments on Recent German Literature (1767–1768) [excerpts on language]', in *PW*, 33–64; The second edition has not been translated; here I have had to make translations myself. On the publishing history of *Fragments*, see Proß, 'Anmerkungen [*Über die neuere deutsche Literatur*]', in *HWP*, I, 724–733; Ernest A. Menze and Karl Menges, 'Commentary to the Translations', in *HEW*, 268–274; Stefan Greif, '3.2.2 *Über die neuere deutsche Literatur*', in *Herder Handbuch*, 431–443.

[6] Cf. Karl Menges, 'Herder on National, Popular and World Literature', in *A Companion to the Works*, 188–212 (189–195). I will return to the topic of Herder's distinctively 'German' patriotism in Chapter 5.

[7] As he programmatically argued in the introduction to the First collection, *literature* included language, *aesthetics*, history and philosophy, as they all formed a single interconnected system, Herder, 'Fragments I', in *HEW*, 95/in *HWP*, I, 76. See also Björn Hambsch, '...*ganz andre Beredsamkeit': Transformationen antiker und moderner Rhetorik bei Johann Gottfried Herder* (Tübingen, 2007), 185.

[8] For a recent discussion of these essays from the viewpoint of Herder's evolving hermeneutics, see Gjesdal, *Herder's Hermeneutics*, ch. 2. See also Stefan Greif, 'Herder's Aesthetics and Poetics', in *A Companion to the Works*, 142–164 and Ulrich Gaier, 'Myth, Mythology, New Mythology', in *A Companion to the Works*, 164–188.

what Michael Sonenscher has termed a broader 'anti-Rousseauian strand of historical speculation' in the middle of the eighteenth century.[9] Herder's interest in the origins of poetry can be described as part of this movement. He also very well understood its political implications. If it was the human capacity for poetry that demonstrated the dignity of human nature and had, from the earliest times, sustained human societies, one could hope that some form of poetry could also supply a remedy to the 'current malaise of the world'.

I will begin by briefly outlining the challenge posed by Rousseau's approach, proceeding then to describe Herder's different starting point in his early essays. I will then move on to discuss the three main alternatives to Rousseau's account that were relevant to Herder's endeavour at this moment. The first two – Isaak Iselin's and Antoine-Yves Goguet's philosophical histories of humanity – he explicitly commented on. The third was the Anglican clergyman John Brown's account of the origins of poetry, as spelled out in his *Dissertation on the rise, union, and power, the progressions, separations, and corruptions, of poetry and music* (1763).[10] Although Herder knew and had discussed several of Brown's works in his early writings and correspondence,[11] it is unclear whether Herder had read Brown's *Dissertation* by the time of writing *Fragments*.[12] Nevertheless, the parallels between their ideas are remarkable. Both Brown and Herder traced all human culture *and* politics back to humans' original creative agency. I conclude by briefly outlining Herder's understanding of literary and linguistic patriotism in *Fragments*, specifying the ways in which it could be seen as a response and projected remedy to 'the current malaise of the world'.

---

[9] Sonenscher, *Sans-Culottes*, ch. 3. (168).

[10] I am very grateful to Michael Sonenscher for drawing my attention to Herder's parallels with Brown at an early stage of my research on Herder's political thought.

[11] For discussion, see below.

[12] Johann Georg Hamann had taught Herder English in Königsberg, so in principle he could have read it in the original. The German translation of Brown's *Dissertation* appeared in 1769 as *Dr. Brown's Betrachtungen über die Poesie und Musik nach ihrem Ursprunge, ihrer Vereinigung, Gewalt, Wachstum, Trennung und Verderbniß. Aus dem Englischen übersetzt und mit Anmerkungen und zween Anhängen begleitet* von Johann Joachim Eschenburg. Eschenburg's translation also incorporated comments on Brown's considerably revised new edition of the *Dissertation*, which was published under the title *The history of the rise and progress of poetry, through its several species* (London, 1764). The French translation of Brown's second work was published in 1768 as *Histoire de l'origine et des progrès de la poésie dans ses différents genres.*

2.1   The Challenge of Rousseau's Conjectural History for Herder

There is no need to give a full outline of Rousseau's account of humans' exit from the state of nature in *Second Discourse* here, given the extensive and excellent scholarship available on this topic.[13] However, a brief summary can still help us spell out the degree of actual divergence already apparent between Rousseau and Herder in this early period.

Rousseau's *Second Discourse* bluntly rejected various theories of sociability as defended in early modern theories of natural law. Piece by piece Rousseau contested the evidence for the psychological features and powers that were usually invoked in refuting Thomas Hobbes's pessimistic views of human nature, and yet sought to show man's 'natural goodness'.[14] He denied the indirect (needs-based) and direct (affectionate) sociability of savages as well as their capability of performing complex mental operations. Neither Hobbes nor his critics, according to Rousseau, had convincingly elucidated the nature of man, and thus had offered theories that were easy to turn into instruments of man's enslavement. Rousseau himself purported to 'set aside all facts' and, thereby, precisely offer a set of more plausible 'conjectures based solely on the nature of man and of the Beings that surround him'.[15]

Natural man, Rousseau argued, was selfish, yet good because he led a self-sufficient existence. He had no needs beyond the physical ones and he never compared himself with anyone nor considered any other being to be his 'spectator'. According to Rousseau, 'man's first sentiment was that of his existence, his first care that of his preservation (self-love or *amour de soi*)'. Self-sufficient existence was also the source of the greatest contentment. Without foresight, man did not even fear death.[16] Self-sufficient man had no 'interest' in others, but thanks to his instinct of pity he was also wary of harming them; he had a natural aversion to witnessing another being's suffering.[17]

---

[13] See, e.g., Arthur M. Melzer, *The Natural Goodness of Man: On the System of Rousseau's Thought* (Chicago, 1990). On Rousseau's critique of modern natural law and his refutation of the principle of sociability, see Kapossy, *Iselin contra Rousseau*, 207–222. On Rousseau's alternative conjectural history (grounded on a more capacious form of pity developed through love) as set out in his *Essay on the Origin of Languages* (which was published posthumously as late as 1781), see Sonenscher, *Sans-Culottes*, 30–33; see also ibid., 110–133 and 146–164 and Sonenscher, *Jean-Jacques Rousseau*, chs. 4–5.

[14] Melzer, *The Natural Goodness*, passim; Kapossy, *Iselin contra Rousseau*, 207–218.

[15] Rousseau, 'Second Discourse', 132.   [16] Ibid., 142–143.

[17] Ibid., 218, 153. This brief account is largely indebted to Melzer's analysis of Rousseau's conception of self-love in *The Natural Goodness*, 35–48.

Change in human nature – one that resulted in creating Hobbesian man – occurred because of man's free will and 'perfectibility', the capacities that enabled him to respond to new circumstances.[18] When human beings were pushed out of the tropical forest due to their expanding numbers and natural catastrophes, they needed to cooperate for survival, and thus came into closer contact and communication with each other. Consequently, their ability to reason started developing, suggesting new means of self-preservation. This gradually led to the creation of human language,[19] the invention of tools and the establishment of fixed dwellings, and finally family. Much of the intellectual progress, of course, was initially admirable. In the conditions of sustained communal life, which gradually emerged due to the progress of language, humans became capable of forming abstract ideas of regularity and proportion and acquired new notions of 'beauty and merit'.[20] When applied to other human beings, these ideas engendered personal preferences and 'moral love'. Love and leisure, Rousseau maintained, gave rise to song and dance, which enabled humans to further distinguish themselves through their natural talents. Thanks to the rise of the arts, they generally began to esteem each other according to their natural talents. Instead of, however, accepting others' judgement of themselves, they now felt 'amour-propre' growing in them, this 'relative sentiment, factitious and born in society, which inclines every individual to set greater store by himself than by anyone else'. They sought recognition of their superiority from others.[21] The moral consequences were harsh:

> This was the first step at once towards inequality and vice: from these first preferences arose vanity and contempt on the one hand, shame and envy on the other; and the fermentation caused by these new leavens eventually produced compounds fatal to happiness and innocence.[22]

A striking feature of *Second Discourse* was that Rousseau referred neither to other-regarding affections and sympathy, nor to aesthetic sensibility as foundations of morality. He presented morality as a purely social institution based on man's self-interest and the natural and unreflective sentiment of pity.[23] The maxim that pity gave to man, Rousseau argued, was not the 'subtle maxim of reasoned justice, *Do unto others as you would do unto you*', but the 'less perfect, but perhaps more useful' one of – *Do your*

---

[18] Rousseau, 'Second Discourse', 140–141; 159.   [19] Ibid., 146–150.   [20] Ibid., 162–165.
[21] Ibid., 218n; 153–155.   [22] Ibid., 165–166.
[23] Ibid., 163. For a more detailed discussion, see Keohane, *Philosophy and the State*, 439.

own good with the least possible harm to others.[24] He did not specify how this maxim could be identical to the 'wish that others be happy'. Furthermore, Rousseau's whole argument was designed to show that the idea of common interest and pity played only a very limited role in the psychology of civilised man. Although man did experience pity in modern theatres in modern times it did not have any significant effect on the actions of civilised man. Similarly, the rise of amour-propre and deception made it hard for humans to perceive instances of common interest. True, Rousseau claimed that morality began to enter into human actions after the rise of amour-propre, but he was referring to a false morality that had nothing to do with the instinct of pity. False 'morality' was based on the 'idea of consideration', which in turn was grounded in the perceived reciprocity of amour-propre: 'everyone claimed a right to it [consideration], and one could no longer deprive anyone of it with impunity.'[25] The 'first duties of civility' required everyone to forbear intentional affronts, because they were now qualified as cases of 'contempt shown to [some]one's person', which was 'often more unbearable than the harm itself' and thus punished 'in a manner proportionate to the stock he [the person] set by himself'.[26] Although fear of vengeance was a rather unreliable constraint on one's amour-propre, it managed to discipline humans to a certain extent at least.

Along with offering a minimalist account of the foundations of morality, Rousseau thus specified the conditions under which selfish passions could provide some stability in society, particularly at an early stage of its development. He even affirmed that the period of human history in which this kind of 'morality' regulated human interactions was the 'happiest and most lasting epoch' in human history, 'occupying a just mean between the indolence of the primitive state and the petulant activity of our *amour-propre*' that unfolded fully only when the notion of property was invented.[27]

Nevertheless, such a condition was not sustainable. The culprit was the perfectibility of man itself.[28] Humans began to feel conjugal and paternal love through the habit of living together, but they also acquired artificial needs, becoming dependent on the conveniences that 'weaken the body and mind'. This dependence was a true 'yoke', since it was 'much more

[24] Rousseau, 'Second Discourse', 154.   [25] Ibid., 166.   [26] Ibid.   [27] Ibid., 167.
[28] For a helpful discussion about the three 'states of mankind' in Rousseau's conjectural history of humanity as well as about the analytical and historical bifurcation of this process that Rousseau laid out in his *Second Discourse*, on the one hand, and his *Social Contract* (1762) and *Considerations on the Government of Poland* (published posthumously in 1781), on the other, see Sonenscher, *Sans-Culottes*, 30–34, 110–164.

cruel to be deprived of them than to possess them was sweet'.[29] Private property or institutionalised (artificial) inequality was established with the division of labour and the development of the arts of metallurgy and agriculture. Due to the inequality of various talents (strength, skill, inventiveness), 'one soon earned much while the other had trouble staying alive'. A general dependence followed, whereby man was subjugated to 'those of his kind': 'rich, he needs their services; poor, he needs their help, and moderate means do not enable him to do without them. He must therefore constantly try to interest them in his fate and to make them really or apparently find their own profit in working for his.'[30] This was the beginning of modern commercial society, a type of society based on mutual needs and dependence.

As we have seen, in addition to satisfying new 'needs', men also pursued 'consideration' and 'superiority' (distinction). The interaction between the pursuit of material needs and these passions in the framework of a full-blown property system was what inspired men's ultimately fatal ardour and resulted in the fundamental falseness and conflict of commercial society:

> Here are all natural qualities set in action, every man's rank and fate set, not only as to the amount of their goods and the power to help and to hurt, but also as to mind, beauty, strength, skill, as to merit or talents, and since these are the only qualities that could attract consideration, one soon had to have or to affect them; for one's own advantage one had to seem other than one in fact was. To be and to appear became two entirely different things, and from this distinction arose ostentatious display, deceitful cunning, and all the vices that follow in their wake.[31]

Non-productive trades, such as those of artists and scientists, were fully integrated into commercial society. As we saw above, Rousseau regarded the arts and sciences as expressions of love and as pastimes that quickly degenerated into instruments of attracting esteem. With the growth of inequality and the establishment of private property, some poor men learned that they could flatter the rich through art and thereby capitalise on their talent, whether real or affected. Even scientists could cherish the hope of being funded by the rich who might wish to earn esteem through supporting their work. The rich on the one hand, and the artists and learned, on the other, thus necessarily corrupted each other.[32]

---

[29] Rousseau, 'Second Discourse', 164–165; cf. 155.   [30] Ibid., 170.   [31] Ibid.
[32] Rousseau develops this genealogy most clearly in 'Observations', 45f. Cf. also 'First Discourse', 16–19, 22f. and 'Last Reply', 65.

Furthermore, humans' pursuit of superiority instilled in them 'a black inclination to harm one another', an inclination that was 'all the more dangerous as it often assumes the mask of benevolence in order to strike its blow in greater safety.'[33] Insofar as the poor had no other pacific means of sustaining themselves than serving the rich, they were in the power of the rich who could make use of them for fulfilling their own desire for superiority and power. Yet they could likewise gang up with other poor people and subject the rich to 'banditry'.[34] Despite humans' attempts at deceiving each other about the reciprocity of their interests, this system of mutual dependence and non-transparency in intentions and qualities necessarily gave rise to 'the most horrible state of war' between the rich and the poor. Political societies were established through fraudulent social contract between the two warring classes in society; a degree of peace was guaranteed in them initially, but since the inequality of property was instituted by laws, the same competitive and deceitful game continued in an only slightly less openly aggressive form within political societies.[35] For Rousseau, there was thus no hope that any kind of art could somehow directly help remedy the 'current malaise of society'.

2.2 Herder's Earliest Essays on the Origins of Poetry

Herder never fully accepted the value in the theoretical construction of the 'state of nature' and in his later writings mounted a direct attack on the concept.[36] However, as we shall see, this did not mean that he regarded the search for the 'origins' of human culture and society as useless. Rather, he rejected purely conjectural accounts of these origins.[37] For Herder, the historical sources (*Urkunden*) or 'facts' as Rousseau had labelled the information derived from such sources, were highly important. Of course, no proper 'reports' (*Nachrichten*) were available on these earliest times, but there were other kinds of important historical sources – the earliest forms of human poetry that had subsequently been recorded in written documents.[38] Although Herder was also willing to engage in theological

---

[33] Rousseau, 'Second Discourse', 171.   [34] Ibid.   [35] Ibid., 175, 182.
[36] See Chapters Four and Seven for further analysis.
[37] On young Herder's self-distanciation from the theoretical constructions about the first man by a broad range of contemporary philosophers, see Wolfgang Proß, 'Nachwort', in *HWP*, III/1, 839–1040 (897–905).
[38] Herder, 'Versuch einer Geschichte der lyrischen Dichtkunst', in *HWP*, I, 8–61 (11); Herder, 'Essay on a History of Lyrical Poetry', in *HEW*, 71.

speculation about the meaning of such documents,[39] his main approach initially was a synthetic one. Already in his earliest unfinished essays,[40] he sought to combine and synthesise some of the current conjectural inves-tigations into the history of the human mind and religion with a compar-ative approach and philological study of ancient poetry and 'literary documents' such as the Bible.[41]

Early on, Herder treated questions about the origins of poetry and religion as belonging to one and the same broader area of enquiry into the origins of human civilisation, and sought to mediate between the Platonic (and Stoic) and Epicurean (and Lucretian) positions on these issues.[42] Briefly stated, the question was whether poetry and religion originated in divine inspiration or were to be seen as human inventions. If the former origin was true, then early works of poetry were also in some sense models for the later works. If, however, the opposite origin was believed, then the primitive and crude style of these early works tended to be highlighted. By Herder's time, there was an increasing consensus that settling the matter involved examining the actual early 'documents' and determining the ways in which they were to be interpreted, which enabled combining elements from both sides of the controversy. For example, in pondering the question about the origins of poetry, Herder drew on the rising tide of Homer studies in Britain and Switzerland, particularly on Thomas Blackwell's *Enquiry into the Life and Writings of Homer* (1735) and Johann Jacob Bodmer's and Johann Jacob Breitinger's various studies of poetics.[43] He also engaged substantially with Robert Lowth's and David

[39] On Herder's relationship to contemporary theological interpretations of the 'tree of knowledge', see also Proß, 'Nachwort', in *HWP*, III/1, 897–905.

[40] Herder, 'Von der Ode. Dispositionen, Enwürfe, Fragmente (1764–1765)', in *FHA*, I, 57–101/ 'Fragments of a Treatise on the Ode', in *HEW*, 35–52; 'Versuch einer Geschichte der lyrischen Dichtkunst (1764)', in *HWP*, I, 9–61/'Essay on the History of Lyrical Poetry', in *HEW*, 69–84; '(Von der Veränderung des Geschmacks)', in *FHA*, I, 149–161/'On the Transformation of Taste of Nations in the Course of Ages' (1766), 65–68; Herder, '(Von den ältesten Nationalgesängen)', in *SWS*, I, 148–152.

[41] For an overview of the wide range of authors and works relevant to Herder in this enterprise, see Proß, 'Anmerkungen [*Geschichte der lyrischen Dichtkunst*]', in *HWP*, I, 694–724. For a good introduction into the epistemological foundations of Herder's aesthetics and poetics in general, see Greif, 'Herder's Aesthetics'. For a broader pan-European background and specification of the uses to which Biblical history was put in debates about sociability, see Robertson, 'Sacred History' and Robertson, 'Sociability in Sacred Historical Perspective'. On Herder's Biblical studies more generally, see Rudolf Smend, 'Kommentar. Herder und die Bibel', in *FHA*, V, 1309–1322; Christoph Bultmann, 'Herder's Biblical Studies', in *A Companion to the Works*, 233–245.

[42] The best ancient source on this controversy is Cicero's *De natura deorum* (43 BC).

[43] Bodmer's weekly journal *Die Discourse der Mahlern* (from 1746 *Der Mahler der Sitten*) was modeled on *The Spectator*. Bodmer's most important writings were the treatises *Von dem Einfluss und Gebrauche der Einbildungs-Krafft* (1727) (co-authored by Johann Jacob Breitinger), *Von dem*

Michaelis' Biblical hermeneutics, sharing many of Michaelis's arguments against Lowth's residual Platonism in his insistence on the divine origin and exemplary brilliance of Hebrew poetry.[44] Like Michaelis, he instead maintained that all earliest examples of fine arts – including the Bible – needed to be viewed in historical context, as reflecting the modes of thinking of an uncivilised, sensuous people.[45] Furthermore, Herder was also sympathetic to David Hume's radically naturalist perspective as elaborated in his *History of Natural Religion* (1757), as well as Edmund Burke's account of the sublime and beautiful in his *Philosophical Enquiry into the Origin of Our Ideas of the Sublime and Beautiful* (1757).[46]

As we will see, Herder ultimately combined insights from both sides of the controversy. Whilst accepting the unmistakably primitive style of ancient poetry (including the Bible), and other fine arts, he also highlighted the dignity of human nature as expressed in these early creative acts of humanity. Johann Georg Hamann's evocative characterisation of poetry as the 'mother-tongue of the human race' in his *Aesthetica in nuce* (1760/2) clearly heavily inspired Herder here. Although he did not endorse Hamann's distinctive theologico-philosophical account of original poetry as translation from the divine into human language,[47] he attempted to prove the more general point about poetry as an expression of the 'divinely' creative power of humanity.

Herder's earliest reflections on the history of poetic art were focussed on the 'ode'. Herder used the term 'ode' to mean a 'poem that expresses a

---

Wunderbaren in der Poesie (1740) and *Critische Betrachtungen über die poetischen Gemälde der Dichter* (1741).

44 Robert Lowth, De *sacra poesi hebraeorum: praelectiones academicae oxonii habitae* (London, 1753). Lowth's lectures were republished, edited and commented on by the Göttingen scholar David Michaelis in *De sacra poesi hebraeorum: praelectiones academicae oxonii habitae, Notas Et Epimetra Adiecit*, Joannes David Michaelis, 2 vols. (1758–1761). On Lowth and Michaelis, see Michael Legaspi, *The Death of Scripture and the Rise of Biblical Studies* (Oxford, 2010), ch. 5; on Michaelis, see Avi Lifschitz, *Language and the Enlightenment: The Berlin Debates of the Eighteenth Century* (Oxford, 2012), ch. 4. See also Menges, 'Commentary to the Translations', in *HEW*, 52.

45 Herder, 'Versuch einer Geschichte der lyrischen Dichtkunst', in *HWP*, I, 17.

46 For discussion, see Proß, 'Anmerkungen. [*Geschichte der lyrischen Dichtkunst*]', in *HWP*, I, 693–724 (particularly 718–719). On Hume's *Natural History of Religion*, see Robertson, *The Case for the Enlightenment*, 308–334; on Burke's *Philosophical Enquiry*, see Richard Bourke, *Empire and Revolution: The Political Life of Edmund Burke* (Princeton, 2015), 119–159.

47 See Pierre Pénisson, 'Nachwort. *Die Palingenesie der Schriften: die Gestalt des Herderschen Werks*', in *HWP*, I, 864–924 (909); Proß, 'Anmerkungen. [*Geschichte der lyrischen Dichtkunst*]', in *HWP*, I,; Stefan Greif, '3.1 Einleitung. Ästhetik, Poetik, Literaturkritik', in *Herder Handbuch*, 387–395, 390–391; Greif, '3.2.2 *Über die neuere Literatur*', 435. On Herder's parodistic self-distanciation from Hamann's *Aesthetica in nuce* (1760/2) in his *Dithyrambische Rhapsodie*, see Hans Graubner, '3.2.1 Dithyrambische Rhapsodie über die Rhapsodie kabbalistischer Prose', in *Herder Handbuch*, 395–421.

certain feeling and is meant to be sung'; as such, he emphasised, it also seeks to excite feelings and stir a sympathetic connection (*Sympathie*) between singers.[48] In an early collection of fragments known as *Fragments of a Treatise on the Ode* (1762–1765), Herder described the ode as 'the firstborn child of poetic sensibility', the work of an 'odic genius' that shakes the 'living' to the 'nervous core' and as such serves as the 'fountainhead' of all fine arts.[49] Thereby, Herder was already locating the origin of all human cultural and social development in the ode. Pointing to the universal occurrence of this form of poetry, he accepted that the particular types of sensibility that different nations developed in their distinctive and geographical settings necessarily also had an impact on their 'odes'. Furthermore, the 'ode' later became part of a heritage cultivated by religious leaders, which meant that an examination of its earliest form was a challenging task:

> Of how many unrevealed secrets and fertile developments it would be a pregnant seed, if it were analyzed by the master of the mainsprings of our heart, a genius who perceives poetic art in its youthful fire, in manly contest and triumph. But observe the difficulties! The fountainhead of poetic art is part of the most sacred darkness of the East, of the Orphic and the Eleusinian mysteries, of the priestly oaths of Druids and Bards.[50]

In a text entitled *An Essay on a History of Lyrical Poetry* (1764), Herder explained the rationale for such a search for the origins of poetry: 'Lacking the origin', Herder wrote, 'we obviously miss a part of its history [. . .], especially the most important part of the history from which, in the end, everything is derived.'[51] It was important to go back to an invention's earliest origins in order to avoid constructing one-sided accounts of its nature. Like Rousseau, Herder thus demanded that, when studying the history of mankind, one needed to uncover the earliest form of a phenomenon under study as it was only on this basis that one could arrive at a proper 'genetic explanation' for the developments that followed.[52] The hypothesis of the divine origin of poetry, while popular with early humans themselves, explained nothing to modern men, and was incompatible with

---

[48] He provides this definition in 'Von der Ode', 59, 67, 70.
[49] Herder, 'Fragments of a Treatise on the Ode', in *HEW*, 50/in *FHA*, I, 78–79.
[50] Herder, 'Fragments of a Treatise on Ode', in *HEW*, 36/in *FHA*, I, 78–79.
[51] Herder, 'Essay on a History of Lyrical Poetry', in *HEW*, 70/in *HWP*, I, 10; cf. Herder, 'Fragments', in *PW*, 53/in *HWP*, I, 150.
[52] Herder, 'Essay on a History of Lyrical Poetry', in *HEW*, 70/in *HWP*, I, 10; cf. Herder, 'Fragments', in *PW*, 53/in *HWP*, I, 150.

the actual ways in which things evolved.[53] According to Herder, nothing was ever invented at one single moment in time and nothing was perfect at the beginning. Chance played a significant role, 'a number of causes worked together, alongside and following one another, so secretively that even the inventor himself often could not account for them'.[54] Yet, as we shall see, this did not mean that odes were purely human inventions; they were human inventions, but it was a deeper emotional and creative energy that expressed itself in them.

Herder's view of the feelings that were expressed in the early odes was roughly as follows. In a Humean vein, Herder particularly emphasised 'pressing need' as the source of these feelings. Religion, too, was such a common need. Odes were basically prayers sung in unison and at moments of common need.[55] As sensuous beings, early humans could not have any abstract ideas about order in the world. Furthermore, they were also more prone to experiencing unpleasant sentiments than pleasant ones in such a situation. Thus, it was not a divinely inspired admiration for order in the world (as Shaftesbury, for example, had argued in a Platonic and Stoic vein), but rather the unpleasant sentiments of fear and anger that were expressed in these early songs, using a sensuous language.[56] The early songs thus did not directly express 'perfection', but were merely 'sensuous' and 'powerful'.[57] The point of these songs was to 'move' and 'stir, excite passions'.[58] Further, 'hymns', a subset of odes extolling the deeds of divine beings, also portrayed virtue as it was understood in this period:

> And what more can we ask of hymns than that they ... sing the virtue of their age! [...] because it [their virtue] was also related to strong passions, vindictiveness, partisanship, ambition and cruelty: so you don't have to weigh it in any bowl other than the culture of that time, and with no other weights than political and poetic virtue.[59]

In another early essay, Herder also expressed the wish that Isaak Iselin's *History of Mankind* would be 'enlivened' in this respect, particularly 'what concerns this remarkable moment, the one in which the transition from a fictional state of nature to the first documented descriptions of primitive

---

[53] Herder, 'Essay on a History of Lyrical Poetry', in *HEW*, 74, 76–79/in *HWP*, I, 16–21; cf. Herder, 'Fragments', in *PW*, 55–59/'Fragmente I', in *HWP*, I, 153–156.

[54] Herder, 'Essay on a History of Lyrical Poetry', in *HEW*, 71–73/in *HWP*, I, 11–13; cf. Herder, 'Fragments', in *PW*, 53–55 'Fragmente I', in *HWP*, I, 150–152.

[55] Herder, 'Geschichte der lyrischen Dichtkunst', in *HWP*, I, 29 (there is no English translation of the second half of the text.)

[56] Ibid.   [57] Ibid., 40.   [58] Ibid., 41.   [59] Ibid., 48.

societies took place'.[60] Herder further refined this idea in both *An Essay on the History of Lyrical Poetry, Fragments* and *On the First Documents of the Human Race*. The search for these origins, he argued in *Fragments*, was common to all peoples, each one of which possessed shared cosmogonies and legends, poets telling stories about the creation and origins of institutions or customs. In modern times, however, it was possible to 'combine' this kind of ancient poetry with philosophy, and 'turn what they both supply into history'.[61] Indeed, as we shall see, this was precisely what he himself was doing, and what he also called on others to do. In *Fragments*, too, he acknowledged Iselin's account, while also pointing out other important sources of inspiration for him: while Isaak Iselin had already 'illustriously' worked on such a 'plan' of earliest history, Antoine-Yves Goguet's *The origins of laws, arts and sciences, and their progress among the most ancient nations* (orig. 1758) had 'collected materials' for it 'with great industry'.[62] In order to gain a clearer understanding of what was at stake here for Herder, let us have a closer look at the arguments of these works that were relevant to Herder's endeavour.

2.3   Iselin's Response to Rousseau

As we saw in Chapter 1, Herder rejected Iselin's early *Philosophical and Patriotic Dreams* (1755, 1758) as being based on 'idealistic Grecianism'. Iselin's *Philosophical History of Mankind* (1764),[63] however, developed a very different position on human history. Here, Iselin elaborated on human anthropology and the philosophically possible primitive state of nature whilst also comparing the available information on the savage and barbarian stages of human history with that on the 'civilised' stage. In what follows, I will provide a brief overview of Iselin's account of the first two. We will return to his broader vision of the dynamics of universal history in Chapter 4.[64]

As Béla Kapossy has shown in fascinating detail, Iselin's mature work was a direct response to Rousseau's *Second Discourse*. Iselin understood very clearly that countering Rousseau required engaging with the latter's purely

---

[60] Herder, 'Von den ältesten Nationalgesängen', in *SWS*, XXXII, 152; cf. Herder, 'Über die ersten Urkunden des menschlichen Geschlechts. Einige Anmerkungen', in *FHA*, V, 9–179 (16).
[61] Herder, 'Fragments', in *PW*, 53/in *HWP*, I, 150.   [62] Ibid.
[63] *Philosophische Muthmassungen über die Geschichte der Menschheit*, 2 vols. (Frankfurt and Leipzig, 1764) (II edition 1768, III edition 1784).
[64] For a comprehensive systematic comparison of various aspects of Herder's and Iselin's philosophy of history, see Wolfgang Proß, 'Geschichte als Provokation zur Geschichtsphilosophie', in *Isaak Iselin und die Geschichtsphilosophie der europäischen Aufklärung*, ed. Lucas Marco Gisi and Wolfgang Rother (*Studien zur Geschichte der Wissenschaften in Basel. Neue Folge* VI) (Basle, 2011), 201–265.

imaginary state of nature and his corresponding account of the development of the human mind and sociability.[65] As seen above, Rousseau had granted savages the sentiment of 'pity', but denied its efficacy in a civilised society. Combined with his rejection of natural sociability, this led to a highly critical view of the underlying moral psychology of modern societies. In the first and second book of his *History of Mankind*, Iselin mounted a direct counterattack on Rousseau. He argued that humans were endowed with self-perception and an 'internal sentiment' (*innerliche Empfindung*) that was the source of all their powers.[66] They also had a natural propensity to take pleasure in 'anything that increases their mental activity', and were capable of forming not only sensuous ideas but also 'inventing' new ones through their creative imagination (*Dichtungskraft*).[67] Since humans were also endowed with foresight and their 'invented' ideas afforded them stronger and more lasting pleasure than the merely sensuous ones, they were naturally inclined (*Neigung*) towards acquiring an ever greater number of ideas and intellectual pleasure.[68] They also possessed a 'dark feeling of pleasure in another human being's pleasure as well as compassion for his sadness' as a fundamental drive of the human soul (*Grundtrieb der menschlicher Seele*), hence having a rudimentary disposition for sociability.[69] By highlighting these psychological traits, Iselin sought to shore up a broader argument about humanity's potential for an increase in true knowledge, moral progress, and eventually self-determination and self-government.[70]

Iselin granted that there was no reliable historical information about the state of nature. His ideas about this state – a state of 'perfectly simple mores' (*der Stand der vollkommen einfältigen Sitten*) as he also characterised it – were more like 'philosophical hypotheses than historical truths'.[71] However, from the first philosophical principles the 'rest would easily follow'. For example, one could safely assume that humans' 'inexperienced senses' would lead them to adopt 'an entire chaos of imagined and chimerical ideas', which in turn would serve as the basis for their 'way of thinking' and action (inclinations), and be shared by entire nations for

---

[65] Kapossy, *Iselin contra Rousseau*, 231.   [66] Iselin, *Über die Geschichte der Menschheit*, I, 3–4.
[67] Ibid., 7–11.   [68] Ibid., 14, 25.
[69] Iselin, *Über die Geschichte der Menschheit*, I, 128, 129–130. For Iselin, the propensity to take pleasure in ideas was also responsible for the emergence of 'national spirit'. He maintained that the 'common character' of these habitual notions and inclinations provided a further source of addiction to them, ibid., 97. For a detailed reconstruction of Iselin's history of the human mind, see Kapossy, *Iselin contra Rousseau*, 231–240; see also Proß, 'Geschichte als Provokation', 242–247.
[70] Kapossy, *Iselin contra Rousseau*, 264–265.   [71] Iselin, *Über die Geschichte der Menschheit*, I, 161.

centuries.[72] They would demonstrate a strong attraction to music and dance 'without any regard to its quality', as it helped to increase their ideas without requiring any strong effort in exercising their powers.[73] They would also develop rudimentary forms of maternal and familial love. Their current enjoyments as well as self-love would often overwhelm all other ideas, but gradually their attention would fall on what brought them greater enjoyment and they would develop ideas about property.[74] Invoking the authority of the Bible and natural historians (first of all, Count of Buffon), Iselin emphasised the completeness of human beings at this early stage.[75] External circumstances, however, would have a major impact on the ways in which humans further developed. In favourable circumstances, in mild climates and fertile lands, humans would learn to cognise perfection and develop ideas about order early on, whereas in colder and mountainous territories, they would 'stay as rude as their nature'.[76] Drawing on Strabo, Iselin also distinguished between 'peaceful herders', on the one hand, and hunters, on the other – it was only the latter who became violent to each other and other societies.[77] The peaceful herders, however, were soon overrun by the hunters, which led towards the establishment of slavery and inspired new ideas of political subordination and obedience.[78] This was Iselin's explanation for the early moral and political corruption experienced by humans.

In contrast to Rousseau, Iselin, however, was generally optimistic about the overall evolutionary dynamics of human history. He famously posited an analogy between evidence of mental development in individuals and within nations (and ultimately the human species).[79] It was 'almost a

---

[72] Ibid., 104. Kapossy, *Iselin contra Rousseau*, 230–232.

[73] Iselin, *Über die Geschichte der Menschheit*, I, 113.   [74] Ibid., 105, 118.

[75] Ibid., 132. Iselin clearly aligned himself with the more optimistic varieties of Christian moral psychology that also sought to incorporate (neo-)Stoic arguments about human sociability to buttress human perfectibility. On a parallel British movement, see Rivers, *Reason, Grace*, II.

[76] Iselin, *Über die Geschichte der Menschheit*, I, 134–161.   [77] Ibid., 150, 194.

[78] Ibid., 149–150.

[79] Ibid., I, 74–76, 108–116, 138–144, 242–243. For Iselin, individual human beings within one nation could reach quite different degrees of rational thinking; it was the 'governing' and most numerous group of people that was representative of the overall state of development of a particular nation. For a broader discussion of this parallelism, see Lucas Marco Gisi, *Einbildungskraft und Mythologie. Die Verschränkung von Anthropologie und Geschichte im 18: Jahrhundert* (Berlin, New York, 2007), 334–357 and Gisi, 'Die anthropologische Basis von Iselins Geschichtsphilosophie', in *Isaak Iselin*, 124–152. As Gisi has pointed out, it is in fact only in the 1768 edition that Iselin distinguished three kinds of human beings and stages of individual and species development. In 1764, Iselin posited a dualistic schema of two 'main classes' of humanity (the 'animal-like' and 'barbarian' sensuous humans, on the one hand, and civilised (*gesittete*) rational humans, on the other). The 1768 edition further distinguished between animal-like human beings led by their senses and 'barbarian' human beings dominated by their imagination (accordingly

general natural law', Iselin argued, that 'man cannot attain a rational state straight away'.[80] A childhood of 'sweet pleasures', he wrote, was followed by a stormy, savage youth.[81] In a similar manner, the period of natural simplicity was followed by that of 'savagery and barbarism' (*Stand der Wildheit und der Barbarey*). Increasing their knowledge, humans would nevertheless gradually progress towards a 'civilised state' (*gesittete Stand*).[82]

2.4   Antoine-Yves Goguet on the Origins of Inventions

Along with Iselin's philosophical history, Herder also mentioned Antoine-Yves Goguet's *The origin of laws, arts, and sciences* as relevant to his own enquiry into the earliest human history.[83] Essentially, Goguet's widely read work can be seen as a compendium-like synthesis of various kinds of historical approaches available in his day – conjectural history, Biblical history, comparative philology and ethnography (he also substantially drew on various new-world travelogues).[84] This does not mean, however, that Goguet would have refrained from taking sides in the controversy over sociability. In contrast to Iselin, Goguet straightforwardly dismissed the views of all those who 'extolled the virtues of primitive ages'. Invoking what was in itself a combination of Augustinian and Epicurean accounts of human nature, Goguet accepted the corrupt nature of man:

> From these facts let us draw this conclusion that men have been essentially the same in all ages. From their birth subjected to the evil tendencies of their corrupt nature, they have laboured at all times to gratify their passions, sometimes with lesser, and sometimes with greater degrees of delicacy, according to the taste and knowledge of the age in which they lived. Mens [*sic*] way of thinking and acting have always born a relation to their circumstances. The apparent simplicity of the first ages, so much celebrated by many

---

also highlighting two kinds of 'uncivilised' stages in human history), Gisi, 'Die anthropologische Basis', 132–134.

[80] Iselin, *Über die Geschichte der Menschheit*, I, 239.   [81] Ibid., 242.   [82] Ibid.

[83] The French original was *De l'origine des lois, des arts et des sciences et de leurs progrès chez les anciens peuples* (Paris, 1758). The English translation was published in 1761 and the German one in 1760/1762. Goguet's relevance for Herder has been highlighted by Proß, 'Anmerkungen. [*Geschichte der lyrischen Dichtkunst*]', in *HWP*, I, 693–998; on Goguet, see Rohbeck, Johannes, 'La philosophie de l'histoire chez Antoine-Yves Goguet: Chronique biblique et Progrés historique', in *Dix-huitième siècle* 34 (2002), 257–266 and Nathaniel Wolloch, '"Facts, or Conjectures": Antoine-Yves Goguet's Historiography', *Journal of the History of Ideas*, 68:3 (2007), 429–449.

[84] On his sources, see ibid., 432–433.

authors, was owing to their ignorance and rudeness. These times would be more truly characterised, by saying that vice then appeared in all its ugliness and deformity.[85]

At the same time, Goguet acknowledged the difficulty of understanding the phenomenon of 'mores': 'Of all subjects we have had occasion to speak upon', Goguet conceded in a footnote, 'there is none more curious and interesting than this of mores [the contemporaneous English translation uses the term 'manners'] and customs; and, at the same time, there is none more difficult for which to give a clear and precise definition.'[86] On the one hand, human opinions and mores were highly diverse, being dependent upon the climate, the degree of knowledge attained, and various kinds of external circumstances.[87] On the other hand, post-diluvian humans also all seemed to agree on some customs at least, which called for further explanation and discussion. When listing such common mores and customs, Goguet mentioned religion and the 'keeping of solemn festivals on some occasions'.[88] He further pointed out the universality of poetry and singing among savage nations, arguing that it was only natural that a savage mind would wish to express its lively sentiments by seeking out 'daring figures, bold and lively images, sublime and soaring expressions'.[89] Goguet also discussed the various hypotheses on the origins of poetry that had been put forward so far, rejecting both the purely utilitarian ones and those that saw its origins in divine enthusiasm and love. Poetry, Goguet emphasised, was used to express all kinds of feelings and existed even where no religious worship was found.[90] Feelings of national self-aggrandisement, gratitude and the simple 'joy' that burst forth after some danger had been avoided could all be seen to prompt nations or their heroes to express their sentiments in poems. Singing and dancing, by contrast, naturally came to accompany the former and were also universal

---

[85] Goguet, *The Origin of Laws*, I, 367. On the different ways in which the Augustinian and Epicurean perspectives were merged in the eighteenth century, see the classic works of Hundert, *The Enlightenment Fable* and Keohane, *Philosophy and the State*.

[86] Goguet, *The Origin of Laws*, I, 367. Like Fontenelle and Iselin, and in contrast to Montesquieu in *The Spirit of the Laws* and Chévalier Jaucourt in Diderot's *Encyclopédie*, Goguet did not seek to distinguish between 'mores' (*moeurs*), manners (*manières*), and customs (*coutumes*). By the 'mores (*moeurs*) of the people', Goguet proposed, 'the way of judging on the morality of human actions' could be understood, while the term 'customs' (*coutumes*) could be used interchangeably with 'manners (*manières*)' or 'way of thinking' (*façon de penser*, translated into German as 'Denkungsart'), ibid.; see Goguet, *Von dem Ursprunge der Gesezze, der Künste und der Wissenschaften; wie auch derselben Wachstum unter den alten Völkern*, trans. Georg Christoph Hamberger (Lemgo, 1760), 334–335.

[87] Goguet, *The Origin of Laws*, I, 327.   [88] Ibid., 327.   [89] Ibid., 341.

[90] Ibid. Proß highlights the significance of Goguet's emphasis on poetry as the most original form of art for Herder, 'Anmerkungen [*Geschichte der lyrischen Dichtkunst*]', in *HWP*, I, 702.

among all nations. None of these contrasting pure hypotheses was thus fully satisfying.[91]

Despite their differing accounts of human nature and sociability, Iselin and Goguet concurred in their generally favourable view of the civilising power of the arts and sciences, and the latter's role in humanity's attaining a correct understanding of morality. Combining the Biblical two-stages history with the Epicurean/Lucretian one, Goguet distinguished only two main developmental stages in the history of human society – a nomadic one during the 'savage' and 'barbarian' period, and a settled one during the period of civilisation (agriculture leading to urbanisation and commerce).[92] According to Goguet, the actual civilisation of humanity only truly took off when mankind entered into the settled stage, the establishment of a proper division of labour and the concomitant invention of writing, which in turn enabled the establishment of written laws and political governments as well as the cultivation of letters. Thereby, a general progress of enlightenment could begin. Like Iselin, Goguet viewed the modern period as the most 'enlightened' one.

2.5 John Brown's Account of the Origins of Poetry, Music (and Laws)

A very different approach – and arguably the one most closely paralleling that of young Herder – was adopted by John Brown in his widely read *Dissertation*.[93] Brown had first made his name by publishing a thorough assessment of Lord Shaftesbury's *Characteristics of Men, Manners, Opinions, Times* (1711), titled *Essays on Characteristics* (1751).[94] In *An Estimate of the*

---

[91] Ibid., 341–346.

[92] This bi-partite schema was also adopted by Edward Gibbon, who greatly appreciated Goguet's work, Wolloch, '"Facts, or Conjectures"', 431. On Gibbon's interest in Goguet, see Pocock, *Barbarism and Religion* (vol. IV = *Barbarians, Savages and Empires*) (2005), 37–64.

[93] For a detailed analysis of Brown's political thought, see Sonenscher, *Sans-Culottes*, 26, 178–195. My discussion of Brown and his relationship to Herder is substantially indebted to Sonenscher.

[94] In a letter to Johann Georg Hamann (January 1767), Herder asked Hamann whether he had Brown's *Essays on Characteristics*, mentioning that 'Brown has illuminated Shaftesbury's principle of ridicule', in *DA*, I, 70. Brown had qualified ridicule as a species of eloquence, disputing its value in finding out about truth. If anything, it was instead a powerful measure of spreading error. Brown also accused Shaftesbury's system of being unable to point out a uniform source of morality for all kinds of character: what motivated persons with weak sense, refined imagination and strongly predominant public affections, had no appeal to those in whom either 'the senses, gross imagination or selfish passions would prevail.' John Brown, *Essays on Characteristics* (London, 1751), 186. Only 'the great Christian principle of universal love', Brown argued, 'forms that perfect virtue in which human weakness is most prone to be *defective*, and which implies and includes every other moral perfection.' Brown, *Essays*, 347, cf. ibid., 230.

Manners and Principles of Our Times published in 1757, Brown had also made a forceful intervention into the debates about public spirit in Britain at the end of the Seven Years' War, adopting a highly critical tone about the waning of patriotism in his contemporary Britain. He admonished his compatriots to 'acknowledge, that the Love of our Country is no longer felt; and that, except in a few Minds of uncommon Greatness, the Principle of Public Spirit exists not'.[95] 'The ruling Character of the present Times', according to Brown, was 'a vain, luxurious, and selfish effeminacy'.[96]

In his *Dissertation*, Brown linked such diagnoses to a theory of the origins of the fine arts in general and poetry in particular. To Brown, an enquiry into the origins of ancient poetry could reveal the human potential, or indeed, provide inspiration for the ways in which modern culture and politics could be reinvigorated. Brown accepted that morality could not be learned from 'savages' or 'ancients' such as Homer, and was critical about those ancient and modern thinkers who had argued that ancient songs taught universal morality either directly or by training human moral capacity and judgement. Homer, Brown argued, was a 'natural', rather than 'moral Painter'.[97] Nevertheless, there was something important that was to be learnt from studying these early songs.

In his *Dissertation* Brown also sought, more clearly than Goguet had, to navigate a middle way between the camps of the Platonists and Stoics (such as Horace, Plutarchus, Lowth) and the Epicureans and Lucretians (such as Voltaire, Hume) on the function and quality of ancient poetry. Drawing extensively on Lafitau's description of the mores of savages in Northern America, Brown attempted to counter the argument, found most recently in Voltaire's *Preface to Oedipus* (1761), that early poetry was first of all a mnemotechnic tool for recording events, histories and laws. Instead, Brown claimed, it was a fully natural outburst of human passion and enthusiasm:

> If the ancient Songs, prior to prose in every Nation, had been coolly composed, for the Sake of Tradition and Information only, they would have been circumstantial and precise: Whereas the contrary appears in their Construction: They are generally vague and enthusiastic; bear all the Marks of being the genuine Effects of savage Passion and Enthusiasm.[98]

---

[95] John Brown, *An Estimate of the Manners and Principles of Our Times* (London, 1757), 64.
[96] Ibid., 67.
[97] John Brown, *Dissertation on the Rise, Union, and Power, the Progressions, Separations and Corruptions of Poetry and Music* (London, 1763), 80.
[98] Ibid., 55.

Indeed, this 'unlettered enthusiasm' was universal across nations, as it did not presuppose 'any Power of abstract Reasoning among the savage Tribes'. 'The Principles of savage Nature (making Allowance for the Difference of Soil and Climate)', Brown stipulated, 'are every where the same.'[99] Mediating between Humean naturalism and Shaftesbury's and Lowth's emphasis on the affects of admiration and rapture as the sources of poetry, Brown saw this kind of raw enthusiasm as first expressed in 'Hymns or Odes', 'Sung by their Composers at their festal Solemnities'.[100] He continued: 'For these, in their simple State, are but a Kind of rapturous Exclamations of Joy, Grief, Triumph, or Exultation, in Consequence of some great or disastrous Action, known, alluded to, or expressed'.[101] Epic poems, a 'Kind of fabulous History', would also naturally arise from these foundations, 'rowling [*sic*] chiefly on the great Actions of ancient Gods and Heroes, and artificially composed under certain Limitations with Respect to its Manner, for the Ends of Pleasure, Admiration, and Instruction'.[102]

Most importantly, Brown emphasised that human culture – religion, morality, society and politics – all sprang forth in a rudimentary joint form in songs and took root in them. Referring to the North American savages, but viewing it as confirmed also in ancient Hebrew, early Greek and Celtic 'bards', Brown argued

> their Songs would be of a legislative Cast; and being drawn chiefly from the Fables or History of their own Country, would contain the essential Parts of their religious, moral, and political Systems. For we have seen above, that the Celebration of their deceased Heroes would of Course grow into a religious Act: That the Exhortations and Maxims intermixed with these Celebrations, and founded on the Example of their Heroe-Gods, would naturally become the Standard of Right and Wrong; that is, the Foundation of private Morals and public Law: And thus, the whole Fabric of their Religion, Morals, and Polity, would naturally arise from, and be included in their Songs, during their Progress from savage to civilized Life.[103]

According to Brown, civilised life and laws were thus grounded in natural passions bursting forth in a combination of poetry, music and dancing, an original form of art. Yet, subsequently this initial unity was dissolved. One of Brown's more original, but also little substantiated, arguments concerned the impact of 'colonialism' on culture. As societies grew and division of labour was established in society, the 'Legislator's and Bard's Character' were no longer 'united in the same Person'.[104] Colonies, too, came to be created in this period, whereby a split emerged between

---

99 Ibid., 56.   100 Ibid., 40.   101 Ibid.   102 Ibid.   103 Ibid., 77.   104 Ibid., 183.

legislation and singing, which in turn had an effect on all of society. 'The Leader of the new Colony not being possessed of the poetic and musical Enthusiasm, can neither have Ability nor Inclination to instil or propagate these Arts among his Followers'. According to Brown, the colonisers, who had departed from their native country 'driven by some Kind of Necessity', 'must betake themselves, for Subsistance, either to Industry or War. The last of these was the chief Occupation of the Roman State: And thus, not because they were a warlike People, but because they were a needy Colony, the musical Arts which were so powerful in early GREECE, were so weak in early ROME'.[105] This observation was also true for the English who were 'a foreign Mixture of late-established Colonies', and therefore had 'no native Music'. Only 'the Irish, Welsh, and Scots', Brown claimed, are 'strictly natives; and accordingly, have a Music of their own'.[106] Offering an array of observations about the history and increasing separation of the 'two Sister Arts' of music and poetry, Brown concluded his discussion of the arts with a proposal for 'the Institution of A Poetic and Musical Academy, for the more effectual Re-union of these two Arts, and their better Direction to their highest Ends' in England.[107]

2.6 Herder on Poetry, Mores and Laws in Fragments

In *Fragments*, Herder only commented on Goguet's, Iselin's and of course, Rousseau's, views on humans' earliest history. He presented Goguet's approach as a middle way between those of Rousseau and (most likely) Iselin, ostensibly siding with Goguet against Iselin and Rousseau: 'Without fancifully making up a Rousseauian condition of nature or exaggerating the picture of a people in a process of becoming', Herder claimed, one must 'pay attention to the voices of the whole of antiquity' as well as their 'echo in the useful work of Goguet'.[108] Herder thereby indicated his agreement with Goguet that it was important not to idealise primitive societies, whereas one also had to acknowledge the existence of poetry at the earliest stages of human history. Yet, ultimately, Goguet had said nothing conclusive about the origins of human poetry, mores and laws; furthermore, as we shall see below, from Herder's perspective, he had failed to identify the devastating consequences of the rise of human division of labour and the art of writing for human creativity in general. Herder thus disagreed with Goguet's account of sociability and his

---

[105] Ibid., 183–184.   [106] Ibid., 184.   [107] Ibid., 238–239.
[108] Herder, 'Fragments', in *PW*, 59/in *HWP*, I, 156.

genealogy of political society. In both these respects, it was instead John Brown's ideas that were closest to those of Herder.

Although Herder did not directly comment on Brown's views on the earliest history of humanity, he described his authorial goals and self-understanding in *Fragments* by invoking the example of 'Browne [*sic*], the republican':

> Allow me to pursue my vision! This universal and unique work would be based on a *History of Literature*, from which it would draw support. Which stage has this nation attained? And which might and should it attain? What are its talents and what is its aesthetic sense? What is its extrinsic state in the sciences and in the arts? [. . .] In short, such a history should aspire to be what it was for the ancients, the voice of patriotic wisdom and the reformer of the people. It should aspire to be for literature what the arbiter of English mores and principles, *Browne*, the republican, was for the state, a voice of patriotic wisdom and reformer of his fatherland.[109]

Indeed, by the time of writing *Fragments*, Herder was already familiar with many of Brown's works. Moses Mendelssohn had (anonymously) reviewed a Swiss writer's letters on Brown's *An Estimate of the Manners and Principles of Our Times* that had been attached to Isaak Iselin's *Philosophical and Political Essays* (1760) in 1761 in *Letters on the Newest Literature*.[110] He had concluded the review with a reference to the 'wisdom of a republican' who can show us the 'opinion of the future generation' on our mores.[111] Herder also referred to Brown when discussing German patriotic writers, praising Friedrich Carl von Moser as a true 'German Browne' and preferring him to Iselin and Wegelin, the Swiss writers.[112] By 1768, Herder had come to 'greatly value' Shaftesbury's philosophy (clearly

---

[109] Herder, 'Fragments I', in *HEW*, 94. In his *Briefe zu Beförderung der Humanität* (1793–1797), Herder lamented the fact that this work had still not been translated into German, Herder, *Briefe zu Beförderung der Humanität*, in *FHA*, VII, 569.

[110] Moses Mendelssohn [Anon.], 'Ueber den in eben diesem Bändchen befindlichen Auszuge aus Dr. Browns Werke von den Englischen Sitten. Iselin, I.: *Philosophische und politische Versuche*. Zurich: Orell 1760: Rezension', *Briefe, die neueste Literatur betreffend* (1761), Literaturbrief 139, 374–384. On Mendelssohn's interest in, and engagement with Brown's *Dissertation* and his later revision of this work in his *History of the Arts*, see Eva J. Engel, '*Habent Sua Fata Libelli*. A Response to John Brown: Moses Mendelssohn on Evolution and Change in Poetry', *Hebrew Union College Annual*, 53 (1982), 165–177.

[111] Mendelssohn, Literaturbrief, 139, 384.

[112] Herder, 'Fragments I', in *HEW*, 152/in *HWP*, I, 132: 'Moser knows the heart and soul of the German language: the Lutheran language of old, the ancient freedom, honesty, and common sense of our fathers: and he can be our *Browne* with more justification than *Iselin* with his Platonic dreams, and *Wegelin*, in Switzerland, with his hypochondriac abundance of virtue.' On Moser's contribution to the debate on German *Nationalgeist*, and Herder's response to this debate, see Chapter 5.

more than Brown himself did), while he also appreciated Brown's discussion of Shaftesbury's principle of ridicule and his general criticism of Shaftesbury's account as 'elitist'.[113] Herder's awareness of Brown's *Dissertation* is most tellingly revealed when his *Treatise on the Origin of Language* (1770/1772) took a critical position to a 'philosophical Englishman' who should have recognised that not just different arts but language itself 'originated from the whole nature of the human being'.[114] The 'philosophical Englishman', in all likelihood, was Brown.[115]

Let us begin the comparison between these thinkers by highlighting their main difference – Herder's distinctive emphasis on the epistemological and linguistic foundations of the human capacity for art. Belief in the coeval origins of language and art was present in Herder's thinking from the outset. The central thesis of Herder's epistemology, as summarised by Stefan Greif, was that 'every human being is originally an artist, who with all his organs of perception and with the aid of his free reason "erfindet" (invents) his own image of nature.'[116] Humans, like all organisms, seek self-preservation in their specific natural environment, developing specific 'organs' that enable them to do so.[117] Human intellect, and language specifically, is precisely such an organ, one among many. Thus, language itself is an expression of human 'art' in general, while art in a more specific sense is in turn an outgrowth of language. In one of his earliest writings, a short school essay titled *On Diligence in the Study of Several Learned Languages* (1764) (*Über den Fleiß in mehreren gelehrten Sprachen*), Herder already examined the relationship between language, mores and 'ways of thought' of different peoples. He emphasised the ways in which

---

[113] Herder to Kant, October 1767, in *DA*, I, 93.

[114] Herder, 'Treatise on the Origin of Language', in *PW*, 104. I will return to Herder's discussion of Brown in the *Treatise* in Chapter 4.

[115] In his prize essay 'Über die Wirkung der Dichtkunst auf die Sitten der Völker in alten und neuen Zeiten' published in 1778, Herder voiced an explicit and even more critical comment on Brown's *Dissertation*. Brown, he argued, had addressed the same topic, but had not been able to properly do justice to it, setting up an 'art-hypothesis' (*Kunsthypothese*) and thus 'touching the best things' only remotely and often also in a 'skewed' manner, ibid., in *FHA*, IV, 150–252 (153). By the 'art-hypothesis', Herder may have meant Brown's idea of an original joint form of 'art' (this is the suggestion of Jürgen Brummack and Martin Bollacher, in 'Kommentar', in *FHA*, IV, 916–970 (945)). However, since he in fact shared this view of the original form of art (himself simply providing a further philosophical grounding for the human capacity for art), it is also possible that what he objected to was not so much the substance of Brown's argument, but his approach – Brown's purely abstract theorising of the topic and his disregard for actual examples of national poetry. See also Chapter 7 for Herder's final comments on Brown.

[116] Greif, 'Herder's Aesthetics', 142.

[117] Herder first formulated his distinctive version of this (fundamentally Stoic) theory of self-preservation in 1769. For discussion, see Chapters 3 and 4.

languages are co-determined by the natural environments in which they emerge as well as reflect and shape the way of thought of the people who speak them. While this idea had begun to find support from a number of literary and biblical scholars, Herder drew a more radical normative conclusion from it: 'If, thus, each language has its distinct national character', he wrote, 'it seems that nature imposes upon us an obligation only to our mother tongue, for it is perhaps better attuned to our character and coextensive with our way of thinking.'[118] While other learned languages held a vast variety of different charms for us, it was only on the basis of our native language that we could truly appreciate and appropriate other languages. Indeed, our dedication to our native language should parallel that to our fatherland:

> Just as the love of our fatherland binds us to each other by heartfelt bonds of affection, the language of our forefathers holds attractions for us also, which in our eyes exceed all others. They impressed upon us first, and somehow shaped themselves together with the finest fissures of our sensibility; or because our mother tongue really harmonizes most perfectly with our most sensitive organs and our most delicate turns of mind. Just as a child compares all images with the first impressions, our mind clandestinely compares all tongues with our mother tongue, and how useful this can be! Thereby, the great diversity of languages is given unity, our steps exploring foreign regions become shorter and more self-assured, when the goal of fatherland remains steadily before our eyes; this way, our diligence is facilitated; I am afloat on a bark that carries me.[119]

In the first collection of *Fragments*, Herder discussed the relationship between language and poetry specifically. Human 'mental forces', Herder argued, manifest themselves first in the creation of language, which is also why one could only truly 'decode' the human soul or, indeed, that of a nation, on the basis of its language.[120] At the centre of Herder's discussion of language here was a philosophical history or as Herder also called it – a 'novel' (*Roman*) – of the life periods of language. In constructing this kind of philosophical history, Herder creatively applied Iselin's parallelism between individual and collective life-stages to the progressive development of language and literature.[121] The earliest stage of history was a

---

[118] Johann Gottfried Herder, 'On Diligence', in *HEW*, 29–34 (30).   [119] Ibid., 32–33.

[120] Herder, 'Fragmente I', in *HWP*, I, 76. Herder described this kind of decoding as 'semiotics' (*Semiotik*).

[121] Herder, 'Fragments I', in *PW*, 59/in *HWP*, I, 144 and 148, cf. ibid., 156; cf. Herder, 'Fragments', in *HEW*, 104–106. For other contemporary examples of this kind of parallelism as applied to the history of language, see Menze and Menges, 'Commentary to the Translations', 283–284.

'condition of *primitive nature* (*rohe Natur*)', as there was no separation of arts yet, no division of labour in society.[122] Restating the ideas he had already set out in *Essay on the History of Lyrical Poetry*, Herder emphasised the particular prominence of strong emotions in this period: 'Horror, fear, amazement, and marvelling', he wrote, 'must be the most frequent emotions, as with children.'[123] The 'rapid needs' of early men, he continued, would be 'registered through short and powerful accents of shouting', while 'unarticulated noises would transform themselves into rough and monosyllabic words'.[124] 'Climate and religion are not yet relevant', Herder argued, 'for both the hot Easterners and the savage Americans confirm what [he] has to say.'[125] The next evolutionary step of an evolving language saw it entering 'boyhood' as humans began to give names to things, mainly by imitating their natural noises and developing new concepts by way of metaphorical extensions from the sensuous ones.[126] At this stage language was 'full of images and rich in metaphors', it was an age of poets.[127] As the 'oldest languages' known to us show, early humans also 'painted' in sounds like the oldest forms of writing 'paint in pictures'. 'Poetic speech' was initially identical with singing, while singing, in turn, was accompanied by bodily gestures, which 'paint' things in their own way. Early languages, Herder continued, had 'much living expression', and 'were formed immediately according to living nature'; indeed, in this childhood period of language, humans seem to have had a great degree of understanding for animal language, which was the seed of the art of poetry.[128] Put simply, 'language was singing and speaking nature'.[129] At that time, human languages and cultures also acquired distinctive individual traits, whilst singing further helped to preserve and transmit individual cultures to future generations.[130]

The subsequent developments already caused language to become distanced from nature. In Herder's view, human language gradually became more orderly, and instead of 'painting' words through all sorts of media, humans began to express themselves in the form of prose. This was the 'manly age' of human language; in this period, inversions were reduced,

---

[122] Herder, 'Fragments', in *PW*, 59/in *HEW*, 104/in *HWP*, I, 146; 156.
[123] Herder, 'Fragments', in *PW*, 60/in *HWP*, I, 157.
[124] Herder, 'Fragments', in *PW*, 60/in *HWP*, I, 145–146, 156–158.
[125] Herder, 'Fragments', in *PW*, 61/in *HWP*, I, 158.
[126] Herder, 'Fragments', in *PW*, 60/in *HEW*, 106/in *HWP*, I; 146.   [127] Ibid.
[128] Herder, 'Fragments', in *PW*, 61/in *HWP*, I, 158.
[129] Herder, 'Fragments', in *PW*, 62/in *HWP*, I, 159.
[130] Herder, 'Fragments', in *PW*, 60/in *HEW*, 106/in *HWP*, I, 158; 146–147.

civic and abstract notions accepted, rules established.[131] In human history, this was a period when the arts and sciences became differentiated from each other, accompanied by a general emergence of the division of labour in society. Compared to the next stage, the 'old age' of language, it was still a period of linguistic beauty. It was solely in this last stage, which Herder also characterised as a 'philosophical age', that language became subjected to the rules of correctness, synonyms were distinguished from each other, and language began to gradually lose its 'attraction'.[132] 'The more language becomes art', Herder argued, 'the more it is removed from nature'.[133]

This kind of history of the evolution of language served as a deeper foundation for Herder's study of the relationship between poetry, mores and laws. In the second collection of *Fragments*, Herder used Christian August Clodius's *Versuche aus der Literatur und Moral (Essays on Literature and Morality)* (1767–1769) as a reference point for outlining his own project of studying what he called the Greek *Ethopöie (ethopoeia)* – character formation in Greek poetry.[134] Herder declared that Clodius had no understanding of the ways in which Greek *ethopoeia* had worked, as he was missing the connection to the history of human understanding. A history of literature, in Herder's view, could only be written as a 'specialised chart in the history of human understanding' (*Spezialkarte in der Geschichte des Menschlichen Verstandes*),[135] and indeed, one could add, history of ethics, society and politics.[136] The account he offered paralleled that of Brown in its rough outline.

Early poetry, Herder restated his main point, was focused on what is great and novel, early humans being moved by fantasy and passion.[137] Indeed, it was in the Homeric world and age that mores were 'truthfully

---

[131] Herder, 'Fragments', in *PW*, 61–62/in *HWP*, I, 159.

[132] Herder, 'Fragments', in *HEW*, 108/in *HWP*, I, 147–148; cf. 164. Herder also hypothesised that a similar process could be distinguished in the mental development of an individual person, Herder, 'Journal meiner Reise', in *HWP*, I, 457. It needs to be emphasised that this correlation between certain types of inclinations and the level of development of thinking is only one element in the complex causal nexus influencing human (ethical) history. For Herder's ideas on the different types of histories of the human mind and the difficulties in establishing a unified theory, see Wolfgang Proß, 'Nachwort', in *HWP*, II, 1175–1204.

[133] Herder, 'Fragments', in *HEW*, 106/in *HWP*, I, 147.

[134] On Clodius and *ethopoeia*, see Proß, 'Anmerkungen [*Über die neuere deutsche Literatur*]', in *HWP*, I, 725–783 (769–770); on Herder's concept of *ethopoeia*, ibid., 730–731.

[135] Herder, 'Fragmente I', in *HWP*, I, 253.

[136] Ibid., 254. Cf. Herder's prize essay 'Über die Wirkung der Dichtkunst'. For a discussion of this essay, see Chapter 6.

[137] Herder, 'Fragments', in *PW*, 60/in *HWP*, I, 157.

sung' and as such 'merely ennobled' (*bloss veredelt*), but not transformed (*umgeschaffen*):

> *The world*, the *age* renders *poetic mores*, in which the passions are effective and the entire human soul reveals itself: virtue is here not the fine notion of self-conquest, or -restraint, the attainment of the purity of the soul, but that of efficacy and self-elevation; the moral sentiment is as yet nothing but humanity, *Humanität* in the broadest sense of the term, and the highest reason would be identified with prudence and wisdom in human life. Such an age that lies between the savagery and the enervated political or moral civilisation, such an age would have mores for the poet. In such an age, Homer would be able to sing about the deeds of the people and the passions of the war-lords, about actions and world affairs.[138]

Homeric poetry, Herder argued, successfully showed the human soul 'in its naked beauty'; it did not seek to bend or transform it in any way. There was no difference between the way in which humans acted in Homer's epics and in actual life, indeed, poetry and human action co-created each other. In poetry, mores were represented in a lively manner, 'in action' and in bold pictures (*kühne Bilder*). As such, they were not a 'dead painting' (*tote Gemälde*), that is, imitation of nature, but nature itself in action (*Handlung*). Herder also contrasted a 'policed poetry' (*polizierte* Dichtung) with poetry as an 'active painting' (*handelnde Gemälde*), maintaining that the latter alone, setting various kinds of human powers in action, was also able to affect (*rühren*) and arouse (*aufwecken*) the feelings of the audience.[139] Poetic mores (*poetische Sitten*) revealed human moral feeling, *Humanität*, in a straightforward manner, and there was no need for a higher reason that was detached from the prudence and practical wisdom of human life.

Herder's understanding of *ethopoeia* encompasses his views on the relationship between nature and culture, on the one hand, and between morality and tradition, on the other.[140] First, Herder saw poetry and mores (*Sitten*) as directly grounded in nature. Positioned between 'savagery' and 'enervated political or moral civilisation', early poetry manifested and supported strong, healthy human mores. Second, he saw the creation of poetry as a starting point for a national tradition. By linking the capacity for art to the more fundamental capacity for language, he provided a deeper philosophical justification for the theses that Brown, too, had put forward. Third, he viewed Homeric *ethopoeia* as comprising the

---

[138] Herder, 'Fragmente II', in *HWP*, I, 260.
[139] On Herder's distinction between 'painting' and 'action', see also Greif, '3.2.2 *Über die neuere Literatur*', in *Herder Handbuch*, 431–443 (434–438).
[140] See also Proß, 'Anmerkungen [*Über die neuere deutsche Literatur*]', in *HWP*, I, 731.

formation of not only the ethical character of a people but also its political principles and laws. Here, the parallels between Herder's and Brown's accounts are particularly evident. Like Brown, Herder insisted that it was during language's age of 'boyhood' that 'laws' originated: 'oracles sang and the voices which the god sang were called sayings (*phata*), the laws sang and were called songs (*nomoi*), the prophets and poets sang and what they sang were called speeches (*epea*)'.[141] Embracing a similar understanding of the natural foundations of political society, Herder maintained that political principles (*Triebfeder des Staats*) were an integral part of poetry and aesthetic and moral taste, or indeed, of a united 'feeling of humanity':

> Insofar as the feeling of beauty would be the dominant taste, feeling of humanity [Gefühl der Menschheit], and the *political principle*, poetry will also be the more efficacious, the more widely pleasant, and useful, and the poet would also as a poet be a noble citizen. The better he would command the lever of the progress of mores [Sitten], the better he would be able to influence the national mores [Nationalsitten], the more the latter would be poetic (emphasis added). [142]

By invoking the term 'political principle', Herder was most likely making a critical reference to Montesquieu's theory of the principles of government. Although not entering into a direct debate with Montesquieu yet,[143] Herder proceeded to exemplify his understanding of early Greek political principles by discussing Homer's achievement. Homer, Herder argued, was the most exemplary 'creator of mores' (*Sittenerschaffer*). Everything in his poetry was 'human' (*menschlich*), whereby also the whole constitution of the state was grounded in 'freedom, honour and passion'.[144] His ethics served as the foundation of society and politics alike. Modern forms of poetry as mere imitations or idealisations could not fulfil that function.[145]

Like Brown, Herder in *Fragments* also took an interest in the effects of 'colonialism' on culture and politics. However, while Brown in his *Dissertation* had dealt with the impact of the actual emigration of people from their native country, Herder discussed self-colonisation, enervation and servility as emerging through the natural dynamics of the development of language and thinking. For Herder, there was thus no need to distinguish

---

[141] Herder, 'Fragments', in *PW*, 60/'Fragments', 106/in *HWP*, I, 158; 146–147.
[142] Herder, 'Fragmente II', in *HWP*, I, 261.
[143] On Herder's relationship to Montesquieu, see Chapter 3.
[144] Herder, 'Fragmente II', in *HWP*, I, 263. Cf. Herder, '[Aus:] *Von Deutscher Art und Kunst*', in *HWP*, I, 475–572 (478) on Ossian as a possible 'creator of mores'.
[145] Cf. Herder's elaboration of similar ideas in his 'Über die Wirkung der Dichtkunst', 151, 156, 169–170.

between indigenous or settler peoples at an early stage of human history; what was more important was the way in which peoples at a later historical stage came to relate to their cultural heritage. Insofar as human languages and thinking had gradually become ever more abstract and refined, and division of labour had emerged between different arts and professions in society, there was an increasing weakening of the intensity of feeling, which in turn undermined the efficacy of (moral) motivation. When 'art-poets' (*Kunstpoeten*) succeeded nature-poets (*Naturdichter*), feeling was replaced by the imagination. Yet when art-poets were replaced by 'scholarly rhyme-sters' (*wissenschaftliche Reimer*), rule-based thinking imposed itself on art.[146] These models were inevitably based on distinct national traditions, in the case of European cultural history specifically on ancient Greek, Roman and French ones, which further contributed to self-alienation where other European peoples, including Germans, were concerned. The recent setting up of new models had not improved the situation. Even when more recent literary critics and art-poets had rejected the neo-classicist models in Germany, Herder argued, they had only implanted 'colonies of true Greek and British taste in [literary] criticism in Germany'.[147] Most importantly, the newer authors still painted sentiments and actions according to a 'beautified ideal of nature' (*ganzverschönerte Ideal*).[148] Instead of 'true mores', they only reflected a 'policed way of life' (*politische Lebensart*).[149] What was missing was 'poetic spirit'.[150] As a result of these processes, Herder concluded, modern poets were incapable of forming mores; laws, too, became rules imposed from above, thus needing extra enforcement.

In the second collection of *Fragments*, Herder presented a series of parallels between ancient and modern authors and artists (e.g. Homer and Bodmer, Theocritus and Gessner, Aisop and Lessing, etc). Through careful comparison of, and commentary on, these different parallels, Herder sought to do justice to each individual author's characteristic features. Nevertheless, his overall argument was that it was impossible for modern authors or artists to 'imitate' any ancient examples or even 'nature' itself. Herder's characterisation of the Zurich professor and literary critic Johann Jacob Bodmer's approach to poetry illustrates well the scope of his concerns and criticism. Aligning himself with British literary critics, Bodmer, too, had from the 1720s onwards pleaded for human imagination to be freed from the straightjacket of French neoclassicism. He had also compared poets with 'painters' – both imitated nature and sought to

---

[146] Herder, 'Fragments of a Treatise on the Ode', in *HEW*, 44/in *FHA*, I, 89.
[147] Herder, 'Fragmente II', in *HWP*, I, 270.   [148] Ibid., 313.   [149] Ibid.   [150] Ibid., 227.

engage the imagination and arouse affects, while poetry, further, was capable of painting 'possible worlds'. In the debate between the leading German neo-classicist Johann Christoph Gottsched's followers and Bodmerians, Herder clearly sided with Bodmerians. At the same time, he was critical of Bodmer's late *Noachide* (1765; earlier version: *Der Noah* 1750) (and Salomon Gessner's *Idyllen* (1756) – another example of the Swiss literary tradition).[151] Engaging in a discussion that would take a new direction in his *First Critical Grove* (*Erstes kritisches Wäldchen*), Herder saw both of them as remaining true to the model of 'imitation of nature' and hence as static and full of 'decor of words' (*Wortschmuck*) and comparisons.[152] The ability to arouse vivid imagination and sympathy, he maintained, could only result from a lively presentation of action. Bodmer's novels could not achieve as much, and actually just 'prattled all the sympathy out of us' (*schwatzt er uns aus aller Sympathie völlig hinaus*)'.[153]

2.7 Literary and Linguistic Patriotism in Fragments

Given that the 'current malaise of the world' was grounded in a certain evolutionary dynamic of the development of human language and thinking, could there be any remedy to it at all? Herder clearly believed so. In *Fragments*, he had already begun to sketch an outline for a programme of cultural regeneration for Germany, envisioning it as having an impact on contemporary politics as well. As his account of early Homeric *ethopoeia* revealed, it was poets who originally created the national ways of thought, 'mores', laws and, indeed, political societies themselves. Poetry was the foremost vehicle of social cohesion and patriotism, but it was also the first and most significant expression of the human capacity for language and art, giving expression to humanity's inner feelings. As such, it was nothing less than 'speaking and singing nature'.[154]

Yet, did not restoring this kind of unity between poetry and politics entail returning to an earlier period of individual human completeness and

---

[151] Ibid., 269–283; 307–317.
[152] Here, Herder was drawing on Gotthold Ephraim Lessing's *Laokoon: An Essay on the Limits of Paintings and Poetry* (*Laokoon: über die Grenzen der Malerei und Poesie*) (1766). On Herder's engagement with Lessing's aesthetic views, see Gregory Moore, 'Introduction', in *Johann Gottfried Herder: Aesthetic Writings*, ed. and trans. Gregory Moore (*SWA*) (Princeton, 2006), 1–30 (10–11).
[153] Herder, 'Fragmente II', in *HWP*, I, 278–279.
[154] Cf. Herder's elaboration of these ideas in his 'Über die Wirkung der Dichtkunst', in *FHA*, IV, 154–158.

undifferentiated society? Did not Herder himself strongly reject such a possibility? Indeed, Herder rejected it, but he also claimed that such a return was not necessary. Instead, he argued, it was necessary and possible for modern Germans to restore a connection to themselves as 'moderns'. As we saw above, already in his *On Diligence* – one of his earliest essays – Herder had envisioned a modern dedication to fatherland as including both love of one's own language and 'diligence' in learning foreign languages, so as to be more aware of the peculiarities and charms of one's own one. In the third collection of *Fragments*, he highlighted the intimate connection between 'thought and expression', urging modern poets to write in a language in which they have the 'widest perception and mastery over the words':[155]

> Truly, the poet who will be master of expression must remain faithful to his soil: here he can plant graphic expressions, for he knows the land; here he can gather flowers, for the earth is his; here he can dig into the depths, and search for gold, and raise mountains, and channel streams, for he is the master of the house. Genuine characteristics express themselves only in the mother tongue.[156]

Writing in the mother tongue, German poets could make productive use of the idiosyncrasies of their language, and further develop the national treasure-trove of idioms and metaphors. In order to write effectively, however, it was necessary to combine both analytical and synthetic skills, bring together philosophy, aesthetic 'genius' and historical knowledge. It was also here that Herder's own literary parallels could serve as a useful inspiration. Careful study of ancient poetry could reveal the ways in which ancient poets successfully aroused passions, and their approach could be emulated to a certain extent. Drawing on Edward Young's distinction between 'imitation' and 'emulation' in his *Conjectures on the Original Composition* (1759), Herder highlighted the need to 'emulate the man', rather than the 'composition'.[157] As his analysis of Thomas Abbt's writing style revealed, it was possible to write in a manner that would speak to the heart, rather than the intellect.[158]

In the third collection of *Fragments*, Herder also included a separate essay titled 'On the Modern Usage of Mythology' (*Vom neuern Gebrauch der Mythologie*). Here, his argument was straightforward: modern poets could make use of ancient mythology as a 'poetic tool'. As Herder

---

[155] Herder, 'Fragments', in *HEW*, 206.   [156] Ibid., 210.
[157] Herder, 'Fragments', in *HEW*, 173. See also Menze and Menges, 'Commentary', 312.
[158] See Chapter 1 for Herder's relationship to Thomas Abbt.

memorably put it, 'ancient mythology could serve as poetic heuristics, so that we may become inventors of ourselves'.[159] A modern poet who wished to create a modern 'world of images' could well use the 'ancient myths':

> Let the ancient images be applied to more recent events. One informs them with a new poetic sense, changes them here and there to achieve a new purpose; as master of the house and owner, one composes and separates, goes forward and turns aside, steps back or stands still, to make use of everything as household goods, to satisfy one's needs, comfort, and adornment, as one sees fit and as it fits the fashion of the day.[160]

Thus making a plea for intertextuality and free use of ancient myths for contemporary purposes, Herder sought to stimulate the imagination and inventiveness of modern poets. And yet, he also believed that at a deeper level, the 'purposes' of ancient and modern poets were still the same – national self-awareness and patriotic cohesion. He was not as yet asking questions about the implications this kind of national self-affirmation and patriotism had on inter-group relationships. Patriotism, for him, was grounded in the human capacity for language and art, which revealed the dignity of human nature. Working out a specifically modern form of patriotism was as much a noble calling as it was a practical need.[161]

2.8 Conclusion

These early investigations into the origins of the 'current malaise of the world' subsequently fed into a variety of relatively independent projects. First, during the 1767–1769 period Herder drafted what he called a 'metaphysics of the fine arts', setting out the sensuous origins of different arts in his *Critical Groves* (*Erstes Kritisches Wäldchen*).[162] Second, Herder continued to investigate in a more systematic manner various other national traditions of poetry alongside the Greek and German ones, including what he called the 'Oriental' tradition. Indeed, as mentioned at the beginning of this chapter, he initially wished to provide an all-encompassing theological,

---

[159] Herder, 'On Recent German Literature [Third Collection]', in *HEW*, 228.

[160] Ibid., 229; cf. 231.

[161] Herder, 'Fragmente', in *HWP*, I, 312–313; for discussion, see Greif, '3.2.2 *Über die neuere Literatur*', 436–440.

[162] For an overview of Herder's aesthetic theory in the *Critical Groves*, see Norton, *Herder's Aesthetics*, chs. 4 and 5; Gregory Moore, 'Introduction', in *SWA*, 1–30; for an introduction into Herder's notion of 'force' as underlying poetry, see the still valuable study of Robert Clark, 'Herder's Conception of "Kraft"', *Modern Language Association*, 57:3 (1942), 737–752.

philosophical and philological view of the earliest state of humanity, but renounced this goal, while completing the second edition of *Fragments*.[163] However, Herder continued to work on separate drafts on the earliest human history and 'documents' as well returned to these questions in several essays in the 1770s and early 1780s.[164] As we will see, he subsequently came to elaborate on the differences between Hebrew, Greek and Roman 'ethopoeia' in a number of writings, now also comparing them to 'Northern poetry' – the poetry of various kinds of northern peoples from the Scots to the Germans. Whilst it is beyond the scope of this book to give a systematic overview of these further developments in Herder's aesthetics, hermeneutics and Biblical studies, we shall, in the next chapters, return to Herder's discussion of different national traditions of poetry insofar as it informed his views on the history of Europe.

Even sooner, however, Herder returned to the question of the origins of human civilisation in connection with his study of Montesquieu's *The Spirit of the Laws*. Criticising Montesquieu's overly legalistic approach, he hoped that his own ideas on the origins of poetry and mores would be able to serve as a grounding for a more substantial 'metaphysics for the formation of peoples'. Thereby, these ideas acquired a direct practical dimension, playing an important role in Herder's thinking on the challenges of moral and political reform in Europe and in particular, Russia. In the longer term, they further fed into a new broader research programme that Herder came to pursue in the following years – a philosophical history of mankind. These will be the themes of the next two chapters.

---

[163] Proß, 'Anmerkungen [*Über die neuere deutsche Literatur*]', in *HWP*, I, 729.
[164] See, in particular, his 'Älteste Urkunde des Menschengeschlechts (1774–1776)', and 'Vom Geist der Ebräischen Poesie' (1782–1783) both in *FHA*, V, 179–659 and 661–1309.

CHAPTER 3

Montesquieu's System and Reforms in Russia

In May 1769, Herder departed on a sea voyage to accompany his friend Gustav Berens, a young Riga merchant, on his business trip to Holland and France. During the trip, Herder kept a philosophical diary, which was posthumously published as *Journal of My Travels in Year 1769* (*Journal meiner Reise im Jahre 1769*).[1] Although most of the journal was written in Nantes and Paris in 1769,[2] the central axis of Herder's reflections is the potential for educational, moral and political reforms in Russia, Livland and Riga. In the journal, Herder mused about becoming 'a genius of Livland', 'a second Zwingli, Calvin and Luther of this province' as well as, more generally, a 'preacher of the virtue of his own age' (373–374). He also hoped to gain 'the ear of the greats' in Russia to enlighten the ruler(s) about the true foundations of political reforms (373–374, 411). Accomplishing these goals would entail delving into two kinds of studies. On the one hand, one would need to study 'the human soul in itself and in its phenomenal forms [*in ihrer Erscheinung*] on this earth', so as to understand what 'can make humans happy here'. On the other hand, it was necessary to 'summon up one's courage to consider things from the viewpoint of politics, the state and finances' (373–375). Indeed, nothing less than developing the outlines of a 'second *Montesquieu* for practical application!' (*Ein zweiter Montesquieu, um ihn anzuwenden!*) would be needed in order to achieve as much (428).

Considering Herder's self-image as a moral and political reformer as well as his interest in European politics in general, it is only natural that Herder in this period returned to reading Montesquieu's *The Spirit of the Laws* (1748), the most authoritative philosophical 'handbook' of politics in his

---

[1] Johann Gottfried Herder, 'Journal meiner Reise im Jahre 1769', in *HWP*, I, 355–465. [Unless otherwise stated, all translations from German and French in this chapter are mine.] Parenthetical page numbers refer to this text in this chapter.

[2] Wolfgang Proß, 'Anmerkungen. [*Journal meiner Reise*]', in *HWP*, I, 804–820 (818).

time.[3] *Journal of My Travels* records much of this engagement; some additional separate notes on Montesquieu are now standardly published as an appendix to *Journal of My Travels*. And yet, Herder's ultimate verdict on Montesquieu in his notes was highly critical: *The Spirit of the Laws* is a 'metaphysics for a dead lawbook' (*Metaphysik für ein totes Gesetzbuch*), rather than a 'metaphysics for the formation of peoples' (*Metaphysik zur Bildung der Völker*).[4] At the same time, Herder also extended this criticism to modern states and argued that there was 'no longer a fatherland, no citizens in our modern European states'.[5] How and why had Herder arrived at such a highly critical opinion of Montesquieu and why did he nevertheless maintain that a 'second *Montesquieu*' was needed to devise proper reforms? Why had he also come to deny patriotism to modern monarchies and what kinds of problems did he have in view specifically when criticising contemporary states?

Herder's relationship to Montesquieu has previously been viewed through the prism of the rise of 'historicism' in his thought and his supposed methodological divergence from Montesquieu.[6] Yet, as we shall see, the direct impetus for Herder's return to Montesquieu in 1769 was political, coming from the publication of Catherine II of Russia's *Nakaz*, or *Grand Instructions to the Commissioners Appointed to Frame a New Code of Laws for the Russian Empire*.[7] Herder was highly critical of Catherine's reform plans and planned to respond to the latter by writing a book entitled *On the true Culture of a Nation and particularly of Russia* (*Über die wahre Kultur eines Volks und insonderheit Rußlands*). Furthermore, he

---

[3] For an overview of Herder's engagement with Montesquieu in different periods, see Moritz Baumstark, 'Vom "Esprit des lois" zum "Geist der Zeiten". Herders Auseinandersetzung mit Montesquieu als Grundlegung seiner Geschichtsphilosophie', in *Sattelzeit: Historiographiegeschichtliche Revisionen*, ed. Elisabeth Décultot and Daniel Fulda (*Hallesche Beiträge zur Europäischen Aufklärung*) (Berlin/Boston, 2016), 54–82.

[4] Johann Gottfried Herder, 'Gedanken bei Lesung Montesquieus (Blätter zum *Journal der Reise*)', in *HWP*, I, 468–473 (470).

[5] Ibid., 471.   [6] See, e.g., Meinecke, *Historism*; Baumstark, 'Vom "Esprit des lois"'.

[7] [Catherine II], *Ihrer Kaiserlichen Majestaet Instruction fuer die Verfertigung des Entwurfs zu einem neuen Gesetz-Buche verordnete Comission* (Moscow, 1767). The original was published in two languages, German and Russian. In the same year, also a separate German edition was published. An English translation was published in 1768. On debates about Catherine's attempt to adjust and apply Montesquieu's ideas on depopulation in Russia, see Graham Clure, 'Rousseau, Diderot and the Spirit of Catherine the Great's Reforms', *History of European Ideas*, 41:7 (2015), 883–908. For a contextualisation of Herder's ideas about the reform of Russia in Enlightenment debates about Russia and civilisation, see Reto Speck, 'The History and Politics of Civilisation: The Debate about Russia in French and German Historical Scholarship from Voltaire to Herder' (unpublished PhD dissertation Queen Mary University of London, 2010), 210–264, and Speck, 'Johann Gottfried Herder and Enlightenment Political Thought: From the Reform of Russia to the Anthropology of Bildung', *Modern Intellectual History*, 11:1 (2014), 31–58.

believed that Montesquieu's own approach was at least partly responsible for what he saw as Catherine's misguided application of Montesquieu's ideas and thus sought to offer the empress an alternative and philosophically more deeply grounded instruction for reform (410–412).[8] As I will seek to show, Herder had two kinds of reasons for being critical about both Montesquieu's and Catherine's ideas.

First, I will argue that Herder's ambition to provide a 'second *Montesquieu*' was grounded in his evolving philosophical outlook, which was continuous with his understanding of the history of the human mind, language and poetry as reconstructed in Chapter 2. Previous studies have examined Herder's views on the soul-body relationship as well as outlined his new metaphysics of 'force'.[9] It is also well-known that in this period, Herder seriously pondered humanity's place in nature, coining a new approach best described as 'philosophical anthropology'.[10] My argument (developed in the first section of the chapter) is that Herder's philosophical anthropology and particularly his insights about the foundations of morality and society developed in tandem with his deepening criticism of Montesquieu. Indeed, we need to have a close look at Herder's evolving understanding of the concepts of 'moral instinct', 'mores' and 'natural laws' in order to understand this criticism, whilst this criticism in turn enables us to see what was at stake for Herder in developing these ideas. Whilst Herder did find certain congenial elements in Montesquieu's *Spirit of the Laws*,[11] he was puzzled to see Montesquieu offer a strikingly thin account of human sociability, never properly exploring how humans could *be* 'happy' in their political societies.[12] It was also in Montesquieu's relative

---

[8] Herder's ideas for this work are incorporated in Herder, 'Sammlung von Gedanken und Beispielen fremder Schriftsteller über die Bildung der Völker', in *SWS*, IV, 469–478 (472–478).

[9] For the most recent discussion, see Nigel DeSouza, 'The Soul-Body Relationship and the Foundations of Morality: Herder contra Mendelssohn', *Herder Yearbook*, 21 (2014), 145–162 (145–161); Nigel DeSouza, 'The Metaphysical and Epistemological Foundations of Herder's Philosophical Anthropology', in *Herder: Philosophy and Anthropology*, 52–71; Nigel DeSouza, 'Herder's Theory of Organic Forces and Its Kantian Origins', in *Kant and His Contemporaries*, ed. Corey Dyck and Daniel O. Dahlstrom, 2 vols. (Cambridge, England, 2018), II, 109–130.

[10] On the concept of philosophical anthropology, and Herder's way into this 'discipline without name', see Wolfgang Proß, 'Nachwort', in *HWP*, II, 1128–1229. See also Ralph Häfner, *Johann Gottfried Herders Kulturentstehungslehre: Studien zu den Quellen und zur Methode seines Geschichtsdenkens* (Hamburg, 1995) and Zammito, *Kant, Herder*, 326–332.

[11] I would like to thank Wolfgang Proß for sharing his concept note for an evolving article on the topic of 'Herder, Natural Law, and Stoicism' with me, and for pointing out the need to consider Herder's relationship to Montesquieu's understanding of natural laws. I am very grateful to Professor Proß for a stimulating email discussion on this theme.

[12] Montesquieu famously stipulated in his Preface to *The Spirit of the Laws*: 'If I could make it so that everyone had new reasons for loving his duties, his prince, his homeland and his laws and that each could better feel his happiness in his own country, government, and position, I would consider

neglect of the 'natural' foundations of mores and laws that Herder found a deeper explanation for Catherine II's misguided application of Montesquieu's ideas. This, I suggest, was what Herder sought to articulate when complaining that *The Spirit of the Laws* was a 'metaphysics for a dead lawbook', rather than 'a metaphysics for the formation of peoples'.

Second, it is quite clear that the 'dead lawbook' to which Herder referred was the one that Catherine II had expected her legal commission to draft. According to Herder, what was needed instead was a 'living lawbook' that would be truly suited to the current character of the people. The lawbook had to be based on recent advances in the science of commerce and government, but also a profound knowledge of local history. In the second section of the chapter, I will thus reconstruct Herder's analysis of the economic and political situation in Russia. I argue that Herder here in many ways still regarded Montesquieu as an 'example' to be followed, albeit 'without his system' (412). The 'relations' in which laws stood with economic activities and social relationships were to be specified. As Montesquieu had suggested, commerce played an increasingly important role in the modern era, whereas not every kind of commerce suited every kind of state. Ambitious legislation, he had maintained, could here do more damage than good. Montesquieu's specific distinctions between monarchical and republican commerce, however, had met with serious criticism by the time of Herder's reading of *The Spirit of the Laws*.[13] As we will see, Herder was aware of some of this criticism. He also engaged with the history of Baltic trade in particular. On this basis, he hoped to provide some practical counsel to the governing elites of Riga as well as the Russian empress.

3.1   Applying Montesquieu

3.1.1   Montesquieu and the Foundations of the Russian 'Monarchy'

Catherine II's *Nakaz* has been characterised as 'perhaps the least original piece of political theory published during the eighteenth century'; what she offered was basically a compilation of excerpts taken from Montesquieu, Beccaria and Justi.[14] Indeed, *Nakaz* essentially proposed an ambitious

---

myself the happiest of mortals', Montesquieu, *The Spirit of the Laws*, xliv. As we will see, Herder did not think Montesquieu actually succeeded in (or even actually intended) studying the conditions of happiness.

[13] On French debates on Montesquieu's idea of monarchy, see Sonenscher, *Before the Deluge*, ch. 3.

[14] Clure, 'Rousseau, Diderot', 886.

reform programme to create a proper Montesquieuian monarchy, a government by laws in Russia, based on the new code of laws. Drawing on Montesquieu, Catherine argued that Russia was climatically a 'European power', whereas the mores of the people in Russia in pre-Petrine times had been corrupted through 'the fusion of different peoples' and 'the conquest of foreign territories', and were thus 'quite unsuitable' to its European location and climate.[15] Thus, Catherine presented herself as completing what Peter I had begun: the re-Europeanisation of Russia. She declared that the goal of sovereign rule in Russia was to achieve 'glory for the citizens, Empire and the Regent' and thereby to instil a 'spirit of freedom' in the people.[16] In a Montesquieuian vein, Catherine also stipulated that 'the intermediate powers, subordinate to, and depending upon the supreme power, form an essential part of monarchical government'.[17] These powers would have the right to remonstrate were they to think that the laws issued by the sovereign would contradict the 'fundamental laws' of the realm. In Russia, the 'political body' that would have such powers should be the Senate instituted by Peter I, to which, in turn, various juridical collegia and courts would be subordinated.[18] The nobility should be animated by true honour consisting in love of the fatherland, zeal of service and the diligent obedience to all laws and duties.[19] The laws should take into account the character of the people and they should be promulgated in the common vernacular tongue, their style should be simple, concise and easily understandable; indeed, every citizen should have a book of laws and be able to buy it 'at as small a price as a catechism'.[20] A moderate government would also require that no citizen would be deprived of their life, honour or property without due juridical process,[21] whilst torture should be abolished.[22] *Nakaz* also contained lengthy sections on the nobility, towns, agriculture, commerce and the 'enlargement of the population' of Russia.

These instructions were prepared for the representatives of estates whom Catherine had ordered to assemble in Moscow in 1767; the representatives continued their session in St. Petersburg in 1768. The estates in the Baltic

---

[15] [Catherine II], *Ihrer Kaiserlichen Majestaet Instruction*, 4; cf. Montesquieu, *The Spirit of the Laws*, XIX: 14, 315–316. For a discussion of Montesquieu's position, see Speck, 'The History and Politics', 127.

[16] [Catherine II], *Ihrer Kaiserlichen Majestaet Instruction*, 5.

[17] Ibid., 6–7; cf. Montesquieu, *The Spirit of the Laws*, II: 4, 17–20.

[18] [Catherine II], *Ihrer Kaiserlichen Majestaet Instruction*, 6, 19.

[19] Ibid., 72–73. Here, Catherine departed from Montesquieu who made a sharp and provocative distinction between love of the fatherland as the principle of republics and honour as that of monarchies.

[20] Ibid., 82–85.   [21] Ibid., 21.   [22] Ibid., 23.

provinces also had to send their representatives to the legislative body. From the viewpoint of the Baltic elites, Catherine's programme was particularly ambitious, even dangerous, since it became obvious that her goal was to treat all Russian territories in a uniform manner. Her *Nakaz* also contained a special section on the government of cities and towns in Russia. After her visit to Riga in 1764, Catherine had begun to search for ways in which to improve the government of Riga and also other, smaller, Livonian cities. However, these reform efforts came to a halt on the outbreak of the Russo-Turkish war in 1768.[23]

It is thus important to realise that Herder's *Journal of My Travels* was written just a year after Catherine's legislative commission had been cancelled. Herder may well have believed that Catherine had just postponed her reform plans due to war.[24] In any case, Herder's opinion of Catherine's philosophical vision for legislation was devastating. As we shall see below, Herder shared some of the same perspectives held by the commercial elites in Riga and highlighted the heterogeneity of Russia as an empire. More fundamentally, however, he maintained that Catherine had completely misunderstood Montesquieu. The greatest problem in the empress's approach, according to Herder, was that she ignored Russia's actual despotism with regard both to its form and principle of government. In Herder's view, Catherine counted on the principle of 'honour' in Russia, whereas in fact simply no sign of its existence could be found in 'the language, nation, and the empire' (426). Russia's actual principles of government were ambition and slavishness, fear and hope, flattery 'in order to become great'. Its *'politesse'* was that of crude despotism, expressing itself in 'crude honour' in 'drinking and kisses', and hence 'either crude habit or ultimately deception' (Herder repeated the same word 'crude' (*grob*) four times in the same sentence) (426). The empress did not regard herself as a 'despot', yet failed to see 'the despots above herself' – the members of the imperial court. (427) The Senate could not function as an 'aristocratic republic' or a Montesquieuian 'depositary of laws', as she hoped it would do, because, as Herder asked: 'did these lords [the appointed members of

---

[23] On Catherine's reform ideas in the Baltic provinces and as seen from the Baltic perspective, see Mati Laur, 'Der Aufgeklärte Absolutismus der Kaiserin Katharina II im Baltikum', in *Narva und die Ostseeregion*, ed. Karsten Brüggemann (Narva, 2004), 185–192 and Lea Leppik, 'The Provincial Reforms of Catherine the Great and the Baltic Common Identity', *Ajalooline Ajakiri: The Estonian Historical Journal*, 1/2(139/140) (2012), 55–78 (61–62).

[24] As Reto Speck has noted, Herder seems to have consistently supported Catherine's plans of Russia's expansion to the Black Sea and the Eastern Mediterranean, 'The History and Politics of Civilisation', 226-228.

the Senat] represent the empire? Were they taken from the country's nobility as a whole?' Most importantly, they lacked the power and motivation to withstand the monarch, if needed, as they were slaves themselves; 'the empire they served' was the palace [of the empress], the goods, luxury, needs, the holdings (*Parten*) that they have received through gifts' (427). No new codebook could therefore achieve an extensive reform of government in such a situation.

As this criticism shows, Herder well understood the fundamental principles of Montesquieu's account of monarchy, showing how it was inapplicable to Russia.[25] Indeed, as we shall see below, Herder was also largely following the analytical map that Montesquieu had charted in order to capture the most characteristic aspects of the states in which he travelled (France and Netherlands).[26] This did not, however, mean that Herder's goals were limited to teaching a correct 'application' of Montesquieu. In a number of respects, Herder argued, Montesquieu's own approach invited such misapplications. As the debate about monarchical patriotism had already revealed, Montesquieu had set up a narrow scheme of three forms and principles of government, paying little attention to mixed forms and more complicated cases (425).[27] He had posited an abstract theory of forms of government and sought to derive explanations from principles, but how had he arrived at this theory? Did he not model it on the basis of a very limited number of empirical cases, taking only minimal interest in contexts he was less familiar with? Even within Europe, Montesquieu had disregarded a vast number of relevant examples, and overlooked much of the historical evolution of those forms of government that he focused on. Could French honour, Herder asked, even be found in Prussia or Spain? Even though in each case the answer was the same – no – there were different reasons for that. And if honour could not be found in these countries, what did that mean for their forms of government? Was not Prussia most accurately to be described as a despotic monarchy? And had not France itself even seen a kind of despotism for a period, a monarchical despotism during the times of Richelieu and Louis XIV? (425)

---

[25] On the complexity of Montesquieu's work in general and on his idea of monarchy in particular, see Sylvana Tomaselli, 'The Spirit of Nations', in *The Cambridge History of Eighteenth-Century Political Thought*, ed. Mark Goldie & Robert Wokler (Cambridge, 2006), 7–39 and Sonenscher, *Before the Deluge*, ch. 2. On Montesquieu's views on Russia, see Speck, 'The History and Politics', 125–128.
[26] Herder particularly faithfully followed Montesquieu in describing the French mores, see Herder, 'Journal meiner Reise', in *HWP*, I, 428–436.
[27] On this debate, see Chapter 1.

A proper application of Montesquieu, thus, needed a 'second *Montesquieu*', a philosophy of laws that would go beyond Montesquieu in important aspects (428). When Herder set out to work out the foundations of the 'second *Montesquieu*' during his stay in Nantes, he became increasingly critical of not only Montesquieu's theory of the principles of government but also of the situation in modern European states in general. His critical attitude is captured in his crucial question: '*the natural and civil history of laws* (*Natur- und Civilgeschichte der Gesetze*): why must they contradict each other? And religion as well? Why should there be three kinds of training (*Erziehung*) that are opposed to each other?' (471) A few paragraphs below, Herder explicated what was at stake here:

> Our distinct reason only weakly rules the body; instinct does it livelier and better. Habits, mores [*Sitten*], moral instincts constitute a healthy state of a political realm. To solely follow the laws, and have no mores, is to wish to solely follow cold reason, and not to enjoy the entire sensitive man [the fullness of one's sensual nature]. A conflict between reason and instinct is a wretched condition of humanity. Conflict between laws and mores places a state in a wretched condition. Having no mores is as hapless as having no instinct-forces; in such a weakly, languishing condition are our European states. Laws only command us weakly and do not make us happy; they are [their ambition is] limited to not making us unhappy; the habits are dead politically; there is no longer a fatherland, no longer any citizens [in these states] (471–472).

3.1.2   A 'Metaphysics for a Dead Lawbook'

Although Montesquieu himself did not use the phrases 'natural' or 'civil history of laws' in *The Spirit of the Laws*, in Book One, entitled 'Of Laws in General', he discussed the relationships between moral, religious, natural and civil laws.[28] This account, I will seek to show, was what Herder must have had in mind when raising the question about different kinds of 'training', and when identifying a conflict between reason and (moral) instinct in modern societies. It is necessary to lay out Montesquieu's discussion of these different laws in some detail in order to see the point of Herder's criticism.

Montesquieu began by defining laws as 'the necessary relations deriving from the nature of things', describing how the divinity, the material world,

---

[28] Montesquieu, *The Spirit of the Laws*, I, 3–9. Cf. also Part V of *The Spirit of the Laws* [1748], in which Montesquieu discusses the relationships between different kinds of laws and uses the term 'natural law' to denote the natural dispositions of humans.

the 'intelligences superior to man', the beasts and humans all have their distinctive laws.[29] In characterising divine laws, he emphasised God as the creator and upholder of the material world and its laws; these laws, he argued, are rooted in God's wisdom and power but operate without needing interference by an intelligence. In addition to the mechanical laws governing the movement of bodies, Montesquieu also referred to 'relations of justice' or 'equity' (*équité*) underlying social life and fundamental to any kind of positive law. Such relations included obedience to the laws of society, and the reciprocity of both beneficent services (and gratitude) as well as harm. These relations were also grounded in divine wisdom but were not followed uniformly by finite intelligences.[30] Finally, Montesquieu also invoked the notion of 'natural laws' not with a view to the fundamental laws of physics but, more specifically, as related to the particular 'nature' of beasts and humans. 'Beasts' were guided by natural laws because they preserved their existence and species by the attraction of pleasure. Since they did not have knowledge, they could not and did not need to have positive laws. Humans, Montesquieu argued, were different. Because of his/her intelligence, a human being 'constantly violates the laws God has established and changes those he himself establishes'. God has revealed laws of religion to 'call him back', just like philosophers have 'reminded him of himself' in their laws of morality, i.e. reminding him of the essential rules of justice prescribing sociability. Finally, political and civil laws were needed so that man would not 'forget his fellows'.[31] These kinds of 'reminders' and warnings are the 'three kinds of training' that Herder was referring to in his comment.

In the next chapter titled 'On the laws of nature', Montesquieu, however, also described human 'laws of nature' proper that were 'so named because they derive uniquely from the constitution of our being.'[32] In contrast to relations of equity, humans did not violate these laws. Rather, these were laws of behaviour, indeed, certain propensities to act, that resulted from the distinctive way of thought of primitive but developing human beings. As such, Montesquieu stipulated, they preceded all prescriptive and corrective laws. Thus Montesquieu sought to keep separate what previous natural lawyers (e.g. Samuel Pufendorf) had tended to conflate, suggesting a certain history of natural laws, i.e. an evolutionary account of the different stages in which mankind had evolved since the 'state of nature'.[33] Rules of equity were

---

[29] Montesquieu, *The Spirit of the Laws*, I:1, 3.   [30] Ibid., I: 1, 3–4.   [31] Ibid., I:1, 5.
[32] Ibid., I:2, 6.
[33] Cf. Rousseau's distinction between the two kinds of natural law (that of the 'Modern Philosophers' and 'Roman Jurists') in the preface to *Discourse on the Origins of Inequality* (paragraphs 6–8), 126–127. On this distinction, see Victor Gourevitch, 'Introduction', in Jean-Jacques Rousseau,

immutable moral norms, but humans would only gradually come to follow them, insofar as they originally, at the beginning of human history, were sensuous beings incapable of 'speculating', i.e. abstract thought. They would think of 'the preservation of their being before seeking the origin of his [their] being.'[34] Tacitly picking up the theme of the history of the human mind previously pursued by Fontenelle and Condillac, Montesquieu thus also suggested an evolutionary account of human society based on the history of the human mind.[35]

Montesquieu distinguished four kinds of 'natural laws' in total that captured the propensities of primitive human beings. Directly challenging Thomas Hobbes's account of the 'state of nature', Montesquieu began by emphasising the timidity of primitive men, which led to the first 'law' of seeking to maintain peace among themselves. Further, Montesquieu argued, 'man would add the feeling of his needs to the feeling of his weakness', thus leading to the law of seeking nourishment for himself. Third, despite their timidity, humans would nevertheless approach each other, due to 'the pleasure one animal feels at the approach of an animal of its own kind'. This pleasure would further be increased between the individuals of opposite sex, whereby the third natural law would be to make a 'natural entreaty to one another'. Finally, by gaining some knowledge, humans would develop a 'desire to live in society' as a fourth natural law.[36]

Despite this defence of basic sociability, Montesquieu rather strikingly associated the rise of society with that of a 'state of war' at the beginning of chapter three of Book One. He wrote: 'As soon as men are in society, they lose their feeling of weakness; the equality that was among them ceases, and the state of war begins.' As they began to 'feel their strength', societies entered into war, yet this also awoke individuals' sense of their individual strength, which led to a state of war between individuals. 'These two states of war', Montesquieu concluded, 'bring about the establishment of laws among men'.[37] Montesquieu suggested that civil and political laws had emerged in response to, and as a correction of, a 'state of war'.

In Montesquieu's account, the 'natural' and 'civil history of laws' were thus in tension with each other; as such, it must have captured Herder's eye. It remained unclear what the first civil and political laws were grounded in;

The Social Contract and Other Later Political Writings, ed. and trans. Victor Gourevitch (Cambridge, 1997), ix–xxxi (x–xi).
[34] Montesquieu, *The Spirit of the Laws*, I:2, 6.
[35] I would like to thank Wolfgang Proß for pointing out these parallels to me.
[36] Montesquieu, *The Spirit of the Laws*, I:2, 7.   [37] Ibid., I:3, 7.

with characteristic brevity, Montesquieu presented them as creations of (limited) human reasoning and specified that their 'spirit' consisted in the 'various relations that the laws may have with various things', such as 'the physical aspect of the country', 'the way of life of the peoples', 'their religion', 'commerce', 'mores', 'manners', etc. He maintained that the laws were also 'related to one another, to their origin, to the purpose of the legislator, and to the order of things on which they are established', without giving much further information about this 'order of things'.[38] Herder concluded that Montesquieu had actually only studied the 'properties' (*Eigenschaften*) of laws, seeking to reduce the great variety of existing laws to a few fundamental principles and forms of government so as to determine their metaphysical 'essence'.[39] As we saw above, Herder of course had noted that Montesquieu paid ample attention to distinct kinds of psychological drives or indeed, 'mores', as underlying the various forms of government in the rest of *The Spirit of the Laws*; he must have also been aware of Montesquieu's understanding of 'mores' as capturing the 'internal conduct' and 'actions of man', rather than relating to 'external conduct' and 'actions of the citizen' as manners and laws did.[40] Nevertheless, Herder seems to have felt that Montesquieu's position about the origins and foundations of mores and laws themselves, and hence also of human societies, remained elusive.

3.1.3 'Moral Instincts' and the 'General Economy of Nature'

Herder's own views about the foundations of human societies were anchored in his theory of the soul-body relationship. The variety of intellectual pursuits in which Herder engaged in the formative years of 1764–1769 is remarkable, yet it is also fair to say that this relationship had come to occupy centre stage in Herder's philosophical studies early on. As Marion Heinz and Nigel DeSouza have shown, Herder developed his conception of the human soul by engaging with Leibniz's conception of the close relationship between soul and body, whilst rejecting the latter's doctrines of the windowlessness of monads and pre-established harmony.[41] Highly significant for him were also Kant's various pre-critical writings of the mid-1750s (*The Universal Natural History and Theory of the*

---

[38] Ibid., I:3, 9.   [39] Herder, 'Gedanken bei Lesung Montesquieus', 471.
[40] Montesquieu, *The Spirit of the Laws*, XIX:16, 317.
[41] For discussion, see DeSouza, 'The Soul-Body Relationship', and DeSouza, 'The Metaphysical and Epistemological Foundations'; see also Adler, *Die Prägnanz des Dunklen*, 63–88; Heinz, *Sensualistischer Idealismus*, 1–26; Zammito, *Kant, Herder*, 310–315; Noyes, *Herder: Aesthetics*, ch. 1.

Heavens (1755) and *Physical Monadology* (1756)), which inspired him to try to reconcile Newton and Leibniz.[42] John Zammito sums up this endeavour as follows: 'He [Herder] sought to explain both the physical and the moral world, both nature and spirit, in attractive and repulsive forces that were unanalyzable but actual, efficient causes'.[43]

By 1769, Herder, in a neo-Platonic vein, viewed human souls as divine emanations of God, which in turn have forming power themselves.[44] Yet, whilst God as an infinite being was inwardly present in everything, the sphere of human souls was limited to that of the body. Only in one's body, Herder argued, was the soul inwardly present, and it was only through the senses that it could attain knowledge, and through physical feeling that the soul was present to itself.[45] Herder's 'philosophical anthropology' was grounded on this metaphysics, whilst also incorporating insights from ancient and modern natural philosophy and history, including, prominently, the 'genetic epistemology' of Étienne Bonnot de Condillac and Charles Bonnet.[46] As humans, for Herder, were an integral part of a general 'household of nature', comparisons with animal souls were highly relevant. It was on the basis of such a metaphysics and philosophical anthropology that the foundations of morality and indeed, even politics, were also best described.

In order to specify Herder's understanding of 'moral instinct' and sociability in this period, let us briefly elaborate on his relationship to three of his major sources of inspiration: Leibniz, Bonnet and Samuel Reimarus. During 1768–1769, Herder engaged seriously with Leibniz's *Nouveaux Essais sur l'entendement humain* (*New Essays on Human Understanding*) (posthumously published in 1765). In this work, Leibniz distinguished between two kinds of innate truths, those 'known in natural light' (and as such distinctively knowable), and those known through natural feeling or instincts. According to Leibniz, the latter were known insensibly and in a confused manner, whereas the internal light of reason could bring them into focus and determine their role in divine order. Leibniz's claim was that God had engraved in humans' minds moral 'instincts which lead,

---

[42] See Heinz, *Sensualistischer Idealismus*, chs. 1 and 2; Proß, 'Nachwort', in *HWP*, III/1, 925–945; DeSouza, 'Herder's Theory of Organic Forces', 116–117. Zammito, *Kant, Herder*, 316.

[43] Zammito, *Kant, Herder*, 316.

[44] DeSouza, 'Herder's Theory of Organic Forces', 117–118, 120.

[45] Heinz, *Sensualistischer Idealismus*, 102–108; see also Nigel DeSouza, 'The Ontological Foundations of Herder's Concept of Sympathy', in *Herder on Empathy*, 37–49.

[46] Proß, 'Nachwort', in *HWP*, II, 1134–1175; cf. Häfner, *Johann Gottfried Herders Kulturentstehungslehre*, passim and Zammito, *Kant, Herder*, 326–332.

straight away and without reasoning, to part of what reason commands'. He conceded that these instincts were not universally followed due to the impact of our passions, prejudices and contrary customs. Nevertheless, the 'largest and soundest part of the human race' clearly bore witness to them.[47]

In a fragment titled *Truths from Leibniz* (*Wahrheiten aus Leibniz*), Herder summarised Leibniz's main points about innate truths and principles that were expressed as 'habitudes' and 'dispositions'. He noted that for Leibniz, instincts could be both theoretical (as in arithmetic) and practical, and that Leibniz distinguished between immediate natural feelings and instincts, on the one hand, and the 'principle of humanity' that is a 'principle of instinct developed with the help of natural light', on the other.[48] As examples of human instincts, Herder basically reproduced the list of fundamental drives that Leibniz had presented (Leibniz in turn invoked the core ideas of the Stoics as mediated by Cicero in *On Duties* and *On Moral Ends*): the 'instinct of society' (*Instinkt zur Gesellschaft*) or philanthropy (tender feeling for members of one's own species), parental and filial love (Greek: *storgē*), regard for dignity and propriety, concern for one's reputation, even beyond death, fear of conscience, and of the future. Herder also paraphrased Leibniz's reflection about this list: 'They are all realities (*Realitäten*), but [as such still] only aids to reason, nature's good advice. Custom, education, tradition, reason, contribute much, but [are] all rooted in nature. – It is true that without reason these aids would not suffice to give a complete certitude to morals, but what needs to be illuminated is still a sentiment, a dark feeling of an inborn truth.'[49]

In pondering the relationship between Montesquieuian 'laws of (human) nature' and moral instincts, Herder could also draw on and develop further Charles Bonnet's ideas.[50] Charles Bonnet had first elaborated on the notion of moral instinct in his *Essay on Psychology or Considerations about the Operations of the Soul, Habits and Education* (*Essai de psychologie ou considérations sur les opérations de l'âme, sur l'habitude et sur l'éducation*)

---

[47] Gottfried Wilhelm Leibniz, *New Essays on Human Understanding* (Cambridge, 2012), Bk I, ch. II, 92–93.

[48] Herder, 'Wahrheiten aus Leibniz', in *HWP*, II, 32–48 (43).

[49] Ibid., 43–44; cf. Leibniz, *New Essays*, 43–44.

[50] For the significance of Bonnet's ideas on the overall chain of beings in the development of Herder's broader understanding of the 'economy of nature', see Proß, 'Nachwort', in *HWP*, III/1, 951–953; for a comparison of Bonnet's and Herder's conceptions of the human soul, see Ralph Häfner, '"L'âme est un neurologie en miniature": Herder und die Neurophysiologie Charles Bonnets', *Der ganze Mensch: Anthropologie und Literatur im achtzehnten Jahrhundert*, ed. Hans-Jürgen Schings (Stuttgart, Weimar, 1994), 390–409 (390–395).

(1755). According to Bonnet, all living beings had a distinct kind of 'sensibility' relating to their natural neurological dispositions, whereas they also developed certain 'habits' in their distinctive environments. Their brains acquired a special kind of 'tone' (*ton*) through sensuous interaction with the environment, whilst their 'habits' would be 'the true source of tastes, affections, inclinations, mores, and character'.[51] Nevertheless, habits ultimately either enhanced or suppressed the more fundamental 'moral instinct', which was independent from them. As Bonnet specified, the latter should be regarded as a distinct 'sentiment' of the natural 'relations' obtained between different individual beings, according to 'their nature and merit'; 'the ideas of justice and injustice, decency and indecency, virtue and vice, good and bad can be reduced to those of order and disorder'.[52]

In his *Essai analytique sur les facultés de l'âme* (*Analytical essay on the faculties of the soul*) (1760), Bonnet also directly engaged with Montesquieu's discussion of natural laws.[53] Bonnet noted that whilst Montesquieu had contrasted humans with animals, emphasising human fallibility and free will as the reasons why humans 'constantly violate the laws God has established', he had also granted that humans like animals follow 'invariable natural laws' resulting from 'their particular nature'. Yet Bonnet was critical about the ways in which Montesquieu further developed his argument. Instead of thus opposing humans and animals in terms of their fallibility, he argued, Montesquieu should have traced in greater detail how humans, too, express their nature. According to Bonnet, an intelligent being's 'nature' comprised

> its ideas, its inclinations, its affections, in one word, its individual character. Its character forms its moral or intellectual essence. A being is intelligent not because it has a capacity to be so, but because it has [acquired] knowledge (*notions*) and acts according to what it cognises.[54]

Montesquieu had compared an abstract notion of natural law (i.e. rules of equity) with the actual actions of intelligent beings, and had thus seen a

---

[51] Charles Bonnet, *Essai de psychologie ou considérations sur les opérations de l'âme, sur l'habitude et sur l'éducation* (London, 1755), ch. 29, 109.

[52] Ibid., 181–183.

[53] Charles Bonnet, *Essai analytique sur les facultés de l'âme* (Copenhagen, 1760), ch. 27. On Bonnet's criticism of Montesquieu's notion of 'relation' and his ideas about the 'natural laws' of humans and beasts more broadly, see Céline Spector, 'De l'union de l'âme et du corps à l'unité de la sensibilité. L'anthropologie méconnue de *L'Esprit des lois*', *Les études philosophiques* (Paris, 2013), 106 (3), 383–396.

[54] Bonnet, *Essai analytique*, 544.

contradiction between the two. However, 'abstractions do not exist in nature', Bonnet argued, only particular beings with particular 'determinations' do. Thus, 'accepting that the world is created by an intelligent being, and the activity of the soul is by nature undetermined', that it is necessary to have 'motives of the will' and that 'the degree of intelligence of each individual being depends on the circumstances in which it is placed', one can see that these beings can also have their particular laws. Thus, the intelligent beings, too, were in fact also led by a desire for happiness, seeking to realise what they regarded as such. Their ideas of happiness in turn could also exhibit a certain regularity, being framed in relation to the circumstances in which they exist.[55]

Finally, a highly significant source of inspiration for Herder was Samuel Reimarus's *General Observations on the Instincts of Animals, Chiefly on their Instincts to Artifice, for the Better Understanding of Connections between the World, the Creator and our Selves* (*Allgemeine Betrachtungen über die Triebe der Thiere, hauptsächlich über ihre Kunsttriebe zum Erkenntniss des Zusammenhanges der Welt, des Schöpfers und unser selbst*) (1760, 1762).[56] Reimarus sought to show that there was a fundamental difference in the 'forces' of animals and humans. Whereas animals had 'determined animal instincts to artifice' (*Kunsttriebe*), humans possessed 'raw undetermined, but also higher natural forces' (*rohe unbestimmte, aber auch höhere Naturkräfte*). For Reimarus, here, the Stoic doctrine of *oikeiōsis* served as a direct inspiration in this, as proven in his quoting a large section of the letter CXXI of Seneca's *Moral letters to Lucillus*.[57] In this letter, Seneca refers to each animal's ability to feel its 'constitution' and its corresponding striving to preserve it. Reimarus directly approved of this idea, and in a Stoic vein posited the idea of a general 'economy of nature' in which each individual animal and species had enough capabilities and skill to preserve themselves and achieve the well-being that corresponded to their needs and way of life. Whilst humans seemingly lacked that skill, their higher kind of undetermined natural forces (the physical form of which was erect posture) enabled them to replace it functionally by developing reason and virtue and by achieving human well-being based on the former. As Wolfgang Proß has demonstrated, in this work Reimarus notably distanced himself from his

---

[55] Ibid., 545–546.   [56] The translation of this title is from Noyes, *Herder: Aesthetics*, 39.
[57] Lucius Annaeus Seneca, *Moral letters to Lucilius* (*Epistulae morales ad Lucilium*), trans. Richard Mott Gummere, *A Loeb Classical Library edition*, 3 vols. (London, 1917–1945), III, 396–410. I am very grateful to Wolfgang Proß for drawing my attention to this citation and for sharing the draft article titled 'Progressive Humanität: Zur Anthropologie des Naturrechts in Herders Geschichtsphilosophie' with me. The article contains an extensive discussion of Seneca's ideas and points out their significance for the development of those of Herder.

earlier physico-theological account in *Die vornehmsten Wahrheiten der natürlichen Religion* (1754, 1766) (*The Most Excellent Truths of Natural Religion*), which emphasised the cognition of divine moral order and the excellence of God as the goals of human development. In his *General Observations*, Reimarus instead understood 'reason' to mean the distinctively human techniques and 'self-productions' that all take specific forms under the influence of *causae secundae* such as clime and environment, thereby ruling out the specification of rational moral norms in abstract.[58]

In a fragment titled *Principles of Philosophy* (*Grundsätze der Philosophie*)[59] as well as his two famous letters to Moses Mendelssohn on the vocation of man written in the same period, Herder drew on these ideas to develop his own position on the foundations of morality.[60] Rejecting Mendelssohn's Leibnizian account where man's vocation was endlessly seeking the moral perfection of the soul, Herder presented a strikingly naturalist view of human perfection and vocation. On the one hand, he endorsed the general Stoic understanding of human sociability embraced by the authors discussed above, on the other, he further expanded on the conclusions that Reimarus had already drawn about human 'reason'. Herder wrote to Mendelssohn from Riga before departing on his sea voyage, stating he was ready to accept that the aims of self-preservation and 'enjoyment' (*Genuß*) were shared by animals and humans alike.[61] It was 'nature's end' that plants, animals and humans would all develop 'skills' (*Fertigkeiten*) to be 'applied in this life', in order to achieve 'limited enjoyment within the limits of one's constitution'.[62] Described this way, striving for happiness could thus be accepted as the most fundamental moral instinct; the forces of attraction and repulsion governed the logic of human action as much as that of any other being.[63] At the same time, and in line with the Stoic account of *oikeiōsis*, Herder used the term 'self-preservation' here in an extended sense, as

---

[58] Proß, 'Anmerkungen', in *HWP*, III/2, 217–220.
[59] Herder, 'Grundsätze der Philosophie', in *HWP*, II, 52–56. On this fragment, see Heinz, *Sensualistischer Idealismus*, 81–108.
[60] Herder to Mendelssohn, Riga, early April 1769, in *DA*, I, 137–143; Herder to Mendelssohn, Paris, 1 December 1769, in *DA*, I, 177–181. On this famous controversy, see in particular Marion Heinz, 'Die Bestimmung des Menschen: Herder contra Mendelssohn', *Philosophie der Endlichkeit: Festschrift für Erich Christian Schröder zum 65: Geburtstag*, ed. Beate Niemeyer and Dirk Schütze (Würzburg, 1991), 263–285; Proß, 'Kommentar', in *HWP*, II, 885–895; DeSouza, 'The Soul-Body Relationship'.
[61] Herder to Mendelssohn, in *DA*, I, 140–141; see also Proß, 'Kommentar', in *HWP*, II, 887–893.
[62] Herder to Mendelssohn, in *DA*, I, 141, cf. ibid., 178. Proß also highlights the close parallels between these ideas and those of Diderot in latter's *De l'interpretation de la nature*, Proß, 'Kommentar', 887–889.
[63] Heinz, 'Die Bestimmung des Menschen', 272.

relating to the preservation of one's distinctive constitution, which involved the development of one's capacities in a specific environment, so as to satisfy one's needs at a certain period of life (*Lebensalter*).[64] Thus, Herder argued in *Principles of Philosophy*, human (moral) instincts included such instincts as the sexual drive and various kinds of social drives that all served the broader goal of 'self-preservation'. Herder also used the opportunity to restate his opinion here on Rousseau's rejection of sociability as a central aspect of human self-preservation; in Herder's view, Rousseau's account of natural man was simply 'void'.[65]

Like Reimarus, but even more directly, Herder simultaneously questioned the possibility of attributing to humans a literal 'moral sense', an instinctive capacity of detecting the right and wrong in human affairs. He also emphasised the impossibility of determining the nature of 'virtue' in the abstract, describing the human pursuit of perfection as follows: since the human soul cannot have any ideas (*Vorstellungen*) after the death of the body, and it is impossible to be happy without a body, the only possible vocation of man can be to 'be more perfect in this world' through the various powers of the body.[66] For Herder, there was an internal striving in humans towards having perceptions about things that would harmonise with their essence, which in turn would provide pleasure and enable them to preserve themselves and collect ideas, so as to become more perfect.[67] Human bodies, like those of animals, existed in highly variable physical and geographical conditions, as did human sensations and ideas (*Vorstellungen*), which were also coloured by these conditions. Although humans thus were fundamentally disposed to seek a certain kind of harmony with those similar to themselves, leading towards a general affirmation of sociability, it was impossible to determine the precise content of morality or supreme happiness in an abstract way. Hence even notions like 'virtue' or 'perfection' were only abstractions from the real processes going on in the human soul in response to external stimuli. There is more to life, Herder declared, than this 'merely deducted concept of human weakness (*ein abgezogner Begriff der menschlichen Schwachheit*)'.[68]

---

[64] Herder to Mendelssohn, in *DA*, I, 140. On Stoic oikeiōsis, see Jacob Klein, 'The Stoic Argument from Oikeiōsis,' *Oxford Studies in Ancient Philosophy*, 50 (2016), 143–200.

[65] Herder, 'Grundsätze der Philosophie', 55. On Herder's alternative to Rousseau's conjectural history, see Chapter 2.

[66] Herder to Mendelssohn, in *DA*, I, 142.

[67] Herder to Mendelssohn, in *DA*, I, 140–141; Mendelssohn, 'Grundsätze der Philosophie', 55. Proß points to parallels between Herder's interpretation of Leibnizian 'inné' with the Stoic 'tonos' (Latin: 'conatus'), see Proß, 'Anmerkungen', in *HWP*, II, 852.

[68] Herder to Mendelssohn, in *DA*, I, 142.

Nothing is more revealing about Herder's position on moral sense than his famous attack on Friedrich Justus Riedel's account of the 'three fundamental forces of the soul' (the *sensus communis* for truth', the *conscience* for good', and the *taste* for beauty') in his draft titled *Viertes kritisches Wäldchen* (*Fourth Critical Grove*), written in 1769.[69] Positing humans' sensuous (aesthetic) disposition, their pursuit of perfection and 'enjoyment' (*Genuβ*), and the interaction between their internal forces and the environment, as his basic starting points in this essay, Herder set out to highlight the ways in which different human senses acquire specific 'habits' (*Gewohnheiten*) through repetitious practice (*Übung*). Initially aligning himself with Bonnet's central point, Herder maintained that humans learn only as much as they need to learn in order to preserve and enjoy themselves in a specific environment, 'collecting concepts and making judgements, and drawing conclusions based on the latter'.[70] In his view, however, these concepts and judgements were strictly speaking individual, whilst habit and similarities of circumstances helped to create certain kinds of national 'common sense'. What it thus ruled out, however, was 'common sense' as an unmediated feeling and judgement shared by all humans: 'Is the common sense of a Greenlander or Hottentot in respect to its objects and applications the same as ours? And the common sense of a ruler [the same as] that of a scholar?'[71]

Regarding matters of morality, Herder also made it clear that humans needed concepts in order to make judgements. Since concepts bore the imprint of the context in which they were formed, and related to the latter, the actual concrete judgements of our conscience and taste could not be regarded as universal. Whilst there was a fundamental similarity of disposition in humans and a possibility of detecting aberrations from the 'economy of nature', it was impossible to determine the precise content of conscience in the abstract.[72] For Herder, humans instead developed specific 'mores' (*Sitten*), particular sentiments and habitual principles as well as action-prompting judgements in their specific environments. Once they had attained a certain level of civilisation, humans could of course also rationally illuminate their 'mores' and work them into ethical principles (*sittliche Grundsätze*). At the same time, conversely, these ethical principles could also again 'cloud and embed themselves' in single impressions and

---

[69] He targeted two of Riedel's works: *Theorie der schönen Künste und Wissenschaften: Ein Auszug aus den Werken verschiedener Schriftsteller* (1767) and *Ueber das Publicum: Briefe an einige Glieder desselben* (1768). The *Fourth Critical Grove* remained unpublished during Herder's lifetime.

[70] Herder, 'Viertes kritisches Wäldchen', in *HWP*, II, 86–87.   [71] Ibid., 87.   [72] Ibid.

sentiments, so that we came to regard them as unmediated feelings. In this case, these impressions and sentiments only reflected the judgements on the basis of which the ethical principles have been formed.[73] Morality, however, originated in moral sentiments and was stabilised in mores, just as mores, in turn, were rooted in human nature and natural sociability, humans' fundamental disposition to preserve themselves and the species.

3.1.4 *Mores and Civil/Political Laws*

As we have seen, in this period Herder took great interest in different attempts to show the foundations of morality and sociability in human nature. But how did he characterise the relationship between moral instincts and mores, on the one hand, and civil and political laws, on the other? An elaboration of the notion of 'moral instinct' and its relationship to laws appears in Part Three of Jean-Baptiste-René Robinet's *Of nature* (*De la nature*) (1763), and Herder had made a short paraphrase of it in this period.[74] Robinet accepted that laws became necessary as societies grew more complex and unequal; however, he maintained that their purpose – just like that of religious rites – was not to suppress or transform human beings but to support morality and guarantee 'freedom'.[75] As the example of ancient lawgivers showed, he wrote,

> the laws that were proposed for this purpose did not make up a new yoke, but were a simple expression of moral sentiments. The first legislations should not be judged on the basis of the code of law of policed nations, in which reason too often seeks to dominate nature; instead it was their [ancient lawgivers'] duty to show us how important it is to never contradict the virtuous movements that originate in our natural constitution.[76]

This was, in all likelihood, also Herder's position. In raising the question of the conflict between 'natural and civil history of laws', I suggest that

---

[73] Ibid., 88.

[74] The paraphrase is reprinted as '*De l'instinct moral*, par Robinet', in Proß, 'Anhang. [*Aus Herders Nachlaß*]', in *HWP*, II, 1226–1229; cf. Jean-Baptiste-René Robinet, *De la nature* 2 vols. (Amsterdam, 1766 (3rd edition)), I, 227–252. On Herder's interest in Robinet's broader ideas, see Proß, 'Nachwort', in *HWP*, II, 1199.

[75] Robinet, *De la nature*, 244.

[76] Ibid., 245. Robinet also quoted Ovid's *Fasti*, chapter III: 'inde datae leges, ne firmior omnia posset, coeptaque sunt pure tradita sacra coli. exituir feritas, armisque potentius aequum est, et cum cive pudet conseruisse manus; atque aliquis, modo trux, visa iam vertitur ara vinaque dat tepidis farraque salsa focis.', ibid. For Herder's short paraphrase of these ideas, see '*De l'instinct moral*', HWP II, 1228; Cf. Montesquieu, *The Spirit of the Laws*, 'One must put oneself in mind of what independence is and what liberty is. Liberty is the right to do everything the laws permit [—]', XI: 3, 155.

Herder applauded Montesquieu's interest in the developmental laws of human society but was struck by his emphasis on the ways in which humans constantly violate the immutable 'rules of equity'. Even more importantly, despite his granting of a rudimentary individual 'desire for society' as a natural law, Montesquieu located the origins of laws in a form of unsocial sociability, the propensity of human groups for external, but increasingly also, internal, conflict. For Montesquieu, positive laws were therefore primarily of a corrective nature; their relationship to natural laws and mores remained unclear. Robinet's and Herder's view was different. Resisting Montesquieu's rather sceptical conclusions about the conflict between the three kinds of training, Herder instead sought to show that political and civil laws could have a more harmonious relationship with 'natural laws', mores and religion, that is, express and solidify the fourth natural law, i.e. man's natural desire for society. 'Having no mores' was an artificial and unhappy condition, one that could only come into being when our internal feelings were suppressed by the 'wish to follow solely cold reasoning'.[77] This condition, he believed, was characteristic of highly civilised modern European states, the citizens of which had adopted abstract ideals of virtue. However, Catherine II was now also seeking to establish a similar situation in Russia through her desired new code of laws. Thus, when commenting on Montesquieu's ideas in his notes, Herder expressed his dissatisfaction with what he saw as Montesquieu's generally legalistic approach. What was needed instead was a metaphysics for a legislator who would be interested in how civil and political laws could make the people truly happy, i.e. enhance the ends of natural law:

> Laws of the world; laws of bodies; laws of human and animal nature[s], I wish to call upon you for succor in the darkness of my labyrinth, [to show me] how the laws of nations are to be formed so that they, like you, will be valid and effectual, make people happy, reach their goal! Laws of bodies first, for they are the best known. Attraction and repulsion! I cannot explain them, but I detect them. They have in all probability formed a body [I observe], they preserve it; they are its essence, its nature; what do I know – To give such laws of attraction and repulsion to a people that would be so natural to its essence, that have originally formed this people, preserved it in the same way as these laws have preserved a body, that is true legislation. I know nothing as yet, attraction and repulsion are abstract expressions, they are nothing but words, collected concepts. What have I said now when I say that they have formed a body, they preserve it, etc. Nothing but that it is according to these laws that the body was formed and preserves itself, that

---

[77] Herder, 'Gedanken bei Lesung Montesquieus', 468–473, 471.

is, it is a simple essence that posseses a limited power/force to build itself a body. It attracts as a limited force, as a limited force it is also repealed, and attains a sphere; this is where its formation is, the formation of a body.[78]

Herder believed that in order to discover how laws can make a people 'happy' it was necessary to study the most 'lively' (*lebendige*) peoples, that is, 'savage' and 'half-savage' peoples who were beginning to be civilised (*gesittet*)'.[79] The formation of mores and laws through early *ethopoeia*, i.e. a poetic creation, was thus highly relevant in this respect. As we saw in Chapter 2, Herder had argued in *Fragments* that there was no separation between ethical and political principles in early cultures. Political principles were directly rooted in poetry and a people's aesthetic and moral tastes, and thus the first poets were also simultaneously the first legislators. Montesquieu, in Herder's view, had completely neglected such processes, hardly paying any attention to 'savage peoples' in Asia, Africa, America. This was a profound flaw in his approach, Herder insisted, since

> it is precisely in the example of the savage peoples [...] that one can best study mores [*Sitten*], habits, and characteristics [of a people]. Written law is a shadow, living ethics [*Sitte*] and habits [*Gewohnheit*] are the body; the latter is a picture, the former a caption. And these living pictures Montesquieu studied and knew too little. He was too little of a human being, and too much of a citizen of a monarchical state, too little of a natural philosopher and too much of a President, to study them [these pictures] in their true power [*Kraft*]. His book is thus a metaphysics for a dead lawbook, not a metaphysics for the formation of peoples.[80]

3.2 Chances of Reform in Modern Europe, Russia and Riga

3.2.1 *Economic and Cultural Situation in Modern Europe*

Herder's emphasis on the need to study the foundations of national mores in early poetry did not preclude him from acknowledging the specific character of the modern era; indeed, it was precisely his goal to show the relevance of poetry, philosophy and the 'beautiful sciences' (*schöne Wissenschaften*) in general to reforming modern societies as well. These ideas were to be implemented in an ambitious programme of school

---

[78] Ibid., 472–473. My translation includes (but has also slightly modified) Zammito's translation of a section of this paragraph in *Kant, Herder*, 333.
[79] Ibid., 470.   [80] Ibid.

education put forth in *Journal of My Travels*.[81] For a political reformer, however, it was also important to understand the 'needs of our age' more broadly. It was necessary to delve into the cultural, economic and political history of a particular country, and here, Herder believed, Montesquieu could still (at least initially) be his general guide (412).

What was Herder's view of modern society and politics in 1769? As we saw in Chapter 1, Herder had already in 1765 aligned himself with Hume's and Hamann's characterisations of the modern age as one of international commerce, modern liberty, and growing refinement in the arts and manners.[82] By 1769 his views had not changed, but he now further elaborated his position on this matter. Herder understood that a crucial question here was what kind of commerce was to be accepted and seen as beneficial. The question of a desirable form of commerce for Russia was not an easy one to solve. In *The Spirit of the Laws*, Montesquieu had distinguished between economy-based trade as suitable to republics and luxury-based trade as suitable to monarchies. The difference between the two, as Michael Sonenscher has shown, consisted in whether trade encompassed the whole of society or just a specialised segment of it, serving the needs of a nobility legally and economically separated from the rest of society.[83] From Montesquieu's perspective, however, Russia was neither a proper monarchy nor a republic. At the same time, the Baltic provinces it had conquered at the beginning of the eighteenth century comprised a number of Hanseatic cities, including, most prominently, Riga, and as such had a long history of participating in pan-European 'trade based on economy'. Herder, albeit not coming up with a definitive vision of the future of Russia's trade, provided a thoughtful commentary on the possible directions in which it could develop.

Herder's interest in the history of commerce was most likely prompted by conversations with the 'circle' around the Berens family in Riga, including the merchant Gustav Berens, whom Herder was accompanying on his journey to Holland and France. As we saw in Chapter 1, Johann Georg Hamann had already befriended another member of Berens family, Johann Christoph Berens (who was Gustav's cousin) during his time in Riga and had been a tutor to Johann Christoph's younger brother Georg. The wealthy patriciate Berens family was highly interested in introducing

---

[81] On this programme, see Rainer Wisbert, '4.2. Kulturpolitische und pädagogische See-Träume', in *Herder Handbuch*, 600–609.

[82] See Chapter 1.

[83] On this distinction and its repudiation by Montesquieu's contemporary readers, see Sonenscher, *Before the Deluge*, 166–171 and ibid., ch. 3.

new economic thought to Riga and the Russian Empire more broadly: it had also been at the family's suggestion that Hamann not only travelled to England in the early 1750s but also translated Louis-Joseph Plumard de Dangeul's treatise on commerce. By 1769 Herder had already read various kinds of works representing what had come to be called the new 'science of commerce' in this period, including Hamann's *Supplement to Dangueil* [*sic*].[84] Further, in 1769, Herder read Jacques Accarias de Sérionne's *Commerce de la Hollande* (1767). During his sojourn in Nantes, he completed the translation of the introductory chapter of *Commerce de la Hollande*. In a letter to the publisher Johann Friedrich Hartknoch from August 1769, he urged the latter to have the whole work or Sérionne's earlier *Intérêts des nations de l'Europe* (1766) translated.[85] In his *Journal of My Travels*, he also referred to *Commerce de la Hollande* as the main source for his thinking on the current situation of commerce in Europe (416).

Both Plumard de Dangeul and Sérionne represented the views associated with the so-called Gournay circle in France, among whom the most widely read and translated author was François Vernon de Forbonnais (Plumard de Dangeul's cousin). The Gourney circle advocated the spread of 'industry' and international commerce, attempting to show the legitimacy and benefits of commercial activity; they accordingly also celebrated the decline of the military and feudal spirit in Europe. More specifically, authors associated with the circle sought to find ways in which France could keep pace with Britain as a commercial rival. There were also subtle disagreements between individual authors in this respect: whilst Forbonnais ruled out straightforward commercial reciprocity and 'cosmopolitanism' based on it, Plumard de Dangeul and Sérionne emphatically maintained the compatibility of patriotism and cosmopolitanism, arguing that France's catching up with Britain by way of emulation would have beneficial effects for all of Europe.[86] Their view was that states could combine different kinds of

---

[84] See Chapter 1.

[85] As Herder wrote to Hamann from Nantes in August 1769: 'Was meinen Sie zu dem *Commerce de la Hollande* – ob das Werk nicht für unsre Zeiten, wo alles Commerziert, Vom Könige bis zum Oberpastor, zu übersetzen wäre; oder wenn das nicht, wegen seines zu partikularen Inhalts, nicht wenigstens das *Interét des nations* von demselben Verfasser? Kennen Sie diesen dem Namen nach?' Herder, in *DA*, I, 159. In fact, a German translation of *Intérêts des nations de l'Europe* had been published in 1766 as *Vortheile der Völker durch die Handlung* in Leipzig; a German translation of *Commerce de la Hollande* was published in 1770.

[86] On Forbonnais, see Sonenscher, *Before the Deluge*, 174–176, 179–189. On the reception of Forbonnais in Germany, see Marco Cavarzere, 'The "New Science of Commerce" in the Holy Roman Empire: Véron de Forbonnais' *Élemens de commerce* and his German Readers', *History of European Ideas*, 40 (2014), 1130–1150. On Sérionne, see Hervé Hasquin, 'Jacques Accarias de Sérionne, économiste et publiciste français au service des Pays Bas autrichiens', *Études sur le XVIIIe*

commerce based on their distinctive advantages. These authors basically sought to drop Montesquieu's distinction between two kinds of trade, arguing that the world of states was differentiated enough to also accommodate highly differentiated and segmented forms of markets, which meant that ruthless competition was not necessary.[87] In their view, trade could thus well be reciprocal: in particular, they encouraged commercially less advanced states to carry goods that they had produced themselves and thus develop their own 'economic trade', instead of leaving trade to other countries (such as Holland or Britain).[88]

Accarias de Sérionne also aligned himself with the French foreign minister Étienne-François de Choiseul's grand project of European balance of trade that the latter had begun to advocate during the Seven Years' War in order to bolster the newly established Franco-Austrian alliance.[89] In order to promote commerce (and peace) at the international level, Sérionne argued, the existing trade privileges had to be abolished, whilst it was also equally important to foster broad international alliances. In his *Intérêts des nations de l'Europe* – which was published in 1766 with a dedication to the Russian empress – Sérionne had already advocated that the special privileges of the Dutch in the carrying trade in France and those of the English in Russia be abolished, emphasising its benefits for European peace.[90] Even Holland, he argued, would not be totally ruined by these measures. Whilst its share of carrying trade would no doubt be considerably reduced, it would still be able to continue to offer its services, whilst also acting as a financial centre of Europe.[91]

Herder's comments on the history of European commerce in his *Journal of My Travels* largely followed the spirit of Sérionne but did not share his

---

siècle (Brussel, 1974), I, 159–170. On Plumard de Dangeul and the reception of Sérionne in the Netherlands, see Koen Stapelbroek, 'Dutch Decline as a European Phenomenon', *History of European Ideas* 36:2 (2010), 139–152 (141, 145–146).

[87] I would like to thank Michael Sonenscher for making this point at the Cambridge Political Thought and Intellectual history seminar discussion.

[88] Antonella Alimento, 'Raynal, Accarias de Sérionne et le Pacte de Famille', in *Autour de l'abbé Raynal : genèse et enjeux politiques de l'Histoire des deux Indes*, ed. Antonella Alimento and Gianluigi Goggi (Ferney-Voltaire, 2018), 33–45.

[89] Koen Stapelbroek, 'The International Politics of Cameralism and the Balance of Power: Dutch Tranlations of Justi', in *Cameralism and Enlightenment*, ed. Ere Nokkala and Nicholas B. Miller (Routledge, 2019), 99–124. I am grateful to Koen Stapelbroek for sharing the preprint of this chapter with me. See also Alimento, 'Raynal, Accarias de Sérionne' on the development of Choiseul's and Sérionne's plans.

[90] Accarias de Sérionne, *Intérêts des nations de l'Europe, dévélopée rélativement au commerce* (Leiden, 1766).

[91] Ibid. In his *Commerce de la Hollande* he further elaborated on this argument.

optimism.[92] He also sought to tease out from Sérionne's ideas more specific views on the cycles of trade in the Baltic Sea region. Sérionne had devoted an entire chapter to Hanseatic commerce in *Commerce de la Hollande*. Herder agreed with Sérionne that in order to understand the current situation, one had to examine the factors that had facilitated the rise of Holland's distinctive commercial spirit and the decline and defeat of Hanseatic commerce. Herder, like Sérionne, underlined the successful way that Dutch commercial spirit had counteracted the dominant spirit of 'feudal wars' in Europe, whilst also being fundamentally different from the 'spirit of discovery' of Spain and Portugal. The latter had 'gained nothing from their discoveries', whereas Holland, by contrast, had worked itself up from the marshes. Yet Herder did not think that any writer had so far managed to capture the reasons why the Hanseatic cities had lost their distinctive patriotic *and* commercial 'spirit' in this process; new writings on this subject were badly needed (414). In any case, he hinted, their spirit had differed from that of the Dutch. Herder, most likely drawing on Montesquieu's and Sérionne's characterisations of Dutch commercial spirit as one of 'strict justice', was also highly critical of the necessary moral consequences of the narrow 'commercial spirit' of the Dutch, which, he implied, lacked precisely the element of patriotism: 'everything in Holland', Herder argued, 'is for sale: talents, which thus also become industry, erudition, which also becomes industry, humanity, honnêteté, everything is formed by the commercial spirit' (418).

Endorsing Sérionne's history of the decline of Dutch commerce, Herder claimed that all European countries had in the long run learned from Holland, having started to trade themselves, too. There was thus no way for the Dutch to maintain their dominant position in the 'economic trade' of Europe; in Herder's view, there was not much sense in Sérionne's musings about Holland's potential discovery of a 'fifth continent' as a solution to its current plight either. However, Herder agreed with the latter that there was no reason why it could not still maintain its role as a financial centre and currency exchanger (416–417). Most importantly from our viewpoint, Herder seems to have supported Choiseul's and Sérionne's attempts to further encourage Russia to take its fleet's navigation and commerce in its own hands; he must have here also seen a new

---

[92] Indeed, by 1769, it was clear that Sérionne's and Choiseul's grand project would not be materialised in any foreseeable future. Choiseul's negotiations with Russia to reach the signing of a trade treaty between France and Russia had failed, and the empress renewed Russia's trade treaty with England in 1767. For discussion, see Alimento, 'Raynal, Accarias de Sérionne'.

and increasing role for the former Hanseatic cities and other Baltic seaports in the Russian Empire.[93]

With regard to possible future developments in European commerce, Herder sketched a number of scenarios in telegraphic style:

> But what will succeed the commercial spirit of Holland? The spirit of dissension, that is, of economic inner commerce of each state? For a while, I believe this will be the case, and everything in Europe points to it. Or the spirit of parties, that is, of incitement? This is an inevitable consequence of the former. One of the great nations of international trade, for instance England, will stir up another one, that is savage, and destroy itself in the process – and could not this nation be Russia? For a while I believed it, everything in Europe points to it.[94]

The reference to 'economic inner commerce' probably hinted at Sérionne's vision of future Europe. Each country would participate in the general 'economy' of Europe, building up its own capacity for 'economic commerce', trading, first and foremost, in the goods produced by itself. Yet this kind of development was bound to alarm the dominant commercial superpower – Great Britain. Indeed, as we have seen, the entire project was designed precisely to counter British dominance in European and global commerce. Thus, Herder quite plausibly suspected that Britain could resort to quite different political measures, instigating subversion by 'savage nations'. Here Herder was possibly also endorsing Sérionne's strictures about Britain's strained relationships with its colonies as contributing to its potential fall (420). He was probably also referring to Britain's support for Russia in the Russo-Turkish War (1768–1774), regarding this as a highly risky enterprise, one that could result in an even more rapid destruction of Britain in such a war (418). Indeed, hinting a few paragraphs below at Britain's exorbitant public debt, Herder highlighted that there were both internal as well as external reasons for its possible collapse (420). As a third possible development, Herder presented 'full savagery, irreligion, conquest of (barbarian) peoples' (418). It is

---

[93] It is highly likely that this was also precisely the political agenda of his friend and travel companion Gustav Berens and the whole Berens family.

[94] Since this is a complicated paragraph to translate, I provide the German version here: 'Was wird aber auf den Handelsgeist Hollands folgen? Geist der Parteien [Parthe (in *FHA*, IX/2, 941; older editions also have 'Parteiung' here], d.i. der Ekonomischen innerlichen Handlung eines jeden Landes? Auf eine Zeitlang glaub ichs, und es lässt sich dazu an in ganz Europa. Oder der Parteien, d.i. der Aufwieglung? Dies ist auf das eben genannten unvermeidlich. Eines der grossen Völker im Ekonomischen Handel z.E. England wird ein anderes aufwiegeln, das wild ist, und dabei selbst zu Grunde gehen – könnte dies nicht Russland sein!' (418). I would like to thank Koen Stapelbroek for helping me to search for the best translation for this passage.

also possible that here he was referencing Rousseau's prediction in *The Social Contract* that Russia would seek to subjugate European states exhausted in the Seven Years' War. As Rousseau put it:

> The Russian Empire will try to subjugate Europe and will itself be subjugated. The Tartars, its subjects or neighbours, will be its masters and ours. This revolution to me seems inevitable. All the Kings in Europe are working in concert to hasten it.[95]

Herder was thus certainly less optimistic than Sérionne about the future of Europe. The excess of refinement in modern times, Herder continued a few lines below, was also likely to evoke a counter-reaction in European states: 'one widespread calamity, a barbarian invasion combined with a general Moravian spirit at pulpits' could lead people to view 'learning and lack of religion and philosophy as reasons for general corruption' (418). This could also lead to a kind of savagery or 'ignorance from piety', the burning of libraries and departure from all learning, as a reaction to its 'overly finely cultivated reason'. This development was even most likely, Herder maintained, being 'contained in the nature of things' (419).

Herder's phrase 'nature of things' referred to the state of 'enlightenment' (*Aufklärung*) in Europe. Enlightenment had become a goal in its own right and not a means to achieve happiness, as it should have. Herder detected signs of corruption, and indeed, reaction to overly cultivated enlightenment all over Europe. Turning his attention away from the question of the future of European commerce, he proceeded to evaluate the general situation of mores in different European states. Not only was Holland in a state of decline economically as well as culturally, but also Britain's commerce was soon going to be ruined by its public debt.

The signs of 'corruption' (*Verfall*), however, were perhaps even greater in France. Without delving into the situation of French commerce, Herder provided a short commentary on the cultural history of France. He emphasised the degree to which French culture was modelled on foreign influences. Most importantly, the French had copied Italian literature and theatre, just adding 'taste' to it. As the French 'philosophical language' was furthermore particularly rich in abstractions as well as capable of 'creating ever new abstractions', this had led to a certain 'approximation of cold reason', an increased coldness of imagination and affections, so that by his time the French 'taste' had come to be 'reduced to what Montesquieu called political honour' (422). The arts and letters had been able to serve as

---

[95] Rousseau, 'The Social Contract', 73. See also Clure, 'Rousseau, Diderot', 883–908.

political drives in ancient Greece,[96] and even in Rome they had been able to guarantee moderation. In France, purely political honour was expected to serve as such now, the arts and sciences aspiring only to formal beauty or brilliance. There was accordingly an increasing shallowness of spirit palpable everywhere, even in the greatest of the recent French works: Diderot's *Encyclopédie* was just a compendium, Rochefoucault spread denigrating 'half-truths', and Montesquieu, Herder asked, could he be regarded as 'free from *faux-brillant?*' (425). Even Rousseau's human philosophy, Herder continued, merely sought to find paradoxes in all things, to impress and shock, whereby, however, 'the beautiful becomes exaggerated; the truthful becomes too abstract, and is not true any more' – indeed, such a spirit ultimately makes Rousseau 'unusable and harmful, despite all his greatness' (424).

Herder's understanding of the current state of commerce, mores as well as the arts and sciences in different European countries was thus generally pessimistic at this point. Herder's prognosis for Russia, by contrast, was certainly not negative. Russia belonged to a different category than the states just discussed; indeed, various kinds of scenarios were possible for it. In all his writings of this period, Herder categorised Russia as largely 'half-savage', thus setting it apart from the rest of Europe. As we saw above, 'half-savage' peoples in his view harboured great potential. Indeed, as I will argue below, Herder did hope that economic, cultural and political reforms could help turn Russia into a 'happy' society. As Herder's interest in Sérionne reveals, this by no means involved isolating Russia from the rest of Europe. He even advocated linking it more closely with Europe, thereby hoping to preclude the most negative scenarios of violent retaliation or indeed, conquest, from materialising.

3.2.2   Political and Educational Reforms in Russia

What counsel would a 'second *Montesquieu'* then give to Catherine II in Herder's view? Russia was, of course, a very special case of a 'half-savage' country, considering that its geographical location was within Europe. Furthermore, reforms had already been attempted in Russia. The process of the 'formation of mores', however, had taken a curious turn in Russia so far. Before Russia had properly developed a national character and 'mores', Czar Peter I had submitted its culture to foreign cultural models and invited a large group of foreigners to the country to help him implement

---

[96] Cf. Chapter 2.

these models. Herder did not approve of these steps, yet celebrated Peter I's bold, even childish innovative spirit. In his view, Peter had felt 'within himself what his nation was and could become'.[97] It was now the task of the succeeding monarchs and reformers to set his endeavour on the right foundations and 'make the forces of a young half-savage nation into those of an original people [*Original Volk*]'. This was possible solely through 'culture' (*Cultur*) and the 'improvement of mores' (*Verbesserung der Sitten*) achieved through education (366–367). Instead of devising a new code of law, one had to begin by establishing or reforming public institutions, courts, schools, universities, museums and libraries.[98]

Herder insisted that it was also vital to recognise that Russia's regions and peoples were highly heterogeneous.[99] Insofar as positive laws had to harmonise with the natural ones concerning the ways in which human language and thinking develop, each of Russia's different regions was also to have its own laws appropriate to its 'level of culture'. While the sea coast of Russia in the Northwest was 'fully cultivated (*ganz cultiviert*), the inner lands were half-cultivated (*halb cultiviert*) and the borderlands fully savage (*wild*)' (412).[100] The nations in the latter would need 'laws of humanity' as known from 'the earliest rude times', Herder argued, whilst laws in the half-cultivated areas would need to be modelled in part at least on the Eastern empires like Persia, Assyria, Egypt, China and Japan, rather than European states. And finally, there would need to be special laws for the fully cultivated 'capital' and 'commercial cities', by which he clearly meant the Baltic cities such as Riga (412). In any case, Herder maintained, one could only 'gradually move towards freedom', drawing inspiration from 'individual families in individual provinces', and 'individual examples in individual families' (411).

Thus, despite putting forward a penetrating criticism of the current form and principle of government in Russia, Herder cherished great hopes for the future and the different regions of that country (418).[101] Russia could still be 'formed' (*gebildet*) and educated (410), and it was worthwhile asking what 'pastors, philosophers and in particular, monarchs' could do in order to unify the three kinds of training or education (religious, philosophical/natural and civil) in it.[102] Ancient lawmakers like Lycurgus in Sparta were paramount examples here because they had known how to rely on habits (*Gewohnheit*), vivacious drive (*lebendige Trieb*), and healthy nature (*gesunde*

---

[97] Herder, 'Sammlung von Gedanken', 474.   [98] Ibid., 477.   [99] Ibid., 473.
[100] Herder used the German terms 'cultivierte' and 'gesittete' interchangeably here, using them to mean basically 'cultivated' or 'civilised'.
[101] Herder, 'Sammlung von Gedanken', 473.
[102] Herder, 'Gedanken bei Lesung Montesquieus', 471.

Natur) in creating 'mores'.[103] Although modern legislators were no longer 'bards' themselves, the 'formation' of the people – Herder was already using the term 'Bildung' here – had to draw on the history of the human mind, language and sentiments, on the one hand, and on the particular linguistic, literary, economic and political history of their country, on the other (374).[104] The role of philosophers, thus, was highly significant, but instead of abstract theorising, they needed to study national culture, language and practical politics so as to achieve a deeper and livelier form of understanding of these matters. Only such an understanding, Herder suggested, could truly contribute towards awakening 'national feeling' (*Nationalgefühl*) in the people at large.[105] As Herder put it, it was necessary for a moral and political reformer to 'see with the spirit of Montesquieu, write with the fiery pen of Rousseau, and have the luck of Voltaire to gain the ear of the greats' (411). 'Hume and Locke, Montesquieu and the brothers of Mably are there', Herder continued, and 'the Empress. . .could be caught out by the weakness of her Code of law' (411). Only on this basis was it possible for the modern rulers to 'know' (*kennen*) and 'feel' (*fühlen*) the culture (*Kultur*) of their people.[106] Devising reforms thus required not just a proper metaphysical foundation but also profound insights into a nation's particular cultural and civil history, both synchronically, in terms of its different component peoples (*Nationen*), regions and ranks, and diachronically, over a long span of time. The projected result of such an effort, Herder mused, would be 'a marvel' (*Wunderwerk*) of a code of law for 'all these different peoples, for each according to its way of thinking and its national feeling'.[107]

3.2.3   Commerce and Modern Mores in Livland

As is already obvious, Herder's special interest lay in the province of Livland and the city of Riga. With its German-speaking higher estates (nobility and the patriciate in towns) and distinctive legal autonomy approved by Peter I in 1710, Livland (like Estland) in Herder's view was characterised by a peculiar combination of 'barbarism and luxury, ignorance, and pretensions to taste, freedom and slavery'. The main challenge for a reformer in Livland was thus to 'destroy this barbarism, oust ignorance, spread freedom and culture' (373). Invoking Livland's 'barbarism and luxury', Herder

---

[103] Ibid., 471–472. Cf. his description of his own calling in such terms in 'Sammlung von Gedanken', 478.
[104] Cf. Herder, 'Sammlung von Gedanken', 473–474.   [105] Ibid., 473.   [106] Ibid.
[107] Ibid.

highlighted the economic dependence of the Baltic nobility on the institution of serfdom, indeed, of 'slavery' (*Sklaverei*), as it was also known in this period. Despite all his interest in Montesquieu, Herder ignored the role of the Baltic nobility in preserving the local autonomy and separate jurisdiction in the Baltic provinces. By 'freedom', Herder meant the self-governing institutions of cities, particularly in the Hanseatic cities (of Russia's Baltic provinces), among which Riga was the largest and wealthiest. To him it was the commercial cities that were these provinces' most distinctive aspects; it was their spirit that he was also predominantly interested in further developing and reforming.

Of course, Herder registered his awareness of the grave problems of 'freedom' in Riga in the *Journal of My Travels*. The city's incorporation into the Russian Empire had led to a multiplication of offices, and an opposition between the different bodies and agents: 'empress and city, court and city; officers of the crown and those of the city; titular councillors and the city; nobility and the city, parasites (*Schmaruzer*) and the city; city councillors and the city – what a state [*welcher Zustand*]!' (415). The city could only escape this 'hell between freedom and orderly service [of the crown]' and become 'happy', Herder insisted, if it stopped being a 'pseudorepublic, a *Republica in a republ. (sic)*', and embraced the role of a 'servant with privileges and ranks [*Dienerin mit Vorzüge und Range*]' (416). 'The city's special institutions, liberties, departments and force (*Gewalt*)' as well as independent budget (*Casse*) were to be preserved, whereas the city councillors were also to 'gain a rank' in the empire, by being led by a president who would also represent the city at the imperial level (415). With some support from powerful local families, Herder mused, he could perhaps make his way to the empress herself and convince her of the necessity of such reforms (416).

According to Herder, the goal of these reforms – general happiness – could not be attained without parallel moral and educational reforms. The mores (*Sitten*) in Riga had become 'soft', which had further brought along 'weakness, falsehood, inactivity and political servility' (414). The golden age of the Hanseatic cities was long past, and commerce was languishing in the Baltic cities. As we saw above, even Dutch commerce was in a state of decline and the future of the currently dominant British trade was also anxiously discussed. The question that interested Herder most here was whether anything could be done to awaken a modern version of the Hanseatic spirit in the Baltic cities (414). For Herder, the answer here again was education. Drawing on examples from the 'history and politics of Livland and Russia', he argued, one could educate as well as motivate

(381). With regard to Riga, the programme of education drafted in 'Benefit of the People' still applied, and could be developed further.[108] To a certain extent, Rousseau could still be a 'teacher of human education', while 'social education' entailed the reformer's delving into the 'needs of society' (379). In describing this task, Herder used the terms 'nationalise' or 'national education' and dreamt of making Rousseau's 'humanly savage Emile' a 'national child of Livland', i.e. educating the Livonians so that they would emulate Emile in their mores (381). In a draft entitled *On the Formation of Peoples* written in the same period Herder further distinguished four different, yet related and necessary, *means* of formation (*Bildung*) – religion, poetry, belle esprit, philosophy – that all needed to be combined with 'government'.[109] A 'second Montesquieu', he believed, would know how to creatively combine all these means to eradicate the traces of a previously dominant military spirit of the nobility in the countryside as well as encourage the formation of a modern version of patriotic commercial spirit in former Hanseatic cities (381).[110]

3.3 Conclusion

Herder's hopes to become a Livonian reformer or 'gain the ear of the greats' in Russia never materialised. He never even returned to Riga, Livland or anywhere else in the Russian Empire. Russia's recent history and prospects figured only marginally in his subsequent writings. Perhaps the most systematic later discussion of this topic can be found in Herder's *Adrastea* (1802). Herder here repeated his positive views of Peter I as a bold reformer whilst also developing a more specific account of the *stasis* and dynamism of cultures as a general logic of cultural development.[111] Pre-Petrine Russia served there as an example of a culture in *stasis* – a culture that has got stuck at a certain level of development, and that would need a powerful new impulse to return to the path of natural dynamism.[112]

---

[108] See Chapter 1 for this programme.
[109] Herder, 'Über die Bildung der Völker', in *SWS*, XXXII, 231–233.
[110] On Herder's understanding of the role of the Christian religion in modern society, see Chapters 1, 5 and 6.
[111] Johann Gottfried Herder, 'Adrastea (Auswahl)', in *FHA*, X, 408–426.
[112] Speck, 'The History and Politics', 246–247, 264–272; see also Dreitzel, 'Herders politische Konzepte', in *Johann Gottfried Herder*, 287. As Speck has argued, throughout his life Herder also recommended moving the capital of Russia to the Black Sea, whereby new trading routes and connections would be opened up, which in turn would be beneficial not only for Russia's Baltic provinces but for the entire Europe and the world; ibid., 226–228.

However, Herder continued to follow the developments in Riga and Livland quite closely. He maintained contacts with several of the members of the patriciate elites in Riga (most importantly, his publisher Johann Friedrich Hartknoch) and corresponded with a number of local country pastors, asking them to collect Latvian or Estonian folk songs for him. He also reviewed A. W. Hupel's *An das Liefländische Publikum* in 1772, now also directly expressing his views on the misery of indigenous peasants (*Landvolk*) and the institution of 'serfdom' – which he straightforwardly characterised as the 'worst kind of bondage, slavery'.[113] He also seems to have kept an eye on Catherine's subsequent reforms in the Baltic provinces. Catherine indeed returned to her reform plans after the end of the Russio-Turkish war in 1774. In 1775, she proclaimed a general *Order for the Administration of Governorates* to determine more precisely the position – rights and obligations – of each juridical body (towns, estates, institutions, individuals) in the general state machinery of her empire.[114] The reforms entered into full force in the Baltic provinces in 1883. Now these provinces, too, had to apply an all-Russian model of government. In 1785, the *Charter to the Nobility and the Charter to the Towns* were implemented, regulating the self-government of the nobility and that of the towns respectively.

Formally, the reform era did not last long, as the old system (with some modifications) was restored soon after the accession of Paul I to the throne of Russia in 1796. However, some of the processes that had been launched could no longer be reversed.[115] One of such changes was perhaps also the mental change. Indeed, one of the most important contemporary reflections of these reforms was a small work entitled *Bonhommien* published by Herder's friend and supporter in his Riga years, Johann Christoph Berens (shortly before his death in 1792).[116] Berens's goal was

---

[113] Johann Gottfried Herder, '[Review of] August Wilhelm Hupel, *Kleine Nachrichten, vermischte Sachen: An das Lief- und Ehstländische Publikum* (Riga, 1772)', in *SWS*, V, 346–350 (348–349).

[114] On the so-called Regency period in Russia's Baltic provinces, see Leppik, 'The Provincial Reforms', 55–78. As a result of this order, one overall governor-general (George Browne) was appointed for both Livland and Estland, customs borders between Livland and Estland (and the rest of Russia) were abolished, and most importantly, the feudal tenure estates with formal service obligation were re-organised into hereditary tenure estates, while poll tax for each male peasant and craftsman was also established in the Baltic provinces, ibid., 64–65.

[115] Leppik, 'The Provincial Reforms'.

[116] Johann Christoph Berens, *Bonhommien: Geschrieben bei Eröffnung der neuerbauten Rigischen Stadtbibliothek* (Mitau, 1792). Berens, in turn, drew heavily on Herder. For Berens's own engagement with Herder, see Thomas Taterka, 'Humanität, Abolition, Nation'. Baltische Varianten kolonialkritischen Diskurses der europäischen Aufklärung um 1800', in *Raynal—Herder—Merkel*, 183–251 (183–212).

essentially to draft a modern 'Bürger-Catechismus' or catechism of 'town morality' (*Stadtmoral*) for his native Riga. Celebrating the opening of a new building for the city library, Berens buttressed the distinctive link between enlightenment (various kinds of learning) and patriotism in modern 'civic/burgher patriotism' (*Bürgerpatriotismus*). The central virtue in this 'catechism' was public spirit. As a prominent tradesman and public figure in the city, Berens went out of his way to impress upon his compatriots an understanding that even when their city was losing some of its older autonomy and needed to adapt to the new situation in which it found itself due to Catherine's reforms since 1783, it was highly important for the burghers to continue to pursue their distinctive ethics of rightful acquisition, industry and commitment to the public good. Local traditions should not be forgotten and the distinctive public spirit was not to be lost, whilst one also had to embrace the new opportunities that the city's inclusion in a large structure of government would offer.[117]

In his *Letters for the Advancement of Humanity* (1795), Herder included long excerpts from this book, presenting Berens's ideas as an exemplary model of 'civic/burgher patriotism'.[118] Berens's ideal of public spirit resonated with his own efforts to negotiate between monarchism and republicanism, central reform initiatives and local self-government, all being guided by patriotism. It is thus perhaps no exaggeration to argue that Herder's political ideals had already crystallised in some sense in Riga. In her 1830 memoir of her late husband, Caroline Herder made exactly this point:

> In Riga he still found beautiful remnants of the spirit of the old Hanseatic cities: a perhaps frustrated (*durchkreutzte*) and often inhibited, but still lively community spirit, animated and effective for the good of the whole. Here his most characteristic principles about civil and state relations were awakened and nurtured. This common spirit (*Gemeingeist, commun [sic] Spirit*) made a lasting impact upon him, he liked to talk about it and wished to awaken it in every town, every village, every institute, every school. His view of life expanded, with the increased knowledge of life on a large scale, he attained higher ideas of civic [*bürgerliche*] freedom, civic well-being and noble, wise effectiveness.[119]

---

[117] On Berens's his role in masterminding Catherine II's 'League of Armed Neutrality' with Spain, Britain and France in 1780, see Bičevskis and Taimņa, 'Johann Georg Hamanns kameralwissenschaftliche Studien'.

[118] Herder, 'Briefe zu Beförderung der Humanität', in *FHA*, VII, 411–434. See Chapter 8 for further discussion.

[119] Maria Carolina Herder, *Erinnerungen aus dem Leben Johann Gottfried Herders*, 2 vols., ed. Johannes Müller (Stuttgart and Tübingen, 1830), I, 97–98.

And yet, having never returned to Riga or Russia, Herder's focus in the following decades came to be on the cultural and political situation in the Holy Roman Empire and Europe more broadly. He revisited Rousseau's and Montesquieu's discussion of the exit from the state of nature, and also engaged with some more specific ideas by Montesquieu on German freedom. As we shall see in Chapter 4, for Herder in the following years the various historians who had taken inspiration from Montesquieu – Ferguson, Hume, Millar, Robertson in Scotland, and Justus Möser in Germany – became even more important. None of the aforementioned authors, however, seemed to be fully capable of providing something like a 'second *Montesquieu*' in Herder's view. Indeed, whilst he did not engage with any of Montesquieu's specific ideas in detail in his *Ideas*, he continued to call for the appearance of such a figure:

> Oh would another *Montesquieu* feast us with the spirit of laws and governments on our Globe, even if just focusing on the centuries best known to us! Not according to the empty names of the three or four forms of government that are nowhere alike, and never remain the same; not according to the clever principles of states; for no state is founded on one word-principle [*Wortprincipium*], and still less could any state adhere to them invariably at all times, and under all circumstances; not from detached examples, taken from all nations, times, and climes [. . .], but only through a philosophical, lively representation of civil history [*bürgerliche Geschichte*], in which, uniform as it appears, no scene occurs twice; and which, fearfully instructive, completes the picture of the vices and virtues of mankind and their governors, according to place and time always changing, always the same.[120]

---

[120] Johann Gottfried Herder, *Outlines of a Philosophy of the History of Man*, ed. and trans. T. H. Churchill (London, 1800), 250–251 (I have considerably modified the translation). For the German original, see Johann Gottfried Herder, *Ideen zur Philosophie der Geschichte der Menschheit*, *HWP*, III/1, 339. For Herder's later views on Montesquieu, see Herder, 'Adrastea', *FHA*, X, 34–37. Here Herder reiterated some of his critique of Montesquieu from a moral point of view.

CHAPTER 4

The Bildung *of Humanity and Modern Virtue*

In 1771, Herder settled in a small town Bückeburg in the Duchy of Schaumburg Lippe, where he stayed for the next five years (1771–1776). He published a lot in this period, but there is one work in particular that has received wide attention among his commentators – his highly ironical, indeed, iconoclastic, *This Too a Philosophy of History for the Formation of Humanity* (1774).[1] In this piece, Herder lashed out against both the masterminds as well as the substance of 'the Enlightenment'. Just as Rousseau in the 1750s and early 1760s had attacked the *philosophes*,[2] Herder now turned against the entire 'eighteenth century'.[3] Indeed, whilst Herder, in his *Journal of My Travels*, was still criticising Montesquieu in particular, he now did not seem to spare anybody and anything in this century from his sharp invectives. In Herder's view, contemporary philosophers blindly celebrated the achievements of their century, neglecting both the rise of new kinds of evils in their times and the loss of highly valuable features developed in previous periods.

Why did Herder adopt this highly critical tone and what kind of positive vision did he put forward in this work, if at all? Scholarly answers to this question have been rather polarised. The classic view, as influentially expounded by a long line of interpreters since the late nineteenth century, is that during the Bückeburg years Herder renounced his earlier theological freethinking in favour of a new pious religiosity, a Hamannian 'fatalism full of faith and piety'.[4] These developments also enabled him to break the shackles of 'the Enlightenment' so as to lay foundations for a

---

[1] Herder, 'This Too a Philosophy', in *PW*, 297.
[2] Cf. the statement of Rousseau in the *'First Discourse'*, 8: 'National hatreds will die out, but so will love of fatherland'.
[3] This parallel is pointed out by Joannis D. Evrigenis and Daniel Pellerin, 'Introduction', in *Johann Gottfried Herder: Another Philosophy of History and Selected Political Writings*, ed. and trans. Evrigenis and Pellerin (Indianapolis and Cambridge, 2004), ix–xxxix (xxxii–xxxv).
[4] Haym, *Herder*, I, 574.

132

new historical outlook.[5] Whilst disagreeing with the classical scholarship about the extent of Herder's religious transformation, Frederick Beiser has also identified drastic changes in Herder's moral and political views in this period: Beiser suggests that by then Herder's distinctive kind of enlightened reform thinking was replaced by a radical (but still 'internal') critique of the Enlightenment (rationalism) and modern European absolutism, whilst an increasingly strong tendency to relativism is palpable in his thought.[6] The more recent historiography, by contrast, has sought to show that we should not read too much into Herder's supposed religious conversion in Bückeburg.[7] The metaphysical foundations of his 'historicism' had in fact been laid earlier.[8] Furthermore, instead of Hamann, several other important influences on Herder in this period have been dissected.[9]

This chapter will seek to strike a middle ground between these two views. It will revisit Herder's main philosophical works of the 1770s to specify the target and theoretical foundations of his radical criticisms of modern European societies and morality, as well as explore his alternative account of moral psychology and modern moral virtue in this period. More specifically, I will juxtapose *This Too a Philosophy of History* (written in 1773) with Herder's *Treatise On the Origin of Language*[10] (*Über den*

---

[5] Meinecke, *Historism*, 341–342.

[6] Beiser, *Enlightenment, Revolution*, 201–209; cf. Beiser, *The German Historicist Tradition* (Oxford, 2011), 132–142.

[7] For critical evaluations of Herder's supposed religious conversion in Bückeburg, see John Rogerson, 'Herders Bückeburger "Bekehrung"', in *Bückeburger Gespräche über Johann Gottfried Herder 1979*, ed. Brigitte Poschmann (Rinteln, 1980), 17–30, and Tino Markworth, 'Zur Selbstdarstellung Johann Gottfried Herders in den ersten Bückeburger Jahren', in *Bückeburger Gespräche über Johann Gottfried Herder 1988*, ed. Brigitte Poschmann (Rinteln, 1989), 81–97; see also idem, 'Unterwegs zum Historismus. Der Wandel des geschichtsphilosophischen Denkens Herders von 1771 bis 1773', in *Johann Gottfried Herder – Geschichte und Kultur*, ed. Martin Bollacher (Würzburg, 1994), 51–59.

[8] See, e.g., (in chronological order), Proß, 'Nachwort', in *HWP*, II, 1128–1216; Michael Maurer, 'Die *Geschichtsphilosophie* des jungen Herder in ihrem Verhältnis zur Aufklärung', in *Johann Gottfried Herder, 1744–1803*, ed. Gerhard Sauder (Hamburg, 1987), 141–155; Jürgen Brummack, 'Herders Polemik gegen die "Aufklärung"', in *Aufklärung und Gegenaufklärung in der europäischen Literatur, Philosophie und Politik von der Antike bis zur Gegenwart*, ed. Jochen Schmidt (Darmstadt, 1989), 277–293; Adler, Die Prägnanz des Dunklen, 150–172; Heinz, 'Historismus oder Metaphysik?; Jochen Johannsen, '1.4.1 *Auch eine Philosophie der Geschichte der Bildung der Menschheit*', in *Herder Handbuch*, 160–170.

[9] John Zammito, 'Herder and Historical Metanarrative: What's Philosophical about History?', in *A Companion to the Works*, 65–91; Proß, 'Die Ordnung der Zeiten', 9–73; idem, '"Diversus cum diversis"'. For a detailed revision of the classical view of the crucial impact of Johann Georg Hamann on Herder's theology, see Claas Cordemann, *Herders christliche Monismus: Eine Studie zur Grundlegung Johann Gottfried Herders Christologie und Humanitätsideal* (Tübingen, 2010), 159–256.

[10] Johann Gottfried Herder, 'Treatise on the Origin of Language', in *PW*, 65–166.

Ursprung der Sprache) (written in 1770 and published in 1772) and *On the Cognition and Sensation of the Human Soul* (*Vom Erkennen und Empfinden der menschlichen Seele*) (1774, 1775, 1778).[11]

In my reading of these works, I emphasise Herder's continuing anthropological interests and practical concerns in this period. As seen in previous chapters, Herder was increasingly critical of modern European societies and morals in the 1760s. Riga and Russia were a special case. However, he was still adamant to demonstrate humans' fundamental natural sociability. His evolving philosophy of language, as we shall see, was also very much a philosophy of human sociability and the history of human thinking. These topics continued to interest him in *This Too a Philosophy*, but an important transformation occurred in this work. He ventured radical criticisms of European large monarchies, whilst putting forward a religiously framed understanding of the education of humanity by Providence. Christianity also played a special role in this history. Such a historical understanding was supposed to give practical guidance to modern Europeans, leading to an emergence of a new understanding of moral virtue as Christian virtue. This kind of practical attitude did not change in the 1770s, rather, it only solidified. This chapter and Chapters 5 and 6 will attempt to prove as much.

This chapter is divided into four sections. In the first, I will outline the foundations of Herder's analysis of human nature, morality, and sociability as laid out in his *Treatise on the Origin of Language*. As we shall see, there is a strong continuity between Herder's writings of the 1760s and the *Treatise* as far as Herder's views on human nature, morality and sociability are concerned; essentially, it can be seen as a sequel to Herder's engagement with Rousseau and Montesquieu in the second half of the 1760s. Herder still continued to wrestle with Rousseau's challenge in *The Second Discourse*. Nevertheless, there were also subtle changes that we can associate with Herder's engagement with Montesquieu's and Adam Ferguson's ideas. Drawing on Ferguson, who, too, was a perceptive reader of Rousseau and Montesquieu, Herder came to accept the unsocial sociability of tribal groups. In *Treatise* Herder thus further substantiated his theory of the

---

[11] Herder, 'On Cognition and Sensation, the Two Main Forces of the Human Soul (1775) [preface]', in *PW*, 178–186; idem, 'On the Cognition and Sensation of the Human Soul (1778)', in *PW*, 187–246. The essay was considerably reworked over the course of four years (1774, 1775 and 1778), and was twice submitted to the prize essay competition of the Berlin Academy of Sciences (1774, 1775). For detailed reconstructions of the emergence and philosophical contexts of the three versions, see Heinz, *Sensualistischer Idealismus*, 109–113; Heinz, '1.2.4. *Vom Erkennen und Empfinden der menschlichen Seele*', in *Herder Handbuch*, 122–140; Proß, 'Nachwort', in *HWP*, II, 1128–1216; Proß, 'Kommentar', in *HWP*, II, 1005–1010.

natural dynamic of the development of human language and mind in history, acknowledging that an increase in abstract ideas and a corresponding enervation was inevitable as a result of these processes. However, he also made a striking claim about the providentially envisioned re-unification of mankind at a higher level. As we shall see in the next sections, *This Too a Philosophy* will build on these views to develop an account of moral virtue based on love of humanity, whilst Herder, in his *On the Cognition*, embedded this vision in a new kind of philosophy of life.

In the second section, I will specify the main points of Herder's criticism of his contemporaries' cosmopolitan philosophies of history in *This Too a Philosophy* and *On the Cognition*. I argue that Herder's polemic against contemporary philosophers was meant to serve as a wake-up call to modern intellectuals. Herder's criticisms were targeting not just their excessive 'rationalism' but also their ideas about modern liberty and morality. He thus considerably qualified his fundamental embrace of modern liberty in his earliest essays on patriotism and highlighted the problematic aspects of modern forms of government. His polemic was an attempt to look beyond the mere surface of modern liberty. It was meant to serve as a warning concerning its underlying tensions and potential instability. As such, it was not, however, a full-scale rejection of modern values, including liberty. Herder rather sought to caution against various forms of modern self-complacency and ethical and political blind spots. In these years, Herder seriously engaged with the ideas of Scottish moral and political philosophers, such as David Hume, John Millar, William Robertson, and, most importantly, Adam Ferguson. This engagement enabled him to considerably refine his understanding of the underlying mechanisms of modern corruption. The bulk of Herder's specific criticisms of modern society and morality resonated with those of Ferguson.

In the third section, I will outline Herder's theologically grounded approach to the history of humanity in *This Too a Philosophy*. Herder's new religiosity led him to view historiography as a tool for sustaining faith in human sociability. Herder's discussions of Oriental and Northern 'patriarchy' were particularly significant in this respect. At the same time, he continued to insist on happiness as a universal and universally achievable goal. The section will also examine the particular developmental logic that Herder put forward about human and European history. Here, we can appreciate the precise ways in which Herder's new emphasis on Providence in history and his understanding of the moral core of Christianity are essential to understanding his account of the process of the formation of humanity (*Bildung der Menschheit*) in *This Too a Philosophy*. He strongly qualified his understanding of the historical process itself, putting special emphasis on Christianity as a new, universal kind of religion.

The fourth section will focus on Herder's account of modern virtue sketched in *This Too a Philosophy* and *On the Cognition*. It will argue that he now put particular emphasis on human freedom and self-determination as the core of Christian virtue. As we shall see in Chapter 5, in his various smaller essays of the 1770s and when discussing German 'national spirit', he also analysed various kinds of political, legal and cultural changes that the adoption of Christianity introduced into Europe. In this chapter, we will limit ourselves to specifying his novel understanding of modern virtue as based on Christian love of humanity.

4.1   Language and Sociability

In the last weeks of 1770, during his stay in Strasbourg, Herder hastily penned an essay entitled *Treatise on the Origin of Language*, which he submitted to the Berlin Academy of Sciences essay competition. The essay was awarded first prize by the academy. In *Treatise* Herder rejected the two main competing theories on the origin of language (human convention versus divine instruction), advancing the strikingly original thesis that human language is grounded in the unique constitution of the human soul.[12] Although Herder's central focus lay in the question of the origins of language, he drew on various contemporary theories of cognition and natural law to work out a broader account of human history.[13] Indeed, in this essay, Herder also made a new attempt to refute Rousseau's account of early human history.[14] In contrast to his earlier discussion of Rousseau in *Fragments*,[15] he now experimented with a purely conjectural approach, further developing the argument about self-preservation and happiness as well as adopting important insights on sociability from the Scottish

---

[12] For a concise overview of the most important scholarly discussions of *Treatise* and a summary of the main arguments in the essay, see Ralf Simon, 'Sprachphilosophie: *Abhandlung über den Ursprung der Sprache* 1.3.2', in *Herder Handbuch*, 143–160. See also Jürgen Trabant, 'Herder and Language', in *A Companion to the Works*, 117–140. For competing accounts submitted to the Berlin Academy as well as a subtle reconstruction of Herder's unique naturalism, see also Lifschitz, *Language and Enlightenment*, ch. 3.

[13] For broader context, see Proß, 'Anmerkungen [*Über den Ursprung der Sprache*]', in *HWP*, II (1987), 905–983; idem, 'Nachwort', in *HWP*, II, 1128–1229.

[14] For a detailed reconstruction of his critique of Rousseau's account of human nature and sociability in this work, see Nigel DeSouza, 'Language, Reason and Sociability: Herder's Critique of Rousseau', *Intellectual History Review*, XXII (2) (2012), 221–240; cf. Beiser, *The German Historicist Tradition*, 120–127.

[15] See Chapter 2.

Enlightenment, most importantly, from Adam Ferguson. Let us briefly spell out his main ideas in this connection, so as to achieve a better understanding of the ways in which his ideas on the progressive development of humanity evolved in the early 1770s.

4.1.1 Herder's Theory of the Natural Mental and Moral Progression of Humanity

Systematically answering the questions posed in the Berlin Academy essay competition (65; 127),[16] Herder's treatise was divided into two sections. In the first, Herder laid out the preconditions of language, distinguishing between the 'natural language' shared by all beings in the world and expressed in different degrees of complexity by different animals, including humans; and the human language, or language proper. In the second, he conjectured the genesis of particular languages, including modern ones. As we will see, here Herder further developed his ideas about the relationship between human and animal self-preservation as discussed in Chapter 3. Whilst he earlier had emphasised the parallels between humans and animals in this respect, he now advanced a distinct claim that humans possessed 'reflective awareness' (*Besonnenheit*) or a capacity to perceive their perceptions, and that their self-preservation hinged on this capacity.

Throughout *Treatise* Herder's central tool for describing and explaining the origin of language was the concept of 'natural law'. As we saw in Chapter 3, Herder shared Bonnet's and Robinet's dynamic understanding of this concept and used it to designate the necessary consequences of sentient life force unfolding and operating in interaction with the external environment and other beings. Understanding the human soul as a set of necessarily unfolding 'creative forces', Herder in *Treatise*, too, sought to provide a naturalistic explanation for these forces' various empirical manifestations, including, specifically, reflective awareness, human language and sociability.

According to Herder's first 'natural law', the human being was a 'freely thinking, active being, whose forces operate forth progressively', and who as such was destined to be a 'creature of language' (127). Here, Herder returned to Reimarus's *General Observations on the Instincts of Animals*,

---

[16] The question posed by the Berlin Academy of Sciences in 1769 was as follows: 'En supposant les hommes abandonnés à leurs facultés naturelles, sont-ils en état d'inventer le langage? Et par quels moyens parviendrons-ils d'eux-mêmes à cette invention?', Simon, 'Sprachphilosophie', 143. Parenthetical page numbers in this section refer to Herder, 'Treatise on the Origin of Language', in *PW*, 65–167.

invoking Reimarus's distinction between animal and human 'forces of representation'.[17] In contrast to animals, he argued, humans had no determinate 'circle', nor did they develop a specific kind of 'ability for' or 'drive to art' for preserving themselves in this circle (instinct) (77–87). Rather, they were organised so as to 'receive "a larger prospect"' (82).[18] This kind of natural 'weakness' and 'neediness', however, immediately brought them into a state of reflective awareness (*Besonnenheit*). No single act of human cognition was thus performed by man 'entirely like an animal', since even his sensations were already conditioned by the *distinctive character of humanity* (82–84, cf. ibid. 128–132).

Herder acknowledged that historically, it must have taken time for humans to become capable of active 'taking-awareness' (*Besinnung*) (88), i.e. develop an ability to 'separate off, stop, and pay attention to a single wave [of sensation], and be conscious of its own attentiveness' (87).[19] Nevertheless, as soon as this occurred, language had also 'inwardly' emerged. Humans became busy seeking 'characteristic marks' in the waves of sensuality they received. Thanks to the 'characteristic marks', humans could recognise the same object upon a new encounter, drawing on these marks as their 'inner language' in the process (87–90). The impressions received through the sense of hearing in particular provided the first characteristic marks, as this sense fundamentally acted as a 'middle and unifying sense', absorbing and assimilating the impressions of our different senses (109, 106–112). Awareness – the chain of thinking – became thoroughly linguistic, making humans capable of steadily comparing and processing collected ideas (130, 127–132). Due to its dialogical character (replying to external sounds) and human natural sociability,[20] the inner language, finally, served as the basis for spoken language in society.[21]

Herder, through this account of human nature, now directly rejected Rousseau's theory of natural man as an 'animal' endowed with the moral faculties of freedom and perfectibility and reasserted his view of humanity's original dignity on systematically naturalistic grounds. On the one hand, humans were continuous with the other species in seeking self-preservation.

---

[17] See also the discussion of Herder's use of Reimarus in Chapter 3.

[18] Cf. Lifschitz, *Language and Enlightenment*, 183–184 and DeSouza, 'Language, Reason, and Sociability', 224–226.

[19] Compare Herder's views on the emergence of active 'taking-awareness' in human history: 'Let one allow the human being as much time as one wants for this first distinct taking-awareness [*Besinnung*]' (128).

[20] Human sociability will be discussed in the next subsection.

[21] Trabant, 'Herder and Language', 124–133.

On the other hand, they pursued it in a distinctively 'human' manner from the outset. Humans were capable of preserving themselves in the natural environment because of reflective awareness and capacity for thought and language. From this characteristic a further distinctive feature of humanity resulted, namely, its being 'always in the process of perfection' and its capacity for creating culture as a means of both adaptation to and transformation of external circumstances (130).

Herder here further invoked Adam Ferguson's anti-Rousseauian insight, in *Essay on the History of Civil Society*, that for man there could not possibly be a 'state of nature' as distinguished from a state of art or culture.[22] He also explicitly endorsed the view of John Brown that all arts were originally united, evolving from a single source.[23] However, he deepened these insights by restating the argument, developed in rudimentary form in his earlier essays, that human language is, specifically, the vehicle for creating culture. Indeed, Herder insisted (referring in all likelihood to Brown) that 'the philosophical Englishman' should have recognised that not just different arts but language itself 'originated from the whole nature of the human being' (104). It was fundamentally through this capacity that human survival could be achieved: 'fall in ruins or else create language for thyself! And if, now, in this pressing circle of needs all forces of the soul bring themselves to conscious control, if the whole of humanity struggles to be human – *how much can be invented, done, ordered* (134)!'

Herder also restated the 'novel' (*Roman*) of the development of language that he had first put forward in *Fragments*, to provide an overview of the stadial history of language and thinking.[24] Further developing another theme that had also already briefly come up in *Fragments*, he posited a strong contrast between the intensely strong forces of the soul of savages when compared to modern, civilised men and pointed to the progressive development of the division of labour between men in society as the key element in this process. The original development of language, he made clear, resulted from the particular kind of psychic integrity and intense sensitivity that typified humans at the beginning of history, in an age when

[22] Adam Ferguson, *An Essay on the History of Civil Society*, ed. Fania Oz–Salzberger (Cambridge, 1995), 12. On Ferguson's own response to Rousseau, see Iain McDaniel, 'Philosophical History and the Science of Man in Scotland: Adam Ferguson's Response to Rousseau', *Modern Intellectual History*, 10:3 (2013), 543–568.

[23] Brown, *Dissertation*. See Chapter 2 for a comparison between Brown and Herder.

[24] Due to the focus of this work, he dwelled on the poetic origins of language in particular; see 'Treatise on the Origin', 102, 112–113, 118–121.

there was no division of labour between humans.[25] Gradually, however, humans began to specialise in narrower areas of action and hence also representation. They were increasingly capable of abstract thought, yet this had the drawback that the ever larger number of people engaging in thinking lost certain other powers that had enabled them to preserve themselves in the natural environment:

> We human beings of society can only ever imaginatively project ourselves into such a condition [of a natural human being] with trembling [. . .]. Our society, which has brought many human beings together so that with their abilities and functions they should be one, must consequently distribute abilities and afford opportunities [to people] from childhood on in such a way that one ability gets developed in preference to another. In this way, the one human being becomes for society entirely algebra, entirely reason, so to speak, just as in another human being society needs only heart, courage, and physical force (134).[26]

In contrast to Rousseau (and like Iselin), Herder hence viewed progressive development as an essential element of the divine plan for mankind. Yet he also pointed to a distinctive logic that language had developed in such a way as to be conducive to ever more abstract and rule-governed thinking, which in turn resulted in inefficacy of action. He made clear that this process was still ongoing, thus suggesting that the problems in modern society were a consequence of the European peoples reaching a motivationally weak 'old age'.

4.1.2   Human Sociability and National Groups

The other three of Herder's natural laws in *Treatise* described the relationship of human language to sociability. His second natural law amplified the first, stating that 'the progressive formation of a language' was 'natural, essential and necessary' for man as a 'creature of herd, of society' (139). In sum, Herder presented two kinds of arguments for human natural sociability. First, he like Reimarus, insisted on the foundations of sociability in the 'needs of life', taking these needs to be common to both humans and

---

[25] As Herder put it: '[T]he whole undivided human soul [. . .] ever lives whole in a circle of needs, of dangers, of pressing demands, and hence ever feels new and whole [. . .] and has enough sensuality, and so to speak, instinct in order to *sense* the whole sound and all the self-expressing characteristic marks of living nature as wholly as we are no longer able to, and, when the taking of awareness then isolates one of these characteristic marks, in order to *name* it as strongly and inwardly as we would not name it', ibid., 138.

[26] Cf. a similar statement in 'On the Cognition (1778)', 227.

animals and reflected in certain fundamental features of their physiological and cognitive make-up. Just like animals, but to a much greater extent, he argued, humans sympathetically 'participate' (*teilnehmen*) in external objects through their delicate nervous systems.[27] Secondly, Herder referred to a distinctively human kind of sociability grounded in the specific 'domestic economy of human sensuous and cognizing [nature], of his cognizing and willing nature' (83). It was this kind of sociability that was the key factor of Herder's 'second natural law'.

It is highly likely that a major inspiration for this idea came from the Third Earl of Shaftesbury's portrayal of natural sociability in *Sensus Communis* and *The Moralists*.[28] It was in this period that Herder intensively studied Shaftesbury and expressed his admiration for him in his letters to Kant.[29] Following Shaftesbury, Herder maintained that human weakness and neediness – which, as we saw above, Herder believed resulted from the distinctive character of the human forces of representation – also necessitated sociability. Humans needed communal lodging, help and support, particularly during times of pregnancy and infancy (139). Our feelings corresponded to this situation. Born without instincts, humans had strong social feelings reinforced by their reflective awareness. There was an immediate parental love (Greek 'storge'), Herder claimed, that came as 'close to instinct, as could be the case with a creature possessed of awareness' (140). Furthermore, human parental love could not be explained through any Epicurean calculation because contrary to what Epicureanism predicted, it was strengthened by pains, troubles and dangers (140).[30]

The core idea of Herder's second natural law was that human sociability facilitates the continuous and progressive development of human language, whilst through language, in turn, social interaction acquires a specific character. Necessarily growing up in families – here Herder again directly took issue with Rousseau's *Second Discourse* – humans acquired a 'familial way of thinking' communicated to them through the early impressions that accompanied the learning of a language. The question as to why humans developed language could not therefore arise at all. Humans simply learned language from their parents or the society around them

---

[27] For Herder, this was evidenced by humans' sharing of the 'animal language', thanks to which they unthinkingly express, communicate, and share their sensations of pain and pleasure, or passions in general (65–74).

[28] For a detailed reconstruction of Herder's use of Shaftesbury in his refutation of Rousseau's denial of natural sociability, see DeSouza, 'Language, Sociability', 236–239.

[29] Herder to Kant, Riga, November 1768, in *DA*, I, 119.

[30] The same argument can be found in Ferguson's *Essay*, 23–24.

(142). Therefore, even if deeply 'individual', language came to be shared, stabilised and ordered through communication and habit. Thereby language became what Herder called the 'tribal core', a bonding agent between individuals and families, and indeed generations, one which transmits the prejudices of the forefathers to subsequent generations.[31]

This special kind of bonding, through 'language and upbringing', entailed the division of mankind into groups. This is the point of Herder's third natural law, which posited that the emergence of a 'formation of different national languages' was inevitable since 'the whole human species could not possibly remain a single herd' (147). Herder backed up this claim by borrowing Ferguson's ideas about the 'unsocial' aspect of human natural sociability. Adam Ferguson's account, in its turn, can be seen as expanding Montesquieu's reference to early group antagonism in Book One of *The Spirit of the Laws*.[32] In *Essay on the Civil Society*, Ferguson argued that humans were prone both to friendship and animosity, concord and discord. Human rivalry, for him, was a source of positive energy in society as well as a guarantee of liberty. Most importantly for the present context, Ferguson particularly emphasised that due to this propensity to rivalry, sociability was also strongly limited to one's own society: on the one hand, humans were drawn to society through their 'parental affection' and 'propensity [. . .] to mix with a herd'[33] as well as their distinctively human nature that consisted in reason, culture and language; on the other hand, this very sociability motivated, and was reinforced by, animosity to other groups. For Ferguson, national animosity resulted from deep-seated prejudices that neighbours harboured against each other without any real 'opposition of interest'. The nations of North Africa, Ferguson argued, were engaged in almost perpetual wars even when they had 'no herds to preserve, nor settlements to defend'. The 'unselfish' character of such wars was best proven in the quarrelling nations' 'mutual reproaches of perfidy and injustice': 'The charge of cowardice and pusillanimity, qualities which the interested and cautious enemy should, of all others, like best to find in its rival, is urged with aversion, and made the ground of dislike.'[34] Hence, what truly was at stake for such nations in these quarrels was 'the

---

[31] Herder, 'On the Cognition (1778)', 212, cf. ibid., 141.
[32] For a brief reconstruction of Montesquieu's account, see Chapter 3. On Ferguson's account of unsocial sociability, see Iain McDaniel, 'Unsocial Sociability in the Scottish Enlightenment: Ferguson and Kames on War, Sociability and the Foundations of Patriotism', *History of European Ideas*, 41:5 (2015) (special issue: *Sociability in Enlightenment Thought*, ed. Eva Piirimäe and Alexander Schmidt), 662–682; see also McDaniel, *Adam Ferguson*, 64–83.
[33] Ferguson, *Essay*, 21.   [34] Ibid., 27.

point of honour and a desire to continue the struggles the fathers main-tained'.[35] This very honour, in turn, served as a central token of the value of one's own group, whilst being perpetuated in songs and other kinds of national heritage.[36]

Herder restated Ferguson's views on the dynamics of human sociability almost verbatim. As he put it, an 'Englishman correctly notes' that it is not 'merely selfishness and security of possession' that is at stake in national quarrels because the 'fact, that our neighbour is not as brave as we are, is no reason for hatred, but we should quietly rejoice about it' (152).[37] He insisted that dissension and mutual animosity were not grounded in the selfish interest in the security of 'goods in possession', but in a 'more noble human weakness than base vice': the group members' national feeling of honour or pride in their tribe and a commitment to the 'shade of their fathers' (152, 153). To this justification of national quarrels as originating in sociability, Herder added another argument about the importance of this behaviour for the development of distinctive languages and the for-mation of humanity (*Bildung der Menschheit*) in general. He claimed that this kind of dissension also directly served the purpose of mankind's progressive development, as the military rivalry that it provoked facilitated internal and intergenerational cohesion and a strong national and linguistic character (160). Thereby, language itself and the whole poetic tradition became a national treasure, fostering the divergence of the languages and lifestyles of neighbouring nations far beyond what the differences in their natural habitats could have brought about (151).

Yet Herder's aim was not to celebrate this diversification absolutely. Just as he, in *On Diligence* and *Fragments*, had ultimately pointed to the need to learn from other nations by learning their languages, he now pointed at the formation of a dynamic world community through the influence of languages upon each other. As he put it in his formulation of the fourth natural law: 'Just as in all probability the human species [*Geschlecht*] constitutes a single progressive whole with a single origin in a single great household-economy, likewise all languages too, and with them the whole chain of civilization [*Bildung*]' (154). The interaction and progression Herder had in view in the *Treatise* were primarily cultural. He posited

---

[35] Ibid.   [36] Ibid., 77.
[37] Characterising the Scottish authors as 'Englishmen' was a common mistake in the eighteenth century. Michael Forster cites Ulrich Gaier's conjecture that the 'Englishman' might be David Hume; see ibid. Wolfgang Proß also refers to Hume in his comments to 'Über den Ursprung der Sprache'; see his 'Anmerkungen', in *HWP*, II, 979. I have not found any direct parallels between Hume's and Herder's ideas in this connection.

that at some point 'all little, so-called barbarous nations' 'get stuck in their own circle' and need the transfer of 'tradition from people to people' (160). Through the transfer of tradition, a 'chain of a certain perfection of art' came into being, one 'progressing over everything':

> The Arabic language is certainly a hundred times finer than its mother in the first, primitive, beginning; our *German* certainly finer than the old *Celtic*; the grammar of the *Greeks* was able to be and become better than the Eastern grammar, for it was the latter's daughter; the *Roman* grammar more philosophical than the *Greek*, the *French* more than the *Roman*. Is the dwarf on the shoulders of the giant not always taller than the giant himself? (161).

Herder described this kind of transfer of tradition as initially emerging through the conquest and imitation of other nations, including the adoption of their religion. Yet he also suggested that cultural interaction caused nations' warlike inclinations and general cults of heroism to recede. 'We Germans', he argued, 'would still, like the Americans, live quietly in our forests, or rather still roughly be at war and be heroes in them, if the chain of foreign culture had not pressed so near to us and compelled us with the force of whole centuries to participate in it' (160–161. Translation slightly modified.).

As we have seen in this section, Herder's *Treatise on the Origin* essentially presented a morally optimistic picture of human civilisation and society, arguing that humans were endowed with the capacities for reason, language and sociability. Herder thus provided an elaborate philosophical justification for his rejection of Rousseau's critique of natural sociability. Like Ferguson, Herder acknowledged the natural limits of the scope of human sociability, and argued that the main reason for international conflict was precisely human sociability and the 'noble weakness' of national honour. At the same time, he celebrated clear indications of the gradual broadening of the scope of sociability through cultural interaction. Yet this celebration remained morally ambivalent, since he also indicated the corresponding weakening of human sensations through the development of ever more abstract language and thinking, one that in turn was further reinforced through the progressive development of the division of labour in society. As we will see in the next sections, in *This Too a Philosophy*, Herder spelled out the implications of this moral ambivalence.

4.2 Herder's Critique of Enlightened Narratives

Let us now turn to Herder's *This Too a Philosophy* and Herder's critique of the philosophy of history espoused by his contemporaries. At first sight, there seems to be a radical break between *Treatise* and *This Too a Philosophy* in every respect, including Herder's approach to modern politics. Herder in this work yet again adopted a critical Rousseauian tone, turning against contemporary 'Enlightened narratives' (J. G. A. Pocock), the philosophical histories reconstructing the emergence of a system of strong sovereign states supported by a commercial civilisation and shared manners.[38] However, as I seek to show in this section, there was in fact more continuity between Herder's views in these two works than has usually been assumed. First of all, Herder continued to invoke his earlier criticisms of his contemporaries' moral inertia and the widening gap between law and ethics. He also found further inspiration in Ferguson's ideas in many respects. Indeed, on closer sight it will emerge that the bulk of his criticisms of his contemporary philosophies of histories resonated with Ferguson's critical remarks about modern civilised monarchies in the latter's *Essay*. Like Ferguson, he also criticised the ethic of (European) cosmopolitanism that the contemporary philosophical histories had put forward.[39] Herder rejected all existing variations on this theme, arguing that they were based on fundamentally misleading accounts of human cognition, sociability and morality. As such, he maintained, these theories of history also misinterpreted the long-term political consequences of the changing moral fabric of society.

Herder identified the first of the typical 'Enlightened' narratives in the political and historical writings of Voltaire, David Hume, John Millar and William Robertson.[40] All these thinkers contrasted modern European societies with ancient Oriental despotisms and medieval barbarism, highlighting the progress of reason and the arts and sciences, as well as the increasing containment of unsociable human passions in structures of transactional, secondary order, in modern Europe. One way or another, they also emphasised the role of modern commerce in this. The unruly and violent nobility was gradually pacified, and a more orderly form of civil

---

[38] Pocock, *Barbarism and Religion, II: Narratives of Civil Government*, 20–21.
[39] On this ethic, see Karen O'Brien, *Narratives of Enlightenment: Cosmopolitan History from Voltaire to Gibbon* (Cambridge, 1997).
[40] The works he mentioned specifically included the following: Abbé Bazin [Voltaire], *La philosophie de l'histoire* (1765); Voltaire, *Siècle de Louis XIV* (1751); David Hume, *The History of England from the Invasion of Julius Caesar to the Accession of Henry VII* (1754–1762); David Hume, *Essays, Moral, Political and Literary* (1741–1742, 1753); John Millar, *The Origin of the Distinction of Ranks, or, an Inquiry into the Circumstances which give rise to Influence and Authority in the Different Members of Society* (1771); William Robertson, *The History of the Reign of the Emperor Charles V. With a View of the Progress of Society in Europe, from the Subversion of the Roman Empire to the Beginning of the Sixteenth Century* (1769).

administration then emerged in the modern state. Also more generally, they argued, the modern age was characterised by increasing civility in social relations, which in turn fostered the development of the arts and sciences. As a result, a general 'polite' and 'civilised' way of behaviour had become the norm, undermining strong national characters and national prejudices. It further contributed to the flourishing of commerce and seemed to impose limits upon politics as well. Since commerce required a high degree of civil liberty, it could also be hoped that monarchs would limit their own power, guaranteeing the rule of law, which then would unleash economic productivity. Furthermore, commerce could also contribute to pacification on the international scene because the ever more technological character of modern war rendered the security and power of states increasingly dependent on their economic success. Although several of the authors whom Herder saw as representative of this argument were far from blind to the limitations of modern commercial civilisation and international order, and even expressed serious doubts with regard to its sustainability in the future, they did celebrate the advent of modern commerce, civility and politeness as key elements in contributing towards the goals of civil liberty and a more enlightened and pacific humanity.[41]

A related, but ethically distinct, 'Enlightened narrative' was outlined in Iselin's *Philosophical Conjectures on the History of Mankind* (1764).[42] As we saw in Chapter 2, in his early essays and *Fragments*, Herder was rather sympathetic to Iselin's attempt to offer a series of philosophical conjectures about the 'state of simple mores' as a counter-narrative to Rousseau. In the early 1770s, however, he revised his overall assessment of Iselin's work, focusing on his account of documented history, particularly the contrast he developed between barbarism and civilisation.

For Iselin, true freedom and moral virtue required a historical interaction between the originally genuinely sociable, but politically despotic, Oriental societies and the fierce and unsociable republican Northern societies in temperate climates. In mild climates and fertile lands, such as those of Oriental agrarian kingdoms, Iselin argued, human reason developed relatively smoothly, thus favouring the emergence and spread of ideas

---

[41] For an analysis of this thesis in its original, 'neo-Colbertist', form, see Hont, *Jealousy of Trade*, 24–30. For Hume's critique of the thesis in this basic form and for his sharp observations about the corruption of modern commerce through 'jealousy of state', see ibid., 9–11.

[42] Three editions of Iselin's book were released: in 1764, 1768 ad 1770 (1764, 1768, 1770). Alongside the 1764 edition, I also provide some references to the considerably expanded 1770 edition here (the 1784 reprint).

of 'perfection, order and justice' and sociability based on them. In the harsher climate of the North, by contrast, early humans were almost totally overwhelmed by numerous chimerical ideas, and thus neither arts nor sociability developed to any significant degree. Nevertheless, it was precisely in the sociable societies that despotism arose, whilst the unsociable 'barbarian' ones proved favourable to the development of a rudimentary idea of republican freedom.[43] Considering individual and social freedom to be interdependent, Iselin claimed that achieving freedom in society required the historical interaction of the two types of sociability and types of learning developed in these societies as well as finally their fusion in a new form of polity in Europe.[44]

As Béla Kapossy has shown,[45] despite his stronger emphasis on human natural sociability, Iselin thus to a large extent concurred with Hume's and Voltaire's relatively positive verdicts on modern commercial civilised monarchies. He too celebrated the gradual recession of 'barbarian' unsociability and 'national hatred' in Europe, and emphasised the contribution of modern 'civil administration' [*Policierung*] as well as enlightenment to this still uncompleted process.[46] The last chapter of the second volume of Iselin's *History of Mankind* followed Hume's *History of England* particularly closely.[47] Iselin put forward an account of moral virtue that emphasised the crucial significance of an increase in learning (*Wissenschaften*) and the development of human intellectual capacities more generally to achieve stable sociability and cosmopolitan moral virtue as well as political freedom and peace in Europe.[48] According to Iselin, true virtue could only be based on 'wisdom' (*Weisheit*), a correct philosophical understanding and love of true principles of humanity (*Menschheit*). For him, Europe was currently solely approaching the age of 'manly years'; most of the work in eradicating still widespread prejudices and remnants of a barbarian law of nations was still ahead.[49]

---

[43] Iselin, *Über die Geschichte* (1764), II, book IV (Oriental despotisms), book V (Greek and Roman history), book VI (Middle Ages); the same books were numbered as VI, VII, VIII in *Über die Geschichte* (1784).

[44] Ibid., book VII; 248–249. Kapossy, *Iselin contra Rousseau*, 256, 278–304.

[45] Kapossy, *Iselin contra Rousseau*, 272–278.

[46] Iselin, *Über die Geschichte* (1764), I, 181–186; (1784), I, 271–283; II, passim.

[47] Iselin, *Über die Geschichte* (1764), II, book VI; (1784), II, book VIII. Kapossy, *Iselin contra Rousseau*, 300.

[48] Iselin, *Über die Geschichte* (1764), II, 251, 257–267; (1784), II, 461–480.

[49] Iselin, *Über die Geschichte* (1764), II, 286–294; (1784), II, 461–480; cf. Kapossy, *Iselin contra Rousseau*, 256, 291–295 and idem, 'Iselins „Geschichte der Menschheit" als Friedensschrift', in *Iselin und die Geschichtsphilosophie*, 100–123.

4.2.1   *Modern Morality and Sociability*

In *This Too a Philosophy*, Herder passionately rejected both these kinds of narratives. The central passage in which he lashed out against modern cosmopolitans deserves to be quoted in full:

> We love *all* of us, or rather no one *needs* to love the other. We *socialize with each other*; are completely each other's *like – ethically proper, polite, blissful!*; indeed have no *fatherland*, no *our-people* for whom we live, but are *friends of humanity* and *citizens of the world*. Already now all of Europe's regents do so, and soon we will *all* speak the French language! And then – bliss! – the Golden Age begins again *'when everyone in the world had one tongue and language! there will arise a single flock and shepherd!'* National characters, what has happened to you? (329)[50]

As we can see from this passage, Herder viewed the neglect or derision of national sentiments as revealing the way in which modern philosophers were contributing to human self-alienation and disregard for others. By extolling enlightened self-interest and civility, or indeed, directly preaching the lofty ideal of 'citizenship of the world', modern philosophers failed to notice the fatal weakening of fundamental human sociability.[51] Furthermore, even if philosophers (like Iselin) sincerely preached genuine love of mankind, these ideals had no impact on people's actions: 'Precisely because these *first principles* are so *commonplace*, pass as *playthings* from hand to hand and as *platitudes* from *lip* to *lip* – precisely for this reason, it proves probable that they *cannot* any longer achieve *any effect*. Does one *use* what one *plays* with?' (321).

The mere spread of abstract ideals, Herder insisted, was no sign of moral progress, quite the contrary. Referring to the proliferation of such abstract

---

[50] Parenthetical page numbers in this and the next sections of this chapter refer to Herder, 'This Too a Philosophy', in *PW*.

[51] A few years later, Herder expressed the same idea even more forcefully: 'Universal human reason, as we would like to understand the term, is a cover for our favourite whims, idolatry, blindness, and laziness.' Herder, 'On the Cognition [1778]', in *PW*, 223. The problem was not just modern self-complacency and self-admiration but fundamental moral regress. Here, Herder harked back to his earlier criticism of abstract morality, and developed it in new directions. As we saw in Chapters 1 and 3, in his earlier works Herder had applied Rousseau's educational ideas, agreeing with Rousseau that abstract moral terms were motivationally inert, or lacked a real connection to sentiments and the capacity for action. In *On the Cognition*, Herder further emphasised the ways in which modern education continued to produce unhappy and immoral human beings. Children who were taught abstract concepts too early, he argued, develop in a one-sided manner: they either become 'weak', 'enervated', and 'idle speculators', or, conversely, 'sentimentalizers' who merely resist the formers' *word-mongery* and *active lies*, but have no true understanding of morality. Either way, these children would not be able to lead healthy lives involving being active and being happy, ibid., 224–228.

idioms and the spread of '*one sort of education, philosophy, irreligion, enlight-enment, vice*', he declared: '*Freedom, sociability*, and *equality* as they are now *sprouting up* everywhere – they have caused harm and will cause harm in a thousand *misuses*' (350). As the glaring contrast between Frederick of Prussia's professed humanitarian ideals and his actual aggressive foreign policy had revealed, it was precisely due to their abstract and 'refined' quality that these idioms could easily be misappropriated to support 'reason of state' politics:[52] 'The universal dress of *philosophy* and *love of humankind* can hide oppressions, attacks on the true, personal *freedom of human beings* and *lands, citizens*, and *peoples*, of just the sort Cesare Borgia would wish for' (349, 351).[53]

4.2.2   Modern Slavery and Self-Deception

Drawing on this criticism of the accounts of sociability and morality underlying contemporary Enlightened narratives, Herder also attacked philosophical historians' generally positive verdict on modern civilised monarchy and its potential contribution to peace. The two supposed pillars of modern virtue according to these philosophical histories – an increased freedom of the mind and increased political freedom – he argued, were largely phantoms of these philosophers' minds. In fact, modern civilised monarchies were verging on despotism:

> every classical humanist [*Schöndenker*] who considers our century's civil administration [*Policierung*] the non plus ultra of humanity has an oppor-tunity to reduce whole centuries to *barbarism, miserable state authority, superstition* and *stupidity, lack of ethics* and *tastelessness* [. . .], and to rave about our century's *light*, that is, about its *superficiality* and *unrestraint*, about its *warmth* in *ideas* and its *coldness* in *actions*, about its seeming *strength* and *freedom*, and its real *weakness-onto-death* and *exhaustion* under *unbelief, despotism*, and *luxury*. All the books of our *Voltaire* and *Hume*, *Robertson's* and *Iselin's* are full of this.[54]

---

[52] As Michael Sonenscher has shown, another prominent example of a theory using the Fénelonian term *friend of mankind* to denote 'a mixture of war propaganda, crude power politics and high moral principle' was marquis de Mirabeau's famous *L'ami des hommes* (1765); see Sonenscher, *Before the Deluge*, 199.

[53] Compare Herder's similar insights in *On the Cognition* (1778): 'In one age, all the wise men gape upwards, look towards the sky and count the stars, and are for the rest nowhere less at home than in their fatherland, in their city. At another time people conduct crusades for the golden fleece of tolerance, universal religion, and love of humankind – perhaps just as fancifully as the crusaders seeking the holy grave and the system of foreign worlds', 230 (translation slightly modified).

[54] Herder, 'This Too a Philosophy', 307.

This may sound like yet another Rousseauian insight in Herder's philosophy of history. Yet, a closer look at Herder's argument again reveals fundamental differences between his and Rousseau's views. For Rousseau, despotism was the necessary outcome of the 'progress of inequality' arising out of the institution of property and division of labour.[55] This led to nothing less than 'the most horrible state of war' between the different ranks of society. Through property-based contract and the establishment of political societies, dependence and inequality were only magnified in the long run, leading to the 'state of Master and Slave' as the final stage of the progress of inequality.[56] Finally, with one state necessitating the creation of others, mankind was also divided into different societies, which remained in a 'state of nature' among themselves, this state being 'even more fatal among these great Bodies than it had previously been among the individuals who made them up'.[57]

Herder, in *This Too a Philosophy*, saw the cause of modern despotism as neither the inflation of amour-propre nor the resulting fundamental antagonism of modern commercial society, but rather as a general complacency, a loss of feeling and energy in the people. As we saw in Chapter 3, Herder had already been concerned in his *Journal of My Travels* about the widening gap between laws and mores in modern societies. In *This Too a Philosophy* he now introduced a slightly different but related argument, aligning himself with Adam Ferguson's warnings about the rise of despotism in modern centralised states. In his *Essay on the History of Civil Society*, Adam Ferguson famously discussed the rise of modern 'imbecillitas', which 'mankind generally flatters [...] under the name of *politeness*', as an effect of modern regular government and luxury.[58] This order was one of 'mere inaction and tranquillity', 'the order of slaves, not that of free men'.[59] This psychological state, Ferguson argued, had clear political consequences. It enabled the rise of a new kind of military despotism that in turn would attempt to bestow a false 'order' on society.[60] Like Ferguson, Herder also argued that there was a specific kind of despotism emerging in the modern state, a despotism fostered by

---

[55] Rousseau, 'Second Discourse', 111–188 (171).   [56] Ibid., 173–175, 182.

[57] Ibid., 174. For an analysis of Rousseau's discussion of the divided condition of mankind, see Sonenscher, *Before the Deluge*, 222–239.

[58] Adam Ferguson, *An Essay on the History of Civil Society*, ed. Fania Oz–Salzberger (Cambridge, 1995), 242.

[59] Ibid., 254.

[60] Ibid., 254–256. Montesquieu had already pointed to a 'new disease' spreading across Europe: 'Each monarch keeps ready all the armies he would have if his peoples were in danger of being exterminated; and this state in which all strain against all is called peace', *The Spirit of the Laws*,

the effects of modern technology and luxury on the human mind. Instead of liberating man from the bonds of nature, the advancement of technology had made certain key human virtues redundant. Manliness, courage, and self-reliance were now replaced by extensive reliance on technology and guidance from superiors. The invention of the gun, for example, had turned armies into mere *puppets of movement* (316). The situation was aggravated by a new obsession with luxury as the source of state income and ultimately the basis for technological achievement and military prowess (317, 326). Far from supporting true liberty, these developments facilitated the transformation of all of society into a 'machine' led by one. Instead of citizens, there were now 'cogs in a machine', a 'forced-together pile', remaining in place through '*fear* or *habit* or *luxury* and philosophy' (319).

Herder thus agreed with Ferguson that these developments opened the gate to the rise of universal despotism.[61] On closer perspective, he suggested, a 'state of war' would also continue to exist between such 'machines'. A certain equilibrium, called 'balance of power', had been achieved in Europe, yet the states continued 'rubbing' against each other, waging 'passionless' wars. Even worse, the monarchs now knew how to stir up 'enthusiasm' in support of the 'state's cause' by corrupting the natural inclination of patriotism.[62] This kind of enthusiasm, however, was hardly a passion that would support moral freedom.

Drawing on the abbé de Raynal's and Diderot's critique of the modern states system and colonialism,[63] Herder also criticised the ruthless colonial politics of commercial monarchies: using the excuse of fostering trade, almost any sort of action was seen as morally justified, leading to the devastation, enslavement or corruption of the whole world. This, in turn, had repercussions for the relationships between European states in colonies: 'the remotest cause' could thus lead to a 'universal bloodletting in all

---

224. On Ferguson's attempt to amend Montesquieu's theory of 'false honour' as the guarantee of moderate government in modern monarchies, see Iain McDaniel, 'Honour and Pride in Adam Ferguson's Conception of Modern Patriotism', in *Human Nature as the Basis of Morality and Society in Early Modern Society*, ed. Juhana Lemetti and Eva Piirimäe (= *Acta Philosophica Fennica*, 83 (2007)), 105–120.

[61] See the final chapter entitled 'Of the Progress and Termination in Despotism' of Ferguson's *Essay*. My discussion of these ideas is indebted to McDaniel, *Adam Ferguson*, 64–83.

[62] Ibid., 326–327.

[63] See Guillaume Thomas Raynal, *A Philosophical and Political History of the Settlements and Trade of the Europeans in the East and West Indies*, 6 vols. (London, 1798). Herder's engagement with Raynal is highlighted by Proß, 'Anmerkungen [Auch eine Philosophie der Geschichte]', in HWP, I, 848–863 (850 and 862–863); cf. Dreitzel, 'Herders politische Konzepte', 276–277; on his complex relationship to Raynal's work, see also Noyes, *Herder: Aesthetics*, 183–185.

parts of the world' (327). Furthermore, the highly-praised modern 'system of trade' had replaced just one form of slavery with another: whilst slavery was disappearing in Europe because of its economic inefficiency, non-European and non-Christian peoples were turned into slaves in Europe's 'silver mines and sugar mills' in the rest of the world.[64] Herder's verdict was harsh: '*Three parts of the world laid waste* and *civilly administered* by us, and we through them *depopulated, emasculated,* sunk in luxury, oppression, and death – that is rich and happy trading' (328).

4.3   Christianity in Human History

Albeit more radical than previously, Herder's criticisms of modern morality and politics in *This Too a Philosophy* were still in many ways continuous with his earlier views on these issues. What was new about *This Too a Philosophy* was the more strongly theologically loaded language that Herder used there. Herder had only adopted the theological perspective marginally in his earlier discussions of human history; now he used it to buttress the sceptical point that humans could have only limited understanding of the historical process. Only God could have an overview of it all (299). This did not mean, however, that Herder avoided making guesses about God's aims in history.[65] Indeed, in many ways, his goal was precisely to show that the inclinations that humans developed in different societies were *all* justified and necessary for the (ethical) formation of humanity. The phrase 'formation of humanity' (*Bildung der Menschheit*) in the title of the work is significant in this respect. First, Herder acknowledged that all kinds of historiography had an educational, 'formative' impact; so did his. Second, the historical process itself could be seen as a continous and providentially designed 'formation of mankind'. Herder's ideas about human history in an early introduction to this essay are revealing in this respect. His main question originally concerned determining the ways in which Providence sought to 'form' and educate humanity:

> Is there, historically and physically, a certain progress in the inclinations of the human species? Can one observe in the bond between the diverse periods, connections, and revolutions of the peoples of this earthly sphere

---

[64] This was specifically the upshot of Herder's criticism of the Scottish philosopher John Millar in his review of Millar's *Observations Concerning the Distinction of Ranks*; in *FHA*, IV, 849–853.

[65] Cf. Bertrand Binoche, 'Herder in 1774: An Incomplete Philosophy of History', in *Companion to Enlightenment Historiography*, ed. Sophie Bourgault and Robert Sparling (Leiden, 2013), 189–216.

a thread and plan of formation (*Bildung*) for developing in the human heart little by little certain inclinations and forces for which people previously and on another path saw no clear trace?[66]

Without presupposing God as a direct agent in the historical process, this question implied a divine intention behind the rise and fall of different national cultures. Herder now also turned to 'documented' history, renouncing the conjectural approach. He invoked the Creation narrative as laid out in the earliest Oriental cosmogonies (including the Book of Genesis of the Old Testament) as the most important source of information about the earliest, foundational period (272–273) and interpreted the rest of human history as revealing 'God's course in nature' (314) and 'through the nations' (340).[67] The 'formation of humanity', for Herder, began in the Orient (Hebrew culture being the best-known, but also the latest, example in the early period), moving from there to Egypt and Phoenicia, to Greece, and Rome. Then, the 'northern [European] nations' entered onto the stage, merged with 'southern [European] peoples' under Roman government, then also absorbed Arab influences due to the Moorish conquest of Spain, before finally transforming into the peoples of modern Europe. Apart from the Oriental and 'northern peoples' who were original, 'patriarchal' peoples, the rest of the significant peoples in human history built on the culture of a preceding one, yet never 'became what the other was' (339–340).

Herder even acknowledged in *This Too a Philosophy* that this process could in a certain sense be characterised as a 'chain of perfection'. The 'chain of perfection', he specified, was not to be understood as an uninterrupted or unilinear process, as there were different stages in it, between which there were '*resting places, revolutions!, changes!*' (299). Nevertheless, he affirmed that true progress or '*progressive development*' was there (292) and could be discerned through careful imaginative reconstruction of the

---

[66] Herder, 'This Too a Philosophy of History for the Formation of Humanity [an early introduction]', in *PW*, 268–271 (269–270). Wolfgang Proß points out that this question was directly inspired by Herder's reading of Raynal's *Philosophical and Political History*, 'Anmerkungen [*Auch eine Philosophie der Geschichte*]', 850.

[67] Here he was developing further an argument expressed in *The Oldest Document of Human History* (*Älteste Urkunde des Menschengeschlchts*). In this work, which was written in parallel to *This Too a Philosophy* and was published in 1774/1775, Herder seriously qualified (and ostensibly directly rejected) his naturalistic account of the origin of language in the *Treatise*, maintaining that divine revelation – happening *via* natural phenomena – occurred at the beginning of human history, 'Älteste Urkunde', 276–278; 289–290. As we will see below, alongside this new theological interpretation of the earliest human history and the rise of the Christian religion, he nevertheless also continued to invoke naturalistic explanations for human evolution and interaction.

different national inclinations as well as through a genuinely historiograph-ical act of '*binding together* the most disparate scenes without *confusing* them' (299).[68] For Herder, this was 'God's revelation' in human deeds, his spirit building a 'temple', a body for himself, in human history (340–341).

Herder thus suggested that it was possible to give a plausible, albeit of course only humanly limited, interpretation of God's intentions in history, one that at the same time was aware of the interpreter's particular stand-point in this process. On the one hand, this interpretation had to accept the insignificance of a single human being, or indeed, a single generation or 'century', in the complex edifice of history. On the other hand, Herder acknowledged that 'I too mean something in my place' (357, 334–337), thus accepting the continuing relevance of a human viewpoint *for humans*, and God's benevolent providence in this respect. At each singular point in history, he maintained, humans still pursue happiness according to the needs and ideas of their time and place (335). Furthermore, precisely such a tentative narrative of God's purposes in history could also serve as an 'encouragement to hope, to act, to believe, even where one sees *nothing* or *not everything*' (299).

4.3.1   National Happiness and Self-Preservation

Viewed from the perspective of the evolution of his thought, Herder's emphasis on national happiness and his tentative hope to provide moral encouragement ring a more familiar tone than his (qualified) scepticism about an 'overall view of history'. Indeed, despite this scepticism, we can still identify many themes familiar from his earlier work in Herder's new narrative. As we saw in Chapter 3, Herder had already in his *Journal of My Travels* devised a programme of research based on the conclusions of his engagement with the 'vocation of man'.[69] Happiness and virtue, Herder stipulated there, could be achieved in each period of history.[70] In *This Too a Philosophy*, he turned this insight directly against one of the prize questions set by the Berne *Patriotic Society*: '*Which was probably the happiest people in history?*' (296).[71] This question was premised on the idea that the greatest happiness depended on the greatest virtue and hence

---

[68] On Herder's 'genetic method', cf. Hans Dietrich Irmscher, 'Aspekte der Geschichtsphilosophie Johann Gottfried Herders', in *Herder und die Philosophie des deutschen Idealismus*, ed. Marion Heinz (Amsterdam, 1997), 5–47 (36–39).

[69] Herder, *Journal meiner Reise*, 374.   [70] Ibid., 375.

[71] Cf. the main question of Herder's first draft of *This Too a Philosophy*: 'What sorts of virtues or unvirtues have governed human beings at all times, and has the tendency of human beings been

could be reformulated as 'Which people, in history, might have been the most virtuous?' Now, 'for both these ideas', Herder argued in an early draft of *This Too a Philosophy*, 'we not only still lack a correct criterion, but it could even perhaps be that human nature had such a flexibility and mutability as to be able to develop (*ausbilden*) for itself [...] the most diverse ideals of its actions into what is called *virtue* and the most diverse ideals of its sensations into what is called *happiness*'.[72]

In the published version of *This Too a Philosophy*, Herder explained this claim at greater length, again developing an insight that derived from Ferguson's philosophy of history. Ferguson had emphasised that there could be no substantive conception of one single kind of happiness, since happiness resulted more from the activity of the mind than from the attainment of certain specified ends.[73] Herder insisted in the same spirit that happiness was nothing but 'the *sum* of "*satisfactions of wishes, achievements of purposes*, and *gentle overcoming of needs*", which [...] all *shape* themselves according to *land, time,* and *place*' (296, cf. 294). Human nature, hence, could not possibly be a 'container of an absolute, independent, unchangeable happiness as the philosopher defines it', but contained seeds for very different constellations of inclinations and needs arising in response to external occasions, i.e. geographical, social, and historical circumstances (296). At a given moment, each nation – just like each individual – could attain a certain kind of happiness, as one did not need to satisfy all dispositions of the heart. Rather, 'if only *a few* get satisfied the soul quickly forms *a concert* for itself from these awakened notes and does not feel the unawakened ones except insofar as they *silently* and obscurely support the sounding song' (297).[74] As previously, in *Journal of My Travels*, Herder in *This Too a Philosophy* was thus absolutely adamant that the historical process was not to be understood as a 'striving for greater

---

improved or worsened with time, or always remained the same?', Herder, 'This Too a Philosophy [an early introduction]', in *PW*, 268–271, 268.

[72] Ibid., 270 (I have slightly modified the translation here).

[73] Cf. Ferguson's views on happiness: '[Happiness] arises more from the pursuit, than from the attainment of any end whatever; and in every new situation to which we arrive, even in the course of a prosperous life, it depends more on the degree in which our minds are properly employed, than it does on the circumstances in which we are destined to act, on the materials which are placed in our hands, or the tools with which we are furnished', *Essay*, 51; see also ibid., 59–63 on the different kinds of national felicity. The importance of Ferguson's ideas for understanding Herder's conception of happiness in the *Ideas* is emphasised by Proß in 'Nachwort', in *HWP*, III/1, 917 and in 'Anmerkungen [*Ideen*]', in *HWP*, III/2, 456, 474, 489. For a comparison of Herder's conception of happiness with that of Iselin, see Proß, 'Nachwort', 912–919.

[74] For a discussion of Herder's notion of national happiness (including its relationship to individual happiness), cf. Patten, 'The Most Natural State', 669–679.

virtue or happiness of the individual' (298). Humanity only ever remained humanity; 'a *double creature*' that could be 'modified a thousandfold', yet one that nevertheless 'inwardly' remains 'only *one measure* and *mixture of forces*' (334–335).

Herder's famous claim about 'nationalism' was embedded in this discussion of happiness. It was out of 'care' for us and our happiness, Herder argued, that nature had limited the human view, created a *horizon* for us beyond which we were not supposed to look or even suspect the existence of something further:

> everything that is still *similar* to my nature, that can be *assimilated* to it, I covet, strive for, make my own; *beyond that,* kind nature has armed me with *feelinglessness, coldness*, and *blindness*; this can even become *contempt* and *disgust*, but only has the purpose of forcing me back *on myself,* of making me satisfied on [sic!] *the center* that bears me. [. . .] Thus all pairs of nations whose inclinations and circles of happiness *collide* – it is called *prejudice!, mob-thinking!,* limited *nationalism*! Prejudice is *good* in its time, for it renders [humans] *happy* (297).

This passage essentially further develops the argument from *Treatise*. In both works Herder emphasised the positive impacts that national prejudices and even animosity could have in terms of generating a sense of national cohesion and happiness. In *Treatise*, he used a distinctive kind of idea of sociable dissension and rivalry to explain the prime differences that historically arose between nations. In *This Too a Philosophy* he now explicitly maintained that there are two principles that govern both nation-building as well as interaction between nations, those of assimilation and dissimilation. Nations emerged from human sociability and sympathy for what was similar to us. At an early stage of social and cultural differentiation, however, there arose directly contrasting conceptions of happiness that occasioned fundamental distrust and even hatred between nations. Herder viewed it exemplified in the ways in which the agricultural Egyptians distrusted shepherding Hebrews or trading Phoenicians.[75] However, nations could also learn from each other as long as the elements learned could be 'assimilated' to the original national character. Beyond that, however, there was coldness and sometimes even disgust.

It is important to highlight that in a few years, in his *On the Cognition and Sensation*, Herder came to explicate the deeper naturalistic foundations of this account. Here, following up his own programmatic call in *Thoughts*

---

[75] For discussion, see the next section.

on Montesquieu, Herder sought to develop a 'natural philosophy' (*Naturlehre*) of the forces governing individual souls, starting from analysing the ways in which our souls 'feel' themselves living in our bodies.[76] In the second and third edition of this work (1775 and 1778), Herder incorporated a modified form of Albrecht von Haller's theory of irritation in his analysis of the soul.[77] He argued that there was a strong parallelism between the ways in which the material forces of attraction and repulsion, the living forces of expansion and contraction, and those of the soul operated, all of them being modifications of the one dynamic thought of God (God's thought-force).[78] Irritation was both the first sign of life in a living animal body as well as the origin of sensation in humans, whilst the self-feeling of the human soul was also based on this phenomenon.[79] According to Herder, the physiological phenomenon of irritation involved a relationship of attraction and repulsion: we were drawn to what was similar to us and rejected what was dissimilar to us. As we have been put in this 'circle of sensation and similarity' by God, Herder argued, God gave us 'no other key for penetrating into the inside of things than [our] own impress or rather the reflected image of His mind in my Mind'.[80] As Marion Heinz explains, Herder here essentially presented a theory of life, according to which different living beings receive irritations from what is fundamentally similar to them, appropriating in their various kinds of mental acts what they 'need'.[81] Thereby, all beings pursue self-preservation both as individuals and as members of a species. In so doing they are also 'used' by higher forms of life for the purposes of their self-preservation, thus also contributing to a divine order of the '*progressive formation, renewal, refinement* of all beings'.[82]

Hence, in *On the Cognition and Sensation*, Herder stated that human happiness was both universal and individual. All individual forces were modifications of divine ones, yet they also took an individual form,

---

[76] Herder, 'On the Cognition (1775)', 181. Herder explained: 'The soul with all its forces feels itself living in its body; even its forces of cognition and volition are only results, aggregates, of this connection; it is only *present* in the universe through action and reaction on this body full of sensations, full of irritations, it otherwise lacks even self-consciousness', ibid., 182.

[77] 'On the Cognition (1778)', 189–201. Herder describes his reworking of Haller's ideas as 'Haller's physiological work raised to psychology, and enlivened with a mind like Pygmalion's statue', 'On the Cognition (1778)' 196–197.

[78] DeSouza, 'The Ontological Foundations', 46 and *passim*.

[79] Herder, 'On the Cognition (1778)', 182, 208–210.   [80] Ibid., 187–188.

[81] Heinz, '1.2.4. *Vom Erkennen und Empfinden*', 130–135; see also Niels Wildschut, 'Analogy, Empathy, Incommensurability: Herder's Conception of Historical Understanding', in *Herder on Empathy*, 158–182 (160–166).

[82] Herder, 'On the Cognition (1778)', 187–188, 192–193.

depending on the ways in which humans as finite beings interact with the external world. Thus, there were also inevitably different degrees of similarity between individual beings. 'Sons of a single tribal father who share a more [sic!] identical organisation in one sort of world and climate', Herder argued, 'inevitably think more similarly to each other than antipodes in ethics and sensation'. However, 'laws, government, manner of life count for still more, and in this way a people's manner of thought, a daughter of the whole, becomes also the witness of the whole'.[83] A major source of such similarity was language that, as Herder argued in the 1775 version, was the 'offprint' of 'our inner structure of sensation' and 'thoughts'.[84] Language, he explained in 1778, was in fact what awakens our *inner elasticity* and *activity*. Some sort of language, certain ready-made 'thought-formulas', would be needed to awaken our inner activity.[85]

In both *This Too a Philosophy* and *On the Cognition*, Herder also drew methodological conclusions for historical interpretation from these ideas. Insofar as we wish to understand other human beings, we need to 'feel into' them. But what did he mean by invoking this expression? In *On the Cognition*, Herder dwelt on our 'living reading' of literary works (so as to discover the authors' 'souls' in the language they use). In *This Too a Philosophy*, he focused on the ways in which historians should study and narrate history. He emphasised the need to familiarise oneself with all aspects of a nation's culture before one can capture any of it in words. Indeed, as Wolfgang Proß has shown, the famous injunction 'feel yourself in everything, only now are you on the way towards understanding the word' (292) was meant as a criticism of Montesquieu's theory of the principles of government. Whilst Montesquieu had sought to encapsulate the character of nations in one 'word', e.g. 'honour' or 'virtue', Herder admonished that one had to begin by closely studying the historical nations' ways of thought (*Denkarten*) as influenced by their 'mode of life, habits, needs, peculiarities of land and climate' as well as distinctive 'constitutions' (*Verfassungen*) and 'history' (291–292).[86] Just as with the formation of nations, this investigation relied on the human capacity for sympathy. However, here sympathy was to be both regulated and cultivated. A proper historical understanding entailed a distanciation from one's own immediate responses of sympathy or antipathy so as to be able

---

[83] Ibid., 220.   [84] Ibid., 221, fn. 42.   [85] Ibid., 211–212.
[86] Proß, '"Diversus cum diversis"', 142–143; cf. Adler, *Die Prägnanz des Dunklen*, 166–172; idem, 'Nation. Johann Gottfried Herders Umgang mit Konzept und Begriff, in *Unerledigte Geschichten: Der literarische Umgang mit Nationalität und Internationalität*, ed. Gesa von Essen und Horst Turk (Göttingen, 2000), 39–56.

to closely examine the relationships between different factors in determining the shape of a particular culture. At the same time, a new form of cognitive sympathy would thereby arise, one that would seek to view the world through the eyes of a particular people living in these particular conditions. On the one hand, this would be made possible by the fundamental sameness of the subject and object, the shared 'humanity' of both, also allowing the use of 'analogy' as a heuristic tool for discovering deeper analogies between 'us' and 'them' which initially would be eclipsed from our view. On the other hand, these attempts could only ever be partially successful, insofar as humanity had historically diversified into distinct types of national culture, which each had developed as a reflection of their characteristic ways of thought and inclinations.[87]

4.3.2   *Civilisation and National Inclinations*

Let us now turn to Herder's account of the moral purposes of a narrative of God's revelation in history in *This Too a Philosophy*. What kind of narrative did he put forward, exactly? And in what way could it serve as an encouragement to 'believe, act and hope'?

To a certain extent, Herder's model for describing the historical process in *This Too a Philosophy* can be characterised as cyclical.[88] Different representative nations around the Mediterranean Sea and in Europe, for him, embodied mankind's development through 'childhood', 'youth', 'manliness' and even 'senility'. Herder took the metaphors of life stages from Iselin, whilst also factoring in 'senility' in a Rousseauian vein. As we shall see, these metaphoric descriptions point to certain fundamental cognitive dispositions and ways of thought that Herder introduced as 'necessary' both for the self-preservation of those peoples and the ethical formation of humanity more generally.[89] At the same time, Herder also organised human history into three epochs: the ancient, middle and new ones. Whilst the first epoch (antiquity) ran through the whole lifespan of an individual, constituting the first cycle, the second and third were stages of one and the same lifespan and cycle.

According to Herder, the earliest period in the first epoch was the one of patriarchal nomadic Oriental nations. It is necessary to dwell somewhat

---

[87] For discussion, see also Wildschut, 'Analogy, Empathy', 158–182.

[88] See also Proß, 'Nachwort', in *HWP*, III/1, 856–864; cf. idem, 'Anmerkungen', in *HWP*, III/2, 456 on the model Herder embraced in the *Ideas*.

[89] Herder points out that 'the greatest part of the nations of the earth is still in childhood', interpreting these nations as 'remains' and 'monuments' of 'the oldest times of *human childhood*' (341).

longer on this period, since here we can also best see the function that Herder's novel kind of historiography was supposed to serve. Herder began by decisively embracing the view of monogenetic origins of the human species against Voltaire,[90] invoking the 'short and apocryphal' account of the 'oldest book' (the story of Creation in the Hebrew Old Testament and other, fragmentary, Oriental accounts), as his most important source, whilst also insisting that the information it provided was confirmed by some recent investigations into the matter (272–273). Developing a delicate 'double seed of the whole species' in man and woman, he argued, '*creating Providence*' initiated a '*heroic period of the patriarchal age*', during which humanity was 'rooted' and 'grounded' in its 'first inclinations, mores and institutions' (274).[91] This view certainly resonated with his argument, in *The Oldest Document of Human History*, that natural law (*Naturrecht*) was grounded in divine revelation *in* natural phenomena at the beginning of human history. The ethical content of 'natural law' was nothing but religion and familial love. Spoken and written language also originated both in this earliest revelation.[92] Yet even according to a human 'raisonnement à la Voltaire', Herder continued, it was clear that '*the shepherd's life in the fairest clime of the world*' should be seen as 'a chosen *garden of God* for raising the first, most delicate *human plants!*' (275).

Herder's point was clear: religious sentiment, the '*feeling of God*' had to be inculcated as deeply as possible in humanity, laying foundations for the most important inclinations of '*wisdom* instead of science, *piety* instead of wisdom, *love of parents, spouse, children* instead of politeness and debauchery, [with] *ordering of life, rule and regency for God over a* house as the original model of all civil ordering and institutions'. (274) Genuine forms of religion and sociability were revealed in this early period. These foundations '*cast firm in eternal forms* what was *right* and *good* or at least *seemed* so' (277). Although Hume, Voltaire and Montesquieu had all invariably criticised Oriental despotism, Herder insisted, they had based their accounts on 'exaggerated, violent phenomena of realms mostly in the state of decay' (276). Instead of stigmatising such 'enthusiasm and child's sense' with our own worst fears of '*deception* and *stupidity, superstition* and *slavery*', '*priest-devils* and *tyrant-ghosts*', it was important to appreciate them as 'God's creation', as 'a *vehicle*, the sole *vehicle, of everything good*' (279). These sentiments were grounded in the early human beings' typical forms of cognition, and as such had to benefit the good of humans and their

---

[90] On this opposition, see Noyes, *Herder: Aesthetics*, 152.   [91] I have modified the translation here.
[92] Herder, 'Älteste Urkunde', 289–290.

happiness. Indeed, it was best to compare the Orientals with children, or more precisely, with what each of us remembered from our childhood. Thereby, Herder suggested, we could perhaps more easily bracket our prejudices and appreciate the necessity and usefulness of such sentiments at such an age (276–277).

However, Herder also sought to show that in a certain sense, this earliest period revealed something deeper about humanity and the human condition that modern people, too, needed to appreciate. Although it was impossible to recreate such sentiments in their original form in a later period, one could recognise through a historical representation that these 'strongest, eternal, almost divine *traits* which *bless* or *ruin* our whole life' should never be completely forsaken (227). The 'word weaving' from this distant period (the scripture) could still help kindle the 'spirit of fire and flame' in modern peoples, whilst a historical representation of this period would also drive home the point that religion can never be eliminated from children's education (337–338). Furthermore, this kind of thinking had by no means disappeared from the world at large, as 'the greatest part of the nations of the earth is still in childhood, all still speak *that* language, have *those* ethics, provide the paradigms of *that* level of civilisation (*Bildung*) – wherever you travel and listen among so-called savages there resound *sounds for the elucidation of scripture!*, *there waft living commentaries on revelation!*'(341). As we shall see in Chapter 5, Herder further developed this idea in his discussion of folk song and German 'national spirit'.

Could other periods of history also 'elucidate scripture' according to Herder? Not in the same way. The earliest period clearly enjoyed a privileged status here. However, each period was certainly worthy of being studied in as close detail as possible. Different cultures developed opposing tendencies in humanity, which was instructive about the vast potential of human nature. From the perspective of divine 'revelation' *in* history, however, it was also possible to show the logic of Providence in bringing forth inclinations that were necessary for the overall 'ethical' progression of the human species. National cultures built on one another, but also 'cured' the vices of a previous culture, generating new and previously unknown virtues and vices. Furthermore, whilst in each period it was possible to attain happiness, cultures differed in terms of their stability and also relationships to other cultures. They also all contained in themselves the seeds of their decay or possible abuse, albeit to a varying degree. For example, as we shall see, the original cycle of humanity's development lasted longest and was the most stable one; the later one was characterised by much more frequent change from the outset.

The Oriental period was followed by that of 'boyhood', the age of ancient agricultural Egypt and trading Phoenicians, both of which in contrasting ways exemplified the progressive development of arts and social differentiation, and the emergence of corresponding forms of civil administration (280–286). Without grazing pastures, the Egyptians had to develop a form of land ownership and the art of agriculture. This led to a differentiation of social ranks and a consciousness of one's standing in society, but also to the 'cultivation of justice, order, civil administration' (280–281). It was only natural that such a culture viewed foreign cultures – both the shepherding ones as well as the trading ones – with utmost suspicion, even hatred (281). The Phoenicians, at the same time, 'became to a certain extent their [the Egyptians'] *opposite in formation* (*Bildung*)', embarking on trade, developing a rudimentary form of republican freedom, and opening up to communication with other peoples through trade (284–285).

The Greek period, representing the time of humanity's 'youth', synthesised much of these earlier foundations, giving rise to distinctive inclinations towards 'Greek *lightness, gentleness, patriotism*' as well as '*the beautiful idea of a republic in a Greek sense*' and a new type of Greek '*universal spirit*' – '*their division* into peoples, *republics, colonies*, and yet the *common spirit* of these; *feeling of one nation, of one fatherland, of one language!* (286–287). The Greeks, at the same time, borrowed so much of their religion from the Orient, but with its 'holy veil taken away', putting everything '*on display* in the *theater* and the *market* and the *dancing place*', whereby religion became a fable, mythology (288). As we shall see in Chapter 6, Herder later elaborated on this fundamental problem in Greek culture in his prize essay on poetry's impact upon mores.

Finally, Herder identified humanity's period of 'manhood' in the history of ancient Rome, emphasising that it was the Romans' '*disregard for sensual gratifications*', '*heroic courage*', and rational planning that sustained their laws and constitution as well as their empire (289–290). Initially positively transforming '*the national manner of thought*' of each of its subjugated peoples and teaching them the '*art of statecraft, military art,* and *international law of peoples*', the Roman empire in its late period sank into a condition of exhaustion, enervation and death (290, 300).

A new cycle started after the Germanic conquest of Roman territories. The 'northern peoples', Herder argued, were essentially '*patriarchies as they were able to be in the north*'.[93] The northern climate had 'hardened human

---

[93] Herder refers to the following tribes: '*Goths, Vandals, Burgundians, Angles, Huns, Heruli, Franks* and *Bulgarians, Slavs* and *Lombards*' (301).

beings', and accordingly no 'Oriental shepherd's life' was possible there. Thus their condition remained '*more primitive*, their small societies were *more separated* and *wilder*, but human bonds [were] still in *strength*, human *drive* and force in fullness' (300). When 'this sea of northern peoples' began to move, waves of peoples were crushing into other peoples, 'the wall and dam around Rome was torn apart' (300). The northern European peoples mixed with the southern ones, and gave birth to a new kind of 'world' that stretched from the Mediterranean to the Black Sea, and from the Atlantic to the North Sea (301). Combined with the distinctive new 'yeast' of the Christian religion, the 'fermentation of northern-southern fluids' in the different European nations in this period gave rise to distinctively 'manly' Gothic 'inclinations and virtues of *honor* and *freedom*, of *love* and *bravery*, of *politeness* and *word*' in the next (301, 309). The modern European nations, finally, as we saw above, exhibited characteristics of an aged individual person, being prone to 'rationalizing', cold calculation and motivational weakness (308, 319; cf. 348).

These two ordering schemata (epochs and cycles) were unified in yet another of the metaphors Herder used to characterise European history: that of a growing tree. From the Oriental nations to the Romans, Herder argued, national cultures were like a tribal stem, solid and undiversified. The European nations in the middle period, by contrast, could be compared to the 'strongly striving, entwined *branches*' (331). None of them was in itself firm like a stem, but each was all the more 'extensive, airier, higher!' (310). The modern period, finally, was like the crown of a tree, consisting of 'airy, wide-spread *twigs*' swaying around in '*heavenly air*' (331).

This tree analogy very clearly reveals that Herder also posited a certain kind of continuity between the two cycles. Hence, he did not fully discard the idea of progressive development expressed in *Treatise of the Origin*, transforming it into a spiral one instead (299, 310, 331). As we have seen, in both cycles, for him, different nations represented stages of the development of the mind and character of mankind (by analogy to those of an individual human being). Yet he also identified an overall (although fractured) increase in abstract thinking and scope of cognition in history that in turn correlated with a progressive diversification of powers, an increasing division of labour in society, and a corresponding weakening of the intensity of feeling (292, 300, 348–352). As we know, Herder had already elaborated this kind of correlation in his *Journal of My Travels* when developing the typical developmental stages of individual psychology and in *Treatise* when describing the differences between the 'natural state' and modern societies. In *This Too a Philosophy*, Herder now specified its two key cycles, the second cycle starting at a significantly higher level of human thinking than the first one (348–349).

As argued above, Herder's thoughts on national happiness and virtue in *This Too a Philosophy* were embedded in his discussion of the first stage of human history, and his examples refer to the contacts and conflicts between the Orientals, Egyptians, Phoenicians, Greeks and Romans. The wider context of these remarks was his criticism of the two kinds of basic mistakes that modern philosophers of history committed when they discussed these early nations. They either searched for a 'favourite nation', a moral example among them, forgetting that virtues and vices were intricately interwoven in each national character (294–295). Or else they arrogantly looked down on them all, contrasting the strong and rough feelings of early sensuous nations (particularly the Orientals or Egyptians) with an '*ideal silhouette* of virtue from the compendium of [their] century' (294, cf. 332). In specifying the principles of nation-building and interaction between nations, Herder attempted to show that this kind of moral criticism was misplaced: these principles were necessary and 'natural' in their particular historical circumstances. Yet what happened to national prejudices and sentiments during the next stages of civilisation, the medieval European and modern cycles of development, was a different story. A further 'revelation' according to Herder was hidden here.

4.3.3   Christianity and Love of Humanity

In order to understand Herder's argument about the second cycle (and the second and third epoch) of human history, we first need to have a closer look at his conception of the role of the Christian religion in the historical process.

Wilhelm Schmidt-Biggemann has suggested that in his Bückeburg period Herder renounced his earlier account of history as a 'natural process' in favour of one in which Providence intervened in history through religious revelation.[94] Indeed, as we have seen above, Herder's four 'natural laws' served as the basic explanation for historical development as a 'natural' process in *Treatise on the Origin*. There was no discussion of the role of revelation or the Christian religion in human history. In *This Too a Philosophy*, by contrast, Herder not only presented historical epochs as forms

---

[94] Wilhelm Schmidt-Biggemann, 'Elemente von Herders Nationalkonzept', in *Nationen und Kulturen: Zum 250. Geburtstag von Johann Gottfried Herder*, ed. Regine Otto (Würzburg, 1996), 27–34; 28–29, 33.

of 'revelation' but also presented the emergence of Christianity as a kind of miracle, 'certainly the strangest event in the world!' (303).

This is not to say, however, that he sought to replace a naturalist approach with a theological one; rather, as we have seen above, he sought to achieve a continuity between these two perspectives. Furthermore, whether Herder really meant to claim that the emergence of Christianity could not be explained in natural terms need not be settled here. What is important in the present context is that Christianity for him was fundamentally different from any home-grown 'national religion'.[95] Whilst the latter were 'full of *images* and *disguises*, full of *ceremonies* and *national customs*, on which the essential duties always only *hung* and were *added*', the Christian religion was the '*first* that taught such *pure spiritual truths* and *such heartfelt duties, so completely without husk* and *superstition, without ornamentation* and *force*, that meant to improve the human heart so exclusively, so *universally*, so *entirely* and *without exception*' (303).

In clear polemical opposition to deists like Voltaire, who rejected Christianity precisely for its superstition and ornamentation, Herder labelled Christianity itself *the most human-loving deism*. In the teaching of Christ, he maintained, the Christian religion appeared as pure ethical thinking. For such a way of thinking to be possible, 'the human race had to be prepared [. . .] for so many millennia, to be *gradually drawn forth* from childhood, barbarism, idolatry, and sensuality' (304). In its purity and universality, the Christian religion was 'certainly religion of the *universe*' (304). Hence Christianity in its moral core was the '*true religion of humanity, the drive of love,* and *bond of all nations into one army*' (303).

In this view, Herder in a way concurred with Rousseau's characterisation of Christianity in the *Geneva Manuscript* (which was unknown to Herder). Rousseau, too, maintained that it was only Christianity that 'sufficiently generalised [. . .] the healthy ideas of natural right and of the common brotherhood [*fraternité*] of all men'.[96] Yet there is a striking contrast between the two authors in terms of their evaluation of the impact of Christianity on politics. Rousseau was adamant that 'the gentle laws of brotherhood which [the God of the wise] imposes on us, the social virtues of pure souls, which are the true cult he wants from us, will always escape the multitude'.[97] In the process of getting transformed into a religion for

---

[95] Cf. ibid., 32.
[96] Jean-Jacques Rousseau, 'From the early version of the Social Contract known as the Geneva Manuscript', in *The Social Contract*, 153–161 (158).
[97] Ibid., 156.

the multitude, he argued, Christianity had necessarily changed in character, becoming 'the most violent despotism in this world'.[98] Rousseau concluded that it was therefore necessary to 'leave aside the sacred precepts of the various Religions whose abuse causes as many crimes as their use may prevent'.[99]

In contrast to Rousseau, Herder consistently emphasised the universal moral message of Christianity. True, Herder, too, argued that in a sense, Christianity built on the Roman ideas of '*international law among peoples* previously unheard of on that scale', which widened the horizons of nations (304). In contrast to this 'philosophical' law that had no real impact on people's actions, however, Christianity addressed both the mind and the heart, opening up a prospect of the reunion of mankind. This could not be achieved in any other way than through becoming a religion for distinct peoples. Whilst Christ's teaching stood outside the natural course of things, its impact on this world could only be played out in accordance with it: When *in the whole analogy of nature* has the deity acted otherwise than through nature? (305) Therefore, Christianity, this 'purest theory of truths and duties', 'could [not] exist, be *applied*, without being mixed with more earthly materials [. . .] [such as] *each people's manner of thought, its ethics and laws, inclinations and abilities* – cold or warm, good or bad, barbaric or civilized [*gebildet*] – everything as it was' (305). Thus it penetrated all the matters of the 'northern-southern' nations, being the 'sole means of progress' in the Gothic period of European history (306).

Nevertheless, the early stage of sensuous and imaginative thinking in the Christian period of European history was distinct from its ancient counterpart precisely due to a higher degree of abstraction and refinement in thinking. 'In comparison with the ancient world [. . .] *the strength of each individual national character had been lost*', yet 'precisely in this *mixture* a *substitute* and *progress* towards a *greater whole*' could be beheld: 'Despite all the barbarism, the cognitions which got treated *scholastically* were *subtler* and *higher*, the *sensations* which got applied *barbarously* and *in a priestly way* were more *abstract* and *higher* – from these two things flowed the *ethics*, their image' (310–311).

According to Herder, this 'subtlety' was reflected in the way in which the individuals and groups of peoples related to each other. It was now 'so many *brother nations* and *no monarchy* on earth!' – 'all of one *German race*, all in accordance with *one ideal of constitution*, all in *faith in one religion*, each *fighting with itself* and with its *members*', whilst also being '*driven and*

[98] Rousseau, 'The Social Contract', 145.   [99] Rousseau, 'Geneva Manuscript', 157.

moved by one holy wind, papal respect' (311–312). In this respect, Herder argued, 'the papacy with all its violence became in the hand of fate the machine for [...] the *universal recognition of people who should be Christians!, brothers!, human beings!*'", establishing a 'still *higher connection*' between humans than the Roman '*international law of peoples*, and *universal recognition of the Romans*' (312). In the short run, the Christian religion had enabled the rise of a new form of despotism, whilst also introducing a genuine and practicable ideal of 'brotherhood of nations' in Europe, one that could hopefully be properly realised by future generations.

4.4   Modern Virtue

What, then, had gone wrong in European history for Herder? How did he characterise the role of Christian virtue in his own society? As we saw in Herder's critique of modern civilised monarchy, he did not believe that modern cosmopolitanism was animated by genuine Christian sentiments. Whilst celebrating the Reformation as one of the most important achievements and Luther as one of the greatest reformers in European history, Herder did not think Christianity had managed to continue serving as a source of morality and politics in modern times (354; cf. 312).[100] The main reason for this, in his view, was a dissociation between thought and sensation (feelings), religious faith included. Abstract thinking had been entirely cut off from its sensuous roots, as all received knowledge was gradually 'cast into *method*, into scientific form' (339). According to Herder, this created the conditions for the technological boom in Europe, which in turn transformed the nature of all of society. Modern 'simple, mechanical inventions' (315) radically increased the (necessarily progressive) division of labour, rendering a distinctively mechanical 'spirit' to modern commerce, warfare, and politics in general (316). Furthermore, by recruiting modern philosophy to directly support the cause of this spirit, '*clarity* and *mechanical skill*' were disseminated everywhere (324).

For Herder, Europe's relationship to the rest of the world was highly unstable. As we saw in Chapters 1 and 3, Herder, at an early point in his intellectual biography, already feared that excessive 'enlightenment' in Europe would provoke a violent reaction and a relapse into a form of

---

[100]   In addition to Luther, Herder explicitly referred to Gustavus Adolphus and Peter the Great as great reformers, proceeding to discuss also Frederick of Prussia and Voltaire (354–356).

pious 'savagery'.[101] Herder voiced similar fears about the future of Europe in *This Too a Philosophy*. The ways of Providence, Herder argued, often seemed to go 'over the corpses' and in so many cases nothing but further decay seemed to result from decay. For example, it was quite probable that the spread of modern 'mechanical' inventions would lead to a new 'act' in the play. Europe's exploitation of other parts of the world would occasion the latters' revolts, which in turn would bring about the collapse of the entire European states system (352).

Although *This Too a Philosophy* was certainly the most sinister-sounding of Herder's works, these fears and pessimism about Europe's future did not come with any kind of total resignation and fatalism, let alone moral nihilism. Even if human power to bring about significant moral and political reforms was severely limited, Herder argued, one had to hold on to 'the poles around which everything turns – *truth, consciousness* of *good intention, happiness of humanity!*' (356). Herder's historiography was designed to drive home the point that a relationship to God, and in modern Europe, Christianity, could and had to be the foundation of all morality, whilst it was not to be a form of mere inward piety, but one of active sociable disposition. This did not imply that it was exclusively Christians who could develop such a disposition, as also shown by Herder's reference to Socrates as a primary example of an 'enlightener' (342–343).[102] Nevertheless, active Christian virtue was simply the most direct and as we shall also see, 'purest', way to achieve it.

By invoking Socrates as his primary example, Herder indicated that it was possible to pursue and approximate these ethics in various kinds of societies. At the same time, he also acknowledged that the moral challenges of modern times needed to be met by the figure of a 'Socrates of our age' (342–349). The situation a modern Socrates faced, he argued, was much more difficult than that of his historical precursor as he lacked the latter's certainty in analysing the practical challenges of his age. The complexity of the modern world made virtuous acting intellectually far more demanding, especially because one now sought to take into account not only the immediate effects of one's actions on one's own society but also those on other societies. Ancient Socrates had already missed out on the joy of seeing the beneficial results of his action; the situation was in some ways worse in modern times. Good results would evolve only gradually and no

---

[101] See, in particular, Herder, '*Journal meiner Reise*', 419.
[102] Cf. Herder, 'On the Cognition (1778)', 222.

immediate rewards would and could be expected for a modern reformer personally (342–344).

The crucial challenge for modern people, Herder insisted, was not to make virtue a 'plaything'. This was best avoided when one studied particular cases and problems by using one's healthy understanding. Invoking ideas that he had expressed in his more optimistic reform period, Herder thereby called on the moderns to appreciate that Greek civic wisdom had never been purely universal, but had always related to the particular case and situation (323–324). Even if it was clearly so much more difficult to reason in this way in modern complex conditions, Herder maintained, there was no alternative to trying to do so. Recognising the very real danger that even the most well-meaning moral education would be subjected to abuse and utilised to justify selfish actions, Herder also advocated a strict separation of virtue and honour. Whilst thinkers like Iselin and Abbt had emphasised the importance of public recognition of merit for supporting the motivation for patriotic action, Herder in 1774 insisted that true and efficient moral education could only be achieved through *humility* and *hiddenness*. The most important thing was to follow virtue in one's own actions and to teach fellow human beings to love virtue mainly by one's 'quiet, godlike example' or gentle convincing (346).

Taking into account the general nature of modern developments, Herder concluded, it was only to be expected that there was less virtue in the modern world than previously. Nevertheless, he called not only on a few intellectuals but on 'all ranks and classes of *justice*, of *religion*, of the *sciences*, of individual *arts*' to follow the pull of virtue. He pointed to the special responsibility of the '*regents*' or '*guardians* of the *peoples*', who 'by *mere intention* and *encouragement*' could already do so much not only for their 'own flock', but also for the 'greater whole of humanity' (345–346). In particular, Herder encouraged the 'father[s]' and 'mother[s] in the poor huts' to do what they must – to *educate* (*bilden*) – whilst fully acknowledging the difficulties of modern life, i.e. its unpredictability and the heterogeneity of modern ethics and the general conditions of life (346).

Herder, using this analysis of virtue, was pointing towards Archbishop Fénelon's evocative analysis of 'pure virtue' or love of mankind.[103] As we have seen above, he did not believe that there was more virtue in the world than previously, quite the contrary. Although humans had been capable of

---

[103] Cf. Herder's own reference to Fénelon: 'Maybe, and certainly, infinitely fewer now have this virtue à la Fénelon than there were once Spartans, Romans, and *knights* who represented the sensuous bloom of their *world*'s and *age*'s *spirit*' (348–349). (I have slightly modified the translation here.)

virtue and happiness during each period of history, there were different ways of pursuing it. Nevertheless, he did argue that, in principle, a deeper understanding of 'pure virtue' had and could be reached in the modern period. Modern thinking, if animated by the sentiments of the Christian religion, and based on the effort to understand particular cases, could lead to a new kind of virtue – the highest, noblest, and purest kind of virtue. As such, Herder conceded with a dint of irony, it would even in some respects be superior to the 'virtue of other ages which, *awakened* by *promptings* and *rewards*, was in the end only *a citizen's appurtenance* and noble finery of the *body!*' (345). In an earnest spirit, Herder continued:

> So this always seems certain to me: the *fewer entirely* and *greatly* good people there may be in our century, the harder the *highest virtue* must *become for us*, and the *quieter,* the *more hidden* it now *can only* become – *where it exists,* then that much *higher, nobler,* perhaps at some time *infinitely useful* and *consequence-bearing,* [a] virtue [it is]! By our for the most part *abandoning* and *renouncing* ourselves, being unable to enjoy a number of immediate *rewards*, strewing the seed out *into the wide world* without seeing where it falls, takes root, whether even there it even eventually bears fruit *for the good*. [...] Entrust the seed to the wafting zephyr – it will carry it that much further; and when at some time there awaken all the germs to which the *nobler part of our century* also quietly and silently made its contribution – in what a blessed age my view loses itself! (347; cf. ibid. 345–346).

For Herder, there was as yet no indication that such a 'blessed age' really was approaching. Yet, if 'the *refinement* and the *purifying progress* of *concepts of virtue* from the *sensuous ages of childhood up through all of history*' as well as 'their *spreading about* and *progress into a wider world*' are clear, Herder asked, can't we also ask ourselves whether 'all this [is really] *without a purpose?, without an intention?*' (349). There was no other option for a modern human being than to acknowledge the 'limitedness of my point on the earth, the *binding* of my looks, the *failure* of my purposes' and still to trust that 'I am nothing but the *whole is everything*' (357). Even if we were completely unable to understand or prophesy how 'all the *light* and the *human disposition* that we were working for' could really be brought 'to *warmth,* to *permanence*, and to *complete bliss*', we had to 'work with courageous, happy hearts even *right in the middle of the cloud*' (353).

4.5   Conclusion

Although Herder in *This Too a Philosophy* was sceptical about any kind of direct patriotic commitment to a modern state, he did not think that the corruption of modern European society was a reason for withdrawing from society altogether. Already in the *Treatise*, Herder viewed reflective awareness as part of human self-preservation and sociability, whilst he later came to emphasise the universalistic aspirations inherent in Christianity. Indeed, he was adamant that embracing the right kind of Christian and humanistic spirit was exactly what was needed for 'reforms from below'; whilst a continuing commitment to one's closest family and society was an indispensable part of an ethic prescribed by it.

Let us conclude this chapter with a brief description of how Herder attempted to combine this double emphasis on natural sociability and Christian universalism in *On the Cognition*.[104] Here, for the first time, Herder made an attempt to theorise human freedom and self-determination in some detail. He first turned his polemic against both rationalists and sentimentalists in morality. In a Shaftesburian vein, he made clear that the deepest core of morality consisted in aiming at achieving order in man's natural inclinations and passions.[105] Herder emphasised that it could by no means involve suppressing one's natural inclinations or sensations as demanded by rationalist accounts of morality, 'because the best cognition arose from all of them [sensations] and continues to live in them'.[106] Yet this did not mean that we 'could heed every insistent knocking and welling of your [our] heart, every echo of an irritated fiber, as though it were the voice of God, and follow it blindly'.[107] Hence, what true 'cognition' achieved was to 'purify' (*läutern*) man's natural inclinations and feelings: 'The dross gets burned off but the true gold should remain. Every force and every irritation that sleeps in my breast should awaken and take effect only *in the spirit of my Creator*'.[108]

This kind of purification for Herder involved establishing 'order' (*Ordnung*) in one's inclinations, based on a living cognition of natural order as the realisation of divine thought-force and the special place of humanity in it. In order to achieve as much, humans would need to 'observe the great analogy of creation' consisting in sympathetic connections between all kinds of beings, particularly with those of one's kind. Humans should recognise that

> *self-* and *other-feeling humanity* (once again expansion and contraction) are the two expressions of the elasticity of our will; *love* is the noblest cognition,

---

[104] On the subtle differences between his ideas on virtue in the three different editions, see Heinz, *Sensualistischer Idealismus*, 109–174. In my brief summary here, I am drawing on the 1778 version.

[105] On Shaftesbury's significance for Herder, see Heinz, *Sensualistischer Idealismus*, 133–137.

[106] Herder, 'On the Cognition', 213.   [107] Ibid., 215.   [108] Ibid., 213.

as it is the noblest sensation. To love the great Creator in oneself, to love one's way into others, and then to follow this sure pull – that is moral feeling, that is conscience. It stands opposed only to empty speculation, but not to cognition, for true cognition is *loving*, is *feeling* in a human way.[109]

In outlining this kind of active and knowing formation of one's own character, Herder also described it as accepting one's 'servitude'. Harking back to Luther's denial of free will, on the one hand, and developing further the Spinozist doctrine of *amor dei*, on the other,[110] Herder highlighted the active and liberating element in such voluntary servitude: 'Hence it is truly the first seed of freedom to feel that one is not free, and with *which* bonds one is bound. [. . .] The deeper, purer, and diviner our cognition is, then the purer, diviner, and more universal our efficacy is, too, hence the freer our freedom.'[111] Furthermore, this activity and freedom, as we have seen, were by no means limited to the interior of one's self. Ordering one's inclinations and the formation of character had to lead to practical efficacy and active disposition in society. Every such reformer simply had to be prepared that it could take centuries for their teachings to have an impact on society. Nevertheless, Herder argued, 'a true *thought* or a *good* sensation is never lost. What is true and good is bound up with the sensorium of the creation, the great spirit on whose robe nothing comes to grief.'[112]

---

[109] Ibid., 213–214.
[110] Ibid., 216. For discussion, see Heinz, '1.2.4. *Vom Erkennen und Empfinden*', 137–138.
[111] Herder, 'On the Cognition', 215–216.   [112] Ibid., 222.

CHAPTER 5

German Freedom and Modern Liberty

As seen in Chapter 4, in the 1770s Herder advocated a distinctive form of modern virtue based on the Christian love of humanity and an affirmation of our 'freedom in bondage'. However, he also continued to think of himself as a German patriot. In a letter to Friedrich Nicolai, written from Paris in April 1769, Herder stated:

> my patriotism for Germany only grows stronger in direct relation to my experience of places and events, instead of weakening as in the cases of other expatriates. I am learning to be a better judge of and gaining a better overview of German literature, whilst I become acquainted with other peoples, and whilst I am at a remove from German truculence, as I wander amongst other nations in the hopes of dedicating myself more fully and completely to my fatherland.[1]

Although Herder sought to distance himself from the internal quarrels of his fellow nationals, his thinking on German issues was stimulated by an important controversy among German-speaking authors – the debate about German 'national spirit' (*Nationalgeist*) in the 1760s. As Chapters 1 and 2 have shown, Herder had already indicated his awareness of this debate in *Fragments* and approvingly analysed the writing style of two of its leading voices, Thomas Abbt and Friedrich Carl von Moser. He also closely followed the latest developments in German academic historiography and imperial history (*Reichsgeschichte*), and embarked on a serious study of German political history. One of the outcomes of this study was an essay entitled *How the German Bishops Became an Estate of the Realm* (*Wie die deutschen Bischöfe Landstände wurden*)[2] that Herder wrote for Göttingen

---

[1] Herder to Friedrich Nicolai, 30 April 1769, in *DA*, I, 175. Unless otherwise indicated, all translations from German or French in this chapter are mine.
[2] Johann Gottfried Herder, 'Wie die deutschen Bischöfe Landstände wurden', in *SWS*, V, 676–698. The translation of the title of this essay is from Clark, *Herder: His Life and Thought*, 197–199. Clark briefly discusses this essay to shed light on Herder's controversy with Spalding over the office of the

University's essay competition in 1774. In this little known essay, Herder spelled out his views on the ancient German constitution and the history of the Holy Roman Empire. In another important prize essay written five years later (*On the Influence of Governments on the Sciences, and of the Sciences on Governments* (1779/1780)) he returned to the political history of wider Europe, whilst also voicing some opinions about that of Germany specifically.[3]

These essays on German and European history have received only very limited attention in specialised studies of Herder. However, over the recent decades, a number of scholars have shed light on the role played by the institutions of the Holy Roman Empire in German political and intellectual life more generally.[4] In this context, scholars have also revisited the German debates on imperial patriotism (*Reichspatriotismus*)[5] and have begun to take interest in Herder's views on the history of the Holy Roman Empire. Engaging with this research, Markus Hien has recently argued that there was a 'novel form of national and political ego-narrative' emerging in the Holy Roman Empire following the Seven Years' War, one that hoped to promote a 'third way' in Germany that would lie between its current fragmented state and the centralism exemplified in the developments in France.[6] According to Hien, this political vision highlighted the positive aspects of the imperial constitution and developed in tandem with visions of cultural revival. In Hien's discussion, Herder emerges as one of its main architects.[7]

Alexander Schmidt, for his part, has situated Herder's essay *On the Influence of Governments* in a broader European discussion on the

---

pastor in a modern state. A longer discussion can be found in Heinz Stolpe, *Die Auffassung des jungen Herders vom Mittelalter* (Köln, Vienna, 1955), 442–454, 469–477.

[3] Johann Gottfried Herder, 'Vom Einfluß der Regierung auf die Wissenschaften, und der Wissenschaften auf die Regierung', in *FHA*, IX/2, 294–391.

[4] See, first of all, Georg Schmidt, *Geschichte des Alten Reiches: Staat und Nation in der Frühen Neuzeit: 1495–1806* (Munich, 1999) and the articles in Dieter Langewiesche and Georg Schmidt (eds.), *Föderative Nation: Deutschlandkonzepte von der Reformation bis zum Ersten Weltkrieg* (Munich, 2000) and Georg Schmidt, Martin van Gelderen and Christopher Snigula (eds.), *Kollektive Freiheitsvorstellungen im frühneuzeitlichen Europa (1400–1850)* (Munich, 2006).

[5] Alexander Schmidt, 'Ein Vaterland ohne Patrioten? Die Krise des Reichspatriotismus im 18. Jahrhundert', in *Die deutsche Nation im frühneuzeitlichen Europa: Politische Ordnung und kulturelle Identität?*, ed. Georg Schmidt (Munich, 2010), 35–64.

[6] Hien, *Altes Reich und Neue Dichtung*, 28–29. (My translation.)

[7] See Markus Hien, 'Mascovisch richtig oder voltärisch schön? Herders „idiotistische Geschichtsschreibung" im Wettkampf der Nationen', in *Sattelzeit: Historiographiegeschichtliche Revisionen*, ed. Elisabeth Décultot, Daniel Fulda (*Hallesche Beiträge zur Europäischen Aufklärung*) (Berlin/Boston, 2016), 83–101; Hien, *Altes Reich*, 151–186. Among contemporary scholars, only Hien has highlighted the central importance of *How the German Bishops* for understanding Herder's political views; see his *Altes Reich*, 172–178.

relationship between learning and political government, reading it as an answer to Rousseau's *First Discourse*. In providing his response to Rousseau, Schmidt argues, Herder was heavily drawing on Hume's and Robertson's accounts of the impact of the arts and sciences on government, thereby also indicating his (qualified) support to modern large and 'civilised' monarchies. Schmidt has also pointed out the essay's very different tone and ideas compared to Herder's views in *This Too a Philosophy*.[8]

This chapter and the next will seek to further specify Herder's accounts of German and European history, on the one hand, and of the history of German literature, on the other, so as to better situate them in his broader programme of reform thinking. As we saw in Chapter 4, in the 1770s Herder voiced sharp criticisms of large European monarchies. Whilst acknowledging the rise of the rule of law *within* them, he highlighted the continuing 'state of war' *between* them. He also deplored the rise of new forms of colonialism and imperialism in the extra-European world. Furthermore, he recognised that the laws and mores of modern states did not fully align, thus also casting doubts on the stability of 'modern liberty'. Instead of making continuous progress in all aspects of social life, modern monarchies were likely to give rise to new forms of military despotism.

But what kind of patriotism did Herder envision as possible or desirable in Germany, and what hope did he have for its emergence there? This chapter will focus on his discussion of the political history of Germany, the next on the literary one. Here, my main questions are as follows: What did Herder believe was particular to German history when compared with that of other large states in Europe? Did he embrace a conception of ancient German freedom and could he be qualified as a *Reichspatriot* (patriot of the Holy Roman Empire)? Was there a contradiction between his views in *How the German Bishops* and *This Too a Philosophy*, on the one hand, and *On the Influence of Governments*, on the other?

I begin by outlining the debate on German national spirit and Herder's earliest views on German political history, highlighting the relevance of Justus Möser's *History of Osnabrück* (*Osnabrückische Geschichte*) (orig. 1768) to the development of Herder's views on German history. I argue that Herder sought to understand the causal mechanisms that had led to the formation of modern European states, and specified the particular historical trajectories that the latter had traversed. He initially closely followed the debate on German 'national spirit' and set out his own view of the history of the Holy Roman Empire. I will also briefly return to Herder's engagement with

---

[8] Schmidt, 'Scholarship, Morals and Government', 267.

Montesquieu here, tracing his deepening criticism of the latter's ideas. I argue that both Justus Möser and Herder were fascinated by Tacitus's account of ancient German freedom but rejected Montesquieu's emphasis on the central role of nobility in pre-Christian German societies. Like Möser, Herder highlighted the original egalitarian nature of the ancient German constitution. Developing further his earlier views on 'ethopoeia' (see Chapter 2), he underlined the central lawkeeping role of priests and poets in this society. The developments that followed the Germanic conquest of Gaul had led to the rise of a distinct form of feudal despotism, rather than 'Gothic liberty'. Herder particularly emphasised the role of the Christian bishops in this process. The form of government that had emerged relied on a mixture of German and Roman principles and ways of thought. What was problematic about it, however, was not simply its mixed character, but its despotism and bellicosity. Roman ways of thought gained the upper hand in Frankish polity, and a peculiar friction emerged between military and ecclesiastical estates. The German case was specific, since the German emperors' military ventures in Italy had precluded the consolidation of territorial power as had happened in France or Spain. Following Möser, Herder in 1774 acknowledged the value of the constitution of the Holy Roman Empire in terms of limiting the power of territorial rulers.

At the same time Herder was, as his 1779 essay reveals, also willing to accept the benefits of large civilised European monarchies, and to a certain extent he here restated his 1765 views on modern liberty. As Schmidt has also highlighted, Herder now drew strongly on Scottish Enlightened narratives, offering a sophisticated account of Europe's post-medieval political history. In this essay, Herder clearly adopted a very different tone than was characteristic of his writings of 1774 and there is certainly a tension between *This Too a Philosophy* and *On the Influence of Government*. As we shall see, this can partly be explained by the different focus of these essays. While the former focused primarily on moral virtue and the impact of mores on political government, the latter discussed the relationship between political government and sciences (learning). In any case, the 1779 essay reveals there is little evidence for viewing Herder as a *Reichspatriot* in any strong sense. While Herder continued to identify as a 'German patriot' and often used the concept 'Germany' to denote the contemporary Holy Roman Empire, he was highly critical of its current constitution specifically and believed that Germany, in contrast to Britain or France, had not seen a similar flourishing of 'useful sciences', including those of commerce. I will thus seek to show that even in the 1770s, despite his criticisms of many problematic aspects of modern trade, Herder did not actually renounce his fundamentally positive view of commerce. He sought to show that the celebrated 'German freedom' in the Holy Roman Empire created as many problems as it prevented. The Germans were no less bellicose than other European states, but unlike their large neighbours in Europe they did not even develop the sciences of government and commerce properly. More generally, this meant that they could not partake of the benefits of modern liberty. The German imperial government was thus badly in need of reforms, yet the question was how the latter could be achieved and what kind of political ideal was to be pursued.

The chapter consists of three sections. First, I will outline the debate on the German national spirit in the 1760s and young Herder's views on the history of German people and the Holy Roman Empire. Second, I discuss Justus Möser's and Herder's views on the ancient German constitution. Third, I provide a reconstruction of Herder's ideas on modern European history and the special status of the Holy Roman Empire.

5.1 Herder and the Debate on the German National Spirit

5.1.1 *The Debate on the German National Spirit*

During the 1760s, a heated debate arose among German intellectuals on the question of defining the German 'national spirit'. In many ways, it was an extension of the debate on modern patriotism (see Chapter 1) except that here the focus shifted to the 'German' question specifically. Considering the political context of these discussions – the ongoing Seven Years' War, in which the German dynasties of Hohenzollern and Habsburgs were on opposite sides – it was a logical development.

One German author in particular did much to shift the issue of the German constitution to the forefront – Friedrich Carl von Moser, son of the famous Imperial lawyer Johann Jacob Moser. In a minor work entitled *The Lord and the Servant* (*Der Herr und der Diener*) (1759) Moser compared the servility of German ministers to the British ideal of 'public spirit', which combined patriotism and independent thinking. Two years later he published another long essay with an emphatic title *Heartfelt Thoughts* (*Beherzigungen*) (1761), in which he specifically addressed the relationship of the growth in Prussian patriotism to Christianity.[9] Translating the dynastic conflict of the

---

[9] Moser was initially an admirer of Frederick the Great, but had come to the conclusion that Frederick lacked true commitment to Protestant Christianity, despite the efforts of a number of hired pens seeking to present Frederick as a defender of the Protestant cause. In 1764, Moser was granted a yearly

Seven Years' War into something like a national crisis, Moser bemoaned the unity of 'Germany' being violated by German territorial rulers.[10] Pointing at Frederick the Great's contempt for Christianity and his 'aggression' against German 'brother-states' in the Holy Roman Empire, Moser accused Frederick of setting up an 'un-Christian government'. 'Patriotism' or 'political virtue' in a state governed by such a monarch was a sign of man's fallen nature, a new kind of 'political superstition' in which God was replaced by the state as an object of veneration. In contrast to Christian virtue and true patriotism grounded in it, Moser argued, 'political virtue' was based on (alleged) utility and involved hatred against anyone outside one's own political community. It did not therefore deserve to be called 'virtue' at all. Tacitly invoking Montesquieu's distinctions between 'political' and 'moral virtue' as well as 'false honour' and 'true honour', Moser insisted that the new kind of patriotism was a 'political principle', not true virtue:

> in the new monster of 'political virtues', God is completely forgotten, common good only weakly considered, fellow citizens made respectable only from the selfish side and the main focus laid on the advantages of the ruler, on the greatness and power of the state, and on the blind obedience and overt diligence of the subjects.[11]

Moser pleaded with his readers that it was vital to revive the true, Christian and brotherly German foundations of the Holy Roman Empire in order to halt the progress of this false morality.[12]

---

pension from the court in Vienna for defending the cause of the Habsburgs as a Protestant writer. On Moser's switch of allegiance see H. H. Kaufmann, *F.C. v. Moser als Politiker und Publizist* (*Quellen und Forschungen zur hessischen Geschichte*, XII) (Darmstadt, 1931), 101–110, cf. also the analysis of Wolfgang Burgdorf, *Reichskonstitution und Nation: Verfassungsprojekte für das Heilige Römische Reich Deutscher Nation im politischen Schrifttum von 1648 bis 1806* (Mainz, 1998), 190–195.

[10] Nicholas Vazsonyi, 'Montesquieu, Friedrich Carl von Moser and the National Spirit Debate in Germany, 1765–1767,' *German Studies Review*, 22:2 (1999), 225–246 (232–236). Vazsonyi points out that Moser's ideas resonated with some of the isolated attempts by German lawyers to respond to Montesquieu's idea of 'spirit of the laws', most notably, Johann Heumann's recent discussion of Montesquieu in his *Geist der Gesetze der Deutschen* (1761), ibid., 231. On Moser in the context of long-term debates on imperial patriotism, see Schmidt, 'Ein Vaterland ohne Patrioten?', 42–44. On Moser's assessment of the Peace of Westphalia as the origin of German absolutism, see Patrick Milton, 'Guarantee and Intervention: the Assessment of the Peace of Westphalia in International Law and Politics by Authors of Natural Law and of Public Law, c. 1650–1806', in *The Law of Nations and Natural Law, 1625–1850*, ed. Simone Zurbuchen (Leiden, 2019), 186–226 (196–197).

[11] Moser, *Beherzigungen* (1761), 328.

[12] Moser's use of the term 'political virtue' was probably inspired by Montesquieu's distinction between political and moral virtue in *The Spirit of the Laws*. However, while Montesquieu had wanted to use the term political virtue to designate republican virtue, Moser ridiculed his contemporaries who admired Frederick and who (like Abbt) wanted to use this term to refer to monarchical patriotism.

This attack upon Frederick II and the growth in Prussian patriotism prompted Thomas Abbt to write a review of Moser's *Heartfelt Thoughts*; he even planned to write a book entitled *Heartfelt Counter-Thoughts* (*Gegenbeherzigungen*).[13] Abbt responded to Moser by elaborating on the relationships between Prussian patriotism and utilitarian political virtue, on the one hand, and those between the former and moral and Christian virtue, on the other.[14] In his review, Abbt also raised a fundamental question about Moser's criticism of Prussian patriotism:

> What kind of man does *Herr von M.* [Moser] want then? A cosmopolitan? He would certainly wish all men well and as far as it depends on him, he would promote their good. A German citizen? In this case he should first show what common laws and duties are shared by the subjects of different German princes. As soon as, however, the subjects of Prussia and Austria become involved, as soon as their rulers have different interests, it is no longer the duty of the Prussian or Austrian subject to study what the German Empire demands of them, but what he owes to his fatherland, that is, to the country whose laws protect him and make him happy. If he fulfils this obligation even at the most challenging of times, then he is a Prussian or Austrian patriot.[15]

Moser could not disagree more. His literary crusade against German factionalism culminated in *On German National Spirit* (*Vom deutschen Nationalgeist*) (1765), which was followed by further clarifications in *Relics* (*Reliquien*) (1766). The famous opening sentences of *On German National Spirit* can be seen as a direct response to Abbt's challenge:

> We are one nation, of one name and language, under one common head of empire, under one single constitution, our rights and duties are determined by the same laws, held together by one major common interest in freedom, united by a national assembly of more than one hundred years standing set up to pursue this goal, the first *Reich* in Europe in terms of internal power and strength, the royal crowns of which glisten on the German heads.[16]

---

[13] See Abbt's letter to Moses Mendelssohn (undated, 1763), Abbt, 'Freundschaftliche Korrespondenz,' in idem, *Vermischte Werke*, ed. Friedrich Nicolai (Hildesheim, 1978; reprint Berlin and Stettin, 1780), II:3, 48.

[14] For a more detailed reconstruction of Abbt's answer to Moser, see Piirimäe, 'Thomas Abbt', 201–209.

[15] Anon. [Abbt], 'Von des Herrn von Moser *Beherzigungen*,' *Briefe, die neueste Literatur betreffend* (1761), XI, Literaturbriefe 178–180, 1–38 (28).

[16] 'Wir sind ein Volck, von einem Namen und Sprache, unter Einem gemeinsamen Oberhaupt, unter Einerley unsere Verfassung, Rechte und Pflichten bestimmenden Gesetzen, zu Einem gemeinschaftlichen grossen Interesse der Freyheit verbunden, auf Einer mehr als hundertjährigen National-Versammlung zu diesem wichtigen Zweck vereinigt, an innerer Macht und Stärcke das

Of course, Moser recognised and indicated that reality in the Holy Roman Empire was the exact opposite of this idealised picture – he granted that the religious split between Catholics and Lutherans, the self-interested behaviour of major territorial states (primarily, Prussia) and general indifference regarding laws had made Germany an object of ridicule by other nations. However, he insisted that Abbt was wrong to dismiss the relevance of the Holy Roman Empire to German patriots with sleight of hand. From a historical point of view, the history of the Holy Roman Empire was that of the German nation; thus the German 'national spirit' should entail a cherishing of the constitution and the distinctive form of freedom it guaranteed. It was thanks to this 'German freedom' that no ruler was an absolute master over his subjects. Moser saw Germans as 'free within the alliance (*Bund*) and protection afforded by laws'.[17] It was just a highly regrettable fact that Germans 'no longer knew themselves'.[18]

In the ensuing controversy, various writers disputed Moser's overly rigid association of the German 'national spirit' with the constitution of the Holy Roman Empire and the behaviour of territorial rulers and their courts. A writer named Johann Jacob Bülau, for example, recommended a much broader comparison of different European 'national characters' that had historically developed in different fields – war and peace, commerce and sciences, religion and law.[19] In his review of Moser's and Bülau's works, the Osnabrück lawyer Justus Möser approved of this criticism and wrote in a programmatic spirit:

> But where do we find the nation? At [royal] courts? No one claims that. In cities, there are misguided and corrupt copies [presumably of the nation], in the army dressed-up machines, in the countryside oppressed peasants. Only at the time when every Frank or Saxon was cultivating a *paterna rura* (his allodial-free hereditary manor, independent from any feudal or manor lord), [...] was it possible to see a nation.[20]

---

erste Reich in Europa, dessen Königs-Cronen auf Deutschen Häuptern glänzen [...]', Friedrich Carl von Moser [Anon.], *Von dem deutschen National-Geist* (Frankfurt/ Main, 1766), 5.

[17] Moser [Anon.], *Von dem deutschen National-Geist*, 8–13.
[18] Friedrich Carl von Moser, *Reliquien* (Frankfurt/ Main, 1766), 239. On discussions about 'German freedom', see Georg Schmidt, 'Die Idee "deutsche Freiheit". Eine Leitvorstellung der politischen Kultur des Alten Reiches', in *Kollektive Freiheitsvorstellungen im frühneuzeitlichen Europa* (1400–1850), ed. Georg Schmidt, Martin van Gelderen and Christopher Snigula (Munich, 2006), 159–189.
[19] Johann Jacob Bülau, *Noch etwas vom deutschen Nationalgeiste* (Lindau am Bodensee, 1766), 53–54.
[20] Justus Möser, '[Review of] Johann Jacob Bülau, *Noch etwas zum Nationalgeiste*' (Lindau am Bodensee, 1766), *Allgemeine deutsche Bibliothek*, VI:1, 4 (1768).

At the same time, Möser did not dispute the role played by the history of the Holy Roman Empire in understanding the current situation in Germany; in his view, it was just necessary to focus on specific German territories and the German peoples who had originally lived in them if one wished to identify something like a historical 'German nation' as well as trace the development of German national character.

5.1.2   Herder on 'Pragmatic' German History

The young Herder initially made no direct comment on the question of German 'national spirit' but asked more generally what a 'German history' might look like. In a minor essay written, during his stay in Riga, in response to Christian Adolf Klotz's *Essay on the History of Taste and Art on the Basis of Coins* (*Beytrag zur Geschichte des Geschmacks und der Kunst aus Münzen*) (1766) and entitled *On Imperial History: A Historical Walk* (*Über die Reichsgeschichte: ein historischer Spaziergang*) (1767/1768), Herder argued that a genuinely 'German history' could neither be written 'à la Grèque nor à la Françoise [*sic*!], despite what our grecianising or frenchifying refined thinkers [*Schöndenker*] demand'.[21] Herder then developed a theme that he had already pursued in *Fragments*, pointing out that, ideally, such a history would need to philosophically study the earliest forms of national mythology and songs.[22] However, since the German songs were all lost and their 'bards' thus 'silent', one then had to rely on descriptions by 'foreigners' who were very different from the Germans – Greeks and Romans who clearly saw the Germans with their own distinctive 'eyes'.[23] An 'internal pragmatic history' in the spirit of the Greeks was thus unattainable for Germans. One also had to accept that while Greek and Roman histories were republican histories (a 'great arena (*Schauplatz*) of Greek culture and freedom' or that of 'Roman spirit of conquest'), German history was largely an imperial history, the history of the Holy Roman Empire and its most peculiar political constitution, 'in which for centuries there had reigned a great chaos, from which in the end dukes,

---

[21] Johann Gottfried Herder, 'Drittes Kritisches Wäldchen', in *SWS* III, 461–471 (463).

[22] Ibid. 'Aus dieser Blume von eigner Nationalmythologie wird mit der Zeit die Frucht reifer wahrer Geschichte, ohne wundersame Einpfropfungen und Bezauberungen, nach dem Laufe der Natur. Und eben das Ordentliche dieses Naturlaufes ergänzet ungemein die Lücken der ältesten Geschichte. Die ersten historisch Dichterischen Mythologisten waren eine Produktion ihres Zeitalters: der Zeitgeist nahm ihnen allgemach immer mehr von ihrem Dichterischen Wunderbaren: sie fanden das Zeitalter der Wahrheit – Wie viel läßt sich nun bei diesem ungestörten Naturlaufe rückwärts schließen?', ibid.

[23] Ibid., 463–464.

counts, lords, bishops and prelates had emerged, making up Germany'.[24] Emperors had only played a very limited role in this. Thus, there was also no point in writing this history in a 'French' manner, like a painter seeking to sketch portraits of 'characters', which also reflected the individuals' morals; a very different approach was needed. If one was also properly interested in studying history, and not in engaging in abstract political reflection, one had to separate historical narration from opinions and conjectures, even though, quite clearly, no meaningful history was possible without the latter.[25] Furthermore, from the point of view of legal and ecclesiastical history, German history also, most distinctly, included the history of another state, Italy.[26] Understanding this entwinement of German and Italian history was a key to German history, even if the resulting mixture was not exactly inspiring or pleasant:

> Priests had served to convert the Germans to follow the Pope, and these Papal Apostles, starting with St. Bonifacius, became the first imperial princes; priests and bishops became the first imperial estates and barons: the first small sovereigns and disturbers of peace. [This was] Not only because Germany, from its inception had adopted an ecclesiastical form before other states did, but also because long afterwards its wars were so often related to priestly disputes and bishops' privileges. And since these higher and juridical clergymen (*Rang- und Rechtsgeistliche*) – two heads, one in and one outside Germany: [it is] no wonder thus that the centre of German deeds and history therefore for so long and so often falls outside of Germany, in Italy, in Rome – one new source of historical confusion! And when this popish-Italian-German story for so long and often again contained nothing but disputes about rank, church and law, [it is] no wonder that these [histories] must also be the driest, most entangled, and often unappealing? And yet they must be.[27]

In order not to 'write a mere history of princes, emperors or popes, but a history of the German people', Herder concluded, it was thus necessary to focus on the history of the latter wherever it took place – be it Italy or Swabia. Also in the early modern period, one had to pay attention to broader developments. For example, the eras of Maximilian I and Charles V coincided with the formation of the modern state, and thus here one

---

[24] Ibid., 466–467.
[25] Ibid., 468. See also Herder's reflections about the relationship between 'history' (*Geschichte*) and 'judgement' (*Urteil*) or 'system' (*Lehrgebäude*) in *The Older Critical Grove* (*Älteres Kritisches Wäldchen*), Johann Gottfried Herder, 'Älteres Kritisches Wäldchen' (1768/1769), in *FHA*, II, 11–23. On Herder's criticism of contemporary universal history as represented by Göttingen-based historians, see Hien, *Altes Reich*, 157–164.
[26] Herder, 'Drittes Kritisches Wäldchen', 468.   [27] Ibid., 468–469.

also had to trace the ways in which politics, literature and religion were transformed, giving rise to a new 'spirit' in Europe.[28]

Far from calling upon the Germans to straightforwardly embrace Moser's 'national spirit' combining Christian virtue with the veneration of the constitution of the Holy Roman Empire, the young Herder thus asked penetrating questions about the identity of German history and, indeed, that of the German people. We will see below how he himself attempted to write such history in the 1770s. Herder's approach resonated most closely with that of Justus Möser who, too, had voiced a call to investigate how the original German peoples' society, institutions and the way of thought had developed over the course of centuries. For both Herder and Möser it was important not only to provide an answer and alternative to Moser, but also to learn from, as well as correct, Montesquieu.

5.2   New Kind of 'German' History

5.2.1   Möser's History of Osnabrück

In 1768 Justus Möser published the first volume of his *History of Osnabrück (Osnabrück Geschichte)*, which provided Herder with an example of how a genuinely 'German' history could be written. Möser invited German historians to programmatically trace the history of the Holy Roman Empire back to the political institutions of the original German peoples. Focusing on his native Prince-Bishopric of Osnabrück in Saxony, Möser himself set out a historical narrative of the transformations of the Saxon 'nation' in German history.[29] As Möser argued in his preface to *History of Osnabrück*, the task of a historian was to delineate the trajectories in which 'humans, rights and concepts have gradually developed'. His broader goal, Möser declared, was to specify the impact that a nation's 'laws, customs, the virtues and shortcomings of rulers, [their] false or good principles, commerce, money, cities, service, nobility, languages, opinions, wars and relations' have on its 'legislative power and state constitution'.[30]

---

[28] Ibid., 469–470.

[29] H. L. Welker highlights the differences between 'Volk' and 'Nation' for Möser. In contrast to 'Volk', 'Nation' was related to political representation; see H. L. Welker, *Rechtsgeschichte als Rechtspolitik, Justus Möser als Jurist und Staatsmann*, 2 vols. (Osnabrück, 1996), 199–201.

[30] Justus Möser, 'Vorrede', in *Osnabrückische Geschichte: allgemeine Einleitung* (Osnabrück, 1768) (unpaginated); cf. Möser, 'Deutsche Geschichte', in: Johann Gottfried Herder, Johann Wolfgang Goethe, Justus Möser, *Von deutscher Art und Kunst* (Leipzig, 1966), 98.

To signpost his admiration for Möser's work, Herder reprinted the long preface of *History of Osnabrück* in his *On German Style and Art* (1773). From Herder's perspective, as we shall see below, Möser's work was significant on two counts in particular. Extensively drawing on ancient and early modern sources (most notably, Tacitus' *De moribus Germanorum* (*On the Mores of the Germans*) and German *Reichspublizistk* and *Reichshistorie*),[31] Möser significantly contributed to the discussions about the German 'national spirit', while also providing a response to Montesquieu's account of the origins of modern monarchy.[32] First, Möser put forward an evocative analysis of the political constitution of the ancient Germans, which served as an inspiration for Herder's own analysis. Second, Möser described the history of the Holy Roman Empire as a series of unintended consequences and complex intertwinements of various national characters. At the same time, Herder was only prepared to share, to a limited degree, Möser's relative optimism about the re-emergence of 'freedom' in German history.

The first volume of *History of Osnabrück* focused on the incremental transformations that the ancient German constitution underwent until the reforms of Charlemagne were implemented. The ancient 'Saxon nation', Möser argued, was composed of freeholders who participated in a 'national assembly' and served in national militia (*Heerbann*). Möser declared that the 'history of Germany would take an entirely new turn', if one traced the history of the 'common landed proprietors' through different historical phases. Such a history would 'construct a body of nation from [these proprietors]', viewing 'the great and small servants of the nation as good or bad accidents to the body'. The territorial estates, first of all the nobility, were thus merely 'servants' or 'accidents' to the nation.[33]

An immediate point of reference for Möser was Montesquieu's very different account. Montesquieu had famously argued that 'the English have taken their idea of political government from the Germans',[34] whilst simultaneously seeking to show that the origins of European monarchies lay in the 'corruption of the government of a conquering people', whereby he was referencing the transformations of the ancient German government after conquering the land of Roman Gaul. As the German conquerors were no longer able to assemble in these large territories they

---

[31] On this intellectual context, see Jonathan Knudsen, *Justus Möser and the German Enlightenment* (Cambridge, 1985), 99–109.
[32] It is beyond the scope of this book to offer a detailed reconstruction of Möser's response to Montesquieu; it would be a worthwhile subject for a future study.
[33] Möser, 'Vorrede'; 'Deutsche Geschichte', 98.
[34] Montesquieu, *The Spirit of the Laws*, XI:6, 166.

began to 'deliberate on [their] business [...] by representatives'.[35] The Gothic model of government that came into being at that point was a mixture of monarchy and aristocracy, eventually evolving into a hierarchy of 'intermediate, subordinate, and dependent powers'.[36]

It is important to note that Montesquieu identified the origins of these powers as lying in the original role played by the nobility in the ancient German constitution. As Michael Sonenscher has clarified, Montesquieu, in the final two books of *The Spirit of the Laws*, sought to show how the juridical power that had initially been vested with kings in the original German polities had been transferred to the nobility in a series of unintended developments.[37] The ancient Germans, Montesquieu argued, drawing on Tacitus and Caesar, were free and martial peoples whose kings and military leaders were merely elected on the basis of their nobility and valour respectively. The kings served double functions, involving jurisdiction and the highest military leadership, and attracted a circle of followers (*comites*).[38] According to Montesquieu, during Tacitus' time the German peoples were basically in a 'state of nature' as described in the third chapter in Book One of *The Spirit of the Laws*.[39] They not only quarrelled with each other but also suffered internal conflict with families constantly waging war on one another over 'murders, robberies, and insults'.[40] They only 'came out of that state of nature'[41] when the Salic Franks established rules or 'settlements' as to how injured parties could gain 'satisfaction' in the form of a graduated fine or 'composition' (blood money) for an injury. While those accused of injury had to pay a fine to the court, called 'fredum', the kings relied on vassals to enforce this system.[42] Originally vassals were paid for this service by lords awarding them rights to shares in plunder, given at will. Having no other 'industry than tending their flocks', Germans originally had no landed property,[43] only tiny strips of land around their huts, called *salus* that were passed along the paternal line (women not being allowed to inherit a *salus*).[44] After their invasion of Roman Gaul, the Franks became more settled, establishing landed property. Now, service came to be paid in land, while

---

[35] Ibid., XI:8, 167.   [36] Ibid., XI:8, 167–168; II:4, 17.
[37] Sonenscher, *Before the Deluge*, 138–139. The following summary rests on Sonenscher's interpretation, ibid. ch. 2.; see also the shorter summary in Sonenscher, *Jean-Jacques Rousseau*, 37–39.
[38] Montesquieu, *The Spirit of the Laws*, XXX:3, 621; XXX:16, 640.   [39] Ibid., XXX:19, 647–648.
[40] Ibid., XXVIII:17, 552.   [41] Ibid., XXX:19, 647–648.
[42] Sonenscher, *Before the Deluge*, 143.
[43] Montesquieu, *The Spirit of the Laws*, XXX:3, 621; XXX:16, 640.
[44] Sonenscher, *Jean-Jacques Rousseau*, 37.

fiefs, in turn, became hereditary. The intrinsic connection between fiefs and jurisdiction, however, was preserved.[45] As Sonenscher has pointed out, Montesquieu located the 'origin of the jurisdiction of the lords' in this development.[46] In keeping with the customs governing the inheritance of *salus*, the fiefs were also inherited solely through the male line, which gradually also became linked to primogeniture. This was the origin of the 'feudal system'. In France, these laws also applied to inheriting the French throne. Through a sequence of steps, thus, the original roles of the nobility and the king were switched – the power to judge became the prerogative of the nobility, while military leadership passed into the hands of the king.[47]

Möser's account, by contrast, notes that ancient Saxons already owned land and enjoyed equal status in the national assembly. They could also try each other in court. The vassals (*comites*) had no special function in lawkeeping, their role was to accompany the chiefs on military adventures. Möser also highlighted the role of German priests in serving as mediators and peacekeepers at the assembly; they bestowed a sacred character to everything related to public affairs.[48] In the first and 'golden' period, as Möser described it, the term 'freedom' was used to designate a 'hateful exception to the common defense',[49] and it was only servants (*Leute, Knechte*) who were free from performing such duties. 'Honour' consisted in doing one's duty. It was bound with the idea of 'common property' and 'fatherland' (*geimeine Eigentum* und *Vaterland*). No free man was bound to follow a lord, while kings were merely elected 'common chiefs' (*gemeine Vorsteher*) who confirmed the verdicts made by their 'juridical peers' (*Rechtsgenossen*), i.e. other commoners.[50] No special enforcement mechanism was needed for maintaining the rule of law.

Following the Frankish conquest of Saxony things changed. Möser highlighted a bifurcation in the history of ancient German constitutions. In Sweden and Poland, he argued, commoners retained their original rights to self-government and justice, whereas in France and Germany they did not.[51] Commoners in Germany gradually lost their right to elect their own judges which they also had previously sent to represent them at the national (imperial) assembly. There the emperor appointed representatives for the commoners, while the position of representative in turn became hereditary.[52] As Möser maintained in his preface, feudalism

[45] Sonenscher, *Before the Deluge*, 143–144.
[46] Montesquieu, *The Spirit of the Laws*, XXX:18, 645; 30:20, 143.
[47] Sonenscher, *Jean-Jacques Rousseau*, 38.   [48] Möser, *Osnabrückische Geschichte*, 72–80.
[49] Möser, 'Vorrede'; Möser, 'Deutsche Geschichte', 99.   [50] Möser, *Osnabrückische Geschichte*, 15.
[51] Ibid., 119.   [52] Möser, *Osnabrückische Geschichte*, 118–119.

emerged during the time of Louis the Pious through the influence of Christian bishops and imperial stewards. The latter encouraged kings to finalise laws in written form, giving kings greater freedom in their interpretation, which then necessitated their enforcement by violent means.[53] Imperial stewards became increasingly important in the empire.

At the same time, bishops and imperial stewards were also given more freedom to hire various kinds of servants for their residences, and freeholders were forced to follow their example. They thus gradually lost their communal 'honour', i.e. the duty of serving in national militia.[54] Emperor Otto the Great established a new system in which fiefs were given to the knights who served him in his foreign wars, as a reward for these services, and an imperial-feudal military system replaced common defence (*Wehre*).[55] Political transformations naturally followed from these economic and social changes.[56] In the third period, which was 'full despotism', the meaning of 'common honour' and the 'true conception of property' were completely forgotten and the 'entire imperial realm was transformed into feudal estates, copyholds, and peasant farms, as it pleased the head of the Empire and his vassals'.[57] Honour became associated with feudal service rather than the common defence of fatherland as before. For Möser, feudalism was thus a royal usurpation of the original rights enjoyed by common freeholders (*Landeigentümer*).[58]

Second, Möser also attempted to show how freedom had re-emerged in Germany. A key to understanding this re-emergence was the 'wonderful narrows and curvatures through which humans have driven forth their proclivity to territorial sovereignty [*Territorialhoheit*]' there.[59] For Möser, the rise of (limited) territorial sovereignty served as a counterbalance to the despotism of emperors in the Holy Roman Empire. At the same time, he also highlighted the impact of 'Christianity, the German heart and an understanding of morality that is supportive of freedom' in this process.[60] 'German genius and industry', Möser maintained, was particularly suited to writing a history that would illuminate such countervailing powers and calculate their effects.[61] Möser concluded his preface by arguing that it was no small matter whether history was properly understood or not. The parties in the recent Seven Years' War had relied on a 'comfortable philosophy' (*bequeme Philosophie*) – that of natural law deduced from abstract

---

[53] Ibid., 42.   [54] Möser, 'Vorrede'; Möser, 'Deutsche Geschichte', 98.   [55] Ibid., 98–99.
[56] Ibid., 100.   [57] Ibid., 38, translation of the citation from Knudsen, *Justus Möser*, 104.
[58] We will return to Möser's views on subsequent developments in the Holy Roman Empire in Chapter 6.
[59] Möser, 'Vorrede'; Möser, 'Deutsche Geschichte', 98, 107.   [60] Ibid., 98.   [61] Ibid., 107.

principles.[62] In Möser's view, the philosopher Christian Thomasius had given a completely new twist to the original principles of the Peace of Westphalia, carelessly encouraging the application of mere 'raisonnement' (*Räsonieren*) to it.[63] Möser's message was rather obvious: it was not absolute monarchy but rather the principles of limited territorial sovereignty and the Imperial constitution that the German representatives had originally sought to defend through the Peace of Westphalia. However, now it was retrospectively interpreted as encouragement towards absolute sovereignty. Characteristically, during the recent Seven Years' War little interest was shown in the ideas of Grotius, since the latter could actually be seen as a countermodel to this kind of abstract thinking, connecting 'history, scholarly erudition, and philosophy'. To Möser, however, things were improving insofar as new legal scholars were emerging who sought to develop the Grotian approach, drawing on legal history rather than sheer sovereign force in solving religious conflicts. The true authority of princes and courts, Möser insisted, depended on their reliance on such advisors. As his model, Möser invoked David Georg Strube, a Göttingen legal scholar, whom he in turn presented as an authentic follower of Hugo Grotius.[64]

5.2.2   Herder's History of the Holy Roman Empire

As we saw in the previous section, Herder had already taken an interest in German history in the late 1760s, before reading Möser's *History of Osnabrück*. However, Möser's account demonstrated that it was possible to use information that Tacitus and other Roman writers had provided on the language, mores, social order and political customs of the German peoples to capture their characteristic way of thought (*Denkart*) and political institutions. Indeed, as we shall see, in his prize essay, *How the Bishops Became an Estate in the Imperial Realm*, Herder subscribed to some

---

[62] Ibid., 105, 108.

[63] On Thomasius, see Ian Hunter, Frank Grunert and Thomas Ahnert, 'Introduction', in *Christian Thomasius: Essays on Church, State, and Politics*, ed. and trans. Ian Hunter, Frank Grunert, and Thomas Ahnert (*Natural Law and Enlightenment Classics*, ed. Knud Haakonsson) (Indianapolis, 2007), IX–XXI. For German assessments of the Peace of Westphalia, see Milton, 'Guarantee and Intervention'. As far as I am aware, Thomasius's and Möser's contributions to these debates have not been discussed in the literature so far. They would clearly merit further study.

[64] Möser, 'Vorrede'; idem, 'Deutsche Geschichte', 108. For the reception of Grotius in Germany, see Frank Grunert, 'The Reception of Hugo Grotius's *De iure belli ac pacis* in the Early German Enlightenment', in *Early Modern Natural Law Theories: Contexts and Strategies in the Early Enlightenment*, ed. Timothy Hochstrasser and Peter Schröder (*Archives internationales d'histoire des idées/International Archives of the History of Ideas*, Vol. 186) (Dordrecht, Boston, London, 2003), 89–105.

key elements in Möser's views about the original German constitution, while also approvingly citing it in a number of contexts. At the same time, like Möser, he rejected Montesquieu's account of the origins of modern monarchy, whilst sharing and following the latter's emphasis on the importance of unintended consequences in human history. Indeed, he here restated in even more stark terms his earlier argument about the positive role that even morally repugnant developments can play in a general scheme of things in the long run. One of these developments was the emergence of an independent estate of clergy in the Holy Roman Empire. As Herder put it in *How the German Bishops*:

> I demand just one [thing]: that the clergy in this political constitution should also be treated as human beings, that is, as (led by) physical drives, not as non-human beings or superhumans. History is the natural philosophy [*Naturlehre*] of succeeding events, but in natural philosophy one does not moralise about how the animal should be according to our desires, but rather [asks] how, whence, and for what purpose it does exist, and then one sees later that there is no absolute poison in Nature which might not on the whole be also a medicament and balm.[65]

First of all, Herder followed Möser in describing the ancient German political institutions as based on 'peace and freedom' (*fredum* and *freiheit*). The ancient German peoples (*deutsche Völker*), Herder argued, in Möser's vein, were originally free peoples who did not recognise any kings or lords, or 'power over laws, body, life and death'.[66] Every free person viewed himself as representing and defending his house and household, as a member of a republic unified in peace (*fredum*) and freedom:

> Peace was the original word [*Urwort*] of their associations [*Innungen*], whims [*Willküren*], languages [*Sprachen*], its laws were habits long approved by himself [the free man], about which he could only be judged as a freeman of his own kind, and when he was judged, his offenses were [regarded as] breaches of the peace that he himself had approved of, his punishment [*Strafe*] and livelihood [*Auskommen*] a substantial blood money [*Wehrgeld*], by which his value was determined, whilst he also served as an instrumental member of a general body of citizens, according to his rank, value and relation to general security [*Mittel der Gesammtbürgschaft nach Stande, Werth und Verhältniss zur allgemeinen Sicherheit*].[67]

War created 'noble houses' (*edle Geschlechter*), Herder continued, but these nobles did not oppress the commoners (*Wehren*). They were companions

---

[65] Herder, 'Wie die deutschen Bischöfe', 679.   [66] Ibid., 680.   [67] Ibid.

of the noblest, the kings, and the bravest, the field commanders, and it was the nobles' privilege to render services to the kings. Among these services, it needs to be highlighted, Herder did not include lawkeeping. As members of one political whole the nobles stood with the leader at the national assembly, alongside the commoners who made up the body of the nation. Otherwise, the nobles were under *ius curiae* (*Hofrecht*). Priests, or 'druids' fulfilled the role of mediating between the two ranks, acting as the 'guarantors of freedom and order, both in the national assembly as well as on the military field'.[68] The authority of the ancient Frankish priests was grounded in the

> sheer awe of an invisible being, the founder of truth and faith. They had incomes, but no goods, made decisions on the holy items which belonged to the nation and which they themselves did not own for that very reason. In the assembly they ruled by [declaring] silence and the interpretation of signs, but not by voting and making proposals: they had no other existence than that which the bond of ranks, honor and peace, promoted.[69]

They participated in military ventures, but carried the flag of holy places and Gods, not that of the king.[70] The priests, rather than the nobility, were thus those who helped to sustain peace and order in society.

Herder posited even more clearly than Möser a strong contrast between the original German and (subsequent) Frankish political constitutions. As soon as the Franks began to learn the art of despotic and military statecraft from the Romans, things began to change in Germany. The Franks conquered the Gallic territories, gaining vast booty. Their chiefs were instituted as kings, and their companions were rewarded with lands.[71] The Franks did not abolish the distinctive jurisdiction of the Gauls but granted the Roman-Gallic bishops a special status, viewing them with 'Frankish eyes' as a valuable rank in the 'nation'.[72] Indeed, bishops did come to serve as a mediating rank between Franks and Gauls, but since they, too, were granted their own laws, they also imported Roman dispositions and ways of thought into the new Frankish monarchy. First, having been born in the bosom of the Jewish religion, Christianity was 'at home with a language of theocracy and priestly religion'. Second, the bishops had already adjusted themselves to Roman military despotism in

---

[68] Ibid., 680, 683.
[69] Ibid., 683. Cf. Montesquieu, *The Spirit of the Laws*, XVIII:31, 307. Herder did not refer to Montesquieu's interpretation of Tacitus at this point.
[70] Herder, 'Wie die deutschen Bischöfe', 683.   [71] Ibid..   [72] Ibid., 680.

the early centuries after Christ. Civil and military authority became discrete during the reign of Constantine and a third authority of clerical authority began to emerge. The clerics had begun to acquire property and continued to do so under the Frankish monarchy, now combining Frankish authority with the Gallic right to property. When commoners began to reclaim their rights, monarchs needed more support and invited not just bishops, but also various other people of Gallic origin to the court, who continued teaching them 'Roman statecraft', speaking 'the language of slavery from the Orient, and all that, in the name of God!'.[73] The bishops gained the upper hand in the *curia palatinatis*, becoming chief justices (*Oberrichter*).[74] In the Frankish state, the need arose to commit laws to paper – and it was the bishops who 'held the pen' of the men whom the king selected to do so. This engendered a fundamental change in the nature of government:

> These [the laws] had lived in the eternal justice-freedom and honor-custom of the nation, in men's memories and mouths, and in the cries of the people, and were holy; arbitration and refined, learned interpretations did not take place: Druids had and suffered no written laws because they were the death of free, true, living laws.[75]

In the new situation, however, bishops gained the right to interpret written law. They felt closer to the Gauls who lived in cities and were associated in guilds, and thus imported Gallic understandings of justice into the monarchical constitution. The episcopal cities grew big again, and with them Gallic arts and crafts (*Gewerbe*), so that the Gauls became richer than the Franks. They served as entrepots between different ranks and served to provide relative safe havens for the development of arts and crafts, as well as concomitant luxury, in an otherwise tumultous situation.[76]

This was a story of the rise and foundations of Frankish despotism; what followed was the unfolding of the latter. Herder divided the rest of the history of bishops into two periods – those of Merovingian and Carolingian kings, during which kings came to be instituted by *misericordia dei*, instead of popular election. They also solidified their rights of legislation, as constant policing was needed in the new situation. This kind of new German-Roman-Frankish type of government witnessed a continuing friction between various kinds of ranks, while the coexistence of the military and ecclesiastical estates in provinces was also most problematic. This was also reflected in the way in which juridical duties were fulfilled. Charlemagne,

---

[73] Ibid., 683.   [74] Ibid., 682.   [75] Ibid., 684.   [76] Ibid., 686.

'an extraordinary person', attempted to create a 'marble temple of legisla-tion' in the hugely expanded Frankish empire, seeking to balance the different powers in his realm, and awarding extensive power to imperial stewards, yet the huge colosseum that he built only lasted the duration of his lifetime. Due to the 'polyp-like' constitution of his empire, in which imperial structures were mirrored in the provinces, the colosseum dissolved into smaller districts with similar structures of government.[77]

We will return to Herder's discussion of Carolingian and post-Carolingian monarchy in Chapter 7. Here it suffices to point out that for Herder, the peculiar 'chaos' of Germany originated in Emperor Otto I's decision to fight for the 'Roman' crown in Italy, which in turn led to the rise of the 'right of the mighty' in the German territories. First bishops, then secular lords, gained increasing power against their imperial superior, rather than being suppressed as happened with their peers in other parts of the former Carolingian empire. The distinctive imperial structure that emerged in Germany, Herder argued using a standard approach of *Reichsgeschichte*, was fortified through the Golden Bull of Charles IV (1356), the 'Perpetual public peace' (*ewige Landfriede*) of Maximilian I (1495) and the electoral capitulation of Charles V (1519).[78] The Westphalian peace did not make any significant alterations to this, indeed, it even 'confirmed and strengthened the imperial constitution and the [fundamental] laws'.[79]

Having thus provided a highly critical history of the rise of the imperial constitution, Herder nevertheless concluded the essay by approving of David Georg Strube's view of its 'ideal' value:

> Our imperial constitution, says a learned, sensible philosopher of German history, our imperial constitution would be perfect to its core if the imperial statutes were duly followed. The disputes that arise between sovereign states are seldom settled without great bloodshed, whereas the disagreements (*Irrungen*) that occur between the German imperial estates should be resolved only through proper knowledge, without leading to the destruction of countries. Insofar as this judicial assistance would also help protect subjects against their authorities, one would prevent both despotic oppres-sion as well as destructive revolts, which the abuse of the highest power induces in many ways.[80]

---

[77] Ibid., 692.   [78] On Herder's reliance on *Reichsgeschichte*, see Hien, *Altes Reich*, 180–181.

[79] Ibid., 696. It is interesting to note that this assessment has now become the mainstream view in contemporary discussions of German history; see e.g., Schmidt, 'Die Idee "deutsche Freiheit"'.

[80] Ibid., 177. Herder cites David Georg Strube, 'Zwey- und zwanzigste Abhandlung. Vom Ursprung der Landes-Hoheit in Teutschland', in *Nebenstunden*, IV (Hannover, 1755), 1–83 (83).

Thus giving the nod to Strube as a 'German philosopher of history' with whom, 'alongside Möser', he would volunteer to 'share the wreath [prize] if it were awarded to [him]' at the essay competition, Herder revealed his own take on the German 'national spirit', too. Friedrich Carl von Moser's vision was clearly too simplistic from the historical point of view as well as too complacent in terms of the existing social and political hierarchies. Justus Möser's approach, by contrast, had no such flaws. Also, Herder's complex account of the history of German bishops was designed to buttress Möser's egalitarian description of the ancient constitution of the German peoples, rejecting Montesquieu's account of the role of the nobility in enforcing the laws and guaranteeing German freedom. Furthermore, he also strongly emphasised the role that German 'priests' or 'druids' had played in upholding German political societies in this early period, thus applying his account of 'ethopoeia' and the foundations of political society in 'legislative songs' to the German case.

Like Möser, Herder also drew a contrast between the original 'German freedom' and the mores and institutions that developed in the subsequent Frankish state. Early on, 'Roman' understandings of law and politics had infiltrated the German realm through Christian bishops, a development for which Herder had little sympathy. This led to the rise of a new understanding of ruler and subjects, whilst also contributing to the emergence of a separate clerical estate that enjoyed the right to hold property. The Frankish conquest of Roman territories, in his view, had further led to profound transformations in wider society as well as in political institutions. Nevertheless, as seen above, Herder was ready to accept some of the positive unintended consequences in the history of the Frankish state in the long run. Most importantly, some of the most negative tendencies – the emergence of a 'right of the fist' (the right of the mighty) and general anarchy during the German emperors' military ventures in Italy – had precluded the consolidation of territorial power that had happened in France or Spain. Herder appreciated this kind of historical idiosyncrasy as a form of 'German freedom' and 'peace'.

However, as we shall see below, Herder did not believe this 'ideal' had ever properly been realised; his optimism regarding the viability of the constitution of the Holy Roman Empire was in fact quite limited. His approving nod to Strube, we may surmise, was meant to encourage a certain understanding of the ethics of the legal profession and the value of a certain kind of legal history and scholarship; he had profound doubts that German princes would be willing to follow the advice given to them.

5.3   The Historical Prospects of Modern Europe and Germany

A few years later, in 1779, Herder entered yet another written submission – on the political history of Europe – to a new Berlin Academy of Sciences essay competition. As in 1770 and 1775 Herder's essay won the competition. This time the essay theme concerned the mutual impact of government and learning (sciences), thus essentially combining the two questions that David Hume and Jean-Jacques Rousseau had famously tackled earlier – its title *On the Influence of Governments on the Sciences, and of the Sciences on Governments* appropriately combined the two different ways in which the arts and sciences and government could be related. While David Hume had first highlighted the stimulating influence of political government upon the arts and sciences in ancient Greek republics, as well as demonstrated how this relationship was inversed in modern 'civilised monarchies',[81] Rousseau, in his *First Discourse*, famously disputed the positive influence of the arts and sciences upon morals and political government (see Chapter 2). As Schmidt has shown, Herder essentially took a 'third' position: he offered a nuanced view of the relationship between political government and the arts and sciences, highlighting the fact that no society could be fully without arts and sciences, whereas different forms of culture and political government fostered different kinds of arts and sciences, while the latter could in turn also influence political government.[82]

Insofar as Schmidt has provided a detailed reconstruction of the core argument of Herder's essay, let us just elaborate on Herder's views of late medieval and early modern European history as expressed here. Most importantly from our point of view, Herder presented an intricate genealogy of modern liberty, highlighting the complex causality and the role of unintended effects in this. The story he presented was thus quite different from what he described in *On Bishops*. Nevertheless, he incorporated at least some of the ideas of the latter. In the vein of Robertson's *History of Charles V*, Herder argued that at the end of the 'middle period', great riches had been amassed in Europe thanks to crusades and trade. What emerged was 'crude luxury' (*grobe Luxus*) that had a corresponding effect on mores.[83] At the same time, during the crusades, ancient texts had been

---

[81] Cf. David Hume, 'Of Civil Liberty', 'Of the Rise and Progress of the Arts and Sciences' and 'Of Refinement in the Arts', in idem, *Essays*, 87–97, 111–137, 268–280 (see also Chapter 1 for young Herder's relationship to Hume).

[82] See Schmidt, 'Scholarship, Morals and Government'.

[83] Herder, 'Vom Einfluß der Regierung', 376.

brought to Europe and ancient ideas were rediscovered. Here Herder notably complemented the argument of rising luxury in the late medieval period with one that resonated with his description of the shadowy impact of 'Roman ways of thought' on European politics in the same period. In this essay he did not, however, blame the Roman-influenced bishops for that, but philosophers. The ancient philosophical ideas of virtue, Herder argued following Hume, merged with the existing beliefs and sentiments in the Renaissance period, engendering the worst form of reason of state politics.[84] 'Had they found a better time, better rulers and constitutions', Herder wrote, these doctrines of 'false politics' would not have emerged:

> Had Machiavelli been a secretary of a Lycurgus or Numa, instead of Borgia, he would not have written his *Prince* in this manner. Had Cicero and Plato fallen into the hands of people other than *idle private individuals*, *inept school teachers*, or opulent *cardinals*, *princes*, *popes*, things may have gone differently, and they would have also had a different impact on government, but what can we do against fate?[85]

Recall that Möser, too, had identified the emergence of a new form of politics based on Roman imperial ideas. In Herder's vision, the Frankish monarchy had introduced Roman ideas of autocracy and law, which in the late medieval period came to be combined with Ciceronian and Platonist ideas. Machiavelli's *Prince*, he implied, was born out of the ambition of an 'idle private individual' to influence the politics of 'cardinals, princes, and popes', justifying their ambitions by drawing parallels between them and Romans. His teaching proved so successful that it led to the rise of early modern 'reason of state' politics more broadly.

The Reformation, Herder continued, added a further twist to these developments. It managed not only to eliminate many old clerical abuses but also to create proper separation between secular and clerical powers. While encouraging people to think for themselves and pursue 'light',[86] the Reformation could not, however, be implemented without the help of 'secular power', resulting in too much in the way of secular politics playing a role in it. Protestantism or reformed religion was often imposed from above, whereas true changes can only be accomplished from within. Thus, its overall effects were ambiguous and in many places it initially generated turmoil, rebellions, repressions and wars.[87] With British history particularly in mind, but also pointing at (presumably German) 'peasant wars', Herder argued that monarchies in the early modern period had basically

---

[84] Hume, 'Of Civil Liberty', 87–88; for discussion, see Hont, *Jealousy of Trade*, 8–11.
[85] Herder, 'Vom Einfluß der Regierung', 378.   [86] Ibid., 378–379.   [87] Ibid.

oscillated between the poles of freedom and despotism. The use and abuse of learning fostered an excessive 'love of freedom' among citizens, and while monarchs were resisting 'foreign bonds', subjects learned to create them. What Herder seems to have meant here was that where monarchs resisted the power of the Pope, rebellious subjects often formed alliances with foreign powers. As circumstances were not suitable for the rise of democracies, Herder argued, aristocracies and monarchies emerged from the turmoil, and subjects gradually learned to use more subtle means to claim their rights – the 'useful sciences' [of government and commerce].[88] In France, however, the Huguenots and the nobility had been repressed through strong centralised power, which led to the rise of a despotism that sought military glory and luxurious pomp. The state had virtually reached the stage of exhaustion and weakness, after which ideas of love of humanity and better government emerged.[89] In Britain, although a succession of remarkably science-friendly monarchs emerged, the country nevertheless oscillated between monarchy and (excessive, partisan-spirited) freedom, eventually tilting towards a monarchy again.

This was Herder's 'Enlightened narrative'. Indeed, Herder now granted that the despotisms that had emerged in early modern Europe had thus gradually become ever more 'lawful', having been turned into monarchies 'almost against the will of the rulers'.[90] He even acknowledged the relative pacification of Europe through these developments (albeit staying silent about colonial conquests).[91] The military and scientific rivalry between the large European monarchies gradually forced the remaining despotisms to emulate the former, whereby 'gross interferences with the rights of peoples (*grobe Eingriffe in die Rechte der Völker*)' were significantly reduced.[92] The rulers have thus been virtually forced to undertake reforms as well as guarantee freedom to their subjects.[93] Herder concluded the essay with an impassioned celebration of the rise of freedom of thought as supporting the power of the ruler in modern monarchies, rather than endangering it – an argument that we also encounter in Immanuel Kant's two essays from 1784, most notably in his famous essay on Enlightenment.[94] A distinctive form of modern liberty had emerged in modern monarchies, while the latter provided an even better – more stable – environment for preserving and developing learning and sciences than the republics in which the arts and sciences had first come to bloom.[95]

---

[88] Ibid.   [89] Ibid., 381.   [90] Ibid., 358, 381.   [91] Ibid., 334.   [92] Ibid., 340.
[93] Ibid., 358, 381.   [94] On Herder's debate with Kant, see Chapter 6.
[95] Herder, 'Vom Einfluß der Regierung', 359–360; cf. Chapter 1.

Strikingly, in this new prize essay Herder did not restate his arguments – so powerfully voiced in *This Too a Philosophy* – about the effects of this new regime on the human mind and morality. The tone of these two pieces of writing is thus very different: while in 1774 he was highly ironic about modern 'achievements', in 1779 he was genuinely positive about them. However, the views that he developed in *This Too a Philosophy* and *On the Influence of Governments* do not directly contradict each other upon closer inspection. The 1779 essay did not discuss virtue, patriotism or indeed, fine arts, just as it did not address the question of the sustainability of modern liberty in the long run. In *This Too a Philosophy* he had looked deeper and further, beyond what was currently visible in modern societies. The 1779 essay avoided asking such questions – presumably for a rather mundane reason: Herder sincerely wished to win the prize from the Berlin Academy of Sciences (which he duly did).[96]

However, Herder did address the state of the German 'national character', delivering a verdict on its current state that was as harsh as his earlier assessment of modern liberty had been. Acknowledging the progress of letters and sciences both in France and England as well as their crucial impact on government, Herder characterised Germany as still being 'in the sixteenth century'.[97] The processes in Germany had been different from the rest of Europe – during the Middle Ages Germany had both endured being conquered whilst also being a conqueror itself, and as such had no proper public spirit. Its constitution did not encourage rulers to invest in useful sciences, nor were conditions in Germany in any way inspiring for literary authors. Using the self-reflexive pronoun in an essay that otherwise was not specifically German-centred, Herder wrote:

> How is it that our literature is such a mixture (*Gemisch*) [. . .]? We are in perpetual conflict with ourselves and with other nations who need and despise us, whom we serve and revere. – As is Germany's history and constitution, so is its literature.[98]

A true German patriot thus had to accept that the reality of Germany was far from what was expected from the 'ideal' of German freedom. In fact, it was the Germans who were still in perpetual conflict among themselves and with others. Herder thus accepted the advantages of large territorial monarchies (including Prussia), in which useful sciences had gradually also softened the mode of government. Instead of solely cherishing the imperial

---

[96] Cf. also Rainer Wisbert, 'Kommentar', in *FHA*, IX/2, 1141.
[97] Herder, 'Vom Einfluß der Regierung', 382.   [98] Ibid., 346.

constitution, Germany, too, needed a more orderly understanding of the role of sciences in government:

> A debris of this old constitution nourishes sciences which are in the most peculiar contradiction with themselves and with this constitution, and which, regardless of the latter, are nevertheless spread, and are handed on. Perhaps we will replace what we did too quickly in this [the sixteenth] century. Building the latter – the sciences and government – on the same principles and unifying them in one work, we shall accomplish it all the more maturely. Neighbouring empires and princes take precedence over us, but we are perhaps too rich to overlook, use, and order our wealth.[99]

Admittedly, it is not quite clear which sciences Herder had in view here. Two related possibilities spring to mind though. One is that it was the philosophy of natural law as taught in German universities. He may have followed Justus Möser here, rejecting this approach for its abstractness and its support of territorial absolutism, thus also acknowledging its tension with the ideas on which the German imperial constitution was based. The other is that Herder, in the paragraph cited above, called for taking the sciences of commerce and government more seriously. For Herder, Germany simply could not afford to continue languishing in the state in which it currently found itself. Herder thus accepted the situation of economic and cultural inter-state rivalry in Europe, and sought to find ways in which Germans could learn from others.

It is instructive to compare Herder's views with those of Justus Möser here. In his preface to *History of Osnabrück*, Justus Möser had discussed the possibility that Germany would have become a 'commercial state' in the early modern period. Tacitly comparing developments in England and the Holy Roman Empire, Möser lamented the fact that the German emperors in the thirteenth and fourteenth centuries had been too 'weak and frivolous' (*schwach und schlüpfrig*) to create a new 'common property' (*gemeine Eigentum*) and fatherland for their subjects. They should have 'bestowed a Magna Carta' upon all associated burghers and cities as well as created a House of Commons for the latter that would have compensated for the disappearance of freeholders. Instead, Möser argued, the emperors 'legislated one imperial law after another' against the associations of burghers.[100] Furthermore, allodial properties were rendered hereditary, reducing the number of available military people, and the establishment of standing armies as a next step. Similarly, the number of taxable people

---

[99] Ibid., 382.   [100] Möser, 'Vorrede'; Möser, 'Deutsche Geschichte', 100.

was initially very low, leading to the gradual evolution of territorial estates (*Landstände*) as the emperor was forced to seek allies.[101]

For Möser, the latter included cities, 'these anomalistic bodies which for so long the Saxons had not been willing to tolerate'. The development of cities changed the Saxon way of thought. Burghers had gradually gained considerable riches, which created confusion in, and overshadowed, the 'concept of honour and property on which the Saxon legislation had rested'.[102] Insofar as the new kind of monied property was largely invisible, the provision of defence was no longer bound up with property, and various kinds of physical and life-threatening punishments were adopted to enforce the duty of military service, which had an impact on everyone's freedom. A 'new conception of constitution [*Verfassung*]' was brought along 'wherein gradually every person was to be accepted as a citizen or a legal peer, exactly as under late Roman emperors, and his obligation and duty was to be founded merely on his quality as a subject'.[103]

Möser made clear that 'freedom' suffered greatly from these new developments, but conceded that 'Germany could have become happy' under this constitution, if it had grounded its greatness immediately in commerce. Implicitly linking up with Hume's similar argument in the *History of England*, Möser acknowledged the special character of the *Hanse* and lamented the fact that the cities had been unable to cooperate sufficiently to make the Imperial Diet recognise the importance of commerce. Individual industry and plain property should have been granted as equally honourable to landed property so as to prevent the fragmentation of the realm into so many rivalling territories. The cities would then have been able to defend their interests in England and later against the Dutch. If they had done so, Möser argued, the Holy German Empire might have become the 'first true commercial state in Europe, and the ruler of two world regions'.[104] In reality, the quarrels between imperial stewards, nobles, and cities continued, until they were solved through the creation of territorial sovereignty, on the one hand, and the rise of a balance of power supervised by the emperor, on the other, in the early modern period of German history.

Möser's account highlighted a high degree of contingency in German history. Germany could have developed in a very different manner, had the

---

[101] Ibid., 101–102.   [102] Ibid., 102.
[103] Ibid., 102, translation from Knudsen, *Justus Möser*, 104–105.
[104] Ibid., 102–103. Cf. the discussion of Hanse in David Hume, *The History of England from the Invasion of Julius Caesar to the Revolution in 1688*, Foreword by William B. Todd, 6 vols. (Indianapolis: Liberty Fund 1983), III, ch. xxxv, 386–387.

emperors adopted a different policy towards city burghers. As we shall see in Chapter 7, Herder subsequently also came to discuss the role of towns and cities in German history, tracing their historical significance and role in much greater detail than Möser did. In 1774 and 1779, he did not as yet discuss this role, but like Möser, was very much interested in understanding the unique character of German history. Furthermore, as Möser's musings about Germany's 'missed opportunities' show, he too considered German developments in a comparative perspective. Herder did not express any similar regrets about Germany's missed opportunities, but was anxious about Germany's backwardness. To this extent, his German patriotism was not just inward-looking; he also recommended that the Germans (in their own way) emulate the large civilised monarchies like Britain. Albeit worried about the possible rise of a new cycle of military despotism and imperialism in advanced modern 'state-machines', he nevertheless wished for Germany to share in the achievements of modern liberty, prosperity and relative international stability (peace).

How could Germany do so? Towards the end of the essay, Herder pointed at ancient Greece as an instructive example in this respect.[105] Greece was a paradigm example of government influence on the arts and sciences. As in his earlier essays, Herder again highlighted the fact that two different models of government and indeed, patriotism, had emerged in Greece. While Lycurgus in Sparta 'drew his people around the stern principle of *sacrifice* and *love for the fatherland*', Solon 'went an entirely different way, and 'sought to pair *riches* with *liberty*, *luxury* [*Üppigkeit*] with *love of the fatherland*'. The Spartan model required putting harsh limits upon everything – just like riches were banned, so were plays, opulent verse, orators and sophists. Spartan science was military science. In Athens, by contrast, 'Solon stirred up all that one would call a *popular science* [*Volkswissenschaft*] – oratory, poetry, philosophy, arts'.[106] Greek theatre and philosophy similarly reflected the Greek constitution and the nature of the people, its 'lightness', which was also answerable for their degeneration into a 'need for the idle state thirsting for entertainment' and 'vacuous chatter about systems and word-stuff', respectively. 'Commerce and prosperity', Herder continued in a more uniformly optimistic manner, 'thrived in Athens and were meant to thrive there according to the plan of the founder'.[107]

[105] On the broader current of the 'Wahlverwandschaft' between ancient Greece and Germany, including Herder's position in this, see Hien, *Altes Reich*, 291–305.
[106] Herder, 'The Influence', 131 (translation modified); Herder, ' Vom Einfluß der Regierung', 308.
[107] Herder, 'The Influence', 132; Herder, 'Vom Einfluß der Regierung', 309–310.

Herder's discussion of the Athenian form of government resonates with the contrasts he drew between austere democratic republicanism and modern liberty in his early essays on patriotism. However, Herder now emphasised the positive impact of Athenian liberty on the arts and sciences. Despite its political shortcomings, the example of Athens revealed that a pairing of luxury, liberty and love of the fatherland was possible in principle. As Herder put it, the arts and sciences of the Greeks were 'daughters of their legislation, their political constitution, in particular of *liberty*, of *work for the common good*, of *universal striving and shared zeal*'.[108] As soon as liberty was lost, the sciences also lost their spirit.[109] Furthermore, even if moderns could never imitate Athens in this respect, they could 'learn from' its example in a more indirect manner. Herder's main point concerned the 'effect' of 'the number and diversity of the competing Greek cities and states' on the sciences. 'So many cities and republics close to each other, connected to each other through language, by the honor of the Greek name, and partly by their tribal type and constitution' competed with each other and 'no one remained a complete stranger to the Muses'.[110] There were clear parallels between the diversity of Greek cities and states and the fragmented state of the Holy Roman Empire. The Greek competition spurred by the 'academy' of '*glory, Greek name, fatherland, liberty*' could thus perhaps nevertheless be emulated by the Germans, too.[111] This system, too, was surely a 'plant' nourished by the Athenian soil and sun, yet perhaps still there was some encouragement for the latter:

> We are a mixture (*Gemisch*) of peoples and languages, subject to a mixture of circumstances and purposes; the pure Greek national character will forever be beyond our reach, we can never achieve their uniformity (*Einfalt*) in learning (*Wissenschaften*) and education (*Bildung*); so let us become what we can be, strive to emulate them insofar as our constitution allows and in this become what they could not be. Perhaps our 'fruits' (*Frucht*) can replace their 'beautiful blossoms' (*schöne Blüte*), just like the duration and spread (*Ausbreitung*) [of our learning] can substitute for what we lack in life and interiority (*Innigkeit*).[112]

---

[108] Herder, 'The Influence', 134; Herder, 'Vom Einfluß der Regierung', 312.
[109] Cf. Herder's similar argument in his 'Ursachen des gesunkenen Geschmacks', 122–127.
[110] Herder, 'The Influence', 133; Herder, 'Vom Einfluß der Regierung', 311.
[111] Herder, 'The Influence', 135; idem, 'Vom Einfluß der Regierung', 313. On similar ideas about the ancient Hebrews in his *Vom Geist der Ebräischen Poesie* (1783), see Chapter 6.
[112] Herder, 'Vom Einfluß der Regierung', 360.

Herder's actual agenda and question was only thinly veiled here: while in Greece institutions had given rise to distinctive arts and sciences, perhaps in Germany this could be achieved the other way around? Remember the dual focus of *The Influence*: it concerned not only the influence of government on the arts and sciences but also that of the arts and sciences on government. The arts and sciences in other parts of Europe, as we saw in our reconstruction of Herder's argument above, had already contributed considerably to the rise of modern forms of government. In Germany, too, things were actually slowly improving, but its imperial constitution was preventing forward movement at the same pace. Was there a way to turn this shortcoming into an advantage, Herder asked. Could it be that precisely this decentralism would enable modern Germans to create a culture that would parallel that of the Greeks in some essential aspects whilst even giving rise to a new form of politics?

5.4   Conclusion

As this chapter has shown, in the 1770s Herder cannot be characterised as a *Reichspatriot* in any strong sense. Rather, he put forward a positive reading of the ancient German constitution, highlighting its egalitarian nature and the role of priests in lawkeeping and in guaranteeing alignment between law and ethics. Although he acknowledged the value of the constitution of the Holy Roman Empire in terms of limiting the power of territorial rulers, he provided a very critical account of the ways in which the original German constitution had developed after the Germanic conquest of Gaul, presenting the Christian bishops' role in this process in negative terms. The resulting new form of government was characterised by a widening gap between law and ethics and a peculiar friction between military and ecclesiastical estates. Last but not least, it was geared towards conquest. In his 1779 essay, Herder was thus quite ready to accept the benefits of modern large civilised monarchies, after all. Germany, in contrast to Britain or France, had not seen a similar flourishing of 'useful sciences', including those of commerce, and thus witnessed continuing despotism in its smaller principalities. To Herder, the celebrated 'German freedom', as supposedly guaranteed by the imperial constitution, was thus highly problematic. Germans were no less bellicose than other European states, but unlike their large neighbours in Europe, they did not as yet partake of the benefits of modern liberty. However, as Herder's tentative comparison between Greek and German decentralism shows, he still cherished some hope for Germany to turn its fragmented political landscape into an advantage as well as pursue some benign forms of commerce. Whilst acknowledging that modern large monarchies could entail certain benefits, he did not wish Germany to blindly copy them. As Markus Hien has also suggested, he was thus envisioning a 'third way' for Germany. Furthermore, as we will see in Chapter 6, Herder did not fail to point out the ways in which they could seek to improve their situation. He was a 'German patriot', after all.

The Vocation of Poets, Pastors and Philosophers

In parallel to his studies of German and European political history, Herder in the 1770s continued to explore the history of German poetry and the relationship between poetry, mores and government. In 1773, he published an edited collection of essays entitled *On German Style and Art* (*Von deutscher Art und Kunst*).[1] Alongside Herder's short essays on *Ossian* and Shakespeare,[2] the collection included a short text by Johann Wolfgang Goethe on German architecture, an anonymous translation of an essay on Gothic art by Paolo Frisi, as well as an excerpt from Justus Möser's *History of Osnabrück*.[3] In this period, Herder also engaged seriously with what he influentially called 'folk songs' – orally transmitted ancient songs sung by the common people.[4] The collection of folk songs titled *Ancient Folk Songs* (*Alte Volkslieder*) was advertised by Herder's publisher in 1774, but for fear of ridicule, Herder never published the manuscript.[5] A revised and toned-down version appeared in two volumes in 1778/1779.[6] Herder further discussed the role of priests and pastors in ancient and modern societies in a collection of letters published in 1774,[7] and in the following years wrote

---

[1] *Von deutscher Art und Kunst. Einige fliegende Blätter* (Hamburg, 1773).

[2] Johann Gottfried Herder, 'Auszug aus einem Briefwechsel über *Ossian* und die Lieder alter Völker', in *HWP*, I, 477–525 (=*FHA*, II, 447–497); idem, 'Shakespear', in *HWP*, I, 526–547; 'Shakespear: 1. Entwurf (1771), in ibid., 547–554; 'Shakespeare: 2. Entwurf (1772)', in ibid., 554–572. An English translation of the 1773 version of the essay can be found in Johann Gottfried Herder, 'Shakespeare', in *SWA*, 291–397. I will be using this translation. Unless otherwise indicated, all translations from German in this chapter are mine.

[3] On this text and Herder's relationship to Möser, see Chapter 5. On Goethe's and Möser's ideas on the parallels between political constitutions and architectural art, see Hien, *Altes Reich*, 142–147.

[4] Ulrich Gaier, 'Kommentar', in *FHA*, III, 839–927 (965–966).   [5] Ibid., 895.

[6] A posthumous and ethnographically structured edition titled *Voices of Peoples* (*Stimmen der Völker*) was published in 1807 (ed. Johannes Müller and Caroline Herder); see Gaier, 'Kommentar', 904–905.

[7] Johann Gottfried Herder, 'An Prediger. Fünfzehn Provinzialblätter' (1774), in *FHA,* IX/I, 67–139.

a series of philosophical essays on religion and the history of poetry.[8] The most well known among these essays is his *On the Spirit of Hebrew Poetry* published in 1783.[9]

The aim of this chapter is to clarify the ways in which Herder's interest in ancient poetry and the responsibilities of various kinds of intellectual and creative professions was related to his commitment to German patriotism. The collection *On German Style and Art* has been described as a 'clarion call to all who were now finally disgusted with the continued domination of Reason in literature'.[10] Indeed, its contribution to the rise of sentimentalism in German literature, and more specifically, the emergence of the Storm and Stress (*Sturm und Drang*) movement is undeniable. Most scholarly discussion has therefore focused on the literary programme it proposed. Considering Herder's leading role in the publication of this collection, it is only natural that questions have been asked about his relationship to the 'German movement' (*deutsche Bewegung*) more broadly.[11] Whilst earlier studies identified aspects of Herder's intensifying national sentiments here,[12] the bulk of contemporary scholarship underscores Herder's comparative approach and continuing interest in universalistic anthropology, his anti-colonial and anti-imperialist goals as well as his distinctive emphasis on the complexities of different kinds of 'modern' receptions of 'ancient poetry', as exemplified in his discussion of folk song, on the one hand, and Shakespeare, on the other.[13]

---

[8] See, most importantly from our perspective, the introductory essays in *Alte Volkslieder*, in *FHA*, III; Herder, 'Von der Ähnlichkeit der Mittleren Englischen und deutschen Dichtkunst, nebst Verschiednem, das daraus folget' (1777), in *FHA*, II, 550–562; Herder, 'Ursachen des gesunkenen Geschmacks bei den verschiedenen Völkern, da er geblühet' (1775), in *FHA*, IV, 109–148; Herder, 'Über den Einfluß der schönen in die höheren Wissenschaften', in *FHA*, IV, 215–232 (English translation: 'On the Influence of Belles Lettres on the Higher Sciences', in *SWA*, 335–346); idem, 'Über die Wirkung der Dichtkunst auf die Sitten der Völker in alten und neuen Zeiten', *FHA*, IV, 150–252. English translation of excerpts from some of these essays can be found in Philip Bohlmann, *Song Loves the Masses. Herder on Music and Nationalism* (Oakland, California, 2017).

[9] Herder, 'Vom Geist der Ebräischen Poesie'. For an interpretation of this work from the viewpoint of the development of his hermeneutics, see Gjesdal, *Herder's Hermeneutics*, ch. 7.

[10] Clark, *Herder: His Life and Thought*, 147.

[11] Dann, 'Herder und die deutsche Bewegung'; Pierre Pénisson, 'Nachwort', in *HWP*, I, 864–920 (900ff.).

[12] See, e.g., Ergang, *Herder and the Foundations*.

[13] See, e.g., Karl Menges, 'Herder on National, Popular and World Literature', in *A Companion to the Works*, 188–212; Wulf Koepke, 'Herder's Views on the Germans and Their Future Literature', in *A Companion to the Works*, 213–232; Stefan Greif, '3.3.1 *Auszug aus einem Briefwechsel über Ossian und die Lieder der Völker, Shakespear, Gefundene Blätter aus den neuesten deutschen Litterannalen, Beiträge zu Lavaters Physiognomischen Fragmenten*', in *Herder Handbuch*, 485–495. On folk songs specifically, see, first of all, Gaier, 'Kommentar', 865–978. Note that Gaier has at the same time also elaborated on the fundamental differences between Herder's approach to folk songs in the

These new lines of interpretation, as we will see, have much to commend them. However, we should not overlook the intensely patriotic tone of Herder's writings as well as his broader interest in German political and cultural history in this period. As I seek to show in this chapter, he delved into the relationship between poetry, religion, mores and politics in various kinds of societies, including, prominently, those of ancient Israel and ancient Germany, but was keen to propose solutions to distinctively modern German and European problems. Ancient Israel and ancient Germany provided a blueprint for the vocation and role of various kinds of creative professions for him. However, he believed that it was also important to understand what had gone wrong in Europe and Germany in particular. I argue that the heart of Herder's argument here was that a gulf had arisen between the creative arts and sciences in Europe in the early modern period. As seen in Chapter 5, this was not an entirely negative development for him. Whilst rivalry between large European states had only intensified thanks to the revival of ancient Roman ideas of government, sciences had come to be seen as an important vehicle for promoting state interests. The cultivation of sciences thus became a matter of 'reason of state', whilst they also came to have an impact on the government, thereby promoting the rise of the rule of law. As we shall see in this chapter, the arts and the 'beautiful sciences' in general underwent a more straightforwardly problematic transformation, however. Poets began to imitate ancient Greek and Roman models, which led to a loss of creativity, and poetry no longer served as a foundation of political society in European states. This was also the reason why there was a gap between the laws and mores; or indeed, proper mores no longer could be found in Germany (and Europe more broadly).

My second main line of argument concerns Herder's desired 'national spirit'. I seek to show that Herder made an effort to reject unreflective kinds of national pride, and envisioned the emergence of a new kind of historical consciousness as an essential part of modern German 'national spirit'. Engagement with history, Herder believed, enabled modern humans to distance themselves from their own prejudices, whilst also revealing some essential universal commitments that they could seek to re-embrace in the current circumstances. Recovering the unity of and the

---

1774 manuscript and the published *Folk Songs* (1778/1779). While the former was still largely committed to the project of the creation of German national literature (whilst also pursuing emancipatory goals), the latter was supposed to stimulate broader intercultural sympathy and recognition of shared common affects and situations (*Grundaffekte und Grundsituationen*) across humanity.

central roles played by various kinds of professions – first of all, poets and pastors – in early human societies was meant to serve as an inspiration for modern poets, pastors and philosophers in their attempts to initiate reforms in their societies. Most importantly, Herder celebrated the genius of Shakespeare. Herder proposed that an engagement with Shakespeare could demonstrate the ways in which modern authors could relate to historical subject matter. Literary studies and historiography also had to fulfil the highly important functions of revealing the historical origins and hence contingent quality of the current ways of thought and showing what was humanly possible. Scholars in these fields were supposed to foster self-reflection and an emergence of historical consciousness. Herder further highlighted the relevance of the Greek principle of emulation for Germans in particular, and envisioned it also as contributing to the social, economic and political reforms in Germany. Although based on historical sources of inspiration, Herder's desired 'national spirit' was clearly forward-looking in its political aspirations. I will conclude with a brief discussion of Herder's ideas on the one possible way in which his ideas could be used for initiating far-reaching reforms in the Holy Roman Empire.

The chapter is divided into three sections. The first will sketch the ways in which Herder's interest in folk songs was embedded in a broader contemporary movement as well as his own anthropological enquiry, highlighting at the same time the political function of this interest. The second will reconstruct Herder's historical account of the impact of poetry on mores, elaborating on the ways in which this history was embedded in his Bückeburg philosophy of history. The third will set out Herder's vision of German 'national spirit' in the 1770s and in 1787.

6.1 Ancient Folk Songs

6.1.1 *Folk Songs from an Anthropological Point of View*

As we shall see below, reviving an interest in ancient poetry and songs in Germany was a key element in Herder's programme of reform. At the same time, Herder's interest in German songs resonated with a number of recent tendencies in German literature and was a logical outgrowth of Herder's aesthetic and anthropological studies. Let us thus start by briefly sketching the ways in which these explorations were grounded in broader trends and Herder's aesthetic and anthropological ideas, proceeding then to explore their political function.

A new surge of patriotic poetry elaborating on themes of German national history, and most importantly the mythological figure of Arminius, had arisen during the Seven Years' War in particular.[14] Several poets further presented themselves as 'bards' who sang for the common people. For example, the poets Ewald von Kleist and Johann Wilhelm Ludwig Gleim had both already pursued the ideal of 'artless simplicity', whilst their approach had also been celebrated by the leading literary critics, such as, most prominently, Gotthold Ephraim Lessing. As Ulrich Gaier reminds us, Lessing had already in 1758 posed programmatic questions about the relationship between Gleim's *Songs of a Grenader* (*Grenadierlieder*) (1758) and the various kinds of German 'bards' from earlier periods.[15] Lessing also published a couple of Lithuanian[16] songs (*Dainos*) in *Letters on the German Literature*, praising their 'naïve humour' (*naïve Witz*) and 'attractive simplicity' (*reizende Einfalt*). According to Lessing, these simple songs showed that 'lively sentiments' (*lebhafte Empfindungen*) were by no means 'a privilege of civilised peoples'.[17]

Taking inspiration from these developments, Herder sought to situate the phenomenon of folk songs in the history of human civilisation and poetry. He had already commented, in *Fragments*, on Lessing's publication of the aforementioned 'Lithuanian' folk songs, expressing the wish that one would also look up and examine other such 'traces of the footsteps of our ancestors' among other peoples, too.[18] As is well known, the young Herder also closely followed the controversy generated by *Ossian*. In the early 1760s, James MacPherson's alleged 'translations' of original Gaelic poetry were published, immediately attaining wide critical attention.[19] Several important figures, among them David Hume, disputed the authenticity of the supposed originals, whilst others stood up in their defence. A collection of MacPherson's translations appeared as *The Works of Ossian* in 1765, including also a *Critical Dissertation on the Poems of Ossian* by Hugh Blair. In 1768, Michael Denis published a German translation, which Herder also very critically reviewed in *Allgemeine Deutsche Bibliothek*.[20]

---

[14] See Hien, *Altes Reich*, 127–129.
[15] Gotthold Efraim Lessing, 'Vorbericht', in *Preussische Kriegslieder in den Feldzügen 1756 und 1757, von einem Grenadier* [J. W. L. Gleim] (1758), cited from Gaier, 'Kommentar', 848–850. As Gaier points out, Herder uses the same examples at the beginning of his preface to *Alte Volkslieder*.
[16] Herder himself referred to 'Latvian' *Dainos*, see Gaier, 'Kommentar', 892.
[17] Gaier, 'Kommentar', 851.   [18] Herder, 'Fragmente II', in *FHA*, I, 285.
[19] For an overview, see Wolf G. Schmidt, *'Homer des Nordens' und 'Mutter der Romantik'. James MacPherson's 'Ossian' und seine Rezeption in der deutschsprachigen Literatur*, 4 vols. (Berlin, 2003/ 2004).
[20] On Herder's life-long relationship to *Ossian*, see Gaier, 'Kommentar', 857–859. For a more detailed overview of Herder's engagement with *Ossian*, see Clark, *Herder: His Life and Thought*, 143–146.

Whilst Herder had already encountered some Ossianic songs in his Riga period, he read Denis's translation on his sea voyage from Riga to France. As he confessed in his 'Correspondence on *Ossian*', this setting was also absolutely fitting for such a reading, making him particularly responsive to the charm of such poetry. Travelling in a small group of people on a ship, subjected to strict routine and rules 'as in a republic of Lycurgus', he found himself 'in the middle of a huge spectacle of a totally different, lively and spinning nature, floating between abyss and sky, every day surrounded by the very same infinite elements, only very rarely getting a glimpse of a distant coast, a new cloud, a new ideal world region'.[21] This, Herder argued, enabled him to listen to Ossian with an 'inner ear'. Such a sensitivity, however, was precisely what was missing in Denis's translation, which served as a focal point of his 'Correspondence on *Ossian*'. Indeed, the latter begins with a discussion of Denis's translation, so as to draw attention to the difference between 'our Ossian' that 'is colouring in' (*ausmalend*) every detail, and uses Klopstockian hexameter, and the 'true Ossian' that is 'brief, strong, manly' and speaks in 'disjointed pictures and sentiments'.[22] Herder accordingly proceeded to discuss the philosophy of translation, and the ways in which an 'authentic' translation could be achieved.[23]

The Ossianic songs had a lasting impact on Herder, but more importantly, they served as an excellent source material to analyse the psychology, language and even history of 'an uneducated, sensuous people'. Of course, he did not think that the Ossianic Scots represented a fully primitive or 'savage' (wild) people. Rather, Herder's characterisation of Ossian's manner of thought in 'Correspondence on *Ossian*' is continuous with his insights into Homeric (or early Hebrew) poetry in *Fragments* as well as his general history of the human mind and language as sketched in the former and in *Treatise*:

> Travelogues have shown us how strongly and starkly savage peoples express themselves. The things they want to say they express in a sensuous and clear manner, in a lively manner, conveying their spoken intention instantly and exactly; not through shadowy concepts, half-ideas and the symbolic reasoning of a written culture (they do not know even this word [reason] in their language, as they have almost no *abstracta*).[24]

Another important work that Herder cited and discussed was Thomas Percy's *Reliques of Ancient English Poetry* (1765).

[21] Herder, 'Auszug aus einem Briefwechsel über Ossian', in *HWP*, I, 486.   [22] Ibid., 477–478.

[23] For discussion of Herder's philosophy of translation, see Clémence Couturier-Henrich (ed. and introd.), *Übersetzen bei Johann Gottfried Herder* (Heidelberg, 2012).

[24] Herder, 'Auszug aus einem Briefwechsel über Ossian', 501.

In short, Homer and Ossian were both able to connect 'the soul and mouth' in a firm manner. They saw, felt and expressed themselves '*impromptu*'.[25] Further refining his concept of 'painting with words and movements', Herder here also posited a theory of the wild soul's creation of a 'picture' through vivid imagination, the elements of which it in turn expressed in a broken style, through 'leaps and bounds' (*Sprünge und Würfe*).[26] According to Herder, the 'songs of all savage peoples' depicted 'a living world' thanks to the force (*Kraft*) of the soul directly expressing itself in poetry in this early period of a people's development: 'You know, the more savage, that is, the more lively, freely efficient a people are (. . .), the more savage, that is, the more lively, free, sensuous, lyrically acting must also be its songs, if it has them!'[27] This could also well be illustrated by bringing examples from contemporary wild peoples, examples from 'Lapland and *Estland*, in Latvian and Polish, Scottish and German'.[28] All these peoples Herder occasionally qualified as 'northern peoples'.

The manuscript of *Ancient Folk Songs* was organised as an anthology of songs, consisting of four chapters, each preceded by an introductory essay.[29] Whilst the first was an introduction to the theme of folk songs in general, the second discussed the translatability of Shakespeare and the third the common origins of the English and German peoples.[30] The fourth essay was titled 'An Excursus into Songs of Foreign Peoples', introducing a collection of songs from the 'northern peoples' living along the southern coast of the Baltic sea.[31] In this essay, Herder directly attacked the idea that ancient (Greek and Roman) poetry served as a model for its modern counterpart, essentially demonstrating the similarities between the poetry of these peoples with that of the ancient Greeks and Romans. Precisely because of this sensuous quality of the folk songs, Herder argued, there was much to be learned from them. The Greeks and Romans, too, had been 'half-savage peoples' just like contemporary 'northern peoples' when they 'sowed the seeds of their most beautiful blossoms and branches'.[32] This, as various commentators have pointed out, was

---

[25] Ibid., 504; cf. ibid., 502.   [26] Ibid., 514–515.   [27] Ibid., 482.   [28] Ibid., 506.

[29] On the genesis and complex publication history of this manuscript, see Gaier, 'Kommentar', 892–906.

[30] See also Herder, 'Von Ähnlichkeit der mittleren englischen und deutschen Dichtkunst' (1777).

[31] On Herder's engagement with the poetry of these 'northern peoples' (and the twentieth-century scholarship on this subject), see Kaspar Renner, '"Ausweg zu Liedern fremder Völker". Antikoloniale Perspektiven in Herders Volksliedprojekt', in: *Raynal—Herder—Merkel*, 107–141.

[32] Herder, 'Ausweg zu Liedern fremder Völker', in *FHA*, III, 59–68 (63); cf. Bohlmann, *The Song Loves the Masses*, 39. (I have modified Bohlmann's translation.)

Herder's way of disputing contemporary veneration of Greek and Roman art as universal models to be imitated.[33]

Herder also believed that there were deeper philosophical reasons for taking an interest in this little-known poetry. 'We know more peoples living on the earth than the ancients did', Herder wrote, 'yet how do we know these peoples, our human brothers?'[34] He then continued: '[Is it] Only from the outside through copper engravings or reports that are similar to the former? Or [is it] as humans who have language, souls, sentiments? [As] our brothers?'[35] What was needed was to study these peoples as one would study nature (*Naturkunde*). Instead of producing external descriptions of these peoples' appearance, customs and mode of living as was common in ethnographic studies, one had to note what 'characterised them on the innermost inside' (am innigsten *charakterisiert*) as well as 'place oneself there' (*sich dahin ein zu setzen*), indeed, penetrate deepest (am tiefsten zu *dringen*) into the soul of these peoples.[36] This implied 'fully familiarising oneself' with their language and 'way of thought' (*Denkart*) as well as 'showing' the true 'natural history' of such peoples in the actual 'monuments' (*Denkmale*) that they have created, i.e. their 'folk songs, mythologies, fairy tales, prejudices, that shape their character'.[37] Such an endeavour was essential for all pastors who wanted to truly know their flock, but not just for them.[38]

6.1.2 German Folk Songs: Patriotic Point of View

Alongside this general goal of enlarging one's understanding, and feeling for, humanity, Herder pursued a different but related goal of reviving German poetry. In his 'Correspondence on *Ossian*'and preface to *Ancient Folk Songs*, Herder strongly lamented the current state of German culture and politics. He pointed to the traces of an earlier sensuous way of thought and expression in old church songs and particularly in Luther but suggested that they

---

[33] See, e.g., Menges, 'Herder on National, Popular and World Literature', 202.
[34] Herder, 'Ausweg zu Liedern fremder Völker', 59.   [35] Ibid., 60.
[36] Ibid., 61; cf. Renner, '"Ausweg zu Liedern fremder Völker"', 119–120.
[37] 'Ausweg zu Liedern fremder Völker', 61–62. On the seminal inspiration of this research programme for new kinds of poetry in the Baltic context, see Liina Lukas, '"…mit Treue, Lust und Liebe". Einfühlung in das Volkslied', in *Herder on Empathy*, 272–296. Lukas and several other commentators have also pointed out the political and emancipatory goals of Herder's engagement with Latvian and Estonian folk songs; see e.g., ibid., 281 and Renner, '"Ausweg zu Liedern fremder Völker"', 121, 130.
[38] Herder, 'Ausweg zu Liedern fremder Völker', 62.

had later all but disappeared.[39] He thus hoped that 'Ossian, the songs of wild peoples, skalds, romances, and provincial history could lead us to a better path', whilst there were already certain indications that a 'manly, strong, firm German tone' would again be found in contemporary lyrical poetry.[40] He also mused that the German ode could again resume some of its original features – 'feeling for the entire situation! Conversation of the human heart – with God! with itself! With all of nature! Harmony! It will be what it was. Not a numerically transcribed artificial piece of harmony! Movement! Melody of heart! Dance!'"[41]

In the preface to *Ancient Folk Songs*, Herder assumed a much more pressing tone, directly reflecting on the relationship between German political history and the current status of German folk culture among the educated segments of society: 'A great people and empire! or rather, a people and empire of ten great peoples! – do you have no folk songs?'[42] Whilst the English and the 'more northern British people' (the Scots) had long shown appreciation for their ancient poetry, the Germans had only recently acquired a 'juvenile national pride without weight and force'.[43] Most importantly, the British people had a 'national way of thought', and thus venerable national authors such as Chaucer, Spencer, Shakespeare, Milton and others had already gathered songs for the '*nation*!, *people*! a body that is called *fatherland*!' – something that 'we Germans (as much as we prattle, sing or write about it) do not as yet *have*, perhaps never will have'.[44] In contrast to British authors, German intellectuals did not seem to take much interest in the songs of their ancestors. There were, however, clear historical reasons for this regrettable neglect in Herder's view – Germany has been 'a mother and servant to foreign nations, their regent and lawgiver, decider of their fate, and almost always at the same time their bleeding slave and exhausted wetnurse'.[45] Indeed, Herder continued, the 'true history of the German national spirit' (*würkliche Geschichte der deutschen Nationalgeist*) was as yet to be written.[46] Emphasising the complexity of this task, he compared Germany with a wild thornbush that had ramified into numerous offshoots. Germans, Herder continued, were 'ashamed of everything that is patriotic', aping foreign models in all kinds

---

[39] Herder, 'Auszug aus einem Briefwechsel über Ossian', 518–520.   [40] Ibid., 521.

[41] Ibid., 523.

[42] Herder, 'Vorrede [Alte Volkslieder]', in *FHA*, III, 15–25 (20); Bohlmann, *The Song Loves the Masses*, 31.

[43] Ibid., 18; cf. Bohlmann, *The Song Loves the Masses*, 28 (the translation is entirely mine).

[44] Ibid., 20.   [45] Ibid., 23; cf. Bohlmann, *The Song Loves the Mases*, 32.   [46] Ibid., 22.

of fine arts.[47] In Herder's view, Germany had acquired a 'hireling's spirit' (*Mietlingsgeist*) so that the connection to the trunk (the *Stamm*) and root was cut through: 'How happy I would be if some really precious national fragments would be rediscovered, to prove me wrong about it!'.[48] Herder's view was clear: there was immense value in the currently despised 'raw songs of a raw people' (*rohe Gesänge eines rohes Volks*). These songs, he suggested, are the 'remnant pieces of folk songs that are still alive', surviving fragments of ancient treasures that perhaps still could spark 'the German patriotic spirit' (*Deutsche Vaterlandsgeist*).[49] It was a most urgent task to search for these 'surviving fragments of a lively way of thinking of the people (*lebendige Volksdenkart*)', as the latter were 'rolling into the abyss of amnesia at an accelerated pace'. Nothing less than 'the light of so-called culture was eating up [everything] around it, like cancer!'.[50]

As we have just seen, Herder in this period took a strong interest in the ways in which German and English literary history were intertwined, hence in some sense encouraging Germans to partake of the already-quite-strong British national pride. Also more generally, he hoped that all kinds of philosophically reflected encounters with the poetry of early peoples, whether it was 'foreign' or 'one's own' would contribute to provide a 'remedy and counter-medicine' for the self-alienation and imitation of Greek and Roman cultural models current in Germany.[51] However, reconnecting with one's own cultural heritage would be most productive here, insofar as it would stimulate patriotism as well as help create an appreciation for and perhaps even regenerate a bit of that 'lively way of thought' that was encapsulated in the ancient metaphors, images and myths of one's linguistic community.

6.2   Poetry, Mores and Politics

The strong, heated sentiment evinced by Herder's discussion of folk song and German national spirit was not meant to serve as an invitation to straightforwardly embrace a cult of northern peoples or ancient Germans. As we shall see below, during the middle and second half of the 1770s and even into the early 1780s, in a series of prize essays and philosophical writings, Herder systematically sought to amend his theory of the

---

[47] Ibid., 13.   [48] Ibid., 23; cf. Bohlmann, *The Song Loves the Mases*, 32 (the translation is mine).
[49] Ibid., 16.   [50] Ibid., 23; cf. Bohlmann, *The Song Loves the Mases*, 32 (the translation is mine).
[51] Herder, 'Ausweg zu Liedern[?] fremder Völker', 62.

relationship between poetry, mores and politics in the light of his Bückeburg philosophy of history. His key ideas in this respect were expressed in a Bavarian Academy of Sciences prize essay *On the Impact of the Art of Poetry on the Mores of Peoples in the Ancient and Modern Times* written in late 1777 and published in 1781.[52] In this essay Herder provided a comprehensive overview of the relationship between poetry, religion and mores in different national traditions. Indeed, as Clark has argued, Herder's essay on the impact of the art of poetry can be seen as forming the theoretical groundwork to *On German Style and Art* and the project of folk songs of 1773/1774.[53] However, it would also make sense to read this essay together with Herder's evocative analysis of Hebrew poetry, mores and politics published in 1782/1783 in which Herder articulated some of his key political ideas.[54]

In alignment with his new emphasis on fathoming the intentions of divine Providence in the unfolding of human history, Herder, both in *On the Impact of the Art of Poetry* and *On the Spirit of Hebrew Poetry*, highlighted the special status of ancient Hebrew poetry. In the spirit of *This Too a Philosophy*, he argued the necessity of recognising the distinctive type of early education that Oriental patriarchal society, and more specifically early Hebrew polity, had provided to 'humanity'. In *On the Spirit of Hebrew Poetry*, he even offered a qualified endorsement of Anglican clergyman and professor of theology Robert Lowth's views on the 'divine' character of Hebrew poetry.[55] The Hebrew language, he argued, exemplified in the 'purest' form the human capacity for creating and ordering poetic images. This capacity was not only created by God but was first awakened by him in the specific circumstances of the Orient. Herder's emphasis on the particular purity of Hebrew poetry did not, however, mean that he believed it should have been read and interpreted differently from other kinds of poetry. Herder never renounced his view that the Old Testament, too, was created by humans and constituted a historical

[52] Johann Gottfried Herder, 'Über die Wirkung der Dichtkunst auf die Sitten der Völker in alten und neuen Zeiten', in *FHA*, IV, 149–215; for a commentary on the prize competition and Herder's participation in it (Herder was awarded the prize in 1778), see Jürgen Brummack and Martin Bollacher, 'Entstehung und Textgrundlage', in *FHA*, IV, 930–931; 812–813).
[53] Clark, *Herder: His Life and Thought*, 252.
[54] For a more detailed analysis of this work, see F. M. Barnard, *Herder on Nationality*, 17–37. Barnard reads this essay as expressing Herder's most fundamental political commitments. I agree that here Herder for the first time reveals his commitment to the republican ideal of 'the government of laws, not men'. However, I think that Herder's discussion of Hebrew republicanism needs to be contextualised in his Bückeburg philosophy of history and should also be seen as reflecting his aspirations at political reform in Germany (*pace* Barnard's rejection of this connection).
[55] Herder, 'Vom Geist der Ebräischen Poesie', 663.

document. Rather, as several commentators have argued, such 'secularisation' of the Bible allowed other kinds of poetry to be regarded as 'sacred', too.[56] Although the earliest Hebrew 'natural poetry' was for Herder the first and purest among various national traditions, all kinds of 'natural poetry originated in and expressed religious experience, the feeling of the presence of the divine spirit within nature,[57] whilst also serving as a foundation for the 'ethopoeia' of distinct nations.

We will discuss these other kinds of national traditions below. However, it is important to dwell a little longer on the Hebrew tradition, as in both essays Herder invoked this tradition to highlight the moral and political function of poetry.[58] The great Hebrew poet-legislators Moses, David and Solomon, Herder argued, had inaugurated the Hebrew 'national art of poetry' (*Nationaldichtkunst*),[59] imprinting on their compatriots' minds the idea of the Hebrew people as 'God's people' (ein Volk *Gottes*).[60] Moses was the first to establish the closest connection between God, the people and the land, encapsulating the mores, laws, and the earliest history of the Hebrews in his powerful songs, whilst King David, similarly, always presented himself in his songs as 'God's servant and helper, the caretaker of God's people, a flock which is herded by the Lord himself, and that should therefore also be exemplary in its mores'.[61] In the vein of his Bückeburg philosophy of history, Herder sought to make a point that Providence chose the Hebrews to communicate to humanity the idea of the higher calling of poetry – 'the idea of the [formation of] mores, the *entire* heart of the people in the *innermost* sense' (*Sitten, das* ganze *Herz des Volkes im* innigsten *Verstande*):[62]

> The poetry of other peoples soon became fable, lies, mythology, often horror and disgrace; this is and remains *of God*! the daughter of heaven, the bride of his honor and avenger of his name. If, among all peoples, *poets* became the first idolaters, flatterers of the people and princes, jesters

---

[56] For a summary of this strand of scholarship, see Ulrike Wagner, 'Herder's Reinvention of Religious Experience', in *Herder and Religion*, ed. Staffan Bengtsson, Heinrich Clairmont, Robert E. Norton, Johannes Schmidt and Ulrike Wagner (Heidelberg, 2016), 57–74 (66). We will return to this question in Chapter 5.

[57] Herder, 'Vom Geist der Ebräischen Poesie', 698.

[58] In *On the Spirit of Hebrew Poetry* Herder again expressed a positive view of John Brown's hypothesis of the common origin of all arts, but criticised his inclusion of 'legislators' in this discussion, 'Vom Geist der Ebräischer Poesie', 1157. He now made it clear that Brown's argument about the unity of all art forms applied only to natural poetry, whereas the moral poetry of legislators was already a more developed form of poetry.

[59] Herder, 'Über die Wirkung der Dichtkunst', 159.   [60] Ibid., 160–161.   [61] Ibid., 163.

[62] Ibid., 169.

(*Tändler*), and finally corrupters of mores (*Verschlimmerer der Sitten*), so that almost nothing could remain sacred to them, here *poets* were precisely those who were zealous *against* idolatry, self-fame, flattery and softness of mores: their poetry was the altar of *the single God of truth and virtue.*[63]

Also the Hebrew politics was exemplary in Herder's view. As he argued in *On the Spirit of Hebrew Poetry*, Moses' legislation was to be regarded as the 'oldest example in the written form' of the truth that 'health, mores, political order and religious service are all of one piece'.[64] Furthermore, Herder did not conceal his admiration for the fundamental principles of politics in the Hebrew community: first, its republicanism or, as he characterised it, 'nomocracy', the government of laws, not men; and second, its federal nature. Indeed, Moses had succeeded in enabling freedom in a political society, and achieving unity in multiplicity.[65]

The Mosaic republican and federal tradition, Herder made clear, was thus superior to the Greek one precisely because in the latter, religion 'had become a *mythology* [*Mythologie*] with regard to its impact and value, a foreign and worn-out every-day fairy-tale [*Alltags-Geschichte Märchen*], its political science mere rhetoric [*Rednerei*], the philosophy sophistry.' In the Greek tradition, everything was just a game, superficial and shiny, and indeed, this kind of mythology came to be used to promote idolatry or superficial pleasure (*Ergötzlichkeit*). It was this kind of poetry, Herder argued, that Plato wanted to banish from his polity, and rightly so.[66] There was even less to be imitated in Roman poetry, as the latter had from the earliest stage been 'rude', related to physical vigour and war, commemorating the deeds and mores of the 'fathers'. The Roman polity had been established on 'constitution [*Einrichtung*], law, political religious customs [*politische Religionsgebräuche*]'.[67] The Romans never developed an 'art of poetry' comparable to the Hebrews Greek ones, indeed, the art of poetry 'never became a principle [*Triebfeder*], even less a foundational pillar of their [Roman] state'.[68] The art of oratory and legal force fulfilled the place of poetry. They thus had no idea of the purposes that this kind of art could serve in a polity, and when they began to imitate the Greeks, they either pursued it for mere entertainment, or tailored it to the crude tastes of the Roman people. Herder acknowledged that highly talented individuals had emerged in Rome, whilst disputing the impact of poetic education

---

[63] Ibid., 166.   [64] Herder, 'Vom Geist der Ebräischen Poesie', 929.   [65] Ibid., 1043ff.
[66] Herder, 'Über die Wirkung der Dichtkunst', 174.   [67] Ibid., 177.   [68] Ibid., 183.

on the people at large. When Rome, finally, became more 'fine', the Romans' art of poetry also adopted new and finer forms, yet its impact was already negligent by then.[69]

According to Herder, this special calling of Hebrew poetry paved the way for the rise of Christianity at a later point in history. The simple divine wisdom of Christianity, he argued, draws on the understanding of the central role of religious feeling for poetry, and 'pulls juice from this root in its images and language'.[70] In Hebrew poetry, this idea was both powerfully 'revealed' (*enthüllet*) and 'attractively veiled' (*reizend verhüllet*) in the form of a 'national art of poetry', because only in this way could it be imprinted deep onto the human heart, which cannot initially speak the language of abstraction. From this specific 'place' and 'time', however, it was meant to be communicated to other peoples in due time, in the form of the teaching of Christ.[71]

6.2.1 Poetry, Religion and Fatherland

According to Herder, there was, however, also a significant parallel between ancient Hebrew and ancient German understandings of the vocation of poets and priests in society, which in turn was revelatory about the more general role that the latter should play in society. In 1774, soon after having published *This Too a Philosophy* and the first part of *The Oldest Document*, and in parallel to writing his essay *How the German Bishops*, Herder got into dispute with Johann Joachim Spalding, the leading rationalist theologian in Berlin. In his 'Fifteen Provincial Papers' (*Fünfzehn Provinzialblätter*), Herder sought to counter Spalding's recent suggestion that in a modern society, Lutheran pastors were to be regarded as contractual state officials.[72] In Herder's view, this was a most serious misinterpretation of the authentic role of preachers. Spalding had been misled by various kinds of criticisms by David Hume and Voltaire regarding the abuse of power by 'priests' as a separate estate. Whilst the clerical estate had indeed been prone to corruption in various cultures, it was important not to let these examples overshadow the original idea and function of that estate as revealed by Herder's philosophy of history of mankind. Religion could not be merely rational, it could only be embraced

---

[69] Ibid., 180–184.   [70] Ibid., 166.   [71] Ibid.

[72] Herder, 'An Prediger. Fünfzehn Provinzialblätter', 124. On Herder's ideas about modern preachers more generally, see Kaspar Renner, 'Herder und der geistliche Stand. Neue Perspektiven für die germanistische Forschung', *Deutsche Vierteljahrsschrift für Literaturwissenschaft und Geistesgeschichte* 89 (2015), 198–234.

through receiving the 'light and image' through revelation which would awaken 'divine feelings' in human beings.[73] Religious faith required training, albeit this training had to be of the gentlest possible kind. This, Herder argued, was clearly revealed in the early 'patriarchy' of primitive cultures. The first educators were always 'fathers and mothers' in their households.[74] As Herder argued some years later in his essay on the 'Influence of Government', it was the parents of each generation who first taught their children religion as well as the 'arts and sciences', whereas the earliest priests had the special role of reminding parents of this important task, that is, teaching the teachers.[75]

In his *Fifteen Provincial Papers*, Herder buttressed this point by invoking Justus Möser's account of early Saxon mores in his *History of Osnabrück*. According to Möser's account of 'northern patriarchy', Herder argued, it was the 'pater familias' who acted as a true 'priest' of God in his household, keeping justice in the name of God. True, as Möser also highlighted, during Tacitus' period a separate estate of 'priests' had already existed alongside the commoners and nobles in ancient German societies. However, there was no contradiction here. In the most original, authentic sense, priests were 'gift-bringers from God to the people – *teachers of revelation*, spreaders of the purest means of education, and so far chosen intermediaries – messengers and instruments of God'.[76] Thereby they also fostered a sense of common spirit within society. German priests did so by 'keeping a balance' between the two other estates of the 'national assemblies', ensuring also that everything in these societies was sacred – all public matters alongside streams, forests, valleys, etc. This, Herder argued, showed the actual responsibilities of poets and the clerical estate specifically:

> *Poetry* was originally *theology*, and the noblest, highest poetry, like musical art, will always remain *theology* in its essence. *Singers* and *prophets*, the most sublime poets of the Old Testament drew flames from the holy fire. The oldest, most venerable poets of paganism, *lawgivers*, *fathers* and *educators* of men, *Orpheus* and *Epimenides* and all the fable-names of primeval times, sang (about) gods and made the world happy. What the *Miltons* and *Klopstocks*, *Fenelons* and *Racines* felt in their purest moments of sunshine was religion, was only the echo of the divine voice in nature and writing.[77]

---

[73] Herder, 'An Prediger. Fünfzehn Provinzialblätter', 108 and 121.
[74] Ibid., 124. Herder clearly did not associate 'patriarchy' with the subjection of women, but rather sought to portray 'fathers and mothers' as jointly fulfilling the role of 'patriarchs'.
[75] Ibid., 296–302.   [76] Ibid., 120.   [77] Ibid., 127.

In Herder's view, as we see in this citation, theology, poetry and legislation were actually ultimately the offsprings of one divine spirit. Herder thereby both restated and expanded his earlier argument about poetry as the foundation of society (see Chapter 2), underlining its particular relationship to religion. Priests were to be recognised as poets and vice versa, indeed, the two estates were initially inseparable. True, Jesus Christ did not belong to this order – he was beyond any traditional ranks, and his example was to be followed by all human beings.[78] Nevertheless, it was necessary to have a special profession in society who would be devoted to spreading the spirit of his teaching. Herder's message was clear: this kind of calling was still relevant in modern society where Christian preachers, in their own way, could fulfil the authentic role of poets and priests, providing humans with the deepest and most important kind of moral training whilst also upholding the true spirit of laws.

The northern peoples, obviously, did not adopt Christianity straight away; their poetry and theology first served the need of their own society. In *On the Impact*, Herder highlighted the role of the 'bards and heroes' of the 'northern peoples' in resisting Rome, once again expressing the wish that the ancient songs of Germans would be rediscovered.[79] Combining the information derived from Tacitus, Bartholin and Mallet, Herder viewed the Scandinavian peoples as a subset of the 'Germans' or 'northern peoples'. The spectacular love of freedom, loyalty, and valour of all these 'northern peoples', he argued, could be seen as an expression of the powerful impact of their songs; whilst they also directly praised the magic power of singing in their songs. Compared to the 'Germans', the Britons, the Gauls, the Irish and the Scots seemed to have a less 'hard' and 'wild' character and were more receptive to the 'magic of solitude and love, courage and mercy', which was why the Ossianic songs had once been able to sustain not only military valour but also resistance to a tyrant, and still had a powerful effect on the modern reader. It was also providentially necessary, Herder argued, that these peoples had to 'remain so long in the state that we call wildness', so as to be capable of adopting Christianity.

In just a couple of brief remarks, Herder here introduced a novel argument, emphasising the exemplary way in which Christianity had spread in northern Europe. He maintained that northern 'simplicity' and 'healthy strong heart' (*gesundes, starkes Herz*) guaranteed that Christianity found its way into these northern peoples' 'songs and customs', the Bible was translated into the 'verses' of their language, whilst the legends of

---

[78] Ibid.   [79] Herder, 'Über die Wirkung der Dichtkunst', 185.

saints were woven into their 'songs of the fathers'.[80] Instead of a narrow
'national art of poetry', northern peoples thus developed a 'wonderful
mixture and composite form'.[81] He did not spend much time discussing
simultaneous developments in southern Europe, whereas he quite clearly
believed that Christianity had more strongly taken root among northern
peoples than southern European peoples.

The defining feature of various European traditions of poetry, for
Herder, was thus precisely their syncretic character. Herder's comments
on the developments in the rest of Europe – and in later centuries, in
Europe in general – were invariably positive. He moved on to point out
the beneficial impact of Arabic poetry on the peoples of southern Europe,
culminating in the rise of a distinctive 'oriental-spiritual' phenomenon of
chivalry (*Rittergeist*), which further contributed to the rise of a novel
understanding of love and a closer communication and relationship
between men and women. He also highlighted some positive side-effects
of crusades in bringing European nations together under a single flag
bearing a cross.[82] Throughout this 'middle' period, Herder further argued,
Christianity had a powerful impact on people's mores through songs (*die
Lieder*). Not only were the ancient Hebrew hymns and psalms as contained
in the Old Testament wonderfully capable of offering consolation and
encouragement, but also church songs, even 'language of the monks'
(*Mönchssprache*) had a powerful effect on people's hearts. Bohemian
brothers and Luther, too, famously used songs for inculcating mores.
Choral singing, Herder concluded, was an excellent way of opening up
human hearts to mutual brotherly sentiments.[83]

Where, exactly, had things gone wrong then? Clearly, the problem was
not the multiplicity and fusion of different poetic traditions. Rather, it was
the interruption of the spontaneous dynamics of their evolution. Herder's
argument was straightforward: the emergence of the neo-Latin and neo-
Greek art of poetry was the culprit here. It created a gulf between the
educated and the common people, as a result of which poetry lost its most
important function – to form mores and political principles. Common
people were despised as barbarians, and so were the mother tongues that
they spoke. Poets began to imitate ancient models, theorise about their art
and follow abstract rules, whereby poetry became 'amusement, beautiful
art, play'. Different influences converged to suppress 'freedom, nature,
peculiarity of mores in all estates', thus weakening all 'forces' (*Kräfte*). The
Moors were driven out of Spain, 'vassals were humiliated and provinces

---

[80] Ibid., 188.   [81] Ibid.   [82] Ibid., 194–195.   [83] Ibid., 196.

unified', and instead, a 'political order' was established and everyone was resting at the feet of a single person – the monarch.[84] Gallantry and religion were replaced by abstract and sometimes openly atheist philosophy. Discoveries of the new world, book printing and a general 'culture of sciences' managed to bring estates, princes, monarchies and entire world regions together, whereas poetry only lost *'penetration, depth* and *determinacy'* (*Eindrang, Tiefe* und *Bestimmtheit*).[85]

Commenting one by one on different national literary traditions in modern Europe – Italian, French, English/British and finally, German – Herder was particularly critical of the Italian and French traditions, as in the latter poetry had degenerated into entertainment. In the English tradition, he briefly highlighted Shakespeare, presenting him as emerging from the 'remains of the time of chivalry'. With an entire world full of characters, forces, passions, mores and facts in his soul, Shakespeare continued to have an impact on the following generations, even though in order to fully comprehend and properly apply his genius, another genius was needed.[86] However, even in Britain, after Shakespeare, genius was replaced with 'taste', and poetry lost much of its warmth. Nevertheless, Herder was relatively positive about the moral weeklies of Pope, Addison and Steele, and even more positive about the English realistic novel, embodied, first of all in Henry Fielding's *Tom Jones*.[87] He also discussed political satire as a supporting feature of British freedom, acknowledging its considerable impact, yet also pointing out its 'exaggerated' nature and the mutual nullification of the usage of the same weapon by opposing parties.[88]

The poverty of the German literary tradition, according to Herder, reflected Germany's dire political situation – it was a literature of a 'divided country, a bay of small monarchical islands', in which 'one province was hardly able to understand another; in which mores, religion, interest, degree of cultivation [*Bildung*], and government [*Regierung*] inhibited and modified even the best kind of effect'.[89] In contrast to other European nations, 'throughout the medieval period, Germans had either been forced abroad or overrun by other peoples, whilst Germany never had the opportunity to collect itself or find a voice for its own distinctive art of poetry'.[90] Indeed, later on, German authors did not write for the people, but for scholars and critics, whilst all that was left for the people was only spiritual poetry. Whilst

---

[84] Ibid., 198.   [85] Ibid., 199–201.
[86] Ibid., 204. We will return to Herder's discussion of Shakespeare below.   [87] Ibid., 207.
[88] Ibid.   [89] Ibid., 209.   [90] Ibid.

numerous German authors had 'wished' to influence mores, their poetry was either overly pious or sternly moralistic, engendering a reaction in the recent fashion of 'bardic singing' (*Bardengesang*), an 'ancient monument, sacred to the virtue and mores of our fathers'.[91] In the second, printed version of the essay, Herder also distanced himself clearly from this recent 'addiction to bards [*Bardensucht*]' that was only the most recent example of a general German 'addiction to strangers' (*Fremdensucht*). Furthermore, reflecting critically about the patriotic literature written during the Seven Years' War, Herder also noted the irony of writing 'patriotic' poetry in a war in which 'Germans were fighting Germans'.[92]

The ending of the version of the essay that Herder submitted to the prize competition was relatively ambiguous about the prospects for the revival of truly effective poetry in Germany. If God inspired a poet, the poet would certainly create a public for himself, but as long as poets arose from among human beings, not much was to be expected from a people among whom 'religion, people, fatherland were suppressed, hazy names'.[93] In the printed version, he was already more explicit about his hopes, relating these to the 'lessons' learned: 'We go slowly, but more surely,' he mused, 'we arrive late, but perhaps more directly and closer to the goal.' Pointing at 'two or three more recent works' (presumably, Goethe's *Götz von Berlichingen* (1773) and *Sorrows of the Young Werther* (1774)), Herder encouraged German writers to 'feel, completely feel [*fühlen, ganz zu fühlen*], and give others, living nature, truth, love, action'.[94] If the German authors would learn to feel themselves, their 'sympathy with their brothers would bring along [other] loving poets' who would [also] be able to 'capture truth, religion, simplicity'.[95] Such divinely inspired art of poetry, in turn, would also not fail to have an impact both on 'single human beings and peoples'.[96]

6.3   Reviving Modern German Poetry

How exactly could this original unity of purpose of educating professions be regenerated in a modern society with its mixed populations, fragmentation of the arts and sciences, and differentiation of ranks? As seen above, Herder accepted that modern (German) culture was necessarily mixed and fragmented. However, he believed that a common written language still served as a vehicle for creating spiritual unity in Germany. Modern

---

[91] Ibid., 211–212.   [92] Ibid., 940.   [93] Ibid., 212–213.   [94] Ibid., 941–942.
[95] Ibid., 942.   [96] Ibid., 943.

intellectuals could creatively engage with the history of their nation and create dialogue among themselves. Modern (linguistically defined) peoples had to be aware of the mixed origins of their culture, whilst also pursuing 'unity in multiplicity'. Indeed, as I hope to show below, Herder's goal was nothing less than cultivating a novel understanding of the modern self and modern 'peoplehood'. With this idea, Herder was emphatically not encouraging reviving certain customs, rituals or aesthetic models, but rather self-reflection and critical self-interrogation as well as innovative 'use' of historical knowledge in thinking through and creatively developing one's social and professional roles, including aesthetic self-expression.

True, as we have seen in previous chapters, Herder's historical accounts were not neutral across different national traditions, and he never recommended totally abstaining from moral judgement. For a modern scholar it was important to bracket one's initial responses, and explore the historical ways of thought of one's linguistic community as best as one could, by using cognitive empathy, analogical thinking as well as by tracing their complex genealogies and upshots. Ultimately, however, one could not escape judging these phenomena from the viewpoint of 'humanity' (*Humanität*). In his prize essay titled 'On the Influence of Belles Lettres on the Higher Sciences' (*Über den Einfluß der schönen auf die höheren Wissenschaften*) (written in 1779 and published in 1781 together with *On the Impact*) Herder explored the distinction between 'belles-lettres' (literature) and the 'higher sciences', meaning thereby various kinds of *humanities*. He insisted that belles-lettres were more fundamental than the higher sciences insofar as they engaged the sensuous part of the soul. However, they both served the same moral purpose – to serve mankind in all its professions and forms. It was to buttress this idea, Herder introduced the term 'humaniora'.[97] The 'humaniora' also included the sciences insofar as they were based on 'the feeling of humanity':

> I do not care to repeat myself and celebrate once more the ancient poets, orators, historians, and philosophers, *for whom all the branches of science were happily still one*. Among the moderns, too, each higher science has possessed *fine* geniuses, who have pursued it in the true spirit of humanity, just as there has been no shortage of poets who were more than poets and impressed this extra dimension on their works.[98]

As we shall see in Chapters 7 and 8, *Humanität* became a central concept for Herder in his mature years.

---

[97] Herder, 'On the Influence of Belles Lettres', 344. [98] Ibid., 345.

6.3.1   Modern Selfhood and Peoplehood

Herder's first and most important reflections on the issues of modern selfhood and peoplehood in the 1770s can be found in his essay on Shakespeare. For Herder, Shakespeare provided a model of a distinctively 'northern' and indeed, 'modern' engagement with the ancient poetry of one's people as well as the historical experience of others. Herder wrote the first version of the essay already in 1771; a second draft version appeared in 1772, but it was the third, considerably revised, version that was published as part of *On German Style and Art* in 1773.[99]

Herder's essay on Shakespeare is groundbreaking in many respects.[100] By seeking to 'explain him [Shakespeare], feel him as he is, use him, and – where possible – bring him to life for us Germans',[101] the essay fostered the rediscovery and indeed, the rise of a cult of Shakespeare in Germany. In Herder's own thinking, it can be seen as foreshadowing Herder's understanding of the process of civilisation in *This Too a Philosophy*. Conceived as a new kind of parallel between 'ancient' and 'modern' drama, and emphasising the contrasts between the original Greek poetry, on the one hand, and the French and the later, German, contemporary imitations, on the other, the essay raised penetrating questions about the changing standards of aesthetic taste in history. It also identified a new, more authentic understanding of 'modernity' in Shakespeare. Furthermore, as Wolfgang Proß has argued, the essay can also be seen as Herder's first attempt to articulate a novel understanding of the historical process as well as a historian's relationship with their material. According to Proß, Herder's emerging philosophy of history is particularly evident in the 1773 version, in which Herder characterises Shakespeare's subject matter as 'history of humanity', and Shakespeare himself as 'the translator of all languages and characters and passions of humanity, and detective of the thread of all events, which fate has thrown [at the characters]'.[102]

Herder's essay on Shakespeare also invoked some of the central themes of his evolving philosophy of life and a novel understanding of the complex relationship of self- and other-feeling that he came to develop in *On the*

---

[99] For a detailed comparison between the three extant versions of his essay on Shakespeare, see Gjesdal, *Herder's Hermeneutics*, ch. 5.

[100] For a broader discussion of Herder's aesthetic views in this period, see Gregory Moore, 'Introduction', in *SWA*.

[101] Herder, 'Shakespeare', in *SWA*, 291.

[102] Proß, 'Anhang. Amerkungen [Aus: *Von Deutscher Art und Kunst*]', in *HWP*, I, 820–849 (820).

Cognition.[103] On the one hand, Shakespeare showed a strong self-feeling, an understanding of his own 'place' and society, and aimed to cultivate it. Herder had no doubt that Shakespeare was a 'genius' as an individual,[104] but he also saw in him an embodiment of the collective creativity of the English nation, which did not 'care to ape the Greeks' but set out to 'invent its own drama'.[105] Shakespeare, Herder argued, 'was confronted with nothing like the simplicity of national manners, deeds, inclinations, and historical traditions that formed Greek drama'.[106] The northern manners, as we have seen above, were complex fusions of the original German mores, Roman, Arabic, and Christian influences. Now, Shakespeare 'was endowed with divine powers to summon from completely different material and by quite different means precisely the same effect [as the Greek drama had], *fear* and *pity*, and to a degree of which the earlier treatment and material were scarcely capable'. But just like Sophocles was teaching and cultivating *Greeks*, Shakespeare was teaching and cultivating 'northern men'.[107]

At the same time, Shakespeare also reached out to the whole world. According to Herder, not only was the society that surrounded Shakespeare in his native England internally much more complex than the Greek one(s), he was also aware of a much wider arena of human history. Shakespeare's work, quite differently from Sophocles in 'whose characters a single tone predominates', encompassed 'only separate events from the book of events, of Providence, of the world, blown by the storm of history; individual impressions of peoples, estates, souls, all the most various and independently acting machines, all the unwitting, blind instruments – which is precisely what we are in the hands of the Creator of the world – which come together to form a single, whole dramatic image, an event of singular grandeur that only a poet can survey'.[108] In this respect, Herder extolled Shakespeare's ability to be 'true to Nature' in his own special way, tossing 'his world events and human destinies through all the time and places in which – well, in which they occurred': 'Thus we see that the whole world is merely the body belonging to this great spirit: all the scenes of Nature are the limbs of this body, just as every character and

---

[103] See Chapter 4.

[104] As Moore reminds us, Herder's understanding of the concept of 'genius' was indebted to Edward Young's *Conjectures on Original Composition* (1759). For Young (following Shaftesbury), the genius was the original creator, whose work grew from the 'vital root of Genius'. It was a 'Promethean figure who imitated no models, but only nature', Moore, 'Introduction', 17–19.

[105] Herder, 'Shakespeare', 297.   [106] Ibid., 298.   [107] Ibid.   [108] Ibid., 299.

way of thinking is a feature of this spirit – and we might call the whole by the name of Spinoza's vast God: "Pan! Universum!"'[109]

For Herder, the Shakespearean relationship to one's national community and the world was to serve as a model for how the modern spectator or reader should relate to their own world.[110] Indeed, Herder suggested that everyone could recognise in Shakespeare their own ability to be transported in space and time and imagine the experience of a different being in a different situation: 'Have you never known situations in your life when your soul sometimes dwelled wholly outside you?'[111] The poet's task, Herder argued, is 'to transport you' to his world, thereby enabling one's own soul, too, to 'create its own space, world, and time'.[112] This kind of 'transport', indeed, a form of cognitive empathy stimulated by literature, was meant not only to arouse the imagination, and perhaps also sympathy and identification with the other, but also reflection about oneself. According to Herder, this was nowhere clearer than in the way in which Shakespeare treated folk poetry. Shakespeare drew on it and incorporated it directly in his work, but he also gave it an individual twist, enlightening the reader/spectator about their own prejudices. Why has no one inquired, Herder asked, 'how, by what art and manner of creation, was Shakespeare able to transform some worthless romance, tale, or fabulous history into such a living whole?' None of his plays is purely of one genre, whilst the 'empty locos communes' are put into 'the mouths of children and fools'.[113] History was his subject, but never just history or 'historical truth' – his purpose was not merely to give support to a 'living tradition' or 'national feeling', even though he certainly 'made it easier to imagine certain stories, strengthen the deceit here and there'.[114] Indeed, the 'historical illusion' emerging from an imagined progression of events as brought forth through forces (*Kräfte*) was essential for philosophising about history, and this kind of illusion itself was modelled on the way in which we create an illusion of our life as individuals. Shakespeare not only mastered all of that but achieved much more than that: he also 'painted history' and thereby achieved the highest degree of 'theatrical illusion', creating lively dialogue and action between characters, not just 'one action',

[109] Ibid., 303. On this reference to Spinoza, cf. Proß, 'Anhang. Amerkungen [Aus: *Von Deutscher Art und Kunst*]', 834–836, 840; Greif, '3.3.1 *Auszug aus einem Briefwechsel*', 493–494.
[110] Cf. Greif, '3.3.1 *Auszug aus einem Briefwechsel*', 487.
[111] Herder, 'Shakespeare', 305 (I have slightly modified the translation).   [112] Ibid.
[113] Ibid., 306. Stefan Greif correctly notes that Herder's discussion of the newer folk song in *Shakespeare* was intended precisely to 'question the latently chauvinistic "self-description" (Lotman) of a language community', '3.3.1 *Auszug aus einem Briefwechsel*', 487; cf. Gaier, 'Kommentar', 876.
[114] Herder, 'Shakespear [sic!]: 2. Entwurf', in *HWP*, I, 561.

but a progressive event (*evenement*).[115] This, however, was nothing but 'moral philosophy and history for education, and human poetry, and intuitive sensation of all hearts, and passions and actions', 'the liveliest, fullest and most instructive history of human nature!'[116] Awareness of the history of one's people and its cultural heritage was thus ultimately to serve the higher purpose of enlightenment about human nature and human interaction, a deeper understanding of one's self and one's people in inter-action with other selves and peoples.

6.4   Conclusion

As seen in this chapter, in the 1770s Herder was drawn to the idea that a certain revival of German poetry might initiate a process of moral and political reform in Germany. Whilst engaging with early forms of poetry and religion, and highlighting the moral and political role of poets and priests in ancient Israel and ancient Germany (Saxony) in particular, Herder sought to analyse the republican and federal political systems of these societies as models of 'unity in multiplicity'. At the same time, he paid serious attention to the ways in which modern, 'northern' traditions had emerged. He highlighted the moral core of Christianity, and its special relationship to the Hebrew tradition, on the one hand, and to the modern European national traditions, in the other. His key idea was that the revival of Greek and Roman models of poetry in the early modern period had interfered with the natural evolution of these traditions, having created a wedge between religion and poetry as well as the culture of the elites and the people, which in turn was conducive to modern mechanical forms of government. However, modern historical consciousness – as exemplified in Shakespeare – also had an enormous moral and political potential. Modern authors, pastors and cultural elites more broadly could cultivate new reflective forms of art and philosophy that would enhance the human capacity for self-determination as well as genuine sociability. This ethic would be fully in line with Christian morality, whilst also enhancing the status of their particular cultural and political community in international contexts.

An opportunity arose for Herder himself to try and propose a way in which this new programme of action could be institutionalised in the Holy Roman Empire. In an essay entitled *The Idea for the First Patriotic Institute for Germany's Universal Spirit*, written in 1785 and published in late 1787,

---

[115] Ibid., 562–563; 571.   [116] Ibid., 572; cf. Herder, 'Shakespeare', in *SWA*, 307.

Herder suggested a way in which Germany's imperial constitution (*Reichsverfassung*) could acquire a new life and 'soul'.[117] He proposed that a 'German academic assembly' (*Teutsche Akademie*) would be created that would act as a unifying, coordinating body above all existing societies and academies, thereby helping 'not only to spread, but unite light'.[118] Different provincial societies would send their representatives to participate in this assembly, in which common matters would be jointly discussed. This assembly, or indeed, a parliament of scholars, could thus serve as the 'heart' of the artificial 'body of the state' of 'our fatherland', which so long has 'not always recognised its own forces [*Kräfte*]'.[119] Such a body, Herder argued, would first of all seek to unify and purify the standards of the written German language, foster the 'patriotic study' of German history as well as promote 'an active philosophy of nation-building and happiness',[120] highlighting the values of the common good and one single common interest of Germany. It would also publish a 'yearbook of German national spirit', which would publish the reports by different members of the institute on their attempts to promote the common cause.[121] The internal 'firmness' (*Festigkeit*), order (*Ordnung*) and lawful freedom (*gesetzesmäßige Freiheit*) that this kind of assembly would help to create, Herder mused, would also be expressed in external power.[122] All 'leading nations' in different historical periods had ruled not only through military might but also 'through language and culture'.[123]

This institute never materialised. As Herder himself mentioned in his correspondence, the idea to write this essay had come from Margrave Carl Friedrich of Baden, one of the leading members of the German League of Princes (*Fürstenbund*) formed in 1785 under the leadership of Frederick the Great of Prussia.[124] Herder could not decline the offer, being currently involved in a project of reforming Weimar's antiquated school and university education. However, he was never very optimistic about the willingness of the German princes to actually invest their energy into it. He

---

[117] See also Dreitzel, 'Herders politische Konzepte', 268–268; Schmidt, 'Scholarship, Morals and Government', 270–271; Hien, *Altes Reich*, 307–308; Noyes, *Herder: Aesthetics*, 248–250. Noyes reads this essay as part of Herder's response to Kant. I do not find this interpretation implausible (cf. my interpretation of Herder's controversy with Kant in Chapter 7), but I think that its most immediate point of reference is clearly the imperial constitution of the Holy Roman Empire.

[118] Johann Gottfried Herder, 'Idee zum ersten patriotischen Institut für den Allgemeingeist Deutschlands (Herbst 1787)', in *FHA*, IX/2, 565–580 (571, 566).

[119] Ibid., 565–566.   [120] Ibid., 573–576.   [121] Ibid., 576.   [122] Ibid., 565.

[123] Ibid., 569.

[124] On the historical context of this plan, see Hans Tümmler, 'Johann Gottfried Herders Plan einer Deutschen Akademie (1787)', in idem, *Weimar, Wartburg, Fürstenbund 1776–1820: Geist und Politik im Thüringen der Goethe-Zeit. Gesammelte Aufsätze* (Bad Neustadt, 1995), 39–52.

was sceptical about the purposes of the *Fürstenbund* from the outset, and feared that the alliance was created to enhance the power of the Prussian monarch. This, indeed, was very much the case. We will learn about his philosophical reasons for this scepticism in Chapter 7. For Herder, the reforms that one could really put one's stakes on were increasingly only those 'from below'.

State-Machines, Commerce and the Progress of Humanität *in Europe*

In 1782, Herder embarked on a new project on philosophy of history, which eventually materialised as his most systematic and voluminous work, *Ideas for the Philosophy of History of Mankind*. The work was published in four instalments (1784, 1785, 1787, 1791). One further instalment was planned, but Herder never completed it. As Wolfgang Proß has highlighted, Herder's new approach to the philosophy of history centred on what he called the 'natural laws of humanity', viewing humanity as both embedded in and standing at the apex of a complex evolving system of natural forces. Crucially, Herder also came up with ideas for a global universal history, laying out the ways in which the human species had diversified itself into different peoples, which in turn traversed different paths of historical development. Such an approach to history, Herder suggested, could also be reconciled with an emphasis on human freedom, including moral and political freedom. Humans were both 'natural beings' as well as the 'first being[s] set free by creation'.[1]

From the second instalment (1785), Herder, in *Ideas*, picked up a heated debate with Immanuel Kant concerning universal history. Kant, too, had begun to ponder the underlying logic of human history in the same period. Kant's minor essay, entitled *Idea for a Universal History with a Cosmopolitan Purpose* (*Idee zu einer allgemeinen Geschichte in weltbürgerlicher Absicht*), appeared in November 1784, and then in January and November 1785 Kant further published two highly critical reviews of the first and second instalments of Herder's *Ideas*.[2] Herder learned of Kant's essay and (anonymous) review of the first instalment simultaneously in early 1785.

---

[1] For a systematic overview of the main themes in this work, see Wolfgang Proß, '1.4.2. *Ideen zur Philosophie der Geschichte der Menschheit*', in *Herder Handbuch*, 171–215.

[2] Immanuel Kant, 'Reviews of Herder's *Ideas for the Philosophy of History: Parts I and II*', in Kant, *Anthropology, History, and Education*, ed. Günter Zöller et al., trans. Mary Gregor et al. (Cambridge, 2007), 121–142. On these reviews, see Haym, *Herder*, II, 275, 279; Hans S. Reiss, 'Introduction to Reviews of Herder's *Ideas on the Philosophy of Mankind* and *Conjectures on the Beginning of Human*

Upon reading them, he became outraged. In a letter to Johann Georg Hamann, Herder sarcastically commented that Kant's argument in his essay was essentially that 'man is created for the species and the most perfect state-machine at the end of all time'.[3] In another letter, addressed to Friedrich Heinrich Jacobi, Herder argued that Kant's central thesis was not just ridiculous but also detestable. By using 'political antagonism and the most perfect monarchy, indeed, the co-existence of many most perfect monarchies that are ruled by pure reason in corpore' to explain the development of human forces (*Kräfte*) and, ultimately, morality, Kant's essay for Herder reeked of 'wretched ice-cold, slavish enthusiasm [*hundelende Eiskalte, Knechtsschwärmerei*]'.[4]

Why did Herder react so strongly to Kant's ideas? The Kant–Herder debate has received considerable attention in scholarly literature.[5] Whilst Kant had published his *Critique of Pure Reason* in 1781 and was rethinking his moral philosophy and views on studying nature and history from the perspective of critical philosophy,[6] Herder's *Ideas* are best understood as both a radicalisation and culmination of his long-term efforts to articulate a naturalist philosophy of humanity. As several scholars have suggested, the fundamental differences between the student and his former academic teacher came to a head in this controversy. Most fundamentally, Kant was a dualist on body and soul as well as on nature and morality, while Herder was an anti-dualist and radical naturalist. In contrast to Kant, Herder viewed humans as belonging to the realm of nature and human history as part of natural history. These differences had a bearing on their understanding of human history as well as moral and political views. Kant and Herder, it has been shown, vehemently disagreed about the methodology of philosophy of history, and held contrasting views about the relationship between nature and culture, morality and happiness, about

---

History', in Kant, *Political Writings*, ed. Hans S. Reiss and trans. by H.B. Nisbet, 2nd, enlarged edition (Cambridge, 2000), 250–272 (195).

[3] Herder to Hamann 14. February 1785, in *DA*, V (1979), 106.

[4] Herder to Jacobi, 25. February 1785, in *DA*, V, 109.

[5] The classic study of the controversy is Hans Dietrich Irmscher, 'Die Kontroverse zwischen Kant und Herder über die Methode der Geschichtsphilosophie (orig. 1987)', reprinted in idem, *Weitstrahlsinniges Denken: Studien zu Johann Gottfried Herder*, ed. Marion Heinz and Violetta Stolz (Würzburg, 2009), 295–334; see also Sharon Anderson-Gold, 'Kant and Herder', in *A Companion to the Philosophy of History and Historiography*, ed. Aviezer Tucker (Oxford, 2008), 457–467.

[6] For the central tenets of Kant's philosophy of life, and its relationship to Herder's ideas, see John Zammito, *The Genesis of Kant's Critique of Judgement* (Chicago, 1992).

the course and possible goal of human history, and about the role of the modern state.[7]

This chapter will further elucidate these differences by seeking to reconstruct the development of Herder's political thought in the 1780s and by showing that he intentionally attempted to devise an alternative vision to that of Kant. Thereby, I hope to highlight certain elements of Herder's account that have so far remained hidden from our view – first of all, his ideas on individual self-determination, and his history of modern liberty and enlightenment. I begin by discussing the moral aspects of Herder's naturalism as laid out in the first instalment of *Ideas*. I argue that Herder here refined his distinctive understanding of human sociability and self-determination (freedom and morality), further deepening his debt to the Stoic understanding of self-preservation. Herder reinterpreted the Stoic strands in early modern natural law in a vitalist idiom, erasing the strict boundaries drawn between the laws of humans and animals, and viewing all living beings as demonstrating a number of functional similarities in the ways in which they relate to themselves, the members of their species and those of other species.[8] Both humans and animals were naturally sociable and 'sympathetic'. They also recognised a rudimentary degree of similarity and reciprocity to other members of their species. Humans, however, developed reason and worked out rules of equity for themselves. Since morality and happiness were grounded in human capacities for sympathy and equity, they were achievable for all humans, whereas they also took very different forms in different conditions and traditions. Nevertheless, there was a universal element in these different iterations of moral virtue, consisting in sociability and equity.

Kant's essay was based on very different foundations. He invoked a distinctive understanding of human 'unsocial sociability' and viewed morality as a late development in human history. Moreover, he underlined the key role of the modern state in facilitating this development. Herder rejected all the constitutive elements of Kant's account of universal history

---

[7] See Marion Heinz, 'Kulturtheorien der Aufklärung: Herder und Kant', in *Nationen und Kulturen: Zum 250. Geburtstag Johann Gottfried Herders*, ed. Regine Otto (Würzburg, 1996), 139–152; Allen Wood, *Kant's Ethical Thought* (Cambridge, 1999), 229–249; Wood, 'Herder and Kant on History'; Sikka, *Herder on Humanity*, 44–84; Muthu, *Enlightenment against Empire*, chs. 4–6; Noyes, *Herder: Aesthetics*, 226–255.

[8] On vitalist natural philosophy, see, e.g., Peter Hanns Reill, *Vitalizing Nature in the Enlightenment* (Berkley, 2005); cf. idem, 'Eighteenth-Century Uses of Vitalism in Constructing the Human Sciences', in *Biology and Ideology from Descartes to Dawkins*, ed. Denis R. Alexander and Ronald L. Numbers (Chicago, 2010), 61–87; Stephen Gaukroger, *The Collapse of Mechanism and the Rise of Sensibility: Science and the Shaping of Modernity, 1680–1760* (Oxford, 2012).

(his ideas on sociability, morality and the role of the modern state). As I seek to show, he at the same time offered an alternative account of the origins of political government and domination (*Herrschaft*) and the conditions for achieving morality. Herder yet again highlighted the new kind of 'despotism' of modern 'state-machines' and put forward a penetrating critique of Kant's proposed solution to the problem of war in universal history, a strong federation of states with coercive powers. Herder believed that a Kantian 'state of states' would be nothing but a most horrifying form of universal despotism. Since my main goal will be to elucidate Herder's position, I will not be defending Kant against Herder's reading of his ideas, nor will I be able to discuss Kant's responses to Herder.[9]

The main focus in this chapter will be on Herder's alternative vision of the development of culture and *Humanität* in Europe. I intend here to set out his theory regarding the role of commerce in European history and his vision of the possible future pacification of Europe. I argue that in order to provide a conclusive response to Kant, Herder sought to refine his own account of the history of modern 'state-machines' and political government in Europe and proposed an alternative vision of the prospects for greater peace in Europe and the world. First, Herder attempted to discern what he called the 'natural laws' of historical development so as to demonstrate that a 'learning process' was well under way in human history. He suggested that there was an underlying logic to the historical process consisting in a form of historical justice. This logic could also be grasped and knowingly followed by individual agents. Second, and more importantly for the general theme in this book, he offered an original account of the ways in which European states had attained their current degree of lawful government and prosperity. This account has received almost no attention in previous scholarship.

As will emerge in this chapter, Herder's account was a peculiar combination of pessimism and optimism about the historical prospects of modern societies to achieve good government and peace. In contrast to Kant, Herder located the origins and foundations of modern European 'state-machines' in a distinctive type of political government that developed after the Germanic

---

[9] See Immanuel Kant, 'Conjectures on the Beginning of Human History', in *Political Writings*, 221–234 and Kant, *Critique of Judgement*, trans. James Creed Meredith (Oxford, 1992), 92–100. On the importance of Herder's work for Kant's concerns with history, see Zammito, *The Genesis of Kant's Critique* and Karl Ameriks, 'The Purposive Development of Human Capacities', in *Kant's Idea of a Universal History with a Cosmopolitan Aim: A Critical Guide*, ed. Amélie Oksenberg Rorty and James Schmidt (Cambridge, 2009), 46–67.

conquest of Roman territories and in the Carolingian period specifically, highlighting this form of government as a novel type of military despotism. Herder acknowledged that these state-machines had undergone several important developments in modern times but maintained that their machine-like and expansive nature had fundamentally remained the same. Furthermore, whilst Herder did not deny various kinds of modern achievements, such as the rule of law or the increasingly orderly conduct of wars, he believed that these achievements only exacerbated the general waning of cultural creativity and agency in modern times, and thus were undermining themselves in the long run.

However, there was also a different line of development in European history that Herder sought to trace in *Ideas*. In contrast to Kant (and to some extent to his own previous views in the late 1770s), he no longer identified the origins of modern rule of law in the intensified rivalry between early modern states and rulers' economic policies but in much more long-term European developments. For Herder, the 'modern' ideal of liberty was in fact already born in the medieval period. The realisation of modern liberty had become possible not only because rulers had wisely come to allow their subjects to pursue their individual interests without arbitrary interference but also because these subjects had initially practised self-government in cities. Drawing on new elements in William Robertson's 'Enlightened narrative' of Europe's history, Herder claimed that the interplay between civil and clerical authorities in the post-Carolingian period enabled the relatively autonomous growth of cities, which had established institutions of self-government as well as achieved the rule of law and security of property in their territories, hence allowing them to become havens of industry, commerce and even mutual aid and security. At the same time, they also created extensive pan-European networks, such as, most importantly, the Hanseatic League. Herder's emphasis on the role of commercial cities in European history constituted not only a significant revision of his views in the 1770s but also a theoretical refinement of his previous celebration of 'modern liberty' in the former Hanseatic city Riga in 1765.

This historical vision, further, had major implications for his understanding of Europe's current predicament and future. On the one hand, Herder suggested that the 'Hanseatic league' could still serve as an example for a future European union. On the other hand, Herder made an equally original point by arguing that an improving understanding of the true 'art of government' and growing international trade would gradually empower the colonised and subdued peoples in Europe. This, he proposed, would ultimately undermine and dismantle the existing imperial state-machines, enabling these peoples to revive their traditions of self-government. In any case, a far-reaching restructuring of the whole political landscape in Europe was unavoidable in Herder's view.

The chapter consists of three sections. In the first, I will outline the basic features of Herder's naturalism and his account of the natural foundations of sociability, morality and *Humanität* in the first instalment of *Ideas*. In the second, I contrast Herder's and Kant's philosophical histories of culture, morality and political government, reconstructing Herder's critique of Kant's account. In the third, I turn to Herder's alternative vision of the development of culture and *Humanität* in Europe, discussing his theory of the role of commerce in European history and his vision of the possible future pacification of Europe.

7.1 Foundations

7.1.1 Herder's Naturalism and Concept of Humanität

In contrast to *This Too a Philosophy*, which emphasised the limits of the human ability to understand the aims and course of Providence in history, Herder confidently presented his approach in *Ideas* as grounded in the suppositions that God as an 'almighty power, goodness and wisdom' is 'in all his works', and that a proper study of the perceptible phenomena created by divine forces (*Kräfte*) could reveal God's plan for the world (ix).[10] This physico-theological starting point, at the same time, was compatible with what Wolfgang Proß has characterised as Herder's novel and 'radically naturalist' interpretation of human culture and history more broadly: for Herder, the latter were an integral part of one single process of nature in which the basic living force was diversifying itself so as to reach a state of stability in organised forms of various degrees of complexity.[11] The first instalment of *Ideas* accordingly outlined a sweeping account of the universal history of planet Earth, viewing it as part of a system of celestial bodies and

---

[10] Johann Gottfried Herder, *Outlines of a Philosophy of the History of Man*, ed. and trans. T. Churchill (London, 1800). Here and below in this chapter, parenthetical numbers refer to *Outlines* and *Ideen*, in *HWP*, III/1. The references to these two editions are separated by a slash (/). Since *Outlines* is the only complete English translation, I generally refer to this edition. However, I have had to modify the translation on several occasions and where possible, I am also using F. M. Barnard's translation in Johann Gottfried von Herder, 'Ideas for a Philosophy of History [1784–1791]', in *J. G. Herder on Social and Political Culture* (henceforth abbr. as *Ideas*), which contains excerpts from books 3–9. References to Barnard's translation (if applicable) are given in footnotes.

[11] Proß, '1.4.2. *Ideen*', passim; 'Nachwort', in *HWP*, III/1, 839–1040 (984–1006); see also Zammito et al., 'Johann Gottfried Herder Revisited', 664; Beiser, *The German Historicist Tradition*, 149–154.

cosmic forces, on the one hand, and as a complex system of bodies in itself, on the other. 'If our philosophy of the history of humanity would in any measure be deserving of that name', Herder declared in the opening sentence of the work, it 'must start with heaven' (1/17. Translation modified.).

As Nigel DeSouza has recently shown in fascinating detail, Herder's radical naturalism was both deeply indebted to Kant's pre-critical metaphysics and also went far beyond it.[12] While Kant had sought to explain the history of the cosmos through the dynamic principles inherent in dead matter, Herder expanded this idea to include the organic world and posited forces operating in an analogous manner at all levels of nature. Here he clearly spelled out the metaphysical view that had gradually begun to take shape in his earlier philosophical writings, that there is fundamentally just one force, that of God, which permeates nature (the created world) and diversifies itself into various modifications of different degrees of complexity, from the forces of attraction and repulsion to those associated with the elasticity of fibres, irritability of muscles and sensitivity of nerves. In so doing, these modifications of the divine force also take a huge variety of ascending forms of inanimate and animate organisation through the scale of beings all the way up to human beings.[13]

The guiding principle of Herder's approach was accordingly the idea that the complexity of the external phenomenal form and organisation of natural being reflects the internal complexity of force, while at the same time enabling a respective degree of complexity in its sensuous and representative capabilities, including self-awareness. By thus examining our constitution, it was also possible to detect our purposes:

> I wish I could extend the word humanity [*Humanität*], so as to comprise in it every thing I have thus far said on the noble formation [*Bildung*] of man to reason and freedom, finer senses and impulses, the most delicate yet strong health, to the population and rule of the Earth: for man has no more dignified word for his destiny than what expresses himself (man), within whom the image of the Creator lives imprinted as visibly as it can. We need only delineate his form [*Gestalt*], to lay out his noblest duties (98/142. Translation modified.).

Herder's unifying approach to nature and culture incorporated important new ideas developed in the field of natural history. He adopted and developed further the distinctive methodological principles of this field. Central among them was analogical reasoning, which essentially consisted

---

[12] DeSouza, 'Herder's Theory of Organic Forces', 109–130.   [13] Ibid.

in examining the form, behaviour and habitats of different species, alternating between different levels of complexity so as to detect more fundamental functional similarities and differences between them. By using analogical reasoning, a student of nature could explain both the constitution as well as behaviour of different species by treating the constitution not as a static entity but as something that changes over time in response to changes in the environment.[14]

As Dalia Nassar has argued, Herder, however, moved beyond this kind of one-directional influence, highlighting as early as in *Treatise on the Origin* that an 'animal's *very structure* , its build [*Bau*], is in dialogue with its environment, such that this structure both serves its environmental needs and is served by its environment'.[15] Furthermore, in order to understand Herder's distinctively normative approach to humanity's status in nature, we also need to appreciate that in substantial elements it was indebted to ancient Stoic ideas of natural law, which he in turn sought to accommodate in his broader vitalist metaphysics. As seen in Chapter 3, in developing his ideas of an animal's relationship to environment in *Treatise on the Origin*, Herder had harked back to Seneca's and Reimarus's ideas of *oikeiōsis*.[16] Indeed, the idea of *oikeiōsis* enables us to make sense of Herder's account of the system of nature he developed in *Ideas* as well. Although the ancient accounts of the process of *oikeiōsis* vary in detail, their authors broadly concurred in viewing it as a gradual process of appropriating what is commensurate with one's faculties and needs. As Jacob Klein has argued, the Stoic authors all point to a complex capacity for self-perception that precedes and explains an animal's earliest impulses, enabling it to display purposeful behaviour in relation to the environment. This behaviour also includes other-regarding activities such as concern for offspring and in some cases cooperation with other species.[17] While the perceptions and representations of animals consist in non-propositional knowledge and evaluations of the environment, those of humans can be verbally articulated and hence made propositional.[18]

The Stoics simultaneously also emphasised that the good of human beings consisted in a 'life regulated by reason', presupposing their rational

---

[14] For an introductory overview of the uses of the analogical method, see Reill, 'Eighteenth-Century Uses', 83–87.

[15] Dalia Nassar, 'Hermeneutics and Nature', in *The Cambridge Companion to Hermeneutics*, ed. Michael Forster and Kristin Gjesdal (Cambridge, 2017), 37–64 (55).

[16] See Chapter 3 and Piirimäe, 'Introduction', 14–18.

[17] Klein, 'The Stoic Argument', 152, 161, 186, 195.   [18] Ibid., 149.

understanding of their own constitution and the cosmos as a whole. Young human beings thus both gradually acquired growing self-awareness and the ability to understand their relationships to each other and the environment, but in order to achieve virtue, a grown-up human being would also have to attain a state of mind in which he would be fully free from the disturbing effects of the passions. Varying accounts existed of humans' capacity to attain this kind of 'right reason', although they all agreed on this being the moral goal of humanity.[19] For most ancient Stoic authors, only Gods and sages were capable of attaining right reason, for others (among them Cicero, the most important mediator of ancient Stoic thought for early modern readers), the virtue of justice as based on human rational capabilities was fundamentally attainable to all humans. According to Benjamin Straumann, the Ciceronian account in turn came to serve as a foundation for Hugo Grotius's influential account of sociability in *On the Law of War and Peace* (*De iure belli ac pacis*).[20]

As we will see, Herder offered a vitalist reinterpretation of this account. Like the Stoics and Grotius, Herder viewed sociability as a universal principle of action of all natural beings. In Herder's scale of beings, as presented in *Ideas*, humans represented the most developed life form on earth, essentially a 'middle ring' between animals and divine beings. On the one hand, they shared a number of fundamental features and desires with animals, among them, most importantly, the fundamental desire of preserving one's constitution, which encompassed both the desire for self-preservation as well as the sociable inclinations that help to preserve the species. All sensitive beings also possessed a capacity for sympathy grounded in the constitution of their nervous system – the sense of hearing enabled them to share in other sensitive beings' feelings, which in all of nature functions best at the intra-species level. As the most delicate beings in nature, humans were the most sensitive to the pain of other creatures as expressed in sound (98–101/142–147). On the other hand, humans related to their environment through reflective awareness (*Besonnenheit*), making it possible for them to develop language and thinking. Reason itself, Herder argued, should be seen as an adaptive capacity enabling humans to preserve themselves and their species. Combining the sensations of their tactile and visual senses thanks to reflective awareness,

---

[19] Ibid., 149, 190–195.
[20] Benjamin Straumann, 'Appetitus societatis and oikeiosis: Hugo Grotius's Ciceronian Argument for Natural Law and Just War', *Grotiana, New Series* 24/25 (2003/2004), 41–66 (53, 59).

humans also developed various higher kinds of sympathy, enabling them to create and sustain complex cultural worlds (89–93/131–135).[21]

Herder's understanding of morality was grounded in this account of natural sociability. While he, in *On the Cognition*, had emphasised the noble calling to follow the pull of true 'cognition and love', so as to purify one's inclinations and form one's character in the divine image (see Chapter 4), Herder now specified that the upright position of the human body and the correspondingly larger and more complex brain enabled and manifested (according to the logic of his naturalism) the complex forces of the human soul. Thanks to their physical and physiological complexity, Herder argued, humans were capable of 'creating unity from the symmetry of the two ears and two eyes', that is, seek consistency (101–102/147).[22] Indeed, 'nature' itself prompted humans to work out and seek agreement about moral norms, on which they could then also draw when regulating their necessarily partial and culturally based sympathies:

> But as the mere with-feeling [*Mitgefühl*] of man cannot be extended to encompass everything and may only serve as an obscure and often impotent guide to man, a limited, complex being, in everything remote; his guiding mother has subjected the numerous and lightly interwoven branches of the with-feeling to her more unerring standard: this is the 'rule of justice and truth' [*Regel der Gerechtigkeit und Wahrheit*] (101–102/147. Translation modified.).

According to Herder, humans could reflectively recognise fundamental similarities as well as seek to distinguish between true and false, which translated into a sense of reciprocity in their dealings with each other. The essence of the 'great law of equity [*Billigkeit*] and reciprocity [*Gleichgewicht*]' written in all human hearts was thus: 'Do not unto others what they should not do unto you; but what others should do unto you, do unto them too' (101–102/147).[23] 'All [natural] right [i.e. laws] of humans, nations and animals [*alles Menschen-, Völker- und Tierrecht*]', he stipulated, is based on the 'similarity of sentiment, unity of design among different persons, and equal loyalty in an alliance' (102/148. Translation modified.).

By invoking the rule of equity, Herder harked back to the arguments of early modern natural lawyers, who in turn often quoted various ancient

---

[21] On Herder's account of the emergence of different cultures in *Ideas* (and its relationship to his views in the *Treatise on the Origin*), see Proß, '1.4.2. Ideen', 191–192.

[22] For discussion, see ibid., 194–197.

[23] *Ideas*, 270. I have considerably modified the translation here so as to bring out the juridical origins of this term and the connection to Hugo Grotius's notion of *aequitas*, as highlighted by Wolfgang Proß in 'Anmerkungen [*Ideen*], in HWP, III/2, 301–304; Proß, 1.4.2. *Ideen*, 195; Proß, 'Kolonialismuskritik aus dem Geist der Geschichtsphilosophie', 17–73.

authors to support arguments about sociability as a general principle. In so doing they, too, referred not only to animals' desire for society but also to their special relationships with, and avoidance of harm to, members of their own species. For example, when developing his defence of human natural sociability, Hugo Grotius cited among others Marcus Terentius Varro's reference to an old proverb that 'a Dog will not eat Dog's Flesh' and Juvenal's remark that 'Tigers live peaceably together, and that the wildest Beasts spare those of their own Species'.[24] For Grotius, too, these were examples of a desire for society common to humans and animals, but he took care to emphasise that humans had a separate 'Faculty of knowing and acting, according to some general Principles, so that what relates to this Faculty is not common to all Animals, but properly and peculiarly agrees to Mankind'.[25] To this Grotius's most prominent eighteenth-century commentator Jean Barbeyrac further added a clarification that this does not mean that humans and animals follow the same kind of natural law ('a Right common to humans and animals').[26] Herder, however, affirmed exactly that. Characteristically, Herder identified the analogous principles underlying the interactions between natural beings, while still seeking to highlight the distinctive features of human cognition and volition.

In Herder's view, then, even non-human animals possessed an instinctive understanding of the fundamental similarity and thus equality of all members of one's species, an understanding that informed a further sense of reciprocity. Humans, however, had this understanding inscribed in their natural sentiments as much as in their reason (a developed capacity), distinctively developing a reflective understanding of equity, which enabled them to 'become sincere brothers and associates' for each other (102/148). At the same time, Herder acknowledged that humans might also deviate from nature due to various kinds of imaginary ideas they developed, up to a point at which they become prepared to eat the flesh of another human being. Yet even an 'inhuman monster who eats the flesh of his own brother', Herder argued, still demonstrates a rudimentary sense of

---

[24] Hugo Grotius, 'The Preliminary Discourse,' in *The Rights of War and Peace*, ed. and with an Introduction by Richard Tuck, from the Edition by Jean Barbeyrac (Indianapolis, 2005), §7, 82.

[25] Ibid. §7, 84–85.

[26] In a note, he argued: '[...] our Author only affirms that the Principle of Sociability has so real a Foundation in the Nature of Man, that we find some faint Tracks of it even amongst irrational Animals, in regard to those of their own Species. He does by no means pretend either that there is any Right common to Men and Beasts, or that any certain Consequences can be drawn from the Actions of Brutes, for proving any one particular Thing conformable or contrary to the Law of Nature'. Ibid., §7, 83, fn. 2.

reciprocity, expecting to be 'eaten in turn' (102/148. Translation slightly modified.).[27] The fundamental disposition towards equity thus never fully disappeared in humans, even though it may be overrun by false ideas and misguided education (92/135). It was the task of a developed form of human reason to lead human beings back to their own internal voice of equality and reciprocity between themselves.

It is important to point out that Herder's substantive understanding of justice in *Ideas* was closer to the ancient Stoics than to Grotius. However, here too, the footnotes that Grotius provided seemed to support the idea that Grotius was continuing in the same tradition, and as we shall see in Chapter 8, Herder explicitly hailed Grotius as his most important source of inspiration when thinking about international justice. In fact, for Grotius, sociability was the foundation of 'strict justice' specifically,[28] whereas in a footnote, he also referred to Seneca's much broader account of reciprocity.[29] Seneca, he argued, made an 'excellent application' of this principle by describing the human urge and duty to reciprocate good offices with gratitude, and characterising the entire social interaction as an exchange of mutually beneficial offices for the sake of maintaining society between equals.[30] Grotius also referred to Marcus Aurelius's similar understanding of the desire for society.[31] Encouraging reciprocity both in terms of mutual love as well as abstaining from harm, Herder's formula of equity clearly echoes those of Seneca and Marcus Aurelius. Indeed, human justice for Herder entails much further-going duties than Grotius's account of natural right. Whilst he did not follow the Stoics in explicitly calling for expanding one's circle of moral concern, he presented various examples of human associative obligations as the 'most powerful strivings of our *self-determination*' (*die kraftvollesten Bestrebungen der Selbstbestimmung* (Herder's emphasis)):

> men have renounced the unsteady reins of blind appetite, and voluntarily assumed *the bonds of matrimony,* of social friendship, of succour, and fidelity, in life and death; [...] they have given up their own wills, and chosen to be governed by laws, so as to establish and defend with their life's blood *the rule of men over men* [*Regierung der Menschen über Menschen*] (Herder must have thought self-rule here), though it still remains far from

---

[27] Cf. Sonia Sikka, 'On Extending Sympathy: Herder, Mencius and Adam Smith', in *Herder on Empathy*, 206–230 (221).
[28] Grotius, 'The Preliminary Discourse', §8, 85–86.   [29] Ibid., §8, 86, fn. 2.
[30] See Hans Blom, 'Sociability and Hugo Grotius', *History of European Ideas*, 41 (*Sociability in Enlightenment Thought*, ed. Eva Piirimäe et al.) (2015), 589–604 for an argument about the way in which sociability was a remedy to the original elitist tendencies in Grotius's early views.
[31] Grotius, 'The Preliminary Discourse', §7, 84, fn. 6.

perfection; [...] noble-minded mortals have sacrificed themselves for their *country* [*Vaterland*], and not only their lives at a tumultous moment, but, what is far more magnanimous, have devoted their lives' labour [...] to conferring peace and happiness [...] on a blind ungrateful multitude; [...] divine philosophers have voluntarily submitted to slander and persecution, poverty and want, so as to *promote truth, freedom and happiness* among the human species (94/137. Translation modified.).

In discussing various kinds of 'self-determination', Herder was developing further his earlier conception of 'freedom in bondage' that we touched upon in Chapter 4. It was precisely by following their natural other-regarding feelings, and consciously embracing the commitments arising from them, that humans exercised self-determination and formed their own character. In *Ideas*, Herder also emphasised the compatibility of this approach with the Christian understanding of virtue. In discussing *Humanität*, he presented 'religion as the highest humanity of mankind', highlighting our proclivity to trace the connection between cause and effect, and to 'divine it where it is not apparent'. Prompted by fear, the earliest humans pursued such understanding, and thus, the 'first and last philosophy is religion' (103/149). This pursuit of knowledge in itself was already an 'unerring monument of [...] the power of man to know and worship [God]'. However, even more importantly, religion entailed 'an exercise of man's heart and the purest direction of its capacities [*Fähigkeiten*] and forces [*Kräfte*]' (103/150). As in *On the Cognition*, Herder again restated his view of morality as consisting in 'freedom' and self-determination in the spirit of God: 'since man is created free, and subject to no other law on the earth than the one he has imposed on himself, he must soon become the most savage of all creatures, if he does not quickly perceive the law of God in all of nature, and strive as a child to imitate the perfection of the father' (103/150. Translation modified.). Whilst animals were 'born servants' in the system of nature, obedience from fear of punishment was characteristic of 'brutish men'. The truly human being, by contrast, would obey freely from love and goodness (104/150).

All in all, it thus needs to be emphasised that Herder, in the first instalment of *Ideas*, put forward an evocative account of the natural foundations of morality, reinterpreting classical Stoic (and Christian) themes in a vitalist vein. On the one hand, he posited a substantial continuity across nature as far as the principles of sociability were concerned. On the other hand, he maintained that humans were distinct insofar as their distinctive higher physical constitution (with its correspondingly high degree of internal complexity) enabled them to knowingly work out, embrace and follow the rules of equity. Although there was thus a rudimentary sense of reciprocity shared by all living beings, humans naturally applied this sense more broadly when making various kinds of judgements. Indeed, there was also a strong element of moral autonomy that he sought to accommodate in this system. Humans specifically had to learn to apply this sense through accumulated experience, based on trial and error in specific natural and cultural contexts, and were capable of 'self-determination' based on their moral sentiments and judgements; this was the specific moral aspect and calling of *Humanität*.[32]

7.2 Herder's Critique of Kant

7.2.1 *Kant's Idea for a Universal History*

In his earliest response to Herder, published in January 1785, Kant famously attacked Herder's 'hypothesis of invisible forces', dogmatic 'metaphysics' and the method of analogy he used for creating his system.[33] Kant had, already in November 1784, proposed his own rivalling philosophy of history in *Idea for a Universal History*. Indeed, when writing this essay, Kant was already aware of Herder's work and sought to provide an alternative to it.[34] Let us very briefly recall the key arguments of his early philosophy of history here.

As the essay title suggests, Kant's aim was to provide an idea for writing universal history. While Kant would come to demonstrate the purely rational source of the supreme principle of morality in *Groundwork of the Metaphysics of Morals* (1785), his argument in *Idea for a Universal History* presupposed this account. Kant stated at the beginning of the essay that he was going to focus on the '*appearances*' of free will, that is, human actions. Kant famously maintained that freedom of will could not be proven in the natural world (the realm of causal determination), it was not a *phenomenon*, but a *noumenon* (something posited by our reason). As rational beings, humans were, for Kant, able to determine themselves, and they were self-determining when they obeyed the law that their own reason

---

[32] Cf. Adler, 'Herder's Concept of Humanity', in *A Companion to the Works*, 93–116 (101).

[33] Kant, 'Review of J. G. Herder's *Ideas*', 132–133.

[34] Kant heard about Herder's *Ideas* from Johann Georg Hamann in August 1784, Haym, *Herder*, II, 275, 279; Reiss, 'Introduction to Reviews', 195. In December, he also published another essay, entitled *Answer to the Question: What Is Enlightenment*.

gave them (doing so from respect for the law). However, humans could not observe freedom in the phenomenal world.

The starting point of *Idea for a Universal History* was the assertion that the realm of human history is highly disappointing from both theoretical and moral points of view. Even a cursory look at it showed that 'everything at large is woven together out of folly, childish vanity, often also out of childish malice and rage of destruction'. Thus, 'there is no other way for the philosopher', Kant continued, 'than to see whether he can discover an aim of nature in this nonsensical course of things human'.[35] Indeed, particularly in order to retain moral hope and confidence in the validity of practical principles it was essential to develop a case for the natural teleology of history.[36]

Kant's proposed scheme of natural teleology was simple. Various kinds of observations showed that 'all natural predispositions of a creature are determined sometime to develop themselves completely and purposively'.[37] In humans, however, all predispositions related to reason could 'develop completely only in the species, but not in the individual'. Furthermore, a human being was destined to 'produce everything out of himself', and it appeared that he was to participate 'in no other happiness or perfection than that which he has procured for himself'.[38] Reason was the basis of freedom of will, which in turn is essential for morality, whilst morality was the sole actual basis for lasting happiness. It is indeed strange, Kant admitted, that 'the older generations appear to carry on their toilsome concerns only for the sake of the later ones [...] and that only the latest should have the good fortune to dwell in the building on which a long series of their ancestors (to be sure, without this being their aim) had labored'.[39] However, this perspective enabled at least some conciliation. Human morality and (morally based) happiness, too, were to be fully attained in the species only, which was 'immortal'.[40]

Alongside these central suppositions of natural teleology, Kant also ventured another hypothesis about the actual mechanism of human

---

[35] Kant, 'Idea for a Universal History with a Cosmopolitan Aim', in Kant, *Anthropology, History, and Education*, 108–123 (109).

[36] Ibid., 110. For a discussion of the 'status' of natural teleology in Kant's philosophical framework, cf. Henry Allison, 'Teleology and history in Kant: the critical foundations of Kant's philosophy of history', in *Kant's Idea for a Universal History*, 29–45. It needs to be pointed out that Allison highlights Kant's 'purely theoretical' approach to history, which I think is not plausible given Kant's explicit mention of 'practical principles'.

[37] Kant, 'Idea for a Universal History', 110.   [38] Ibid., 110.   [39] Ibid., 111.

[40] For a concise overview of the interpretative debates about the consistency of Kant's philosophy of history with his critical philosophy as a whole, see Anderson-Gold, 'Kant and Herder', 460–462.

antagonism that 'nature' used for achieving this destiny. Kant believed this mechanism was sustained by what he famously called human 'unsocial sociability':

> The human being has an inclination to become *socialized*, since in such a condition he feels himself as more a human being, i.e. feels the development of his natural predispositions. But he also has a great propensity to individualize (isolate) himself, because he simultaneously encounters in himself the unsociable property of willing to direct everything so as to get his own way, and hence expects resistance everywhere because he knows of himself that he is inclined on his side toward resistance against others.[41]

Humans thus had a desire to be with other human beings, but they also had a tyrannical disposition to impose their ideas on others. Furthermore, they were aware of a similar disposition in others, and thus entered into a vicious rivalry with them, being driven by 'ambition, tyranny and greed'.[42] This fundamentally antagonistic disposition could, however, yield positive results when law and order were guaranteed by a sovereign.[43] In a civil society, humans would be able to exercise and practise skill and discipline – the two key aspects of Kant's notion of culture – whereby they would further develop 'taste' and 'progress in enlightenment'.[44] As a result of these developments, Kant argued, 'a beginning is made towards the foundation of a mode of thought which can with time transform the crude natural predisposition to make moral distinctions into determinate practical principles and hence transform a *pathologically* compelled agreement to form a society finally into a *moral* whole'.[45]

Over time, as members of civil societies, humans would thus also arrive at an increasingly correct understanding of the nature of 'just civil constitution' guaranteeing equal freedom (i.e. rights) to all and the methods of putting it into practice. They would come to see that the development of reason and morality require the establishment of such a constitution, which in turn depends on achieving lawful order and peace at the international level. 'The human being', Kant famously declared, 'is an *animal which*, when it lives among others of its species, *has need of a master* [...]

---

[41] Ibid., 111. On this account, see J.B. Schneewind, 'Good Out of Evil: Kant and the Idea of Unsocial Sociability', in *Kant's Idea for a Universal History*, 94–112; cf. Allen Wood, 'Kant's Fourth Proposition: the Unsociable Sociability of Human Nature', in *Kant's Idea of a Universal History*, 112–128.

[42] Kant, 'Idea for a Universal History', 111   [43] Ibid., 111–112.

[44] Ibid., 112–113; 117. Compare also Kant's famous discussion of enlightenment in 'What is the Enlightenment?'.

[45] Kant, 'Idea for a Universal History', 116.

who ...necessitates him to obey a universally valid will with which everyone can be free. But where will he get this master? Nowhere else but from the human species. But then this master is exactly as much an animal who has need of a master.'[46] The (political) states, he further claimed, had remained in a state of nature among themselves. Wars and preparation for war constantly interrupted and interfered with the development of culture and the process of *enlightenment* that was necessary for moral education and for achieving a fully free civil constitution. The only secure way to achieve lawful order and international peace was to establish an international federation of states (*Völkerbund*) with coercive powers.[47]

The 'idea for a universal history' that Kant proposed in his essay for historians specifically was that a philosophical history could trace the gradual improvement of the 'civil constitution and its laws and [. . .] the relations of states' over different periods.[48] For Kant, there were already several indications that states might also enter into new kinds of relationships among themselves. First, thanks to the progressive importance of commerce as a source of state revenue, rulers were increasingly compelled to leave their subjects as much freedom as possible, while the inevitable progress of enlightenment (*Aufklärung*) in such conditions led the public to press for reforms. At the same time, however, rulers were forced to extract ever more revenue from society in order to sustain increasingly expensive warfare, which would at some point lead towards a general situation of exhaustion. Mounting public debt, further, saw rulers come to regard wars as increasingly dubious enterprises.[49] Thus, Kant argued, it was not entirely groundless to cherish a 'chiliastic' expectation that 'the purpose of nature is at least fairly well safe-guarded (if not actually furthered) even by the ambitious schemes of various states'.[50] The increasing interrelatedness of modern states would thereby ultimately lead to the establishment of informal mediating institutions between states, and finally, to that of a 'great federation of nations', in which 'every state, even the smallest, could expect its security and rights not from its own might, or its own legal judgement, but only from this great federation of nations (*Foedus Amphictyonum*), from a united might and from the decision in accordance with laws of its united will'.[51] Although Kant did not envision a clear path towards this kind of union, he nevertheless hinted that it is likely that states would ultimately be

---

[46] Ibid., 107–121, 113.   [47] Ibid., 114.   [48] Ibid., 118–120.   [49] Ibid., 118.
[50] Ibid., 116–118.   [51] Ibid., 114.

compelled to enter into such a union, just as savage individuals had been compelled to enter into a civil union. Once properly instituted, it would, however, 'preserve itself like an *automaton*'.[52]

Hence Kant essentially recommended that empirical historians trace the ruptured, yet in broad outline 'regular course of improvement of state constitutions in our part of the world'.[53] It would be worthwhile, he wrote, to further determine how this factor, and the laws and mutual relations between states 'through the good they contained' have 'served for a while to elevate and exalt nations (*Völker*) (and with them also arts and sciences)'. True, the faults of these constitutions historically undermined them, but the 'germ' of enlightenment was always preserved and developed further with each revolution, preparing the stage for a subsequent stage of enlightenment. It was also to be expected, Kant does not forget to add, that 'our part of the world' – in which this improvement was most visible – would also 'probably someday give laws to all the others'.[54]

7.2.2   *Herder's Response to Kant*

Herder's outrage at Kant's essay and review of the first instalment of *Ideas* probably partly resulted from his feeling that Kant had stolen his own key idea of applying a form of natural teleology to history, albeit with heavy qualifications (as a hypothesis and guideline for writing history, rather than as part of a broader natural philosophy). Even more importantly, however, Herder resisted what Kant had turned this idea into. As we will see in Chapter 8, Herder would come to attack Kant's very different understanding of 'self-determination' in his *Letters for the Advancement of Humanity*. In *Ideas*, he mainly focused on Kant's approach to politics. He detected that Kant's hypothesis of 'unsociable sociability' disputed the significance of human sociable inclinations for cultural agency,[55] social cohesion, peace and morality. Herder also understood that Kant affirmed a quasi-Hobbesian account of sovereignty. While human cultural agency was triggered by need as well as mutual competition and antagonism, the best conditions for it were created in those states that realised the external freedom of all. Yet this condition of freedom was to be guaranteed by a strong sovereign authority and required the establishment of an international state in order to be stable. Furthermore, Kant, just like Hobbes, could not imagine any constitutional limits to sovereign power. He did,

---

[52] Ibid., 115.   [53] Ibid., 119.   [54] Ibid.
[55] I am borrowing Muthu's apt term here, see Muthu, *Enlightenment against Empire*, 7.

however, imagine 'economic' limits while also proposing an international state as the only true guarantee of international peace.

Herder seized the opportunity to respond to Kant's vision of the possible historical development of political and moral progress in the second instalment of *Ideas*. The overall topic of this part of his work is the physical and cultural diversification of the human species into different nations under varying external conditions (climate, geographical habitat, mode of life (*Lebensart*) and through 'traditions of education'. Books Eight, Nine and Ten in particular deal with themes highly relevant to making the case against Kant's idea of a universal history. In Book Eight, Herder offered a detailed account of the epistemological and moral-psychological foundations of human sociability and cultural agency (human sensuality (*Sinnlichkeit*), imagination, practical reason, sentiments and drives), while also explaining the diversity of national characters and conceptions of happiness by tracing the creative unfolding of the human forces (*Kräfte*) in different external conditions. In Book Nine, provoked by Kant's third proposition according to which man 'should produce everything out of himself',[56] Herder proceeded to discuss the role of various kinds of 'tradition' (*Tradition*) (language, political government, arts and sciences and religion) in the education of humanity (understood as the sum of the generations of human beings, organised into families and nations) (251–256/340–347). In Book Ten, he elaborated on the earliest human history on the basis of sacred history.[57] Let us reconstruct his key arguments against Kant step by step.

7.2.3   Sociability, Morality and the Modern State

In Book Eight, Herder targeted the premises of Kant's legitimation of the modern state: his theory of unsocial sociability, cultural agency and civilisation. A major theme in this book is Herder's defence of natural sociability and nature's benevolence regarding the possibility of satisfying the universal natural goal of happiness. Herder here, even more clearly than in his earlier account of natural sociability in *Treatise on the Origin*, emphasised the pacific nature of humanity, also distanced himself critically from Rousseau's account of 'state of nature' or 'natural man' one more

---

[56] Cf. Beiser, *The German Historicist Tradition*, 157; see also Proß, 'Anmerkungen [*Ideen*]', in HWP, III/2, 491–493.

[57] It was this chapter in particular which Kant answered in his *Conjectures*. For reasons of space, I will leave out a discussion of this chapter. I have discussed it briefly in my article 'State-Machines, Commerce and the Progress of Humanity', 170.

time (cf. Chapters 2 and 4).[58] In terms of their physical and physiological make-up, mental capacities, and due to the circumstances surrounding birth and infancy, Herder argued, humans were a sociable species designed to live in peace with each other (209/284–285).[59] The feelings of love that a mother and father have for their children, and the necessarily weaker love of the latter for their parents, constituted the very basis of human sociability, while broader groups of tribes, and finally nations, originated in the education fathers sought to give to their sons (211–218/288–296).[60] Although early humans sought self-preservation and happiness (as all humans do), Herder argued, this was in itself not a source of antagonism between them either individually or even in groups: since nature had secured widely diverse kinds of enjoyments for the 'diverging species' of humanity, chances of the self-preservation and pursuit of happiness of different human groups colliding with each other were minimal (209–211/286–287).[61] The fierce tribal wars in fact also originated in human sociability: Herder here again invoked Ferguson's key ideas to set up an alternative to Kant's emphasis on the prevalence of individual unsociable propensities. Following Ferguson, Herder argued that such wars in fact originated in one of the noblest forms of human feeling, that of companionship and friendship among those who shared common perils and endeavours, which gave rise to the feeling of wounded tribal honour or hurt tribal friendship (217/296).[62] At the same time, Herder endorsed Rousseau's distinctive emphasis on the transformative power of private property upon human dispositions, using it to bolster his attack on Kant. Herder argued that it was a fundamental misconception to 'set up the malicious discordant disposition of men crowded together, of rival artists, opposing politicians, envious authors, for the general character of the species' (210/286).[63] The pervasive antagonism between individual human beings emerged only at a higher stage of civilisation (*Cultur*), that is, with nations that had invented private property and agriculture and thereby thoroughly transformed their natural environment and their entire mode of life (207–208/283–284).[64]

Fortunately, there was no predetermined progression towards this condition in human history. Herder cautioned against simplistic applications of the standard division of nations into hunters, fishers, pastoralists and

---

[58] See the detailed commentary on this chapter in Proß, 'Anmerkungen [*Ideen*]', in HWP, III/2, 446–490.

[59] Herder, *Ideas*, 304.   [60] Ibid., 305–306.   [61] Ibid., 305.

[62] Ibid., 306. Herder here reiterated the argument which he had made, relying on Ferguson's ideas, in *Of the Origin of Language* and *This Too a Philosophy*, see Chapter 4.

[63] Ibid., 304.   [64] Ibid., 303–304.

agriculturalists for determining the rank of a people in a single hierarchy of civilisation (*Cultur*) or when it was assumed that a given way of living would automatically bring about a higher level of civilisation (202/276–277).[65] There was a significant diversity in the mores, customs and arts of different peoples who fell into the same category in this scheme, which resulted primarily from their varying living conditions (climate and geography). In many cases, there simply was no existing impetus for progress to a further level of civilisation. Clearly, a human being living on an isolated island with a mild climate and 'feeding on roots, herbs, and fruits' would remain contented with his lot once natural indolence and this contentment had 'begotten the child called convenience' (202/277).[66] Instead, different external causes had to combine in order to propel the development of civilisation, among which Herder particularly emphasised the proximity of men and animals on our large continents, and the resulting practices of hunting and the domestication of animals (202–208/276–284).[67]

Herder's final and most important point was that man's happiness was in no way enhanced by the development of civilisation. Kant agreed, of course, that there was no linear growth of morality and happiness in universal human history. Rather, Kant hinted that unsocial sociability under the conditions of stable political government fostered the develop-ment of moral freedom by activating humans' 'crude disposition' for moral discrimination – one consisting in humans' ability to restrain themselves, although not for moral purposes as yet. So far in human history, however, the outcome had been ever more civilisation (social decorum and propri-ety), but no real 'moralisation'.[68] Kant's hope was that this might change, once stable civil freedom was achieved and humans would properly have a chance to enlighten themselves, thereby moving closer to a situation in which they could seriously pursue moral freedom and the ideal of moral happiness resulting from everyone's acting on the basis of moral law.

Herder passionately rejected this understanding of moral happiness. Emphasising humans' active forces of the mind as the source of their cultural agency, he associated happiness with the natural exercise of these very forces

---

[65] Ibid., 302.   [66] Ibid.
[67] Ibid., 302–304. For a discussion of Herder's comparison between Eurasia and the Americas in terms of the number of animals available for domestication and the resulting differences between the development of civilisation (and ultimately the ability of self-defence) in these two parts of the world, see Muthu, *Enlightenment against Empire*, 240–241. However, as will become evident below, I do not agree with Muthu's claim that for Herder, agriculture as such rendered nations bellicose, see ibid., 242.
[68] Kant, 'Idea for a Universal History', 116; cf. 111.

and a simple sensation of existence accompanying it in all natural and cultural conditions (218–224/298–305).[69] Thus, he argued, 'large, complex state-machines' by no means formed the necessary preconditions for achieving virtue or happiness. On the contrary, they instead created substantial obstacles to realising these goals. Here Herder again reiterated his earlier argument, developed first in *Treatise on the Origin*, that thanks to the increasing division of labour in human societies, the forces of the soul were no longer fully put to use, leading to a significant decrease of the original intensity of sensation, and finally to servility and inertness, which in turn paved the way for despotism and empty moral cosmopolitanism (207–209; 220–221/283–284; 300).[70] Herder also drew on this theory in *This Too a Philosophy*, where he had further launched a devastating attack on modern civilised monarchies, associating their rise with the progress of technology and luxury that had made certain key human virtues redundant and facilitated the transformation of the entire society into a 'machine' led by one individual.[71] When responding to Kant in *Ideas*, Herder similarly lashed out against the contemporary ideal of a 'modern well-ordered state', indeed, the idea of a 'state-machine that is ruled by the thought of one'. Without mentioning the benefits of modern large states that he had acknowledged just a few years earlier (see Chapter 5), Herder pointed to the increased danger of oppression they represented: 'in large states, hundreds must pine with hunger, that one may feast and carouse: thousands are hunted and oppressed to death, that one gratified fool or philosopher may gratify his whims' (223/304).[72] He again highlighted the long-term psychological effects of the realisation of this ideal and ironically associated it with the increased happiness of being able to 'serve in this machine as an unthinking component'. He also invoked anew the theme of moral inefficacy, memorably contrasting the happiness of the intellectually over-refined 'citizen of the world', who was in love with the 'name' of mankind, with that of a savage who actively exercised his powers (*Kräfte*) in loving his wife, children and in being active for his tribe, and who as such was willing to 'receive a stranger in his poor hut as his brother, and with a calm benevolence' (222–223/304. My translation.).[73]

---

[69] Herder, *Ideas*, 307–311. For discussion, see Proß, 'Nachwort', in *HWP*, III/1, 912–925 and Sikka, *Herder on Humanity*, 53–58; cf. Wood, *Kant's Ethical Thought*, 226–233. For Herder's very similar ideas on this subject already in the 1760s, see Marion Heinz, 'Die Bestimmung des Menschen: Herder contra Mendelssohn', in *Philosophie der Endlichkeit: Festschrift für Erich Christian Schröder zum 65. Geburtstag*, ed. Beate Niemeyer and Dirk Schütze (Würzburg, 1991), 263–285.

[70] Herder, *Ideas*, 309–311. [71] Herder, *This Too a Philosophy*, 319; for discussion, see Chapter 4.

[72] Herder, *Ideas*, 310. [73] Ibid., 310.

7.2.4   *The Origins and Progress of Political Government*

In the next book, Book Nine, Herder was primarily interested in the positive contribution of different traditions to educating humanity and the relationship of these traditions to each other. However, he also tried to account for the possible aberrations from the human striving for *Humanität* in certain forms of tradition. Political government for him represented a distinctive and highly mutable form of tradition. It is in Book Nine, too, that Herder's most direct answer to Kant's political ideas can be found, largely developed in his notorious chapter four on governments. Herder himself regarded this chapter as a *caput mortuum*.[74] As he complained to Hamann, he had revised and shortened it a number of times in order to properly answer 'Mr Immanuel [Kant] and the public that demands [to read about] universal history, and for whom everything in miserable history (*leidige Geschichte*) is hinging on the government'.[75] The final published version turned out in some ways to be even more opaque than the earlier ones, and much of Herder's critique of Kant's political cosmopolitanism, including an entire section on the 'imperfection of all ways of the human formation [Bildung] on earth', was omitted from the published version.[76] The philosophical history of political government that Herder presented there was highly fragmentary. Nevertheless, I believe it is possible to reassemble Herder's main argument here.

Herder distinguished a total of three 'degrees of government'. The first two were 'natural', while the third was invented. The first consisted simply in the 'ties of the law of nature' as constituted through human natural sociability and as expressed in family relations (244–245/330–331).[77] The second was also natural and characteristic of hunting, fishing and shepherding nations. Individuals in such groups did not need much of each other's assistance for most of the time, yet had to elect leaders for their common undertakings. Even 'the elected judges of a community', Herder argued, emerged as late as at this stage of government. This form of authority was originally temporary and lasted only as long as was necessary for carrying out the specific joint venture (244–245/330–331).[78] At the end of the second stage of development, however, humans reached a crucial crossroads at

---

[74] *Caput mortuum* (dead head) was the term alchemists used for referring to the worthless residue of a chemical process.

[75] Herder to Hamann, 23. April 1785, in *DA*, V, 121.

[76] Herder, 'Nachlaß', in *SWS*, XIII, 464–470; reprinted in Herder, *Ideen*, in *HWP*, III/1, 1135–1139.

[77] Herder, *Ideas*, 317–319. (The translation of the term 'Grad der Regierung' is from *Outlines*.)

[78] Ibid., 318.

which they were forced to invent political institutions. 'Nature extended the bonds of society only to families', Herder wrote, while 'beyond that, she left mankind at liberty to knit them, and to frame their most delicate work of art, the state, as they thought proper. If they framed it well, happiness was their reward; if they chose, or endured tyranny and bad forms of government, they had to bear their burden' (248/335).[79] Human nature certainly did not necessitate political government, let alone a monarchical or despotic form of government (domination). No nation knowingly gave away its freedom. Sometimes it occurred through loss of vigilance or even laziness, while in most cases despotism originated in conquests. (246/334).[80] Hereditary government (*Erbregierung*) or the right to dominate (*herrschen*) was based not on natural right, but on 'forcible conquests' and tradition (245–246/332).[81]

Herder's critique of Kant famously culminated in a direct rejection of what he took to be Kant's morally repulsive Hobbesianism:

> The maxim that 'man is an animal who needs a master when he lives with others of his species, so that he may attain happiness and fulfil his destiny on earth', is both facile and noxious as a fundamental principle of a philosophy of history. The proposition, I feel, ought to be reversed. Man is an animal as long as he needs a master to lord over him; as soon as he attains the status of a human being he no longer needs a master in any real sense. Nature has designated no master for the human species, brutal vices and passions render one necessary. [—] A father who brings up his children in a manner which keeps them under age for the rest of their lives and hence in need of a tutor and guardian, is rightly considered a bad father. [—] Let us apply this line of reasoning to the educators of mankind, to fathers of fatherlands and their pupils. Either the latter are incapable of improvement or it must have become perceptible during the thousands of years that they have been governed as to what has become of them, and to what purposes they have been trained by their teachers (249/336–337).[82]

Previous scholarship has mainly focused on the first half of this quotation, discussing the question as to whether Herder was rejecting all political government, or perhaps only modern absolute monarchies.[83] The ambiguity of Herder's meaning is further exacerbated by Herder's following remarks: 'Nature educates families, the most natural state (*der natürlichste Staat*), therefore, is also *One people* (*Ein* [sic!] *Volk*), with One national

[79] Ibid., 322. The translation is mine, combining phrases from *Ideas* and *Outlines*.
[80] Ibid., 320–321. I am using the translation of *Outlines* here.   [81] Ibid., 319–320.
[82] Herder, *Ideas*, 323–324. (The translation is modified and from *Ideas*.)
[83] See, e.g., Beiser, *Enlightenment, Revolution and Romanticism*, 211–213.

character (*mit Einem* [sic!] *Nationalcharakter*). This it retains for thousands of years and can be developed most naturally, if its compatriot [mitgeborene] prince only wishes so.' (249/337).[84]

What kind of political community did Herder have in view here? As a careful reading of Herder's argument in the previous quoted section suggests, Herder did not regard it as possible to answer the question about political obligation and the aims of political government in the abstract only: he instead calls for the empirical history of political government and its main purposes in different contexts to be studied. We will specify this history in the next section. It is, however, important to highlight already now that the famous remark about the 'most natural state' being 'one people [*Volk*], with one national character' (249/337)[85] most likely aims to contrast two kinds of historical polities in respect of their aims and stability: the modern European externally oriented, expansive and aggressive monarchies, on the one hand, and internally oriented and self-contained ancient kingdoms in which compatriot prince[s] cultivated the 'national character' of the people, on the other (249/338).[86] Albeit in some sense it is beyond doubt that for Herder 'national character' was necessary for a political community to be 'alive' rather than 'dead', it is still an open question as to what a 'natural state' would mean in European context. As we will see below, he also envisioned the rise of a novel kind of federative union in Europe. A more detailed answer to this question will be given in Chapter 8.

What is clear already here, in any case, is that for Herder the modern state-machines grounded in, and geared towards, foreign conquest were fundamentally unstable in themselves:

> Nothing therefore appears so directly opposite to the aim of government as the unnatural enlargement of states, the wild mixing of various human races [*Menschen-Gattungen*] and nations [*Nationen*] under one sceptre. The human sceptre is far too weak and slender for such incongruous parts to be engrafted upon it: glued together indeed it may be into a fragile machine, called state-machine [*Staats-Maschine*], but [it is] destitute of internal life and sympathy between parts. [—] Like Trojan horses these machines get close to each other, mutually promising eternity, yet without national character [*National-Charakter*], there is no life in them and for those thus forced together it is only the whim of fate that dooms them to immortality:

[84] Herder, *Ideas*, 324. (The translation is entirely my own here.)
[85] Ibid. (I have modified the translation.)   [86] Ibid.

since precisely the art of politics [*Staatskunst*] that brought them about, is also the one that plays with peoples and humans as with lifeless bodies (249–250/337–338).[87]

One of Herder's main points against Kant, hence, concerned the origins and stability of the modern state, and by implication, the possibility of heightened cultural agency in them. While Kant, too, had criticised modern monarchies for their bellicosity, he nevertheless seemed to think that internally they offered the best chance for the development of culture. Herder disagreed, making clear that in some essential respects, European monarchies were still continuing the tradition of barbarous government. They hampered the energies of their populations, while also denying them any proper representation, let alone political participation. As we will see below, this also necessarily affected the stability of modern liberty and political government.

Herder also clearly distanced himself from the ideal of enlightened paternalist monarchism. It is impossible to tell whether he, mistakenly, also read Kant as supporting this idea.[88] In any case, in voicing this criticism Herder revealed his own republican and constitutionalist sympathies. He passionately emphasised that the people itself had to be active in seeking enlightenment and happiness, and not only by engaging in public debate[89] but by taking active responsibility for their situation and social life around them.[90] He cautioned against evaluating constitutions on the basis of the rulers' capacity to contribute to public enlightenment and happiness, regarding this as an 'arbitrary' aspect of their rule.[91] The only essential point of view from which all citizens should and would view forms of government instead, Herder argued in a draft version, was to what extent the constitution enabled limiting the possible 'damage to the

---

[87] Ibid., 324. (I have extensively modified the translation.)

[88] While Kant indeed neglected the need for any constitutional limits to the power of monarchs, he did not demand that monarchs should directly promote their subjects' moral virtue and happiness. Also, Kant acknowledged that a 'perfect solution' to the master's possible abuse of power did not exist, see Kant, *Idea*, 113, see also Kant's defence of his own views in his 'Review of Johann Gottfried Herder, *Ideas for a Universal History of Mankind* (Part Two) (Riga and Leipzig, 1785)', idem, *Political Writings*, 219.

[89] This was obviously Kant's view in his 'Answer to the Question: What is Enlightenment', in idem, *Practical Philosophy*, 11–23.

[90] Herder, 'Nachlaß', 453–454, 456; reprinted also in Proß, 'Anmerkungen [*Ideen*]', in *HWP*, III/2, 509–510.

[91] Herder, 'Nachlaß', 453. While this was not a Kantian idea, Gottlieb Hufeland, a young professor at the University of Jena, had sought to show that on Kantian premises it was the duty of rulers to promote their subjects' moral virtue and enlightenment, see Maliks, *Kant's Politics*, 32–35. It is possible that Herder was here trying to answer Hufeland's ideas in particular.

machine' that a bad ruler might do.[92] At the same time, Herder left it open as to what exactly these limitations might consist of.

7.2.5   The Problem of War

Herder also found the idea that modern monarchs would come to appreciate their true self-interest in international affairs and join together to form a strong international federation fundamentally implausible. Considering Kant's own emphasis on enlightenment, Herder was astonished that he envisioned the emergence of an international federation as a likely or, indeed, desirable prospect in the current situation of only relative pacification. In a section he ultimately omitted from publication, he directly invoked the abbé de Saint-Pierre as his ally against Kant:

> The abbé de Saint-Pierre, one of the most philanthropic dreamers who has ever written with truly-good purposes, and who has repeatedly been copied by new and worse [authors], wanted to get rid of war in Europe and tirelessly continued making proposals for a European Diet; yet he was not enough of a dreamer to desire his perpetual peace from the political state-machines as such, but made hundreds of other suggestions in all his writings to show how the evil passions of both high and low status individuals might be extinguished, active education improved and general reason made truly effective; had this happened, perpetual peace would have been achieved even without a European Diet.[93]

As Herder's resentment in his private letters reveals, what most disturbed him about Kant's account was precisely his self-avowedly '*chiliastic*' expectation that 'the purpose of nature is at least fairly well safe-guarded (if not actually furthered) even by the ambitious schemes of various states' and by European colonialism.[94] Herder did not dispute Kant's view of the increasing interdependence of European monarchies. He too acknowledged that a standard version of despotism as 'unbound license' (*ungebundene Willkühr*) had become impossible in European states that found themselves in 'a most artificial condition in respect to each other'.[95] As we have seen in Chapter 5, he was willing to accept that modern monarchies currently guaranteed a degree of liberty and rule of law. He did not deny that sciences had influenced government, and that government, in turn, fostered the development of (some) sciences. He was, however, systematically concerned about the situation of the fine arts, 'fine sciences' and people's mores in modern societies. He voiced these concerns yet again in *Ideas* when

---

[92] Herder, 'Nachlaß', 453.   [93] Ibid.   [94] Kant, *Idea*, 118–119.   [95] Herder, 'Nachlaß', 455.

critiquing Kant. Insofar as Kant seemed to suggest that 'enlightenment' would require first of all distinct kinds of political settings (domestic and international), he had not taken seriously the need for sentimental enlightenment and hence neglected the danger that modern lawful monarchies might give rise to new forms of despotism and imperialism.

Furthermore, as Herder's draft versions reveal, he also clearly rejected the union of state-machines as a solution to the Kantian problem (without directly mentioning Kant), labelling it ironically as 'Achaean league[s] of the rulers of the world'.[96] For Herder, the danger that the strong central authority of such a league might abuse its power was evident, while it was not clear how a weaker union could be kept together. Either there was one 'ruler of the world' or this league was bound to collapse through internal disagreements. While modern monarchies were 'rubbing against each other' like huge machines or lifeless Trojan horses within Europe,[97] they gave full vent to their aggressive disposition in colonial politics.[98] Fortunately, however, the formation of such a 'league' seemed to be an impossible goal thanks to Nature's wonderful arrangement in which nations were separated from each other:

> . . .not only by woods and mountains, seas and deserts, rivers and climates, but also more particularly by languages, inclinations and characters. . . . No Nimrod has yet been able to drive all the inhabitants of the World into one Park for himself and his successors; and though it has been for centuries the object of a united Europe to take the form of a despot, compelling all the nations of the Earth to be happy in her way, this happiness-dispelling deity is yet far from having obtained her end (224/305).

Nonetheless, Herder's message to his contemporaries was far from pessimistic. It was possible for the subjects of modern monarchies to 'undo the damage' resulting from the barbaric 'art of politics' using the positive means (*Hülfsmittel*) that human culture provided.[99] True, in the present situation, Europeans only needed to adopt the maxim of serving the state when it was strictly necessary, while using every opportunity for directly 'serving the freedom, enlightenment and happiness of man'.[100] True patriotism was not devotion to the 'state', but to humanity. This, however, did not mean that humans were to declare their love for the abstract idea of humanity or envision abstract utopian fantasies; what truly helped humanity was true 'civic enlightenment' (*bürgerliche Aufklärung*) and 'active human help' in concrete situations.[101] Thereby humans would achieve

---

[96] Ibid.   [97] Ibid., 456.   [98] Ibid., 451, 455.   [99] Ibid., 456.   [100] Ibid.
[101] Ibid., 469.

more radical reforms. 'We are certainly tied to a chain of tradition binding so many centuries [...]', Herder boldly and at this point cryptically insisted in a draft version, 'yet humankind [*Menschheit*] with all its rights and duties remains eternally young [...], shakes off the old prejudices and learns, even if against its will, reason and truth.'[102] Therefore, it was also highly unlikely that modern European state-machines would continue to be able to preserve themselves in their present form for long. A look at the history of human societies demonstrated that such 'instruments of human pride were made of clay' and were hence bound to collapse sooner or later (250/337–338).[103]

7.3   Herder's Alternative to Kant

Let us now turn to Herder's own account of the history of humanity, searching for the continuities or ruptures with his views in the 1770s. In the third and fourth instalments of *Ideas*, Herder outlined the history of individual nations and cultures, including their political government. While the third instalment focused on ancient cultures, the fourth was devoted to European history.[104] At the end of the third instalment, in chapter fifteen, he also attempted to answer Kant's new response to his criticisms in the latter's review of the second instalment of *Ideas*. Herder now came up with a new argument about the progress of *Humanität* in European history. As we will see, Herder's and Kant's divergence concerned the origins, nature and future prospects of modern state-machines specifically, not the possibility of enlightenment and even progress of *Humanität* in Europe. Whilst Herder did not deny that such progress had happened and was further possible in Europe, he sought to show that its substance, underlying causes and historical prospects were very different from those highlighted by Kant.

7.3.1   *Natural Laws of History*

In his review of the second instalment of Herder's *Ideas* and in direct response to Herder's critique of his own *Idea*, Kant reiterated his earlier view that the only morally encouraging way of making sense of human history was to posit, and empirically illustrate, humanity's ability to work

---

[102] Ibid., 457.   [103] Herder, *Ideas*, 324.
[104] See also the illuminating discussion by Proß, 'Anmerkungen [*Ideen*]', in *HWP*, III/2, 722–746.

its way towards a new political condition in which the development of moral freedom in each individual human being would become possible:

> But what if the true end of Providence were [. . .] the ever continuing and growing activity and culture which are thereby set in motion, and whose highest possible expression can only be the product of a political constitution based on concepts of human right, and consequently an achievement of the humans themselves? [—] Does the author really mean that, if the happy inhabitants of Tahiti, never visited by more civilised nations, were destined to live in their peaceful indolence for thousands of centuries, it would be possible to give a satisfactory answer to the question of why they should exist at all, and of whether it would not have been just as good if this island had been occupied by happy sheep and cattle as by happy human beings who merely enjoy themselves?[105]

We saw in the previous section that Herder vehemently rejected the idea that refining the art of political government as such could contribute towards heightened cultural activity, and thereby, ultimately, moral perfection and happiness. In Book Fifteen, at the end of his discussion of ancient nations and cultures in the third instalment, Herder reiterated these views in response to Kant's continuing disagreement with him, emphasising that each people pursued *Humanität* in its own distinctive way, and that there was no increase or approximation of morality in history, human nature itself ever remaining the same mixture of good and bad (437/578). Furthermore, Kant's view completely ignored the fact that all human beings were moral and cultural beings seeking self-preservation and self-constitution, in accordance with what was possible for them in their 'time and place' (438–442/580–585).

However, Herder now made clear that this did not rule out the pursuit of ever purer and nobler forms of *Humanität* throughout history by people developing, and critically engaging with, their own traditions. Kant's argument entailed that happiness could only be achieved in states with a distinct kind of 'constitution ordered in accordance with concepts of human right', while all of human history and interactions between nations were to be measured according to their contribution towards the progress of such a constitution. In Herder's view, this perspective disregarded the value of self-determination for all human beings and undermined the notion of their equal worth. It was necessary to understand that all humans possessed resources for recognising each other as equals. Instead of glorifying the progressive development towards a certain form of political organisation

---

[105] Kant, 'Review of Johann Gottfried Herder', 219–220.

and thereby establishing new hierarchies among different nations and cultures, history had to teach moderation and reciprocity with others. 'Human nature' itself, Herder maintained, 'is constructed on this principle, so that no individual can suppose himself to exist for the sake of another or of posterity' (464/613). Humans developed what was possible to develop in given circumstances, what the 'place and time' allowed them to develop (392/522). Of course, individuals and even peoples existed who manifestly failed to respect the principle of equity (*Billigkeit*), a kind of 'practical reason' that taught them the 'measure of the actions and reactions of similar beings for general security'. Nevertheless, even so they had exercised at least some degree of self-determination by following the norms of their culture. Furthermore, their example was instructive for others, indeed, it showed precisely that erring against reciprocity was bound to have consequences for everyone involved. The history of humankind could be seen as the field in which the Goddess of justice – *Nemesis* – ruled, punishing those who violated the law of equal respect and reciprocity. Indeed, by understanding the realm of history as ruled by *Nemesis*, humans could also increasingly correct the excesses of their imagination about the differential worth of different individuals, social groups and nations, and reflectively clarify the implications of the rule of justice for concrete human and inter-societal relationships (436, 440, 443–450/581, 584, 585–595).[106]

7.3.2   *The Lessons of Ancient History*

What, then, was Herder's own vision of the history of political government? As we will see, Herder consistently sought to explain the genesis of different forms of culture as well as political government by reference to the specific climatic and geographical conditions in which distinct societies had emerged; at the same time, he also attempted to evaluate the latter from various viewpoints, such as, for example, stability, cultural dynamism and brilliance, and most importantly, equity (*Billigkeit*). This principle, furthermore, was to be applied both to the domestic as well as international institutions and practices. Let us set out some broader lines of argument in Herder's vastly complex discussion of the history of political government in the ancient world, up to the entry of the German peoples in the arena of history.

Right at the beginning of the third instalment, Herder clarified that it was the 'half-savage hunters and nomads' in the harsh climate and 'cold, steep,

---

[106] On the idea of Nemesis in Herder's thought, see Proß, 'Geschichtliches Handeln'.

broken land' of northern Asia that first developed bellicose dispositions.[107] It was also in this context that ideas of leadership and submission soon degenerated into crude hereditary-based nomadic despotism, the paradigmatic example of which was the Tatarian war-lordship. In the South, by contrast, the story unfolded very differently: here 'migrating colonies, led chiefly by the rivers, gradually headed towards the sea, and assembled in towns and countries (*Länder*), while a milder climate awakened in them more refined ideas' (289/392). People living in the South had more time for leisure, men's drives were also more stimulated, awakening the passions (and, one might add, inventiveness leading to new modes of subsistence such as agriculture), which however led to individual conflicts and necessitated the establishments of laws and various kinds of institutions, political and religious (289/392). Yet since many of these countries soon degenerated through luxury and despotism, they were easy prey for northern nomads.

At the same time, Herder posited a stark contrast between South and East Asia, on the one hand, and the Near East (West Asia and Egypt), on the other. In South and East Asia, geography supported the formation of stable national borders, and hence 'national characters' – a population's morals, customs, and distinctive ways of thinking – were fixed and fortified at an early stage. National characters were here supported and cultivated by political leaders, yet these states were also bound to be stuck at a certain stage of civilisation. The greatest kingdom of East Asia – China – developed from a semi-Tatar despotism into a rigid 'state-machine' built on a strict kind of subordination and 'childish obedience' reinforced by moral maxims (290–292/392–396). Yet being contained in natural geographic borders, it did not pursue aggressive expansion. Only one single people, the Mongols, were a threat to China, and even if they conquered the Chinese state for a period, they did not alter the Chinese constitution or national character (296/400).

In the Near East, by contrast, various empires arose close to mountains from which numerous primitive nomadic nations continuously descended to attack and overrun these empires, to found new ones themselves. In the Near East, hence, most nations developed a particularly bellicose mindset, combining an originally nomadic form of government and wandering disposition with flourishing arts and trade; as a result there was constant

---

[107] 'Necessity and the circumstances of the country rendered men barbarous: a thoughtless way of life, once become habitual, confirmed itself in the wandering tribes, or those that separated from them; and fashioned amid rude manners that almost eternal national character, which so completely discriminates all the northern Asian tribes from the nations of the south.' (289/392. I have modified the translation.)

shifting of borders, one empire being replaced by another (316–317; 323/
425–427; 434). However, there were also 'states springing up from one
root' in the Near East. These were states that 'were able to maintain
themselves for ages': such states, Herder argued, could be subdued, 'but
the nation preserves itself', remaining true to the old morals of their
fathers – as happened to the Hebrews and the Egyptians (350; 325/468/
436. Translation modified.). Like China, the ancient kingdoms of these
nations had originally ascribed great importance to the formation of morals
(*Sitten*) through education, understanding that this was 'the spring of their
internal strength'. This was in stark contrast to modern European states
that were based only on money or mechanical political arts, while the early
kingdoms drew on religion as a particularly suited 'drive' at this level of
civilisation (350/468). Yet since it was typical of all human inventions,
whether political or religious, that they necessarily stagnate and degenerate
after a few generations, these state religions, too, were turned into vehicles
of oppression and ignorance in due time (351–352/469–470), rendering
these states prey to aggressive empires in their neighbourhood.

In discussing ancient republicanism, Herder distinguished between the
Greek and Roman variants. The Greeks, who as a nation were formed in a
specific coastal and insular geographic environment, represented the first
example of an open culture in which, thanks to the impact of multiple
cultural sources, a uniquely dynamic national culture was formed. This
dynamism was also expressed in Greek political life. Although Herder, as we
have seen, was no uncritical admirer of Greek republicanism, he celebrated
its fundamental tendency: 'the period of Greek republics', he argued, was
the first step towards the maturity of the human spirit (*Mündigkeit des
menschlichen Geistes*) in the important matter of how humans should govern
humans' (373/497. Translation modified.). Using this unmistakably
Kantian terminology against Kant himself, Herder here again sought to
correct Kant's emphasis, in his 1784 essay on the process of enlightenment,
on modern monarchies as the most suitable environment for public
debate:[108] Herder once again reiterated his point, as made earlier in *This
Too a Philosophy* and *On the Influence of Government*, that the origins of
critical philosophical reflection about politics lay in Greek republics.
Ancient legislators who filled public posts, and enjoyed the trust of their
fellow citizens, were capable of directly shaping the laws and mores, indeed,
the 'political culture' (*politische Cultur*) of their societies; they at the same
time admirably 'declined the supreme power (*Oberherrschaft*), both for

---

[108] See Kant, 'Answer to the Question: What is Enlightenment', 23.

themselves and for posterity; and applied all industry, all their knowledge of men and the world, to the commonwealth (*Gemeinwesen*)' (373/498).

Furthermore, the Greeks had invented and tested, although not fully developed, 'the two poles, round which the entirety of the cultivation of humanity's morals [*alle Sittencultur der Menschheit*] revolves': first, that of patriotism as the voluntary submission to laws as cherished in Sparta, and second, that of the enlightenment (*Aufklärung*) as pursued by the Athenians (375/499–500. Translation modified.). Spartan commitment to 'the harsh patrician laws of [their] small country' demonstrated the highest possible political virtue that humans could 'invent and practice for their happiness and freedom'. This commitment, however, had unfortunately never been associated with the 'pure law of all of humanity' as yet (375/499–500). The Athenian principle of enlightenment, similar to the Spartan principle of patriotism, was unrivalled in its brilliance so far. When the political government was designed so as to enhance the 'enlightenment of the people' in 'matters that are most important to it', then 'Athens was the most enlightened city in the world', and no other city – 'neither Paris nor London, neither Rome nor Babylon, and still less Memphis, Jerusalem, Peking and Benares, can compete with it' (375/500. Translation modified.). It was to Athens, Herder declared that 'we ever remain indebted with regard to civic enlightenment' (376/501). In line with his earlier views in *On the Influence of Governments*, Herder maintained that it was Athenian political institutions – including, prominently, the art of public oratory that he had been so critical of in his early essays on patriotism – that had encouraged and enabled this degree of enlightenment. However, in Athens, too, not all the forces awakened were grounded in *Humanität*. Indeed, the very political institutions (Athenian democracy) that had encouraged Greek enlightenment also offered prominent opportunities for undermining those very institutions. This instability was exacerbated through external threats as well as internal Greek rivalry. Thus, Herder concluded, the Greek example makes it amply clear that the 'health' and 'permanence' of a state depended on the degree in which its institutions were 'grounded in *Humanität*, that is, reason and equity' (396/527. Translation modified.).

With regard to the Romans, Herder restated his view, already developed in several earlier writings, that Rome was a military state through and through. It was fundamentally a 'rudely composed living machine [. . .] within the walls of one city' (404/538), which through its artificial division in different classes, and an ever-increasing number of various superior offices and honours was geared towards external military conquests and empire, and which finally collapsed under its own weight (404–405/538). Furthermore, the celebrated Roman law was only suitable for governing the city of Rome alone; as soon as it was applied in a wider area, it corrupted the original character of the conquered nations and became an instrument of oppression (433/574).

It was mainly based on this empirical history of the ancient world that Herder, in Book Fifteen at the end of the third instalment, attempted to spell out the 'natural laws of history'. He also, however, made some comments on the relevance of these examples for modern peoples, thus specifying some of the characteristics of modern societies more broadly. Whilst emphasising the fundamental equal worth of human beings and even cultures, he highlighted that humans were not fully tied to any of the traditions they created. Greeks and Romans, in particular, were shining examples of how it was possible to 'shake off the yoke of ancient forms of government and traditions' (441/584). However, their examples were not positive in all respects, and, indeed, their eventual corruption and disappearance could encourage moderns to pursue even more pure forms of *Humanität* (441–442/583–585). Now assuming a much less critical tone regarding modern societies than when discussing the relationship between the modern state and morality and happiness, Herder acknowledged that modern times created more favourable conditions for the pursuit of *Humanität*. Although in some sense modern societies had made it more difficult for individuals to achieve moral efficacy and happiness, it was nevertheless possible to detect the growth of *Humanität* in these societies. It was perhaps as yet not stable, but the overall logic of history was becoming evident. Just like the laws of attraction and repulsion that produced order out of chaos in nature, Herder argued, so were human societies moving towards a greater degree of 'order' both within *and* between themselves. Even if humans' destructive powers would never entirely disappear, they 'must not only yield in the course of times to preserving powers, but must ultimately serve the formation [*Ausbildung*] of the whole' (443/585). The number of destructive demons in history was decreasing, both at the individual and state level, which made it possible collectively to defeat them. Likewise, the perfection of sciences (and their inventions) enabled humans to increasingly master unruly natural elements like fire and oceans, while even the wildest human activities like war had been transformed into ordered and systematic practices (447–450/591–595).

Herder also attempted to justify this vision by describing it in terms of a mathematical theory of nature according to which a certain 'maximum' or 'minimum' of some characteristic was necessary for all natural objects to achieve a harmony or equilibrium of their internal powers in order to sustain themselves. Human societies, too, were striving for the highest possible harmony of various kinds of 'cooperative powers', anchored in a certain maximum that best sustains this society (e.g. the political morality of the Chinese or the 'maximum of sensual beauty both in arts and manners, in science and in political institutions in Greece') (451–452/ 597)). Next to these maxima, however, there could be significant short-comings in other respects, e.g. in the form of government of a society. The happiness of society, Herder argued, depended only on the 'most perfect bond of union' of forces achieved in it (453; cf. 451/599; cf. 597). As soon as societies became internally unbalanced, mainly due to the passions of powerful individuals, they were bound to oscillate from one extreme to the other, thereby destroying the overall balance between them, too: 'Thus Rome had disturbed the peace of the Globe for more than a thousand years; and half a World of savage nations was requisite for a slow restora-tion of its quiet.' (456/603). The historical process, Herder emphasised, could by no means be expected to resemble the 'peaceable progress of an asymptote', but rather the course of a pendulum striking from one extreme to another, finally achieving a state of balance (456; cf. 451/596; cf. 603).

For Herder, moral learning was thus in fact possible in history, and here humans' aesthetic, compassionate as well as 'calculating' judgement of history was of great help. What emerged was a clear preference for the pacific way of life and mutually beneficial international communication and exchange, indeed, commerce:

> The more reason increases among men, the more one will learn from early youth to understand that . . . it is more laudable . . . to form, than to ravage a nation, to establish, rather than destroy cities. Industrious Egyptians, ingenuous Greeks and commercial Phoenicians not only come across as more beautiful, but they also enjoyed a much more pleasant and useful life than the destructive Persians, conquering Romans and stingy [*geizige*] Carthagineans (445; cf. 454/589; cf. 601).

At the present level of culture, Herder argued, it was possible to detect retrospectively that nations had achieved good government and longevity in human history by pursuing pacified forms of industry and internal harmony, while dire consequences necessarily followed from the destruction of balance and order within or between societies (445–446; 441–442, 462–467/589; 584–585, 612–619). Herder also discussed commerce in this context. European commerce was in all respects incomparably larger than that of earlier individual nations (459/607), and although still widely believed to be 'the greatest [form of] self-interest [*grösseste Eigennutz*]', it was in reality a major vehicle of communication, exchange and interaction between nations (446/590. My translation here.). Here Herder probably drew on the abbé de Raynal's highly critical, but not entirely pessimistic, analysis of modern commercial politics: in *History of the Two Indies*, Raynal had laid bare the causes of the decline of various formerly successful modern commercial polities, while continuing to emphasise the beneficial nature of commerce rightly pursued.[109] 'Every commercial nation [*handelnde Nation*] in Europe,' Herder argued in the same vein, 'is now bitterly lamenting, and will do so even more in the future, what they formerly destroyed out of superstition or jealousy'. Subscribing to the widespread contemporary critique of overseas' trading companies and maritime commercial powers, Herder voiced a more positive hope that these policies would soon be abandoned because of their ultimately self-defeating consequences, whereby 'conquering seafaring' would give way to a 'commercial seafaring', 'based on reciprocal justice [*Gerechtigkeit*] and leniency [*Schonung*], on a progressive emulation to excel in arts and industry, in short, on humanity and its eternal laws' (446/590. Translation modified.).[110]

Even in terms of the principles of war and politics in modern times, Herder believed it possible to determine that a certain new 'level of culture' had been reached in Europe over time. Nations had been brought closer to each other, even if through the destructive power of war at first. Since the Romans, no civilised [*cultivierte*] European nation had built its entire organisation [*Einrichtung*] on wars and conquests, and the rude German settlers also gradually learnt to value 'arts-based industry [*Kunstfleiss*], farming [*Landbau*], commerce and sciences' (446/590). Similarly to his 1779 essay on political government, he now was again echoing ideas developed in the 'Enlightened narratives' of David Hume, William Robertson and Isaak Iselin. Herder argued that the 'growing true enlightenment' (*wachsende wahre Aufklärung*) was even reflected in the increasing 'reasonableness' (*Vernunft*) and 'mildening' (*Milderung*) of the art of war and politics (448–450/592–595).[111] Not the gradual improvement of

---

[109] On Raynal's analysis of modern commercial politics, see Iain McDaniel, 'Enlightened History and the Decline of Nations: Ferguson, Raynal, and the Contested Legacies of the Dutch Republic', *History of European Ideas*, 36:2, 203–216 (211–215). As mentioned in Chapter 4, Raynal was an important source of inspiration for Herder's critique of European colonialism and imperialism in *This Too a Philosophy* as well, whereas he did not then invoke the more hopeful elements of his account.

[110] I am grateful to Wolfgang Proß for suggesting this translation to me.   [111] See Chapter 5.

political constitutions and the growing chances for men to enlighten themselves, but the 'natural laws of history' fostered hopes for a more harmonious international order. While for Kant human 'natural instincts' had so far continued to rebel against the demands of morality, and only a 'crude disposition to morality' was activated through civilisation, Herder sketched an optimistic vision of a broader collective learning process well under way in European history. This learning process in his view made it possible to hope for a 'natural' non-political solution to the problem of war. As we shall see in the next section, Herder believed that Europe, in particular, had very good chances of realising this solution. However, it entailed profound transformations or, indeed, the dismantling of modern state-machines from within.

7.3.3   The Historical Prospects for True Modern Liberty and Peace in Europe

Although the fourth instalment of Herder's *Ideas* was published in 1791, its manuscript was already finished by autumn 1788 and hence pre-dated the French Revolution.[112] Also, since it concluded with the period of the Reformation and Renaissance, it did not directly address contemporary politics; in consequence, Herder's original views on modern developments can only be distilled from his sketch of the overall plan of the work.[113] Nevertheless, as Herder's analysis concluded that the period of *Völkerwanderungen* and the era of Germanic conquest had laid the foundations for subsequent developments, the fourth instalment provides important information about Herder's views on the trajectory of Europe's history and its future prospects.[114] Just as in the 1770s, Herder was again particularly interested in the contingent intersections between various chains of events and tendencies in European history. Quite expectedly, political developments played a rather ambivalent, and certainly not a central, role in his narrative of the formation of the European common spirit, while he singled out Europe's distinctive geography and climate, the impact of the common religion of Christianity, the cultivation of the arts and sciences, and above all, freedom and commerce in cities as the key factors in this process. In what follows I will focus on Herder's specific

---

[112] Proß, 'Nachwort', in *HWP*, III/1, 1012.
[113] Proß, 'Dokumentarischer Anhang', in *HWP*, III/1, 1157f. On this plan, see below.
[114] For Herder, Europe now constituted a new centre for humanity's development, taking over from the ancient states which ended in a *stasis* (China) or downfall (Egypt, Rome, etc.), Proß, 'Nachwort', 1013.

view of the rise of a form of modern liberty in Europe and his ideas on the contribution of commerce to Europe's common spirit in particular.

As we saw in Chapter 4, Herder had already in *This Too a Philosophy* presented modern Europe as a particular kind of international community united through common 'German' origins and the adoption of the Christian religion. In *Ideas*, he deepened this line of argument, claiming that the foundations for the emergence of the distinctive culture and spirit of the 'European republic' were laid by the fusion of the 'ancient' Mediterranean civilisation and the northern 'barbarian' cultures, which in turn had been made possible by Europe's distinctive geography.[115] In Herder's vision there was a continuous 'descending plane' from the 'vast, elevated region, Asiatic Tartary' westwards towards the sea, which explained why Europe was exposed to the 'pressure' and influx of various kinds of northern-eastern peoples (479–480/637–638). Internally, however, Europe possessed a particularly rugged terrain and intersected geographical space, with various rivers, lakes, seas, coastlands, which contributed simultaneously to national diversity, on the one hand, and communication and commerce between various regions and peoples within Europe, on the other, while also connecting Europe to the world. All of this, Herder argued, led to highly distinctive processes of ethnogenesis in Europe, so that instead of strong 'national trunks' (*Stammesbildung*) characteristic of ancient nations, the emerging European nations developed 'milder' and mixed forms of national character, which enabled the rise of a 'European common spirit [*Allgemeingeist*]' (488/649. Translation modified.). Through appropriation of the remnants of the Mediterranean ancient civilisation, and the new universalistic religion of Christianity, Europe gained unique chances to develop a new kind of international ethic.

Yet, Herder also did not fail to spell out the developments that initially hampered the realisation of this potential: first, the continuing relevance of Roman imperial structures and law for the development of ecclesiastical hierarchy, and second, the transformation of the original German system of government based on common property and freedom into a 'Tartarian

---

[115] Europe's geographical space and climate, Herder argued, were determined by a 'huge mound of rocks, known by the names of Mustag, Altai, Kitzigtag, Ural, Caucasus, Taurus, Haemus, and farther on by the Carpathian Mountains, the gigantic Alps and the Pyrenees'. The climate in Europe was milder than at the other side of Ural and Altai, yet nevertheless there was a distinctive continuity between northern Europe and 'Tartary', explaining the German nations' and 'Tartarians' rather similar 'vandal-gothic-scythian-tartarian way of life' in the early period (one distinct from other, less adventurous nations such as Slavs or Fennic peoples which hence also easily fell prey to the former) (468; 479–80; 481–484; 487/623; 637–638; 640–643; 647–48. Translation modified.).

imperial constitution' in the large post-Roman 'cultivated' or 'miscultivated' space. These developments brought along what Herder called 'phantom-monarchies' of the spiritual and lay kind, or as he also put it, a double 'barbarism' of popes and priests, on the one hand, and of kings and knights, on the other (560/740).

As we have seen in Chapter 5, Herder had already in the 1770s claimed that medieval European states were based on a new combination of Roman and German principles that emerged when the German peoples had established new states in conquered Roman territories. In *Ideas*, Herder renounced Möser's theory of ancient Germans as settled peoples and now followed Montesquieu[116] in comparing Germans to Tartars in terms of their nomadic lifestyle. He maintained that the German peoples who conquered Roman territories were fundamentally European 'Tartars', barbarous and bellicose peoples. When Germans came to serve in the Roman army, they, moreover, added a distinctively Roman type of militarism to their original national character.[117] More generally, however, Herder restated his admiration for the ancient German constitution, and did not endorse Montesquieu's emphasis on the special role of nobility in law enforcement.[118] The Germans, Herder argued, had devised a distinctive ideal of government known as 'German peoples' government' (*Deutsche Völkerverfassung, Gemeinverfassung*) to govern themselves, and these principles were admirable in their own right. Originally, the German tribes were 'free nations' who only selected leaders to accomplish specific tasks. Also, the territories conquered remained in the shared ownership of the nation as a whole. However, things changed radically after their conquest of Roman lands. During the subsequent conquering and settling down in the vast territories of the Roman Empire, most people became 'landholders [*Landeigentümer*] of their newly acquired possessions', while continuing to owe specific duties, particularly military service and council, to the commonwealth. They soon lost their common spirit, no longer participated in the assemblies of the nation, and began to hire 'knights' to serve in the military instead of them, which gradually led to the freemen's loss of rights and possessions. Since knights were rewarded with land by the kings, their power gradually increased both relative to the kings, who were soon impoverished, as well as to the common people, so that finally there were only 'noblemen' and their 'servants' (*Knechte*) (558–559/737–738).

---

[116] Cf. Montesquieu, *The Spirit of the Laws*, XVIII:10–22, 290–301.
[117] Herder had emphasised the early Roman influence in the 1770s already.   [118] See Chapter 5.

Herder made it clear that the German peoples originally had no concept of the territorial state, conceiving of the relationship of the king and his people as a personal one. While Charlemagne continued to rely on these 'German' elements of personal loyalty in his administration, he also strengthened royal and imperial authority, building a central power structure like that of Rome. For governing vast territories, 'viceroys, dukes, and counts' were needed. A 'state-machine' was thereby emerging, with the king seen as an 'abstract token' exemplifying the idea of the 'artificial machine' (*Kunstmaschine*) of the state. Charlemagne, an extraordinary figure, had for a moment been capable of really breathing life into the imperial structure thus created and had made use of this structure to keep external danger away. After his death, however, the imperial structure soon fragmented into feuding islands of 'satrapism' (542–545; 558–559/717–721; 738–739). Here, Herder was again arguing very clearly in line with Möser's account of the rise of feudal despotism (see Chapter 5).

Herder further buttressed this account with a novel argument that emphasised the peculiar kind of military despotism of European monarchies. In the Carolingian period, a 'singular metamorphosis' happened, he argued, essentially consisting in a 'monstrous' combination of Tartarian and Roman elements of political government. In a Tartarian form of government, the king's dignity also transferred to the members of his household – his satellites, domestics and servants. This was also the case with the Germans. In the Carolingian and post-Carolingian states, the idea of the king's dignity was turned into a 'naked reality'; 'the household of the regent was made the sum and substance of the kingdom' (560/740). The various kinds of personal services provided to the king became hereditary dignities and offices, and celebrated as though they were services to the state, while the household members (*Knechte*) themselves began to claim to represent the body of the nation. A singular kind of 'barbarous pomp', further, came to envelop them all. These claims, Herder stipulated, were totally absurd, since 'no free member of [this body] had been [the king's] servant, but only a comrade and co-fighter, and could not allow himself to be represented by any of the king's domestics'. The emerging monarchies completely renounced the original German principles. It was also a form of government of which 'neither Greeks nor Romans, neither Alexander nor Augustus', had known anything (538–545/717–721). This, Herder clarified, was the origin of European 'state-machines'.

Modern European monarchies, Herder maintained in discussing subsequent developments, originated in this system of government and had preserved its core element: the 'artificial' and 'outward-projected' (i.e.

aggressive) structure that was not in any way suited to energising the common people. Likewise, the popish government in no way managed to fulfil the universalistic and impartial role it should have assumed as a spiritual authority. Yet, this kind of situation in fact also harboured a potential for a new kind of good in itself. It was precisely due to the specific balance of power that had emerged between the lay and spiritual 'phantom-monarchies' that Europe as a whole could avoid the two extremes of rude despotism and an ecclesiastical state (631–632/830). This was in fact a totally novel argument in Herder's work, explaining the distinct character of European culture and its sociological basis. In stark contrast to the general thesis of *This Too a Philosophy*, Herder was now maintaining that in the long run, this fortunate balance of powers enabled the rise of cities as havens of industry and commerce, bringing along 'a third estate' (*dritte Stand*), that of 'science, of useful activity, of emulative industry in the arts', which alone could be the 'life-blood of this great active body' of Europe (627/824):

> With them [cities] were founded constitutions that first gave public spirit room to breathe; in them, aristocratic-democratic bodies were formed, the members of which watched over each other, were often mutual enemies and opponents, and on this very account unavoidably promoted common security, emulative industry and common exertion. Within the walls of a city, all that could awaken and give consistency to invention, diligence, civil liberty, economy, policy and order, according to the times, was condensed together in a narrow space; the laws of many cities are masterpieces of civic wisdom. Through the means of cities, the nobles as well as commoners enjoyed the first title of common liberty [*gemeinschaftlicher Freiheit*], citizenship [*Bürgerrecht*] (627–628/824–825. Translation modified.).

Like William Robertson (and Adam Smith on whom Robertson was actually drawing), Herder here outlined the pivotal role of the southern European towns in preserving and developing Roman arts and trade following the German conquest. 'The cities of Europe,' Herder argued, gave rise to 'an advanced political economy, without which this country would still be a desert' (604–605/795–796. Translation slightly modified.).[119] Emerging luxury awakened industry and encouraged not only trade and the establishment of manufactures but also agriculture in the surrounding countryside. This generated ever more order, security of

---

[119] On Robertson and Smith, see István Hont's brilliant reconstruction of Smith's ideas (which, as Hont suggests, were in turn borrowed and popularised by Robertson) in *Jealousy of Trade*, 354–388.

private property and lawful government all over the country in the long run (604/795–796).[120]

In the short run, however, the southern cities also degenerated into tyranny or fell prey to conquest because of their growing riches. In this context, Herder saw the development of the chivalric spirit in European monarchies as a welcome countervailing development (605/796), while squarely rejecting William Robertson's view that the Crusades had unintentionally contributed to freedom in cities and to the liberation of serfs in the countryside.[121] Herder, while not denying that the Crusades had led to the widening of horizons, cultural contacts and increased the riches of cities, instead deemed their overall impact to have been highly negative. It was the Crusades in particular that had contributed to increased rivalry among European princes, had nourished the taste for luxuries both among rulers and their subjects, and had even led to a reckless aggressive competition for any kinds of resources at the global level (619/814).

According to Herder, a different process had unfolded, however, in Northern Europe. The Crusades had played an important role in leading to the German conquest and colonisation of the north-eastern regions at the Baltic Sea, which in turn led to the enslavement of indigenous peoples, such as Latvians, Curonians and others (476–477/634). However, new kinds of cities had also emerged in this region. Merchants who 'first travelled about as pilgrims' created fraternities, while 'danger and necessity by sea and land extended the union higher and farther, till at length, under the protection of European Christendom, such a widespread *commercial republic* [*Handelsrepublik*] arose, as the World had otherwise never seen' (582/767).

Here, Herder thus could hark back to and further substantiate, his early enthusiasm about Riga's (historical) 'commercial spirit', which, he believed, had once coincided with the 'public spirit'. Like their southern counterparts, he stipulated, the northern cities, particularly those united in the Hanseatic League, contributed to the rise of industry, the rule of law and security of property. Herder made a further bold move by suggesting that cities constituted the specific context in which the principles of the original German constitution had been applied and developed with success (561/742).[122] While the German constitution had undergone

---

[120] As Smith and Robertson highlighted, this helped to undermine the power of the nobility in the long run, see ibid.

[121] On the central importance of this idea in Robertson's narrative, see J. G. A. Pocock, *Barbarism and Religion*, II: *Narratives of Civil Government* (Cambridge, 1999), 281.

[122] On Justus Möser's views on cities, see Chapter 5.

problematic transformations at the level of the state, it was highly suitable for small municipalities. According to Herder, the European cities thus had implemented

> the old German principles that everyone should be tried by one's peers, that the chairman of the court only draws the [his] right from the assessors [*der Vorsitzer des Gerichts von den Beisitzern das Recht nur schöpfe*], that restitution is to be made for every crime only on the basis of its being an offence to the community, and that an offence is not to be judged by the letter of the law, but by the actual consideration of the case: these, with a number of customs, respecting the administration of justice, confraternities and other matters, testify to the clear understanding, and equitable [*billige*] spirit of the Germans' (561/742).

Herder pointed out that universities, monasteries, guilds and other kinds of corporate bodies had also emerged along with cities in the medieval period. All these 'Gothic institutions' had been vital for the preservation, indeed, development of the arts and sciences in this turbulent period. Furthermore, universities had fulfilled a particularly important role not so much 'as schools, but as political bodies', providing support to rulers in their attempts to weaken the power of the nobles as well as that of the pope (629/827). Herder acknowledged that there was a need for reforms in these institutions in contemporary times, but his main goal here was to encourage further reflection about the sociological basis of European culture as well as 'modern liberty' more generally. As we have seen, his claim was that the public spirit and a degree of self-government was essential for the latter.

7.4   Conclusion

Herder spent the period of spring 1788-summer 1789 travelling in Italy. He returned to Weimar just a few days before the outbreak of the French Revolution.[123] Herder initially hoped to continue working on the final, fifth, volume of *Ideas*, but his worsening health did not allow him to do so. Since this final volume never materialised, we cannot lay out in any detail what Herder's view of the development of European politics might have been. There are, however, a few hints concerning his likely thoughts. The development of modern European trade and the concomitant rise of the European 'third estate' were to serve as the central themes of the final instalment. Herder also planned to discuss the impact of the Reformation

---

[123] Nowitzky, 'Biographie', 35–36.

on modern politics, including the English 'bill of rights', while intending an entire book to focus on the relationship of the arts, letters and sciences to the idea of the balance of power and law of nations. The following one was in turn set to discuss the relationship of the general spirit of industry and trade to money, luxury and taxes concomitant with it. As a sequel to this, another book focusing on Europe's different 'others' was planned, starting with Russia, and finishing with a general European 'colonial system'.[124] The concluding book, finally, was supposed to show the growth of *Humanität* 'at the individual level, in respect of religion', as well as in respect of 'state constitutions, trade, arts, sciences'.[125]

Based on Herder's remarks on humanity's moral learning process in chapter fifteen, we can suppose that Herder would have paid considerable attention to the rise of competitive and aggressive trade in the post-Renaissance period. This kind of trade, as we have seen above, was highly problematic, but he qualified it as a very recent and thus also hopefully transient phenomenon. Herder's theory of the natural laws of history enabled him to express confidence in humanity's providentially guaranteed ability to restore the natural tendency of commerce to promote harmony among nations in the long run. A further hint was hidden in Herder's discussion of Hanseatic cities specifically. The northern cities, Herder argued, had established a 'true commercial state based on genuine principles of mutual aid and security', which as such served as a 'model of the future situation for all trading European peoples [*Völker*]', exemplifying the principles on which Europe as a common system (*Gemeinwesen*) was truly based (600/790). Going beyond all national and religious differences, the Hanseatic cities had 'grounded a union of states in mutual utility, emulating industry, honesty, and order' (623/825. Translation modified.). In contrast to state-machines, these kinds of corporate bodies had succeeded in creating a long-lasting pan-European league. The question was whether this kind of league could also be established by modern Europeans based on the moral foundation of *Humanität*.

Despite his growing optimism about the progress of *Humanität* in Europe, it was clear that Herder did not think that European monarchies would be able to sustain themselves in their current machine-like form for long. Furthermore, it was precisely commerce that he saw as undermining the imperial 'state-machines', despite the arts of war and government becoming more 'mild'. In some ways, he thus also already anticipated

---

[124] Proß, 'Dokumentarischer Anhang', 1157.   [125] Ibid., 1158.

the French Revolution. However, his particular acumen was expressed in his statements about the likely 'awakening' of the Slavic nations and the eventual collapse of Europe's multinational empires. Curiously, previous scholarship has hardly noticed that here, too, Herder emphasised the emancipatory potential of trade and international commerce more broadly:

> The wheel of changing time would continue to revolve, and as these nations inhabit for the most part the finest region of Europe, if it were completely cultivated and its trade [*Handel*] opened; while it cannot be supposed, but that legislation and politics in Europe, instead of a military spirit, must and will more and more promote quiet industry, and peaceful commerce [*ruhige Verkehr*] between different peoples [*Völker*], these now deeply sunk, but once industrious and happy people, will awake from their deep and long slumber, will be freed from their chains of slavery and will use their beautiful areas from the Adriatic Sea to the Carpathian Mountains, from the Don to the Moldau as their property and can celebrate on them their old festivals of peaceful industry and trade (483–484/642–643. Translation slightly modified.).

Any more specific guidance as to how this might happen, whether it would involve also violence, maybe even wars at first, and what kind of future form of government these newly liberated peoples should establish on their historical territories, was not forthcoming from Herder in *Ideas*; just as he did not specify what their relationship to the descendants of their former conquerors was to look like. It remained a suggestive hint only.

CHAPTER 8

Perpetual Peace and Purified Patriotism

In summer 1792, Herder began to collect materials for *Letters for the Advancement of Humanity*. He followed contemporary developments in France closely, providing an explicit commentary on the Revolution in the manuscript of the first series of *Letters* penned that same year.[1] As he wrote to his friend Johann Wilhelm Ludwig Gleim, 'The times do not permit us to remain silent; they tear our mouths open.'[2] However, the political situation intensified in 1793 and Herder never published this early draft. The published *Letters* (1793–1797) thus engage mostly with aesthetic, moral and historical reflection.[3] Nevertheless, as John Noyes has observed, 'the *Letters* never strayed far from the topic of the French Revolution, even if it is often absent from the surface of the text'.[4]

Invoking the personal example and 'patriotic and humane' philosophy of Benjamin Franklin, Herder, in the first *Letter*, programmatically voiced an aspiration to create a universal 'league of humanity' that would unite 'all thinking humans' in history.[5] Indeed, as Wulf Köpke has put it, *Letters* is best read as 'Herder's attempt to initiate a conversation [among individuals and peoples] that would contribute to reason and justice, humanity and peace despite the partisanship, chaos and atrocities that had followed the

---

[1] Hans Dietrich Irmscher, 'Herders Humanitätsbriefe', in *FHA*, VII, 809–840 (811). English translations of some of the excerpts of these early letters can be found in *PW*, 361–369. Unless otherwise indicated, all translations from German in this chapter are mine.

[2] Herder to Ludwig Gleim, 12. November 1792, in *DA*, VI, 292.

[3] For an overview of the wide range of themes and authors discussed in this work, see Christoph Binkelmann, Violetta Stolz, '1.4.3. *Briefe zu Beförderung der Humanität*', in *Herder Handbuch*, 216–232.

[4] Noyes, *Herder: Aesthetics*, 276.

[5] Herder, *Briefe zu Beförderung der Humanität* = FHA, VII, 13–14, 139. The parenthetical page numbers in this chapter refer to this edition. Wherever possible, I also add a reference to translated excerpts in *PW*, separating the references to these two editions by a slash (/). If there is just one number, the reference is to *FHA*, VII.

French Revolution'.[6]At the same time, Herder was also clearly writing as a 'German' and as such was still addressing and educating the German public first of all. Another of his self-avowed goals was to create what he called the '*Athanasium* or *Mnemeion* of Germany' in which German examples of patriotism and *Humanität* would be remembered and evaluated. He also sketched a set of letters on the situation of Germany – the Holy Roman Empire – in the period of 1796–1797, but did not publish them.

The aim of this chapter is to lay out Herder's political vision in the French Revolution era. Whilst there are valuable studies of Herder's humanitarianism and his vision of perpetual peace, much less has been said about his ideas on patriotism and the future of Germany in this period.[7] The more precise interconnections between Herder's humanitarian aspirations and patriotic commitments have thus not been worked out so far. Furthermore, as I seek to show, Herder continued his debate with Kant, which also helps to shed light on this question. The chapter will thus discuss Herder's political vision by tracing his engagement with the French Revolution and his debate with Kant in parallel; indeed, its central argument is that these two revolutions form an essential historical context for understanding Herder's political ideas in these years.

Although Herder adopted a conciliatory approach to most Enlightenment thinkers after the French Revolution, he continued to regard Kant's ideas and influence with considerable ambivalence.[8] This is somewhat puzzling. In his 1792 draft manuscript, Herder made some rather hopeful remarks about the possible political applications of Kant's moral philosophy. During 1793–1797, Kant indeed disclosed his republican sympathies, including his positive view of the French Revolution, and substantively amended his theory of international peace. In many ways,

---

[6] Wulf Köpke [Koepke], 'Humanität in Goethes Weimar. Herder nach der Französischen Revolution', in "*Verteufelt human*"?: *zum Humanitätsideal der Weimarer Klassik*, ed. Volker C. Dörr, Michael Hofmann (Berlin, 2008), 47–68 (68) (my translation).

[7] See, e.g., Noyes, *Herder: Aesthetics*, 246–296; Proß, 'Geschichtliches Handeln'.

[8] Cf. John Pizer, 'The German Response to Kant's Essay on Perpetual Peace: Herder contra the Romantics', *The Germanic Review: Literature, Culture, Theory*, 87(4) (2008), 343–368; Isaac Nakhimovsky, *The Closed Commercial State: Perpetual Peace and Commercial Society from Rousseau to Fichte* (Princeton, NJ, 2011), 22–23, 36–37; Vicki Spencer, 'Kant and Herder on Colonialism, Indigenous Peoples, and Minority Nations', *International Theory*, 7:2 (2015), 360–392; Noyes, *Herder: Aesthetics*, 276–296. Tellingly, Friedrich Schiller and Johann Wolfgang von Goethe were also absent from Herder's discussion of German literature. On Herder's estrangement from Schiller and Goethe in these years, see Gerhard Sauder, 'Die Darstellung von Aufklärung in Herders *Adrastea* und die Kritik Schillers und Goethes', *Aufklärung und Weimarer Klassik im Dialog*, ed. Andre Rudolf and Ernst Stöckmann (Tübingen, 2009), 169–185.

the gap between Kant's and Herder's political views could be seen as narrowing, rather than widening in this period.[9] Nevertheless, when Herder listed and commented on a number of classical authors as his 'prophets of peace' in the published *Letters*, Kant was strikingly absent from them.[10] Furthermore, as we will see, Herder consistently criticised several ideas typically associated with Kant without mentioning him by name. Indeed, Herder developed an increasingly critical attitude towards Kant's moral and political thought. This did not mean that Herder renounced his humanitarian aspirations; quite the contrary. He just developed a very different kind of humanitarianism than Kant.

I will thus begin by laying out Herder's initial thoughts on the French Revolution, proceeding to discuss his engagement with Kant's evolving philosophy of history, including his theory of peace. My argument is that Herder consistently contrasted his ideas with those of Kant and Kantians, seeking to provide a morally more encouraging and practically more effective humanitarian philosophy of history.[11] Second, I will seek to demonstrate that this kind of philosophy of history informed Herder's ideas of purified patriotism and German patriotism, including German 'self-constitution'. As Herder himself put it, 'history is the study of *Humanität*' and as such 'an instrument of the most authentic patriotic spirit [*Werkzeug des echtesten Vaterlandsgeistes*]' (278).

More specifically, I will seek to show that Herder strongly sympathised with the French attempt to 'regenerate' the nation politically; he fully shared the broad republican principles espoused by the revolutionaries and regarded the revolution as an attempt to restore a 'living constitution' based on natural order.[12] Similarly, he endorsed the Kantian emphasis on the dignity of an individual human being and the Kantian goal (but not the means and description) of enlightenment. At the same time, he detected certain parallels between the problematic aspects of the French and the 'Kantian' revolutions. His worries about the outbreak of the Revolutionary wars were reflected in his concern about 'dogmatic' applications of Kant's ideas and the 'fighting' around them. He came to believe

---

[9] Muthu, *Enlightenment against Empire*, 257; cf. Zammito, *The Genesis of Kant's Critique*. On the evolution of Kant's political views, see Maliks, *Kant's Politics*.
[10] This is also highlighted by Nakhimovsky, *The Closed Commercial State*, 36–37.
[11] For Herder's other 'absent interlocutors' in this period, see Proß, 'Geschichtliches Handeln'.
[12] Although Herder owned Friedrich Gentz's translation of Edmund Burke's *Reflections on the Revolution in France* (1790), he never discussed it in his correspondence and writings. Arnold, 'Herder und Friedrich Gentz', *Herder-Yearbook: Publications of the International Herder Society*, X (Columbia, 1992), 80–98.

that Kant's philosophy of history and theory of republican peace could unwittingly exacerbate, rather than curb, what he called a 'swindle of freedom' (*Schwindelgeist der Freiheit*) (779), that is, republican moral absolutism and imperialism. Kant's solution, in Herder's opinion, did not adequately resolve what he saw as the main problem of modern society – the gap between professed principles and action, law and ethics. The revolution had once again revealed this gap in a particularly striking manner. Legal and institutional solutions were not enough. From Herder's perspective, Kant's theories of a modern representative republic and republican peace also relied mainly on an institutional mechanism and rational enlightenment but neglected the most important preconditions for their realisation – the dispositions of purified patriotism and peace.

Herder grounded his understanding of a truly humanitarian philosophy of history in his previous investigations into the natural foundations of morality and the individual capacity for self-determination, which he continued to interpret in a Stoic-Christian vein. He further elaborated on the ways in which humans could cultivate their 'sensus humanitatis' through reflective engagement with history, severely criticising various instances of European colonial imperialism. John Noyes has recently dissected an important underlying theme in this criticism, namely, Herder's rejection of Kant's Eurocentrism.[13] This was clearly one of Herder' intentions. However, Herder simultaneously and indeed primarily, also sought to guide European nations – above all, the German – in cultivating a new ethic to enable the simultaneous pursuit of domestic reforms and international cooperation. On the one hand, he provided a complex overview of how European nations had evolved and interacted over centuries, highlighting the emergence of international and transnational forms of community in Europe. On the other hand, his vision of purified patriotism included an element of constitutional patriotism. It thus essentially spelled out what could be termed a novel understanding of national self-determination in which cultural and political aspects were seen as equally important. At the same time, he also provided a perceptive analysis of the ways in which patriotism can morph into what he called 'national delusion', and voiced highly critical views on the current German constitution.

The chapter is divided into three sections. The first lays out Herder's initial, relatively optimistic stance towards the French Revolution. The second focuses on his discussion of the Kantian revolution, whilst also

---

[13] Noyes, *Herder: Aesthetics*, 276–296.

reconstructing Herder's alternative vision of the 'spirit of history' and perpetual peace. The third discusses Herder's idea of modern patriotism in the French Revolution era. The chapter concludes with Herder's assessment of Germany's prospects during the Coalition wars and around the turn of the century, up until his death in 1803.

8.1   Early Comments on the French Revolution

Herder is known to have welcomed the French Revolution with excitement and sympathetic concern.[14] However, in a short essay 'Tithon and Aurora' published in *Scattered Leaves (Zerstreute Blätter)* in 1792, Herder seemingly took a stance for 'evolution' as the only truly appropriate course of human affairs, inviting regents to take charge of the gradual evolution of society and the political institutions.[15] Each individual had to invent ways in which new forces would be awakened in their estate in society. Yet it was also important to realise that the life cycle of 'states' was shorter than that of 'land' and 'people': 'Whilst the land and the people never really become old, or become so only very late, the states [*Staaten*] as human institutions and children of the times, and as such often offsprings of contingency, can fortunately also have old age and youth, and thus an ever-lasting unnoticeable progression towards growth, fruition or dissolution.'[16] Violent upheavals of the state, Herder claimed, happened when the rulers attempted to preserve outdated modes of politics, and were not careful to reform the institutions and 'awaken the sleeping forces' in the people as they should. Such upheavals were characteristic of human politics in a barbarous age, and not much good had emerged from most of them. However, when a political upheaval actually took place, the 'state' was not allowed to restore the previous institutions but was forced to seek to 'retain or restore the natural order, the healthy activity of all its parts as well as the vibrant circulation of all its fluids, and not fight against the nature of things. Sooner or later, even the strongest machine will yield [to nature] in this fight'.[17] This was nothing but a 'regeneration' of life forces in the dead body of a state, and there were

---

[14] For an overview of Herder's relationship to the French Revolution, see Günter Arnold, 'Die Widerspiegelung der Französischen Revolution in Herders Korrespondenz', in *Impulse. Aufsätze, Quellen, Berichte zur deutschen Klassik und Romantik*, ed. Walter Dietze and Peter Goldammer (Berlin and Weimar, 1980), III, 41–89 and Hans-Wolf Jäger, 'Herder und die Französische Revolution', in *Johann Gottfried Herder, 1744–1803*, ed. Gerhard Sauder (Hamburg: Meiner, 1987), 299–307.

[15] Herder, 'Tithon und Aurora', in *FHA*, VIII, 221–239 (231). See also Köpke, 'Humanität in Weimar', 52–53.

[16] Herder, 'Tithon und Aurora', 236–237.   [17] Ibid., 225.

positive examples of this in history. Interestingly, Herder in this essay also praised the Glorious Revolution for having helped England to achieve its 'living constitution' in the 'most peaceful manner' and cited the view of the 'good-willed bishop Berkeley' of 'America' as a place in which Europe can truly 'regenerate' itself.[18] He pointed out that these positive developments often depended on small circumstances and single individuals, yet were possible more generally because human 'art and science' (*Kunst und Wissenschaften*) never died, but only regenerated themselves, attaining new forms.

It was this conception of a politics of 'regeneration' and 'rejuvenation' that Herder hoped to be realised in France, too. In the draft of the first series of *Letters*, Herder presented a series of a fictitious letters exchanged among a group of friends about the goal and course of the historical process and the significance of the French Revolution in world history.[19] The bulk of the letters expressed positive ideas and tentative hopes. He restated his earlier account of European political history, as developed in *Ideas*, but now presented the recession of the barbaric spirit of conquest and war and the abolition of old privileges of kings and the nobles as representing the inevitable course of history. In fact, there was only one rank to be accepted in the state – 'the people (not the rabble)' (*Volk (nicht Pöbel)*) (767–768/362). In a set of particularly hopeful letters, Herder thus expressed his full support for 'France' in its attempts to 'give itself a constitution' (*Verfassung*) (785) and thereby to regenerate itself (783). Referring to the discussions in the National Convention (elected by universal manhood suffrage in a two-stage voting process in September 1792),[20] Herder hailed the fact that more than a thousand well-selected individuals were now publicly discussing 'the tasks, details and doubts regarding the constitution [*Einrichtung*] of the entire nation, its full organisation [*völlige Organisation*] and fundamental rebirth [*Wiedergeburt von Grund aus*]', which was bound to have consequences for all European nations and the entire human species:

> The constitution [die *Konstitution*] that the National assembly (*Nationalversammlung*) is working on is an unsolved, until now unprecedented problem; [regardless of whether] those who seek to resolve it do not

---

[18] Ibid., 232; 237–239.
[19] Cf. Jäger, 'Herder und die französische Revolution', 302. According to Hans Dietrich Irmscher, this series of letters was written from November to December 1792, Hans Dietrich Irmscher, 'Herders Humanitätsbriefe', in *FHA*, VII, 809–840 (811).
[20] On the composition of, and debates in, the National Convention, see Peter McPhee, *The French Revolution 1789–1799* (Oxford, 2002), 100–101.

succeed or, conversely, meet with success is *the* struggle, *the* victory, even the failure of this most complex, difficult problem of humanity not worth the attention of anyone who does not want to be considered to be an animal? [my emphasis] (783)

The contrast made in this passage between a human-oriented constitution and an animal-oriented one is closely reminiscent of Herder's 1785 debate with Kant. However, now the emphasis was on a 'nation' that was deliberating on a possible 'living constitution' for itself. Without clearly endorsing any designated procedure for drafting or ratifying a constitution or pondering upon the question of how exactly a 'nation' can be a political actor, Herder was celebrating the fact that the French nation could now be 'active' to an unprecedented degree, and was seeking a return to the principles of natural order. What he meant, essentially, was that the true leaders of the nation could now take action to create *humane* political institutions. In the early draft of *Letters*, Herder also expressed a strong preference for the idea of meritocracy or more precisely, 'aristo-democracy'. The true meaning of the term 'aristo-democrats' (*Aristodemokraten*), Herder wrote, was 'noble, great, wise men' trained by 'education and experience' who were 'arranged as heads and leaders of the people by God and the state' (768/364).[21] Hereditary government in Europe had had its time.

Acknowledging that the state needed to distribute its powers, Herder underscored that such a distribution should not rely on hereditary offices because this would preserve an element of 'despotism' in the political system. (785/366) Thus Herder also criticised the 'limited monarchy' concept that was still the preferred option of many theorists in summer 1792. Such a monarchy, Herder argued in one of his most radical letters, would only be an 'irregular vacillation' from the pole of despotism towards that of republicanism. The earlier the republic (*Republik*) or a 'system common to all' (*das jedermann gemeinsame Wesen*) was established, the better (785/366). Indeed, Herder continued, the crucial issue for France was whether it was possible to establish a republic 'in such a large territory of lands and former provinces as France'. Although the size of French territory and the differences between its regional customs and habits might pose considerable challenges to this process, France should continue this experiment since 'the largest realms have long, albeit unhappily, persisted under the most miserable constitution, despotism, or what is still worse, aristocratic despotism'. Were France to succeed in this attempt, Herder

---

[21] I have modified the translation here.

concluded, it would revolutionise all of European political theory since the time of Aristotle (785/366).[22]

Turning to Germans specifically, Herder presented France as a useful laboratory for new ideas and policies that could also be tried out *mutatis mutandis* in Germany. The juridical side of this process of regeneration in France should not concern 'us' Germans, he maintained, since 'we' are not sufficiently familiar with the political circumstances there, just like it was none of 'our' business to tell the French how they should proceed. At the same time, Germans could well evaluate the principles espoused in this process as well as 'learn from the French' in some other respects (784). For example, it was highly instructive for Germans to observe the developments in France bearing in mind the degree of 'corruption' and slavery that the French had previously endured, particularly since this corruption had exerted a profound impact on German culture as well (782–783). Herder also touched on France's economic situation in this early draft. As a 'nation that constitutes a political whole' (*eine Nation, die ein politisches Ganze konstituiert*), France obviously faced the need to invent a 'just' and 'sparing' taxation system, in the same way that it was an open question whether its 'economistic' system would persist and how it would affect France's success as a 'trading state' (786/367).[23] 'In Germany,' Herder continued, 'we can await the solution to these questions with great tranquillity, since so few of our territories are genuine trading states and our taxes, means of livelihood, and products, are of a completely different type than they are in France' (786/367).

Some of the participants in Herder's fictitious conversation, however, were less optimistic. One of the concerns that Herder sought to express through their voices was that the French may have gone too far in their celebration of popular self-government. He was worried that the revolutionaries had begun to pursue popular self-government as an absolute or indeed, single most important, value. In one letter Herder accordingly pointed out that Rousseau's idea of the 'rule of the people' has been

---

[22] This discussion is reminiscent of Thomas Paine's interpretation of the term 'republic' and republicanism in his *Rights of Man*, Part 2 (1792), in Thomas Paine, *Philosophical Writings*, ed. Bruce Kuklick (Cambridge, 1997), 155–264 (176–181). Like Paine, Herder also regarded the people as the author of the French constitution, and (ideally) did not see any role for hereditary offices in a republican system. Although Herder did not make use of the term 'representation' or 'representative government' in this context, it is likely that it is precisely what he had in view when presenting France as experimenting with a new kind of republicanism.

[23] As Isaac Nakhimovsky has pointed out, the term 'economistic system' (*Ökonomistische System*) in this period commonly referred to physiocratic system, physiocrats being widely called 'economists', Nakhimovsky, *The Closed Commercial State*, 15.

implemented without any regard to the fact that the 'people have remained uneducated for centuries' within European despotisms (774). In another more directly critical letter, he compared current German bureaucratic rule with the 'even more oppressive yoke of popular rule by numerous municipalities' in France, expressing his relief that Germans can observe the 'French shipwreck in an open and alien sea from a safe coast', at least as long as 'our evil genius does not push us against our will into the [same] sea' (782). In a further letter, Herder also expressed the concern that French Revolutionaries were chasing a 'swindle of freedom' (*Schwindelgeist der Freiheit*) that had already contributed to 'deception and disorder' at home and was likely to instigate 'bloody wars directed against peoples and regents' abroad (779). This was not an unsubstantiated worry, as we shall see below.

Herder also voiced perceptive comments about France's international standing, revealing his awareness of the ongoing debates in France. The National Assembly had declared in its decree of 22 May 1790 that 'the French nation renounces the undertaking of any war with a view to making conquests, and that it will never use its forces against the freedom of any people'.[24] Most theorists of the French Revolution initially rejected revolutionary imperialism, albeit on different grounds.[25] Jacobins like Robespierre and Saint-Just also initially strongly denounced territorial conquest as an act of violence, and hence rejected the violent export of republican institutions, too. Instead, it was best to adhere to the principle that 'every people, however small the country it inhabits, has an absolute right to be its own master'.[26] The Jacobins were aware of the precarious nature of setting up a solitary republic surrounded by monarchies and thus they initially supported an isolationist approach in order to preserve France in the interests of humanity.[27] Yet soon the more bellicose view got the upper hand among a significant number of revolutionaries, including the Jacobins, despite their initially strongly pacific commitments; the argument arose that changes in the international environment were paramount for the republic's survival. This advocacy of war resulted from changing opinions as to what the interests of France and humanity demanded; the Jacobins also initially suggested that France would not actually need to fight, since it could count on foreign 'peoples' (as opposed to their tyrannical rulers) laying down arms to join the

---

[24] McPhee, *The French Revolution*, 93 (the translation of the declaration is also by McPhee); T. C. W. Blanning, *The French Revolutionary Wars* (London, 1996), 49.
[25] Blanning, *The French Revolutionary Wars*, 48–51; Hont, *Jealousy of Trade*, 493.
[26] Lazare Carnot's report in the name of the diplomatic committee concerning the annexation of the Principality of Monaco, cited from Hont, *Jealousy of Trade*, 513.
[27] Ibid., 510–511.

cause of the humanity of the French people instead.[28] When it turned out not to be that simple, very different justifications were invented to legitimise conquests, from the idea of 'natural borders' to that of 'fraternity and assistance to all peoples who wish to recover their liberty' as stated in the declaration of the National Convention of 19 November 1792.[29]

Like the Jacobins, in June 1791 Herder already expressed his regrets that France was not an island like Great Britain, and thus most likely faced an intervention by neighbouring monarchical states.[30] Would other European states allow France to 'clean out its old, entirely autonomous throne?', Herder asked in a similar vein in the early draft of *Letters*. Or will they still resort to 'the fruitful fiction of a balance [of power]' to prevent France from doing so? (785/366) Referring to emigrant conspiracies and the increasing fears about foreign intervention in France in the second half of 1791 and early 1792,[31] Herder did not hold back in expressing his indignation: 'But what may be the result of this strange, extremely strained, crisis in which without right or authority masters of foreign houses interfere in the administration of a house that is foreign to them, shelter and arm its deserters and traitors?' (785–786/366. Translation modified.) Writing shortly before the outbreak of the first Coalition war, Herder further asked apprehensively: '*How, in the case of successful resistance, would France behave according to its first principles which say that it has renounced the system of conquest?*' Will France be able to 'afford the first example of a right and just war, for whose running its [France's] own constitution has made itself a pledge and watchman?' (786/366–367) As these comments show, Herder well understood the challenges that Revolutionary France was facing in this difficult period.

8.2 New Debates with Kant

Herder concluded his critical examination of recent developments in France in 1792 with a set of questions about what consequences the establishment of a republican form of government might have for French religious practices, literature and arts, whilst also considering the

---

[28] Blanning, *The French Revolutionary Wars*, 59.   [29] Ibid., 92.
[30] Dieter Lohmeier, 'Herder und der Emkendorfer Kreis', in *Nordelbingen: Beiträge zur Kunst- und Kulturgeschichte: Im Auftrag der Gesellschaft für Schleswig-Holsteinische Geschichte*, ed. Olaf Klose and Ellen Redlefsen, XXXV (Heide and Holstein, 1966), 46; cited from Arnold, 'Die Widerspiegelung der französischen Revolution', 44–45.
[31] McPhee, *The French Revolution*, 92–94; Blanning, *The French Revolutionary Wars*, 56–59.

relationship between culture and politics more broadly. In this context, he also discussed philosophy's role in society. As we saw in Chapter 1, Herder had already seriously engaged with this issue in his early professional years in Riga, having set out to develop a sociable and 'human' philosophy in the spirit of Abbt, Hume, the young Hamann and the pre-critical Kant himself. Now Herder addressed the same issue by reflecting on Kant's 'Critical revolution' in philosophy, raising questions about the role and responsibility of practical philosophy and philosophical history more broadly. As we will see below, these questions would come to occupy much of Herder's theoretical attention in the following years.

For Herder, the two revolutions – the French and the Kantian one – were developing in close synergy. Just as in his evaluation of the French Revolution, Herder initially sought to distinguish between the true idea of the Kantian revolution and its corrupted versions. However, Herder's discussion of the Kantian revolution was considerably less enthusiastic even in 1792, whilst he only grew more critical of Kant's ideas later. During 1793 Herder suffered a deep crisis, being dismayed by the execution of Louis XVI in January 1793 and the unleashing of the 'Reign of Terror' that autumn.[32] Herder was also concerned about the rise of French republican imperialism. Of course, Kant was not responsible for these failures. Yet Kant's views, in a different manner, also developed in a direction of which Herder could not fully approve. As I hope to show below, Herder was provoked by a number of new ideas that Kant and his followers put forward in this period.[33] He provided a series of penetrating criticisms of these ideas, whilst developing his own moral and political ideas as clear alternatives to them.

8.2.1   Herder's Comments on Kant in 1792

The Kantian revolution in German political thought was largely inspired by the influential explanation of Kant's critical philosophy in 1786/1787

---

[32] Arnold, 'Die Widerspiegelung der französischen Revolution', 50–54.

[33] On Kant's political thought, see Pauline Kleingeld, *Kant and Cosmopolitanism: The Philosophical Ideal of World Citizenship* (Cambridge, 2012); Georg Cavallar, 'Kant and the Right of World Citizens: An Historical Interpretation', in *Critique of Cosmopolitan Reason: Timing and Spacing the Concept of World Citizenship*, ed. Rebecka Lettevall and Kristian Petrov (Oxford, Bern, 2014), 141–180; idem, 'Cosmopolitanisms in Kant's Philosophy', *Ethics and Global Politics* 5:2 (2012), 95–118; Sankar Muthu, 'Conquest, Commerce and Cosmopolitanism in Enlightenment Political Thought', in *Empire and Modern Political Thought*, ed. Sankar Muthu (Cambridge, 2012), 199–231.

by Karl Leonhard Reinhold, philosophy professor at Jena.[34] By the early 1790s, a number of young philosophers adopted Kant's distinctive style of philosophising about religion, morality and politics. Kant himself openly avowed his unequivocal republicanism as late as in 1793, inspiring his followers to formulate more radical theories even before that.[35]

In the 1792 draft Herder was still mostly worried that Kant's followers – and Karl Leonhard Reinhold in particular – might abuse his philosophy. Mocking Reinhold's 'conversion' to Kantianism,[36] Herder diagnosed the emergence of new forms of scholasticism and Cartesianism both in terms of argumentation and expression, and warned that the new 'sectional spirit' would yield nothing but ignorance and lack of originality. He was concerned about whether a 'transcendental school' inimical to *popular philosophers* (*populare Philosophen*) was not 'drawing philosophy into the darkness again', positing an 'extramundane type of human freedom' and 'a pure *must*' (*ein reines Soll*) unrelated to any human drives or motives (792). For Herder, the spread of Kantian transcendentalism potentially represented the return of the kind of abstract and dogmatic metaphysics that he and Kant had together sought to combat in the 1760s.

These views prefigure Herder's critique of Kant in his two-volume *Metacritique of Critique of Pure Reason* (*Eine Metakritik zur Kritik der reinen Vernunft*) (1799) and *Calligone* (*Kalligone*) (1800).[37] However, at this point, Herder was still hopeful that Kant's true teaching could be clearly dissociated from that of his disciples, similar to his defence of the core ideas of the French Revolution in the face of their misguided application by a 'maddened people'. Kant's own spirit, Herder argued, was originally completely free of all dogmatism and arrogance, and open to learning from, and discussing, the thought of other great thinkers. During the most prosperous years of his life, Kant was 'a true teacher of humanity', making it now impossible to imagine him leading a new sect of scholastic thinking. Here Herder welcomed the inspiration Kant had recently provided for 'various

---

[34] On Reinhold and his relationship to Herder and Kant, see Martin Bondeli, 'Von Herder zu Kant, zwischen Kant und Herder, mit Herder gegen Kant—Karl Leonhard Reinhold,' in *Herder und die Philosophie des deutschen Idealismus*, ed. Marion Heinz (Amsterdam, Atlanta, 1998), 203–34.

[35] For a reconstruction of Kant's philosophy as responding to his contemporaries' questions and adaptations of his own ideas, see Maliks, *Kant's Politics*.

[36] See, in particular, Karl Leonhard Reinhold, *Briefe über die Kantische Philosophie*, vol. 2 (Leipzig, 1792).

[37] On *Metacritique*, see Marion Heinz, 'Vernunft ist nur Eine – Untersuchungen zur Vernunftkonzeption in Herders Metakritik', in *Herders Metakritik: Analysen und Interpretationen*, ed. Marion Heinz (Stuttgart-Bad Cannstatt, 2013), 163–194; on *Calligone*, see idem, 'Sympathie. Zur Palingenesie stoischen Denkens in Herders *Kalligone*', in *Herder on Empathy*, 50–73.

salutary attempts' at 'ordering the *human sciences*, morality, natural right and right of nations according to strict notions', and expressed the hope that these principles would become 'fact/acts' (*Tathandlungen*) and gradually even 'accepted maxims' (798).[38] Herder also raised a number of further questions that Kantian philosophy needed to solve in future philosophical investigations, concluding on a positive interrogative note: '[What consequences would it have] if his [Kant's] *Critique of Practical Reason* and the *Moral Philosophy* based on it would form the basis of a natural right and right of nations? If it were universally recognised? Widely practiced?' (800). As yet, Kant had not spelled out his views on morality and Christian religion or on the modern constitutional republic and republican peace.

8.2.2   Radical Evil

In 1793, Kant published his *Religion within the Boundaries of Mere Reason*. Now, finally, Kant was directly adressing the topic of the origin of 'evil' that Herder had asked him to do already in the late 1760s.[39] Kant distinguished between an 'original predisposition to good' in human nature and the 'not yet demonstrable' idea of 'radical evil' in human nature as consisting in the fundamental propensity (*Hang*) of all human beings to transgress moral law when its commands conflict with our inclinations grounded in our desire for happiness.[40] Kant did not thereby argue that moral evil was located in our natural inclinations themselves, ascribing this view to the Stoics instead.[41] His claim was rather that a human being was evil insofar as he or she has incorporated the desire for happiness rather than respect for moral law into his or her maxim. Pointing out that humans were fully responsible for their propensity to do so, Kant in his own way endorsed the Augustinian doctrine of original sin. At the same time, he pointed out that the propensity was activated in social context,

---

[38] Fact/act [*Tathandlung*] was a term coined by Johann Gottlieb Fichte. Although Herder was never close to Fichte and never expressly commented on the latter's work, this sentence indicates that he may have favourably viewed Fichte's early work, which in many ways paralleled his own. For the development of Fichte's republicanism and the similarities between early Fichte and Herder, see Nakhimovsky, *The Closed Commercial State*, ch. 1.

[39] See the beginning of Chapter 2.

[40] Immanuel Kant, 'Religion within the Boundaries of Mere Reason (1793)', in *Religion and Rational Theology*, ed. A. Wood and G. di Giovanni (Cambridge, 1996), 39–216 (74–77) (6:25–29).

[41] Ibid., 101–102 (6:58–59). As we have seen throughout this book, Herder highlighted very different strands in Stoicism and accordingly could not have agreed with this interpretation.

hence, as Allen Wood has pointed out, also identifying it with what he earlier had called 'unsocial sociability'.[42]

In order to combat this evil in ourselves, Kant argued, it was necessary to posit the idea of, and indeed, establish, an ethical community of rational human beings united by a system of shared ends and the common goal of the highest good (morality). For Kant, this ethical community was to be understood as an enduring and ever-expanding society, specifically designed for the preservation of morality by counteracting evil with 'united forces'. As Wood explains, as a pure idea, this community would be grounded solely on ethical laws of reason. However, in order to be effective in this fight against evil, it had to exist on earth, as a human institution – it had to take the form of a 'church'. As an ideal, it could thus be described as a 'church invisible' – the 'mere idea of a union of all upright human beings under direct yet moral divine world-governance'.[43] For weak human beings, such a church could only come into being historically, and would need to conceive of itself as receiving its laws directly from God, through revelation. The actual existing churches on earth, Kant maintained, have historically fallen short of the actual ideal of a truly ethical community, but can and should gradually approximate this ideal.[44]

For Herder, this analysis of moral psychology was an anathema. A hidden polemic with Kant's ideas runs all the way through the published *Letters*. As he claimed at the beginning of *Letters*, the 'universal league of all thinking humans' that he was seeking to establish was also the 'true invisible church uniting all human beings in different times and places'. Thereby, Herder signalled his intention to propose an alternative, more inclusive view of humanity (13–14).[45] The final collection culminates in an attack on what he describes as a 'hypothesis of the radical evil basic force in the human mind and will' (746/420). Throughout the work, Herder was also at pains to emphasise the holism and continuing integrity of human nature, rejecting what he saw as Kant's dualist account. In the Fourth Collection of his *Christliche Schriften* (*Christian Writings*) published in exactly the same year as the final Collection of *Letters* (1797),

---

[42] Allen Wood, *Kant and Religion* (Cambridge Studies in Religion, Philosophy, and Society) (Cambridge, 2020), ch. 3.

[43] Kant, 'Religion', 135 (6:101).

[44] For discussion, see Wood, *Kant and Religion*, 164–168. This theological notion had been previously elaborated by St Augustine, Luther, Melanchton, and Lessing; see Köpke, 'Humanität in Weimar', 56–58.

[45] On the theme of 'invisible church' in Herder's thought, cf. Johannes Schmidt, 'Herder's Political Ideas and the Organic Development of Religions and Governments', in *Herder on Empathy*, 231–257.

Herder implicitly accused Kant and Kantians of positing a split within human nature (as well as in the human species) and hence reviving the idea of an evil spirit (devil). This, he ironically maintained, had been achieved with the help of 'pure reason' or more precisely, dogmatic thinking inspired by the former. Authentic forms of religion – from the natural religion to the Christian religion (in its true form) – in fact did not know such a force alongside the divine one, instead encouraging a positive and holistic idea of man, which in turn inspired mutual love and fidelity in human relationships. In Herder's interpretation, Kant had essentially denied the existence of natural sociable feelings in man, seeking to estab- lish a purely artificial form of sociability via 'pure reason'. For Herder, this was a deeply implausible and morally repulsive idea of humanity.

Herder like Kant conceived of morality in terms of self-determination (*Selbstbestimmung*), yet for Herder, humans were to determine themselves in accordance with 'nature' rather than through 'pure reason' alone (746–753/420–424).[46] We have seen throughout this book how Herder, in various places, emphasised the need for humans to purify and enhance their existing sociable feelings and commitments. This idea of morality was grounded in his neo-Spinozist metaphysics, according to which the 'divine' and 'natural' realms were inseparable. God was an active dynamic being immanent in nature. Human souls carried the imprint of the divine and were free insofar as they *knowingly* pursued beauty, goodness and truth. Herder thus emphatically declared in his concluding remarks in *Letters* that 'the divinity itself guides every honest man to learn to obey the great law of *Humanität*' (805). Within a few years, Herder would more clearly express this in *Metacritique* (1799), now again targeting the Kantian idea of self- determination: 'Self-determination in accordance with the laws of nature, not outside these laws, is the highest freedom, in that it creates and organises laws in accordance with the laws of nature'.[47] Self-determination was the 'highest' kind of natural 'force' in humans insofar as it consisted in a knowing understanding of 'natural laws', which essentially captured the ways in which natural forces interacted with each other.

---

[46] Herder, 'Von Religion, Lehrmeinung und Gebräuchen', in *FHA*, IX/1, 725–858 (810–831). I am very grateful to one of the anonymous reviewers for pointing out this further source on Herder's polemic with Kant's idea of radical evil. On Herder's critique of Kant's concept of Christianity more broadly, cf. Johannes Schmidt, 'Light or Nature/Light of Reason. Herder's and Kant's Religion Essays', in *Herder and Religion*, 153–166.

[47] Herder, *Metakritik*, in *SWS*, XXI, 229. Cf. Chapter 4 on his similar statements in *On the Sensation and Cognition*.

In *Letters*, Herder expressed a similar idea by identifying human voluntary and rational 'self-constitution' according to the 'sacred, inviolable laws of society' as the central element of humanity (*Humanität*) (153).[48] Here Herder was again directly harking back to the Stoic sense of 'humanity' that was based on the belief that human reason was part of the divine, as indicated by his proceeding to cite passages from Marcus Aurelius's *Thoughts to Myself*. What impressed him in the Stoic account was also the emphasis on 'active reason' (*tätige Vernunft*) and sociability. At the same time, Herder further restated his view of Christian virtue as not only compatible with these ideas of humanity but also as providing the 'purest' and most direct inspiration for it. Our commitment to society, Herder maintained, is demanded by 'our very nature, our Christian vocation', which consists in 'joining the battle for victory' so as to 'be a free, happy species, which, without fear of a sovereign hangman-spirit [*Machthabende Henkergeist*], does good for the sake of good, from an inner desire, from innate character and higher nature' (747/421. Translation modified.). Contesting Kant's interpretation of the concept of 'autonomy', he was adamant that '*Christianity commands the purest humanity on the purest path*, humanly and intelligibly to all, humbly, not with *proud autonomy* [*stolzautonomisch*], not even as a *law* [my emphasis both times] but as a gospel of hope [*Evangelium*] for the happiness of all' (752/424).[49] The hypothesis of 'radical evil', by contrast, implied a very different understanding of humanity. Instead, it 'now puts it [our species] in the place of fallen angels, now abases it under their guardianship and sovereignty [*Oberherrschaft*]' (748/421).

Herder was thereby pointing at a certain parallelism between the Augustinian view of human depravity and original sin and its corresponding advocacy of submission to earthly sovereigns, on the one hand, and the Kantian idea of 'radical evil' and constitutional republicanism, on the other. This kind of criticism may look surprising, considering Kant's own explicit emphasis on the value of individual autonomy and his attack on hereditary privilege in his *On the Common Saying: 'This May be True in Theory, but Does not Apply in Practice'* (1793). However, Kant had simultaneously continued to advocate for the need for a strong sovereign power to guarantee 'external freedom' and 'right' (*Recht*), i.e. a system of law

---

[48] Cf. Köpke, 'Humanität in Goethes Weimar', 61–65.
[49] For a discussion of Herder's views on the relationship of Christianity to a purely 'human religion' (*Menschenreligion*), see Johannes Schmidt, 'Herder's Religious Anthropology in his Later Writings', in *Herder: Philosophy and Anthropology*, 185–203.

grounded in reason.[50] While not specifying a theory of obligation at this point, he put forward a theory of the state based on 'rational' rather than actual consent. He designated a form of government that guarantees 'right' as 'patriotic government', contrasting it with a 'paternalistic' one in which a benevolent ruler would impose his view of happiness on his subjects.[51] Albeit thus ostensibly attacking Hobbes, he denied the subjects' right of resistance, even against unjust rulers, maintaining that even imperfect forms of lawful order are to be preferred to a situation in which there is no order whatsoever.[52] For Kant, rulers were obliged to govern in a republican manner, whilst individuals merely had the right and duty to criticise public institutions and policies. This did not mean that the French Revolution was to be reversed; if a revolution had already taken place, its consequences were to be accepted. Thus, Kant affirmed the fundamental legitimacy of the republican constitution that the French were seeking to devise and implement, but rejected the idea that the people – the actual physical individuals – could ever legitimately take action outside the established legal order. For Herder, this view reeked of Hobbesianism while being grounded on Kant's quasi-Augustinian moral psychology.

8.2.3   War and Peace

Herder was also never able to reconcile himself to Kant's paradoxical notion of war as supporting cultural and political development. Although Kant clearly regarded peace as a central political value, he did not absolutely condemn warfare in earlier historical periods. In the years following their mid-1780s dispute, Kant further refined his views on the potential progression of culture and enlightenment. In his *Conjectures on the Beginning of Human History* (1786), written directly in response to Book Ten of Herder's *Ideas*, for example, Kant attempted to combine a Rousseauian account of human perfectibility with a four-stage theory of human civilisation, presenting human autonomy as an end-result of the civilisation process.[53] Here, however, Kant emphasised – even more

---

[50] For discussion, see Maliks, *Kant's Politics*, 50–52.
[51] Immanuel Kant, 'On the Common Saying: That May Be Correct in Theory, but It Is of No Use in Practice,' in *Practical Philosophy*, 273–310 (290–291).
[52] Ibid., 298–300. For the evolution of Kant's views on this issue in debate with his radical republican followers in the later 1790s, see Maliks, *Kant's Political Thought*, ch. 4.
[53] Immanuel Kant, 'Conjectures on the Beginning of Human History', *Political Writings*, ed. H.S. Reiss and trans. H.B. Nisbet, 2nd, enlarged edition (Cambridge, 2000), 221–234. For reconstructions of Kant's argument in *Conjectures*, see Sonenscher, *Sans-Culottes*, 195–201; Muthu, *Enlightenment against Empire*, 125–133.

forcefully than in *Idea for a Universal History* – the instrumental value of war to domestic freedom and cultural development, and indeed, even peace, in certain contexts and historical periods:

> We need only to look at *China*, whose population may expose it to occasional unforeseen incursions but not to attack by a powerful enemy, and we shall find that, for this very reason, it has been stripped of every vestige of freedom. So long as human culture remains at its present stage, war is therefore an indispensable means of advancing it further; and only when culture has reached its full development – and only God knows when that will be – will perpetual peace become possible and of benefit to us.[54]

Herder's view was very different; furthermore, as we will see below, he believed that Kant's perspective could be misused for justifying wars in a revolutionary period in particular. The opening sentences of the Tenth Collection of his *Letters* make this very clear: 'But why must peoples have impact on peoples in order to disturb each other's peace?', Herder asked. 'It is said that this is for the sake of progressively growing culture; but what a completely different thing the book of history says!' (671/380. Translation modified.). Proceeding to criticise all violent 'impositions' of foreign culture upon conquered nations, Herder resolutely protested against the view of wars as tools of Providence (673/382). In the same Tenth Collection, Herder further presented a comprehensive assessment of what he called the 'recent talk on plans *for perpetual peace*' (713/400).[55] Although he did not directly mention Kant in this context, it seems likely that he was referring to Kant's essay *Toward Perpetual Peace* (1795) and the resulting German debates.[56]

Let us briefly recall Kant's and his followers' main arguments here. Already in *On the Common Saying* (1793) Kant had substantially revised his theory of how to solve the problem of antagonistic 'masters' at the international level. Here he explicitly acknowledged that a lawful federation of states based on 'publicly enforceable' right would be the only solution to this situation, whilst also admitting that a 'universal cosmopolitan commonwealth under a single ruler' would create the danger of a powerful despotism.[57] However, Kant further maintained that a beneficial end-result could be achieved through increased warfare, leading to rising

---

[54] Kant, 'Conjectures', 232. See also Schmidt, 'Sources of Evil', 53–54.
[55] Various German essays on perpetual peace are reprinted in *Ewiger Friede? Dokumente um eine deutsche Diskussion um 1800*, ed. Anita and Walter Dietze (Munich, 1989).
[56] See also Pizer, 'The German Response to Kant's Essay', 358–359; Nakhimovsky, *The Closed Commercial State*, 36–37; Maliks, *Kant's Politics*, 158–162.
[57] Kant, 'On the Common Saying', 308.

public debt. Kings and populations of monarchies would end up in a state of 'sheer exhaustion', which in turn would lead to the establishment of a republican state constitution either through reform or popular resistance (as we saw above, he denied its legitimacy). The establishment of such a constitution would cause a crucial change in respective states' foreign policies, since 'the head of state, for whom war really costs nothing' would no longer have the 'decisive vote as to whether there is to be war or not, but instead the people, which pays for it'.[58]

Kant famously further elaborated on these ideas in *Toward Perpetual Peace*.[59] Alongside putting forward a purely normative account of republican principles and peace, he also discussed the conditions for establishing a republican form of state and indeed, peace. In so doing, he was spelling out a theory of modern representative republics embedded in a commercial society, flatly contradicting the claims that republics were suited solely for 'angels':

> The problem of establishing such a state, no matter how hard it may sound, is *resolvable* even for a nation of devils (if only they have understanding) and goes like this: 'Given a multitude of rational beings all of whom need universal laws for their preservation but each of whom is inclined covertly to exempt himself from them, so to order this multitude and establish their constitution, that, although in their private dispositions they strive against one another, these yet so check one another that in their public conduct the result is the same as if they had no evil dispositions'.[60]

War itself forces people to submit to the constraint of public laws, i.e. establish a state, whilst states, too, are also 'approaching in their external conduct what the idea of right prescribes'. In both cases, it is not internal morality that forces humans or states to do so; 'on the contrary, the good moral education of a people is to be expected from a good state constitution'.[61] Of course, Kant emphasised the crucial role of enlightenment, that is, the 'public use of reason' in this moral learning process. Nevertheless, he did not think that republics

---

[58] Ibid., 308.
[59] Kant, 'Toward Perpetual Peace' and 'The Metaphysics of Morals', in *Practical Philosophy*, 311–352 and 353–604.
[60] Kant, 'Toward Perpetual Peace', 335. For a discussion of whether, in Kant's view, these self–maintaining systems would come about automatically or would require a benevolent legislator to establish them, see Paul Guyer, *Kant on Freedom, Law and Happiness* (Cambridge, 2000), 13. Guyer suggests that Kant must have distinguished between the motives of subjects in adhering to a constitution, and those of a ruler in establishing one. While it is perfectly possible for the subjects of a just state to be ruled solely by self-interest, such a state can only be instituted and maintained by what Kant in *Perpetual Peace* calls 'moral politicians'. Paul Guyer, 'The Crooked Timber of Mankind', in *Kant's* Idea for a Universal History, 129–149 (131).
[61] Kant, 'Toward Perpetual Peace', 336–337.

would need any further moral grounding. 'Nature' itself 'irresistibly wills that right should eventually gain supremacy'.[62]

Kant regarded both the republican form of government and peace simultaneously as normative goals and 'ends of nature'. According to Kant, the aim of republican government was to guarantee citizens' rights and property in the territory of a particular state, and thus it was not mandated to enter into aggressive wars.[63] At the same time he also introduced an empirical claim, arguing that the people, when allowed to determine the foreign policy of their country, would most likely be 'hesitant to begin such a bad game [war], since they would have to decide to take upon themselves all the hardships of war'.[64] Kant did not clearly acknowledge the actual empirical nature of this argument and its further preconditions, but proceeded to discuss the ways in which 'nature' contributes to the realisation of peace. In this context, he maintained that the 'spirit of commerce, which cannot coexist with war' will 'sooner or later [take] hold of every nation'.[65] As this claim shows, Kant essentially regarded the spirit of commerce as a precondition to allow for the emergence of irenic dispositions among populations of republican states.

In further elaborating on the ways to achieve international peace Kant also restated the claim (first made in *Idea for a Universal History*) that the only *rational* way of solving the problem of war at the international level was by creating an *international state* with coercive powers. However, he also maintained that this state could only be achieved gradually. No state may legitimately force other states to join a federation of states. Kant thus underlined this federation's voluntary nature and accordingly also the value of national autonomy. In such a league, he argued, humans would have an opportunity to cultivate morality, and hence improve their conception of international and even cosmopolitan right (the rights of individuals outside their own states) as well. Thus, it could also be hoped that the states that joined the federation would in the distant future still decide to create an 'international state', one in which it would also be possible to achieve the widest conceivable realisation of moral agency, the highest good of a 'moral commonwealth', the world in which all agents act morally.[66]

---

[62] Ibid., 336.
[63] Arthur Ripstein, *Force and Freedom: Kant's Legal and Political Philosophy* (Cambridge, MA, 2009), 228ff; Maliks, *Kant's Politics*, 162–166.
[64] Kant, 'Toward Perpetual Peace', 323.   [65] Ibid., 334–337
[66] For discussion, see Kleingeld, *Kant and Cosmopolitanism*, 47–58; Maliks, *Kant's Politics*, 154–158 and 162–167 and ch. 5 as a whole.

Kant's German followers like Johann Gottlieb Fichte and Friedrich Schlegel developed this argument further, claiming that a voluntary world federation or non-coercive 'republic of republics' was not an unrealistic ideal at all, considering that true morality would be able to develop within republics.[67] Johann Gottlob Heynig, a student and follower of Fichte in Jena, went even further, accusing Kant himself of placing too much confidence in current despotisms, once 'allied with a mighty republic'.[68] The preliminary articles of Kant's *Towards Perpetual Peace*, Heynig argued, would be redundant as soon as republics were created everywhere, while this could by no means be expected from despots, but only from populations themselves, among whom the 'first seed of peace should be sown'.[69] Thus restating what was fundamentally a Jacobin position about the right of resistance, Heynig also envisioned the emergence of a cosmopolitan 'people', among whom all 'national religions' and separate languages would disappear, giving way to a general 'republican civil society'.[70]

Fichte, Schlegel and Heynig followed Kant and explicitly ruled out 'forcing' other states (or nations) to join the federation. Yet Heynig's direct plebiscitary model had a structural affinity with the radical cosmopolitan vision espoused by Anacharsis Cloots in France in 1792. The Kantian vision of constitutionalist republican monarchism espoused by Fichte and Schlegel could also be modified so as to encourage republican imperialism. Thus Joseph Görres, a young journalist from the city of Koblenz in the Rhineland argued in his essay *General Peace, an Ideal* (1798) that perpetual peace would only be realised if all lands became republics, allowing that, if necessary, a cosmopolitan republic of republics (*Völkerrepublik*) could be forcefully imposed by a 'lawfully organised state' on its surrounding barbarian neighbours.[71] Görres even sent his essay directly to the Directory to persuade the French to guarantee the newly acquired liberty of the Rhineland by annexing that territory to the French Republic.[72]

Writing in 1796–1797, Herder could not as yet be aware of Görres's vision. However, he anticipated the possibility that various kinds of philosophical histories of mankind focusing on the progress of political

---

[67] Johann Gottlieb Fichte, 'Grundriß des Völker- und Weltbürgerrechts' and Friedrich Schlegel, 'Versuch über den Begriff des Republikanismus, veranlaßt durch die Kantsche Schrift "Zum ewigen Frieden"', both in *Ewiger Friede?*, 177–192 and 161–177; cf. Nakhimovsky, *The Closed Commercial State*, 59–61; Maliks, *Kant's Politics*, 158–162.

[68] Johann Gottlob Heynig, 'Frieden durch antidespotische Volksaufklärung', in *Ewiger Friede?*, 257–271.

[69] Ibid., 264.   [70] Ibid., 270.

[71] Joseph Görres, 'Der allgemeine Frieden, ein Ideal', in *Ewiger Friede?*, 512–532.

[72] Nakhimovsky, *The Closed Commercial State*, 60; Pizer, 'The German Response', 357.

constitutions could provide inspiration for republican imperialism. In the Tenth Collection, he celebrated the fact that a 'certain recovery from the basest kind of reason of state' could be registered in the public opinion of modern Europe, but he was apprehensive about a new 'dazzling phantom' (*Glanzphantom*) rising in historiography and public opinion, namely, 'the *calculation of undertakings towards a future better republic, towards the best form of the state, indeed of all states*' (734/413. Translation modified.). In Herder's view, this phantom was particularly dangerous since it 'obviously introduces into history a nobler yardstick of merit than the one that those arbitrary reasons of state contained' and as such 'blinds [us] with the names of "freedom", "enlightenment", "highest happiness of the peoples"'. It hence remained only to wish that it 'never deceived'. Clearly, 'the so-called best form of government' [—] cannot 'suit all peoples, at once, in the same way'. For Herder, any attempt to use military force in spreading freedom and republicanism was thus doomed to failure: 'The happiness of one single people cannot be imposed on, talked onto, loaded onto the other and every other. The roses for the wreath of freedom must be picked by a people's own hands and grow up happily out of its own needs, out of its own desire and love' (734/413). Putting too much trust in republican institutions, on the one hand, and encouraging a certain vision of historical progress, on the other, the Kantian view of perpetual peace to Herder sounded like a thinly veiled encouragement towards republican imperialism.

8.2.4   The Native American Arrangement for Peace

Herder also contested Kant's presentation of his idea of perpetual peace as an attempt to end the savagery between European states; in Herder's view, Kant's comparison of Europeans with Native American savages in *Towards Perpetual Peace* was demeaning for the latter. As Kant had ironically argued, 'the difference between the European and the American savages consists mainly in this: that whereas many tribes of the latter have been eaten up by their enemies, the former know how to make better use of those they have defeated than to make a meal of them, and would rather increase the number of their subjects, and so too, the multitude of their instruments for even more extensive wars, by means of them'.[73] Instead of hastening to leave such a condition of lawless freedom, 'each *state* [in Europe] puts its majesty (for the majesty of the people is an absurd expression) just in its not being subject to any external lawful coercion at

---

[73] Kant, 'Towards Perpetual Peace', 326.

all'.[74] Herder responded by arguing that it was precisely the American 'savages' who had in fact been the first to attempt to create a lasting institutional solution to the problem of war. In elaborating this argument, Herder drew on the Jesuit missionary Georg Heinrich Loskiel's account of the Iroquois arrangement for guaranteeing peace among Native American nations.

Herder's version of the story is as follows. Native Americans waged bloody wars with each other until they were brought to the verge of mutual destruction. At this point the Iroquois asked their age-old enemy, the Delawares, to disarm and to become the neutral arbiter of conflicts between different Indian nations. This nation, which according to its own testimony had so far always been the 'victor over the Iroquois', was henceforth called the 'woman', while the Iroquois and other nations amongst whom it was to arbitrate were called 'men'. It was agreed that where aggression occurred towards the 'woman', all men would run to defend her, just like the female nation and arbiter among male nations would try its best to 'preserve the peace' among them. While 'she' would not always succeed, 'she' would at least 'have the power to address [the warring nations] and remind them that 'their wives and children were bound to die unless they stop' (714/401). The arrangement was cemented by means of three wampums, i.e. belts of mussel-shells, which signified the Delawares' new commitments: to disarmament, to a 'purifying oil' and 'medicine' to turn the remaining nations' hearts to good, and to agriculture as their occupation (715/401). They also invented new titles for each other; the Delawares were called *sister-children* by the Iroquois, and the three Delaware tribes called each other *fellow female playmates*. However, Herder pointed out, these 'public titles' were 'only used in their councils' and when they had 'something important to say to each other' (715/402). The professed principles and ideals thus never became truly internalised among the peoples. The collapse of this friendly arrangement was inevitable as 'the Europeans pressed closer'. Soon *men* began to demand that the woman-nation, too, participated in defence. 'It was their [*men's*] intention', Herder wrote, 'first of all to shorten her skirt, then to take it away entirely and put the war ax in her hand' (716/403). Herder concluded: 'A foreign, unforeseen dominant force disturbed the savages' beautiful peace project among each other; and this will always be the case as long as the tree of peace does not bloom for the nations with firm, inextirpable roots *from within to outside.*' (716/403)

[74] Ibid., 326.

As Claudia Taszus has observed, Herder's account diverges considerably from that of Loskiel's original. In Loskiel's account different savage nations assume varying hierarchical positions in the system, but Herder depicts them as equals.[75] Clearly, this suggests that Herder intended his story to serve as a parable for a broader message rather than merely a piece of accurate information on Native Americans. It has therefore been argued that Herder wished to set up the Native American system as an 'ideal vision' for mankind.[76] However, there is little supporting evidence for this interpretation; instead, it is more plausible that Herder viewed it as a relatively successful model, which nevertheless failed in the end because of the persistent gap between declared principles and actual sentiments, on the one hand, and the precarious international situation, on the other.

Herder briefly also discussed two European parallels to this arrangement, showing how they, too, failed due to the same reasons. Firstly, the pope in Rome had once been supposed to play the role of the *woman* in Europe, yet instead had turned out to be one of the major initiators of conflict. Second, no *real* nation in Europe could fulfil the role of a 'woman' either, particularly as long as 'dark cabinets initiate and continue wars' in Europe (716/402). As this remark shows, the whole parable may have been a veiled reference to the initial anti-militarism of the French Republic. It was quite clear that external pressures had forced the French to militarily resist illegitimate interference by foreign powers. Yet this military self-defence had all too soon given way to a remilitarisation of society and foreign conquests motivated by republican enthusiasm. France's revolutionary wars for Herder served as a straightforward counter-example to Kant's empirical argument that the people's reluctance 'to call down on themselves the miseries of war' in a republic would be sufficient to guarantee its peacefulness, or indeed, inspire the creation of a gradually (peacefully) expanding federal association.[77]

---

[75] Claudia Taszus, 'Die Sieben Friedensgesinnungen Johann Gottfried Herders und ihre Stellung innerhalb der 'Briefe zu Beförderung der Humanität'' (unpublished diploma dissertation (Diplomarbeit), Friedrich-Schiller-Universität Jena, 1991). I am very grateful to Claudia Taszus for sending me a copy of the manuscript.

[76] See e.g., J. M. van den Laan, 'Johann Gottfried Herder on War and Peace', *Monatshefte* 101 (Madison, 2009), 335–346 (341).

[77] Empirical argument, however, was just one aspect of Kant's theory of republican peace; the more important constitutionalist arguments Herder did not tackle.

8.2.5   The Spirit of History

In various places in the published collections of *Letters*, Herder also tackled the topic of history-writing, turning his polemic directly against the kind of history Kant had recommended. As seen above, Kant, in *Towards Perpetual Peace*, had refined his argument of the natural mechanism of unsocial sociability that fostered peace contrary to the actual propensities of human beings. At the same time, he highlighted the development of human reason in this process and the growing understanding of the true principles of political right. From Herder's perspective, Kant was setting up an implausible opposition between irrational and selfish beings in the past, on the one hand, and rational moral beings who would emerge in the future, on the other. In what is quite evidently a direct rejoinder to Kant's moral philosophy, Herder contrasted his preferred 'spirit of history' with all kinds of attempts to reduce humanity to one single principle:

> [The spirit of history] knows that in human nature the principles of *sensuality*, of *imagination*, of *selfishness*, of *honor*, of *sympathy with others*, of *godliness*, of the *moral sense*, of *faith*, etc. do not dwell in separated compartments, but that in a living organization that gets stimulated from several sides, many of them, often all, cooperate in a living manner. [—] Let each human being chew as he can, history treats human beings not as word-mongers or critics, but as agents of a moral law of nature which speaks in all of them, which initially warns gently, then punishes harder, and richly rewards every good disposition through itself and its consequences. Does this *spirit of human history* not appeal to you? (736–737/415; cf. 750/423)

Herder elsewhere characterised his own preferred 'spirit of history' as based on a '*sensus humanitatis, sense [Sinn] and sympathy [Mitgefühl] for the whole of humanity*' (742/420). This kind of spirit, he argued, rested on two different kinds of psychological capacities: first, a certain 'flexibility of spirit, in order to place oneself in bygone ages (*Biegsamkeit des Geistes, sich in vergangene Zeiten zu setzen*), that is, an ability to leave aside one's own prejudices and develop an understanding of a foreign cultural context,[78] and second, a 'scale of judgement' (*Waage des Urteils*) and 'moral sense' (*moralischer Sinn*) (339). By using the term 'sense' Herder did not wish to characterise this 'spirit' as merely intuitive or unmediated. In fact, what was needed was a kind of cognitive empathy combined with historical judgement and moral reflection. In order to understand 'events, actions or

---

[78] On Herder's ideas about historical understanding, see Wildschut, 'Analogy, Empathy' and Proß, '"Diversus cum diversis"'.

institutions,' Herder explained, the historian would need to reconstruct the 'opinions and principles of peoples' as well as 'trace their origin and legacy genealogically [*genealogisch*]' (339). However, as a next step, he also needed to apply his moral judgement and thereby cultivate his *human feeling* (*Menschengefühl*), since 'history's highest *interest*, its *value* rests on this human sensibility [*Menschenempfindung*], the *rule of right and wrong*' (733/411–412).[79]

Herder sought to exemplify this approach by discussing the ways in which Machiavelli's *Prince* should be interpreted. He pointed out the existing amount of confusion about this work, regarded by some as a satire, by others as a corrupting textbook, and by yet others as 'a wavering, softheaded mixture of the two'. In fact, Herder continues, 'Machiavelli knew history and the world well, he was an honest man and fine observer, and a warm friend of his fatherland'. He also knew 'the value and form(s) of different states', as his *Discourses on Titus Livy* reveal (340). Misguided interpretations of Machiavelli resulted from the fact that contemporary authors did not properly register the opposition between politics and morality that was prevalent in Europe in Machiavelli's time. Religion itself was separated from morality, whilst the idea of the 'reason of state' had first developed in the politics of the Catholic Church (the Pope). Yet these principles were also brought to France, Spain and Germany, and came to be widely accepted in Italian city-states (341). Machiavelli thus described the prince as an 'individual creature of a [distinct] species'. For him, the task of history was to narrate the 'natural data of humanity (*Naturbegebenheiten der Menschheit*)' without evaluating these data in any way. According to Herder, thus, while Machiavelli did not invent the maxims of reason of state (*Staatsräson, la ragione del stato*), his *Prince* was undeniably a 'purely political masterpiece for his contemporary Italian princes, according to their principles,' written in order to serve a higher political purpose of 'driving the barbarians out of Italy' (342).

This was Herder's attempt to show 'flexibility of spirit' in placing himself in Machiavelli's shoes. For Herder, this kind of historical understanding of Machiavelli as a child of his time, did not prevent a historian from assessing the moral value of his teaching. In the Tenth Collection of *Letters*, Herder returned to this topic and revealed his opinion of Machiavelli: 'Who can read Machiavelli's *Prince* without horror? Even if he had been successful in everything, would he be a worthy prince?'

---

[79] Cf. Johann Gottfried Herder, 'Adrastea', in *FHA*, X, 41–42. On Herder's understanding of historical empathy in *Adrastea*, see also Schmidt, 'The Organic Development', 232–233.

(733/411). Machiavelli's history represented a form of 'cold calculating reason', yet it had also come to be 'warmed up' when applied in practice. Essentially, Machiavelli managed to combine the Popish 'reason of state' with a warm idea of the fatherland: 'The Athenians, the Romans – what did they not include in the *good of their fatherland*, in their *glory*, and hence in their *right*? What did the pope, the clergy, the Christian kings not permit themselves in the interest of the alleged goods of their realms? [—] Forgotten in this spirit is humanity, which, according to it, lives merely *for the state*, that is, for kings and ministers.' (734/412)

Such a reading of Machiavelli enabled Herder to buttress his point that Kantian history of humanity, while seemingly noble and warm, did not fundamentally differ from Machiavelli's: 'a history that calculates everything as applicable to each country with a view to this utopian plan [of achieving republican freedom] in accordance with unproven first principles is the most dazzling deceptive history' (734/413. Translation modified.). We saw above how this critique warned against the possible abuse of Kant's 'history of constitutions' as inspiration for republican imperialism. In the context of discussions about historiography, Herder thus showcased the actual complexity of human history as a bulwark against such misapplications. The dazzling history of constitutions, Herder warned, would be nothing but a 'foreign varnish that robs the forms [*Gestalten*] of our world and the preceding world of their true stances, even of their outlines. Many works from our time will, in twenty years, come to be read as either well- or poorly-intentioned feverish fantasies; more mature minds already now read them this way' (735/413. Translation modified.). Instead, history should remain faithful to the original spirit of Herodotus and his distinctive 'sense of humanity', which 'regards all peoples [without bias] and sketches each one in its place, in accordance with its ethics and customs' as well as 'observes how everywhere only *moderation* has made peoples happy' (735/413).

8.2.6   Dispositions of Peace

Herder's conclusion in *Letters* was unequivocal: if a true *Anti-Machiavelli* was to be set up and worshipped, it had to be an author who could transcend his own times by synthesising existing moral knowledge (343). This author, Herder suggested in the Tenth Collection, was the natural lawyer Hugo Grotius. Grotius had indeed declared that he used 'the testimony of philosophers, historians, poets, finally also of orators' to prove the existence of the law of nature he described (§40). In contrast with

Rousseau's remark, in *Emile*, that Grotius had 'just embellished and covered' his (Grotius's) fundamentally Hobbesian principles 'with the help of poets',[80] Herder rallied to defend and praise Grotius on exactly this point: 'Indeed, you [Grotius] only collected materials for it [his treatise on the law of nations], and not only from Italy and your own times, but first of all from the good ancients, from the laws of reason and equity, from religion itself; from all this a law of nations [*Recht der Völker*] gradually emerged that could not have been known in barbarous times.' (345).[81]

Herder's praise of Grotius also sharply contrasts with Kant's dismissive remark in *Perpetual Peace* (1795) about Grotius, Pufendorf and Vattel as 'sorry comforters' whose philosophical and legal codes have served to legitimate, rather than restrain military aggression.[82] Herder thus celebrated Grotius as the first author to embrace an open and eclectic spirit conducive to mutual understanding among human beings from different periods and cultures about international relations. Even though Grotius was unable to 'unite religions,' he 'united human principles', so that 'what has been written ever since about the right of peoples (*Recht der Völker*), about natural and rational right (*Natur- und Vernunftrecht*) follows in his footsteps' (342–343). According to Herder, Grotius's *De jure belli ac pacis* lay open on the table in the Swedish king Gustavus Adolphus's tent in camp, at the very moment the king himself was killed on the field of battle. Indeed, Herder continued, the fact that 'a number of the noblest men in Sweden, France, Holland and Germany had also loved and honoured him [Grotius]' gave hope that one day all future European generations would prove themselves his ally and confederate (*Verbündete und Verbundene*)' (344). The gradual recognition of these principles and an ability to properly apply them could only be achieved through humanity's learning process.

Herder's 'spirit of history' was fundamentally a form of moral education to enlighten humans about their moral potential and the principles of *Nemesis*. It also entailed acknowledging human fallibility and most importantly, partiality

---

[80] 'The science of political right [*le droit politique*] is yet to be born, and it is to be presumed that it never will be born. Grotius, the master of all our learned men in this matter, is only a child; and, what is worse, a child of bad faith [*enfant de mauvaise foi*]. When I hear Grotius praised to the skies and Hobbes covered with execration, I see how few sensible men read or understand these two authors. The truth is that their principles are exactly alike. They differ only in their manner of expression. They also differ in method. Hobbes bases himself on sophisms, and Grotius on poets. They have everything else in common', Rousseau, *Emile*, 458.

[81] For the central importance of Grotius to Herder's account of equity, see Chapter 6 and Wolfgang Proß, 'Anmerkungen [*Ideen*], III/2, 301–304. See also idem, 'Kolonialismuskritik', 17–73 and idem, '*Ideen zur Philosophie der Geschichte der Menschheit*', 210.

[82] Kant, 'Toward Perpetual Peace', 326.

(244). Humans were necessarily prone to delusion [*Wahn*] and prejudices grounded in self-love and self-interest, while their sympathy with distant others was rather weak and motivationally unreliable (686/384; cf. *Outlines*, 159. Translation modified.). In a fictitious continuation of the dialogue between Ernst and Falk originally written by Gotthold Ephraim Lessing, Herder called for the combined efforts of poetry, philosophy and history to enlighten humans about such dispositions, whilst also providing inspiration as to how to cultivate countervailing sentiments. Poetry was to incite human imagination, philosophy to teach humans firm principles and history to provide them maxims as to how to apply them. Yet all these branches of human activity were to be moved by one and the same drive (*Antrieb*) of humanity (140).

Herder listed '*Las Casas, Fénelon,* [. . .] two good St. *Pierres* [the Abbé de Saint-Pierre and Bernardin de Saint-Pierre], many an honest *Quaker, Montesquieu, Filangieri*' (689/386) as example authors of this kind of *humane* history guided by human feeling (*Menschengefühl*) and the rule of right and wrong (*die Regel des Rechts und Unrechts*) (733/411; cf. 688/386). Each one had characteristically focused on particular cases of injustice in human history. By applying their moral judgement to these cases, their readers could cultivate better dispositions. Seeking to take into account the joy and sorrow of all parties involved in an action, humans cannot but help noticing: 'No human being can live *for himself alone*, much as he might wish to do so. The capacities that he attains, the virtues or vices which he performs, to a lesser or greater degree will bring pain or joy to others' (124; cf. ibid., 750/423). At the same time, sustained engagement with history would also convince humans that there is a measure of 'justice' in it, one that corresponds to an understanding of 'just deserts' as expressed in the indeterminate 'rule of justice' in our breast. Herder yet again invoked the name of a Greek goddess *Nemesis* as a shorthand for this kind of growing moral and historical understanding. Nemesis, Herder explained, is the principle that demonstrates that no single act of cruelty remains unpunished, just like every act of human goodness is amply paid back (735/413; 747/421–422).

This kind of moral training via history, according to Herder, would contribute to the rise of what he called 'dispositions of peace' (*Friedensgesinnungen*) (720/404). These dispositions would reflect as well as sustain something like an overlapping consensus between different nations regarding the ways in which 'nations should take effect on each other' (114/380). Herder listed 'horror of war', 'reduced respect for heroic glory' and the rejection of 'false statecraft that places a regent's glory and his government's fortune in expansion of borders, in capturing or seizing foreign provinces, in increased income, sly negotiations, in arbitrary power, cunning, and deception' as examples of such dispositions. On a constructive side, these dispositions would also include attitudes such as 'purified patriotism' (*geläuterte Patriotismus*), a '*common feeling* so that every nation empathise with the position of every other one', and finally, 'love of useful activity' in promoting human well-being (720–726/404–409. Translation modified.). Emphasising that these dispositions could only emerge gradually, Herder warned that people should not lose hope when not witnessing any real progress towards the realisation of their goals. Changes in dispositions were slow and the precise ways and forms in which they would take effect could not be predicted (725–727/408–410).

8.3 Purified Patriotism

As seen above, Herder also mentioned 'purified patriotism' among the emerging dispositions of peace in Europe. What did he mean by this term? How did he construe patriotism in these turbulent years? Herder's final comprehensive discussion of this issue is an essay entitled *Have We Still Got the Public and the Fatherland of the Ancients?*, published in the Fifth Collection of *Letters* in 1795, the year of the Basel peace treaty (and of the publication of Kant's *Perpetual Peace*). As in his earlier essay on the same topic, Herder approached this problem from a broader historical perspective. However, instead of juxtaposing 'ancient' republican and 'modern' monarchical peoples, he now offered a much more complex argument about the formation of various kinds of national, transnational and international 'publics' and the ideal of a 'moral fatherland'. As I hope to show below, he thereby sought to carve out a sophisticated alternative to Kant's ideas on enlightenment, perpetual peace and constitutional republicanism. His broader goal was to provide guidance to the German people as to how to pursue national self-determination in a self-reflective and historically informed manner.

8.3.1 Ideal and Real Publics

Herder began by making the distinction between 'real' and 'ideal' forms of public. The former, he explained, was a public that was physically present, whereas an 'ideal public' was an imagined community. In both cases, however, one assumed the existence of a 'reasoning moral being that sympathetically observes our thoughts, our behaviour, our actions – one that is able to judge their merit or demerit, that approves or disapproves, and one whose taste we are also allowed to strive to instruct, teach, form and further develop'. (302) In making this argument, Herder sought to highlight the historicity of human existence as well as critically reflect on the very possibility of his own historical enquiry and practical goals. He argued that one could also distinguish between different kinds of 'ideal publics'. On the one hand, each nation could be seen to exist as an 'ideal public' lasting from generation to generation, united through the use of common language. On the other hand, each nation had developed very different cultural and aesthetic traditions that also presupposed or facilitated the rise of very different 'real' and 'ideal' publics. A historical enquiry into these different traditions was possible and pertinent precisely because modern individuals and peoples could also be seen as an 'ideal public' for some historical peoples (Herder specifically discussed the ancient Hebrews, Greeks, Romans and the 'so-called barbars of the Middle Ages' as 'part of us' and as 'our ancients'), which in turn invited comparisons between their distinctive forms of public and those of the moderns. This was exactly what Herder also set out to do in the first section of this essay: comparing the publics of the modern 'us' – that is, modern Germans – with those of the different significant ancient 'them'. However, he also showed that there were distinctive kinds of transnational 'ideal publics' that had emerged in European history and that had gained strength in recent times, giving rise to something like a current 'European' public. Awareness of the existence of these kinds of public, in turn, was essential for Germans' contemporary forms of self-purification, self-constitution and regeneration.

As we can see, Herder's starting point in describing the process of enlightenment was very different from that of Kant. For Kant, political concepts such as rights based on equal external freedom were universal by nature, even though humans only gradually became fully aware of, and capable of applying, these concepts. As Kant argued in his essay on the enlightenment, the process of enlightenment was greatly enhanced in modern monarchies in which there were no 'insurmountable barriers' to people's freedom of *spirit*, as opposed to smaller republics in which there was a greater degree of civic freedom (*bürgerliche Freiheit*) but also always the danger that the different ideas expressed in the public would destabilise society and politics. An enlightened sovereign ruler, by contrast, would not fear criticism or public debate, since obedience to laws would be guaranteed in any case. Distinguishing between their own responsibilities as holders of distinctive offices and as citizens of a state, individual members of the public would learn to assess public matters from a general point of view, critically examining all kinds of established traditions and institutions.[83] Enlightened rulers would derive guidance from the results of this critical enquiry, 'finding it profitable to treat the human being – now seen as more than a machine – in accordance with his dignity'.[84]

Herder's view of the process of enlightenment as well as of moral and political reforms highlighted the broader psychological (sentimental) aspects of this process. We have seen above how he criticised Kant's quasi-Hobbesian account of 'patriotic government' and exclusive emphasis on rational enlightenment and constitutionalist republicanism sustained by a 'spirit of commerce'. However, Herder's concerns ran even deeper. He believed that Kant overlooked the ethical nature and continuing political relevance of already existing sentimental solidarities and communal identities – whether at the national or international level. The people were not just individual 'critics' but living human beings who spoke distinct languages, expressed themselves in different art forms and pursued various kinds of individual and communal goals. At the same time, different forms of transnational public had already emerged, which further influenced their self-understanding.

8.3.2 Language, Politics and Philosophy

As already indicated, an important theme that Herder powerfully took up in this essay was the role of language in creating a sense of unity among its speakers. This theme had been missing in the 1765 essay on patriotism. Nevertheless, as we saw in Chapter 2, even in his earliest essays Herder had already analysed the formative power of language and poetry. This topic is one of the most consistent themes in his thinking. The 1795 essay tackles it on the example of the ancient Hebrews, thus linking up with Herder's discussions of the earliest Hebrew culture in his *Impact of Poetry* and *On the Spirit of Hebrew Poetry* that we discussed in Chapter 6. Here, Herder's argument is that the Hebrews emerged as 'one people', a 'genetic individual' at the earliest stage of their historical existence. This was possible because their legislators spoke in the name of God to the Hebrews as to 'one person', 'one moral essence' whose existence extended over generations (303). The prophets regarded the people as a whole as 'servants' and 'lost children of God'. Nevertheless, Herder suggested that this kind of public should not be regarded as peculiar only to the Hebrews – each people could actually cultivate such a public through its language:

---

[83] Kant, 'Answer to the Question: What Is Enlightenment', 18–19.
[84] Ibid., 22 (translation modified).

> Language is a divine organ of instruction, punishment and guidance for
> everyone who has the sense and ear for it. The bond between the tongue
> and the ear builds an audience, in this way we hear thoughts and advice, we
> make resolutions, and share instruction, suffering and joy with one another,
> anyone who has been brought up in the same language, anyone who has
> poured his heart into it, learns to express his soul in it and belongs to the
> people of this language (304).

The Hebrew case was nevertheless paradigmatic for Herder because it
enabled him to show how language and poetry functioned as a reservoir
of moral instruction and training. Herder thereby wished to make clear
that language and poetry itself could also be regarded as a 'voice of God'
(306). He yet again emphasised the human capacity for language as the
most fundamental human trait, whilst also presenting loyalty to one's
language and linguistic community as a moral, divinely ordained duty.
In a similar vein, he also insisted on the inevitably 'poetic' nature of
language and thinking and the value of all kinds of creative and aesthetic
self-expression, whilst also presenting it as an educated professions' moral
duty to seek to creatively develop the existing forms of fine arts, including,
most prominently, poetry.

Juxtaposing contemporary Germans with the ancient Hebrews, Herder
accepted that they had nothing comparable in terms of a linguistic public.
Germans were separated from each other geographically and politically,
spoke different dialects, and often did not 'understand each other even in
written texts'. Furthermore, as the upper ranks of society in Germany had
adopted a foreign language (the French language) for education (306), the
Germans were 'alienated from their own souls' (328). There was thus no
'common patriotic training, no inner co- and together-feeling, no father-
land-public' in Germany (306). However, Herder did not view this
situation as unreformable. As we have seen in previous chapters, throughout his entire life, he insisted on the need for and possibility of a revival of
the German language and literature. Yet again, he urged Germans to find
their way back to their common language, to cherish as well as cultivate it
as other important nations had done with their languages. A 'national
language, one *developed* in the highest sense of the word' was what was
needed in Germany. Only by purging the language of the 'oppressive
adornment' of the 'imperial and courtly style' (*Reichs- und Hofstil*),
Herder argued, could the German language yet again become a 'language
of reason, vigour and truth' (337/116). It was now time for the wider
German public, this 'sleeping God' to 'wake up from its slumber' and
demonstrate that it was 'no barbar so that it would also not be treated as a

barbar'. The Germans were to show that their language was nothing less than 'the sister of Greek, the queen and mother of many nations' (328).

Herder's overall comparison between the Greek and German publics strikes a very different chord, however. Herder maintained that the Greeks developed a distinctive kind of public culture and politics that could not be recreated in a modern setting. In Herder's view, this fact was not to be regretted. Expanding on his critique of ancient liberty in his 1765 essay on love of the fatherland, Herder maintained that this liberty was problematic even in ancient times, insofar as it made 'proclamations of war and peace, verdicts upon life and death, merit and rewards' to depend on the 'judgement of the ear' of an 'uneducated (*unerzogene*) people' (308). The ancient Greek republics, particularly Athens, provided an array of 'frightening-beautiful' examples in this respect. Herder did not mention Socrates here, but we may presume that Socrates' death was never too far from his mind when discussing the shortcomings of Athenian democracy. So were, presumably, the shortcomings of the French experiment with direct democracy. Herder here went as far as to argue that even 'the public festivities related to religious and state-matters, public games, dances, contests and competitions, perhaps even the entire Athenian theatre', would perhaps not be missed too much by moderns (308), yet again indicating his suspicion of external ceremonies as vehicles for achieving deep-grained humanitarian dispositions.

For Herder, there was nevertheless at least one important parallel between Greeks and Germans with regard to philosophy. Whilst the earliest legislators in Greece were also wise men, Socratic philosophy was not designed for use with the broader public, but for private societies or individuals. This, Herder maintained, was also the true purpose of philosophy – 'self-formation' (*Selbstbildung*). As we saw in Chapter 1, Herder, in his early essays of 1765, had emphatically defended the possibility of a sociable kind of philosophy – one that would serve the people, speak to their heart and thereby initiate reforms from below. In 1795 Herder still wholeheartedly embraced and sought to promote this ideal of practical philosophy but introduced an important qualification, highlighting the tension between philosophy and the opinion of the wider public (313). According to the original Socratic understanding, Herder argued, the teacher of philosophy was only to serve as a 'midwife of our ideas, a co-helper of our own active forces' (*eine Hebamme unsrer Gedanken, ein Mithelfer unsrer eigenen, arbeitenden Kräften*), so as to foster our 'self-directed processing of the human spirit and will' (*eigne Bearbeitung des menschlichen Geistes und Willens*). This kind of processing could not 'depend on the voice of the public' and indeed, it was rather the latter that directly hindered it (313). Philosophy teachers could not teach their students truth and morality, as wisdom could only be pursued 'autonomously' (*autonomisch*) (314). Nevertheless, they would create philosophical schools. As long as philosophy teachers regarded themselves as merely 'helping hands' (*Handleiter*), they would always have a powerful impact on the souls of their students, in inspiring ideas and ideals in them, which in turn would also slowly spread into the wider world through their schools of philosophy. Thereby, a 'hidden, silent public for philosophy' would be created – one that can 'never be found in a market-place or in one single school in a visible form' (314). Thus insisting on one basic philosophical method, on the one hand, and a plurality of philosophical schools, on the other, Herder sought to stake out his own vision of the role of practical philosophy in general enlightenment. Agreeing with Kant about the importance of independent thinking, he was not proposing it as a general approach for each single individual in every single matter. What Kant was calling for was really an enlightenment of philosophers, rather than that of the wider public. In Herder's view, philosophers could best influence the public in an indirect manner, via their schools. Here Herder also qualified his warnings against philosophical schools as expressed in the draft version of *Letters*. He acknowledged that philosophical schools were potentially of immense practical value in mediating philosophical ideas and ideals to a wider public but that one nevertheless needed to guard against their transformation into dogmatic sects.

8.3.3   Christian and European Publics

Herder maintained that the edifying, unifying and pacifying power of religion was also to be recognised. Again, he was also implicitly opposing Kant's view. Kant's positing the 'kingdom of ends' on the Earth as a morally necessary idea was not really an affirmation of Christian morality as Herder understood it. Herder, by contrast, maintained that the Christian religion had already contributed and still was contributing to the formation of a novel kind of moral public. Whilst earlier religions had focused on 'external ceremonies', Christ sought to promote 'spiritual exercises' and the 'following of the strictest equity and forgiving love among human beings' (317). Each Christian congregation, Herder argued, could thus be seen as part of this intergenerational 'spiritual congregation' (*Geistesversammlung*), a 'moral institute' (*moralisches Institut*) lasting until 'the end of times'. This ideal Christian public was a worthy goal to be pursued and as such was to be kept free from doctrinal conjectures and quarrels (318).

Thanks to Christianity, Herder argued, something like a 'common culture of peoples' (*eine gemeinschaftliche Kultur der Völker*) had already emerged in Europe. Although Christianity had led to an increase in disputes and the need for compromises between nations, at a deeper level it had already served as 'a peacemaking bond' (319). Mutual rights and duties had become recognised in principle and practice, even though they were not yet being 'applied in a sustained manner' (*bleibendes Gebrauch*) (319). European peoples had also been drawn together ever more closely through mutual needs, inventions, modern science and academic learning. A 'larger and finer public sharing in quarrels and peace, love and suffering' was thus developing in Europe 'in the midst of all the rubbing between peoples, societies, guilds and members'. Furthermore, this 'raw art, the industry emerging from need' had begun to spread to other parts of the world, for better or worse (320). All these transnational kinds of modern publics already existed alongside national publics.

Celebrating the invention of the printing press, Herder also wholeheartedly defended freedom of speech as a central value, provided 'one in doubtful issues writes under one's own name and offends no one personally' (324). However, like in *Ideas*, Herder also sought to show that this form of liberty was in fact grounded in self-governing institutions that had emerged in an earlier period. This was yet another corrective to Kant's vision of enlightenment. Herder here reiterated his view that the modern public sphere was not a new development emerging thanks to rulers' and citizens' enlightened self-interest, but rather had roots in medieval associations. As such, it in all likelihood also continued to presuppose the existence of independent associations in order to flourish. In a rather cursory manner, Herder pointed out that the most remarkable original institution in this respect were 'guilds' (*Zünfte*) and various kinds of semi-independent corporations that in difficult times had managed to establish 'safe havens' for human 'industry, activity, inventions and the spirit of humans'. 'Schools and universities,' Herder maintained, functioned in much the same way as guilds. Offering safe space for the pursuit of learning behind their walls, even against the arbitrary will of rulers, they also served as the most powerful vehicles for spreading ideas (320–321). This impact was only increasing in recent years. It was not just the likes of religious reformers, such as Wiclef, Hus and Luther, who spread their teaching through universities, but a general academic rivalry had also arisen among lecturers, faculties and universities. Much was thus to be expected from these 'watchtowers and lighthouses of learning' (*Wacht- und Leuchttürme der Wissenschaft*); they were also to serve as the 'last free spaces, and a protective force of the sciences' (*Freistätten, und eine Schutzwehr der Wissenschaften*) during tumultuous times (322). German universities, too, had already made impressive progress and were perhaps the only German institutes honoured abroad (322). Clearly, Herder regarded this as an important development to build on when fashioning a new form of German national public.

8.3.4 Modern 'Moral Fatherland'

According to Herder, Germany had undergone two parallel processes. On the one hand, Germans had lost touch with their national language and literature. On the other hand, a multilayered and complex transnational public had gradually emerged in Europe, despite its continuing bloody wars. Germans formed an element of this public. Yet, they were also to reconstitute themselves as a nation in modern times. Creating a vibrant national public was an important part of Herder's vision, whilst he also demanded practical efficacy, action, social and political change. This required rethinking the essence of the modern 'fatherland'. In the second part of *Do We Still Have the Public*, Herder yet again undertook a thorough examination of the psychological nature of ancient and modern love of country, including the domestic and international implications of these aspects.

In conformity with his theory of the importance of understanding the true meaning of concepts through rediscovering their sensuous origins, Herder began by laying out the original meaning of the idea of fatherland in ancient societies. He pointed out that it had never designated just physical belonging or rootedness, vehemently disputing the idea that humans were somehow wedded to the soil on which they were born. Although 'there have been and still are enough harsh laws about such servitude and serfdom', Herder wrote, the 'whole course of reason, of culture, even of industry and of utilitarian calculation leads towards the gradual unshackling of these slaves' (330/110). In contrast to plants or animals, humans were free to choose the place where they lived. The term 'the land of the fathers' was invented by early nomadic societies in order to designate the land where they buried their fathers. What was important was the social bond, which only came to include a particularly close relationship to land within agricultural societies. As Herder explained: our affection for the fatherland was grounded in our first experiences in the small society around us, *the father's house, the father's field, family* (330–331/110).

According to Herder, Greek patriotism, too, was based on this kind of natural family spirit. Greek states – or rather, cities (*Städte*) – originated in such small communities, and their legislators knew how to preserve a certain closeness to this original way of life. At the same time, they reinterpreted the idea of the 'fatherland' in moral and political terms. Invoking the idea of civic enlightenment, Herder pointed out that Greeks had coined the idea of a *moral fatherland* (*moralisches Vaterland*) as a special kind of community of fate established through *laws* and *civil institutions* (*bürgerliche Einrichtung*). They 'esteemed nothing higher than the achievement of these civil institutions that had made them into Greeks', believing that they were protected by Gods. For Greeks, their institutions, language and culture were immortal, they regarded them as the crown of the universe. In the same spirit, they also glorified their victories over other nations. Similarly, the Romans saw themselves as destined to be the rulers of the world, as entitled to all the victories and glory of the world (331/111).

In modern times, Herder argued, people no longer believed in the divine origins of states: 'Numa's dreams no longer accord with our times'. Hence it was also possible to reject 'glory idly possessed and lazily inherited from our ancestors', as such an understanding of glory would be likely to make people 'vain and unworthy of it' (332/112). Yet the idea of a *moral fatherland* was all the more relevant in modern times. What could and had to be borrowed from the Greeks and Romans was exactly the 'moral tendency of the name of the fatherland', i.e. the idea of the 'fatherland' as a moral and political project to be pursued by various generations through collaborative efforts. It was thus essential that a people would 'seek out what *we* ought to respect and love about the fatherland, that we may love it worthily and purely' (332/112). This ideal, Herder insisted, could in modern times only be 'the institutions or good constitution [*Einrichtung, die gute Verfassung*] under which we would most like to live with what is dearest to us' (333/113):

> Morally we consider ourselves happy in a state [*Staat*] where under a lawful freedom and security [*bei einer Gesetzmäßigen Freiheit und Sicherheit*] we do not make ourselves blush, where we do not waste our efforts, where we and those dear to us are not abandoned but are free to do all our duties as worthy, active sons of fatherland who are recognised and rewarded in the eyes of the mother. The Greeks and Romans were right to [think] that no other human achievement exceeds that of establishing such a union, or strengthening, renewing, purifying, and preserving it. To think, to work, to

accomplish something not only for the common cause of those dearest to us but for all those who descend from us and for the entire, eternal fatherland of mankind – what, compared to this, is a single life but a day's work of a few minutes and hours?' (333/113)

This paragraph is a thinly veiled reference to the legitimacy of the efforts of the French nation to give itself a 'living' constitution based on natural order. Indeed, it seems that by 1795 Herder had regained at least some of his original optimism regarding the French Revolution. The concept of 'moral fatherland' for him encompassed the legal freedom and security of citizens but also their active participation in the community's political life. In making this argument, he acknowledged the interdependence between civil and political liberty (broadly understood), whilst also pondering the form political liberty could take in modern times. For example, Herder underlined the idea that voicing one's critical opinion in the public press was one important way of participation, arguing that silencing such voices would prove lethal to true patriotism (333–334/114). Using the metaphors of 'mother' and 'children' and associating self-respect with the requirement of the state 'not to abandon us', Herder also voiced the idea that in a 'fatherland' everyone should benefit from not just the formal opportunity but also the means for action, as essential for self-respect (333/114) and empowerment of citizens:

> If the state is as it should be it embodies the eye of general reason, the ear and heart of universal equity and goodness, it will hear all of these voices [of different individuals], and awaken and encourage the activity of human beings according to their various kinds of inclinations, sentiments, weaknesses and needs. (131)

Herder was adamant that this kind of 'humanising' of the state machine should not be expected from rulers alone; on the contrary, his point is that it can also start from below. Precisely by cultivating a form of national public and committing themselves to the pursuit of the ideal of moral fatherland, modern citizens could begin to 'humanise' their states. As Herder put it in the first Collection of *Letters*, the ideal of *Humanität* was already being implemented in most different areas of life: in how wars were waged, prisons and hospitals were run, the police was organised and judicial processes were conducted (103). These new principles were not rooted in calculations of enlightened utility (only) but in human moral dispositions. However, Herder granted that they had a particularly close relationship to what he regarded as civic virtues (*Bürgertugenden*) necessary for responsible burghers and officials in commercial cities.

In the Sixth Collection of *Letters*, Herder reprinted large segments of his friend Johann Christoph Berens's book *Bonhommien* (1792).[85] The excerpts that Herder picked from Berens's work extol precisely such virtues. Citing the opinion of his and Berens's friend Johann Christoph Schwarz, the mayor of Riga, Herder claimed that Berens's whole life and thought was best captured through the concept of patriotism (*Patriotismus*) (432). Patriotism, according to Berens, consisted in diligent and honourable public service, on the one hand, and the enjoyment of rightfully acquired prosperity (*Wohlstand, Wohlerworben zu haben*), on the other. It also involved the spreading of practical enlightenment and religion (412). Young burghers would learn an ethic of 'work and patience' as well as cultivate 'precision and trustworthiness', whilst they also needed to understand that they did not live in isolation from the rest of the society. (418). English 'public spirit', according to Berens, had long been known among German burghers under the name of 'the good of the city' (*der Stadt Bestes*). Herder approved of this idea, suggesting that this kind of spirit could also be extended to all of society, if 'theologians, officials and philosophers' would only understand it this way (419–420). Herder here also referred to Berens's own initiatives: in demanding 'freedom and property' for the lowest ranks in his society – the Livonian serfs – Berens had encouraged much broader education (*Bildung*) and transformations in his society (413–415). In some ways, Berens can be seen as a German equivalent of Benjamin Franklin in Herder's thinking – Berens's ideas resonate well with Franklin's socially responsible commercial ethic as discussed in Herder's first Collection of *Letters*.

Perhaps surprisingly, Herder here concluded this presentation of Berens's ideas by pointing to none other than the philosopher Immanuel Kant as an inspiring example in this respect. According to Herder, Kant had powerfully reminded us that we can only pursue 'our freedom' by 'acting according to the demand: do the right thing (*recht zu tun*)' and that we need to *earn* happiness (423). Here Herder also inserted his description of Kant's personality that he had first drafted in the unpublished 1792 version in yet another attempt to rescue the true Kant from the shadow of the old one. Herder sought to clarify that the morality that Kant had once taught him was one of practical efficacy and commitment to improving one's society, rather than a suppression of one's nature. In order to buttress his point, Herder further praised the young Kant's cheerful disposition and ethic of responsibility. The Kant he once knew, Herder wrote, had

[85] On Johann Christoph Berens, see also Chapters 1 and 3.

encouraged 'independent thought (*Selbstdenken*)' and self-reliance, all kinds of 'despotism being fully alien to his mind' (424).

8.3.5   Self-Reflective and Self-Contained National Pride

In thus outlining a humanitarian and sociable vision of modern patriotism as a form of self-determination, Herder did not neglect the question of 'when patriotism stopped being a virtue' (131). As we've seen above, he believed that humans were necessarily prone to developing delusions and prejudices. These prejudices, Herder accepted in one of the earlier letters, were characteristically strong when it came to matters relating to our-selves – our person, rank, nation (46).[86] Herder revisited this theme in *Do We Still Have the Public*. Nearly every ancient nation, he argued, had succumbed to a 'mania of pride in the fatherland, religion, lineage and ancestors' (*Wahn von Vaterlands-Religions-Geschlechts-Ahnenstolze*). As the cases of Greek and Roman patriotism revealed, this mania was prone to develop in a particularly strong manner in those communities that aspired to higher moral standards and regarded themselves as chosen by Gods (332/112). Like in *Ideas,* Herder thus reminded his readers that although the Greeks often used the name of the fatherland in a noble manner, they also often abused it. Sparta's zeal for the fatherland oppressed not only the Helots but also its citizens as well as sometimes other Greeks. Athens, too, 'was often hard on its citizens and colonies', which needed to be 'concealed with sweet phantoms', while the Romans' love of their fatherland 'proved pernicious not only for Italy but for Rome itself and the entire Roman world' (332/112).

Herder observed that the tendency towards aggressive patriotism was also vicious in modern times. 'The good of the fatherland' or 'the glory of the nation' had all too often been turned into a cloak for the 'most tangled, most loathsome state interests, of personal presumptions and of state trickeries' (733/412). Explicitly referring to recent developments in France, Herder also pointed out that abstract words, such as '*rights, humanity, freedom, equality*' could also be used as banners and slogans of quarrelling parties, arousing passions and destroying friendships and families (248–249). Reason of state and patriotism could also be used to justify struggles for

---

[86] Herder's discussion of these ideas was inspired by Johann Jacob Wegelin's essay on the delusions of the people, which he had discussed with a group of friends in Goethe's *Freitagsgesellschaft*, Bermhard Suphan, 'Schlußbericht', in *SWS*, XVIII, 541. See also Johann Jacob Wegelin, 'Von dem Wahnsinn des Volks', in Wegelin, *Briefe über den Werth der Geschichte* (Berlin, 1783), 151–157.

commercial supremacy. No wonder, thus, that the nations suffering under colonial exploitation had been stirred up recently, since no passions were 'as mightily effective in everything living as those that aim at self-defence' (687/385).

For Herder, this was no reason to discard patriotism altogether. The potential for patriotism to be corrupted only pointed to the need to invest one's efforts in 'purifying' and redirecting patriotism. Patriotism necessarily had to increasingly 'clean and purify itself of dross' (722/406). For Herder, the more general human pursuit of self-determination thus translated directly into 'purified patriotism'. As we have seen above, Herder saw individual self-determination as denoting a distinctively human capacity for reflective self-constitution both as an individual and as a member of a human community. It entailed an awareness of fallibility and partiality cultivated through critical engagement with the historical evolution of one's cultural and political community, whilst also encouraging public debates about the ways in which self-government could be achieved. For Herder, these kinds of efforts would also enable a nation to achieve international respect:

> Let Germany be courageous and upright. Courageously and uprightly it once allowed itself be led to Spain and Africa, to Gaul and England, to Italy, Sicily, Crete, Greece, Palestine. Our courageous and upright ancestors bled there – and are buried there. [But] courageously and uprightly, so history shows, the Germans were [also] willing to fight each other for a price, within their fatherland and outside it, friend set against friend, brother against brother; the fatherland was torn apart and remained forsaken. Should not something more than courage and uprightness therefore be necessary for our fatherland? Light, enlightenment, a public spirit; the noble pride not to be governed by others, but to govern oneself like other nations have done since time immemorial; to be Germans on their *well-defended* land (335/115).

As this citation reveals, Herder did not fully dissociate purified patriotism from national pride. However, Herder's goal was to stimulate a form of national pride that would be self-critical as well as self-contained, guarding against any attempts to situate the nation's self-esteem in military or imperial glory. Following the line of argument already introduced by Johann Georg Zimmermann in his *On National Pride*,[87] Herder invoked this idea as an antidote to national delusions and misguided pursuits of

---

[87] See Eva Piirimäe, 'The Vicissitudes of Noble National Pride: Johann Georg Zimmermann's (1728–1795) Theory of Patriotism', *Acta Philosophica Fennica*, 83 (2007) (= *Human Nature as the Basis of Morality and Society in Early Modern Society*, ed. J. Lemetti et al.), 121–142.

national glory. The glory of a fatherland in modern times, he argued, can be no other 'than that this noble mother provide her children with the security, activity, cause for free and charitable exercise – in short, the upbringing – that enables her own protection and utility, dignity and glory' (335/115. Translation modified.). Each nation, Herder emphasised, must 'learn to feel that it becomes great, beautiful, noble, rich, well-ordered, active and happy, not in the eyes of others, not in the mouth of posterity, but only in itself, in its own self; and that both foreign and subsequent respect then follows it as the shadow follows the body' (722–723/406–407. Translation modified.).

This new understanding of patriotism, Herder continued, was also vital for achieving international peace. On the one hand, a general understanding would emerge that any attempts at meddling into the 'self-constitution' of other nations would be ridiculous. On the other hand, this would encourage the rise of a certain 'common feeling', a feeling of solidarity with those nations that are 'disparaged and abused' by foreign nations (723/407). Herder predicted that this sentiment would also extend itself to nations suffering commercial mistreatment: 'trade should, even if not from the noblest motives, *unify* human beings, not divide them'. Drawing on Isaac Pinto's reflections on cosmopolitanism in economic relations, Herder insisted in the spirit of his youthful ideas that trade implied reciprocity of interest, which was why no nation was justified in violating this principle by monopolising certain universal media of trade, such as the seas (724/408).[88] Indeed, it was important to 'awaken the indignation of all nations against [such] a subjugator of the freest element [the ocean], against the robber of every highest profit, the presumptuous possessor of all treasures and fruits of the earth'. (723/407) This indignation must have effect one day, Herder believed. With the view to colonial and imperialist legacies of European states, Herder also emphasised the Europeans' responsibility in contributing to removing the causes of unhappiness everywhere (116, 749–750/423), arguing that 'Europe *must* give compensation for the debts that it has incurred, make good the crimes that it has committed – not from choice but according to the very nature of things' (741/418). Herder thus concluded his essay with an alluring vision of a future international order:

> Cabinets may deceive each other, political machines may be moved against each other until one blows the other to pieces. But *fatherlands* do not move against each other like this; they lie quietly side-by-side and assist each other

---

[88] On Pinto, see Koen Stapelbroek, 'From Jealousy of Trade to the Neutrality of Finance: Isaac de Pinto's "System" of Luxury and Perpetual Peace', in *Commerce and Peace*, 78–109.

as families do. . . Fatherlands against fatherlands in a bloody struggle – that is the worst barbarism of the human language. (338/116).

8.3.6   The Prospects of Germany and Europe

Let us conclude this chapter with a brief overview of Herder's assessment of Germany's political prospects in the post-Revolutionary period. As seen in Chapter 6, Herder, in his *Plan for Establishing a Patriotic Institute*, had hoped to create something like a 'universal' patriotic spirit in the Holy Roman Empire.[89] While he had not been enthusiastic about the chances of realisation for this plan, his hopes about breathing life into the current imperial institutions were completely dwindling by the 1790s. Furthermore, as already indicated, Herder was devastated when his own superior, grand duke Karl August, formed an alliance with the Prussian king to fight against Revolutionary France in summer 1792.[90] In his private correspondence, Herder resented the fact that the German princes invested their energies into fighting against Revolutionary France, whilst also demonstrating their military weakness and inability to collaborate efficiently. Indeed, 'coalition powers' who had joined forces against republican France met with spectacular failures from 1792 onwards. By 1795, after the Basel peace treaty, Germany was split into two zones – the northern zone of neutrality, including Prussia and the Saxon states, and the southern war-zone. In summer 1796, the southern German princes notoriously fled to northern Germany to escape the French armies marching into Bavaria.[91]

Herder's most explicit comments on these developments can be found in his private correspondence as well as some unpublished letters of the Tenth Collection of *Letters*. Originally, Herder had intended the collection to include not only a discussion of peace plans but also a series of letters on the situation in Germany – one on German 'national glory' (*Der deutsche Nationalruhm*), one on national self-defence, one on Justus Lipsius's ideas about the Dutch resistance to Spain in 1584, and one on the concept of 'coalition' (*Koalition*). The tone of these letters is highly ironical. Looking back at various discussions among German intellectuals, Herder poured scorn in the drafted letters on the exaggerated expectations that had initially been raised in princely propaganda regarding military coalitions:

---

[89] On this, see also Hien, *Altes Reich*, 288–291.
[90] Herder to Karl Ludwig von Knebel, 2 May 1792, in *DA*, VI, 265. For discussion, see also Arnold, 'Die Widerspiegelung', 46–48.
[91] On Herder's comments on these events in his correspondence, see ibid., 60–62.

A few years ago, when the word 'coaligned [*coalisierte*] powers' resounded in newspapers and conversations, this unusual word [*coalition*] was disputed in [private] society. [—] One spoke of the often attempted dangerous brotherhood (fraternity) of peoples; of the effects of the court of the Amphictyons and its decline among Greeks, of the Achaean League, the Panaetolium, the unification of Asia and Europe, which Alexander had in mind, [..] of the principles on which the union of the states of Italy, the British empire, the confederation of the Swiss, the seven provinces of Belgium [or] the unfortunate Poland had been founded or not, and finally came to [ponder the situation of] our Germany, which is so close to poor Poland, [asking] how far it [Germany] had succeeded or could hope to succeed in terms of its inner coalescence [growing together].[92]

These endless jeremiads and lamenting, Herder continued, were interrupted when society's attention was directed to a piece of writing entitled *Dangers of Time* (*Gefahren der Zeit*) (1794), in which the Swiss historian Johannes Müller pleaded for southern German states to rally to armed self-defence against the French. Herder approvingly cited three pages from the pamphlet, presenting it as a 'wake-up call' to his fictitious society.[93] Despite this, Herder did not think that there was actually a 'national constitution' to be defended in Germany. The fictitious society, he wrote, could not 'declare war or peace', but agreed on a set of conclusions. The first of them was that

only a nation that has the will, strength and a lasting constitution to protect itself is a nation. A constitution in which individual members challenge and insult with impunity other individual members as well as cause each other harm, but neither can nor wish to defend themselves, is not a national constitution (*Nationalverfassung*).[94]

This is a very clear criticism of the current constitution of the Holy Roman Empire. Furthermore, Herder proceeded to proclaim his disappointment about the current situation of the German language and the German public's relationship to it. The second conclusion of this fictitious society was as follows: 'A nation that neither knows nor loves and honors its own language has deprived itself of its own tongue and brain, the organs for its own formation (*Ausbildung*) and the noblest national honor.' In 1795, Poland had just been partitioned for the third time and now fully disappeared from

---

[92] Herder, 'Briefe zu Beförderung', in *SWS*, XVIII, 346.
[93] See also his self-critical confession to Müller that thanks to the piece, he was forced to realise 'against his will' that his long-standing 'antipathy' towards a 'nation that has now so pitifully shamefully cheated, upset, confused and plundered the world' is 'an awfully a deep-seated hatred', Herder to Johannes Müller, 10. October 1796, in *DA*, VII, 275.
[94] Herder, 'Briefe zu Beförderung', in *SWS*, XVIII, 346.

the map of Europe. In 1797, the year of the peace treaty of Campo Formio and the second Congress of Rastatt, Herder warned that Germany was facing the same fate – the current indifference towards language, religion, even literature was thus to be combatted with all possible means. The only possible solution in this situation was simply fostering 'the great feeling in EVERYTHING that we are one people, one fatherland, one language. That we must honor ourselves in this and strive to learn impartially from all nations, but to be a nation in ourselves. [—].' Nothing but 'respect for oneself' and, in danger, 'the ultimate self-defense' could help here.[95]

In Herder's view, the preservation of national independence was necessary for guaranteeing the nation's potential to properly become self-determined and self-governing in the future. Although the Holy Roman Empire was no less an empty husk than the French ancien régime, the German states were not to surrender to the French revolutionary army. It was still important to defend the 'land of Germans' to make it possible for future generations to properly awaken and regenerate the slumbering German nation. In case of a defensive war, a patriot would not shy away from fighting for his fatherland. His most important goal, however, would be to establish a human-oriented constitution in it.

8.4 Conclusion

As we have seen, Herder like Kant supported the original intentions of the French Revolution but distanced himself from Kantian theories of individual self-determination, republicanism and perpetual peace. He also criticised Kant's view of philosophical history and developed his own alternative view that did not centre on the evolution of political constitutions but on that of human sentiments and different kinds of 'publics'. On this basis, he put forward an evocative theory of 'purified patriotism' that entailed the simultaneous cultivation of both national and European (or even broader, cosmopolitan) forms of public in Germany and a commitment to an ideal of a 'moral fatherland', a set of republican principles.

For Herder, constitutional reform needed to be grounded in a nation's history and 'ethics', whilst leadership in this process was to be taken by the local 'aristo-democrats' and patriotic citizens, who in turn had arisen to prominence as active members of the 'public'. In 1798–1799, Herder had a chance to test these ideas in practice. As the revolutionary army was nearing East Switzerland in early 1798, Herder advised his family friend and protégé

---

[95] Ibid., 348.

Johann Georg Müller, the younger brother of the historian Johannes Müller to stay in his fatherland to discharge his civic duty (*Bürgerpflicht*) despite the personal risks involved. The question for Müller was not whether to rally to arms, but whether to leave the country or use the new opportunities that the collapse of the old system of government in his native Schaffhausen created. Invoking the example of Socrates, Herder and his wife reminded Müller of the particular obligations that a 'free Swiss citizen' has.[96] They encouraged Müller to take up possible new responsibilities in the administration of the reformed state, particularly since, as Caroline put it, the French did not require the Swiss to adopt 'totally new laws, but only the renewal of old ones'. This was a time to lay down old prejudices and 'help creating unity [in Switzerland]'.[97] Müller became a vice-governor of Schaffhausen and a deputy on the church and school board of the newly founded Helvetic Republic. In line with Herder's thoughts about the rejuvenation of states and the French 'self-constitution' in 1792, Caroline wrote to Müller: 'You must help Helvetia to rejuvenate and reinvigorate itself. [—] Declining Switzerland no longer has a living breath, the Spirit of God. Awaken now, dear friends, the old, true spirit of Helvetia, the spirit of loyalty, brotherly love, morality [. . .] An old, decaying corpse can no longer be revived, but a new body can. Instead of the collapsed house build a new, human-brotherly house.'[98]

Obviously, Herder also continued to ponder the fate of Germany and Europe in his final years. On the one hand, he clearly retained his fundamental republican and federalist commitments and belief in the importance of home-grown, historically grounded reforms. In *Adrastea,* the journal that Herder launched in 1801, he once again expressed the hope that the communal self-government and public spirit in medieval German cities could perhaps be regenerated in a novel form in a modern state, thus pointing towards the need to combine civil liberty with various forms of political liberty.[99] On the other hand, he did not rule out that something positive might emerge from Napoleon Bonaparte's 'highest game' for Germany.[100] Now acknowledging the achievements of the enlightened rulers like Frederick the Great of Prussia, Herder further voiced the wish that the 'great peers' of Europe would be capable of agreeing on some basic rules in international relations, for example settling the rules of inheritance for thrones. Like in the 1780s, he made clear that a proper historiography

---

[96] Karoline and J.G. Herder to Johann Georg Müller, 12 February 1798 in *DA*, VII, 365–367.
[97] Karoline and J.G. Herder to Johann Georg Müller, 16 February 1798, in *DA*, VIII, 368.
[98] Karoline Herder to Johann Georg Müller, 29 March 1799, in *DA*, VIII, 42.
[99] Herder, 'Adrastea' [Aurora], 960–961.
[100] Herder to Johann Wilhelm Ludwig Gleim, 27 December 1799, in *DA,* VIII, 111.

based on, and cultivating, *sensus humanitatis* would be essential for achieving more orderly international relations, admonishing the leading intellectuals of the dominant peoples (the British, the French, or indeed, Germans) of different large monarchies to take responsibility for the politics of their states in a self-critical spirit.[101] Public opinion, Herder implied, was an increasingly strong force in European politics. In a controversial article entitled *Atlantis* (1803), Herder at the same time put forward an argument against extreme academic freedom, proposing that some coordination and overseeing should be given to a higher 'council of sensible people' that would represent the public and the state in matters of common interest.[102]

It is quite evident that there was an element of pragmatic and realist thinking in Herder's conception of politics in the early 1800s. He acknowledged in 1802 that Russia had emerged as a new great power, whilst it was not to be expected that the 'Western merchant-nations' would come to help Germany (meaning the smaller German states). It was thus essential that Prussia and Austria would overcome their dualism, constituting an essential 'middle power' that alone would be capable of defending the land of Germans against the 'oppression of foreign nations and languages'.[103] In the poem 'Germania' (*Germanien*), published in a posthumous issue of *Adrastea* (1804), Herder once again reminded Germans of the fate of Poland, thus encouraging them to unite and 'organise themselves as a powerful people'. His realism did not amount to a glorification of power politics, however. Nor did he accept the current system of political government. He made clear that the reorganisation of Germany was to be achieved on a bottom-up republican basis, as 'dynasties [Höfe] had not protected' Germany, just like its 'magnates [Magnaten] would flee from it' in a moment of danger. Casting aside *Deutschheit*, German people and lands should become a 'Germania'.[104]

---

[101] See, e.g., Herder, 'Adrastea', 24–29.
[102] Herder, 'Adrastea', 708, 710. For discussion, see Dreitzel, 'Herders politische Konzepte', 295 and Günter Arnold, 'Kommentar', in *FHA*, X, 980–982.
[103] Herder, 'Adrastea', 433–434; cf. Dreitzel, 'Herders politische Konzepte', 284.
[104] Herder, 'Adrastea', 899–900.

Conclusion

In recent decades, scholars have carved out Herder's novel philosophical anthropology and metaphysics as well as traced his sustained engagement with natural history and histories of the human mind and society, elaborating also on the ways in which his ideas on language, aesthetics and morality grounded his republicanism, anti-imperialism and anti-colonialism. Much less attention, however, has been given to his evolving thoughts on the problems and prospects of modern European politics specifically. And yet, as we have seen in this book, Herder was deeply committed to finding ways to improve modern society and achieve moral and political reform in Russia, Germany and Europe more broadly. In virtually all his major works and a series of minor essays, Herder addressed questions on how to close the gap between moral principles and action, as well as law and ethics, in contemporary societies. Although he certainly had a variety of philosophical interests and theoretical ambitions, many of his literary studies as well as anthropological and historical enquiries can be seen as directly contributing to this practical endeavour.

Herder's approach to politics was embedded in various contemporary debates on modern politics. Herder started off in his youth as an admirer of Rousseau, Abbt and Hume at the same time. At a fundamental level, he like Abbt and Hume welcomed the rise of modern lawful and 'civilised' monarchies in the post-Renaissance period, particularly the new forms of civil liberty that were guaranteed in the latter. At the same time, he adopted much of Rousseau's critical perspective on modern society. He powerfully contrasted the professed ideals and values of the modern elites with their actual individualism and moral inertia whilst also deploring the continuing old and emerging new forms of despotism, military antagonism and imperialism evident in Europe. He also held up a mirror to modern individuals and societies by comparing the attitudes and values that characterised them with those typical of a wide array of earlier human societies. Nevertheless, as this book has shown, his precise diagnosis of, as well as proposed remedy to, what he called the 'current malaise of the world' differed profoundly from what Rousseau had concluded. Herder rejected Rousseau's accounts of sociability and perfectibility, and by implication, his theory of the general will. Herder's alternative to Rousseau's highly demanding political vision was a relatively more optimistic theory of potential gradual reforms from below. He also welcomed initiatives 'from above', insofar as they paid attention to the actual needs of the people.

Herder viewed himself as a 'popular philosopher' in a deeper sense. He was genuinely interested in advancing the cause of the common people. Pondering the possibilities of reform in Russia, Herder engaged seriously with Montesquieu's *The Spirit of the Laws*. Whilst accepting Montesquieu's emphasis on the intricate relationship between laws and mores, Herder maintained that he did not go far enough in exploring the foundations of mores themselves. Montesquieu's theory of principles of government did not pay sufficient attention to how ethics and politics had originally been unified in poetry and religion; neither ethics nor politics could be separated from culture broadly understood. This, Herder believed, rendered Montesquieu's approach susceptible to misguided applications, such as that of Catherine II in her *Nakaz*. Herder accordingly emphasised the need for all reformers to understand the specific historical preconditions for reform. Instead of applying abstract principles to particular cases, they needed to develop a deep understanding of the cultural, economic and political history of their polity and its different regions and of that of Europe more broadly. The patriotic reformers and reform-minded rulers also needed to know how to properly appeal to individuals' hearts and minds.

The young Herder's preferred political model diverged from those put forward by Montesquieu and Rousseau. Neither Montesquieu's theory of 'modern monarchy' nor Rousseau's distinction between 'sovereignty' and 'government' in a modern republic struck a chord with him. He also rejected the ideals of ancient republicanism. Athenian liberty had exerted a powerful impact on cultural development, but it had also engendered political instability and incompetent government. More importantly, it was ill suited to the modern age defined by a high degree of division of labour and luxury. The Spartan-inspired ideal of an austere republic, which some radical Swiss and French thinkers proposed, was even less feasible or even desirable in his eyes. Above all, modern men valued civil liberty, as trade was playing an increasingly important role in modern society. Herder, like many other thinkers in the period of the Seven Years' War and beyond, accepted that Christianity and commerce had substantially transformed Europe's social and political realities. He acknowledged that there were some 'trading states' that were far ahead of others, simultaneously strongly criticising their actual commercial practices – in these states, trade had clearly become an instrument of imperialism and exploitation. Nevertheless, in his more optimistic periods, both in his youth and from the 1780s to the end of his life, Herder hoped that the distortions of commercial reciprocity by powerful states and private commercial companies would soon become self-defeating, and thus encouraged both Russia and the Holy Roman Empire to join the ranks of modern commercial states. He was well aware that the realisation of this hope would require profound changes in human attitudes more generally. His own efforts were very much focussed on achieving this goal.

Responding to Rousseau and Montesquieu, Herder turned to fundamental questions about human nature, sociability and the origins and the evolutionary dynamics of human civilisation. He argued that language was the basis and instrument of human self-preservation, cognition and culture, emphasising also its social function. A distinctive way of thought, mores (*Sitten*) and laws of a people arose in communal singing, in which various kinds of cognitive endeavours were originally combined. Acknowledging the diversification of humanity into distinct groups as well as the necessary rise of group prejudices and animosity in early human history, he identified a tendency to an increasingly abstract way of thinking inherent in the history of language and in the human mind. Insofar as morality for Herder was grounded in sentiments, this went some way towards explaining the gap between professed moral principles and action as well as law and ethics in modern times to him. However, he believed that this tendency also opened up a prospect for a reunification of mankind at a higher level, having prepared mankind for the adoption of the Christian religion (and possibly other universalistic religions). Although Christianity had not yet delivered its original promise of creating a brotherhood of nations, there was hope that it would do so in the future.

Commentators have been puzzled by the relationship between Herder's ideas of the 1760s and those of the 1770s; for example, there is no clear agreement as to what the purpose of his sharp criticism of modern large monarchies was and whether he also proposed a solution to modern problems in this period. A close reading and comparison of Herder's various writings of the 1770s has revealed that, Herder, even in these most pessimistic years, fundamentally welcomed what he saw as the glimmers of civil liberty, order and prosperity in Europe. He disputed, however, that modern 'machine-states' could set a universal standard for all peoples and identified a number of distinctively modern pathologies. Thus he also vehemently criticised (what he saw as) Isaak Iselin's, William Robertson's and David Hume's excessively sanguine assessments of modern commercial society and cosmopolitanism. In so doing, he aligned himself with several idiosyncratic views of Adam Ferguson. First, he was concerned about the weakening of moral sentiments in modern times. He followed Ferguson in elaborating on the devastating effect that modern division of labour and machine-like government would have on people's minds. Second, he revealed and ridiculed the pervasive hypocrisy and the problematic conjunction of trade and imperialism in the modern world.

This study confirms the view that during the 1770s Herder developed a more strongly religious and Christian perspective on human history. As we have seen, Herder suggested that one of the reasons why modern individuals were particularly prone to moral and political apathy was the weakening of religious sentiment or conversely, overstated inward piety that was a reaction to the former. Thus, in the 1770s the crucial question for Herder became whether it was possible to revive a genuinely sociable form of Christian virtue. One of Herder's hopes was that here religion and poetry could yet again unite their forces. He suggested that a renewed form of Christian ethic might emerge in Europe, if modern Europeans would take seriously the foundations of moral virtue in religion and natural sociability as revealed by God in the earliest period of human history. He also sought to show that the original unity between poetry and politics could be restored at a new level and in a new manner in modern European societies. Cultivating a form of sociable and Christian patriotism, the modern intellectuals – poets, pastors and philosophers – could reclaim their leading positions in modern societies. This did not mean they were to serve the 'state', let alone advocate servile commitment to the current policies of the state; on the contrary, their real task was to *educate* humans, so as to teach them ways in which they could achieve freedom and self-determination, which in turn was to lead to an active disposition of doing good in society.

In the 1770s, Herder also pondered German political and literary history. Recent anglophone discussions of his political thought have mostly overlooked his engagement with these topics so far. As we have seen in this book, Herder drew on and developed further some of Justus Möser's ideas, presenting a highly critical view of the history of the Holy Roman Empire. Like Möser, he highlighted the original egalitarian nature of the ancient German constitution and the central law-keeping role of priests and poets. Following some of Möser's emphasis on unintended consequences in human history, he maintained that the conquest of Rome by German tribes and the subsequent Frankish conquests had led to the amalgamation of German and Roman systems of political government and the rise of feudal despotism and antagonism in Europe. German emperors' military ventures in Italy had precluded the consolidation of territorial power as had happened in France or Spain. However, Herder did not give much credit to the idealised vision of a distinctive 'German freedom'; he maintained that it had created as many problems as it prevented. In Germany, the sciences of government and commerce had not developed properly and thus Germans could not properly partake of the benefits of modern liberty. Herder thus encouraged his compatriots to begin cultivating these sciences. Of similar, if not greater importance, however, was the cultivation of the fine arts and poetry in particular.

Delving into the history of poetry, Herder also came up with specific views about the development of poetry in Germany and Europe. The real problem for Herder was that in the early modern period, poets all over Europe began to imitate ancient Greek and Roman models, which dissociated poetry from real-life concerns. Herder closely studied the moral and political role of poetry in different early societies and encouraged scholars to further investigate the latter's traces in the current world – folk songs. This did not mean that these songs were to be seen as new literary models. Rather, they enabled modern humans to appreciate the different modalities of human cognition and sensation as well as belief and sentiment; the songs in one's native language could also reveal deeper national ways of thought that maybe still informed modern linguistic usage and thinking. As such, they could further serve as a resource for the rejuvenation of modern poetry and arts, whilst it was also essential that modern authors and various kinds of professionals would seek to cultivate a self-reflective and critical attitude to national prejudices and traditions.

Herder's mature ideas of the progress of civil liberty and enlightenment in Europe constituted a clear alternative to the currently much better known contemporary vision proposed by Kant. Whilst the controversy between Kant and Herder on the history of mankind has been studied from a variety of viewpoints, this study has sought to further reassemble and analyse Herder's detailed critique of Kant's history of political government as well as his ideas on the prospects for peace in modern Europe. As we have seen, in the 1780s, in response to Kant's vision of the progress of civil liberty and enlightenment in Europe, Herder considerably modified his assessment of the history and prospects of modern liberty. He not only straightforwardly rejected Kant's argument in 1784 that modern civilised monarchies created the best conditions for the development of cultural agency and enlightenment, but also showed the unjustified idealism of his vision of international peace.

Herder's alternative vision was simultaneously more pessimistic and optimistic than Kant's. His pessimism was expressed in that he predicted the likely collapse of modern 'state-machines' and potential revolutions in Europe. The core of his argument was, however, optimistic: he showed that the foundations of modern civil liberty had been laid in the medieval period. The spirit of the original 'German popular constitution' had been revived in a new form in the Hanseatic cities, where civil liberty coincided with public spirit. Commerce and the arts and sciences first began to develop in southern European cities, contributing to the rise of better ideas of government. In northern European cities these ideas were further developed and were combined with ideas about a certain 'universal spirit of Europe'. Kant had thus not properly captured the origins of, and the particular contribution of commerce to the rise of, modern liberty in European history. Herder further held that modern commerce could potentially also have much more extensive impact on modern politics than Kant had envisioned. By fostering the growth of the arts and sciences and peaceful industry among populations, Herder argued, commerce could enable subjugated peoples like Slavs to abolish slavery (serfdom), dismantle the existing fundamentally expansionist imperial state-machines and embrace peaceful national self-government in their historical territories. More generally, Herder called for a cultural revival in European states that would lead to the spread of a new kind of sociable and self-reflective patriotic ethic. Such an ethic, he hoped, would help to gradually restore the foundations of civil liberty in communal self-government as well as ultimately contribute to a more pacific international order in Europe and all over the globe.

Herder's mature understanding of modern patriotism synthesised an emphasis on cultural and historical particularity and on self-determination and progress of *Humanität*, a universal goal grounded in the fundamental human disposition in favour of equity. Herder's peculiar form of vitalist naturalism allowed him to develop a view of history as constant natural evolution. He attempted to accommodate an element of contingency in this historical outlook by elaborating on various kinds of complex interactions and influences between different specific agents (individuals, social groups, nations). Nevertheless, his overall interest lay in tracing the most fundamental underlying continuities based on human nature. He underlined that all humans in all kinds of cultures were and had been capable of individual self-determination; his historical outlook further included a vision of progressive moral learning leading towards a greater degree of it. Whilst the central value of self-determination for Herder has been highlighted by several contemporary scholars, there has not been much engagement with the actual philosophical origins or indeed, more precise meaning, of this idea in Herder's thinking. This study has argued that Herder developed a holistic Stoic-Christian understanding of self-determination 'according to nature', which he in his later years directly contrasted with Kant's idea of moral autonomy. Herder also came to conceptualise modern patriotism as a form of self-determination. He maintained that the moderns would need to develop new self-reflective forms of art and aesthetics, preaching and philosophising, creating a new form of 'public' that would in turn also conceive of itself as part of a wider European and even global one. Herder's German patriotism was conceived in this spirit. He hoped to stimulate the creation of new and vibrant forms of national art and argued the need for public spirit in various kinds of communities: schools, universities, guilds and free associations, cities, states, Europe and mankind.

In his later years, Herder also spelled out the more radical implications of his conception of self-determination for political action. During the French Revolution, he came to argue that there are moments in history when modern 'nations' led by their natural leaders could also cast aside their old and long 'dead' political institutions, so as to give themselves a new 'living' constitution, one that would be grounded in the ethical dispositions and sentiments of the people as well as restore 'natural order', i.e. equality of human beings. In 1792, he thus also celebrated the fact that the French National Convention discussed and deliberated about 'the constitution [*Einrichtung*] of the entire nation' and 'fundamental rebirth', suggesting that this process was edifying not only for the French, but for all nations. He later also welcomed similar developments in Switzerland and hoped that Germany, too, would soon be able to 'self-constitute' itself on a federalist and republican basis. The constitution of the Holy Roman Empire was 'dead' and needed to be fundamentally renewed. In the dire international situation of the first and second Coalition wars, he repeatedly reminded the Germans of the sad fate of Poland and encouraged unity and reform.

Despite this emphasis on the need for 'regenerating' the political institutions of European states, Herder cautioned against exaggerated enthusiasm about abstract constitutional ideals and empty declarations and ceremonies. Whilst he, in the 1780s, had already openly dismissed all forms of hereditary privilege and in the 1790s developed an account of constitutional patriotism centred around republican values, he remained agnostic about the 'best form of government'. He held firm to his belief that all kinds of reforms had to be grounded in local traditions and backed up by public support and appropriate moral sentiments. Just as he in his youth had attacked Montesquieu for embracing an overly legalistic approach, he towards the end of his life criticised Kant for unwittingly encouraging republican enthusiasm and even imperialism. Indeed, as we have seen, he maintained a sustained critical dialogue with Kant through-out the 1790s. 'Civic enlightenment' concerning the merits and demerits of different forms of government was important for Herder, too, but needed to be combined with a 'sentimental enlightenment' including the cultivation of an ethic of social responsibility and activity, on the one hand, and an expansion of citizens' circles of solidarity and concern, on the other.

When Herder advocated the need for a historically informed political judgement and the grounding of laws in the 'mores' and, indeed, 'national ways of thought' of the people, he certainly opened up new ways of thinking about the relationships between states and nations. On the one hand, by drawing attention to valuable forms of national tradition (folk songs) even with the most 'primitive' subjugated peoples, Herder contrib-uted to the rise of national self-consciousness and grassroots reform initia-tives among such peoples. He also predicted the 'awakening' of the Slavic peoples in the Habsburg realm and, in his late years, strongly opposed Joseph II's centralising efforts and linguistic unification projects.[1] On the other hand, Herder himself was primarily interested in achieving moral and political reforms in Russia and Germany (the Holy Roman Empire) and thereby also enhancing the status of these states in the international arena. He maintained that Russian rulers should recognise the heteroge-neity of the Russian Empire, whilst seeking to better integrate its different cities and provinces into it. Although he was highly critical about the constitution of the Holy Roman Empire, his ideas contributed to the strengthening of 'German' national identity. Most importantly, Herder provided a theoretical justification to the idea that there exist various kinds of prepolitical communities (peoples and territories) that survive and can regenerate their political institutions. When, both during and after the French Revolution, Herder admonished the leading intellectuals of the dominant peoples (the British, the French, or indeed, Germans) of differ-ent large monarchies to take responsibility for the politics of their states in a self-critical spirit, he unwittingly strengthened the link between 'the

[1] Herder, 'Briefe zu Beförderung', in *FHA*, VII, 66–67.

state' and 'the nation' (a distinct people).[2] During the Coalition wars, this link was particularly important, insofar as it could also encourage patriotic fighting for states that according to Herder's own classification were 'dead'. Defending the land and the people still remained morally necessary, even though there was no proper living constitution in such a state. Achieving such a constitution, however, was the ultimate goal.

There is no denying that Herder put forward a morally highly optimistic vision of humanity and politics. Albeit Herder briefly acknowledged the need for constitutional limits on government, he never specified the exact nature of such limits, leaving it unclear how political decisions were to be made or the less savoury human tendencies should be neutralised or contained in the political process. He also offered no clear answers to the question of how national self-government should be organised, provided there were many nations living on one territory. He just pointed at the right of subjugated peoples to revive self-government on their historical territories. Last, but least, his fundamental optimism about the future of international politics has not been vindicated. Although he voiced insightful criticisms of the continuing instrumentalisation of patriotism and trade by modern states, he viewed the latter as aberrations from the 'natural laws' of history rather than as endemic aspects of modern politics. As we know, these hopes did not materialise. Even Herder himself adopted a somewhat more pragmatic approach to politics in the early 1800s. Furthermore, it is even possible to argue that it was precisely the Herderian model of 'intense cultural and sentimental-motivational agency' that helped to raise modern international rivalry and power politics to 'unprecedented heights'.[3] As István Hont has described it, the second half of the nineteenth century witnessed the rise of self-avowed 'national states', whilst the ever more intense global economic and military competition between states was interpreted as that between 'nations'. The relationships between different nationalities in states were securitised, minority nations often coming to be seen as jeopardising the social trust and cohesion in such states and as responsible for the social disruptions and national humiliations caused by global competition for economic and military power.[4]

We should not, however, interpret Herder's political ideas through the lens of these subsequent developments. Nor should we see them as his sole, let alone true legacy. As we have seen in this book, Herder identified deep, intractable problems such as those of individualism, moral self-deception, political apathy, exploitative commerce and war in modern European

---

[2] See, e.g., Herder, *Adrastea*, 24–29.   [3] Hont, *Jealousy of Trade*, 141–142, 147ff.   [4] Ibid., 144.

politics, and was genuinely searching for solutions to them. He whole-heartedly sought reforms in Russia and the Holy Roman Empire, advo-cating the ideal of a distinctively 'modern' kind of polity in which the citizens would be enjoying civil liberty, prosperity as well as various kinds of autonomy and self-government. Furthermore, he pursued the vision of a united Europe, in which former empires and 'state-machines' would be replaced by pacific and *humanised* political communities, regarded as their 'own' by their peoples for various reasons, and between which there would be mutual respect and emulation, and, last but not least, reciprocal, rather than competitive, let alone exploitative, trade. He believed that this kind of Europe would have a completely different relationship to the rest of the world than before; indeed, it would even seek to rectify the damage and sufferings it had caused to others. The crucial element, upon which his envisioned grand transformation hinged, was the broader public's moral sentiments, which is why he also tirelessly sought to find ways to contrib-ute to the cultivation of 'purified patriotism' and 'dispositions of peace'. These ideals and aspirations continued to resonate with a number of subsequent thinkers; indeed, they still resonate with many of us.

Epilogue

As Günter Arnold, Kurt Kloocke and Ernest A. Menze have noted, the reception of Herder's thought is a vast and little explored field.[1] Precisely because so many of Herder's ideas have become commonplace, it is now difficult to determine his influence. This applies to his political ideas, too. Moreover, the reception of Herder's political thought in different national contexts was strongly conditioned by what Herder had to say about the history of a particular people or region; so much so that the rest of his political thought was often ignored. However, having now reconstructed Herder's own specific agenda and main concerns, it is possible to better appreciate the inspiration he could or could not provide to the next generations of political thinkers in Europe. Alongside the nationalist mis-appropriations of Herder dating back to the late nineteenth century and culminating in the 1930s in Germany, there have been other, substantively more justified instances of reception and appropriation of his political ideas. The latter are yet to receive the scholarly attention they deserve.[2] Let us conclude this book by briefly sketching some of them.

Perhaps not surprisingly, Herder's political ideas did not find much resonance in Germany in the first decades of the nineteenth century. His reputation was initially severely damaged by his opposition to Kant at the end of the eighteenth and in the early nineteenth centuries. The German Idealists and Romantics sided with Kant in this dispute, meaning that whilst they further developed certain isolated Herderian ideas (on culture, religion, human history or nature), they were dismissive of his broader

---

[1] Arnold et al., 'Herder's Reception', 391.
[2] See, however, Barnard, *Herder on Nationality* and more recently, Proß, 'Herder zwischen Restauration' and Jochen Johannsen, 'Politische Rezeption', in *Herder Handbuch*, 617–677. Isaiah Berlin also had suggestive ideas about Herder's legacy, maintaining that nineteenth-century democratic and peaceful 'populism' was Herder's 'true heir', *Three Critics*, 257.

philosophical outlook and political vision.[3] It is also to be concurred with Wolfgang Proß's assessment that Herder's *political* ideas could not and, indeed, did not find much favour with the emerging German Historical School, notwithstanding the many superficial parallels between them.[4] In contrast to the latter, Herder viewed the amalgamation of Roman and German 'ways of thought' in German history in negative terms, and he also expressed severe criticisms of the modern state. It is likely that the thinkers associated with the German Historical School were also critical of his egalitarianism and sympathetic attitude to the French Revolution.

However, there were other thinkers and schools in the first half of the nineteenth century and beyond who found much appeal in Herder's ideas. Indeed, this study enables us to see how Herder's political thought could be directly relevant to some specific strands of nineteenth-century liberalism, republicanism, socialism and anarchism *at the same time*. Furthermore, we can now also reconsider his relationship to nineteenth-century nationalism and cosmopolitanism. What emerges is that Herder's philosophical ideas in many ways serve as a bridge between typical eighteenth-century concerns (like sociability) and those traditionally associated with the post-Revolutionary period (like individual self-development, constitutional reform, popular sovereignty, nationality and international solidarity).

First of all, as Henri Tronchon's classic study has shown, Herder's thought attracted considerable attention from a wide range of French-speaking intellectuals (including Madame de Staël and the Coppet circle more broadly) during the first decades of the nineteenth century.[5] Among these thinkers, the best-known is Benjamin Constant, whose essay on *The Liberty of the Ancients Compared with the Moderns* was cited in the Introduction. Constant had studied Herder extensively during his stay in Weimar in 1804, drawing important insights from Herder for his ideas on religion. He even wrote an essay on perfectibility that he conceived explicitly as an introduction to Herder's *Ideas for a Philosophy of History*.[6] Indeed, a number of significant parallels emerge in Herder's and Constant's political thinking as well. Let us here venture a brief comparison between Constant and Herder to highlight some of the relevance that the latter's ideas may have had for self-avowed 'liberals' like Constant.

---

[3] Arnold et al., 'Herder's Reception', 394. On Herder and German Idealism, see Heinz (ed.), *Herder und die Philosophie des deutschen Idealismus*.

[4] Proß, 'Naturalism, Anthropology, Culture', 247; cf. Proß, 'Herder zwischen Restauration', 121.

[5] Henri Tronchon, *La Fortune Intellectuelle de Herder en France: La Préparation* (Paris, 1920).

[6] Arnold et al., 'Herder's Reception', 410.

Despite establishing a seemingly stark contrast between ancient and modern liberty, both Herder and Constant recognised the mutual dependence of, and intricate relationship between, civil and political liberty in modern times. The preservation of modern liberty was, for both of them, also closely connected to patriotism, which they further associated with the ideal of self-development. As we have seen, Herder suggested that public spirit and self-government in various sub-state communities in pre-modern times was an important precondition for the rise of modern civil liberty. In the concluding remarks of his famous speech, Constant similarly acknowledged that the people should retain a certain 'right to share in political power' in the modern system. It was not only participation in elections, but more substantially, the exercise of some form of collective self-government at various levels of society (first of all, in towns, but also in the 'smallest villages' and 'workshops') that was needed to stabilise modern liberty.[7] According to Constant, this kind of political liberty further provided the 'most powerful, the most effective means of self-development that heaven has given us'. Our true purpose, after all, was not just 'happiness, of whatever kind' but happiness based on activity and self-elevation.[8]

Similarly, Herder and Constant shared a clear distrust in the ability of abstract provisions of law to guarantee civil liberty in the long run. Both of them were suspicious of the theoretical construct of 'rights' in this context, instead highlighting the characteristic attitudes and values of the moderns as substantiating the idea of 'rights'.[9] Both viewed the progress of *Humanität* and humans' increasing capacity for self-determination as essential elements in providing a remedy to problems that the increased division of labour had created. Both also believed that commerce would gradually take a more regular and reciprocal form, whilst societies would reach a greater rather than smaller degree of equality between human beings in the long run. At the same time, they shared a similar concern about representative bodies as well as single rulers misusing the language of abstract popular sovereignty

---

[7] Constant was here drawing on Jean-Charles-Léonard Simonde de Sismondi's *Histoire des républiques italiennes du moyen age* (1809, 1819). On Sismondi's understanding of modern liberty and its broader significance in debates on ancient and modern liberty, see Michael Sonenscher, 'Liberty, Autonomy, and Republican Historiography. Civic Humanism in Context', in *Markets, Morals, Politics*, 161–211. The relationship of Sismondi's ideas to those of Herder would merit a separate study.

[8] Constant, 'The Liberty of the Ancients', 327.

[9] My interpretation of Constant here draws on Bryan Garsten, 'Benjamin Constant's Liberalism and the Political Theology of the General Will', in *The General Will: The Evolution of a Concept*, ed. J. Farr and D. Williams (Cambridge, 2015), 382–401; idem, 'Representative Government and Popular Sovereignty', in *Political Representation*, ed. Ian Shapiro, Susan C. Stokes, Elisabeth Jean Wood (Cambridge, 2010), 90–110.

and constitutional republicanism so as to justify encroachment on the actual liberties of individuals and the independence of entire peoples, instead highlighting the value of local as well as cultural patriotism. In his pamphlet, *The Spirit of Conquest and Usurpation and Their Relation to European Civilization* (1813), Constant like Herder directly contrasted the patriotism of abstract ideals with the sentimental patriotism grounded in local contexts, using this contrast to buttress his critique of Napoleonic imperialism.[10] Finally, as was true of Herder, Constant's account of local forms of public spirit was intimately tied to his idea of a 'Europe of nations'. Indeed, Constant may have inherited (via Madame de Staël) the Herderian vision of an integrated Europe, bound by mutual commercial ties and a historically emerged cosmopolitan public sphere – a vision of Europe in which self-development, artistic achievement and civil liberty would co-depend on various kinds of vibrant patriotism.[11]

In contrast to French and Swiss post-revolutionary liberals, Kant-influenced German liberals seem to have had little interest in Herder's political ideas.[12] However, a new and more radical strand of republican liberalism developed in the 1830s.[13] In these years, thinkers associated with the 'Young Europe' movement all over Europe began to take sustained interest in Herder's political thought. Herder's ideas resonated with thinkers like Edgar Quinet, Jules Michelet and Victor Hugo who were particularly interested in his philosophy of religion and its implications for societal and political change, including the justifications for revolutionary action. German thinkers were no exception. Most significantly, Ludwig von Feuerbach explicitly referred to Herder as his inspiration in drafting his sensualist anthropology as an alternative to Hegel's approach.[14] Heinrich

---

[10] Constant, 'The Spirit of Conquest', in *The Political Writings of Benjamin Constant*, 44–302 (73–74).

[11] On this vision, see Biancamaria Fontana, 'The Napoleonic Empire and the Europe of Nations', in *The Idea of Europe: From Antiquity to the European Union*, ed. Anthony Pagden (Cambridge, 2002), 116–128.

[12] However, Herder was clearly relevant to Wilhelm von Humboldt's understanding of self-development. For discussion, see Anette Mook, *Die freie Entwicklung innerlicher Kraft: Die Grenzen der Anthropologie in den frühen Schriften der Brüder von Humboldt* (Göttingen, 2012).

[13] Cf. Wolfgang J. Mommsen, 'German Liberalism in the Nineteenth Century', in *The Cambridge History of Nineteenth-Century Political Thought*, ed. Gareth Stedman Jones and Gregory Claeys (Cambridge, 2011), 409–432 (415).

[14] Christine Weckwerth, 'Die Herdersche Philosophie als Aurora der neuern sensualistischen Philosophie – Nachwirkungen Herder in Vormärz', in *Herder Handbuch*, 686–696; on the resonance of Herder with Marx, see John Noyes, 'Herder and Marx', in *Herder und das neunzehnte Jahrhundert*, 179–193.

Heine also studied Herder in Paris, having great sympathy both for his general humanitarianism as well as sharing his interest in Hebrew republicanism.[15]

Perhaps the most explicit follower of Herder, however, was the Bavarian journalist and lawyer Johann Georg August Wirth who invoked Herder's philosophy of culture as a foundation for his democratic republicanism. In May 1832, Wirth helped to organise the Hambach Festival in Bavaria as a reaction to the restrictive measures against political self-expression in South-German states (following the Paris Revolution of 1830). The festival was an international event, including French and Polish guests. In his famous speech held at this festival, Wirth vehemently criticised the German 'kings and aristocrats' for sucking the blood of the German nation, whilst accusing Prussia and Austria of suppressing the liberty of smaller countries of Germany and of making the 'powers of these countries serve the system of princely autocracy and despotic force' all over Europe. The only solution to this situation, Wirth argued, was the establishment of proper German 'popular sovereignty' (*Volkshoheit*). Thereby, Wirth suggested, also the 'most heartfelt confederation of peoples' would be formed in Europe, 'for the people loves, while kings hate, the people defends, where kings perse-cute, the people grants [...] its ardently desired goals of freedom, enlight-enment, nationality [*Nationalität*], and popular sovereignty to a fraternal nation as well'.[16] In the same breath, Wirth highlighted 'freedom of world trade' as 'the exquisite material fruit' of this 'global event', one that would bring along an 'unstoppable advance of civilization' as its 'incalculable spiritual gain'.[17]

Wirth grounded these ideas in Herder's philosophy of self-determination, nationhood and *Humanität*. Soon after the festival, repres-sions started. Wirth was imprisoned. Tried in court in 1833, Wirth held a speech, which lasted altogether eight hours spread over two days.[18] Significantly, the speech was to a large extent an extensive commentary on Herder's philosophy. Drawing on Herder (and criticising the French Jacobins), Wirth emphasised the individual 'internal free self-determina-tion' (*innerlich freie Selbstbestimmung*) as a central precondition for the

[15] On Herder and Heine, see Barnard, *Herder on Nationlity*, ch. 3.
[16] Johann Georg August Wirth, 'Rede von Wirth', *Das Nationalfest der Deutschen zu Hambach* (Neustadt, 1832), 41–43; English translation by Jeremiah Riemer, GHDI – Document – Page (ghi-dc.org) (visited on 28 April 2022).
[17] Ibid.
[18] Elisabeth Hüls, *Johann Georg August Wirth: Ein politisches Leben im Vormärz* (*Beiträge zur Geschichte des Parlamentarismus und der politischen Parteien*, 139) (Düsseldorf, 2004), 332, 341.

establishment of 'free states' (*Freistaaten*) (and universal suffrage) and federations of 'free states', whilst associating its development with what he called the 'humanity's cultural evolution'.[19] In 1848 Wirth attended the Frankfurt National Assembly, but died during it.[20]

Wirth was not only a democratic republican but also a German patriot defending the 'rights of the German people' and the German 'nationality'. Indeed, Herder's thinking was most likely an important inspiration to various kinds of thinkers who began to use the term 'nationality' in the first half of the nineteenth century. Furthermore, he inspired both those who insisted that nationality was an important factor to be taken into account of 'in determining the forms of the state' as well as those who elevated it into the most important principle of political life.[21] As seen above, Herder's criticisms of Catherine II's reform ideas in Russia as well as his warnings against abstract idealism and republican absolutism during the French Revolution were echoed by early nineteenth-century liberals like Benjamin Constant who used these ideas to criticise the misuse of 'ancient liberty' and the construct of 'popular sovereignty' by the Jacobins and Napoleon alike. These ideas were later expanded on, in a different manner, by thinkers who maintained that modern democratic states needed to take culture and national sentiment (as well as cultural differences within one state) seriously. At the same time, as the example of Wirth's political thought shows, the idea of 'nationality' also became a rallying cry for those fighting against the Quadruple Alliance in the Restoration period, inspiring dreams about a Europe-wide federation of peoples.

The attraction of smaller nations' intellectuals to Herder's ideas is well-known. Herder's chapter on Slavs in *Ideas* was widely read and commented on all over the Habsburg and Russian Empires, not least because of its prophetic predictions.[22] His comments on the awakening of Slav peoples

---

[19] *Die Rechte des deutschen Volkes: Eine Verteidigungsrede vor den Assisen zu Landau* (Nancy, 1833), 62–64. In a few years, Wirth also published *Fragmente zur Culturgeschichte*, 2 vols. (Kaiserslauten, 1835/1836), which heavily drew on Herder's work. On Wirth's philosophical interpretation of Herder's *Ideas*, see Proß, 'Herder zwischen Restauration, Vormärz und Reichsgründung', 133–137.

[20] Hüls, *Johann Georg August Wirth*, 529–539. On debates about the identity and 'future' of Germany during the Frankfurt Parliament, see Brian Vick, *Defining Germany: The 1848 Frankfurt Parliamentarians and National Identity* (Cambridge, 2002).

[21] This kind of distinction between two main interpretations of 'nationality' was made by John Emerich Edward Dalberg Acton, 'Nationality [1862]', [reprinted] in Dahlberg-Acton, *The History of Freedom and Other Essays* (1907 (*The Online Library of Liberty*)), 176–191 (185). Acton did not, however, explicitly mention Herder in this context.

[22] See Peter Drews, *Herder und die Slaven: Materialien zur Wirkungsgeschichte bis zur Mitte des 19: Jahrhunderts* (Munich, 1990) and Holm Sundhaussen, *Der Einfluß der Herderschen Ideen auf die Nationsbildung bei den Völkern der Habsburger Monarchie* (Munich, 1973).

were a direct encouragement for the latter, whereas he was also one of the crucial figures to launch a Europe-wide interest in folk songs. He not only inspired social movements to collect these songs but also encouraged modern poets to use them as a resource for their own creative pursuits.[23] Some of Herder's friends or former students in the Baltic provinces of Russia also directly drew on his ideas in criticising the prevailing serfdom and miserable economic and cultural situation of local peasant populations. This misery was increasingly attributed to the historical conquest and colonisation of these territories through Germans as a result of the medieval crusades.[24] Herder's ideas about the inseparability of language and thought, and the value of language and national traditions for individuals' self-respect also soon came to contribute to the rising self-consciousness and linguistic patriotism of even predominantly 'peasant' nationalities, leading the latter to pursue various forms of political self-organisation as well as establish voluntary associations on a national basis. It is important to note, however, that the leading intellectuals of such small nations characteristically did not advocate the creation of 'national states' in the nineteenth century. Rather, these ideas encouraged linguistic and cultural revival programmes as well as sometimes provincial or civic patriotism.[25]

Indeed, it is worth highlighting that Herder's political ideas also continued to have a special appeal to minority nations resisting, and seeking to propose alternatives to, state-induced patriotism in the second half of the nineteenth century. Considering Herder's particular relationship to Riga and Livland, it is perhaps appropriate to dwell a little longer on a notable episode of Herder-appropriation in Riga in this period. In 1864, a Herder statue was erected in Riga, commemorating Herder's arrival there a century earlier, but its erection was also a political act. During the 1860s, the Russian central government, supported by the emerging liberal press in Russia, was actively intensifying its efforts to transform Russia into a modern 'national state'. In Russia's Baltic provinces this involved administrative consolidation and proposals for the abolition of several previously

---

[23] On this process, see Lukas, '…mit Treue, Lust und Liebe'.

[24] For various kinds of political discourses inspired by Herder in the Baltic context, see Taterka, 'Humanität, Abolition, Nation'.

[25] Axel Körner, 'National Movements against Nation States', in *The 1848 Revolutions and European Political Thought*, ed. D. Moggach and G. Stedman Jones (Cambridge, 2018), 345–382 (365–366); On the complex intellectual landscape in East-Central Europe more broadly, see Balàzs Trencsényi, Kopeček M., Falina M., Lisjak L., Baár M.K., and Janowski M., *A History of Political Thought in East-Central Europe* (Oxford, 2018), I.

granted noble and municipal privileges, including the right to use German as the local administrative language. The local Baltic German intellectuals rejected these reform initiatives and proposed alternative reform ideas. The central intellectual authority invoked by the local liberal intellectuals in their counterproposals was, notably, Herder. Various kinds of documents relating to Herder's stay in Riga were published, accompanied by commentaries on and discussions of Herder's ideas. The most important among them was a pamphlet of Jegór von Sivers, a Livonian writer, university lecturer, and nobleman, the title of which can be translated as *Humanity and Nationality: A Livonian Secular Essay in Memory of Herder and in Defence of Livonian Constitutional Law*.[26] Sharply criticising both the centralising and nationalising attempts of the tsarist government as well as the local nobility's clinging to its feudal privileges, Sivers advocated a different, federalist and 'cosmopolitan' solution based what he characterised as Herder's 'republican' understanding of modern politics. Sivers acknowledged that Herder had not known the nineteenth-century idea of a 'principle of nationality' (*Nationalitätsprincip*) but suggested that he would have approved of its original form, which postulated 'the political right of the speakers of the same language to unite themselves into a nation and to choose their form of government independently'. According to Sivers, Herder would have, however, passionately rejected the post-1848 interpretations of the 'principle of nationality' by governments of aspiring 'national states'. Instead of the values of personal growth and formation (*Bildung*), independent activity work (*Selbsttätigkeit*) and self-government, the writers who supported the cause of central government associated the principle of nationality with 'blood, race, and the nationality of the majority of the population'.[27] Adopting such an 'unfree principle of state', they allegedly pursued 'the good of the peoples', whilst actually only provoking national hatreds. Sivers instead suggested as genuine intellectual heir to Herder the 'republican' Mikhail Bakunin, who had distinguished between 'state patriotism' (*Staatspatriotismus*) and 'popular patriotism' (*Volkspatriotismus*). As Bakunin had shown, it was impossible for centralised states to truly fraternise with each other, as the patriotism directed towards them required nothing but fame, dominion and war. True

---

[26] *Humanität und Nationalität: eine livländische Säcularschrift zum Andenken Herders und zum Schutze livländischen Verfassungsrechtes* (Berlin, 1869). On Sivers and the political context of his appropriation of Herder's ideas, see Eva Piirimäe, '*Humanität* versus Nationalism as the Moral Foundation of the Russian Empire: Jegór von Sivers' Herderian Cosmopolitanism', *Ajalooline Ajakiri: The Estonian Historical Journal*, 139/140 1:2 (2012), 79–113.

[27] Sivers, *Humanität und Nationalität*, 40–45.

fraternity, by contrast, could only exist among confederated provinces, territories and nations.[28]

There was an element of irony, however, in Sivers' reform proposals. Sivers did not pay much attention to the practical difficulty of realising this programme in Russia's Baltic provinces, where Germans were just a tiny and mostly highly privileged minority, whilst the Estonian and Latvian majority populations occupied the lowest ranks of society. Although he was far-sighted enough to imagine that the representatives of the latter would be included in the new forms of political representation that he proposed, he did not realise that these ethnic groups had already gradually come to view themselves as distinct nations, based on a new awareness of the value of their folk traditions and the idea that 'their land' had once been conquered and colonised by Germans, which had also led to their individual enslavement (serfdom). As we have seen, both these ideas, too, had been theoretically elaborated by Herder. Furthermore, insofar as the more radical republican political views such as Sivers' were only supported by a small segment of the local Baltic German elites, the representatives of these 'peasant' nations did not believe their situation would improve much under the domination of the Baltic German upper classes. Instead, separate national public spheres emerged based on Herderian ideas in these territories, the representatives of the majority nations coming to voice their own ideas about federalism and 'national self-determination' in the early twentieth century.[29]

During the First World War, Herder's name was yet again frequently mentioned in political debates. Indeed, historians have identified something like the spread of a 'Herderian paradigm in international relations' in these years.[30] Tomáš Garrigue Masaryk (who later became Czechoslovakia's first president) is perhaps its most prominent and well-known promoter. Masaryk had been deeply interested in Herder's ideas on culture and religion in his youth, further drawing on his ideas in discussing what he called the 'problem of small nations' in the early twentieth century.[31] During the Great War, he

---

[28] Ibid., 2.
[29] Kaarel Piirimäe, 'Federalism in the Baltic: Interpretations of Self-Determination and Sovereignty in Estonia in the First Half of the 20th Century', *East Central Europe*, 39 (2012), 237–265.
[30] Xosé M. Nuñez Seixas, 'Wilson's Unexpected Friends: the Transnational Impact of the First World War on Western European Nationalist Movements', in *The First World War and the Nationality Question in Europe: Global Impact and Local Dynamics*, ed. by Xosé M. Núñez Seixas (Leiden, 2020), 37–64 (45–46).
[31] See Tomáš Garrigue Masaryk, *Modern Man and Religion* (Freeport, NY, 1938, reprint 1970), 121–124; on Masaryk's political views, see László Bence Bari, 'New Worlds Tackling on Side-Tracks: The National Concepts of T.G. Masaryk and Oszkár Jászi during the First World War (1914–1919)', in *The First World War*, 115–141.

launched a massive campaign to raise support for the ideal of national self-determination for small nations in Central Europe, presenting the latter as essential elements in the new postimperial international order that he envisioned for Europe. Indeed, Masaryk sought to show that small nations, in particular, would be well disposed to creating conditions for individual self-development, guaranteeing the rights of minorities as well as upholding peace in Europe and beyond. From the viewpoint of international politics, a federation of a small nations in 'Central Europe' could also serve as a reliable barrier against the 'pan-Germanism' of imperial Germany and Austria-Hungary.[32] Expressing some (limited) distance from what he saw as Herder's overly stark contrast between 'natural' (organic) nations and 'artificial' states, Masaryk credited Herder with creating the ideal of national self-determination (Masaryk mostly used the term 'principle of nationality'). Masaryk further endorsed Herder's demand that national sentiment would be purified of great power ideology and imperialist ambitions, insisting that Herder had clearly not advocated anything like 'pan-Germanism'.[33]

Even in Germany, there were some authors who during the First World War (and beyond) came to argue that Herder's thinking provided a powerful alternative to what had come to be mainstream German thinking (including German mainstream socialism). A prominent example in this respect was Gustav Landauer, a socialist who died tragically during the Bavarian Revolution in 1919. In 1914, in his journal *Der Sozialist*, Landauer reprinted sections of Herder's *Letters for the Advancement of Humanity* to buttress the point that a proper understanding of German nationhood had originally involved an aspiration towards a pacific world of autonomous, self-determining 'peoples' (nations) rather than 'states'.[34] This interpretation was also mobilised to criticise German national socialism in the 1930s. In his influential *Nationalism and Culture*, which was originally planned for publication in 1933 in Germany but only first appeared in Spanish and English from 1936 to 1937, the anarcho-syndicalist Rudolf Rocker attempted to uncover the reasons for Germany's turn to national socialism.[35] Offering an idiosyncratic longue durée intellectual history of the main currents of German political thought, Rocker compared Herder

---

[32] Tomáš Garrigue Masaryk, 'Pangermanism and the Zone of Small Nations', *The New Europe: A Weekly Review of Foreign Politics* I, 19 October 1916–11 January 1917 (London, 1917), 271–277 (277).

[33] Tomáš Garrigue Masaryk, 'Pangermanism and the Eastern Question', *The New Europe*, 2–19 (3).

[34] On Landauer's relationship to Herder, see Eugene Lunn, *Prophet of Community: The Romantic Socialism of Gustav Landauer* (Berkeley, 1973), 257–279.

[35] I would like to thank Edward Castleton for drawing my attention to Rocker.

favourably to Kant. In contrast to the latter, Rocker argued, Herder understood that 'an understanding among the nations can only be achieved by
organic-meaning cultural-means, and never by mechanical means, that is,
by the activity of "political machines."' In Rocker's view, Herder clearly saw
that 'the forced organization which constitutes the state maintains itself
primarily by continually creating external interests which run contrary to
the interests of other states'. The only acceptable solution, as already Herder
argued, was moral education from within and 'from below upwards by the
will of the people themselves'.[36] For Rocker, Herder's ideas thus constituted
a much more solid foundation for 'socialism' than Kant's. The authoritarian
character and the contamination of German socialism with 'nationalism',
Rocker argued, owed its origins to Kant's, Fichte's, Hegel's and the German
Romantics' ideas, all of whom had venerated the modern state. Insofar as the
recent League of Nations, too, had been framed along Kantian, rather than
Herderian ideas, it was not surprising that it had failed abominably.
According to Rocker, it would have been more appropriate to have called
it a 'League of States' rather than that of nations, insofar it was made up by
the former, not the latter.[37]

    As we see, Herder's ideas resonated widely across a broad spectrum of
political ideologies in the nineteenth century and beyond. They still continue to inspire thinkers who wish to emphasise the value of cultural
belonging or who are interested in the role that culture plays in politics.
Although such appropriations should not serve as guides to our interpretations of Herder's own ideas and political agenda, they deserve attention as
part of his reception history. While many of Herder's central concerns and
precise arguments inevitably got lost in the reception process, the history of
his political reception helps to highlight both the ambivalence of his political
thinking as well as its deeper consistency. Herder inspired those emphasising the need for a vibrant and culturally distinct public sphere in representative democracies as well as those opposing the top-down 'nationalising'
attempts of 'state-machines' transforming themselves into 'national states'.
His ideas could be used to encourage national self-defence, liberation and
awakening movements but also those for humanitarian cosmopolitanism,
including a pursuit of a federalist Europe of peoples. Indeed, an important
unifying element for all these different parallels and sometimes direct
homages to Herder is a simultaneous commitment to the improvement of
distinct languages, cultures and political societies as well as the pacification

[36] Rudolf Rocker, *Nationalism and Culture* (Los Angeles, 1937), 187.
[37] Ibid.; cf. ibid., 152 and 215.

of Europe (which in some cases amounted to supporting the abolition of states altogether). All these authors sympathetic to Herder believed that it would be necessary and possible to achieve a stable synthesis of cultural attachments and cosmopolitan commitments, combining linguistic-cultural and republican patriotism with humanitarianism. As this study has shown, they were justified in appealing to Herder's authority in voicing these ideals and aspirations. Herder was the first thinker to powerfully articulate them. More importantly, however, we have seen that he would need to be and deserves to be understood in his own terms.

Bibliography

Primary Sources: Johann Gottfried Herder

DA = Herder, Johann Gottfried. *Briefe: Gesamtausgabe 1763–1803*, 18 vols., ed. Wilhelm Dobbek and Günter Arnold (Weimar, 1977–2016).

FHA = Herder, Johann Gottfried. *Werke in zehn Bänden*, 10 vols., ed. Günter Arnold et al. (Frankfurt am Main, 1985–).

'Haben wir noch jetzt das Publikum und Vaterland der Alten? Eine Abhandlung zur Feier der Beziehung des neuen Gerichtshauses [1765]', in *FHA*, I, 40–56.

'Von der Ode. Dispositionen, Entwürfe, Fragmente [1764–1765]', in *FHA*, I, 57–101.

'Wie die Philosophie zum Besten des Volks allgemeiner und nützlicher werden kann? [1765]', in *FHA*, I, 101–134.

'(Von der Veränderung des Geschmacks) [1766]', in *FHA*, I, 149–160.

'Über die neueste Literatur. Fragmente. Eine Beilage zu den Briefen, die neueste Literatur betreffend' (three collections) [1766–1767]', in *FHA*, I, 161–540.

'Über die neueste Literatur. Fragmente. Erste Sammlung. Zweite, völlig umgearbeitete Ausgabe' [1768], in *FHA*, I, 541–640.

'Älteres Kritisches Wäldchen' [1768/1769], in *FHA*, II, 11–23.

'Über Thomas Abbts Schriften. Der Torso einem Denkmal, an seinem Grabe errichtet. Erstes Stück' [1768], in *FHA*, II, 565–608.

'Von der Ähnlichkeit der Mittleren Englischen und deutschen Dichtkunst, nebst Verschiednem, das daraus folget' [1777], in *FHA*, II, 550–562.

'Vorrede [Alte Volkslieder]', in *FHA*, III, 15–25.

'Ausweg zu Lieder fremder Völker [Viertes Buch. Nordische Lieder]', in *FHA*, III, 59–68.

'Ursachen des gesunkenen Geschmacks bei den verschiedenen Völkern, da er geblühet' [1775], in *FHA*, IV, 109–148.

'Über die Wirkung der Dichtkunst auf die Sitten der Völker in alten und neuen Zeiten (1781)', in *FHA*, IV, 149–214.

'Über den Einfluß der schönen in die höheren Wissenschaften [1779/1781]', in *FHA*, IV, 215–232.

'Älteste Urkunde des Menschengeschlechts (1774–1776)', in *FHA*, V, 179–659.

'Vom Geist der Ebräischen Poesie [1782–1783]', in *FHA*, V, 661–1309.

'Briefe zu Beförderung der Humanität [1792/1793–1797]', in *FHA*, VII, 9–806.

'Haben wir noch jetzt die Vaterland und Publikum der Alten? [1795]', in *FHA*, VII, 301–338.

'Tithon und Aurora', in *FHA*, VIII, 221–239.

'An Prediger. Fünfzehn Provinzialblätter [1774]', in *FHA*, IX:1, 67–138.

'Von Religion, Lehrmeinung und Gebräuchen' [1798], in *FHA*, IX:1, 725–858.

'Vom Einfluß der Regierung auf die Wissenschaften, und der Wissenschaften auf die Regierung [1779/80]', in *FHA*, IX:2, 294–391.

'Idee zum ersten patriotischen Institut für den Allgemeingeist Deutschlands [1787]', in *FHA*, IX:2, 565–580.

'Adrastea (Auswahl) [1801–1804]', in *FHA*, X, 9–962.

HEW = Herder, Johann Gottfried. *Selected Early Works, 1764–1767: Addresses, Essays and Drafts; Fragments on German Literature*, ed. Ernest A. Menze et al. (University Park, 1991).

'On Diligence in the Study of Several Learned Languages', in *HEW*, 29–34.

'Fragments of a Treatise on the Ode', in *HEW*, 35–51.

'Do We Still Have the Public and Fatherland of Yore?', in *HEW*, 53–64.

'Essay on a History of Lyrical Poetry', in *HEW*, 69–84.

'On Recent German Literature: The First [and Second and Third] Collection', in *HEW*, 85–234.

HWP = Herder, Johann Gottfried. *Werke in 3 Bänden*, 3 in 4 vols., ed. Wolfgang Proß (Munich, 1984–2002).

'Versuch einer Geschichte der lyrischen Dichtkunst', in *HWP*, I, 9–61.

'Über die neueste Literatur. Fragmente I–II [Zweite, völlig umgearbeitete Ausgabe]', in *HWP*, I, 65–354.

'Journal meiner Reise im Jahre 1769', in *HWP*, I, 355–465.

'Gedanken bei Lesung Montesquieus (Blätter zum *Journal der Reise*)', in *HWP*, I, 468–473.

'Auszug aus einem Briefwechsel über *Ossian* und die Lieder alter Völker' [1773] ('[Aus:]Von Deutscher Art und Kunst'), in *HWP*, I, 477–525.

'Shakespear', in *HWP*, I, 526–547.

'Shakespear: 1. Entwurf (1771)', in *HWP*, I, 547–554.

'Shakespeare: 2. Enwurf (1772)', in *HWP*, I, 554–572.

'Wahrheiten aus Leibniz', in *HWP*, II, 32–48.

'Grundsätze der Philosophie', in *HWP*, II, 52–56.

'Viertes kritisches Wäldchen', in *HWP*, II, 57–240.

Ideen zur Philosophie der Geschichte der Menschheit = *HWP*, III/1–III/2.

PW = Herder, Johann Gottfried von. *Philosophical Writings*, ed. and trans. Michael N. Forster (Cambridge, 2002).

'How Philosophy Can Become More Universal and Useful for the Benefit of the People', in *PW*, 3–29.

'Fragments on Recent German Literature (1767–1768) [Excerpts on Language]', in *PW*, 33–64.

'Treatise on the Origin of Language', in *PW*, 65–166.

'On Thomas Abbt's Writings [Selections Concerning Psychology] (1768)', in *PW*, 167–177.

'This Too a Philosophy for the Formation of Humanity [An Early Introduction]', in *PW*, 268–271.

'This Too a Philosophy for the Formation of Humanity', in *PW*, 272–358.

'On Cognition and Sensation, the Two Main Forces of the Human Soul (1775) [Preface]', in *PW*, 178–186.

'On the Cognition and Sensation of the Human Soul (1778)', in *PW*, 187–246.

'Letters concerning the Progress of Humanity [Excerpts on European Politics]', in *PW*, 361–369.

'Letters for the Advancement of Humanity [Excerpts concerning freedom of thought and expression]', in *PW*, 370–373.

'Letters for the Advancement of Humanity [Excerpt on Patriotism]', in *PW*, 374–379.

'Letters for the Advancement of Humanity (1793–1797): Tenth Collection', in *PW*, 380–424.

SWA = Herder, Johann Gottfried. *Selected Writings on Aesthetics*, ed. and trans. Gregory Moore (Princeton, 2006).

'On the Influence of Belles Lettres on the Higher Sciences', in *SWA*, 335–346.

'Shakespeare [1773]', in *SWA*, 291–397.

SWS = Herder, Johann Gottfried. *Sämmtliche Werke*, 33 vols., ed. Bernhard Suphan (Berlin, 1877–1913).

'Über Vom Verdienste', *Königsbergsche gelehrte und politische Zeitungen auf das Jahr 1765*, in *SWS*, I (Rostock, Greifswald, 1877), 79–81.

'(Von den ältesten Nationalgesängen)', in *SWS*, I, 148–152.

'Drittes Kritisches Wäldchen', in *SWS*, III, 461–471.

'Sammlung von Gedanken und Beispielen fremder Schriftsteller über die Bildung der Völker', in *SWS*, IV, 469–478.

'[Review of] August Wilhelm Hupel, *Kleine Nachrichten, vermischte Sachen. An das Lief- und Ehstländische Publikum* [1772]', in *SWS*, V, 346–350.

'Wie die deutschen Bischöfe Landstände wurden [1774]', in *SWS*, V, 676–698.

Eine Metakritik zur Kritik der reinen Vernunft, 2 vols., in *SWS*, XXI.

Herder, Johann Gottfried. *Another Philosophy of History and Selected Political Writings*, ed. Daniel Pellerin and Ioannis Evrigenis (Indianapolis, 2004).

'Do We Still Have the Fatherland? (1765)', 104–108.

'Do We Still Have the Fatherland of the Ancients? (1795)', 109–117.
'The Influence of Free Legislation on the Sciences and Arts [An Excerpt] [1780]', 130–142.

Herder, Johann Gottfried. *Auszug aus einem Briefwechsel über Ossian und die Lieder alter Völker'* (Hamburg, 1773).
Herder, Johann Gottfried. *Outlines of a Philosophy of the History of Man*, ed. and trans. T. H. Churchill (London, 1800).
Herder, Johann Gottfried. 'Ideas for a philosophy of history', in *Herder's Social and Political Thought: From Enlightenment to Nationalism*, ed. F. M. Barnard (Oxford, 1965).

Other Primary Texts

Abbt, Thomas. 'Vom Verdienste [orig. 1765]', in *Vermischte Werke*, 6 vols. (Frankfurt am Main and Leipzig, 1783), I:1.
'Freundschaftliche Korrespondenz,' in *Vermischte Werke*, 3 vols., ed. Friedrich Nicolai (Hildesheim, 1978; reprint Berlin, Stettin, 1780), II.
'Vom Tode für das Vaterland', in *Aufklärung und Kriegserfahrung: Klassische Zeitzeugen zum Siebenjährigen Krieg*, ed. Johannes Kunisch (*Bibliothek der Geschichte und Politik*, 9) (Frankfurt am Main, 1996), 589–650, 971–1008.
Anon. [Thomas Abbt] 'Von des Herrn von Moser *Beherzigungen*,' *Briefe, die neueste Literatur betreffend* (1761), XI, Literaturbriefe 178–180, 1–38.
'Einige allgemeine Anmerkungen über das Genie der Deutschen und den Zustand der deutschen Literatur,' *Briefe, die neueste Literatur betreffend* (1762), XV, Literaturbrief 245, 53–62.
'Über *Patriotische Vorstellungen und sichere Mittel, arme Staaten zu bereichern*', *Briefe, die neueste Literatur betreffend* (1762), XV, Literaturbrief 253, 137–160.
'Über [Anon = J.J. Wegelin] *Politische und moralische Betrachtungen über die Spartanische Gesetzgebung des Lykurgus*', *Briefe, die neueste Literatur betreffend* (1765), XXII, Litetaturbriefe 320–322, 93–146.
Berens, Johann Christoph. *Bonhommien: Geschrieben bei Eröffnung der neuerbauten Rigischen Stadtbibliothek: Erstes Profil* (Mitau, 1792).
Bonnet, Charles. *Essai de psychologie ou considérations sur les opérations de l'âme, sur l'habitude et sur l'éducation'* (London, 1755).
Bonnet, Charles. *Essai analytique sur les facultés de l'âme* (Copenhagen, 1760).
Brown, John. *Essays on the Characteristics* (London, 1751).
An Estimate of the Manners and Principles of Our Times, 2 vols. (London, 1757).
A Dissertation on the Rise, Union, and Power, the Progressions, Separations, and Corruptions, of Poetry and Music: To Which Is Prefixed, the Cure of Saul: A Sacred Ode (London, 1763).
The History of the Rise and Progress of Poetry, through its Several Species (London, 1764).

Histoire de l'origine et des progrès de la poésie dans ses différents genres (Paris, 1768).

Betrachtungen über die Poesie und Musik nach ihrem Ursprunge, ihrer Vereinigung, Gewalt, Wachstum, Trennung und Verderbniss: Aus dem Englischen übersetzt und mit Anmerkungen und zween Anhängen begleitet (Leipzig, 1769).

Bülau, Johann Jacob. *Noch etwas zum deutschen Nationalgeiste* (Lindau/Bodensee, 1766).

Catherine II, Empress of Russia. *Ihrer Kaiserlichen Majestaet Instruction fuer die Verfertigung des Entwurfs zu einem neuen Gesetz-Buche verordnete Comission Kaiserlichen Universitaets-Buchdruckerey* (Moscow, 1767).

Constant, Benjamin. 'The Spirit of Conquest', in *Political Writings*, ed. and trans. Biancamaria Fontana (Cambridge, 1988a), 44–302.

'The Liberty of the Ancients Compared with that of Moderns', in *Political Writings*, ed. and trans. Biancamaria Fontana (Cambridge, 1988b), 308–328.

Dalberg Acton, John Emerich Edward. 'Nationality [1862]', [reprinted] in *Dahlberg-Acton, The History of Freedom and Other Essays* (1907 (*The Online Library of Liberty*)), 176–191.

Ferguson, Adam. *An Essay on the History of Civil Society*, ed. Fania Oz–Salzberger (Cambridge, 1995).

Fichte, Johann Gottlieb. 'Grundriß des Völker- und Weltbürgerrechts', in *Ewiger Friede? Dokumente um eine deutsche Diskussion um 1800*, ed. Anita and Walter Dietze (Munich, 1989), 177–192.

Görres, Joseph. 'Der allgemeine Frieden, ein Ideal', in *Ewiger Friede? Dokumente um eine deutsche Diskussion um 1800*, ed. Anita and Walter Dietze (Munich, 1989), 512–532.

Grotius, Hugo. 'The Preliminary Discourse', in *The Rights of War and Peace*, ed. and with an introduction by Richard Tuck, ed. Jean Barbeyrac (Indianapolis: Liberty Fund, 2005).

Goguet, Antoine-Yves. *De l'origine des lois, des arts et des sciences et de leurs progrès chez les anciens peuples* (Paris, 1758).

The Origin of Laws, Arts, and Sciences: and Their Progress among the Most Ancient of Nations (1758). [Anonymous translation from French]

Vom dem Ursprunge der Gesezze [sic!], der Künste und der Wissenschaften; wie auch derselben Wachstum unter den alten Völker, trans. Georg Christoph Hamberger (Lemgo, 1760).

Hamann, Johann Georg. *Des Herrn von Dangueil [sic!] Anmerkungen über die Vortheile und Nachtheile von Frankreich und Grossbritannien in Ansehung des Handels und der übrigen Quellen von der Macht der Staaten: Auszug eines Werks des Bernardo de Ulloa über die Wiederherstellung der Manufacturen und des Handels in Spanien; Beylage des deutschen Übersetzers* (Mitau, Leipzig, 1756).

Herder, Maria Carolina von. *Erinnerungen aus dem Leben Johann Gottfried Herders*, ed. Johannes Müller, 2 vols. (Stuttgart and Tübingen, 1830), I.

Heynig, Johann Gottlob. 'Frieden durch antidespotische Volksaufklärung', in *Ewiger Friede? Dokumente um eine deutsche Diskussion um 1800*, ed. Anita and Walter Dietze (Munich, 1989), 257–271.

Hirzel, Johann Caspar. *Die Wirtschaft eines Philosophischen Bauers* (Zurich, 1761).

Hume, David. *The History of England: From the Invasion of Julius Caesar to The Revolution in 1688* (1778 edn.), 6 vols. (Indianapolis, 1983), III.

'Of the Rise and Progress of the Arts and Sciences', in *Essays Moral, Political, and Literary*, ed. Eugene Miller (Indianapolis, 1985), 87–96.

'Of the Rise of Arts and Sciences', in *Essays Moral, Political, and Literary*, ed. Eugene Miller (Indianapolis, 1985), 111–137.

'Of Commerce', in *Essays Moral, Political, and Literary*, ed. Eugene Miller (Indianapolis, 1985), 253–267.

'Of Refinement in the Arts', in *Essays Moral, Political, and Literary*, ed. Eugene Miller (Indianapolis, 1985), 268–280.

Iselin, Isaak. *Philosophische und Patriotische Träume eines Menschenfreundes* (Freiburg, 1755; Zurich, 1758).

Philosophische Muthmassungen über die Geschichte der Menschheit, 2 vols. (Frankfurt and Leipzig, 1764) (II edition 1768, III edition 1784).

'Anrede an die im Jahr 1764 zu Schinznach versammelt gewesene Helvetische Gesellschaft', in *Vermischte Schriften*, 2 vols. (Zurich, 1770), II.

'[Review of] Herder, J.G. *Über Thomas Abbts Schriften; Der Torso Von Einem Denkmal Auf Seinem Grabe Errichtet*', Anhang zum *Nachwort zu dem ersten bis zwölften Bände, Allgemeine Deutsche Bibliothek* (1771), 626–630.

Kant, Immanuel. 'Answer to the Question: What Is Enlightenment', in *Practical Philosophy*, ed. and trans. Mary J. Gregor (Cambridge, 1996), 11–23.

'On the Common Saying: That May be Correct in Theory, but It Is of No Use in Practice', in *Practical Philosophy*, ed. and trans. Mary J. Gregor (Cambridge, 1996), 273–310.

'Toward Perpetual Peace', in *Kant, Practical Philosophy*, ed. and trans. Mary J. Gregor (Cambridge, 1996), 311–352.

'The Metaphysics of Morals', in *Practical Philosophy*, ed. and trans. Mary J. Gregor (Cambridge, 1996), 353–604.

'Religion within the Boundaries of Mere Reason [1793]', in *Religion and Rational Theology* ed. A. Wood and G. di Giovanni (Cambridge, 1996), 39–216.

'Conjectures on the Beginning of Human History', in *Kant, Political Writings*, ed. H. S. Reiss and trans. H. B. Nisbet (Cambridge, 2000), 221–234.

'Idea for a Universal History with a Cosmopolitan Aim', in *Anthropology, History, and Education*, ed. Günter Zöller et al., trans. Mary Gregor et al. (Cambridge, 2007), 108–123.

'Reviews of Herder's *Ideas for the Philosophy of History: Parts I and II*', in *Anthropology, History, and Education*, ed. Günter Zöller et al., trans. Mary Gregor et al. (Cambridge, 2007), 121–142.

Leibniz, Gottfried Wilhelm. *New Essays on Human Understanding* [orig. French 1765] (Cambridge, 2012).

Lessing, Gotthold Ephraim. *Laokoon: über die Grenzen der Malerei und Poesie* (1766).

Lowth, Robert. *De sacra poesi hebraeorum: praelectiones academicae oxonii habitae* (London, 1753).

Lowth, Robert and Michaelis Johannes David. *De sacra poesi hebraeorum: praelectiones academicae oxonii habitae* (*Notas et Epimetra Adiecit* 2) (1770).

Mably, Gabriel Bonnot, Abbé de. *Entretiens de Phocion, sur le rapport de la morale avec la politique* (Amsterdam, 1763).

Phocion's Conversations or the Relation between Morality and Politics (London, 1769).

Mandeville, Bernard. *The Fable of the Bees, or the Private Vices, Public Benefits*, 2 vols., ed. and annot. F.B. Kaye [1924] (Indianapolis, 1988),

Masaryk, Tomáš Garrigue. 'Pangermanism and the Zone of Small Nations', *The New Europe: A Weekly Review of Foreign Politics* I, 19 October 1916–11 January 1917 (London, 1917), 271–277.

'Pangermanism and the Eastern Question', *The New Europe: A Weekly Review of Foreign Politics* I, 19 October 1916–11 January 1917 (London, 1917), 2–19.

Modern Man and Religion (Freeport, NY, 1938, reprint 1970).

Mendelssohn, Moses. 'Über Vom Tode für das Vaterland,' *Briefe, die neueste Literatur betreffend* (1760), LB 181, 39–58.

[Anon.]. 'Ueber Iselin, I.: Philosophische und politische Versuche. Zurich: Orell 1760: Rezension', *Briefe, die neueste Literatur betreffend* (1760), LB (Literaturbrief) 138, 361–373.

'Ueber den in eben diesem Bändchen befindlichen Auszuge aus Dr. Browns Werke von den Englischen Sitten; Iselin, I, *Philosophische und politische Versuche*' (Zurich, 1760), *Briefe, die neueste Literatur betreffend* (1760), LB 139, 374–384.

'Von einer patriotischen Gesellschaft in der Schweiz, zum Besten der Sittenlehre und der Gesetzgebungswissenschaft. Gedanken darüber, Preisfragen dieser Gesellschaft für das Jahr 1763', *Briefe, die neueste Literatur betreffend* (1762), LB 123, 169–182.

'Nachricht', *Briefe, die neueste Literatur betreffend* (1763), LB 262, 136–140.

Millar, John. *The Origin of the Distinction of Ranks, or, an Inquiry into the Circumstances Which Give Rise to Influence and Authority in the Different Members of Society* (1771).

Montesquieu, Charles de Secondat, Baron de. *The Spirit of the Laws*, ed. and trans. Anne M. Cohler, Basia Carolyn Miller and Harold Samuel Stone (Cambridge, 1989).

Moser, Friedrich Carl von. *Beherzigungen* (Frankfurt, 1761).

Von dem deutschen National-Geist (Frankfurt am Main, 1765).

Moser, Friedrich Carl von. *Reliquien* (Frankfurt am Main, 1766).

Möser, Justus. '[Review of] Johann Jacob Bülau, *Noch etwas zum Nationalgeiste* (Lindau am Bodensee, 1766)', *Allgemeine deutsche Bibliothek*, VI:1 (1768).

'Vorrede', in *Osnabrückische Geschichte: allgemeine Einleitung* (Osnabrück, 1768).

'Deutsche Geschichte', in Johann Gottfried Herder, Johann Wolfgang Goethe, *Von deutscher Art und Kunst* (Leipzig, 1966).

Paine, Thomas. *Philosophical Writings*, ed. Bruce Kuklick (Cambridge, 1997), 155–264.

Percy, Thomas. *Reliques of Ancient English Poetry* (1765).

Raynal, Guillaume Thomas. *A Philosophical and Political History of the Settlements and Trade of the Europeans in the East and West Indies* [orig. 1770] (London, 1798), 6 vols.

Reinhold, Karl Leonhard. *Briefe über die Kantische Philosophie*, 2 vols. (Leipzig, 1792), II.

Riedel, Friedrich Justus. *Theorie der schönen Künste und Wissenschaften: Ein Auszug aus den Werken verschiedener Schriftsteller* (Jena, 1767).

Ueber das Publicum: Briefe an einige Glieder desselben (Jena, 1768).

Robertson, William. *The History of the Reign of the Emperor Charles V: A View of the Progress of Society in Europe, from the Subversion of the Roman Empire to the Beginning of the Sixteenth Century* [1769], *in idem, The Works of William Robertson, D.D. to Which Is Prefixed, An Account of the Life and Writings of the Author, by Dugald Stewart*. 8 vols. (London: T. Cadell, 1840) (III).

Robinet, Jean-Baptiste-René. *De la nature* [1763], 2 vols. (Amsterdam, 1766).

Rocker, Rudolf. *Nationalism and Culture* (Los Angeles, 1937).

Rousseau, Jean-Jacques. *Lettres écrites de la montagne* (1764).

Emile, or On Education, ed. and trans. Allan Bloom (New York, 1979).

'Discourse on the Sciences and Arts or First Discourse', in Rousseau, *The Discourses and Other Early Political Writings*, ed. and trans. Victor Gourevitch (Cambridge, 1997), 1–28.

'Observations [to Stanislas, King of Poland]', in *The Discourses and Other Early Political Writings*, ed. and trans. Victor Gourevitch (Cambridge, 1997), 32–51.

'Last Reply', in *The Discourses and Other Early Political Writings*, ed. and trans. Victor Gourevitch (Cambridge, 1997), 63–85.

'Discourse on the Origin and Foundations of Inequality among Men or Second Discourse', in *The Discourses and Other Early Political Writings*, ed. and trans. Victor Gourevitch (Cambridge, 1997), 111–188.

'Discourse on Political Economy', in *The Social Contract and Other Later Political Writings*, ed. and trans. Victor Gourevitch (Cambridge, 1997), 3–38.

'From the early version of the Social Contract known as the Geneva Manuscript', in *The Social Contract and Other Later Political Writings*, ed. and trans. Victor Gourevitch (Cambridge, 1997), 153–161.

'The State of War', in *The Social Contract and Other Later Political Writings*, ed. and trans. Victor Gourevitch (Cambridge, 1997), 162–176.

Schlegel, Friedrich. 'Versuch über den Begriff des Republikanismus, veranlasst durch die Kantische Schrift "Zum ewigen Frieden', in *Ewiger Friede?*

Dokumente um eine deutsche Diskussion um 1800, ed. Anita and Walter Dietze (Munich, 1989), 161–177.

Seneca, Lucius Annaeus. *Moral letters to Lucilius (Epistulae morales ad Lucilium)*, trans. Richard Mott Gummere (A Loeb Classical Library edition), 3 vols. (London, 1917–1945).

Sérionne, Accarias de. *Intérêts des nations de l'Europe, dévélopée rélativement au commerce* (Leiden, 1766).

Commerce de la Hollande ou Tableau du Commerce des Hollandois, 3 vols. (Amsterdam, 1768).

Sismondi, Jean-Charles-Léonard Simonde de. *Histoire des républiques italiennes du moyen age* (1809, 1819).

Sivers, Jegór von. *Humanität und Nationalität: eine livländische Säcularschrift zum Andenken Herders und zum Schutze livländischen Verfassungsrechtes* (Berlin, 1869).

Strube, David Georg, 'Zwey- und zwanzigste Abhandlung. Vom Ursprung der Landes-Hoheit in Teutschland', in *Nebenstunden*, IV (Hannover, 1755), 1–83.

Tucker, Josiah. *Essay on the Advantages and Disadvantages, Which Respectively Attend France and Great Britain with regard to Trade* (London 1749; new edition 1750).

Voltaire, François Marie Arouet de. *Le siècle de Louis XIV* (Berlin, 1751).

Wegelin, Johann Jacob. '[Review of] Thomas Abbt, *Vom Tode für das Vaterland* (1761)', in *Freymüthige Nachrichten Von Neuen Büchern, und andern zur Gelehrtheit gehörigen Sachen*, Achtzehnter Jahrgang, XXXIII (Zurich, 1761).

Politische und moralische Betrachtungen über die spartanische Gesetz-Gebung des Lykurgus (Lindau, 1763).

'Von dem Wahnsinn des Volks', in *Wegelin, Briefe über den Werth der Geschichte* (Berlin, 1783), 151–157.

Wirth, Johann Georg August. 'Rede von Wirth', *Das Nationalfest der Deutschen zu Hambach* (Neustadt, 1832), 41–43; English translation by Jeremiah Riemer, GHDI - Document - Page (ghi-dc.org) (visited on 28 April 2022).

Die Rechte des deutschen Volkes: Eine Verteidigungsrede vor den Assisen zu Landau (Nancy, 1833).

Fragmente zur Culturgeschichte, 2 vols. (Kaiserslauten, 1835/1836).

Zimmermann, Johann Georg. *Von dem Nationalstolze* (Zurich, 1758).

Secondary Sources

Adler, Hans. *Die Prägnanz des Dunklen: Gnoseologie—Ästhetik—Geschichtsphilosophie bei Johann Gottfried Herder* (Hamburg, 1990).

'Nation. Johann Gottfried Herders Umgang mit Konzept und Begriff', in *Unerledigte Geschichten: Der literarische Umgang mit Nationalität und Internationalität*, ed. Gesa von Essen und Horst Turk (Göttingen, 2000), 39–56.

'Herder's Concept of Humanity', in *A Companion to the Works of Johann Gottfried Herder*, ed. Hans Adler and Wulf Koepke (Rochester, NY, 2009), 93–116.

Adler, Hans and Wulf Koepke (eds.). *A Companion to the Works of Johann Gottfried Herder* (Rochester, NY, 2009).

Alimento, Antonella. 'Raynal, Accarias de Sérionne et le Pacte de Famille', in *Autour de l'abbé Raynal: genèse et enjeux politiques de l'Histoire des deux Indes*, ed. Antonella Alimento and Gianluigi Goggi (Ferney-Voltaire, 2018), 33–45.

Allison, Henry. 'Teleology and History in Kant: the Critical Foundations of Kant's Philosophy of History', in *Kant's Idea for a Universal History with a Cosmopolitan Aim: A Critical Guide*, ed. Amélie Oxenberg Rorty and James Schmidt (Cambridge, 2009), 29–45.

Ameriks, Karl. 'The Purposive Development of Human Capacities', in *Kant's Idea of a Universal History with a Cosmopolitan Aim: A Critical Guide*, ed. Amélie Oksenberg Rorty and James Schmidt (Cambridge, 2009), 46–67.

Anderson-Gold, Sharon. 'Kant and Herder', in *A Companion to the Philosophy of History and Historiography*, ed. A. Tucker (Oxford, 2008).

Arnold, Günter. 'Die Widerspiegelung der Französischen Revolution in Herders Korrespondenz', in *Impulse: Aufsätze, Quellen, Berichte zur deutschen Klassik und Romantik*, ed. Walter Dietze and Peter Goldammer, III (Berlin, Weimar, 1980), 41–89.

'Herder und Friedrich Gentz', in *Herder-Yearbook: Publications of the International Herder Society*, X (Columbia, 1992), 80–98.

Arnold, Günter, Klaus Kloocke and Ernest A. Menze. 'Herder's Reception and Influence', in *A Companion to the Works of Johann Gottfried Herder*, ed. Hans Adler and Wulf Koepke (Rochester, NY, 2009, 391–419.

Bader, Veit. 'Review: For Love of Country [Book Review]', in *Political Theory* 27:3 (1999), 379–397.

Bari, Bence László. 'New Worlds Tackling on Side-tracks: The National Concepts of T.G. Masaryk and Oszkár Jászi during the First World War (1914–1919)', in *The First World War and the Nationality Question in Europe: Global Impact and Local Dynamics*, ed. by Xosé M. Núñez Seixas (Leiden, 2020), 115–141.

Barnard, F. M. *Herder's Social and Political Thought: From Enlightenment to Nationalism* (Oxford, 1965).

'Introduction', in *J. G. Herder on Social and Political Culture*, ed. Barnard (London, Cambridge, 1969).

Self-Direction and Political Legitimacy: Rousseau and Herder (Oxford, 1988).

Herder on Nationality, Humanity, and History (Montreal, London, 2003).

Baumstark, Moritz. 'Vom *Esprit des lois* zum *Geist der Zeiten*. Herders Auseinandersetzung mit Montesquieu als Grundlegung seiner Geschichtsphilosophie', in *Sattelzeit: Historiographiegeschichtliche Revisionen*, ed. Elisabeth Décultot and Daniel Fulda (*Hallesche Beiträge zur Europäischen Aufklärung*) (Berlin, Boston, 2016), 54–82.

Beiser, Frederick C. *Enlightenment, Revolution and Romanticism: The Genesis of Modern German Political Thought* (Cambridge, MA, 1992).

The German Historicist Tradition (Oxford, 2011).

Benner, Erica. 'The Nation-State', in *Cambridge History of Philosophy in the Nineteenth Century 1790–1870*, ed. Allen W. Wood and Songsuk Susan Hahn (Cambridge, 2012), 699–730.

Berlin, Isaiah. 'The Counter-Enlightenment' [1973], in Berlin, *Against the Current*, ed. H. Hardy (New York, 1980), 1–24.

'Vico and Herder', in Berlin, *Three Critics of the Enlightenment: Vico, Hamann, Herder* (Princeton, NJ, London, 2000), 3–242.

Bičevskis, Rainis and Aija Taimņa. 'Johann Georg Hamanns kameralwissenschaftliche Studien und Johann Christoph Berens' *Vision von Riga: ein utopisches Projekt aus der zweiten Hälfte des achtzehnten Jahrhunderts*', Forschungen zur baltischen Geschichte, 8 (2013), 127–144.

Binkelmann, Christoph and Violetta Stolz. '1.4.3. Briefe zu Beförderung der Humanität', in *Herder Handbuch*, ed. Stefan Greif, Marion Heinz and Heinrich Clairmont (Paderborn, 2016), 216–232.

Binoche, Bertrand. 'Herder in 1774: An Incomplete Philosophy of History', in *A Companion to Enlightenment Historiography*, ed. Sophie Bourgault and Robert Sparling (Leiden, 2013), 189–216.

Blanning, T.C.W. *The French Revolutionary Wars* (London, 1986).

Blom, Hans. 'Sociability and Hugo Grotius', *History of European Ideas* (Special issue: *Sociability in Enlightenment Thought*, ed. Eva Piirimäe and Alexander Schmidt), 41:5 (2015), 589–604.

Blom, Hans, John Christian Laursen and Luisa Simonutti (eds.). *Monarchisms in the Age of Enlightenment: Liberty, Patriotism, and the Common Good* (Toronto, 2007).

Bohlman, Philip V. *Song Loves the Masses: Herder on Music and Nationalism* (Oakland, 2017).

Bondeli, Martin. 'Von Herder zu Kant, zwischen Kant und Herder, mit Herder gegen Kant – Karl Leonhard Reinhold', in *Herder und die Philosophie des deutschen Idealismus*, ed. Marion Heinz (Amsterdam, Atlanta, 1998), 203–234.

Bourke, Richard. *Empire and Revolution: The Political Life of Edmund Burke* (Princeton, 2015).

Brummack, Jürgen. 'Herders Polemik gegen die *Aufklärung*', in *Aufklärung und Gegenaufklärung in der europäischen Literatur, Philosophie und Politik von der Antike bis zur Gegenwart*, ed. Jochen Schmidt (Darmstadt, 1989), 277–293.

Brummack, Jürgen and Martin Bollacher. 'Kommentar', in *FHA*, IV, 916–970.

Bultmann, Christoph. 'Herder's Biblical Studies', in *A Companion to the Works of Johann Gottfried Herder*, ed. Hans Adler and Wulf Koepke (Rochester, NY, 2009), 233–245.

Burgdorf, Wolfgang. *Reichskonstitution und Nation: Verfassungsprojekte für das Heilige Römische Reich Deutscher Nation im politischen Schrifttum von 1648 bis 1806* (Mainz, 1998).

Carey, Daniel. *Locke, Shaftesbury, and Hutcheson: Contesting Diversity in the Enlightenment and Beyond* (Cambridge, 2009).

Cavallar, Georg. 'Cosmopolitanisms in Kant's Philosophy', *Ethics and Global Politics*, 5:2 (2012), 95–118.

'Kant and the Right of World Citizens: An Historical Interpretation', in *Critique of Cosmopolitan Reason: Timing and Spacing the Concept of World Citizenship*, ed. Rebecka Lettevall and Kristian Petrov (Oxford/Bern, 2014), 141–180.

Cavarzere, Marco 'The *New Science of Commerce* in the Holy Roman Empire: Véron de Forbonnais's Elémens du commerce and its German Readers', *History of European Ideas*, 40:8 (2014), 1130–1150.

Clark, Robert Thomas. 'Herder's Conception of *Kraft*', *Modern Language Association* 57:3 (1942), 737–752.

Herder: His Life and Thought (Berkeley, Los Angeles, 1955).

Clure, Graham. 'Rousseau, Diderot and the Spirit of Catherine the Great's Reforms,' *History of European Ideas*, 41:7 (2015), 883–908.

Cordemann, Claas. *Herders Christlicher Monismus: Eine Studie zur Grundlegung von Johann Gottfried Herders Christologie und Humanitätsideal* (Tübingen, 2010).

Couturier-Henrich, Clémence (ed. and introd.). *Übersetzen bei Johann Gottfried Herder* (Heidelberg, 2012).

Dann, Otto. 'Herder und die deutsche Bewegung', in *Johann Gottfried Herder 1744–1803*, ed. Gerhard Sauder (Hamburg 1987), 308–340.

Dent, Nicholas J. H. and Timothy O'Hagan. 'Rousseau on Amour-Propre', *Proceedings of the Aristotelian Society Supplementary Volume*, 72:1 (1998), 57–74.

DeSouza, Nigel. 'Language, Reason, and Sociability: Herder's Critique of Rousseau', *Intellectual History Review*, 22:2 (2012), 221–240.

'The Soul-Body Relationship and the Foundations of Morality: Herder contra Mendelssohn', *Herder Yearbook*, 21 (2014), 145–162.

'The Metaphysical and Epistemological Foundations of Herder's Philosophical Anthropology', in Herder. *Philosophy and Anthropology* (Oxford, 2017), 52–71.

'Herder's Theory of Organic Forces and Its Kantian Origins', in *Kant and His Contemporaries*, 2 vols., ed. Corey Dyck and Daniel O. Dahlstrom (II=*Aesthetics, History, Politics, and Religion)* (Cambridge, 2018), 109–130.

'The Ontological Foundations of Herder's Concept of Sympathy', in *Herder on Empathy and Sympathy/Einfühlung und Sympathie im Denken Herders*, ed. Eva Piirimäe, Liina Lukas and Johannes Schmidt (Leiden, 2020), 37–49.

Dobbek, Wilhelm. 'Johann Gottfried Herders Haltung im politischen Leben seiner Zeit', *Zeitschrift für Ostforschung*, 8 (1959), 321–387.

Dreitzel, Horst. 'Herders politische Konzepte', in *Johann Gottfried Herder, 1744–1803*, ed. Gerhard Sauder (Hamburg, 1987), 266–298.

Drews, Peter. *Herder und die Slaven: Materialien zur Wirkungsgeschichte bis zur Mitte des 19: Jahrhunderts* (Munich, 1990).

Eggel, Dominic, Andre Liebich and Deborah Mancini-Griffoli. 'Was Herder a Nationalist?', *The Review of Politics*, 69:1 (2007), 48–78.

Engel, Eva J. 'Habent Sua Fata Libelli. A Response to John Brown: Moses Mendelssohn on Evolution and Change in Poetry', *Hebrew Union College Annual* 53 (1982), 165–177.

Ergang, Robert Reinhold. *Herder and the Foundations of German Nationalism* (New York, 1976).

Evrigenis, Ioannis D. and Daniel Pellerin (eds. And trans.), 'Introduction', in *Johann Gottfried Herder: Another Philosophy of History and Selected Political Writings* (Indianapolis and Cambridge, 2004), ix–xxxix.

Fontana, Biancamaria. 'The Napoleonic Empire and the Europe of Nations', in *The Idea of Europe: From Antiquity to the European Union*, ed. Anthony Pagden (Cambridge, 2002), 116–128.

Forster, Michael N. 'Introduction', in *PW*, vii–xxxv.

(ed.). 'Note on Texts and Translations', in *PW*, xiii–xiiv.

After Herder: Philosophy of Language in the German Tradition (Oxford, 2010).

Frazer, Michael L. *The Enlightenment of Sympathy: Justice and the Moral Sentiments in the Eighteenth Century and Today* (Oxford, 2010).

Gadamer, Hans-Georg. *Volk und Geschichte im Denken Herders* (Frankfurt am Main, 1942).

Gaier, Ulrich. 'Kommentar', in *FHA*, I, 811–1334.

'Kommentar', in *FHA*, III, 839–927.

'Myth, Mythology, New Mythology', in *A Companion to the Works of Johann Gottfried Herder*, ed. Hans Adler and Wulf Koepke (Rochester, NY, 2009), 164–188.

Garsten, Bryan. 'Representative Government and Popular Sovereignty', in *Political Representation*, ed. Ian Shapiro, Susan C. Stokes and Elisabeth Jean Wood (Cambridge, 2010), 90–110.

'Benjamin Constant's Liberalism and the Political Theology of the General Will', in *The General Will: The Evolution of a Concept*, ed. J. Farr and D. Williams (Cambridge, 2015), 382–401.

Gaukroger, Stephen. *The Collapse of Mechanism and the Rise of Sensibility: Science and the Shaping of Modernity, 1680–1760* (Oxford, 2012).

Gisi, Lucas Marco. 'Die anthropologische Basis von Iselins Geschichtsphilosophie', in *Isaak Iselin und die Geschichtsphilosophie der europäischen Aufklärung*, ed. Lucas Marco Gisi and Wolfgang Rother (*Studien zur Geschichte der Wissenschaften in Basel: Neue Reihe, VI*) (Basel, 2011), 124–152.

Einbildungskraft und Mythologie: Die Verschränkung von Anthropologie und Geschichte im 18: Jahrhundert (Berlin, New York, 2007).

Gjesdal, Kristin. *Herder's Hermeneutics: History, Poetry, Enlightenment* (Cambridge, 2017).

Goldenbaum, Ursula. 'Einführung', in Jean-Jacques Rousseau, *Abhandlung von dem Ursprunge der Ungleichheit*, trans. M. Mendelssohn, ed. U. Goldenbaum (Weimar, 2000), 1–63.

Gourevitch, Victor. 'Introduction', in Jean-Jacques Rousseau, *The Social Contract and Other Later Political Writings*, ed. and trans. Victor Gourevitch (Cambridge, 1997), ix–xxxi.

Graubner, Hans. 3.2.1 *Dithyrambische Rhapsodie über die Rhapsodie kabbalistischer Prose*, in *Herder Handbuch*, ed. Stefan Greif, Marion Heinz and Heinrich Clairmont (Paderborn, 2016), 395–421.

'Spätaufklärer im aufgeklärten Riga: Hamann und Herder', *Zeitschrift für Ostforschung*, 43:4 (1994), 517–533.

Greenfeld, Liah. *Nationalism: Five Roads to Modernity* (Cambridge, MA, London, 1992).

Greif, Stefan. 'Herder's Aesthetics and Poetics', in *A Companion to the Works of Johann Gottfried Herder*, ed. Hans Adler and Wulf Koepke (Rochester, NY, 2009), 141–164.

3.1 Einleitung. Ästhetik, Poetik, Literaturkritik, in *Herder Handbuch*, ed. Stefan Greif, Marion Heinz and Heinrich Clairmont (Paderborn, 2016), 387–395.

'3.2.2 *Über die neuere Literatur*', in *Herder Handbuch*, ed. Stefan Greif, Marion Heinz and Heinrich Clairmont (Paderborn, 2016), 431–443.

'3.3.1 *Auszug aus einem Briefwechsel über Ossian und die Lieder der Völker, Shakespear, Gefundene Blätter aus den neuesten deutschen Litteraturannalen, Beiträge zu Lavaters Physiognomischen Fragmenten*', in *Herder Handbuch*, ed. Stefan Greif, Marion Heinz and Heinrich Clairmont (Paderborn, 2016), 485–495.

Greif, Stefan, Marion Heinz and Heinrich Clairmont (eds.). *Herder Handbuch* (Paderborn, 2016).

Grunert, Frank. 'The Reception of Hugo Grotius's De iure belli ac pacis in the Early German Enlightenment', in *Early Modern Natural Law Theories: Contexts and Strategies in the Early Enlightenment*, ed. Timothy Hochstrasser and Peter Schröder (*Archives internationales d'histoire des idées/International Archives of the History of Ideas*, vol. 186) (Dordrecht, Boston, London 2003), 89–105.

Guyer, Paul. *Kant on Freedom, Law and Happiness* (Cambridge, 2000).

'The crooked timber of mankind', in *Kant's Idea for a Universal History with a Cosmopolitan Aim: A Critical Guide*, ed. Amélie Oksenberg Rorty and James Schmidt (Cambridge, 2009), 129–149.

Haakonssen, Knud. *Natural Law and Moral Philosophy: From Grotius to the Scottish Enlightenment* (Cambridge, 1996).

Hambsch, Björn. '...*ganz andre Beredsamkeit*': *Transformationen antiker und moderner Rhetorik bei Johann Gottfried Herder* (Tübingen, 2007).

Hasquin, Hervé. 'Jacques Accarias de Sérionne, économiste et publiciste français au service des Pays Bas autrichiens', *Études sur le XVIIIe siècle* (Brussel, 1974), I, 159–170.

Häfner, Ralph. '*L'âme est un neurologie en miniature*: Herder und die Neurophysiologie Charles Bonnets', in *Der ganze Mensch: Anthropologie und Literatur im achtzehnten Jahrhundert*, ed. Hans-Jürgen Schings (Stuttgart, Weimar, 1994), 390–409.

Johann Gottfried Herders Kulturentstehungslehre: Studien zu den Quellen und zur Methode seines Geschichtsdenkens (Hamburg, 1995).

Haym, Rudolf. *Herder nach seinem Leben und seinen Werken dargestellt*, 2 vols. (Berlin, 1958).

Heinz, Marion. 'Die Bestimmung des Menschen: Herder contra Mendelssohn', in *Philosophie der Endlichkeit: Festschrift für Erich Christian Schröder zum 65: Geburtstag*, ed. Beate Niemeyer and Dirk Schütze (Würzburg, 1991), 263–285.

Sensualistischer Idealismus: Untersuchungen zur Erkenntnistheorie des jungen Herder (1763–1778) (*Studien zum achtzehnten Jahrhundert*, XVII) (Hamburg, 1994).

'Historismus oder Metaphysik? Zu Herders Bückeburger Geschichtsphilosophie', in *Johann Gottfried Herder: Geschichte und Kultur*, ed. Martin Bollacher (Würzburg, 1994), 75–85.

'Kulturtheorien der Aufklärung: Herder und Kant', in *Nationen und Kulturen: Zum 250. Geburtstag Johann Gottfried Herders*, ed. Regine Otto (Würzburg, 1996), 139–152.

Heinz, Marion and Heinrich Clairmont. 'Herder's Epistemology', in *A Companion to the Works of Johann Gottfried Herder*, ed. Hans Adler and Wulf Koepke (Rochester, NY, 2009), 42–64.

'Vernunft ist nur Eine – Untersuchungen zur Vernunftkonzeption in Herders Metakritik', in *Herders Metakritik: Analysen und Interpretationen*, ed. Marion Heinz (Stuttgart-Bad Cannstatt, 2013), 163–194.

'1.2.4 Vom Erkennen und Empfinden der menschlichen Seele', in *Herder Handbuch*, ed. Stefan Greif, Marion Heinz and Heinrich Clairmont (Paderborn, 2016), 122–140.

'1.2.2 *Philosophie zum Besten des Volks*', in *Herder Handbuch*, ed. Stefan Greif, Marion Heinz and Heinrich Clairmont (Paderborn, 2016), 58–71.

'Anthropology and the Critique of Metaphysics in the Early Herder', in *Herder: Philosophy and Anthropology*, ed. Anik Waldow and Nigel DeSouza (Oxford, 2017), 30–51.

'Sympathie. Zur Palingenesie stoischen Denkens in Herders Kalligone', in *Herder on Empathy and Sympathy/Einfühlung und Sympathie im Denken Herders*, ed. Eva Piirimäe, Liina Lukas and Johannes Schmidt (Leiden, 2020), 50–73.

Hien, Markus. *Altes Reich und Neue Dichtung: Literarisch-Politisches Reichsdenken zwischen 1750 und 1830* (Berlin, 2015).

'Mascovisch richtig oder voltärisch schön? Herders „idiotistische Geschichtsschreibung" im Wettkampf der Nationen', in *Sattelzeit: Historiographiegeschichtliche Revisionen*), ed. Elisabeth Décultot and Daniel Fulda (Berlin, Boston, 2016), 83–101.

Hont, István. *Jealousy of Trade: International Competition and the Nation-State in Historical Perspective* (Cambridge, MA, 2005).

'The Early Enlightenment Debate on Luxury and Commerce', in *Cambridge History of Eighteenth-Century Political Thought*, ed. Mark Goldie and Robert Wokler (Cambridge, 2006), 379–418.

Politics in Commercial Society, ed. Béla Kapossy and Michael Sonenscher (Cambridge, MA, 2015).

Hüls, Elisabeth. *Johann Georg August Wirth: Ein politisches Leben im Vormärz* (*Beiträge zur Geschichte des Parlamentarismus und der politischen Parteien*, 139) (Düsseldorf, 2004).

Hundert, Ed J. *The Enlightenment Fable: Bernard Mandeville and the Discovery of Society* (Cambridge 1994).

Hunter, Ian, Frank Grunert, Thomas Ahnert (ed. and trans.). 'Introduction', in *Christian Thomasius: Essays on Church, State, and Politics* (*Natural Law and Enlightenment Classics*, ed. Knud Haakonsson) (Indianapolis, 2007), ix–xxi.

Im Hof, Ulrich. 'Mendelssohn und Iselin', in *Moses Mendelssohn und die Kreise seiner Wirksamkeit*, ed. Michael Albrecht et al. (Tübingen, 1994), 61–92.

Irmscher, Hans Dietrich. 'Herder's Humanitätsbriefe', in *FHA*, VII, 809–840.

'Aspekte der Geschichtsphilosophie Johann Gottfried Herders', in *Herder und die Philosophie des deutschen Idealismus*, ed. Marion Heinz (Amsterdam, 1997), 5–47.

Irmscher, 'Die Kontroverse zwischen Kant und Herder über die Methode der Geschichtsphilosophie [1987]', in Irmscher, *Weitstrahlsinniges Denken: Studien zu Johann Gottfried Herder*, ed. Marion Heinz and Violetta Stolz (Würzburg, 2009), 295–334.

Jaumann, Herbert. *Rousseau in Deutschland: Neue Beiträge zur Erforschung seiner Rezeption* (Berlin, New York, 1995).

Johannsen, Jochen. '1.4.1 Auch eine Philosophie der Geschichte der Bildung der Menschheit', in *Herder Handbuch*, ed. Stefan Greif, Marion Heinz and Heinrich Clairmont (Paderborn, 2016), 160–170.

'Politische Rezeption', in *Herder Handbuch*, ed. Stefan Greif, Marion Heinz and Heinrich Clairmont (Paderborn, 2016), 617–677.

Jäger, Hans-Wolf. 'Herder und die Französische Revolution', in *Johann Gottfried Herder, 1744–1803*, ed. Gerhard Sauder (Hamburg, 1987), 299–307.

Kapossy, Béla. 'The Sociable Patriot: Isaak Iselin's Protestant Reading of Jean-Jacques Rousseau', *History of European Ideas*, 27:2 (2001), 153–170.

Iselin contra Rousseau: Sociable Patriotism and the History of Mankind (Basel, 2006).

'Iselins „Geschichte der Menschheit" als Friedensschrift', in *Isaak Iselin und die Geschichtsphilosophie der europäischen Aufklärung*, ed. Lucas Marco Gisi and Wolfgang Rother (*Studien zur Geschichte der Wissenschaften in Basel: Neue Reihe, VI*) (Basel, 2011), 100–123.

Kaufmann, H.-H. 'F. C. Moser als Politiker und Publizist', *Quellen und Forschungen zur hessischen Geschichte*, XII (Darmstadt, 1931).

Kedourie, Elie. *Nationalism* (Oxford, Cambridge, MA, 1993).

Keohane, Nannerl O., *Philosophy and the State in France: The Renaissance to the Enlightenment* (Princeton, 1980).

Klein, Jacob. 'The Stoic Argument from Oikeiōsis', in *Oxford Studies in Ancient Philosophy* 50, ed. Victor Caston (Oxford, 2016), 143–200.

Kleingeld, Pauline. *Kant and Cosmopolitanism: The Philosophical Ideal of World Citizenship* (Cambridge, 2012).

Knudsen, Jonathan. *Justus Möser and the German Enlightenment* (Cambridge, 1985).

Koepke, Wulf. 'Humanität in Goethes Weimar. Herder nach der Französischen Revolution', in *'Verteufelt human'?: zum Humanitätsideal der Weimarer Klassik*, ed. Volker C. Dörr, Michael Hofmann (Berlin, 2008), 47–68.

'Herder's Views on the Germans and Their Future Literature', in *A Companion to the Works of Johann Gottfried Herder*, ed. Hans Adler and Wulf Koepke (Rochester, NY, 2009), 213–232.

Körner, Axel. 'National Movements against Nation States', in *The 1848 Revolutions and European Political Thought*, ed. D. Moggach and G. Stedman Jones (Cambridge, 2018), 345–382.

Laan, J. M. van der. 'Johann Gottfried Herder on War and Peace', *Monatshefte*, 101 (Madison, 2009), 335–346.

Langewiesche, Dieter and Georg Schmidt (eds.). *Föderative Nation: Deutschlandkonzepte von der Reformation bis zum Ersten Weltkrieg* (Munich, 2000).

Laur, Mati. 'Der Aufgeklärte Absolutismus der Kaiserin Katharina II im Baltikum', in *Narva und die Ostseeregion*, ed. Karsten Brüggemann (Narva, 2004), 185–192.

Legaspi, Michael. *The Death of Scripture and the Rise of Biblical Studies* (Oxford, 2010).

Leppik, Lea. 'The Provincial Reforms of Catherine the Great and the Baltic Common Identity', *Ajalooline Ajakiri = The Estonian Historical Journal*, 1:2 (139: 140) (2012), 55–78.

Liebich, André. 'Globalising the 'Principle of Nationality'', in *Nationalism and Globalisation: Conflicting and Complimentary?*, ed. Daphne Halikiopoulou and Sofia Vasilopoulou (New York, 2011), 27–40.

Lifschitz, Avi. *Language and Enlightenment: The Berlin Debates of the Eighteenth Century* (Oxford, 2012).

'Genesis for Historians: Thomas Abbt on Biblical and Conjectural Accounts of Human Nature', *History of European Ideas* (Special Issue: *Sociability in Enlightenment Thought*, ed. Eva Piirimäe and Alexander Schmidt), 41:5 (2015), 605–618.

'Between Friedrich Meinecke and Ernst Cassirer: Isaiah Berlin's Bifurcated Enlightenment', in *Isaiah Berlin and the Enlightenment*, ed. L. Brockliss and R. Robertson (Oxford, 2016), 51–66.

Lifschitz, Avi (ed.), *Engaging with Rousseau: Reaction and Interpretation from the Eighteenth Century to the Present* (Cambridge, 2016).

Lohmeier, Dieter. 'Herder und der Emkendorfer Kreis', in *Nordelbingen: Beiträge zur Kunst- und Kulturgeschichte: Im Auftrag der Gesellschaft für Schleswig-Holsteinische Geschichte*, ed. Olaf Klose and Ellen Redlefsen, vol. 35 (Heide and Holstein, 1966).

Louden, Robert B. *The World We Want: How and Why the Ideals of the Enlightenment Still Elude Us* (Oxford, 2007).

Kant's Human Being: Essays on His Theory of Human Nature (Oxford, 2011).

Lukas, Liina. '...mit Treue, Lust und Liebe: Einfühlung in das Volkslied', in *Herder on Empathy and Sympathy/Einfühlung und Sympathie im Denken Herders*, ed. Eva Piirimäe, Liina Lukas and Johannes Schmidt (Leiden, 2020), 272–296.

Lunn Eugene. *Prophet of Community: The Romantic Socialism of Gustav Landauer* (Berkeley, 1973).

Maliks, Reidar. *Kant's Politics in Context* (Oxford, 2014).

Markworth, Tino. 'Zur Selbstdarstellung Johann Gottfried Herders in den ersten Bückeburger Jahren', in *Bückeburger Gespräche über Johann Gottfried Herder 1988*, ed. Brigitte Poschmann (Rinteln, 1989), 81–97.

'Unterwegs zum Historismus. Der Wandel des geschichtsphilosophischen Denkens Herders von 1771 bis 1773', in *Johann Gottfried Herder - Geschichte und Kultur*, ed. Martin Bollacher (Würzburg, 1994), 51–59.

Maurer, Michael. 'Die Geschichtsphilosophie des jungen Herder in ihrem Verhältnis zur Aufklärung', in *Johann Gottfried Herder, 1744–1803*, ed. Gerhard Sauder (Hamburg, 1987), 141–155.

McDaniel, Iain. 'Honour and Pride in Adam Ferguson's Conception of Modern Patriotism', in *Human Nature as the Basis of Morality and Society in Early Modern Society*, ed. Juhana Lemetti and Eva Piirimäe *(Acta Philosophica Fennica, 83)* (2007), 105–120.

'Enlightened History and the Decline of Nations: Ferguson, Raynal, and the Contested Legacies of the Dutch Republic', *History of European Ideas*, 36:2 (2012), 203–216 (211–215).

Adam Ferguson in the Scottish Enlightenment: The Roman Past and Europe's Future (Cambridge, MA, London, 2013).

'Philosophical History and the Science of Man in Scotland: Adam Ferguson's Response to Rousseau', *Modern Intellectual History*, 10:3 (2013), 543–568.

'Unsocial Sociability in the Scottish Enlightenment: Ferguson and Kames on War, Sociability and the Foundations of Patriotism', *History of European Ideas* (Special issue: *Sociability in Enlightenment Thought*, ed. Eva Piirimäe and Alexander Schmidt), 41:5 (2015) 662–682.

McPhee, Peter. *The French Revolution 1789–1799* (Oxford, 2002).

Meinecke, Friedrich. *Weltbürgertum und Nationalstaat: Studien zur Genesis des deutschen Nationalstaats* (Munich, Berlin, 1907); Eng. Translation: '*Cosmopolitanism and the National State*', trans. Felix Gilbert (Princeton, NJ, 1970).

Historism: The Rise of a New Historical Outlook, trans. J. E. Anderson; with a foreword by Sir Isaiah Berlin (London, 1972; German original 1936).

Meineke, Christoph. 'Die Vortheile unserer Vereinigung: Hamanns Dangeuil-Beylage im Lichte der Debatte um den handeltreibenden Adel', in *Johann Georg Hamann: Religion und Gesellschaft*, ed. M. Beetz and R. Andre (Halle, 2012), 46–71.

Melzer, Arthur M. *The Natural Goodness of Man: On the System of Rousseau's Thought* (Chicago, 1990).

Menges, Karl. 'Herder on National, Popular and World Literature', in *A Companion to the Works of Johann Gottfried Herder*, ed. Hans Adler and Wulf Koepke (Rochester, NY, 2009), 188–212.

Menze, Ernest A. and Karl Menges. 'Commentary to the Translations', in *HEW*, 235–334.

Milton, Patrick. 'Guarantee and Intervention: The Assessment of the Peace of Westphalia in International Law and Politics by Authors of Natural Law and of Public Law, c. 1650–1806', in *The Law of Nations and Natural Law, 1625–1850*, ed. Simone Zurbuchen (Leiden, 2019), 186–226 (196–197).

Mommsen, Wolfgang J. 'German Liberalism in the Nineteenth Century', in *The Cambridge History of Nineteenth-Century Political Thought*, ed. Gareth Stedman Jones and Gregory Claeys (Cambridge, 2011), 409–432.

Mook, Anette. *Die freie Entwicklung innerlicher Kraft: Die Grenzen der Anthropologie in den frühen Schriften der Brüder von Humboldt* (Göttingen, 2012).

Moore, Gregory. 'Introduction', in *SWA*, 1–30.

Muthu, Sankar. *Enlightenment against Empire* (Princeton, 2003).

'Conquest, Commerce and Cosmopolitanism in Enlightenment Political Thought', in *Empire and Modern Political Thought*, ed. Sankar Muthu (Cambridge, 2012), 199–231.

Nakhimovsky, Isaac. *The Closed Commercial State: Perpetual Peace and Commercial Society from Rousseau to Fichte* (Princeton, NJ, 2011).

Nassar, Dalia. 'Hermeneutics and Nature', in *The Cambridge Companion to Hermeneutics*, ed. Michael Forster and Kristin Gjesdal (Cambridge, 2017), 37–64.

Nelson, Eric. *The Greek Tradition in Republican Thought* (Cambridge, 2004).

Neuhouser, Frederick. *Rousseau's Theodicy of Self-Love: Evil, Rationality, and the Drive for Recognition* (Oxford, 2008).

'Jean-Jacques Rousseau and the Origins of Autonomy', *Inquiry*, 54 (2011), 478–93.

Norton, Robert E. *Herder's Aesthetics and the European Enlightenment* (Ithaca, London, 1991).

'The Myth of the Counter-Enlightenment', *Journal of the History of Ideas*, 68:4 (2007), 635–658.

Nowitzki, Hans-Peter. 'I. Biographie', in *Herder Handbuch*, ed. Stefan Greif, Marion Heinz and Heinrich Clairmont (Paderborn, 2016), 23–38.

Noyes, John. *Herder: Aesthetics against Imperialism* (Toronto, 2015).

(ed.). *Herder's Essay on Being: A Translation and Critical Commentary* (Rochester, 2019).

Nuñez Seixas, Xosé M. 'Wilson's Unexpected Friends: the Transnational Impact of the First World War on Western European Nationalist Movements', in *The First World War and the Nationality Question in Europe: Global Impact and Local Dynamics*, ed. by Xosé M. Núñez Seixas (Leiden, 2020), 37–64.

O'Brien, Karen. *Narratives of Enlightenment: Cosmopolitan History from Voltaire to Gibbon* (Cambridge, 1997).

Patten, Alan. 'The Most Natural State: Herder and Nationalism', in *History of Political Thought* XXXI (2010), 658–689.

Pénisson, Pierre. 'Nachwort. Die Palingenesie der Schriften: die Gestalt des Herderschen Werks', in *HWP*, I, 864–924.

Piirimäe, Eva. 'Thomas Abbt (1738–1766) and the Philosophical Genesis of German Nationalism', unpublished Ph.D. Thesis (Cambridge University, 2006).

'The Vicissitudes of Noble National Pride: Johann Georg von Zimmermann's (1728–1795) Theory of Patriotism', in *Human Nature as the Basis of Morality and Society in Early Modern Philosophy*, ed. Juhana Lemetti and Eva Piirimäe, *Acta Philosophica Fennica* 83 (Helsinki, 2007), 121–142.

'Dying for the Fatherland: Thomas Abbt's Theory of Aesthetic Patriotism', *History of European Ideas*, 35:2 (2009), 194–208.

'Monarchisms, Republicanisms, and Enlightenments', *History of European Ideas*, 36:1 (2010), 125–129.

'*Humanität* versus Nationalism as the Moral Foundation of the Russian Empire: Jegór von Sivers' Herderian cosmopolitanism', in *Ajalooline Ajakiri=The Estonian Historical Journal*, 139:140 (1:2) (2012), 79–113.

'Herder and Cosmopolitanism', in *Critique of Cosmopolitan Reason: Timing and Spacing the Concept of World Citizenship*, ed. Rebecka Lettevall and Kristian Petrov (Oxford, Bern et al., 2014), 181–213.

'Philosophy, Sociability and Modern Patriotism: Young Herder between Rousseau and Abbt', *History of European Ideas* (Special issue: *Sociability in Enlightenment Thought*, ed. Eva Piirimäe and Alexander Schmidt), 41:5 (2015), 640–661.

'Herder, Berlin and the Counter-Enlightenment', *Eighteenth-Century Studies*, 49:1 (2015), 71–76.

Piirimäe, Eva and Alexander Schmidt. 'Between Morality and Anthropology: Sociability in Enlightenment Thought', in *History of European Ideas* (Special issue: *Sociability in Enlightenment Thought*, ed. Eva Piirimäe and Alexander Schmidt), 41:5 (2015), 571–588.

'Sociability, Nationalism and Cosmopolitanism in Herder's Early Philosophy of History', *History of Political Thought*, 36:3 (2015), 521–559.

'State-Machines, Commerce and the Progress of *Humanität* in Europe: Herder's response to Kant in "Ideas for the Philosophy of History of Mankind"', in *Commerce and Peace in the Enlightenment*, ed. Béla Kapossy, Isaac Nakhimovsky and Richard Whatmore (Cambridge, 2017), 155–191.

'Human Rights and their Realisation in the World', in *Passions, Politics and the Limits of Society* (*Helsinki Yearbook of Intellectual History*, 1), ed. Heikki Haara, Mikko Immanen and Koen Stapelbroek (Berlin, 2020).

Piirimäe, Eva, Liina Lukas, and Johannes Schmidt (eds.). *Herder on Empathy and Sympathy/Einfühlung und Sympathie im Denken Herders* (Leiden, 2020).

Piirimäe, Eva and Marion Heinz. 'Johann Gottfried Herder', in *Encyclopedia of the Philosophy of Law and Social Philosophy*, ed. Mortimer Sellers and Stephan Kirste (Dordrecht, 2022), 1–5. https://doi.org/10.1007/978-94-007-6730-0_890-1 (online version).

Piirimäe, Kaarel. 'Federalism in the Baltic: Interpretations of Self-Determination and Sovereignty in Estonia in the First Half of the 20th Century', *East Central Europe*, 39 (2012), 237–265.

Pizer, John. 'The German Response to Kant's Essay on Perpetual Peace: Herder Contra the Romantics', *The Germanic Review: Literature, Culture, Theory*, 87:4 (2007), 343–368.

Pocock, J. G. A. *Barbarism and Religion*, II=*Narratives of Civil Government* (Cambridge, 1999).

Barbarism and Religion, IV=*Barbarians, Savages and Empires* (Cambridge, 2005).

Proß, Wolfgang. 'Anhang. Amerkungen [*Geschichte der lyrischen Dichtkunst*]', in *HWP*, I, 693–724.

'Anhang. Amerkungen [*Über die neuere deutsche Literatur*]', in *HWP*, I, 725–803.

'Anmerkungen. [*Journal meiner Reise*]', in *HWP*, I, 804–820.

'Anhang. Amerkungen [Aus: *Von Deutscher Art und Kunst*]', in *HWP*, I, 820–849.

'Anhang. Anmerkungen [*Auch eine Philosophie der Geschichte*]', in *HWP*, I, 848–863.

'Anmerkungen [*Über den Ursprung der Sprache*]', in *HWP*, II (1987), 905–983.

'Nachwort. Herder und die Anthropologie der Aufklärung', in *HWP*, II, 1128–1216.

'Anhang. [*Aus Herders Nachlaß*]', in *HWP*, II, 1217–1229.

'Nachwort. *Natur* und *Geschichte* in Herders *Ideen zur Philosophie der Geschichte der Menschheit*', in *HWP*, III/1, 839–1040.

Proß, Wolfgang/Herder. 'Dokumentarischer Anhang', in *HWP*, III:1, 1043–1158.

'Anmerkungen [*Ideen*]', in *HWP*, III/2.

'Die Begründung der Geschichte aus der Natur: Herders Konzept von 'Gesetzen' in der Geschichte', in *Wissenschaft als kulturelle Praxis, 1750–1900*, ed. Hans-Erich Bödeker et al. (Göttingen, 1999), 187–226.

'Naturalism, Anthropology, Culture', in *The Cambridge History of Eighteenth-Century Political Thought*, ed. Mark Goldie and Robert Wokler (Cambridge, 2006), 218–247.

'Die Ordnung der Zeiten und Räume. Herder zwischen Aufklärung und Historismus', in *Vernunft – Freiheit – Humanität: Über Johann Gottfried Herder und einige seiner Zeitgenossen: Festgabe für Günter Arnold zum 65: Geburtstag*, ed. Claudia Taszus (Eutin, 2008), 9–73.

'Geschichte als Provokation zur Geschichtsphilosophie', in *Isaak Iselin und die Geschichtsphilosophie der europäischen Aufklärung*, ed. Lucas Marco Gisi and Wolfgang Rother (*Studien zur Geschichte der Wissenschaften in Basel: Neue Reihe, VI*) (Basel, 2011), 201–265.

'1.4.2 *Ideen zur Philosophie der Geschichte der Menschheit*', in *Herder Handbuch*, ed. Stefan Greif, Marion Heinz and Heinrich Clairmont (Paderborn, 2016), 171–215.

'Kolonialismuskritik aus dem Geist der Geschichtsphilosophie: Raynal, Herder, Dobrizhoffer und der Fall Paraguay', in *Raynal—Herder—Merkel:*

Transformationen der Antikolonialismusdebatte in der europäischen Aufklärung, ed. Mix York-Gothard and Hinrich Ahrend (Heidelberg, 2017), 17–73.

'Geschichtliches Handeln und seine Nemesis: Visionäre der Geschichte in der Zeit der Französischen Revolution', in *Gestaltbarkeit der Geschichte*, ed. Kurt Bayertz, Matthias Hoesch (Hamburg, 2019), 81–116.

'Diversus cum diversis: John Barclays Icon animorum (1614) und Herders Auch eine Philosophie der Geschichte', in *Herder on Empathy and Sympathy/ Einfühlung und Sympathie im Denken Herders*, ed. Eva Piirimäe, Liina Lukas and Johannes Schmidt (Leiden, 2020), 119–157.

'Herder zwischen Restauration, Vormärz und Reichsgründung—Zur politischen und anthropologischen Interpretation seines Werkes (1805–1870)', in *Herder und das neunzehnte Jahrhundert*, ed. Liisa Steinby (Heidelberg, 2020), 119–148.

Reill, Peter Hanns. *Vitalizing Nature in the Enlightenment* (Berkeley, 2005).

'Eighteenth-Century Uses of Vitalism in Constructing the Human Sciences', in *Biology and Ideology from Descartes to Dawkins*, ed. Denis R. Alexander and Ronald L. Numbers (Chicago, 2010), 61–87.

Reiss, Hans S. 'Introduction to Reviews of Herder's *Ideas on the Philosophy of Mankind and Conjectures on the Beginning of Human History*', in Kant, *Political Writings*, ed. H.S. Reiss and trans. H.B. Nisbet (Cambridge, 2000), 250–272.

Renner, Kaspar. 'Herder und der geistliche Stand. Neue Perspektiven für die germanistische Forschung', in *Deutsche Vierteljahrsschrift für Literaturwissenschaft und Geistesgeschichte 89* (2015), 198–234.

'*Ausweg zu Liedern fremder Völker*. Antikoloniale Perspektiven in Herders Volksliedprojekt', in *Raynal—Herder—Merkel: Transformationen der Antikolonialismusdebatte in der europäischen Aufklärung*, ed. Mix York-Gothard and Hinrich Ahrend (Heidelberg, 2017), 107–141.

Redekop, Benjamin W. *Enlightenment and Community: Lessing, Abbt, Herder and the Quest for the German Public* (Montreal, London, 2000).

Ripstein, Arthur. *Force and Freedom: Kant's Legal and Political Philosophy* (Cambridge, MA, 2009).

Rivers, Isabel. *Reason, Grace, and Sentiment*, 2 vols (II = From Shaftesbury to Hume) (Cambridge, 2000).

Robertson, John. *The Case for the Enlightenment* (Cambridge, 2005), 308–334.

'Sacred History and Political Thought: Neapolitan Responses to the Problem of Sociability after Hobbes', *The Historical Journal*, 56:1 (2013), 1–29 (4).

'Sociability in Sacred Historical Perspective, 1650–1800', in *Markets, Morals, Politics: Jealousy of Trade and the History of Political Thought*, ed. Béla Kapossy, Isaac Nakhimovsky, Sophus A. Reinert and Richard Whatmore (Cambridge, MA, 2018), 53–81.

'Herders Bückeburger *Bekehrung*', in *Bückeburger Gespräche über Johann Gottfried Herder 1979*, ed. Brigitte Poschmann (Rinteln, 1980), 17–30.

Rohbeck, Johannes. 'La philosophie de l'histoire chez Antoine-Yves Goguet: Chronique biblique et Progrés historique', in *Dix-huitième siècle* 34 (2002), 257–266.

Rosenblatt, Helena. *Rousseau and Geneva: From the First Discourse to the Social Contract, 1749–1762* (Cambridge, 1997).

Rouché, Max. *La philosophie de l'histoire de Herder* (Paris, 1940).

Sauder, Gerhard. 'Die Darstellung von Aufklärung in Herders Adrastea und die Kritik Schillers und Goethes', in *Aufklärung und Weimarer Klassik im Dialog*, ed. Andre Rudolf and Ernst Stöckmann (Tübingen, 2009), 169–185.

Schmidt-Biggemann, Wilhelm. 'Elemente von Herders Nationalkonzept', in *Nationen und Kulturen: Zum 250. Geburtstag von Johann Gottfried Herder*, ed. Regine Otto (Würzburg, 1996), 27–34.

Sebastiani, Silvia. 'Conjectural History vs. The Bible: Eighteenth-Century Scottish Historians and the Idea of History in the *Encyclopedia Britannica*', *Storia della Storiographica* 39 (2001), 39–50.

  'National Characters and Race: A Scottish Enlightenment Debate', in *Character, Self, and Sociability in the Scottish Enlightenment*, ed. Thomas Ahnert and Susan Manning (New York, 2011), 187–205.

Schmidt, Alexander. 'The Liberty of the Ancients? Friedrich Schiller and Aesthetic Republicanism', *History of Political Thought*, 30:2 (2009), 286–314.

  'Ein Vaterland ohne Patrioten? Die Krise des Reichspatriotismus im 18. Jahrhundert', in *Die deutsche Nation im frühneuzeitlichen Europa: Politische Ordnung und kulturelle Identität?*, ed. Georg Schmidt (Munich, 2010), 35–64.

  'Scholarship, Morals and Government: Jean-Henri-Samuel Formey's and Johann Gottfried Herder's Responses to Rousseau's First Discourse', *Modern Intellectual History*, 9:2 (2012), 249–274.

  'Sources of Evil or Seeds of the Good? Rousseau and Kant on Needs, the Arts and the Sciences', in *Engaging with Rousseau*, ed. Avi Lifschitz (Cambridge, 2016), 33–55.

Schmidt, Georg. *Geschichte des Alten Reiches: Staat und Nation in der Frühen Neuzeit: 1495–1806* (Munich, 1999).

  'Teutsche Kriege. Nationale Deutungsmuster und integrative Wertvorstellungen im frühneuzeitlichen Reich', in *Föderative Nation: Deutschlandkonzepte von der Reformation bis zum Ersten Weltkrieg*, ed. Dieter Langewiesche and Georg Schmidt (Munich, 2000), 34–61.

  'Die Idee „deutsche Freiheit". Eine Leitvorstellung der politischen Kultur des Alten Reiches', in *Kollektive Freiheitsvorstellungen im frühneuzeitlichen Europa (1400–1850)*, ed. Georg Schmidt, Martin van Gelderen and Christopher Snigula (Munich, 2006), 159–189.

Schmidt, Georg, Martin van Gelderen and Christopher Snigula (eds.). *Kollektive Freiheitsvorstellungen im frühneuzeitlichen Europa (1400–1850)* (Munich, 2006).

Schmidt, Johannes. 'Light or Nature/Light of Reason. Herder's and Kant's *Religion Essays*', in *Herder and Religion*, ed. Staffan Bengtsson, Heinrich

Clairmont, Robert E. Norton, Johannes Schmidt and Ulrike Wagner (Heidelberg, 2016), 153–166.

'Herder's Religious Anthropology in his Later Writings', in Herder. Philosophy and Anthropology, ed. Anik Waldow and Nigel DeSouza (Oxford, 2017), 185–203.

'Herder's Political Ideas and the Organic Development of Religions and Governments', in *Herder on Empathy and Sympathy/Einfühlung und Sympathie im Denken Herders*, ed. Eva Piirimäe, Liina Lukas and Johannes Schmidt, 231–257.

Schmidt, Wolf G. *Homer des Nordens und Mutter der Romantik: James Macphersons Ossian und seine Rezeption in der deutschsprachigen Literatur* (Berlin, 2003), 4 vols.

Schneewind, Jerome B. 'Good out of Evil: Kant and the Idea of Unsocial Sociability', in *Kant's Idea of a Universal History with a Cosmopolitan Aim: A Critical Guide*, ed. Amélie Oksenberg Rorty and James Schmidt (Cambridge, 2009), 94–112.

Shovlin, John. *The Political Economy of Virtue: Luxury, Patriotism and the Origins of the French Revolution* (Ithaca, 2006).

Sikka, Sonia. *Herder on Humanity and Cultural Difference: Enlightened Relativism* (Cambridge, 2011).

'On Extending Sympathy: Herder, Mencius and Adam Smith', in *Herder on Empathy and Sympathy/Einfühlung und Sympathie im Denken Herders*, ed. Eva Piirimäe, Liina Lukas and Johannes Schmidt, 206–230.

Simon, Ralf. '1.3.2 *Sprachphilosophie: Abhandlung über den Ursprung der Sprache*', in *Herder Handbuch*, ed. Stefan Greif, Marion Heinz and Heinrich Clairmont (Paderborn, 2016), 143–159.

Sonenscher, Michael. *Before the Deluge: Public Debt, Inequality, and the Intellectual Origins of the French Revolution* (Princeton and Oxford, 2007).

Sans-Culottes: An Eighteenth-Century Emblem in the French Revolution (Princeton, 2008).

'Liberty, Autonomy, and Republican Historiography. Civic Humanism in Context', in *Markets, Morals, Politics: Jealousy of Trade and the History of Political Thought*, ed. Béla Kapossy, Isaac Nakhimovsky, Sophus Reinert and Richard Whatmore (Cambridge MA, 2018), 161–211.

Jean-Jacques Rousseau: The Division of Labour, the Politics of the Imagination and the Concept of Federal Government (Leiden, 2020).

Speck, Reto. 'The History and Politics of Civilisation: The Debate about Russia in French and German Historical Scholarship from Voltaire to Herder' (unpublished PhD dissertation, Queen Mary University of London, 2010).

'Johann Gottfried Herder and Enlightenment Political Thought: From the Reform of Russia to the Anthropology of *Bildung*', *Modern Intellectual History*, 11:1 (2014), 931–958.

Spector, Céline. 'De l'union de l'âme et du corps à l'unité de la sensibilité. L'anthropologie méconnue de *L'Esprit des lois*', *Les études philosophiques*, 106:3 (2013), 383–396.

Spencer, Vicki. 'Herder and Nationalism: Reclaiming the Principle of Cultural Respect', *Australasian Journal of Politics and History*, 43 (1997), 1–13.

Herder's Political Thought: A Study of Language, Culture and Community (Toronto, 2012).

Spencer, Vicki. 'Kant and Herder on Colonialism, Indigenous Peoples, and Minority Nations', *International Theory*, 7:2 (2015), 360–392.

Stapelbroek, Koen. 'Dutch Decline as a European Phenomenon', *History of European Ideas*, 36:2 (2010), 139–152.

'From Jealousy of Trade to the Neutrality of Finance: Isaac de Pinto's "System" of Luxury and Perpetual Peace', in *Commerce and Peace in the Enlightenment*, ed. Béla Kapossy, Isaac Nakhimovsky and Richard Whatmore (Cambridge, 2017), 78–109.

'The International Politics of Cameralism and the Balance of Power: Dutch Tranlations of Justi', in *Cameralism and Enlightenment*, ed. Ere Nokkala and Nicholas B. Miller (Routledge, 2019), 88–124.

Stapelbroek, Koen and Jani Marjanen (eds.). *The Rise of Economic Societies: Patriotic Reform in Europe and North America* (Houndmills, Basingstoke, 2012).

Sternhell, Zeev. *The Anti-Enlightenment Tradition* (New Haven, 2010).

Stilz, Annie. 'Hume, Modern Patriotism, and Commercial Society', *History of European Ideas*, 29:1 (2003), 15–32.

Stolpe, Heinz. *Die Auffassung des jungen Herders vom Mittelalter* (Cologne, Vienna, 1955).

Straumann, Benjamin. '*Appetitus socialis* and *oikeiosis*: Hugo Grotius's Ciceronian Argument for Natural Law and Just War', *Grotiana New Series*, 24:25 (2003/2004), 41–66.

Sundhaussen, Holm. *Der Einfluß der Herderschen Ideen auf die Nationsbildung bei den Völkern der Habsburger Monarchie* (Munich, Oldenburg, 1973).

Taszus, Claudia. 'Die Sieben Friedensgesinnungen Johann Gottfried Herders und ihre Stellung innerhalb der Briefe zu Beförderung der Humanität' (unpublished diploma dissertation (Diplomarbeit) (Jena, 1991).

Taterka, Thomas. 'Humanität, Abolition, Nation'. Baltische Varianten kolonialkritischen Diskurses der europäischen Aufklärung um 1800', in *Raynal—Herder—Merkel: Transformationen der Antikolonialismusdebatte in der europäischen Aufklärung*, ed. Mix York-Gothard and Hinrich Ahrend (Heidelberg, 2017), 183–251.

Taylor, Charles. *Hegel* (Cambridge, 1975).

Sources of the Self: The Making of Modern Identity (Cambridge, 1989).

'The Importance of Herder', in *Isaiah Berlin: A Celebration*, ed. Edna Margalit and Avishai Margalit (Chicago, 1991), 40–63.

Thaden, Edward C. *Russia's Western Borderlands, 1710–1870*, ed. Marianna Forster Thaden (Princeton, NJ, 1984).

Tomaselli, Sylvana. 'The Spirit of Nations', in *The Cambridge History of Eighteenth-Century Political Thought*, ed. Mark Goldie and Robert Wokler (Cambridge, 2006), 7–39.

Trabant, Jürgen. 'Herder and Language', in *A Companion to the Works of Johann Gottfried Herder*, ed. Hans Adler and Wulf Koepke (Rochester, NY, 2009), 117–140.

Träger, Claus. *Die Herder Legende des deutschen Historismus* (Berlin, 1979).

Trencsényi, Balàzs, Kopeček M., Falina M., Lisjak L., Baár M.K. and Janowski M. *A History of Political Thought in East-Central Europe* (Oxford, 2018), 2 vols., I.

Tronchon, Henri. *La Fortune Intellectuelle de Herder en France: La Préparation* (Paris, 1920).

Tuck, Richard. *The Rights of War and Peace: Political Thought and the International Order from Grotius to Kant* (Oxford, 1999).

The Sleeping Sovereign: The Invention of Modern Democracy (Cambridge, 2015).

Tümmler, Hans. 'Johann Gottfried Herders Plan einer Deutschen Akademie (1787)', in *Weimar, Warthburg, Fürstenbund 1776–1820: Geist und Politik im Thüringen der Goethe-Zeit: Gesammelte Aufsätze* (Bad Neustadt, 1995), 39–52.

Unger, Rudolf. *Hamann und die Aufklärung: Studien zur Vorgeschichte des romantischen Geistes im 18ten Jahrhundert* (Jena, 1911).

Vazsonyi, Nicholas. 'Montesquieu, Friedrich Carl von Moser and the National Spirit Debate in Germany, 1765–1767', *German Studies Review*, 22:2 (1999), 225–246.

Vick, Brian. *Defining Germany: the 1848 Frankfurt Parliamentarians and National Identity* (Cambridge, MA, 2002).

Viroli, Maurizio. *For Love of Country: An Essay on Patriotism and Nationalism* (Oxford, 1997).

Vivian, John. 'Der Einfluß David Humes auf den jungen Herder von 1762–1769: unter besonderer Berücksichtigung der Königsberger und Rigaer Jahre' (unpublished PhD manuscript (University of Jena, 1993)).

Waldow, Anik and Nigel DeSouza (eds.). *Herder: Philosophy and Anthropology* (Oxford, 2017).

Weckwerth, Christine. 'Die Herdersche Philosophie als Aurora der neuern sensualistischen Philosophie – Nachwirkungen Herder in Vormärz', in *Herder Handbuch*, ed. Stefan Greif, Marion Heinz and Heinrich Clairmont (Paderborn, 2016), 686–696.

Wiedemann, Conrad. 'The Germans' Concern about their National Identity in the Pre-Romantic Era: An Answer to Montesquieu?' in *Concepts of National Identity – An Interdisciplinary Dialogue*, ed. Peter Boerner (Baden-Baden, 1986), 141–152.

Wildschut, Niels, 'Analogy, Empathy, Incommensurability: Herder's Conception of Historical Understanding', in *Herder on Empathy and Sympathy/ Einfühlung und Sympathie im Denken Herders*, ed. Eva Piirimäe, Liina Lukas and Johannes Schmidt (Leiden, 2020), 158–182.

Wisbert, Rainer. '4. Kulturpolitische und Pädagogische See-Träume', in *Herder Handbuch*, ed. Stefan Greif, Marion Heinz and Heinrich Clairmont (Paderborn, 2016), 595–622.

'Kommentar. [*Vom Einfluß der Regierung*]', in *FHA*, IX:2, 1140–1190.

Wolloch, Nathaniel. '*Facts, or Conjectures*: Antoine-Yves Goguet's Historiography', *Journal of the History of Ideas*, 68:3 (2007), 429–449.

Wright, Johnson Kent. *A Classical Republican in Eighteenth-Century France: The Political Thought of Mably* (Stanford, 1997).

Wood, Allen W. *Kant's Ethical Thought* (Cambridge, 1999).

'General Introduction', in Immanuel Kant, *Practical Philosophy*, ed. and trans. Mary J. Gregor (Cambridge, 1996), xiii–xxxiii.

'Kant's Fourth Proposition: the Unsociable Sociability of Human Nature', in *Kant's Idea of a Universal History with a Cosmopolitan Aim: A Critical Guide*, ed. Amélie Oksenberg Rorty and James Schmidt (Cambridge, 2009), 112–128.

'Herder and Kant on History: Their Enlightenment Faith', in *Metaphysics and the Good – Themes from the Philosophy of Robert Merrihew Adams*, ed. Samuel Newlands and Larry M. Jorgensen (Oxford, 2009), 313–342.

Kant and Religion (Cambridge Studies in Religion, Philosophy, and Society) (Cambridge, 2020).

Zammito, John H. *The Genesis of Kant's Critique of Judgement* (Chicago, 1992).

'Herder, Kant, Spinoza und die Ursprünge des deutschen Idealismus', in *Herder und die Philosophie des deutschen Idealismus*, ed. Marion Heinz (Amsterdam, 1997), 107–144.

Kant, Herder, and the Birth of Anthropology (Chicago, 2002).

'Die Rezeption der schottischen Aufklärung in Deutschland: Herders entscheidende Einsicht', in *Europäischer Kulturtransfer im 18: Jahrhundert: Literaturen in Europa – Europäische Literatur?*, ed. Barbara Schmidt-Haberkamp, Uwe Steiner and Brunhilde Wehinger (Berlin, 2003), 113–138.

'Herder and Historical Metanarrative: What's Philosophical about History?', in *A Companion to the Works of Johann Gottfried Herder*, ed. Hans Adler and Wulf Koepke (Rochester, NY, 2009), 65–91.

Zammito, John H., Karl Menges and Ernest A. Menze, 'Johann Gottfried Herder Revisited: The Revolution of Scholarship in the Last Quarter Century', *Journal of the History of Ideas*, 71:4 (2010), 661–684.

Zurbuchen, Simone. 'Staatstheorie zwischen eidgenössischer Republik und preussischer Monarchie', *Das Achtzehnte Jahrhundert*, 26:2 (2002), 145–162.

'Theorizing Enlightened Absolutism: The Swiss Republican Origins of Prussian Monarchism', in *Monarchisms in the Age of Enlightenment: Liberty, Patriotism, and the Common Good*, ed. Hans Blom, John Christian Laursen and Luisa Simonutti (Toronto, 2007), 240–266.

Wagner, Ulrike. 'Herder's Reinvention of Religious Experience', in *Herder and Religion*, ed. Staffan Bengtsson, Heinrich Clairmont, Robert E. Norton, Johannes Schmidt and Ulrike Wagner (Heidelberg, 2016), 57–74.

Welker, Karl H. L. *Rechtsgeschichte als Rechtspolitik, Justus Möser als Jurist und Staatsmann*, 2 vols. (Osnabrück, 1996).

White, C. E. 'Scharnhorst's Mentor: Count Wilhelm zu Schaumburg-Lippe and the Origins of the Modern National Army', *War in History*, 24:3 (2017), 258–285.

Yack, Bernard. *Nationalism and the Moral Psychology of Community* (Chicago, 2012).

Index

Milton Keynes UK
Ingram Content Group UK Ltd.
UKHW030258120224
437685UK00004BA/8